The Essays of
Virginia Woolf
VOLUME III

The Essays of
Virginia Woolf

VOLUME III

1919–1924

EDITED BY

ANDREW McNEILLIE

The Hogarth Press

LONDON

Published in 1988 by
The Hogarth Press
30 Bedford Square
London WC1B 3SG

A CIP catalogue record for
this book is available from the
British Library
ISBN 0–7012–0668–3
Text by Virginia Woolf copyright © Quentin Bell and Angelica Garnett 1919, 1920, 1921,
1922, 1923, 1924, 1988

Introduction and editorial notes copyright © Andrew McNeillie 1988
Typeset by Wyvern Typesetting Ltd, Bristol
Printed in Great Britain by
Redwood Burn Ltd
Trowbridge, Wiltshire

Contents

Introduction

As the year 1919 began, Virginia Woolf, approaching her thirty-seventh birthday, was still known to the majority of her readers only as the author of *The Voyage Out* (1915). No doubt there were those among the literati who were familiar with more of her writings, but, with the exceptions of her intimate friends and of the uniquely placed Bruce Richmond, editor of the *Times Literary Supplement* (to which contributions were in those days anonymous), they are unlikely to have recognised much more of her work than did the common reader or humble subscriber to Mudie's Circulating Library.

The Hogarth Press's first publication, *Two Stories*, containing her rhapsodical reverie 'The Mark on the Wall' (and Leonard Woolf's 'Three Jews') had been published in July 1917. (According to the Press's accounts, it sold a mere 134 copies.) This story and *The Voyage Out* were Virginia Woolf's only signed writings to appear between 1908 – and the days of her brief celebrity as a regular contributor to the *Cornhill Magazine* – and May 1919 when The Hogarth Press published *Kew Gardens*.

Yet since 1904 she had published anonymously a vast quantity – more than a quarter of a million words – of journalism, journalism very largely of great brilliance, written from a deeply impasssioned point of view.

In the next few years – those covered by this volume – her relative obscurity came to an end. She published two more novels, *Night and Day* (1919) and *Jacob's Room* (1922), and also *Monday or Tuesday* (1921), a collection of her shorter fictional pieces, including 'The Mark on the Wall', 'Kew Gardens' and 'An Unwritten Novel'; and she engaged, famously, in controversy upon the subject of 'Character in

Fiction' (and less famously but with equal polemical panache, upon 'The Intellectual Status of Women',[1] and upon 'The Plumage Bill').

The *TLS* remained the major outlet for her journalism but she gradually wrote fewer straightforward reviews for the paper and produced, as she much preferred, more extended essays or 'leaders', pieces that with little or no refurbishment could later be included in *The Common Reader: 1st series* (1925). At the same time, some of her most important critical writing and biographical essays began to appear elsewhere. She contributed to the *Athenaeum*, under J. M. Murry's short-lived but culturally enormously successful editorship of that journal, to the newly founded *London Mercury*, edited by J. C. Squire, and to T. S. Eliot's *Criterion*. With Desmond MacCarthy's succession to the literary editorship of the *New Statesman* in 1920, she found more work, some of it in dramatic criticism. Then, from the spring of 1923, following Leonard Woolf's appointment (about which she had mixed feelings) as literary editor of the merged *Nation & Athenaeum*, she turned her industrious hand to all manner of journalistic activity, from essays such as 'To Spain', 'The Patron and the Crocus' and 'Thunder at Wembley' to reviews, notices and occasional 'fillers'. She contributed the first of her articles to *Vogue*; and at the opposite end of the cultural spectrum – far from 'ladies' clothes and aristocrats playing golf'[2] – she wrote for the *Daily Herald*, Labour's newspaper for the working classes, and for the feminist *Woman's Leader*. She also published signed articles in America, in the columns of the *New York Post Literary Review*, the *New York Herald Tribune, Dial* and the *New Republic*.[3] (The first American edition of *The Voyage Out* appeared in 1920.) In time The Hogarth Press would provide another occasional outlet for her essays ('Character in Fiction' was reprinted by the Press as the pamphlet *Mr Bennett and Mrs Brown* in 1924).

There were also significant changes during this time in the Woolfs' domestic circumstances. In July 1919 they acquired at auction Monks House, Rodmell; and in January 1924, after prolonged hunting for a suitable London home, they bought the lease of 52 Tavistock Square, Bloomsbury, and moved there from Hogarth House, Richmond, the following March.

As we know from the previous volumes in this edition, Virginia Woolf's criticism had already begun (more implicitly than explicitly) to state a case for modernism, for a rejection of 'materialism' and conventional methods of character portrayal. She had been profoundly impressed by the psychological realism of the Russians. Now all this was to be developed quite openly in a number of important essays. The first of these, 'Modern Novels', appeared as the leading article in the *TLS* of 10 April 1919. Here she attacked the methods of the Edwardians (H. G. Wells, John Galsworthy, Arnold Bennett), praised Hardy, Conrad and Hudson, and also, significantly, James Joyce (but with reservations that would later become emphatic), and she applauded again the virtues of the Russians. To her it seemed that the mass of recent and contemporary English fiction was quite untrue to 'life itself'.[4] In what has since become a famous passage, representing the mind's surface as the constant recipient of 'a myriad impressions . . . an incessant shower of innumerable atoms',[5] she points to quite another kind of verisimilitude from that cultivated by the Edwardians and those she saw to be their mediocre descendants.

The question of what constitutes 'reality' pervades, via Plato and G. E. Moore, much of Bloomsbury's thinking. Leonard Woolf, in his Apostle paper of 14 May 1904 entitled 'Embryos or Abortions?'[6] pursued it to nineteenth-century France, to Flaubert and to Zola, for example. As students of Bloomsbury, we may also relate it to Post-Impressionism, to the paintings of Cézanne, and the writings of Roger Fry and Clive Bell. But 'Modern Novels', embedded in historic argument, none the less divines its author's future. The creator of *Jacob's Room* and its successors is clearly present in her essay, as in no other piece of criticism to have come from her pen by this date.

It was *Jacob's Room* that provoked Arnold Bennett in March 1923 to make what proved to be a rash criticism of Virginia Woolf. That her latest book was a brilliant piece of writing (we should remember perhaps that he is impaled in its pages[7]), he did not deny. It was original, it was clever, but its characters did not in his opinion 'vitally survive in the mind'.[8] In other words, they were not in his view 'real'; and, for Bennett, that was sufficient to condemn any novel to oblivion. Stung by his criticism, Woolf declared war; not at once, but after some months' rumination.

Her campaign opened in America, in Henry Seidel Canby's *New York Evening Post Literary Review* where 'Mr Bennett and Mrs Brown' appeared in the issue for 17 November 1923. But it soon switched to London when, on 1 December, her article was reprinted by Leonard Woolf in the *Nation & Athenaeum*. Her arguments in this new piece echo many of those in 'Modern Novels'. She attacks the Edwardians, who 'give us a vast sense of things in general but a very vague one of things in particular'; she praises the Russians, who create 'characters without any features at all'[9] (a phrase that might almost have derived from an essay on Post-Impressionist portraiture); and, in the process, she somewhat slights the Victorians, which she does not do in subsequent versions of her argument. Taking a literary historical approach, to which she would later give more emphasis and greater depth, she explains the difficulties facing her own generation of writers. If that generation is, as she suggests, the 'least successful', it is also, to her mind, the 'most interesting' for a century.[10] She predicts that the next chapter in the history of literature will be the 'most epoch-making'[11] there has ever been. And, agreeing as she does with Bennett as to the pre-eminent importance of character in fiction, she urges on the 'perilous'[12] pursuit (perilous because fundamentally subjective) of Mrs Brown, the protean personification of character.

She found an opportunity to return to and develop her arguments when the Cambridge Heretics invited her to address their society in May 1924. Her paper, entitled 'Character in Fiction', was published the following July by T. S. Eliot in the *Criterion*. In renewing her attack on the Edwardian 'materialists', she conscripts (whether they would have volunteered to serve together is certainly arguable) E. M. Forster, D. H. Lawrence, Lytton Strachey, James Joyce and T. S Eliot. But no women, as can hardly escape our notice – not at least in this, the *Criterion* version of her essay. In the draft version (transcribed in Appendix III) her recruits also include Edith Sitwell and Dorothy Richardson. (The latter is discussed in this volume's '*The Tunnel*' and 'Romance and the Heart'.[13]) In neither version do we find the name of Katherine Mansfield (who had died in 1923). Nor in her wider campaign does she salute that most celebrated and pioneering modernist Henry James, on whose wartime essays, letters and ghost stories she writes in this volume. (On the other hand, Samuel Butler and George Bernard Shaw are both mentioned in despatches.) But the citing of honours and the summoning of allies is something of a blind, for Virginia Woolf is speaking, as she acknowledges, primarily for herself.

Her perspective is nonetheless a broad one, her point of view literary- and socio-historical (in a wholly unacademic sense), as might be expected from the daughter of Leslie Stephen. She addresses Bennett once again on the twin issues of character and reality. Her historical theme concerns the shift in *all* human dealings – in religion, conduct, politics – which she perceives to have occurred since the age of Victoria, encapsulated in her provocative assertion that 'on or about December 1910 human character changed'.[14] (1910 was the year in which, we may remember, Edward VII died. It is also the year and December almost the month in which the first Post-Impressionist Exhibition opened at the Grafton Galleries, outraging much of London Society.[15]) In the surviving draft of her essay she elaborates upon the difference between the generations:

No generation since the world began has known quite so much about character as our generation. I am not saying that we are the best judges of character; for that unfortunately does not necessarily follow. What I do say is that the average man or woman today thinks more about character than his or her grandparents; character interests them more; they get closer, they dive deeper in to the real emotions and motives of their fellow creatures. There are scientific reasons why this should be so. If you read Freud you know in ten minutes some facts – or at least some possibilities – which our parents could not possibly have guessed for themselves.[16]

For their part, Virginia Woolf argued, novelists differ from the rest of humanity in finding in character something permanently interesting 'in itself'[17] (readers familiar with G. E. Moore's writings will prick up their ears at that expression). They are further obsessed by the need to impart that 'something', to embody it in writing. The task is extremely difficult, and to show just how difficult, she recounts a scene in a railway carriage with Mrs Brown and a Mr Smith, travelling between Richmond and Waterloo, in one sense, and in another, as she says later, 'from one age of English literature to the next'.[18] (She had already employed the same device, the railway carriage encounter, in 'An Unwritten Novel',[19] and she also has recourse to it in 'Byron & Mr Briggs', here reprinted in Appendix II, of which more later.) The method she employs is tentative and her story 'ends without any point to it',[20] as if, we might suggest, it had been written by Chekhov. (It is essentially the same method, passive and speculative, as 'The Mark on the Wall'.) She admits its inadequacy. But how, she wonders, would Wells, Galsworthy and Bennett have dealt with the subject? With consummate mockery she proceeds to show us. Then – it seems necessary to protest, with something considerably less than justice (though no doubt all's fair in art and war) – she rounds upon Bennett, and, quoting at length from *Hilda Lessways* (1911), allows him to demonstrate with his own pen what she sees to be the essential failure of his method. (Which may be summarised in the declaration: 'one line of insight would have done more than all those lines of description ...')[21] The Edwardians were distracted from Mrs Brown by didacticism and an urge to authenticate. They were not, as for example were Sterne and Jane Austen, 'interested in things in themselves'[22] (again, the Mooreite turn of phrase). To the aspiring novelist of 1910 they set no worthwhile example. Their conventions, she protested, were ruin, their tools death, to the Georgian generation. 'Thus it is,' Virginia Woolf declares, 'that we hear all round us, in poems and novels and biographies, even in newspaper articles and essays, the sound of breaking and falling, crashing and destruction.'[23] She does not despair at this but, on the contrary, she is sanguine, and concludes her essay in the same prophetic vein already encountered in 'Mr Bennett and Mrs Brown'.

(If anyone should have despaired, it was surely Arnold Bennett, recent butt of Ezra Pound,[24] and now of Mrs Woolf, whose onslaught is reputed to have had a seriously damaging effect upon the sales of his books. He never replied to her criticism, either in the *Nation & Athenaeum*, where other writers – neither Wells nor Galsworthy, however – did respond,[25] or in the *Criterion*, although pressed to do so by T. S. Eliot.)

By the end of 1924 and the close of this volume Virginia Woolf had almost completed *The Common Reader: 1st series*. The history of that book's evolution is substantially mapped in these pages. If we may judge by the piece here entitled 'Reading', which was not published in its author's lifetime, she began as early as 1919 to experiment with the ideas that eventually bound her book together. 'Reading' is a kind of reverie, a meditation upon England's past, a species almost of fiction, set in a country house – one of those 'little fortresses of civilisation'[26] that in more barbarous days gave shelter to writers, thinkers, musicians and artists. It draws directly upon a number of earlier articles – 'Lady Fanshawe's Memoirs', 'Trafficks and Discoveries', '*The House of Lyme*'[27] – and anticipates in its interest in 'all the lumber and wreckage and accumulations of time'[28] her *Common Reader* essay 'The Elizabethan Lumber Room'. (Its entomological interlude resounds, with the same loud report of falling timber, in the pages of *Jacob's Room*.[29])

In May 1921 we find her contemplating a critical book also to be called 'Reading'. This she appears to have begun writing in the spring of 1922. Her introductory chapter, 'Byron & Mr Briggs', more or less all that survives of the enterprise, is an especially interesting document. For it is here that she begins to explore, in the person of Mr Briggs, spectacle maker of Cornhill, and his descendants, the nature of the relationship between Dr Johnson's 'common reader' and 'literature'.

'Byron & Mr Briggs' airs some familiar Woolfian ideas and arguments, concerning great critics, scholars and reviewers, the problems of judging contemporary literature, the value of biography, the process itself of reading (and of re-reading). But at its centre stands the common reader and the book. The relationship between the two, as Virginia Woolf represents it, is at once commonsensical and yet also of an emotional and fugitive kind. It is a liaison as difficult to capture in criticism as it is to catch Mrs Brown in fiction. (In the latter case, Virginia Woolf argues, the problem is exacerbated by the failure of the Edwardian example; in the former, by the absence of a contemporary great critic.) Both reader and novelist, or railway carriage eavesdropper, are shown in the essay to be animated by the same desire. They seek 'to make a whole',[30] however partial or fragmentary their knowledge, of the book before them, or of the passenger seated opposite (Mrs Brown is present here in principle rather than by name). They are represented as playing a game, in which the reward for the reader is to experience 'a sense of something very real outside, of something flung by Byron or another into the air',[31] independent of its author and apart from everyday society. In other words, as we may choose to say, the reader seeks to discover a work of art, a thing both rare and durable 'unchanged by the triumphs of science, and never superseded by any new discovery in the art of writing'.[32] This is an essentially hermetic view of the book or literary artefact. (It too – in the idea of 'making a whole', of 'something very real outside' – may be seen in Mooreite, and Platonic, terms.) But at the same time it is a view repeatedly qualified by Virginia Woolf's concern to relate literature to daily life. This we find her doing, for example, in the closing scenes of her essay, where she introduces a party of 'ordinary people'[33] (characters in fact from her own novels – Terence Hewet, Mr Pepper, Clarissa Dalloway, Rose Shaw, Julia Hedge) engaged in a dinner-table conversation about Byron. Her final concern is not with art or with a 'circle round the whole' (by now the discussion has moved on to Shakespeare) but with life itself, with fate, with that which 'opposes itself inexorably to human desires'.[34]

There is not space here in which to attempt to unpack the full significance of 'Byron & Mr Briggs'. But the reader may also profitably peruse it in conjunction with 'Mr Howells on Form' (*II VW Essays*) and with 'How It Strikes a Contemporary', as well as with 'Character in Fiction' and *The Common Reader* itself. 'On Re-reading Novels' also addresses itself to the common reader and does so in a particularly interesting way. For it shows Virginia Woolf, a critic deeply suspicious of theories and theory-mongering (and yet a considerable theoretician in her own oblique fashion), working towards an acceptance of Percy Lubbock's theory of the point of view as expounded in his critical classic

The Craft of Fiction (1921). (For an amusing diversion upon academic literary criticism turn here to 'The Anatomy of Fiction'.)

Nothing could be more refreshingly unacademic than Virginia Woolf's hope, as expressed in the summer of 1923, that what was to become *The Common Reader* should be 'a rough, but vigorous statue testifying before I die to the great fun & pleasure my habit of reading has given me'. She spoke of applying to her essays some 'drastic & spirited treatment'.[35] This was in July. In August we find her toying with the idea of 'embedding'[36] them in conversation, a form already explored in 'A Talk About Memoirs' (*NS*, 6 March 1920), and in 'Byron & Mr Briggs', and which was to appear again in 'Mr Conrad: A Conversation' (*N&A*, 1 September 1923). If she rejected the straightforward collection of articles as 'inartistic' she recognised at the same time the risk involved in attempting the more attractive 'artistic' alternative: it might run away with her.[37]

The Common Reader finally appeared in April 1925.[38] Hard on its heels, in May, was published *Mrs Dalloway*. This had 'branched into a book'[39] in October 1922, and so its writing also stands prominently in the background to this volume. (Drafts for several of the reviews and essays published here occur in the *Mrs Dalloway* manuscript, as indeed they do in that for *Jacob's Room* – see Editorial Note.)

Virginia Woolf's industry was thus as prodigious as ever in the six-year period covered here. In fact her journalism had never before been quite of the same critical stature. Nor had it been so eclectic. As already remarked, a significant factor in this eclecticism was the access she now had to a wider variety of periodicals. She wrote dramatic criticism for the *New Statesman* ('The Higher Court', 'The Cherry Orchard', 'Congreve'); she wrote on the visual arts for the *Athenaeum* ('The Royal Academy', 'Pictures and Portraits') and also for the *Nation & Athenaeum*, to which she contributed notices, again on a Royal Academy exhibition and on a show by the London Group at the Mansard Gallery. ('The Royal Academy' also takes an entertaining smack at imperialism and the British establishment, as does 'Thunder at Wembley', her essay on the British Empire Exhibition.) In 'The Plumage Bill', published by Ray Strachey at the *Woman's Leader,* we have what is perhaps her earliest feminist polemic. Once again she wrote on the Russians ('The Russian Background', 'Dostoevsky in Cranford', 'Gorky on Tolstoy', 'A Glance at Turgenev', 'Dostoevsky the Father'). She wrote an obituary of her aunt, Anne Thackeray Ritchie, and reviewed her correspondence ('The Enchanted Organ'). She wrote on romance and Gothic literature ('Horace Walpole', 'Scott's Character', 'Gothic Romance', '*The Antiquary*'). She wrote on the essay itself, and, in addition to the extended critical articles mentioned earlier, she produced full-length essays on Montaigne, Addison, Defoe, Sterne, Jane Austen, George Eliot. The author of 'How It Strikes a Contemporary' (the title, by the way, was originally Browning's) wrote too upon her own contemporaries and near-contemporaries: Dorothy Richardson, Romer Wilson, Hope Mirrlees, Elizabeth Robins, Joseph Conrad, D. H. Lawrence, Aldous Huxley, Frank Swinnerton, W. E. Norris, J. D. Beresford, Joseph Hergesheimer, Theodore Dreiser. There were biographies to review, good and bad, including accounts of Thomas Coutts, George Meredith, Mrs Humphry Ward, and Miss Mitford, the last so bad it inspired three reviews, one unsigned, 'An Imperfect Lady', in the *TLS*, and two signed, 'A Good Daughter', in the *Daily Herald*, and in the *Athenaeum*, 'The Wrong Way of Reading', a hilarious hatchet job, later incorporated into 'Miss Mitford' in *The Common Reader*. For Leonard Woolf's literary pages of the *Nation & Athenaeum* she not only produced essays and reviews but also numerous notices, and for the paper's 'From Alpha to Omega' column she turned out paragraphs on such subjects as French indifference to the English language, the increasing penetration of the motor-car into rural England, and a new process of making colour film for the cinema.

Her relations at this time with her editors and with Grub Street (or, as she called it, the 'underworld')[40] had, as ever, their moments of animation. For once, Bruce Richmond was an offender. His request that she refrain from using the word 'lewd'[41] in her *TLS* article on 'Henry James's Ghost Stories' earned the fairly predictable response: she complied, while declaring to herself that she would review no more for Printing House Square. Richmond, she opined, 'fondled' his paper 'like an only child',[42] dreaded public criticism and so rewrote her sentences 'to suit the mealy mouths of Belgravia',[43] an exaggeration, as she acknowledged. Nonetheless, such editorial interventions were, at least temporarily, damaging: 'how stiffly one sets pen to paper,' she observed, 'when one is uncertain of editorial approval.'[44] But her resolve to abandon Richmond proved short-lived. (Writing on Henry James did seem to have its peculiar hazards. Her article on his correspondence, again in the *TLS*, was, to her discomfort, attacked in an unlikely corner of *The Times* by the paper's querulous drama critic, A. B. Walkley.[45])

At the *Athenaeum*, Middleton Murry, for his part, proved to be highly accommodating. But perhaps, indeed, he was too accommodating when he asked her to review his own book, *The Critic in Judgment,* and T. S. Eliot's *Poems* – both of which were Hogarth Press publications. A crisis of conscience ensued, leaving her unable to complete the task. What we have in 'Is This Poetry?', the review concerned, is a collaboration with Leonard Woolf, rendered as stylistically bland as possible, and published anonymously.[46] Her reaction to the fact that she found Joseph Conrad's *The Rescue* (1920) a failure and had to say so in the *TLS* led her to proclaim in her diary the nature of her faith as reader and reviewer: 'nothing shakes my opinion of a book – nothing – nothing. Only perhaps if it is the book of a young person – or of a friend – no, even so, I think myself infallible.'[47] Let others chorus like 'obedient sheep', she was 'the true seer, the one independent voice'.[48] But she could be shaken in other ways, as may be seen in the interesting case of Dorothy Richardson's *Interim.* With impeccable tact, she declined to review this book for the *TLS* because, wounded by Katherine Mansfield's treatment in the *Athenaeum*[49] of her own *Night and Day*, she now found herself both looking and hoping for faults in Richardson's work, the motivation involved being, as she surmised, 'an instinct of self-preservation'.[50]

Journalism made taxing demands upon her time and emotions. It kept her from her other writing. Yet if she could and did now begin to call the tune at the *TLS*, as we have seen, she continued to find it difficult to refuse requests for essays, reviews or notices from other quarters. Then there was the need to make money, and she was nothing if not professional. (She would write for *Vogue*, let priggish Logan Pearsall Smith carp as much as he liked.) But her journalism, in the shape especially of her extended essays, was also an end in itself; and in important (non-material) respects it was a means, too, towards the ends of fiction.

A significant number of her contemporary readers (and others since) have preferred Virginia Woolf's essays to her novels. At least one eminent reviewer of the previous volumes in this edition has suggested that essay-writing was her proper *métier,* the occupation that promoted her greatest fulfilment.[51] However attractive and persuasive this view may seem as we read the essays, we can only say that Virginia Woolf did not regard the matter in the same light. As she remarked in her diary, at a time when *Mrs Dalloway* was in early progress:

To get to the bones now I'm writing fiction again I feel my force flow straight from me at its fullest. After a dose of criticism I feel that I'm writing sideways, using only an angle of my mind. This is justification; for free use of the faculties means happiness. I'm better company, more of a human being.[52]

(Not that writing fiction was an everlasting bed of roses.)

As common readers, descendants of Mr Briggs and of Penelope Otway,[53] we will properly have our stubborn preferences. But neither these nor Virginia Woolf's private demarcation disputes, her periodic expressions of frustration or well-being, as she switched between modes of writing, or merely as her moods altered, should obscure from us the important relationship that came to exist between her essays and her fiction, her fiction and her essays. As is abundantly evident from this volume.

1 – Letters to the literary editor of the NS, Desmond MacCarthy, originally published in the NS, 9 and 16 October 1920, reprinted in II VW Diary, App. II.
2 – III VW Letters, no. 1524, to Jacques Raverat, 24 January 1925, on Logan Pearsall Smith's disapproval of her writing for Vogue.
3 – For details of the periodicals mentioned here, see App. IV, Notes on the Journals.
4 – 'Modern Novels', p. 33.
5 – Ibid.
6 – LWP, II O 2. See also the paper 'George or George or Both?'.
7 – Jacob's Room (1922), ch. ix (Penguin, 1965, p. 101): 'For example, there is Mr Masefield, there is Mr Bennett. Stuff them into the flame of Marlowe and burn them to cinders ... Don't palter with the second rate ... Detest your own age. Build a better one ... Useless to trust to the Victorians, who disembowel, or to the living, who are mere publicists.'
8 – Arnold Bennett, 'Is the Novel Decaying?', Cassell's Weekly, 28 March 1923.
9 – For the first quotation, 'Mr Bennett and Mrs Brown', p. 387, and for the second p. 386.
10 – Ibid., p. 388.
11 – Ibid.
12 – Ibid., p. 387.
13 – For VW's only known article dealing with Edith Sitwell, see 'Adventurers All', II VW Essays, pp. 306–10.
14 – 'Character in Fiction', p. 421.
15 – 'Manet and the Post-Impressionists'. Grafton Galleries, 8 November 1910–15 January 1911.
16 – App. III, p. 503, which she qualifies with a manuscript insertion: 'That is a very debatable point ... how much we can learn ... & make our own from science.'
17 – 'Character in Fiction', p. 505.
18 – Ibid., p. 512.
19 – Originally published in the London Mercury, July 1920, now collected in CSF.
20 – 'Character in Fiction', p. 425.
21 – Ibid., p. 429.
22 – Ibid., p. 427.

23 – *Ibid.*, pp. 433–4.

24 – See the poem 'Mr Nixon' in Pound's *Hugh Selwyn Mauberley* (1920), which opens: 'In the cream gilded cabin of his steam yacht/ Mr Nixon advised me kindly, to advance with fewer/ Dangers of delay. "Consider/ Carefully the reviewer."'

25 – J. D. Beresford, 'The Successors of Charles Dickens', *N&A*, 29 December 1923; Logan Pearsall Smith, 'First Catch Your Hare', *N&A*, 2 February 1924; Michael Sadleir, 'Why Only Dickens?', *N&A*, 9 February 1924.

26 – 'Reading', p. 144.

27 – For the first two essays see *I VW Essays* and for the second two, *II VW Essays*.

28 – 'Reading', p. 153.

29 – *Jacob's Room*, ch. ii, p. 21.

30 – App. II, p. 482.

31 – *Ibid.*, p. 485.

32 – *Ibid.*, p. 486.

33 – *Ibid.*, p. 494.

34 – For the first quotation *Ibid.*, p. 497, and for the second, p. 498.

35 – *II VW Diary*, 28 July 1923.

36 – *Ibid.*, 17 August 1923.

37 – *Ibid.*

38 – For details of its contents see Editorial Note.

39 – *II VW Diary*, 14 October 1922.

40 – For a whiff of this environment see *II VW Diary*, 6 July 1920: 'We were at the first Athenaeum lunch – a long single file of insignificant brain workers ... a little dingy & professional, a glimpse into the scullery where the Sullivans & Pounds & Murrys & Huxleys stand stripped with their arms in wash tubs. I see the obvious retort; yet I can't rid myself of the feeling that if Lytton, Roger, Desmond, Morgan, Nessa & Duncan had been there the atmosphere would have been less of the area steps & more of the open air.'

41 – *II VW Diary*, 19 December 1921.

42 – *Ibid.*

43 – *Ibid.*, 3 January 1922.

44 – *Ibid.*

45 – *Ibid.*, 15 April 1920.

46 – In 'Gorky on Tolstoy' she reviewed another Hogarth Press publication: *Reminiscences of Leo Nicolayevitch Tolstoi* by Maxim Gorky, in the *NS*, 7 August 1920.

47 – *II VW Diary*, 23 June 1920.

48 – *Ibid.*, 6 July 1920.

49 – Katherine Mansfield, 'A Ship Comes into Harbour', *Athenaeum*, 21 November 1919.

50 – *I VW Diary*, 28 November 1919.

51 – See P. N. Furbank, 'Invitations to Bliss', *TLS*, 12 December 1986, and 'Scenes from Writing Life', *ibid.*, 9–15 October 1987.

52 – *II VW Diary*, 19 June 1923.

53 – For whom see 'Mr Conrad: A Conversation'.

Editorial Note

At the present stage in the compilation of this edition, a conflict of interest arises between its chronological purpose and the intention to reproduce in their entirety, in volumes IV and V respectively, *The Common Reader*: 1st and 2nd series (1925, 1932). This conflict has been resolved in the following way. Explanatory headnotes are provided at the appropriate chronological points in the text for the 13 articles, of the period 1919–24, which, without, or with only minor, revision, Virginia Woolf reprinted in the first *Common Reader*. (Variants concerned will be dealt with in footnotes to the *Common Reader* articles in Volume IV.) Essays substantially revised, or adapted, for inclusion in *The Common Reader*, appear here in their original form. As far as possible consideration has been given to the ultimate convenience of the reader, who, it is thought, is likely to prefer a greater rather than lesser degree of duplication, if the alternative means accounting for variants by an extensive or complex apparatus. In borderline cases it has generally been decided to err on the side of duplication, while a particularly strong chronological argument may also carry considerable weight, as for example in the case of 'Modern Novels', published here and not accounted for at 'Modern Fiction' in Volume IV. Details of the essays involved are provided below.

Otherwise the volume is compiled upon the principles stated in *I VW Essays*. Of the 136 pieces published here, 80 have not been previously collected. All are reprinted in chronological order from the original source of publication. Source, publication date and bibliographical reference are detailed in the first note to each article; this information has been provided by B. J. Kirkpatrick's bibliography. Departures from Kirkpatrick's sequence have been made in the following cases: 'Reading', an essay first published by Leonard Woolf in *The Captain's Death*

Bed and Other Essays (1950), is reprinted here at the end of 1919, upon the basis of internal evidence suggesting that it was written that year; 'The Compromise' is published at the date of its original publication in the *N&A*, 29 September 1923, and not as listed by Kirkpatrick at the date of its appearance in the *NR*, 9 January 1924; 'Restoration Comedy' is also published at its original date of publication in the *N&A*, 18 October 1924, and not as listed at the date of its appearance in the *NR*, 11 February 1925; the notices of *Memories of a Militant* by Annie Kenney and *Peggy. The Story of One Score Years and Ten* by Peggy Webling, *N&A*, 8 November 1924, are placed before, and not after, 'The Antiquary', November 1924.

'Character in Fiction' is reprinted in the form in which it was originally published in the *Criterion*, July 1924, with footnotes to account for the minor revisions that occur in the pamphlet version 'Mr Bennett and Mrs Brown', Hogarth Press, October 1924. Similarly, 'Indiscretions', *Vogue*, late November 1924, is reprinted here, with footnotes accounting for substantial but minor alterations, arising in the retitled version 'Indiscretions in Literature', *Vogue*, NY, 1 June 1925. The original version of 'On Re-reading Novels', *TLS*, 20 July 1922, is reprinted here; the substantially revised version published by Leonard Woolf in *The Moment and Other Essays* (1947) will appear in *VI VW Essays*.

Headnotes are provided for the following *Common Reader* articles: 'The Novels of Defoe' ('Defoe'), 'The Soul of an Archbishop' ('Archbishop Thomson'), 'Joseph Addison' ('Addison'), 'George Eliot', 'Behind the Bars' ('Lady Dorothy Nevill'), 'Modern Essays' ('The Modern Essay'), 'Laetitia Pilkington', 'Jane Austen at Sixty' ('Jane Austen'), 'Montaigne', 'The Lives of the Obscure' ('Taylors and Edgeworths'), 'The Patron and the Crocus', 'Joseph Conrad', 'Miss Ormerod'. Essays revised or substantially adapted for inclusion in *The Common Reader* and reprinted here are: 'Modern Novels', 'The Wrong Way of Reading' ('Miss Mitford'), 'John Evelyn' ('Rambling Round Evelyn'), 'How It Strikes a Contemporary'. (The contents of *The Common Reader*: 1st series, are: 'The Common Reader', 'The Pastons and Chaucer', 'On Not Knowing Greek', 'The Elizabethan Lumber Room', 'Notes on an Elizabethan Play', 'Montaigne', 'The Duchess of Newcastle', 'Rambling Round Evelyn', 'Defoe', 'Addison', 'Lives of the Obscure: I Taylors and Edgeworths, II Laetitia Pilkington, III Miss Ormerod', 'Jane Austen', 'Modern Fiction', '*Jane Eyre* and *Wuthering Heights*', 'George Eliot', 'The Russian Point of View', 'Outlines: I Miss

Mitford, II Bentley, III Lady Dorothy Nevill, IV Archbishop Thomson', 'The Patron and the Crocus', 'The Modern Essay', 'Joseph Conrad', 'How It Strikes a Contemporary'.)

Drafts of the following published articles occur in the holograph of *Jacob's Room* (Berg Collection, New York Public Library): Part III: 'On Re-reading Novels', pp. 13–58, 67–73; 'Jane Austen Practising', pp. 75–95; 'Romance and the Heart', pp. 173–81; in the manuscript of VW's Diary (Berg Collection): Diary X dated 18 May 1921, 'Patmore's Criticism'; and in the holograph of 'The Hours' (*Mrs Dalloway*) (Department of Manuscripts, British Library): Add.Ms. 51,044: 'Mr Benson's Memories', ff 140–1; Add.Ms. 51, 045: '*Robert Smith Surtees*', f 29; 'Thunder at Wembley' (entitled in the draft 'Nature at Wembley'), ff 33–8; '*Unwritten History*', f 40; '*The Life and Last Words of Wilfrid Ewart*', f 42; '*Before the Mast – And After*', f 58; 'Stendhal', f 61; 'The Weekend', ff 75–7; Add.Ms. 51, 046 (reversed): 'The Lives of the Obscure', f 140; 'Appreciations', ff 137–133; 'Restoration Comedy', ff 120–115; 'The cheapening of motor-cars', f 117; 'Not the least pitiable victims', f 114; 'The Schoolroom Floor', ff 113–110; '*Smoke Rings and Roundelays*', f 109; '*Richard Hakluyt*', f 108.

The following drafts of untraced and perhaps unpublished reviews are to be found in the *Jacob's Room* holograph, Part III: 'Royal Academy, 155th exhibition', pp. 169, 171; '*The Art of Thomas Hardy*' (by Lionel Johnson), pp. 219, 221; '*Maud Evelyn* and *The Sacred Fount*' (by Henry James), p. 273; and in the holograph of 'The Hours' (*Mrs Dalloway*), Add.Ms. 51, 046 (reversed): '*The Passing Years*' (by Lord Willoughby de Broke).

Acknowledgements

My indebtedness to the directors of The Hogarth Press and to Professor Quentin Bell and Angelica Garnett, administrators of Virginia Woolf's literary estate, for retaining me to prepare this edition remains paramount. I am also greatly indebted to the British Academy whose research award has played a vital part in the completion of this volume. My wife, Diana McNeillie, has again read far and wide in pursuit of quotations and references. I have been especially dependent upon and am particularly grateful for her help. I must also thank Nicola Edwards, a true common reader, and my daughter Gail McNeillie, for her secretarial assistance.

I am most grateful to Professor Edward A. Hungerford of Southern Oregon State College for his generous advice and encouragement and to Professor Elizabeth Steele, from whose early advice I continue to benefit. Professor Susan Dick and Professor S. P. Rosenbaum remain invaluable in their support and help. I am also grateful to Anne Olivier Bell and to Professor Quentin Bell for their great encouragement.

Elizabeth Inglis of Sussex University Library has been unstinting in her help and I am especially grateful to her.

I should acknowledge the facilities of the London Library, without which the progress of this project would have been considerably slower; and those too of the British Library and the Bodleian Library. I remain indebted to London University's Librarian and to the staff of the Library's periodicals department.

Acknowledgement is also due to the following: Mrs B. Cantor of the Library, Condé Nast Publications Ltd; Rosemary Evison of the Archives and Library, National Portrait Gallery; Dr E. S. Leedham-Green of the University Archives, Cambridge University Library; Kate Perry of Girton College, Cambridge; Irene L. Schubert of the Periodical Section,

Library of Congress, Washington D.C.; Helen Valentine of the Library, Royal Academy of Arts; and the Archivist at Newnham College, Cambridge.

My thanks also go to the following individuals: Alan Bell, Ted Bishop, Hugo Brunner, Tim Binyon, James McNeillie, Craig Raine, and George Rylands.

For permission to publish the material in Appendices II and III, I have to thank Professor Quentin Bell and Angelica Garnett; acknowledgement is also due to Sussex University Library.

Abbreviations

B&P	*Books and Portraits*, ed. Mary Lyon (Hogarth Press, London, 1977; Harcourt Brace Jovanovich, New York, 1978)
CDB	*The Captain's Death Bed and Other Essays*, ed. Leonard Woolf (Hogarth Press, London, 1950; Harcourt Brace Jovanovich, New York, 1950)
CE	*Collected Essays,* 4 vols ed. Leonard Woolf (vols 1–2, Hogarth Press, London, 1966, Harcourt Brace & World Inc., New York, 1967; vols 3–4, Hogarth Press, London, and Harcourt Brace & World Inc., New York, 1967)
CR	*The Common Reader:* 1st series (Hogarth Press, London, and Harcourt Brace & Co., New York, 1925; annotated edition, 1984), 2nd series (Hogarth Press, London, and Harcourt Brace & Co., New York, 1932; annotated edition, 1986)
CSF	*The Complete Shorter Fiction*, ed. Susan Dick (Hogarth Press, London, Harcourt Brace Jovanovich, New York, 1985)
CW	*Contemporary Writers,* with a Preface by Jean Guiget (Hogarth Press, London, 1965; Harcourt Brace & World Inc., New York, 1966)
DNB	*Dictionary of National Biography*
DoM	*The Death of the Moth and Other Essays*, ed. Leonard Woolf (Hogarth Press, London, and Harcourt Brace & Co., New York, 1942)
G&R	*Granite and Rainbow,* ed. Leonard Woolf (Hogarth Press, London, and Harcourt Brace & Co., New York, 1958)

Kp	B. J. Kirkpatrick, *A Bibliography of Virginia Woolf* (third ed., Oxford University Press, Oxford, 1980)
LW	Leonard Woolf, *An Autobiography*, 2 vols (Oxford University Press, Oxford, 1980)
LWP	Leonard Woolf Papers, Sussex University Library
MHP	Monks House Papers, Sussex University Library
MoB	*Moments of Being,* ed. Jeanne Schulkind (2nd ed., Hogarth Press, London, 1985; Harcourt Brace Jovanovich, New York, 1985)
MoE	*The Moment and Other Essays*, ed. Leonard Woolf (Hogarth Press, London, 1947; Harcourt Brace & Co., New York, 1948)
N&A	*Nation & Athenaeum*
NPD	*Newspaper Press Directory*
NR	*New Republic*
NS	*New Statesman*
QB	Quentin Bell, *Virginia Woolf. A Biography. Volume One. Virginia Stephen, 1882–1912. Volume Two. Mrs Woolf, 1912–1941.* (Hogarth Press, London, and Harcourt Brace Jovanovich Inc., New York, 1972)
TLS	*Times Literary Supplement*
VW Diary	*The Diary of Virginia Woolf*, ed. Anne Olivier Bell (5 vols, Hogarth Press, London, and Harcourt Brace Jovanovich, New York, 1977–84)
VW Essays	*The Essays of Virginia Woolf,* 6 vols
VW Letters	*The Letters of Virginia Woolf*, ed. Nigel Nicolson (6 vols, Hogarth Press, London, and Harcourt Brace Jovanovich, New York, 1975–80)
W&W	*Women & Writing*, ed. Michèle Barrett (Women's Press, London, 1979; Harcourt Brace Jovanovich, New York, 1980)

The Essays

1919

The War from the Street

Mr Metchim has discovered the very important truth that the history of the war is not and never will be written from our point of view. The suspicion that this applies to wars in the past also has been much increased by living through four years almost entirely composed of what journalists call 'historic days'. No one who has taken stock of his own impressions since 4 August 1914, can possibly believe that history as it is written closely resembles history as it is lived; but as we are for the most part quiescent, and, if sceptical ourselves, content to believe that the rest of mankind believes, we have no right to complain if we are fobbed off once more with historians' histories. Less sluggish or less cynical, Mr Metchim here records the history of the war as it appeared to a gentleman living in South London so far as the body is concerned, but populating the whole of England spiritually, constituting, in fact, that anonymous monster the Man in the Street. He is not an individual himself, nor is the anonymous 'you' who merges into the gentleman in South London an individual; both together compose a vast, featureless, almost shapeless jelly of human stuff taking the reflection of the things that individuals do, and occasionally wobbling this way or that as some instinct of hate, revenge, or admiration bubbles up beneath it.

They, the individuals, the generals, the statesmen, the people with names, proclaim war.

How and why, date, &c., will be found in any reliable history[2] ... You felt frightfully strawlike about that time[3] ... You bolted each edition of your paper red-hot as it came out[4] ... You saw ⟨the Russians⟩ yourself pass through London[5] ...

You read several versions of The Truth about Neuve Chapelle, and Real Facts about Neuve Chapelle, and heard many personal tales against people in high positions, and you cursed the Government.[6]

So it goes on. The individuals do the thing, and you in a muddled way reflect what they do in blurred pictures half obliterating each other; little particles of you get somehow broken off and turned into soldiers and sent to France, to reflect rather different things out there, while you, in your vast quivering bulk, remain at home. Soon your mind, if one may distinguish one part of the jelly from another, has had certain inscriptions scored upon it so repeatedly that it believes that it has originated them; and you begin to have violent opinions of your own, which are reinforced by those varieties of you, Jones, Livermore and Algernon Shaw, so that there is a very marked sameness of opinion throughout the jelly. There is a little latitude allowed upon certain points, as, for example, 'the curious incident of the Angels of Mons . . . Jones said that probably wreaths of smoke had been mistaken for Angels; Shaw said that the British soldier was not a fanciful man, and would be far more likely to mistake Angels for wreaths of smoke. You were prepared to open your mind on the matter'.[7] But to have opinions is not your business; for four years and more you are nothing but a vast receptacle for the rumours of other people's opinions and deeds. There has been a great naval battle in the North Sea; they have won; we have won – so at least a friend of somebody's cook says. Your conviction that nothing is ever going to touch you is profound; it is obviously not in the nature of things that you should be touched. But the quality that distinguishes you from your French or Italian counterpart is your humour; all your feelings come out wearing the same livery. The humour of death is much the same as the humour of the allotment garden. But by this time we are analysing you with admiration, and therefore you are not us; and therefore the history, is, as it is always fated to be, your history, not ours.

1 – A review in the TLS, 9 January 1919, (Kp C139) of Our Own History of the War. From a South London View (Arthur G. Stockwell, 1918) by D. Bridgman Metchim.
2 – Metchim, p. 5.
3 – Ibid., p. 6.
4 – Ibid., p. 10.
5 – Ibid., p. 11, adapted.
6 – Ibid., p. 17.
7 – Ibid., pp. 14–15.

Small Talk About Meredith

The limitations which Mr Ellis has imposed upon himself are such that his work can neither be accepted as the final biography of Meredith, nor again as a study possessing the qualities of a work of art. His aim has been to preserve certain facts, about Meredith's early life in particular, which are known to him from his relationship to the poet, and to prove how largely the characters and situations of the novels were drawn from living people and actual events. His critical remarks are sparing, and his narrative is often shrunk to 'biographical links' connecting quotations from all sorts of sources, including a certain number of letters here published for the first time.

A book is thus produced which may be said to be the prelude or pre-natal state of a book rather than a book in being. In one way or another, however, it brings together some facts that have not before been made public or stated with such authority, and has an interest for people who wish to know more about an author than the author himself chose to tell them. To discuss the ethics or the necessity of such publications is none of our business. If it is desirable to know what was the exact social standing of Meredith's father, why his marriage with Peacock's daughter turned out unhappily, what caused his estrangement from his son Arthur, what led him to 'pillory his own relations'[2] in *Evan Harrington* and elsewhere, together with facts of a less intimate nature about the position of his lodgings and the aspect of the various rooms in which he slept, ate and wrote, then Mr Ellis is a guide at once authentic and unobtrusive. In justice to him it must be said that, considering the delicate nature of the office he has assumed, we do not often feel ourselves in the position of listeners at a keyhole. If Meredith were to open the door he would find us for the most part devoutly examining the boots and umbrellas in the hall. Our deductions from these objects would probably provide him with some merriment. For the truth is that, though Mr Ellis makes some damaging statements and the book produces as a whole a disparaging impression, it is necessarily an impression and by no means a conviction. Not only is the evidence slight, but the use made of it in interpreting Meredith's character will differ according to the temperament of the reader and the opportunities he may have had for knowing Meredith in the flesh, or seeing him through the eyes of those intimate with him. For example, it is stated that

Meredith refused the request of his first wife to visit her when she lay dying. Mr Ellis, as he has every right to do, puts his own interpretation upon this. 'He did not go; he had that horror of illness and the circumstances of death which is generally found in a man of imaginative temperament; that is the only excuse that can be offered in mitigation of censure.'[3] Having no further evidence to go upon, but having read *Modern Love*, we could neither agree in the censure nor infer from this fact, or any other adduced in the book, that Meredith was a bitter, hard, implacable man, 'who never forgave what had offended him'.[4] We have in mind, it is true, a very different verdict, passed by those who knew his faults but thought them more than expiated by the depth and passion of the feeling which underlay them. To his friends, we have reason to know, he was a man to be loved, not merely a writer to be admired.[5]

But as to such matters as these Meredith took care that the public should have no evidence to make up their minds upon. Even when, as in the case of his parentage, we have evidence in plenty and know for a certainty that he was born in Portsmouth, the son of a tailor, it is still extremely difficult to decide the chief question of interest – why it was that he was so anxious to conceal the facts. Was it that he was ashamed of them, in which case we must convict him of snobbishness; or that his childhood was unhappy, in which case we must decide where to lay the blame; or, conceivably, that his sense of romance was gratified by the mystery and he was not so eager as Mr Ellis thinks he should have been to correct the rumours of his royal or aristocratic parentage? That Meredith harboured 'a petty and long-brooded animus against his relatives'[6] and gave vent to it in the portraits of Mr and Mrs Strike in *Evan Harrington*, is supported by a suggestion, which is no more than a suggestion, to the effect that Meredith took his uncle's advice in investing some money, and lost it. When Mr Ellis infers that this may have 'brought down upon the uncle his nephew's implacable resentment'[7] and led him after the lapse of many years to make free with the reputation of the Royal Marines in *The Egoist*, the impartial reader will feel that more light has been thrown upon the loyalty of Mr Ellis than upon the disposition of George Meredith.

But these approaches to the keyhole are few, and what we hear is easily transformed according to our prejudices. More substantial and less disputable is the evidence which Mr Ellis supplies that Meredith was no exception, as we were inclined to think him, to the rule that great novelists take their characters from life. Not only characters and places, but even actual incidents and names were introduced, his method being to 'blend the actual traits and facts and names with the entirely imaginary doings of his characters'.[8] Thus a little detective ingenuity shows that Blackburn Tuckham in *Beauchamp's Career* is a portrait of Sir William Hardman, who came from the Bury and Blackburn district of Lancashire and was called Tuck for a nickname. In the same way the Romfreys in that novel derive their characteristics and some of their actions from the Berkeley family,[9] and the list of similar correspondences in each of the novels is long and striking. That Tolstoy employed the method is clear enough; we can guess that it was Jane Austen's;[10] but that Meredith whose characters seem compact of star and sunshine, heroic of stature and inspired of speech, helped himself thus largely from the actual is a little surprising, and suggests that we have only to turn back the pages of history to find Hamlet and Falstaff in the flesh. All depends, of course, upon what you do with your handful of fact. When Meredith was told that George Eliot did not take her characters from life, he replied emphatically, 'Oh I do; but,' he added, 'never till I know them by heart.'[11] No doubt Meredith's heart was much in communication with his brain; but whatever the combination, the absence of any mean, spiteful, or ugly realism in his work is very notable. One might maintain that in his later books he went to the opposite extreme and looked upon life too little and made his men and women too frequently masks for his own face. In support of this view there is among the scraps of all kinds swept up by Mr Ellis an interesting statement by Mr Shaw to the effect that 'owing to leading the literary life in the Surrey hills,' Meredith became 'a walking anachronism' (*'Diana of the Crossways* is fifty years behind *Our Mutual Friend'*), so that Mr Shaw and many others can read 'nothing of his except the poems and *Shagpat'*.[12] But as this can be matched by the equally definite assertion by Stevenson[13] that Meredith, at any rate, is among the immortals, the reader who wishes to make up his mind is constrained to do so for himself.

And that, perhaps, is not the least merit of such a book as this. It shows us the wrong side of the carpet and, fascinating though the wrong side of things always is, it is also a little crude, and ultimately breeds a keener desire than we were conscious of before to look upon the right side. All these half-heard words and disconnected fragments, with their suggestion of Meredith talking somewhere behind a curtain, drive us to the true source of Meredith, which is his writing; for, like all great imaginative writers, he reveals himself there with a completeness and subtlety, for good and for bad, which transcend all the facts that we may be told

7

about him. Nobody can have the sense of *Diana* and *The Egoist* fresh upon him without feeling convinced that he is the greatest authority upon Meredith in existence. In addition to this, there must be scores of people now alive who combine with their reading of Meredith a memory of his actual voice and presence which, too, acts curiously upon the written word. His manner of speaking, it has often been noted, much resembled his manner of writing, and gave currency to the notion that a marked style is always founded upon a marked speech. The high booming voice addressing a silent and invisible audience could be heard beyond the door. There was not, at least towards the end of his life, much trace of the colloquial, or any possibility, should there have been the desire, for give and take. The pitch was too high and the pace too swift for interruption. People who wish great men to be simple were, it is said, frequently annoyed by what they called his habit of talking for effect. Considering how amply their needs are catered for elsewhere, the demand seems a little exacting; and Meredith certainly did nothing to gratify it. He was in no way simple. His talk passed from metaphor to metaphor, built phrase upon phrase, derided, denounced, and extolled with a vigour and gusto which made it appear that, if such brilliance were not natural, it was at any rate extremely enjoyable to himself. At the same time, granting that great men in their old age tend to be a trifle spectacular, his claim that he read character from the slightest hints and constantly observed it, was shown to be true by tokens difficult to describe, but impossible to mistake. His manner might be artificial, but there was nothing frigid about it: everything was alert, and secretly, one guessed, upon the look out. If this vitality and press of ideas, this intense intellectual activity and the sometimes fantastic shapes which it took, were so singular as to rouse suspicion, it can be recorded that, after leaving Meredith's presence, the whole world seemed to have fallen under a ban of silence and stupidity. The people in the train looked only half alive; their talk was as primitive as the talk of sheep. Nevertheless Meredith did not talk incessantly. He stopped quite suddenly, as if something had struck him. His mind seemed to pass into another region. He appeared a little relieved that his visitors must catch their train. Waving an affectionate, but already slightly absent-minded farewell, he turned directly to a consideration of his thought, which he seemed to pursue with the greatest intensity pacing slowly in front of his house alone.

1–A review in the *TLS*, 13 February 1919, (Kp C140) of *George Meredith* [1828–

1909]: *His Life and Friends in Relation to his Work* . . . with Forty-One Illustrations (Grant Richards Ltd., 1919) by S. M. Ellis, a grandson of Meredith's aunt, Catherine Matilda Ellis, *née* Meredith.

VW wrote in her diary on Wednesday, 22 January 1919: 'Two days more were spent in bed, & today counts as my first of complete health. I even wrote a sentence of alterations and additions this morning [to *Night and Day*]. I have a book on Meredith to do for the Times, & we walked this afternoon, so I am back again nearly in my old position.' She again alluded to her article, and implicitly her health, in writing to Katherine Cox on 5 February 1919: 'I should have written to you before, but being limited to one hour's writing a day, and having to use that to polish off an old gentleman whose life I've promised for the Times, I put off good Bruin Cox.' (*II VW Letters*, no. 1016.)

See also 'Memories of Meredith' below; 'On Re-reading Meredith', *II VW Essays*; and 'The Novels of George Meredith', *V VW Essays* and *CR2*.

2 – Ellis, ch. ix, p. 214. Among Meredith's pilloried relations was the author's grandmother, she and her husband being the originals for Major and Mrs Strike in *Evan Harrington* (1860–1). Meredith's father, Augustus Urmston Meredith (1797–1876), originally destined for a medical career, had been compelled by his father's premature death to abandon his studies and take over the family tailors and naval outfitters in Portsmouth. He was a Freemason, dined out with his customers, especially the higher ranking naval officers, kept horses and followed the hunt, and, according to the *DNB*, 'talked like Sidney Smith'.

Meredith had married Mary Ellen, *quondam* Nicolls (d. 1861), daughter of the novelist Thomas Love Peacock (1785–1866), in 1849. Their unhappy marriage, by which they had a son, Arthur Gryffydh Meredith (1853–90), forms the background to Meredith's famous tragic poem *Modern Love* (1862). Meredith married his second wife Marie, *née* Vulliamy (d. 1885), in 1864.

3 – This quotation remains untraced. It does not occur in Ellis.

4 – Ellis, ch. iii, p. 69.

5 – Meredith was a friend of VW's parents. On one occasion at least he read his poetry to Julia Stephen and some of her guests in the garden at Talland House, St Ives; he would also accompany Leslie Stephen's 'Sunday Tramps' on their treks through the English countryside. Leslie Stephen was the model for Vernon Whitford in Meredith's novel *The Egoist* (1879); their relationship is described in Ellis, ch. xii, pp. 263–6.

VW was later to recall 'the roll and roar of Meredith's voice; pointing to a flower and saying "that damsel in the purple petticoat" . . .' and remembered his particular 'growl' (*MoB*, p. 158).

6 – Ellis, ch. vi, p. 134.

7 – *Ibid.*, p. 136.

8 – *Ibid.*, ch. 238, adapted.

9 – For Sir William Hardman and *Beauchamp's Career* (1875–6), *ibid.*, ch. xi, p. 240; and for the Berkeley family – in particular Grantley Berkeley, a younger son of the 5th Earl of Berkeley, and model for Everard Romfrey – *ibid.*, p. 239.

10 – L. N. Tolstoy (1828–1910); Jane Austen (1775–1817).

11 – The source of Meredith's remark has not been discovered. George Eliot (1819–80).

12–Ellis ch. ix, pp. 212–13, quoting a note to the author from G. Bernard Shaw (1856–1950), whose first novel, *Immaturity* (1928), written in 1878, Meredith had turned down on behalf of the publishers Chapman and Hall. Meredith's *Diana of the Crossways* was published in 1885, *Our Mutual Friend* by Charles Dickens (1812–70) in 1864–5. *The Shaving of Shagpat: An Arabian Entertainment* (1856).
13–For Robert Louis Stevenson (1850–94) on Meredith, Ellis, ch. xii, pp. 256–7, where he is said to be 'built for immortality'; and *ibid.*, p. 271.

'The Tunnel'

Although *The Tunnel* is the fourth book that Miss Richardson has written, she must still expect to find her reviewers paying a great deal of attention to her method.[2] It is a method that demands attention, as a door whose handle we wrench ineffectively calls our attention to the fact that it is locked. There is no slipping smoothly down the accustomed channels; the first chapters provide an amusing spectacle of hasty critics seeking them in vain. If this were the result of perversity, we should think Miss Richardson more courageous than wise; but being, as we believe, not wilful but natural, it represents a genuine conviction of the discrepancy between what she has to say and the form provided by tradition for her to say it in. She is one of the rare novelists who believe that the novel is so much alive that it actually grows. As she makes her advanced critic, Mr Wilson, remark: 'There will be books with all that cut out – him and her – all that sort of thing. The book of the future will be clear of all that.'[3] And Miriam Henderson herself reflects: 'but if books were written like that, sitting down and doing it cleverly and knowing just what you were doing and just how somebody else had done it, there was something wrong, some mannish cleverness that was only half right. To write books knowing all about style would be to become like a man.'[4] So 'him and her' are cut out, and with them goes the old deliberate business: the chapters that lead up and the chapters that lead down; the characters who are always characteristic; the scenes that are passionate and the scenes that are humorous; the elaborate construction of reality; the conception that shapes and surrounds the whole. All these things are cast away, and there is left, denuded, unsheltered, unbegun and unfinished, the consciousness of Miriam Henderson, the small sensitive lump of matter, half transparent and half opaque, which endlessly reflects and distorts the variegated process, and is, we are bidden to believe, the source beneath the surface, the very oyster within the shell.

The critic is thus absolved from the necessity of picking out the themes of the story. The reader is not provided with a story; he is invited to embed himself in Miriam Henderson's consciousness, to register one after another, and one on top of another, words, cries, shouts, notes of a violin, fragments of lectures, to follow these impressions as they flicker through Miriam's mind, waking incongruously other thoughts, and plaiting incessantly the many-coloured and innumerable threads of life. But a quotation is better than description.

She was surprised now at her familiarity with the details of the room . . . that idea of visiting places in dreams. It was something more than that. . . . all the real part of your life has a real dream in it; some of the real dream part of you coming true. You know in advance when you are really following your life. These things are familiar because reality is here. Coming events cast *light*. It is like dropping everything and walking backward to something you know is there. However far you go out you come back. . . . I am back now where I was before I began trying to do things like other people. I left home to get here. None of those things can touch me here. They are mine . . .[5]

Here we are thinking, word by word, as Miriam thinks. The method, if triumphant, should make us feel ourselves seated at the centre of another mind, and, according to the artistic gift of the writer, we should perceive in the helter-skelter of flying fragments some unity, significance, or design. That Miss Richardson gets so far as to achieve a sense of reality far greater than that produced by the ordinary means is undoubted. But, then, which reality is it, the superficial or the profound? We have to consider the quality of Miriam Henderson's consciousness, and the extent to which Miss Richardson is able to reveal it. We have to decide whether the flying helter-skelter resolves itself by degrees into a perceptible whole. When we are in a position to make up our minds we cannot deny a slight sense of disappointment. Having sacrificed not merely 'hims and hers', but so many seductive graces of wit and style for the prospect of some new revelation or greater intensity, we still find ourselves distressingly near the surface. Things look much the same as ever. It is certainly a very vivid surface. The consciousness of Miriam takes the reflection of a dentist's room to perfection. Her senses of touch, sight and hearing are all excessively acute. But sensations, impressions, ideas and emotions glance off her, unrelated and unquestioned, without shedding quite as much light as we had hoped into the hidden depths. We find ourselves in the dentist's room, in the street, in the lodging-house bedroom frequently and convincingly; but never, or only for a tantalising second, in the reality which underlies these appearances. In particular, the figures of other people on whom Miriam casts her capricious light are vivid enough, but their sayings and doings never reach that degree of significance which we, perhaps unreasonably, expect. The old method seems sometimes the more profound and economical of the two. But it must be admitted that we are exacting. We want to be rid of realism, to penetrate without its help into the regions beneath it, and further require that Miss Richardson shall fashion this new material into something which has the shapeliness of the old accepted forms. We are asking too much; but the extent of our asking proves that *The Tunnel* is better in its failure than most books in their success.

1–A review in the *TLS*, 13 February 1919, (Kp C141)of *The Tunnel* (Duckworth & Co., 1919) by Dorothy Richardson (1873–1957), author of the twelve-volume novel sequence, *Pilgrimage* (1915–38), the first in which, *Pointed Roofs,* had appeared some six months after VW's *The Voyage Out*, also published by Duckworth's.

About a month later, on Saturday, 22 March 1919, VW recorded in her diary a meeting with Katherine Mansfield: 'At once she flung down her pen & plunged, as if we'd been parted for 10 minutes, into the question of Dorothy Richardson; & so on with the greatest freedom & animation on both sides until I had to catch my train.'

But by the autumn, VW found herself irritated with Mansfield because of her review of *Night and Day* (*N&A*, 26 November 1919). Indeed, it was this review and the literary spite she considered lay behind it, which prompted VW to decline to review Dorothy Richardson's next novel, *Interim*, for the *TLS*: 'The truth is that when I looked at it, I felt myself looking for faults; hoping for them. And they would have bent my pen, I know. There must be an instinct of self-preservation at work. If she's good then I'm not.' VW also declined an invitation from H. W. Massingham to review Richardson's *Deadlock* (1921) for the *Nation* (*II VW Diary*, 21 February 1921). She did, however, review its sequel, *Revolving Lights*, when it appeared in 1923. See 'Romance and the Heart' below. Reprinted: *CW*.

2–For which Richardson preferred the term 'interior monologue', rather than 'stream of consciousness'.

3–Richardson, ch. vi, pt 5, p. 118.

4–*Ibid.*, pt 10, p. 132, which has: 'To write books, knowing'.

5–*Ibid.*, ch. i, pt 2, pp. 3–4; the ellipses are Richardson's.

Lady Ritchie

The death of Lady Ritchie will lead many people to ask themselves what she has written, or at least which of her books they have read; for she was never, or perhaps only as Miss Thackeray for a few years in the 'sixties and 'seventies of the last century, a popular writer. And, unless we are mistaken, they will find themselves, on taking down *The Story of Elizabeth* or *Old Kensington*,[2] faced with one of those curious problems which are more fruitful and more interesting than the questions which admit of only one answer. The first impression of such a reader will be one of surprise, and then, as he reads on, one of growing perplexity. How is it possible, he will ask, that a writer capable of such wit, such fantasy, marked by such a distinct and delightful personality, is not at least as famous as Mrs Gaskell, or as popular as Anthony Trollope?[3] How has she escaped notice all these years? And by what incredible oversight have we allowed passages which can only be matched in the classics of English fiction to be so hidden beneath the modern flood that the sight of them surprises like the flash of a jewel in a dust heap? What are the faults that have neutralised – if they have neutralised – this astonishing bounty of nature?

Some of the reasons at any rate for this neglect are not far to seek, and are to be ascribed more to the fault of the public than to the fault of the writer. Lady Ritchie was incapable of much that appears necessary to ensure popularity. She wrote neither for the busy man who wants to be diverted, nor for the earnest who wishes to be instructed; she offered neither sensation nor impropriety, and her beauty and distinction of manner were as unfailing as they were natural. Such characteristics are not those that appeal to a large public; and, indeed her gifts and her failings were so curiously and so provokingly combined that, while none of her novels can be called a masterpiece, each one is indisputably the work of a writer of genius. But the test of the masterpiece is not, after all, the only test. We can also ask ourselves whether a novelist has created a world which, with all its limitations, is still a habitable place, and a place which but for him would never have come into existence. Now Lady Ritchie's novels and recollections, although it is only honest to admit that they have their lapses, their unbridged abysses and their tracts of obscurity, offer us a world unlike any other when we are setting out upon one of our voyages of the imagination. We doubt whether since the death of George Eliot in 1880[4] the same can be said of the work of any other Englishwoman. It is not only still possible to read with enjoyment *The Story of Elizabeth*, *The Village on the Cliff*, and *Old Kensington*, but as we read them we have the sense that there is nothing quite like them in existence. When we remember that they were published in 1866, 1865, and 1873[5] respectively, we may feel certain that they owe their survival to some real, and to some extremely rare, magic of their own.

We should ascribe it largely to their absolute individuality. Some writers, like Charlotte Brontë, triumph by means of one overwhelming gift; others, like George Borrow,[6] are so queerly adjusted to the world that their vision reveals a new aspect of things; but Lady Ritchie's genius belonged to neither of these classes. It would be difficult to quote any scene in her books as one of surpassing power, or to claim that the reading of her writing has influenced our view of life one way or the other. On the other hand she possessed indisputably what seems to be as rare a gift as any – the gift of an entirely personal vision of life, of which her books are the more or less complete embodiment. She had her own sense of character, of conduct, of what amused her, of what delighted her eye, of trees and flowers and the beauty of the seasons. She was completely and transparently faithful to her vision. In other words she was a true artist; and when once we have said that of any writer we have to draw back a little and look at his work as a whole, with the understanding that whether great art or lesser art it is a thing unique of its kind.

With every excuse for taking shelter behind the great shield of tradition inherited from her father, nothing impresses one more in Lady Ritchie's work than the certainty that every stroke proceeded directly from her own hand; a more natural gift than hers never existed. It came to her directly, and owed nothing to discipline or to the painstaking study of other writers. Not many novelists can have assumed as early as she did complete command not only of their own method, but of their own language. *The Story of Elizabeth*, written in early youth, is as fluent, easy and composed in style as the work of one who has been framing sentences and casting scenes for a lifetime. This early maturity was the result of a great natural gift growing up with all the most polished tools at command in an atmosphere forbidding any but the most sensitive right use of them. Thus endowed, and thus wisely cherished, she rested we will not say indolently, but frankly and simply in her gift. She trusted to her instinct and her instinct served her well. Young writers might do worse than go to Lady Ritchie's pages for an example of the power of an apparently simple and yet inevitably right sense of the use of language. There is no premeditation, no effort at profundity; her prose appears to swim and float through the air rather than to march firmly with its feet set upon the ground. But every sentence is formed; they cohere together; and invariably at the end of a chapter or paragraph there is a sense that the melody has found its way through one variation and another to its natural close. The impression, it may be of the slightest, has been conveyed to us; the scene, it may be of the most transient, lives with the breath of life. She has, in fact, done exquisitely and exactly what she set out to do.

However this was achieved, and her instinct after all was a highly cultivated instinct, no one can read *Old Kensington* or *The Story of Elizabeth* without being aware of a certain spaciousness and composure of manner which are oddly unlike the style of the present time. The style, of course, corresponds to something in the point of view. Her heroes and heroines live in a world of their own, which is not quite our world, but a rather simpler and more dignified place. They do not analyse themselves very much, nor do they complicate their lot by taking upon them the burden of public right and wrong. They are blissfully unconscious even of themselves. Much that a modern writer would dissect into detail is presented to us in the mass. One might suppose that the process of building up such a character as Dolly Vanborough in *Old Kensington* was a simple one calling only for a few strokes of the brush in comparison with the process by which some of our complex young women are now constructed. And yet Dolly Vanborough lives, and the others for the most part merely serve to tell the time of day like efficient little clocks whose machinery will soon be out of order. Like all true creations, Dolly Vanborough and Elly Gilmour, while they pay homage to the conventions of their time have within them capacities for feelings which are never called forth by the story. We could fancy ourselves at ease today with one of these honest, arch, rather reserved young ladies in spite of the fact that she wears a crinoline and has no sort of desire for a vote. Against all probability, indeed, the thing we should find strange in them is not their sentimentality or their extravagance of feeling, but rather their slight hardness of heart, their determination to keep always well within the bounds of common sense.

Here, indeed, lay one of the paradoxes and fascinations of Lady Ritchie's art. With all her power of creating an atmosphere of tremulous shadows and opal tinted lights, with all her delight in the idyllic and the rapturous, the shapes of things are quite hard underneath and have,

indeed, some surprisingly sharp edges. It would be as superficial to sum
her up as a sentimentalist as it was to call her father a cynic. In her case
the sentiment is more hopefully and openly expressed, but her sight is
singularly clear; the shrewd, witty judgement of a woman of the world
smiles constantly upon her own rosy prospects. It is notable that she had
neither heroes nor heroines in the accepted sense of those terms; her hero
is generally a clumsy, ineffective young man who spends too much and
fails to pass his examinations; and the heroine, even the first born of all,
has a thousand follies of a natural human kind. Who, after all, had a
greater delight than Lady Ritchie in the delineation of a fool – a delight
naturally without a trace of cruelty? We need only recall the inimitable
Mrs Palmer, whose mother had been an Alderville, 'and the Aldervilles
are all young and beautiful, helpless, stout, and elegantly dressed'.[7] As
an example of her vein of humour, here is a little scene from *Old
Kensington*:

'Hulloh!' shouted Sir Thomas, as he drove out at the park-gates. 'Look there,
Anley! he is draining Medmere, and there is a new window to the schools. By jove!'
'Foolish young man!' said Mr Anley, 'wasting his substance, draining cottages,
and lighting school rooms!' and he looked out with some interest.
'Then, Uncle Jonah, you are foolish yourself,' said Bell.
'Are you turned philanthropist, Uncle Jonah?' said Mrs Boswarrick. 'I wish
someone would take me and Alfred up. What have you been doing?'
'I make it a rule never to do anything at the time that can be put off till the
morrow,' said Mr Anley apologetically. 'My cottages were tumbling down, my dear,
so I was obliged to prop them up.'
'He bought them from papa,' said Bell. 'I can't think why.'
'It is all very well for bachelors like you and Raban to amuse yourselves with
rebuilding,' said Sir Thomas, joining in from his box in an aggravated tone; 'if you
were a married man, Anley, with a wife and daughters and milliners' bills, you would
see how much was left at the end of the year for improvements.'
'To hear the talk, one oughtn't to exist at all,' says Mrs Boswarrick, with a laugh.[8]

Or if we want to confute a charge of undue sentimentality we can
point to characters like Robert Henley and Rhoda, into whose shallow
depths and twisted motives Lady Ritchie's art strikes like a beam of the
sun.
But many fine talents have come to grief over the novel, which
demands precisely those qualities of concentration and logical construction in which Lady Ritchie was most naturally or wilfully deficient. We
could guess, if we had not good authority for knowing, that in composing her novels 'she wrote fragments as thoughts struck her and pinned
them (with literal not metaphor pins) at parts of her manuscript till it

became a chaotic jumble maddening to the printers'.[9] As Leslie Stephen, one of her warmest admirers, wrote of her –

She showed more perception and humour, more delicate and tender and beautiful emotion, than would have made the fortune of a dozen novelists, had she had her faculties more in hand. Had she, for example, had any share of Miss Austen's gift for clearness, proportion, and neatness, her books would have been much better, as incomparably more successful.[10]

It is true the string does not always unite the pearls; but the pearls are there, in tantalising abundance – descriptions, sketches of character, wise and profound sayings, beyond the reach of any but a few modern writers, and well able to stand the ordeal of printing together in some book of selections.

But the qualities which militated against her success as a novelist did not stand in her way in another branch of literature in which she excelled. The lack of ambition, the childlike candour of mind which had so much rather praise and exalt than weigh and ponder made her singularly happy in her task, or pleasure, of recording the great and small figures of her own past. Here the whimsical and capricious genius has its scope unfettered and exquisitely inspired. We should be inclined to put her at the head of all modern artists in this manner and to claim for her indeed, that she invented an art of her own. For her method is quite unlike the ordinary method. There is no analysis, no criticism, and few good stories – or the stories only become good in the telling. But her skill in suggesting the mood, the spirit, the look of places and people defies any attempt to explain it. How, we ask, from such apparently slight materials are such vivid impressions created? Here is Charlotte Brontë:

My father, who had been walking up and down the room, goes out into the hall to meet his guests; then, after a moment's delay, the door opens wide, and the two gentlemen come in leading a tiny, delicate, serious, little lady, pale, with fair straight hair and steady eyes. She may be a little over thirty; she is dressed in a little *barège* dress with a pattern of faint green moss. She enters in mittens, in silence, in seriousness; our hearts are beating with wild excitement.[11]

Trelawny:

Not very long afterwards came a different visitor, still belonging to that same company of people. I had thrown open the dining-room door and come in looking for something, and then I stopped short, for the room was not empty. A striking and somewhat alarming-looking person stood alone by the fireplace with folded arms; a dark impressive looking man, not tall, but broad and brown and weather beaten, gazing with a sort of scowl at his own reflection in the glass. As I entered he turned slowly and looked at me over his shoulder. This was Trelawny, who had come to see my father. He frowned, walked deliberately and slowly from the room, and I saw him no more.[12]

George Sand:

She was a stout middle-aged woman, dressed in a stiff watered-silk dress, with a huge cameo, such as people then wore, at her throat. Her black shiny hair shone like polished ebony, she had a heavy red face, marked brows, great dark eyes; there was something – how shall I say it? – rather fierce, defiant, and set in her appearance, powerful, sulky; she frightened one a little. 'That is George Sand,' said Mrs Sartoris, bending her head and making a friendly sign to the lady with her eye-glasses. The figure also bent its head, but I don't remember any smile or change of that fixed expression.[13]

We feel that we have been in the same room with the people she describes. Very likely the great man has said nothing memorable, perhaps he has not even spoken: occasionally her memory is not of seeing him but of missing him: never mind – there was an ink-pot, perhaps a chair, he stood in this way, he held his hat just so, and miraculously and indubitably there he is before our eyes. Again and again it has happened to us to trace down our conception of one of the great figures of the past not to the stout official biography consecrated to him, but to some little hint or fact or fancy dropped lightly by Lady Ritchie in passing, as a bird alights on a branch, picks off the fruit and leaves the husk for another.

Something of the kind will perhaps be her destiny in the future. She will be the unacknowledged source of much that remains in men's minds about the Victorian age. She will be the transparent medium through which we behold the dead. We shall see them lit up by her tender and radiant glow. Above all and for ever she will be the companion and interpreter of her father, whose spirit she has made to walk among us not only because she wrote of him, but because even more wonderfully she lived in him. It would have pleased her well to claim no separate lot for herself, but to be merged in the greater light of his memory. Praise of her own work would have seemed to her unnecessary. It would have surprised her, but it would have pleased her, to realise with what a benediction many are today turning to the thought of her, thanking her not only for her work, but thanking her more profoundly for the bountiful and magnanimous nature, in which all tender and enchanting things seemed to grow – a garden, one might call it, where the airs blew sweetly and freely and the bird of the soul raised an unpremeditated song of thanksgiving for the life that it had found so good.

1–An obituary in the *TLS*, 6 March 1919, (Kp C142) of Anne Isabella Ritchie (1837–1919), who had died at her home, The Porch, Freshwater, Isle of Wight, on 26 February 1919. She was the elder daughter of W. M. Thackeray (1811–63). Her sister Harriet Marian ('Minnie') had been the first wife of Leslie Stephen (1832–1904). She was thus VW's aunt, 'touches' of whom (*II VW Letters*, no. 1103) are to be found in the character of Mrs Hilbery in VW's second novel *Night and Day*, published in October 1919. In 1877 she had married her second cousin (Sir) Richmond Ritchie (1854–1912); they had two children, Hester and William.

'And I've just done Aunt Anny, on a really liberal scale,' VW wrote in her diary on Wednesday, 5 March 1919. 'Yes, since I wrote last she has died, a week ago today to be precise, at Freshwater, & was buried up at Hampstead yesterday where 6 or 7 years ago we saw Richmond buried in a yellow fog. I suppose my feeling for her is half moonshine; or rather half reflected from other feelings. Father cared for her; she goes down the last, almost, of that old 19th Century Hyde Park Gate world. Unlike most old ladies she showed very little anxiety to see one; felt, I sometimes think, a little painfully at the sight of us, as if we'd gone far off, & recalled unhappiness, which she never liked to dwell on. Also, unlike most old Aunts she had the wits to feel how sharply we differed on current questions; & this, perhaps, gave her a sense, hardly existing with her usual circle, of age, obsoleteness, extinction. For myself, though, she need have had no anxieties on this head, since I admired her sincerely; but still the generations certainly look very different ways. Two or perhaps three years ago L. & I went to see her; found her much diminished in size, wearing a feather boa round her neck, and seated alone in a drawing room almost the copy, on a smaller scale, of the old drawing room; the same subdued pleasant air of the 18th Century & old portraits & old china. She had our tea waiting for us. Her manner was a little distant, & more than a little melancholy. I asked her about father, & she said how those young men laughed in a "loud melancholy way" & how their generation was a very happy one, but selfish; & how ours seemed to her fine but very terrible; but we hadn't any writers such as they had. "Some of them have just a touch of that quality; Bernard Shaw has; but only a touch. The pleasant thing was to know them all as ordinary people, not great men –" And then a story of Carlyle & father; Carlyle saying he'd as soon wash his face in a dirty puddle as write journalism. She put her hand down I remember, into a bag or box standing behind the fire, & said she had a novel, three-quarters written – but couldn't finish it – nor do I suppose it ever was finished. but I've said all I can say, dressing it up a trifle rosily, in the Times tomorrow. I have written to Hester, but how I doubt the sincerity of my own emotions!'

See the obituary by LW in *The Times*, 28 February 1919, reprinted in App. I. See also 'The Enchanted Organ' below and '*Blackstick Papers*', *I VW Essays*.

2–*The Story of Elizabeth* (1863); *Old Kensington* (1873).

3–Elizabeth Gaskell (1810–65); Anthony Trollope (1815–82).

4–George Eliot (1819–80).

5–The dates of publication for the first and last-named novels are, in fact, as given in n. 2 above and that of *The Village on the Cliff* 1867.

6–Charlotte Brontë (1816–55); George Borrow (1803–81).

7–Ritchie, *Old Kensington* (Smith, Elder & Co., 1873), ch. xxii, p. 191.

8–*Ibid.*, ch. xliii, pp. 392–3, which has: 'To hear them talk'.

9–Leslie Stephen's then unpublished *Mausoleum Book* (OUP, 1977), p. 14, which has: 'at odd parts of her MS.'.
10–*Ibid.*, which has: 'and incomparably more successful'.
11–Ritchie, *Chapters from Some Memoirs* (Macmillan & Co., 1894), ch. v, pp. 60–1, which has 'guests, and then'.
12–*Ibid.*, pp. 58–9. Edward John Trelawny (1792–1881), the friend of Shelley.
13–*Ibid.*, ch. xii, p. 211. George Sand (1804–76). Adelaide Sartoris, *née* Kemble (1814?–79), vocalist and author, sister of Fanny.

'Sylvia and Michael'

The feat that no reviewer of Mr Mackenzie's books can possibly attempt is to explain even in the most compressed form what happens. In *Sylvia and Michael* the reader must be content with the assurance that Sylvia Scarlett is, in the familiar phrase, 'still running'. We leave her, indeed seated upon the shore of a Greek island with her hand in the hand of Michael Fane: but figuratively speaking she is still running as hard as she can; and when the book is shut the eye of imagination sees her whisking over the skyline attended by the usual troupe of chorus girls and nondescript young men doing their best to keep up with her, but more and more hopelessly outdistanced by the speed of her legs and the astonishing volubility of her tongue. The number of volumes still to be run through we guess to be considerable. The race which ends in the Greek island begins in Petrograd and is continued under every condition of discomfort and danger, since not only is she periodically reduced to her last penny, but the European war is blazing and roaring all round her and never ceases to harry her and her companions much as a relentless mowing machine will drive all the small deer of a cornfield into the open.

The gifts which enable Mr Mackenzie to keep so large and various company in such incessant activity, at any rate of the legs, are not negligible, although whether they have anything to do with literature is an open question. They include, to begin with, an astonishing swiftness of eye, so that he has only to be in a room once in order to write a complete inventory of its furniture. And should the room be furnished not only with chairs and tables but with a large and queer assortment of men and women, he will with equal swiftness make an inventory of them too. He rattles off their little distinguishing peculiarities as if his fund were inexhaustible, and the out of the way nature of his discoveries stimulates the imagination to hold itself in readiness for a strange and delightful expedition. So, at an evening party, someone might whisper in your ear, 'That lady is Mère Gontran, and she keeps owls in a shed, and when her collie barks she thinks it is the voice of her dead husband.'[2] One looks at Mère Gontran with a access of interest, and before the interest has died out someone else is introduced, who has some different peculiarity or even little trick of the hand such as plaiting four necklaces in a rope until the string breaks and the green shells fall on the floor, and what can be more natur.l than that the dogs should start fighting in the street at that moment, until someone throws a stone which hits one of them on the hind leg, so that he runs off leaving a trail of blood upon the pavement? Meanwhile, what has become of Mère Gontran? She is no longer there: we may keep on repeating to ourselves, 'She keeps owls in a shed,' but the light of that illumination is not everlasting.

But, though we own to have tried, it would be difficult to burlesque the extreme swiftness with which Mr Mackenzie whisks his figures across the stage. For the sake of such vivacity one is ready to pardon a considerable degree of superficiality. But since Sylvia is not whisked across the stage and has developed a habit of soliloquy in the intervals of activity it is difficult to account for our failure to find her when we come to look for her. But the more she talks the less we see her. '"This Promethean morality that enchains the world and sets its bureaucratic eagle to gnaw the vitals of humanity," Sylvia cried, . . . "No, no it cannot be right to secure the many by debasing the few."'[3] That she says many smart things about war and religion and nationality is undeniable: but in the process of saying them she fades out of existence beyond the power of owl or necklace to revive her, and leaves us wondering why so clever a journalist should think it necessary to get himself up as a young woman. But what is it that this queer combination of movement and brilliancy, platitude and vacancy, reminds us of? Not in the least of Greek islands and besieged cities: but rather of an evening party where conversations are always being cut short, where people look queer in their finery, where great vivacity alternates with empty silences, and where it is the fate of some to be pinned in a corner and discoursed to eternally by a bore.

1–A review in the TLS, 20 March 1919, (Kp C143) of Sylvia & Michael. The Later Adventures of Sylvia Scarlett (Martin Secker, 1919) by Compton MacKenzie (1883–1972). See also 'The "Movie" Novel' – VW's review of The Early Life and Adventures of Sylvia Scarlett – in II VW Essays. Reprinted: CW.

2 – For Mère Gontran and the owls, MacKenzie, ch. ii, p. 41; and the speaking collie, p. 49.

3 – *Ibid.*, ch. v, p. 185.

'Within the Rim'

It would be easy to justify the suspicion which the sight of *Within the Rim* aroused, and to make it account for the tepid and formal respect with which we own to have approached the book. Essays about the war contributed to albums and books with a charitable object even by the most distinguished of writers bear for the most part such traces of perfunctory composition, such evidence of genius forcibly harnessed to the wagon of philanthropy and sullen and stubborn beneath the lash, that one is inclined for the sake of the writer to leave them unread.[2] But we should not have said this unless we intended immediately and completely to unsay it. The process of reading these essays was a process of recantation. It is possible that the composition of some of them was an act of duty, in the sense that the writing of a chapter of a novel was not an act of duty. But the duty was imposed upon Henry James not by the persuasions of a committee nor by the solicitations of friends, but by a power much more commanding and irresistible – a power so large and of such immense significance to him that he scarcely succeeds with all his range of expression in saying what it was or all that it meant to him. It was Belgium, it was France, it was above all England and the English tradition, it was everything that he had ever cared for of civilisation, beauty and art threatened with destruction and arrayed before his imagination in one figure of tragic appeal.

Perhaps no other elderly man existed in August 1914 so well qualified to feel imaginatively all that the outbreak of war meant as Henry James. For years he had been appreciating ever more and more finely what he calls 'the rare, the sole, the exquisite England':[3] he had relished her discriminatingly as only the alien, bred to different sounds and sights and circumstances, could relish others so distinct and so delightful in their distinctness. Knowing so well what she had given him, he was the more tenderly and scrupulously grateful to her for the very reason that she seemed to him to bestow her gifts half in ignorance of their value. Thus when the news came that England was in danger he wandered in the August sunshine half overwhelmed with the vastness of what had happened, reckoning up his debt, conscious to the verge of agony of the extent to which he had committed his own happiness to her, and analysing incessantly and acutely just what it all meant to the world and to him. At first, as he owned, he had 'an elderly dread of a waste of emotion ... my house of the spirit amid everything around me had become more and more the inhabited, adjusted, familiar home';[4] but before long he found himself

building additions and upper storeys, throwing out extensions and protrusions, indulging even, all recklessly, in gables and pinnacles and battlements – things that had presently transformed the unpretending place into I scarce know what to call it, a fortress of the faith, a palace of the soul, an extravagant, bristling, flag-flying structure which had quite as much to do with the air as with the earth.[5]

In a succession of images not to be torn from their context he paints the state of his mind confronted by one aspect after another of what appeared to him in so many diverse lights of glory and of tragedy. His gesture as of one shrinking from the sight of the distress, combined with an irresistible instinct of pity drawing him again and again to its presence, recalls to the present writer his reluctance to take a certain road in Rye because it led past the workhouse gates and forced to his notice the dismal line of tramps waiting for admittance. But in the case of the wounded and the fugitive his humanity forced him again and again to face the sight, and brought him the triumphant reward of finding that the beauty emerging from such conditions more than matched the squalor. '. . . their presence,' he wrote of the wounded soldier, 'is a blest renewal of faith.'[6]

A moralist perhaps might object that terms of beauty and ugliness are not the terms in which to speak of so vast a catastrophe, nor should a writer exhibit so keen a curiosity as to the tremors and vibrations of his own spirit in face of the universal calamity. Yet, of all books describing the sights of war and appealing for our pity, this largely personal account is the one that best shows the dimensions of the whole. It is not merely or even to any great extent that we have been stimulated intellectually by the genius of Henry James to analyse curious shades and subtleties; but rather that for the first and only time, so far as we are aware, someone has reached an eminence sufficiently high above the scene to give it its grouping and standing in the universal. Read, for instance, the scene of the arrival of the Belgian refugees by night at Rye, which we will not curtail and thus rob of its completeness.[7] It is precisely the same little scene of refugees hurrying by in silence save for the cry of a woman carrying her child, which, in its thousand varieties, a thousand pens have depicted during the past four years. They have done their best, and left us acknowledging their effort, but feeling it to be a kind of siege or battering ram laid to the emotions, which have obstinately refused to yield their fruits. That it is altogether otherwise with the scene painted for us [by] Henry James might perhaps be credited to his training as a novelist. But when, in his stately way, diminishing his stature not one whit and majestically rolling the tide of his prose over the most rocky of obstacles, he asks us for the gift of a motor-car, we cannot help feeling that if all philanthropies had such advocates our pockets would never be anything but empty. It is not that our emotions have been harassed by the sufferings of the individual case. That he can do upon occasion with beautiful effect. But what he does in this little book of less than a hundred and twenty pages is, so it seems to us, to present the best statement yet made of the largest point of view. He makes us understand what civilisation meant to him and should mean to us. For him it was a spirit that overflowed the material bounds of countries, but it is in France that he sees it most plainly personified:

... what happens to France happens to all that part of ourselves which we are most proud, and most finely advised, to enlarge and cultivate and consecrate ...[8] She is sole and single in this, that she takes charge of those of the interests of man which most dispose him to fraternize with himself, to pervade all his possibilities and to taste all his faculties, and in consequence to find and to make the earth a friendlier, an easier, and especially a more various sojourn.[9]

If all our counsellors, we cannot help exclaiming, had spoken with that voice!

1–A review in the TLS, 27 March 1919, (Kp C144) of Within the Rim and Other Essays 1914–15 (W. Collins Sons & Co. Ltd., 1918) by Henry James (1843–1916). See also 'The Letters of Henry James' and 'Henry James's Ghost Stories' below; and see 'Mr Henry James's Latest Novel', 'Portraits of Places', I VW Essays; and 'The Old Order', 'The Method of Henry James', II VW Essays. Reprinted: DoM, CE.
2–James's acknowledgements disclose that the title essay had been written in February 1915 'for Miss E. Asquith for a proposed album in aid of the Arts Fund'; it eventually appeared in the Fortnightly Review, August 1917. Of the remaining titles: 'Refugees in Chelsea' appeared in the TLS, 23 March 1916; 'The American Volunteer Motor-Ambulance Corps in France: A Letter to the Editor of an American Journal [unidentified]' was issued as a pamphlet in 1914; 'France' was published in The Book of France, ed. Winifred Stephens (1915); and 'The Long Wards' in The Book of the Homeless, ed. Edith Wharton (1916).
3–James, 'Within the Rim', p. 18.
4–Ibid., p. 19, which has: 'spirit, amid everything about me, had become.'

5 – *Ibid.*, p. 20. James's 'passionate ardour of patriotism' (*DNB*), at the catastrophe of the war had caused him to become, in 1915, a naturalised British subject.

6 – *Ibid.*, 'Refugees in Chelsea', p. 53: 'The strong young men ... mutilated, amputated, dismembered in penalty for their defence of their soil against the horde, and now engaged at Crosby Hall in the making of handloom socks, to whom I pay an occasional visit ... express so in their honest concentration under difficulties the actual and general value of their people that just to be in their presence is a blest renewal of faith.'

7 – *Ibid.*, pp. 57–9: 'It was in September, in a tiny Sussex town which I had not quitted since the outbreak of the war, and where the advent of our first handful of fugitives before the warning of Louvain and Aerschoot and Termonde and Dinant had just been announced. Our small hill-top city, covering the steep sides of the compact pedestal crowned by its great church, had reserved a refuge at its highest point; and we had waited all day, from occasional train to train, for the moment at which we should attest our hospitality. It came at last, but late in the evening, when a vague outside rumour called me to my doorstep, where the unforgettable impression at once assaulted me. Up the precipitous little street that led from the station, over the old grass-grown cobbles where vehicles rarely pass, came the panting procession of the homeless and their comforting, their almost clinging entertainers, who seemed to hurry them on as in a sort of overflow of expression of the fever of charity. It was swift and eager, in the autumn darkness and under the flare of a single lamp – with no vociferation and, but for a woman's voice, scarce a sound save the shuffle of mounting feet and the thick-drawn breath of emotion. The note I except, however, was that of a young mother carrying her small child and surrounded by those who bore her on and on, almost lifting her as they went together. The resonance through our immemorial old street of her sobbing and sobbing cry was the voice itself of history; it brought home to me more things than I could then quite take the measure of, and these just because it expressed for her not direct anguish, but the incredibility, as who should say, of honest assured protection. Months have elapsed, and from having been then one of a few hundred she is now one of scores and scores of thousands: yet her cry is still in my ears, whether to speak most of what she had lately or of what she actually felt; and it plays, to my own sense, as a great fitful, tragic light over the dark exposure of her people.'

8 – *Ibid.*, 'France', p. 89.

9 – *Ibid.*, p. 90, which continues: 'and the great thing is the amiability and the authority, intimately combined, with which she has induced us all to trust her on this ground.'

Dickens by a Disciple

Perhaps no one has suffered more than Dickens from the enthusiasm of his admirers, by which he has been made to appear not so much a great writer as an intolerable institution. People read Dickens who boast with truth that they have read nothing else. Others talk of him in the proprietary way that Yorkshiremen talk of Yorkshire. And on this account it is easy enough to believe that you have read Dickens without having opened him since childhood: you have not merely read him, but you have made up your mind that you do not want to read him again. So, from photographs and coloured postcards one has seen all one ever hopes to see of the Taj Mahal or the Bay of Naples. But, happily for the health of the soul, there exist country inns and wet Sundays; there exist on the solitary shelf of the single sitting room only Edna Lyall[2] and Charles Dickens. Faced with the alternative of counting the raindrops, people have been known to declare that they would rather demolish Dickens, and, proceeding sternly enough to do so, they have emerged at the end of four or five hours protesting that no one has ever read Dickens before. It can only be a question whether any other English novelist, save Scott,[3] has a right to be called Shakespearean. Like Shakespeare and like Scott, his faults are so colossal that, had he been guilty of them alone, one might have inferred the prodigious nature of his merits. The extravagance of a first acquaintance wears away; doubts and difficulties arise; the book marker stays wedged in the mass of *Nicholas Nickleby* for months at a time; the Brothers Cheeryble[4] prove almost insurmountable, and yet the certainty is none the less sure that somehow or other Dickens was a very great man.

Perhaps Mr Crotch is too much of an admirer to help us to interpret this somehow or other more exactly. He has remained rather in the first stage of astonishment when it is natural to speak of Dickens and Shakespeare in the same breath. But, if he is what is called a 'Dickensian', it is by no means true to say of him that he has read no one else. He has read widely in English literature, but he has read always, so it seems, to the glory of Charles Dickens. Great men appear to him either as the forerunners or the successors of his hero; and though this is undeniably true in one sense, it is apt to be false in another. Perhaps Mr Crotch does not exaggerate his hero's debt to the past; though, as is usual in these cases, the links by which Dickens is attached to Richardson and Fielding,[5] the Social Revolution and the battle of Waterloo, the female novelists and the Factory Acts, are of the most elastic description. But what are we to say when he claims that 'Thackeray was so much the creation of the older writer that, had the latter never come to maturity, it is, to say the least of it, doubtful whether *Vanity Fair* or *Esmond* would ever have been given us'?[6] As if it were not enough to make Dickens swallow Thackeray at one gulp, we are bidden to observe how much of

Mrs Gaskell, Kingsley, Wilkie Collins, Charles Reade, Bret Harte and Kipling is directly, though spiritually, the work of Dickens. We admit to have thought that Hawthorne[7] was protected both by the Atlantic and by a certain natural distinction of genius from the infection. But it is not so.

It would be a dull man indeed who did not discern the very spirit of the master in the romances of Nathaniel Hawthorne, with their fresh, almost childlike delight in the frank, unconscious charm of unspoilt natures ... Not less discernible is Hawthorne's indebtedness to him in that early sense of horror which comes upon us in the pages of both with a force all the more compelling because of its swift suddenness.[8]

After this example of the creative powers of Dickens we own to have felt some alarm lest it could be proved that his spirit not only crossed the Atlantic but somehow anticipated its appearance in the flesh. We become nervous whenever a new author is introduced lest he shall be shown to be only Dickens in disguise. Is this, then, the secret of Dickens to which Mr Crotch refers in his title? If everybody is, in a way, somebody else, would it not be simpler to call them all Charles Dickens and have done with it?

But it is easy to poke fun at enthusiasts, and the laugh after all remains with them. In his hunt up and down the centuries, in and out of social, philanthropic, and literary currents, Mr Crotch starts a great many hares which are well worth pursuing, whether we catch them or not. There is the fundamental question of morality. Dickens 'evinced an unique domestic purism undiscoverable anywhere except in England' and, according to Mr Crotch, indisputably to the advantage of his novels. And yet perhaps there is no single characteristic that so alienates the present generation from Dickens and Thackeray as their insistence upon this same 'domestic purism undiscoverable anywhere except in England'.[9] It is not only that by so doing they restrict their sphere: it is that their refusal to say things is, after all, equivalent to saying them rather emphatically. Again, there is the question of democracy and literature. The greatness of Dickens, according to Mr Crotch, lies in his 'quality of looking at life and of judging all institutions from the standpoint of the common man'.[10] On that account both he and Shakespeare are assured of immortality. But Shakespeare's democracy, we feel, was an extremely expansive society by no means limited to the common man. Nor can we be certain that the 'average, wholesome, human son of Adam'[11] appeared to Shakespeare more profound, elemental, and worthy of his study than Lear, who was probably a 'highbrow', and certainly a king. But it is not for the quality of his genius that one likens Dickens to Shakespeare, but for its spontaneity and abundance.

1 – A review in the TLS, 27 March 1919, (Kp C145) of *The Secret of Dickens* (Chapman and Hall, 1919) by W. Walter Crotch, author of several books about Charles Dickens (1812–70).
2 – Edna Lyall, pseudonym for Ada Ellen Bayly (1857–1903), novelist and ardent feminist, author of *Donovan* (1882), a work admired by Gladstone, *We Two* (1884) and *In the Golden Days* (1885).
3 – Sir Walter Scott (1771–1832).
4 – Ned and Charles Cheeryble, characters in *Nicholas Nickleby* (1838–9).
5 – Samuel Richardson (1689–1761); Henry Fielding (1707–54).
6 – Crotch, ch. v, p. 127, adapted. *Vanity Fair* (1847–8), *Esmond* (1852).
7 – Elizabeth Gaskell (1810–65); Charles Kingsley (1819–75); Wilkie Collins (1824–89); Charles Reade (1814–84); Francis Bret Harte (1836–1902); Rudyard Kipling (1865–1936); Nathaniel Hawthorne (1804–64).
8 – Crotch, ch. v, p. 131, which continues: '; and surely no other author knew better than Dickens himself how to show the corroding poison that fanaticism spreads through a nature sweet and lovable.'
9 – *Ibid.*, ch. i, p. 13.
10 – *Ibid.*, ch. vi, p. 152.
11 – *Ibid.*

Washington Irving

It would be strange to complain of an editor for the excellence of his introduction; yet to find that all one's own points have been made already, and some, to be honest, that had escaped one's notice, is to be tempted to sulk in silence. Mr van Doren has said, and said very well, all that there is to be said about Washington Irving. He has pointed out that

he did not find controversy pretty or reform amusing ... He was unfailingly humane, but he was not at all speculative ... He chose his themes because they pleased and amused him ... He would not have admitted that he owed anyone the duty to be stiffly realistic ... In the comfortable middle ground which he took he never suffered from the zeal which makes narrative formless and style cloudy and violent.[2]

We were about to remark that all his stories are really essays when we found that we had been frequently anticipated in that remark too.

It is only left us, therefore, to take up the position which Mr van Doren is denied by the accident of birth. We can state the English point of view. In his polite way Mr van Doren is evidently of opinion that the English influence upon his author was by no means to the good. When he wrote about English customs 'he wrote too often with his eye a little off the object and on the past'; except in 'The Stout Gentleman' he never 'entirely succeeded with a story which had its setting laid in England'.[3] Patriotism in literature is an insidious poison, but we cannot help thinking that *Bracebridge Hall* has a considerable charm independently of its tribute to our island merits. It is easy, of course, to guess how it strikes an American. Here is a native writer, promising to do credit to his country. He takes ship to England; he sees the ruins; he hears the nightingales; the voices of the Sirens were not more seductive.

Accustomed always to scenes where history was, in a manner, anticipation . . . there was something inexpressibly touching in the sight of enormous piles of architecture, grey with antiquity and sinking to decay . . .[4] I shall never forget the thrill of ecstasy with which I first saw the lark rise. . . . The first time that I heard the song of the nightingale I was intoxicated more by the delicious crowd of remembered associations than by the melody of its notes.[5]

Washington Irving is lost to America from that day forwards; and as others, more distinguished, have followed him in varying degrees of desertion, her case, were it not for Walt Whitman,[6] would be hard indeed. Yet the fields of America have, one supposes, their banks of violets, though Shakespeare never saw them; their woods contain at least one bird, the whip-poor-will, though its song never found a path through the sad heart of Ruth.[7] But why the lack of 'the delicious crowd' of associations should be so keenly felt by writers when the objects themselves exist is one of the puzzles of literature. On the face of it, no conditions could seem better fitted to stimulate and initiate; and yet, just for the lack of this soft tint of distance, memory, tradition, the buds are withered and the fountains frozen. To judge at least from the nature of the work they produce, it is for the sake of such amenities as these that American writers have turned, physically and spiritually, to England and outdone the English in the emblems of long-founded civilisation, in culture, urbanity, and slow-flowing melodious prose that slips ever so smoothly in the canals cut by the good English writers of the eighteenth century.

The pleasantness of the product is undeniable. For the first ten or even twenty minutes the gentle undulations of Washington Irving's tales, rippling with his sly sentimental humour, will enchant and even convert a reader from more modern predilections. But the great enemy is only held at bay: our dreams are pleasant, our waking sweet, but it cannot be denied that we have slept. As in conversation, so in literature, excessive politeness that holds everything at arm's length and allows no familiarity begins by conciliating and ends – wherever refuge is to be found. Irving's love of ruins 'grey with antiquity and sinking to decay', his obsession with the past, his passion for buried treasure, and his enthusiasm for ghosts are all ingredients in the sleeping-draught, though he sought them, we believe, in an instinctive and pathetic attempt to provide his native land with an atmosphere in which literature could be produced. He forces us to consider what our natural endowment of ruins and nightingales amounts to. It amounts, perhaps, to no more than a congenial sense that one is not speaking out into the raw air. There is no need to prove oneself literate, to convert others, or to bother too much about the quality of one's own style. Or are the nightingales and the ruins more profoundly ingrained in us than we know? However this may be, Washington Irving produced literature that is by no means to be despised. The episode of the stout gentleman is a first-rate specimen of the English essay; his tales are rich in passages of excellent humour and literary charm; but they compel us to repeat what everyone else has said already, that he never wrote a story in his life.

1–A review in the *TLS*, 3 April 1919, (Kp C146) of *Tales of Washington Irving* [1783–1859]. Selected and edited with an introduction by Carl van Doren.
2–Irving, intro., pp. xxx–xxxi, slightly adapted.
3–For both quotations, *ibid.*, p. xiv; 'The Stout Gentleman' is an essay in Irving's *Bracebridge Hall* (1822).
4–*Ibid.*, p. xiii, quoting Irving's intro. to *Bracebridge Hall*.
5–*Ibid.*, p. xiv.
6–Walt Whitman (1819–92).
7–The reference is to Keats's 'Ode to a Nightingale':

> 'Perhaps the self-same song that found a path
> Through the sad heart of Ruth, when, sick for home,
> She stood in tears amid the alien corn.'

Modern Novels

In making any survey, even the freest and loosest, of modern fiction it is difficult not to take it for granted that the modern practice of the art is somehow an improvement upon the old. With their simple tools and primitive materials, it might be said, Fielding did well and Jane Austen[2] even better, but compare their opportunities with ours! Their master-pieces certainly have a strange air of simplicity. And yet the analogy between literature and the process, to choose an example, of making bicycles scarcely holds good beyond the first glance. It is doubtful whether in the course of the centuries, though we have learnt much about making machines, we have learnt anything about making literature. We do not come to write better; all that we can be said to do is to keep moving, now a little in this direction, now in that, but with a circular tendency should the whole course of the track be viewed from a sufficiently lofty pinnacle. It need scarcely be said that we make no claim to stand even momentarily upon that vantage ground; we seem to see ourselves on the flat, in the crowd, half blind with dust, and looking back with a sort of envy at those happy warriors whose battle is won and whose achievements wear so serene an air of accomplishment that in our envy we can scarcely refrain from whispering that the prize was not so rare, nor the battle so fierce, as our own. Let the historian of literature decide. It is for him, too, to ascertain whether we are now at the beginning, or middle, or end, of a great period of prose fiction; all that we ourselves can know is that, whatever stage we have reached, we are still in the thick of the battle. This very sense of heights reached by others and unassailable by us, this envious belief that Fielding, Thackeray,[3] or Jane Austen were set an easier problem, however triumphantly they may have solved it, is a proof, not that we have improved upon them, still less that we have given up the game and left them the victors, but only that we still strive and press on.

Our quarrel, then, is not with the classics, and if we speak of quarrelling with Mr Wells, Mr Bennett and Mr Galsworthy[4] it is partly that by the mere fact of their existence in the flesh their work has a living, breathing, everyday imperfection which bids us take what liberties with it we choose. But it is also true that, while we thank them for a thousand gifts, we reserve our unconditional gratitude for Mr Hardy, for Mr Conrad, and in a much lesser degree for the Mr Hudson of *The Purple Land, Green Mansions,* and *Far Away and Long Ago.*[5] The former, differently and in different measures, have excited so many hopes and disappointed them so persistently that our gratitude largely takes the form of thanking them for having shown us what it is that we certainly could not do, but as certainly, perhaps, do not wish to do. No single phrase will sum up the charge or grievance which we have to bring against a mass of work so large in its volume and embodying so many qualities, both admirable and the reverse. If we tried to formulate our meaning in one word we should say that these three writers are materialists, and for that reason have disappointed us and left us with the feeling that the sooner English fiction turns its back upon them, as politely as may be, and marches, if only into the desert, the better for its soul. Of course, no single word reaches the centre of three separate targets. In the case of Mr Wells it falls notably wide of the mark. And yet even in his case it indicates to our thinking the fatal alloy in his genius, the great clod of clay that has got itself mixed up with the purity of his inspiration. But Mr Bennett is perhaps the worst culprit of the three, inasmuch as he is by far the best workman. He can make a book so well constructed and solid in its craftsmanship that it is difficult for the most exacting of critics to see through what chink or crevice decay can creep in. There is not so much as a draught between the frames of the windows, or a crack in the boards. And yet – if life should refuse to live there? That is a risk which the creator of *The Old Wives' Tale,* George Cannon, Edwin Clayhanger,[6] and hosts of other figures, may well claim to have surmounted. His characters live abundantly, even unexpectedly, but it still remains to ask how do they live, and what do they live for? More and more they seem to us, deserting even the well-built villa in the Five Towns, to spend their time in some softly padded first-class railway carriage, fitted with bells and buttons innumerable; and the destiny to which they travel so luxuriously becomes more and more unquestionably an eternity of bliss spent in the very best hotel in Brighton. It can scarcely be said of Mr Wells that he is a materialist in the sense that he takes too much delight in the solidity of his fabric. His mind is too generous in its sympathies to allow him to spend much time in making things shipshape and substantial. He is a materialist from sheer goodness of heart, taking upon his shoulders the work that ought to have been discharged by Government officials, and in the plethora of his ideas and facts scarcely having leisure to realise, or forgetting to think important, the crudity and coarseness of his human beings. Yet what more damaging criticism can there be both of his earth and of his Heaven than that they are to be inhabited here and hereafter by his Joans and Peters? Does not the inferiority of their natures tarnish whatever institutions and ideals may be provided for them by the generosity of their Creator? Nor, profoundly though we respect the integrity and humanity of Mr Galsworthy, shall we find what we seek in his pages.

We have to admit that we are exacting, and further, that we find it difficult to justify this, the essential thing, has moved off, or on, and refuses to be contained any longer in such ill-fitting vestments as we provide. Nevertheless we go on perseveringly, conscientiously, constructing our thirty-two chapters after a design which more and more ceases to resemble the vision in our minds. So much of the enormous labour of proving the solidity, the likeness to life, of the story is not merely labour thrown away but labour misplaced to the extent of obscuring and blotting out the light of the conception. The mediocrity of most novels seems to arise from a conviction on the part of the writer that unless his plot provides scenes of tragedy, comedy, and excitement, an air of probability so impeccable that if all his figures were to come to life they would find themselves dressed down to the last button in the fashion of the hour, he has failed in his duty to the public. If this, roughly as we have stated it, represents his vision, his mediocrity may be said to be natural rather than imposed; but as often as not we may suspect some moment of hesitation in which the question suggests itself whether life is like this after all? Is it not possible that the accent falls a little differently, that the moment of importance came before or after, that, if one were free and could set down what one chose, there would be no plot, little probability, and a vague general confusion in which the clear-cut features of the tragic, the comic, the passionate, and the lyrical were dissolved beyond the possibility of separate recognition? The mind, exposed to the ordinary course of life, receives upon its surface a myriad impressions – trivial, fantastic, evanescent, or engraved with the sharpness of steel. From all sides they come, an incessant shower of innumerable atoms, composing in their sum what we might venture to call life itself; and to figure further as the semi-transparent envelope, or luminous halo, surrounding us from the beginning of consciousness to the end. Is it not perhaps the chief task of the novelist to convey this incessantly varying spirit with whatever stress or sudden deviation it may display, and as little admixture of the alien and external as possible? We are not pleading merely for courage and sincerity; but suggesting that the proper stuff for fiction is a little other than custom would have us believe it.

In some such fashion as this do we seek to define the element which distinguishes the work of several young writers, among whom Mr James Joyce[7] is the most notable, from that of their predecessors. It attempts to come closer to life, and to preserve more sincerely and exactly what interests and moves them by discarding most of the conventions which are commonly observed by the novelists. Let us record the atoms as they fall upon the mind in the order in which they fall, let us trace the pattern, however disconnected and incoherent in appearance, which each sight or incident scores upon the consciousness. Let us not take it for granted that life exists more in what is commonly thought big than in what is commonly thought small. Any one who has read *The Portrait of the Artist as a Young Man* or what promises to be a far more interesting work, *Ulysses*, now appearing in the *Little Review,* will have hazarded some theory of this nature as to Mr Joyce's intention.[8] On our part it is hazarded rather than affirmed; but whatever the exact intention there can be no question but that it is of the utmost sincerity and that the result, difficult or unpleasant as we may judge it, is undeniably distinct. In contrast to those whom we have called materialists Mr Joyce is spiritual; concerned at all costs to reveal the flickerings of that innermost flame which flashes its myriad messages through the brain, he disregards with complete courage whatever seems to him adventitious, though it be probability or coherence or any other of the handrails to which we cling for support when we set our imaginations free. Faced, as in the Cemetery scene, by so much that, in its restless scintillations, in its irrelevance, its flashes of deep significance succeeded by incoherent inanities, seems to be life itself, we have to fumble rather awkwardly if we want to say what else we wish; and for what reason a work of such originality yet fails to compare, for we must take high examples, with 'Youth' or *Jude the Obscure.*[9] It fails, one might say simply, because of the comparative poverty of the writer's mind. But it is possible to press a little further and wonder whether we may not refer our sense of being in a bright and yet somehow strictly confined apartment rather than at large beneath the sky to some limitation imposed by the method as well as by the mind. Is it due to the method that we feel neither jovial nor magnanimous, but centred in a self which in spite of its tremor of susceptibility never reaches out or embraces or comprehends what is outside and beyond? Does the emphasis laid perhaps didactically upon indecency contribute to this effect of the angular and isolated? Or is it merely that in any effort of such courage the faults as well as the virtues are left naked to the view? In any case we need not attribute too much importance to the method. Any method is right , every method is right, that expresses what we wish to express. This one has the merit of giving closer shape to what we were prepared to call life itself; did not the reading of *Ulysses* suggest how much of life is excluded and ignored, and did it not come with a shock to open *Tristram Shandy* and even *Pendennis,*[10] and be by them convinced that there are other aspects of life, and larger ones into the bargain?

However this may be, the problem before the novelist at present, as we suppose it to have been in the past, is to contrive a means of being free to set down what he chooses. He has to have the courage to say that what interests him is no longer this, but that; out of 'that' alone must he construct his work. The tendency of the moderns and part of their perplexity is no doubt that they find their interest more and more in [the] dark region of psychology. At once therefore the accent falls a little differently; it becomes apparent that the emphasis is upon something hitherto ignored or unstressed in that relation, a feeling, a point of view suggesting a different and obscure outline of form, incomprehensible to our predecessors. No one but a modern, perhaps no one but a Russian, would have felt the interest of the situation which Tchehov has made into the short story which he calls 'Gusev'.[11] Some Russian soldiers are lying ill in the hospital of a ship which is taking them back to Russia. We are given scraps of their talk; a few of their thoughts; then one of the soldiers dies, and is taken away; the talk goes on among the others for a time; until Gusev himself dies and, looking 'like a carrot or a radish',[12] is thrown overboard. The emphasis is laid upon such unexpected places that at first it seems as if there were no emphasis at all; and then, as the eyes accustom themselves to twilight and discern the shapes of things in a room, we see how complete the story is, how profound, and how truly in obedience to his vision Tchehov has chosen this, that, and the other, and placed them together to compose something new. But it is impossible to say that this is humorous or that tragic, or even that it is proper to call the whole a short story, since the writer seems careless of brevity and intensity, and leaves us with the suggestion that the strange chords he has struck sound on and on. There is, perhaps, no need that a short story should be brief and intense, as there is perhaps no answer to the questions which it raises.

The most inconclusive remarks upon modern English fiction can hardly avoid some mention of the Russian influence, and if the Russians are mentioned one runs the risk of feeling that to write of any fiction save theirs is a waste of time. If we want understanding of the soul and heart where else shall we find it of comparable profundity? If we are sick of our own materialism the least considerable of their novelists has by right of birth a natural reverence for the human spirit. 'Learn to make yourself akin to people . . . but let this sympathy be not with the mind – for it is easy with the mind – but with the heart, with love towards them.'[13] In every great Russian writer we seem to discern the features of a saint, if sympathy for the sufferings of others, love towards them, endeavour to reach some goal worthy of the most exacting demands of the spirit constitute saintliness. It is the saint in them which confounds us with a feeling of our own irreligious triviality, and turns so many of our famous novels to tinsel and trickery. The conclusions of the Russian mind, thus comprehensive and compassionate, are inevitably perhaps of the utmost sadness. It might indeed be more true to speak of the inconclusiveness of the Russian mind. It is the sense that there is no answer, that if honestly examined life presents question after question which must be left to sound on and on after the story is over in hopeless interrogation that fills us with a deep, and finally it may be with a resentful, despair. They are right perhaps; unquestionably they see further than we do and without our gross impediments of vision. But perhaps we see something that escapes them, or why should this voice of protest mix itself with our gloom? The voice of protest is the voice of another and an ancient civilisation which seems to have bred in us the instinct to enjoy and fight rather than to suffer and understand. English fiction from Sterne to Meredith[14] bears witness to our natural delight in humour and comedy, in the beauty of earth, in the activities of the intellect, and in the splendour of the body. But any deductions that we may draw from the comparison of one fiction with another are futile, save as they flood us with a view of infinite possibilities, assure us that there is no bound to the horizon, and nothing forbidden but falsity and pretence. 'The proper stuff of fiction' does not exist; everything is the proper stuff of fiction; whatever one honestly thinks, whatever one honestly feels. No perception comes amiss; every good quality whether of the mind or spirit is drawn upon and used and turned by the magic of art to something little or large, but endlessly different, everlastingly new. All that fiction asks of us is that we should break her and bully her, honour and love her, till she yields to our bidding, for so her youth is perpetually renewed and her sovereignty assured.

1–An essay in the *TLS*, 10 April 1919, (Kp C147) which VW substantially revised and included, under the title 'Modern Fiction', in *CR* 1 (see *IV VW Essays*); see Editorial Note, p. xxiii. See also 'On Re-reading Novels', 'Mr Bennett and Mrs Brown' and 'Character in Fiction' below. Reading Notes (Berg, xxxi).
2–Henry Fielding (1707–54); Jane Austen (1775–1817).
3–W. M. Thackeray (1811–63).
4–H. G. Wells (1866–1946), on whose *Joan and Peter* (1918) VW wrote in 'The Rights of Youth', *II VW Essays*; Arnold Bennett (1867–1931); John Galsworthy (1867–1933), on whose *Beyond* (1917) VW wrote in 'Mr Galsworthy's Novel', *II VW Essays*.
5–Thomas Hardy (1840–1928); Joseph Conrad (1857–1924); W. H. Hudson

(1841–1922), *The Purple Land* (1885), *Green Mansions* (1904), and *Far Away and Long Ago* (1918), for VW's review of which see 'Mr Hudson's Childhood' in *II VW Essays*.

6–*The Old Wives' Tale* (1908); George Cannon appears in the 'Clayhanger' trilogy (*Clayhanger*, 1910, *Hilda Lessways*, 1911, *These Twain*, 1916).

7–James Joyce (1882–1941).

8–*Portrait of the Artist as a Young Man* (1916–17), *Ulysses* (1922). As early as April 1918 Harriet Weaver had approached the Woolfs in the hope that The Hogarth Press might publish the whole of *Ulysses* (of which the first thirteen episodes, and a part of the fourteenth, had started appearing in the *Little Review* the previous month, continuing until December 1920), but for several reasons, legal and practical, this proved impossible. However, VW made reading notes on those episodes that appeared in the *Little Review* March–October 1918. Reading Notes (Berg xxxi).

9–'Youth' (1902); for VW's views upon it see 'Mr Conrad's *Youth*', *II VW Essays*. Thomas Hardy's *Jude the Obscure* (1896).

10–*The Life and Opinions of Tristram Shandy* (1759–67) by Laurence Sterne and *The History of Pendennis* (1848–50) by W. M. Thackeray.

11–For this story see *The Witch and Other Stories* by Anton Tchehov (1860–1904), trans. Constance Garnett (Chatto & Windus, 1918), a volume discussed by VW in 'Tchehov's Questions', *II VW Essays*.

12–*The Witch and Other Stories*, 'Gusev', p. 166: 'Sewn up in the sail cloth he looked like a carrot or a radish: broad at the head and narrow at the feet . . ."

13–*The Village Priest, and Other Stories* by Elena Militsina and Mikhail Saltikov, trans. from the Russian by Beatrix L. Tollemache, with an intro. by C. Hagberg Wright (T. Fisher Unwin, 1918), the title story, by Militsina, p. 34; the ellipsis marks the omission of: 'I would even like to add: make yourself indispensable to them'. The full passage is quoted in 'The Russian View', *II VW Essays*; see also 'The Russian Point of View', *IV VW Essays* and *CR1*.

14–Laurence Sterne (1713–68); George Meredith (1828–1909).

The Novels of Defoe

VW's essay in the *TLS*, 24 April 1919, (Kp C148) on the occasion of the 200th anniversary of the publication of *Robinson Crusoe* was later revised for inclusion, under the title 'Defoe', in *The Common Reader*: 1st series (1925). The reader is referred to *IV VW Essays*, where the revised version, together with variants in the form of footnotes, is reprinted in its place as part of *The Common Reader*.

The Eccentrics

If, in your more ambitious moments, you have coveted a monument in the *Dictionary of National Biography*, you have not, perhaps, wished to see inscribed upon it the single word 'eccentric'. That the efforts and aims of your life, your virtues, learning, and devotion, should be summed up once and for all, briefly and comprehensively, as those of an eccentric does not perhaps seem to you a fitting reward, nor an epitaph to be pointed at with pride by your descendants. Yet considering how small a company it is that comes through the gates of Death wearing this title upon their breasts, and how infinitely more common it appears to be to die a Dean or a Professor, a hero or a Prime Minister, perhaps after all there is something to be said for the eccentrics. If, at the age of forty or thereabouts, other distinctions seem rather to recede than to bestow their brightness on your head, it might be worth while, supposing you are still set upon a title, to see what can be done in the direction of eccentricity. But let us forewarn you of failure.

It is not a profession that can be taken up late in life or practised successfully by the mere will to practise it. You can, of course, walk up and down the Tottenham Court Road wrapped in a towel in imitation of the Greeks; or adopt a panther for a pet; or bury all your gold in a cellar and sit upon the grave. But you will never, we hope, deceive the editor of the *Dictionary of National Biography* by such trumpery devices as these. The quality which marks all true eccentrics is that never for a moment do they believe themselves to be eccentric. They are persuaded – and who shall say that they are wrong? – that it is the rest of the world who are cramped and malformed and spiritually decrepit, while they alone have lived their lives according to the dictates of nature. It must be owned that in the battle of life, the triumph of civilisation, or whatever we choose to call it, they have invariably been worsted. The Government offices are not for them, nor the Houses of Parliament, nor the Woolsack, nor the Judicial Bench. If they appear in any of these places it is in some menial capacity, to sweep the stairs, or to collect the waste paper on the point of a very long stick; or, occasionally, in the dock itself. Even so they will not be arrested for any such crime as murder or felony; they will only have committed what is called a 'nuisance', such as giving away sovereigns in the street or worshipping some peculiar variety of God in the back garden.

For such reasons as these it is extremely rare to find a full and satisfactory biography of an eccentric. His family generally contrives to forget all about him; he only crops up, in our experience, as if by accident in the biographies of his relations, like a weed picked by mistake with the roses, or a dandelion that the wind has wafted to a bed primly sown with prize specimens of the double aster. But it is always worthwhile to make the experiment. Here we will suppose (without too much tasking probability) is the life and letters of some great dignitary in three volumes with an index, bound in blue and stamped upon each volume with some heraldic emblem and a motto protesting loyalty, or tenacity, or integrity to which the hero, as his life convinces us, has more than lived up. But where, then, is his Uncle John with his passion for the baptismal rite, or his Aunt – I forget her name – who knew for certain that the world is shaped like a star-fish? It is no use looking for them in the index; they are not to be found there; but sometimes inadvertently, or perhaps to illustrate some law of heredity or some creditable act of devotion on the part of their nephew, they do stealthily and as if by the back door momentarily creep in. The other day, looking through the life and letters of a famous man who was worshipped with reason and died not only a Canon, but also a Sub-Dean, it was the reward of a wandering attention to light upon the figure of his father, a maker of iron bedsteads in the city of Bristol.[2] As the son was going from good to better and there could be no reason whatever for anxiety about his career, it seemed worthwhile to consider for a moment this maker of iron bedsteads in the city of Bristol. And the reward was instant. All his life he made all their legs of solid iron. It was useless to tell him that science had devised a means of making hollow legs without impairing the virtue of beds; it was useless to prove that his competitors would out-distance him and his family be brought to ruin. It was the state of his soul that he cared for. He could not tolerate hollowness within. The imagination likes to picture him in the decline of his years and the decay of his fortunes, with death only in prospect, repeating over and over the proud boast with which he would front the Recording Angel and claim for himself a superior station in the Heavenly Choir: 'The legs of all my bedsteads were of solid iron!'

Sometimes, though it happens far too seldom, lives have been written of these singular men and women, or, after they are dead, someone half-shamefacedly has put together their papers. Dr Meryon, for example, wrote the memoirs of Lady Hester Stanhope,[3] thus earning our eternal gratitude; and there are three volumes where we could have done with twenty devoted to the superb memory of Margaret Fuller.[4] Neither of these women would have seen any force in the word *eccentric* as applied to herself, though it would not have surprised them in the least, could they have woke a century later, to find Temples dedicated to them, religions ascribed to them, and sects of devotees worshipping their divinity. Lady Hester indeed kept her white horse perpetually in readiness for the Messiah in her stable. How often, sitting alone in her castle at the top of Mount Lebanon, now picking a little bit of meat from one of the innumerable saucers, now sharply reproving some sylph for its antics behind the chest of drawers, and all the time puffing blue clouds of smoke from her hookah, did she not see herself riding into Jerusalem by the side of the Lord and enjoy in fancy the consternation with which Lord Palmerston and Queen Victoria received the news! The fancies of Margaret Fuller were not so much different from other people's fancies; she merely thought herself inspired, married an Italian footman, believed him a Marquis, and perished in shipwreck off the American coast, losing not only son and husband and her life in the waves, but also the manuscripts that were to have made her immortal and – freed the world from death? – proclaimed the truth? – made all men equal and women perhaps a little superior? – or what was it? The waters hold those secrets still. Then there was the friend of Shelley, Elizabeth Hitchener, who left her school to float his little bottles out to sea, and wrote at least one line of an epic,

All, all are men – women and all!

together with some philosophical reflections upon the soul of the horse. And Mrs Grote must not be forgotten, nor can be so long as the English language endures and one has use for the expressive word that was her legacy to the world; or Margaret, Duchess of Newcastle, or Mrs Cameron of Freshwater, or Adolphus Blatt, or Caroline Mew, and others innumerable, for they crowd into the memory as one begins to think of Tennyson[6] and the rest, often so dishevelled, in such dishabille from their long obscurity and fantastic behaviour that we are not certain of remembering even their names. Without names and so strangely inspired, leaving behind them now one line, now one word, and now nothing at all, what whim is it that bids us go seeking them round the corners and just beneath the horizons of so many good books devoted to good men? Surely the world has been right in conferring biographies where biographies are due? Surely the shower of titles and honours has not always descended upon the wrong heads? That the world's estimate has been perverse from the start, and half her great men geese, are themes too vast to be disposed of for ever in one short article. Let a homely figure serve instead of argument. Suppose that you turn on the light in the kitchen when the servants are gone to bed; the beetles slip beneath the carpet, the mice behind the wainscot; nothing remains in the room save the scrubbed deal table and the round white clock. Do you never pause for a moment to wonder where all those nimble lives have gone to and what pranks they are playing beyond your sight, and whether, after all, the solid and the serviceable fulfil every need of the soul?

1–A signed essay in the *Athenaeum*, 25 April 1919, (Kp C149) upon a subject of considerable fascination to VW. 'I think one day I shall write a book of "Eccentrics",' she had noted in her diary on 19 January 1915, 'Mr Grote [sic] shall be one. Lady Hester Stanhope. Margaret Fuller. Duchess of Newcastle. Aunt Julia.' On Sunday, 30 March 1919, she wrote: 'I open this book today merely to note that *Miss Eleanor Ormerod*, destroyer of insects, promises well for Murry: should he take kindly to my first (Eccentrics: I myself rather liked it).' See 'Lives of the Obscure': 'Miss Ormerod', *IV VW Essays* and *CR* 1.

2–The identities of the canon and his bedstead-making father have not been discovered.

3–Dr Charles Lewis Meryon (1783–1877), *Memoirs of the Lady Hester Stanhope* and *Travels of Lady Hester Stanhope* (6 vols, 1845, 1846). For VW on Lady Hester, a niece of William Pitt, summarily described in the *DNB* as 'Stanhope, Lady Hester Lucy (1776–1839), eccentric', see 'Lady Hester Stanhope', *I VW Essays*.

4–Sarah Margaret Fuller (1810–50), transcendentalist, literary critic and editor, author of *Summer on the Lakes in 1843* (1844) and *Woman in the Nineteenth Century* (1845). Her memoirs, edited by R. W. Emerson, W. H. Channing and J. F. Clarke, were published in 1852. She had married in Rome in 1847 the Marchese Ossoli, a follower of Mazzini, and herself took part in the revolution of 1848–9.

5–The line, from Elizabeth Hitchener's 'Ode on the Rights of Women', is quoted in *The Life of Percy Bysshe Shelley* (2 vols, Kegan Paul, 1886) by Edward Dowden, vol. i, ch. vii, p. 314, and by VW in her article 'Shelley and Elizabeth Hitchener', *I VW Essays*. Hitchener, whose dates are not known, published two volumes of verse *The Fireside Bagatelle* (1818) and *The Weald of Sussex* (1822).

6–Harriet Grote, *née* Lewin (1792–1878), biographer, wife of the historian and politician George Grote, both of whom were associated with the Philosophical Radicals. VW liked to think the word 'grotesque' derived from Mrs Grote. For VW on Margaret Cavendish, *née* Lucas, Duchess of Newcastle (1624?–74), author, see 'The Duke and Duchess of Newcastle-Upon-Tyne', *I VW Essays*, and 'The Duchess of Newcastle', *IV VW Essays* and *CR* 1 For VW on her great-aunt, the pioneer photographer Julia Margaret Cameron, *née* Pattle (1815–79), see 'Julia Margaret Cameron', *IV VW Essays*.

'The Obstinate Lady'

It is probable that if Mr Norris chose to write down the names of all the novels he can lay claim to they would overflow the allotted page. Even if we had not very pleasant memories of some of them we could infer from internal evidence the long and distinguished ancestry of *The Obstinate Lady*. She has all the marks of maturity: a few, to be frank, of middle age. Mr Norris learnt his craft in the days when a plot was as necessary to a novel as a spring to a mouse-trap; and in these days we have given up catching mice. Yet if it is the plot that teaches this precision and neatness and rightness we need not plume ourselves too much upon our neglect; nor can we deny that a plot of some kind is an admirable device for making us keep our eyes open.

The Obstinate Lady has earned that title because she will not apply for a divorce from the incorrigible drunkard who is her husband. Indeed, when his sins have found him out, she goes to the length of nursing him herself, and to her charge is committed the necessary bottle of morphia. Touched by her conduct, Jack Maddison revokes his will; everything is left to his wife; and next morning his valet finds him dead in his bed. An overdose of morphia is said to be the cause; the widow alone had access to the drug, and the finger of suspicion, though not of blame, must point in her direction. But our sympathies are stirred and enlisted by many other complications. The trap, for it is scarcely a problem, is set down in the middle of a nicely arranged group of English gentle-people. They have a charming house up the river; the only blot upon their circumstances is the unhappy marriage of their daughter and her obstinate refusal to accept her freedom. Nevertheless, they have weekend parties and picnics on the Thames; and they have befriended, a little incongruously, a promising young poet whose verses are said not to rhyme, but that, we suspect, is a concession on Mr Norris's part to the spirit of the age. We rather believe that the war is another of Mr Norris's concessions. There was no war in the Stanfields' England. But it is all so skilfully combined and touched up that the modern additions are almost imperceptible, and the question of Blanche Maddison's guilt is of moment to a good many people whom we know, not intimately indeed, but well enough to feel concerned. Intimacy, of course, is not in Mr Norris's line. His characters keep their distance, and thus it is quite possible for a savage bull on the one hand and a savage review on the other to settle the question of Kitty Stanfield's affections. Grains of sand had no effect upon those rather solid scales. But everything that Mr Norris tells us, whether about a bull or about a review, or about an overdose of morphia has the advantage of being quite possible. That is one of the good results of having proved your skill so often that you know to a hairsbreadth how far it will serve you. And at the right moment, not noisily, or clumsily, or ostentatiously, but quietly and with an appearance of almost humorous ease, the catch is released, and the trap comes down to perfection upon the very tip of the villain's tail.

1 – A review in the *TLS*, 1 May 1919, (Kp C150) of *The Obstinate Lady* (Hutchinson & Co., 1919), by W. E. (William Edward) Norris (1847–1925). See also 'Mr Norris's Method' and 'Mr Norris's Standard' below; and '*Barham of Beltana*' and '*Lone Marie*' in *I VW Essays*. Reprinted: CW.

The Soul of an Archbishop

VW's review in the *Athenaeum*, 9 May 1919, (Kp C151) of *The Life and Letters of William Thomson, Archbishop of York* (John Lane, 1919) by Ethel H. Thomson, was later minimally revised and included, under the title 'Archbishop Thomson', in *The Common Reader*: 1st series (1925). The reader is referred to *IV VW Essays*, where the revised version, together with variants in the form of footnotes, is reprinted in its place as part of *The Common Reader*.

The Anatomy of Fiction

Sometimes at country fairs you may have seen a professor on a platform exhorting the peasants to come up and buy his wonder-working pills. Whatever their disease, whether of body or mind, he has a name for it and a cure; and if they hang back in doubt he whips out a diagram and points with a stick at different parts of the human anatomy, and gabbles so quickly such long Latin words that first one shyly stumbles forward and then another, and takes his bolus and carries it away and unwraps it secretly and swallows it in hope. 'The young aspirant to the art of fiction who knows himself to be an incipient realist',[2] Mr Hamilton vociferates from his platform, and the incipient realists advance and receive – for the professor is generous – five pills together with nine suggestions for home treatment. In other words they are given five 'review questions' to answer, and are advised to read nine books or parts of books, '1. Define the difference between realism and romance. 2. What are the advantages and disadvantages of the realistic method? 3. What are the advantages and disadvantages of the romantic method?'[3] – that is the kind of thing they work out at home, and with such success that a 'revised and enlarged edition' of the book has been issued on the tenth anniversary of the first publication. In America, evidently, Mr Hamilton is considered a very good professor, and has no doubt a bundle of testimonials to the miraculous nature of his cures. But let us consider: Mr Hamilton is not a professor; we are not credulous ploughboys; and fiction is not a disease.

In England we have been in the habit of saying that fiction is an art. We are not taught to write novels; dissuasion is our most usual incentive; and though perhaps the critics have 'deduced and formulated the general principles of the art of fiction',[4] they have done their work as a good housemaid does hers; they have tidied up after the party is over. Criticism seldom or never applies to the problems of the present moment. On the other hand, any good novelist, whether he be dead or alive, has something to say about them, though it is said very indirectly, differently to different people, and differently at different stages of the same person's development. Thus, if anything is essential, it is essential to do your reading with your own eyes. But, to tell the truth, Mr Hamilton has sickened us of the didactic style. Nothing appears to be essential save perhaps an elementary knowledge of the A.B.C., and it is pleasant to remember that Henry James, when he took to dictation, dispensed even with that.[5] Still, if you have a natural taste for books it is probable that after reading *Emma*, to take an instance, some reflections upon the art of Jane Austen[6] may occur to you – how exquisitely one incident relieves another; how definitely, by not saying something, she says it; how surprising, therefore, her expressive phrases when they come. Between the sentences, apart from the story, a little shape of some kind builds itself up. But learning from books is a capricious business at best, and the teaching so vague and changeable that in the end, far from calling books either 'romantic' or 'realistic',[7] you will be more inclined to think them, as you think people, very mixed, very distinct, very unlike one another. But this would never do for Mr Hamilton. According to him every work of art can be taken to pieces, and those pieces can be named and numbered, divided and sub-divided, and given their order of precedence, like the internal organs of a frog. Thus we learn how to put them together again – that is, according to Mr Hamilton, we learn how to write. There is the complication, the major knot, and the explication; the inductive and the deductive methods; the kinetic and the static; the direct and the indirect with sub-divisions of the same; connotation, annotation, personal equation, and denotation; logical sequence and chronological succession – all parts of the frog and all capable of further dissection. Take the case of 'emphasis' alone. There are eleven kinds of emphasis.[8] Emphasis by terminal position, by initial position, by pause, by direct proportion, by inverse proportion, by iteration, by antithesis, by surprise, by suspense – are you tired already? But consider the Americans. They have written one story eleven times over, with a different kind of emphasis in each. Indeed, Mr Hamilton's book teaches us a great deal about the Americans.

Still, as Mr Hamilton uneasily perceives now and then, you may dissect your frog, but you cannot make it hop; there is, unfortunately, such a thing as life. Directions for imparting life to fiction are given, such as to 'train yourself rigorously never to be bored', and to cultivate 'a lively curiosity and a ready sympathy'.[9] But it is evident that Mr Hamilton does not like life, and, with such a tidy museum as his, who can blame him? He has found life very troublesome, and, if you come to consider it, rather unnecessary; for, after all, there are books. But Mr Hamilton's views on life are so illuminating that they must be given in his own words:

Perhaps in the actual world we should never bother to converse with illiterate provincial people; and yet we do not feel it a waste of time and energy to meet them in the pages of *Middlemarch*. For my own part, I have always, in actual life, avoided meeting the sort of people that appear in Thackeray's *Vanity Fair*; and yet I find it not only interesting but profitable to associate with them through the entire extent of a rather lengthy novel.[10]

'Illiterate provincial people' – 'interesting but profitable' – 'waste of time and energy' – now after much wandering and painful toil we are on the right track at last. For long it seemed that nothing could reward the American people for having written eleven themes upon the eleven kinds of emphasis. But now we perceive dimly that there is something to be gained by the daily flagellation of the exhausted brain. It is not a title; it has nothing to do with pleasure or with literature; but it appears that Mr Hamilton and his industrious band see far off upon the horizon a circle of superior enlightenment to which, if only they can keep on reading long enough, they may attain. Every book demolished is a milestone passed. Books in foreign languages count twice over. And a book like this is of the nature of a dissertation to be sent up to the supreme examiner, who may be, for anything we know, the ghost of Matthew Arnold.[11] Will Mr Hamilton be admitted? Can they have the heart to reject anyone so ardent, so dusty, so worthy, so out of breath? Alas! look at his quotations; consider his comments upon them:

'The murmuring of innumerable bees' . . . The word innumerable, which denotes to the intellect merely 'incapable of being numbered,' is, in this connection, made to suggest to the senses the murmuring of bees.[12]

The credulous ploughboy could have told him more than that. It is not necessary to quote what he says about 'magic casements' and the 'iniquity of oblivion'. Is there not, upon page 208, a definition of style?[13]

No; Mr Hamilton will never be admitted; he and his disciples must toil for ever in the desert sand, and the circle of illumination will, we fear, grow fainter and farther upon their horizon. It is curious to find, after writing the above sentence, how little one is ashamed of being, where literature is concerned, an unmitigated snob.

1–A review in the *Athenaeum*, 16 May 1919, (Kp C152) of *Materials and Methods of Fiction. Revised and Enlarged*. With an introduction by Brander Matthews, member of the American Academy of Arts and Letters (George Allen & Unwin, 1918), by Clayton Hamilton, member of the National Institute of Arts and Letters; the work was originally published in 1908. The same issue of the *Athenaeum* carried articles by: Clive Bell, on 'Cézanne'; and E. M. Forster, on 'St Athanasius' (pt i). Reprinted: *G&R, CE*.

2–Hamilton, ch. ii, p. 37, which continues: 'had therefore best confine his efforts to attempted reproduction of the life he sees about him.'

3–*Ibid.*, p. 43; the fourth and fifth questions are: 'Which method is more natural to your own mind?' and 'Upon what evidence have you based your answer to the foregoing question?'

4–The source of this quotation has not been discovered.

5–Henry James (1843–1916), all of whose later books were dictated to an amanuensis. (From 1907 until his death this was Theodora Bosanquet whose essay on *Henry James at Work* was published by the Hogarth Press in 1924.)

6–*Emma* (1816), Jane Austen (1775–1817).

7–Hamilton, ch. ii, p. 25, has a subheading: 'Every Mind Either Realistic or Romantic'.

8–*Ibid.*, ch. vii, 'Emphasis in Narrative', pp. 139–55.

9–For the first quotation, *ibid.*, ch. i, p. 24; and for the second, p. 23.

10–*Ibid.*, ch. v, p. 79; *Middlemarch* (1871–2) by George Eliot; *Vanity Fair* (1847–8).

11–Matthew Arnold (1822–88).

12—Hamilton, ch. xii, p. 209, slightly adapted. Hamilton quotes these lines from
Tennyson's 'The Princess':

> 'Myriads of rivulets hurrying thro' the lawn,
> The moan of doves in immemorial elms,
> And murmuring of innumerable bees.'

13—For the 'magic casements' from Keats's 'Ode to a Nightingale', *ibid.*, ch. xii, p.
211; and the 'iniquity of oblivion' from Sir Thomas Browne's *Urn Burial*, p. 213.
Style is defined on p. 208 in the following terms: '. . . an utterance has the quality of
style when these two appeals of language – the denotative and the connotative, the
definite and the indefinite, the intellectual and the sensuous – are so coordinated as to
produce upon the reader or the listener an effect which is, not dual, but indissolubly
single.'

'Java Head'

The Three Black Pennys was a very good novel; *Java Head* is a good
novel. But, even so, *Java Head* is quite good enough to deserve that we
should bring forward our reasons for judging it decidedly inferior to its
predecessor. Every writer, after the first flush of youthful experiment,
settles into a manner of his own. It is inevitable; and yet, as the new scene
shapes itself after the pattern of the old, as the sentence takes its
accustomed curve, some little thrill of foreboding may stay the pen in the
air. These easy cadences and facile arrangements are the first grey hairs,
the first intimations of senility. There is only one way to remain young: it
is to cease doing what you have learnt to do easily and perhaps
successfully, and to attempt what you are not certain of being able to do
at all. The odious discipline which we should prescribe for Mr
Hergesheimer is to write a novel in which there is no furniture, no ladies'
dresses, no still life. He should be forced to write of modern people; he
should be required to make them talk. For the comparative failure of
Java Head is due to a self-indulgence which eliminates all that Mr
Hergesheimer finds difficult or repellent and leaves those problems
which he enjoys solving and is certain of solving exquisitely as often as
he chooses.

Again we have America some hundred years ago. The scene is laid at
Salem. The family of Ammidon, with whom the story is chiefly concerned, is a great shipowning family. They trade with the East, and the
beautiful sailing ships laden with picturesque cargoes furl their sails
almost under the windows of the substantial dwelling-house which the

old sea captain, Jeremy Ammidon, has christened Java Head, after the high black rock which was 'the symbol of the safe and happy end of an arduous voyage'.[2] One day his son, the sea captain Gerrit, after being given up for lost, sails into the harbour, and along with his casks and bales brings to shore an unknown bride, a Chinese woman of the highest caste. Exposed to the chatter and gossip of Salem society, Taou Yuen remains imperturbable and alien. The love-making of Edward Dunsack, a merchant trading with China, acquainted with the language and demoralised by the smoking of opium, scarcely rouses her. But through him she learns to suspect her husband's fidelity. He was, she is told, in love with Dunsack's niece. During her visit to the suspected girl Dunsack breaks into the room, and to escape the horrors pressing round her Taou Yuen snatches his opium pills, swallows one after another, and dies in her sleep.

But as in a picture the eye rests on some tuft of daisies or spray of foliage while conscious of the larger lines, so these details are part of the surrounding landscape. At the same time that Taou Yuen loves and dies, the old sea captain Jeremy faces the fact that the slow-sailing ships of his youth and pride are outdone by the new racing clippers, and dies of the shock of finding that without his knowledge two of the company's vessels are engaged in the opium trade. Somehow, too, it is not merely jealousy that has killed the Chinese woman, but America, with its 'unfamiliar circumstances, tradition, emotions'.[3] The presence of a scaffolding of this sort gives Java Head its sobriety and distinction. And, to continue a metaphor which is peculiarly suitable to Mr Hergesheimer, the painting of the little tufts and sprigs is at once loving and precise. Take this, for instance, of the Nautilus coming into harbour: 'The ship moved more slowly, under her topsails and jibs, in a soundless progress with the ripples falling away in water like dark green glass, liquid and still.'[4] Or take one of the many descriptions of the apparel of Taou Yuen. She wore

a long gown with wide sleeves of blue-black satin, embroidered in peach-coloured flower petals and innumerable minute sapphire and orange butterflies, a short sleeveless jacket of sage green caught with looped red jade buttons and threaded with silver, and indigo high-soled slippers crusted and tasselled with pearls. Her hair rose from the back in a smooth burnished loop. There were long pins of pink jade carved into blossoms, a quivering decoration of paper-thin gold leaves with moonstones in glistening drops, and a band of coral lotus buds. Pierced stone bracelets[5]

but it is too long to quote in its entirety; worse, it is too detailed to be seen as a whole. Happily Mr Hergesheimer has himself saved us from uttering the priggish comment which keeps breaking in among these pretty things. 'She is very gorgeous and placid, superior on the surface; but the heart, Gerrit – that isn't made of jade and ivory and silk.'[6] No, the heart is neither gorgeous nor placid. It is very difficult to write beautifully about the heart. When Mr Hergesheimer has to describe not what people wear but what they feel, he shows his lack of ease or of interest by becoming either very violent or very stiff. There is no sense of enjoyment in his dialogue.

The origin of this fault-finding, however, is to be found in the fact that *Java Head* is one of the smaller number of novels which appear to be written by an adult; and therefore we make Mr Hergesheimer responsible for our disappointment instead of saying nothing about it, because it is useless to point out the immaturity of a child. He brings to mind some of the novelists who are undoubtedly mature – Mr Conrad,[7] for example. And one of their peculiarities is that felicities of the kind we have quoted come incidentally on the stretch for something higher and more remote so that we take them in half consciously at the time as part of the general richness, and only in memory go back and distinguish them for their individual beauty. But in *Java Head* we are led up to them; they are the fruit on the topmost branch; there is nothing beyond them. Nevertheless, *Java Head* is a good novel.

1–A review in the *TLS*, 29 May 1919, (Kp C153) of *Java Head* (William Heinemann, 1919) by Joseph Hergesheimer (1880–1954), a prolific author, born in Philadelphia of German and Scottish descent, who attended Pennsylvania Academy of Fine Arts, but then turned from painting to writing. See also '*Gold and Iron*', 'The Pursuit of Beauty', 'Pleasant Stories', below; and '*The Three Black Pennys', II VW Essays*. Reprinted: *CW*.

2–Hergesheimer, ch. ii, p. 40.

3–*Ibid.*, ch. x, pp. 266–7.

4–*Ibid.*, ch. iii, p. 71.

5–*Ibid.*, p. 76, which continues: 'hung about her delicate wrists, fretted crystal balls swung from the lobes of her ears; and clasped on the ends of several fingers were long pointed filagrees of ivory.'

6–*Ibid.*, ch. iv, p. 92.

7–Joseph Conrad (1857–1924).

On Some of the Old Actors

This is one of the primitive biographies, recording every fact, but scarcely attempting composition. It is addressed manifestly to a group of people who have a peculiar relish for old theatre programmes – those 'lovers of the stage and its traditions' to whom the book is dedicated. For many readers, therefore, the interest which certainly exists is of an indirect nature. We are interested that other people should be interested. What is it that holds them spellbound in this vast collection of faded programmes thirty or forty years of age? What is this passion for the stage?

Mr Daly makes no attempt to define, and none certainly to justify. Directly the two small brothers, Augustin and Joseph, are conscious of any desire whatever, they know that they wish to own a theatre. Augustin, the leader in the life-long companionship, set up his first theatre in the back-yard of their house in New York. All the fittings were ready and the opening announced, when 'it suddenly occurred to him that he had no play'.[2] Equally characteristic, though in the circumstances more remarkable, is the fact that 'he was absolutely without ambition to act.'[3] He appeared upon the stage only twice, and to judge by the names of his productions his taste in the drama was so casual and catholic that one can easily believe that he sometimes forgot about the play. His passion was to 'manage the production'.[4] Some desire he had, originally at least, to break with tradition, to eliminate stars, and to found his theatre upon the French model; but this fades into insignificance, if it is not crushed out of existence, by the rapacity of the other appetite. Impelled by this instinct, he possessed two theatres, was building a third, and had three companies to provide for by the time he was thirty-five. The long reel of the names of the forgotten and apparently meretricious dramas with which he kept his companies supplied makes the head spin. Melodrama of the most sensational kind alternated with plays of Shakespeare and Wycherley re-written by Mr Daly so that 'all the gaiety and charm of the situations',[5] robbed of their coarseness, remained. Once set in activity, the machine for producing plays could never stop. If one fails, the gorged and capricious public must be tempted by a fly of a brighter tint or a more audacious shape. For all the insight that Mr Daly gives us into his brother's mind, he might have been one of those men of iron will and instant determination who lead armies to victory or provide a continent with pills.

But a difference, subtle but unmistakable, between this business and other businesses makes itself felt. Mr Daly had no desire to amass a fortune. The gilt and carving – 'the doors were ornamented with wood carving . . . which none of the general public had time to observe'[6] – the curtains specially embroidered at Milan in silk, the carpets of velvet, the crimson satin drop curtains, the first of their kind in existence, were for the theatre alone. Everything was for the theatre. When, reluctantly and with an air of embarrassment, Mr Daly appeared on the stage in answer to calls, 'he is generally dusty, and not infrequently there is a big dab of whitewash or some other colour rubbed from the scene upon some part of his clothing'.[7] He was a reserved and rather unpopular man who worked eighteen hours a day in his theatre and insisted that his rule there was absolute. But beyond the gambler's excitement of throwing gold upon the table and watching it multiply or disappear, we are able to detect now in a name, now in a letter, and now everywhere rather than anywhere in particular what is called 'the glamour of the stage'.[8] The pen of Mrs John Wood at once transports us to a more generous and richly lighted world. 'My dear person,' she writes, 'nothing shall prevent my seeing you. You leave Victoria Station . . . arriving here at one o'clock – where you would behold your Peach blossom on the plank.'[9] She ends her letters, 'Yours muchly Matilda', or 'Yours until we meet and long after'; she signs herself 'Peachblossom' or 'Thalia'. The charm begins to work. We feel, a little prematurely perhaps, admitted behind the scenes; invited into dressing rooms where, among the tinsel and the rouge, the atmosphere is deliciously warm and full of the vibrations of temperament. They talk of 'plays that would add to the incomparable fame of the great Shakespeare himself'.[10] Miss Avonia Jones declares, 'I must tell you that my style is passionate. When I love it must be madly . . . Hate, revenge, despair, sarcasm and resistless love are what I glory in'.[11] Good Miss Jones, Daly calls her, and adds that she enjoys the domestic virtues of a cow. Old Charlotte Cushman, famous in the early part of the century for her representation of Meg Merrilies, complains that 'the trouble nowadays exists in the actors – they lack respect for the profession.'[12] And there are vast numbers of young men and women, conscious of inspiration (or, as one of them puts it, 'I have the volcanic temperature'), who demand that the chief parts shall at once be allotted to them, though, as one lady thinks it necesssary to warn Mr Daly, 'in acting tragic parts my emotion, which is apt to carry me away, may prove perilous to the gentleman who plays with me.'[13] Indeed, their emotion perpetually carries them away, though it proves perilous rather to them than to others. Faithless as they appear in breaking contracts and deserting to the rival manager, they can always be trusted to flock to the support of any of their number who have fallen upon evil days. This is no uncommon predicament. To judge from the frequency of benefits and bankruptcies, to settle down upon their own land, which is said to be their ambition, is the rarest consummation. 'The actor,' said Mr Daly, 'lives and dies in the present.'[14] When the money floods in after a successful season they lavish it childishly and ostentatiously. Even Augustin Daly, though personally abstemious, must indulge a mania for 'extra-illustrating' such books as Knight's Shakespeare, which he swells to forty-four volumes with 3,700 plates, or employ an artist to decorate the margins of books with pen-and-ink drawings, or collect first editions of the Waverley novels which, bound in full levant, with gilt tops and uncut, were destined – so one feels – to remain permanently in that condition. When they come up for auction, as periodically happens, they fetch much less than he gave for them.[15]

For the actor, however, it is not merely bankruptcy of coin that has to be dreaded, but bankruptcy of applause. 'Applause!' Miss Ada Rehan exclaims. 'We must have it!'[16] The public tires or changes its taste. About the year 1894, as Mrs John Wood testifies, the case of the old comic actress, faced with the advent of the problem play, was hard indeed. 'It is not my fault I've not acted,' she writes, '– it's the authors who are to blame. They won't be funny, and they are driving me to tradegy – I can't even spell the word, how shall I act it? But what is to become of me?'[17] Must she really play Emilia in *Othello*? She need not have been alarmed. Mr Daly's prediction that 'musical comedies are destined to be the permanent attraction everywhere'[18] was fulfilled. In the last of his productions a coach-and-four drove across the stage; and the mounting of *The Great Ruby*[19] was magnificent beyond precedent. But the strain was too much for him; a lawsuit threatened; the pecuniary situation was difficult, and in the midst of splendours and embarrassments he died worn out.

1–A review in the *Athenaeum*, 6 June 1919, (Kp C154) of *The Life of Augustin Daly* [1839–99] (Macmillan Company, 1917) by Joseph Francis Daly. The same issue of the *Athenaeum* carried an article by Roger Fry, on 'Art and Science'.
2–*Ibid.*, ch. iii, p. 21.
3–*Ibid.*, ch. ii, p. 13.
4–*Ibid.*, slightly adapted.

5–*Ibid.*, ch. xxiv, p. 365: 'It was now Mr Daly's object to take up the old play [*The Country Wife*, 1675, by William Wycherley, which David Garrick had revived in 1766 as *The Country Girl*] and fit it for his public; and his success showed that coarseness does not add to the humor of a comedy. He edited Garrick's dialogue, but preserved all the gayety and charm of the situations. Before Mr Daly revived the play it had not been seen for nearly fifty years.'
6–*Ibid.*, ch. xxvi, p. 390, slightly adapted.
7–*Ibid.*, p. 387, quoting Leander Richardson in the *Boston Herald*, in 1885.
8–This expression does not occur in Daly.
9–*Ibid.*, ch. vii, p. 269. Mrs John Wood, *née* Matilda Charlotte Vining (1831–1915), actress and theatre manageress, well known to audiences in both New York and London. 'Peachblossom': a favourite part of hers in Daly's *Under the Gaslight; or Life and Love in These Times* (1867). For the other letters referred to below, *ibid.*, pp. 283, 284.
10–*Ibid.*, ch. xiv, p. 183, quoting a letter to Daly from Henry Bergh on the production of the Spanish play *Yorick*, in December 1874.
11–*Ibid.*, ch. v, p. 58. Avonia Jones (1839–67), American actress, wife of the English tragedian G. V. Brooke.
12–*Ibid.*, ch. xi, p. 135, quoting a letter to Daly, dated 7 July 1873, from Charlotte Cushman (1816–76). Meg Merrilies: character in Scott's *Guy Mannering* (1815) which had been adapted for the stage by the author.
13–For the first quotations, *ibid.*, ch. xxxix, p. 509, which has: 'One adult writes that she is desirous of becoming an actress, "not of your limp namby-pamby kind but a whole soul artist whose fate it has been to inherit a volcanic temperature"'; and for the second, p. 510, also adapted.
14–*Ibid.*, ch. xliii, p. 567.
15–For Daly's mania, *ibid.*, ch. xix, pp. 305–6.
16–*Ibid.*, ch. xliii, p. 566. Ada Rehan (1860–1916), immensely popular American actress, a comedienne, and a central figure in Daly's company.
17–*Ibid.*, ch. xliii, p. 575, which continues: 'I thought Emilia in *Othello* would be a nice easy part to begin with. She walks on and off so much I could get used to the stage – and my black velvet train! Think about this and tell me tonight.'
18–*Ibid.*, ch. xliv, p. 578, slightly adapted.
19–*The Great Ruby*, a melodrama by Cecil Raleigh and Henry Hamilton, imported from Drury Lane and performed in New York during Daly's last season, 1898–9. See *ibid.*, ch. xlix.

Joseph Addison

VW's essay in the *TLS*, 19 June 1919, (Kp C155) on the occasion of the 200th anniversary of Addison's death, was later revised for inclusion, under the title 'Addison', in *The Common Reader*: 1st series (1925). The reader is referred to *IV VW Essays*, where the revised version, together

with variants in the form of footnotes, is reprinted in its place as part of
The Common Reader.

Is This Poetry?

There are people who write what they wish to write, though it misses by
a thousand words or exceeds by five hundred and fifty the accustomed
measure. And, when they write, they have for audience in their mind's
eye – five people, three, nobody at all perhaps. But the invisible audience
is the most exacting. The little books issued by the Hogarth Press are, to
judge by the present examples, of this uncompromising nature, designed
to please no one in particular, addressed to no public save that which has
in it the ghosts of Plato and Sir Thomas Browne, and one or two living
writers who are certainly unaware of their distinction. Thus it comes
about that Mr Murry and Mr Eliot, who have nothing in common save
the sincerity of their passion, are issued by the same press and fall to be
reviewed on the same day. 'Reviewed' is written, but it is scarcely felt.
Whether or not it is to be charged to the writer's merit, the reviewer of
these two books must feel himself decidedly more fallible than usual.
Perhaps all writing with an honest intention behind it is thus teasing and
destructive. Perhaps poetry pays less surface deference to rules than prose.

At any rate, to deal with Mr Murry first, we have to recognise in our
own mind as little serenity and certainty as is compatible with what we
have done our best to make a thorough understanding of his work. As a
first step towards understanding, rub out as many years as divide you
from the youth which, stark, stiff, severe, terribly sanguine, has not yet
been absorbed into the main activities of the world. Never again is one so
serious, so uncompromising and so clear-sighted. That is Mr Murry's
position. He stands upright, surveys the prospect, in which as yet he
plays no part, and asks himself, What is the aim of life? What can one
believe?

> Even he, I say, believed, as I believe,
> That we may seek some purpose from our void,
> A clew to grope our way by our own wires
> Back to the one Unchanging Hand that flings
> Us on the stage, and bids us dance a tune,
> Though first uncomprehended, comprehensible,
> To him that seeks believing.[2]

One after another the forms of Ulysses, Helen, and Plato rise before him and give him their versions of the faith upon which the poet makes his comment – but we will not tread out the steps of the argument. At our age we are inclined to say that the argument does not matter, since most certainly nothing can be proved. Yet as we read the strong, egotistical, sunless poem, such is the force of youth that the argument once more seems to matter. Honesty matters, courage matters, – devil take them! one may add, seeing what a springless jolt over the cobbles they are apt to lead one. But does Mr Murry make the journey worthwhile? Is he, that is to say, what, for convenience sake, we call a poet? Does he give us what after all matters so much more than the end of any journey or the truth of any argument? This, indeed, is what we find it difficult to decide. A healthy glow pervades anyone who takes hard exercise, but that you can get to perfection by mastering an Act of Parliament. Poetry – this of course is an individual experience – suddenly bestows its beauty without solicitation; you possess it before you know what it contains. But in *The Critic in Judgment* one feels that one has earned every word that one is given; and the payment is exact; there is no suspicion of gratuity. And yet, how is that without these graces and bounties the poem makes us read it? In part, of course, the subtle English logic carries us along. Beyond that, however, there are passages and phrases where the glow and heat that we require appear, giving us not the easy beauty that we are used to call inspiration, but a more difficult variety born of friction which, from the effort that it exacts, makes us ask in the midst of our exaltation, 'Is this poetry?'

The 'ordinary man', the ghostly master or terror of most writers, would certainly ask the same question about Mr Eliot, and answer it with a decided negative.

> Polyphiloprogenitive
> The sapient sutlers of the Lord
> Drift across the window-panes.
> In the beginning was the Word.[3]

Thus begins one of Mr Eliot's poems, provocative of the question and of the jeering laugh which is the easy reaction to anything strange, whether it be a 'damned foreigner' or a Post-Impressionist picture. Mr Eliot is certainly damned by his newness and strangeness; but those two qualities, which in most art are completely unimportant, because ephemeral, in him claim the attention of even the serious critic. For they are part of the fabric of his poetry. Mr Eliot is always quite consciously 'trying for' something, and something which has grown out of and developed beyond all the poems of all the dead poets. Poetry to him seems to be not so much an art as a science, a vast and noble and amusing body of communal feeling upon which the contemporary poet must take a firm stand and then launch himself into the unknown in search of new discoveries. That is the attitude not of the conventional poet, but of the scientist who with the help of working hypotheses hopes to add something, a theory perhaps or a new microbe, to the corpus of human knowledge. If we accept, provisionally, Mr Eliot's attitude, we must admit that he comes well equipped to his task. The poetry of the dead is in his bones and at the tips of his fingers: he has the rare gift of being able to weave, delicately and delightfully, an echo or even a line of the past into the pattern of his own poem. And at the same time he is always trying for something new, something which has evolved – one drops instinctively into the scientific terminology – out of the echo or the line, out of the last poem of the last dead poet, something subtly intellectual and spiritual, produced by the careful juxtaposition of words and the even more careful juxtaposition of ideas. The cautious critic, warned by the lamentable record of his tribe, might avoid answering the question: 'And is this poetry?' by asking to see a little more of Mr Eliot than is shown in these seven short poems and even 'Prufrock'.[4] But, to tell the truth, seven poems reveal a great deal of any poet. There is poetry in Mr Eliot, as, for instance, in the stanzas:

> The host with someone indistinct
> Converses at the door apart,
> The nightingales are singing near
> The Convent of the Sacred Heart,
>
> And sang within the bloody wood
> When Agamemnon cried aloud,
> And let their liquid siftings fall
> To stain the stiff dishonoured shroud.[5]

Yet the poetry often seems to come in precisely at the moment when the scientist and the science, the method and the newness, go out. A poem like 'The Hippopotamus',[6] for all its charm and cleverness and artistry, is perilously near the pit of the jeu d'esprit. And so scientific and scholarly a writer as Mr Eliot might with advantage consider whether this method was not the method of that 'terrible warning', P. Papinius Statius.[7] We hope that Mr Eliot will quickly give us more and remove our melancholy suspicion that he is the product of a Silver Age.

1–A review, written jointly by VW and LW, and published anonymously in the *Athenaeum*, 20 June 1919, (Kp C155.1) of two Hogarth Press publications: *The Critic in Judgment or Belshazzar of Baronscourt* by John Middleton Murry (1889–1957), newly-appointed editor of the *Athenaeum* (see App. IV), husband, since 1918, of Katherine Mansfield; and: *Poems* by T. S. Eliot (1888–1965), at this date an employee of Lloyds Bank, and assistant editor of *The Egoist*, whose *Prufrock and Other Observations* had appeared in 1917. (His *The Waste Land*, 1922, was published for the first time in Britain by The Hogarth Press in 1923, the type set by VW herself.)

VW wrote of their collaboration on 30 June 1919 to Philip Morrell (*II VW Letters*, no. 1065): 'You are partly right and partly wrong about the article. The truth is that Murry asked me to do it, and I refused; then he insisted, and with the greatest labour in the world I began an article, but broke down. Leonard went on with it; and then we cobbled the two parts together hoping that no one would recognise either of us. It's rather important both for the Hogarth Press and for the Athenaeum that nobody should know this; so please keep the secret. It's such a mixture of Leonard and me both trying not to give ourselves away that we're surprised that you should have suspected either of us. I thought of telling you, but had promised not to, and hoped you'd forget. On the whole its more Leonards work, I think than mine; but I never owned up to Murry that I had to call in help, and would rather he didn't know.'

A year later, she confessed to T. S. Eliot (*II VW Letters*, no. 1138, 28 July 1920): 'it was not I who reviewed your poems in the Athenaeum, but my husband. (I don't think I told Murry this.) We felt awkward at reviewing our own publications, and agreed to share the guilt: he reviewed you, and I reviewed Murry.'

The same issue of the *Athenaeum* carried articles by: Clive Bell, on 'The Artistic Problem'; and Bertrand Russell, on 'The Mystic Vision'.

2–Murry, p. 7, lines spoken by 'Critic'.

3–Eliot, unpaginated, 'Mr Eliot's Sunday Morning Service', first stanza.

4–'The Love Song of J. Alfred Prufrock', written in 1910, and first published in *Poetry* (Chicago) in 1915.

5–*Ibid.*, 'Sweeney Among the Nightingales', last two stanzas.

6–The other works in *Poems* are: 'Whispers of Immortality', 'Le Spectateur', 'Mélange Adultère de Tout', 'Lune de Miel'.

7–Publius Papinius Statius (c. AD 45–96), poet, patronised by the Emperor Domitian, whose work – *Thebais, Achilleis, Silvae* – much influenced by Virgil, is noted for its polish and fluency.

'The Way of All Flesh'

'... like most of those who come to think for themselves, he was a slow grower',[2] says Samuel Butler of Ernest, the hero of *The Way of All Flesh*. The book itself has had the same sort of history, and for much the same reason. For seven years after the first publication in 1903, it sold very slowly. It was reprinted, 'widely reviewed and highly praised',[3] but still hung fire. Then, in 1910, the flames caught; twice in that year it was reprinted, and the impression before us is the eleventh of the second edition. A wise author might choose that fate rather than one of more immediate splendour. No reading public is going to be rushed into buying an author who thinks for himself; its instinct of self-preservation protects it from that folly; first it must go through all the processes of inspection and suspicion. But the public is fundamentally sagacious. It makes up its mind after seven years or so as to what is good for it, and when it has made up its mind it sticks to it with dogged fidelity. Therefore, one is not surprised to find that in the year 1915 'Butler's writings had a larger total sale than in any previous year since their publication.'

Satisfactory as this record is, it is also much in keeping with the character of *The Way of All Flesh*. The book was written very slowly. Butler worked at it intermittently during twelve years. It is thus like a thing that has grown almost imperceptibly, a cactus or a stalactite, becoming a little shapeless, but more and more solid and sturdy year by year. One can imagine that he had grown too fond of it to part with it. Such a work is too uncompromising to make many friends when it first appears. It bears in every part of it the mark of being a home-made hobby rather than the product of high professional skill. All his convictions and prejudices have been found room for; he has never had the public in his mind's eye. So, just as Butler himself would have appeared in a crowd of fashionable people, *The Way of All Flesh* appeared among the season's novels, awkward, opinionated, angular, perverse. Nor, upon re-reading, does it appear that time has softened these qualities, and, to speak the truth, they are not qualities that are admirable in a novel. The note-book which, according to Butler, every one should carry in his waistcoat pocket, has left that secret post of observation and thrust itself forward. Shrewd, didactic passages taken from its pages constantly block the course of the story, or intrude between us and the characters, or insist that Ernest shall deliver them as if they were his own. For this reason Ernest himself remains a sheaf of papers, written all over with the acute and caustic observations of his maker, rather than an independent young man. Such is the penalty that a writer pays for indulging his hobby too far, even though the hobby be, as it was with Butler, the hobby of using his brain. The scene when Ernest attempts the seduction of Miss Maitland is a proof that when Butler's young men and women stepped beyond the circle illuminated by his keen intelligence they found themselves as thin and faltering as the creations of a tenth-rate hack. They must at once be removed to the more congenial atmosphere of the Law Courts. There are certain scenes, it appears, which must be written a great deal too quickly to allow of the deliberate inspection of a note-book, and viewed with a passion imposs- ible to the disillusioned eyes of the elderly. There is a sense, after all, in which it is a limitation to be an amateur; and Butler, it seems to us, failed to be a great novelist because his novel writing was his hobby.

In every other respect his gifts were such as to produce a novel which differs from most professional novels by being more original, more interesting, and more alive. The elderly and disillusioned mind has this advantage – that it cares nothing what people think of it. Further, its weight of experience makes up for its lack of enthusiasm. Endowed with these formidable qualities and a profound originality which wrought them to the sharpest point, Butler sauntered on unconcernedly until he found a position where he could take up his pitch and deliver his verdict upon life at his ease. *The Way of All Flesh*, which is the result, is thus much more than a story. It is an attempt to impart all that Butler thought not only about the Pontifexes, but about religion, the family system, heredity, philanthropy, education, duty, happiness, sex. The character of Christina Pontifex is rich and solid, because all the clergymen's wives whom Butler had ever known were put into her stew. In the same way Dr Skinner has the juice of innumerable headmasters in his veins, and Theobald is compounded of the dust of thousands of middle-class Englishmen. They are representative, but they are, thanks to Butler's vigorous powers of delineation, distinctly themselves. Christina's habit of day-dreaming belongs to her individually, and is a stroke of genius – if Butler did not promptly remind us that it is a little silly to talk about strokes of genius. We should not like to say how often in the course of reading *The Way of All Flesh* we found ourselves thus pulled up. Sometimes we had committed the sin of taking things, like genius, on trust. Then, again, we had fancied that some idea or other was of our own breeding. But here, on the next page, was Butler's original version, from which our seed had blown. If you want to come up afresh in thousands of minds and books long after you are dead, no doubt the way to do it is to start thinking for yourself. The novels that have been fertilised by *The Way of All Flesh* must by this time constitute a large library, with well-known names upon their backs.

1–A review in the *TLS*, 26 June 1919, (Kp C156) of *The Way of All Flesh* (1903; A. C. Fifield, 1919) by Samuel Butler (1835–1902), a writer of seminal importance to Bloomsbury. 'Mr Whitty [of the Women's Co-operative Guild] & another pressed me for copies of Kew Gardens [1919].' VW noted in her diary on Wednesday, 18 June 1919, 'But I don't want them to read the scene of the two women. Is that to the discredit of Kew Gardens? Perhaps a little. I've just been there, in the flesh, & sat under a tree, reading The Way of all Flesh, which I have to review tomorrow.' See also 'A Man With A View', *II VW Essays*; 'The Two Samuel Butlers', *IV VW Essays*; 'Gissing's *By the Ionian Sea*', *VI VW Essays*.

2–Butler, ch. lxi, p. 302.

3–The source of this information, and of that quoted at the end of the paragraph, has not been discovered. It possibly derives from the book's dust jacket.

Forgotten Benefactors

The claims of stupidity and the rights of the average human being have never, in our opinion, had justice done to them. The light of history strikes duly upon the mountain peaks; but what of the flocks and herds, the little villages, the cottages whose bedroom candles feebly penetrate a yard or two of the dark, which lie in the valleys and just at the foot of the hills? It is seldom that anybody concerns himself with them, or sets forth to write a book about nonentities. This was not Mr Bettany's intention when he devoted several years of his life (to judge by the extent of his labours) to Edward Jerningham and his friends. He must be at pains to prove that though Jerningham was not a great writer, still he was a writer; that though his friends were not great men, still some of his acquaintances had certainly been in the same room with men who were. But, having thrown this perfunctory sop to the Muse of History, Mr Bettany devotes himself as completely as we could wish to the service of the insignificant and the unknown. The result is charming. Perhaps we do not read quite as Mr Bettany would have us. Perhaps his labours were designed for a more solemn end than we have always put them to. However this may be, Mr Bettany is one of those rare historians who believe in the importance of men and women and in the individuality of their dogs.

It would be unjust to call Edward Jerningham a stupid man, and still less was he an average man. A friend remarked, 'Mr Jerningham (poor man!) still continues sillier than his sheep,'[2] but this refers to his books and is written by a fellow-author. His books, we have to confess, are unknown to us, but his character is nicely portrayed in an anecdote told by his niece:

Aug. 12th. Last Thursday my Uncle Ed., who appears very light and thoughtless, considering the present circumstances of things, went up to my Father's room after dinner (he appeared a little elevated); but, when he saw my Mother, sitting by the bedside suffering with the gout, and his Brother lying as he does, silent and weak, he was suddenly so struck with the melancholy of the scene that he burst into violent and loud weeping. Edward, who was in the outward room with Frederick, rushed in dreadfully alarmed, supposing my Father was gone, and that the screams came from my Mother. He dragged my Uncle out, who was in a perfect hysteric; but after a few minutes and drinking a glass of water, he returned to the library, quite recovered. Nor should I ever have guessed it by his manner.[3]

Uncle Edward, it appears from another extract, was the best of company, and good-natured in the extreme; if he were rich, she feels certain, he would be 'very generous to us all'; as it is, he is always in difficulties from which he expects her father to extricate him. 'My Uncle talked to all the people he met,' she concludes an account of a walk, 'particularly the children, and gave them halfpence. This is the Jerningham way; I have it quite.'[4]

Edward Jerningham had several affairs of the heart, but never married. He played on the harp; he wrote poetry in the manner of Gray; and it was common for the ladies and gentlemen of his acquaintance, when buried in the country, to entreat him to send them his witty, original letters. But no one ever troubled to keep Edward Jerningham's letters. He, on the other hand, carefully preserved several bundles addressed to him, partly no doubt because of the very kind things his friends said about his poetry, but also because he attached great importance to his friendships. He was always more or less in love.

The Jerningham family is one of those extremely ancient families which have existed in respectable obscurity upon the same spot of England for centuries, marrying into the aristocracy, but acquiring nothing more than an occasional knighthood or baronetcy for themselves. Practically all Jerningham's correspondents bore names which still adorn the columns of the *Morning Post*. The Walpoles, through a marriage with the Fitz-Osberts in the fourteenth century, were his cousins; the Harcourts, the Howards, the Mount Edgcumbes, the Conways, addressed him familiarly as an equal. The pillar-boxes of Mayfair a hundred and fifty years ago are open for our inspection, and the condition of insignificance to which we attach so much importance is almost invariably fulfilled by their contents then, as perhaps we should find it now. Were it not for the astonishing pertinacity of Mr Bettany, some even of the famous names would be gone past recall. Like the population of a deserted graveyard, a Jones would be found beneath a Howard's tombstone, and small boys would be playing marbles indifferently upon the grave of a marchioness. Even Mr Bettany has to own himself defeated again and again in his work of identification. 'I cannot explain this reference. I cannot identify this person,' is the melancholy refrain of many a letter. But he does not easily give up hope. Those dismissed to darkness upon one page sometimes emerge into a faint ray of light upon another. It is proved satisfactorily that Mr Money, who threatened to escape altogether, was at one time occupied at the Tower.[5] But of whose complexion did Mr Jerningham speak disrespectfully in the year 1799? Who was that entertaining lady, la Belle Emilie, and her fair friend 'too incapable of feeling a passion ever to inspire one'?[6] Who was Major Wilson? And what was the Christian name of Miss Carter? Mr Bettany has no idea. Even of a great lady like Lady Harcourt, daughter of George, first Baron Vernon, by his third wife Martha, 'little is known, and therefore little can be said. [. . .] But she seems to have possessed sincere religious feeling'.[7] There can be two opinions even about that. And though Mr Bettany guesses discreetly, we cannot always feel sure that his guess is the right one. 'When I do return home,' writes Lady Harcourt, 'I will not tell Patty a word about the letter you have thought of writing to Madame de Biron; as she could never go into my bed again.' 'Patty was apparently the Countess's favourite bitch' is Mr Bettany's too rash conjecture.[8] On another occasion, however, his caution seems to us excessive. 'The only great event that has happened since my arrival here is the accouchement of Madame Cloe: she has produced three puppies.' 'Presumably Miss Harland's favourite bitch,' Mr Bettany observes.[9] The three puppies, to our mind, put the question beyond presumption, though what position Madame Cloe had in Miss Harland's affections must remain obscure until the great day of identification dawns, upon which occasion Mr Bettany's excitement will be pleasant to witness.

But the book is all the better for having these dark places, and leaving us plenty of scope to guess and speculate and peer after the vanished spectres. Lord Harcourt, indeed, vanished in an extremely abrupt and, to him, unpleasant manner, being found 'in a narrow well, nothing appearing above water but the feet and legs, occasioned, as it is imagined, by his over-reaching himself in order to save the life of a favourite dog, who was found in the well with him, standing on his

lordship's feet'.[10] Surely that end was ordained by a humorous providence for the author of the following sentence. Lord Harcourt had been
dining with the Queen, and wrote to Mr Jerningham:

I shall never forget what her Majesty so justly observed of your works, that she was
sure the author was a man of worth and merit. I was quite struck with the justness
and the propriety of the observation.[11]

From that on an autumn morning he went pompously, considerately,
and appropriately to his death. And Lady Mount Edgcumbe. She was
known, behind her back, as the 'Sea Cowcumber', which phrase,
together with her ladyship's own plethoric and congested style – 'this
week, beyond both, came death (probably) ... and the suspected
character of her daughter, to agonize her heart; herself a most excellent
woman and therefore the more shocked'[12] – somehow produce a sense
of the voluminous peeress, kind-hearted, censorious, garrulous, indiscreet, such as pages of pure English would fail to convey. And there is
war with France, and 'a Duke of Beaufort blowing about in a tent, and a
Lord Uxbridge crammed into a low damp barrack';[13] Heaven protect
the French noblesse, and avert revolution, and send our sons safe home;
poor Lady Clarges' son died a little hero; but the way Lady Jersey is
carrying on with the Prince of Wales is a public scandal, and Lady Emily
has been brought to bed of a boy, thank Heaven, and a thousand loves,
dear Mr Jerningham, and we wish you were here to make one of our
party in the warm South Library.

1–A signed review in the *Athenaeum*, 4 July 1919, (Kp C157) of *Edward
Jerningham and his Friends: A series of Eighteenth-Century Letters.* Edited by Lewis
Bettany (Chatto & Windus, 1919). Edward Jerningham (1727–1812), poet, drama-
tist, and man of fashion, third son of Sir George Jerningham (d. 1774) and his heiress
wife, Mary, *née* Plowden (d. 1785). He numbered Lord Chesterfield (1694–1773)
and Horace Walpole (1717–97) among his friends and, writing in the manner of
Thomas Gray (1716–71), was the butt of much satire.
  The review's title may recall Leslie Stephen's celebrated lecture in which he spoke
of his wife Julia 'without mentioning her name' (see *Social Rights and Duties*, 1896).
  The same issue of the *Athenaeum* carried articles by: T. S. Eliot, on 'A Foreign
Mind', a review of Yeats's *The Cutting of an Agate*; and E. M. Forster on 'The
Extreme Case', a review of a collection of Gauguin's letters.
2–Jerningham, ch. i, p. 4, quoting William Gifford (1756–1826), who, in his *Baviad*
(1794), had satirised 'Snivelling Jerningham' as weeping, at the age of fifty, 'o'er
love-lorn oxen and deserted sheep'.
3–*Ibid.*, p. 11, quoting the diary for 1809 of Jerningham's niece, Lady Bedingfeld.
4–For both quotations, *ibid.*
5–*Ibid.*, ch. iv, p. 78, fn. 4.

6–*Ibid.*, letter from Elizabeth, Countess Harcourt (d. 1826), ? date, p. 79.
7–*Ibid.*, p. 76, which has: 'She composed verses which Horace Walpole admired, was a courtier and an agreeable letter-writer, and seems to have possessed sincere religious feeling. That is practically all that is known about her.'
8–For the first quotation, *ibid.*, p. 80, and for the second, p. 81, fn. 8.
9–For the first quotation, *ibid.*, ch. vi, p. 155, and for the second, p. 156, fn. 3.
10–*Ibid.*, ch. iv, p. 76; Simon, 1st Earl Harcourt (1714–77), Lord Lieutenant of Ireland, October 1772–January 1777.
11–*Ibid.*, p. 78, letter dated 29 March 1773; Harcourt died on 16 September 1777.
12–For the 'Sea Cowcumber', *ibid.*, ch. viii, p. 196, and for the following quotation, *ibid.*, letter dated 9 July 1794, p. 214; Emma, Countess of Mount Edgcumbe (d. 1807), daughter of John Gilbert, Archbishop of York, had married 3rd Baron Edgcumbe in 1761.
13–*Ibid.*, letter dated 20 September 1794, p. 218.

A Positivist

'Alas!' exclaims Mr Harrison, 'I wrote an article in the very first number of the *Fortnightly*, in May, 1865, along with papers by Huxley, Bagehot, Trollope, George Eliot, G. H. Lewes, Lord de Tabley. And soon after came on John Morley, Lecky, Freeman, Swinburne, Meredith, Pater, Leslie Stephen, Herbert Spencer, Mark Pattison, Frederick Myers, Arthur J. Balfour. Ah! we were a poor lot.'[2] 'Alas!' of course, ought to be written 'Lord be praised!' and 'Ah! we were a poor lot' similarly transposed into 'Did the civilised world ever see the like of us?' for self-depreciation and lack of self-confidence are not the faults of Mr Frederic Harrison. If they had been he would not have contributed, at the age of eighty-seven, these very positive and energetic notes upon current policies and literature to the *Fortnightly Review*. He would not have given us the impression that somewhere about the middle of the last century Truth opened her lips and spoke her secrets to a little group of which he is now almost the only survivor. With a little more diffidence he might have mitigated some of his sarcasms against the moderns and – who knows? – have read some of their books. As it is, when someone asked him what he found to read in these days he replied, 'Well! nothing new, unless what deals with the war or standard literature of the old immortals'.[3] Following upon that confession come, as a matter of course, the usual ironies about Cubism and morality and the manners of young women in omnibuses. A less helpful relationship between the generations it would be difficult to conceive.

Such little amenities may pass; but when Mr Harrison delivers himself with his usual vigour upon current questions – the House of Commons, Ireland, Bolshevism, the League of Nations, patriotism, socialism, or whatever it may be – his asperity, combined with his conviction of having been in the right for sixty years or so, gives him the arrogance of a judge rather than the more valuable insight of a fellow sinner. The inevitable result is that although he says much that is sound and much that is trenchant he seems to be talking to someone in the next room, or, more mysteriously, addressing a world that has ceased to exist. Our point will be made clear by quoting him not upon subjects that are controversial, but upon a matter outside controversy – upon the spectacle of London in 1918: –

It shocks, wounds, disgusts me, as if, with the poet, I were in one of the circles of his Inferno. Modern mechanism has brutalized life. And in this rattle and crash and whirl, wild luxury, games, shows, gluttony, and vice work their Vanity Fair with greater recklessness than ever.[4]

We have no wish to be numbered among those who, according to Mr Harrison, pursue the Victorians with cries of 'Go up, ye Baldheads!'[5] but we cannot help wondering how long that remarkable generation will neglect certain aspects of its own morality and society for which we find as many epithets and as severe.

But Mr Harrison has been actively interested in the development of modern thought for at least sixty years; and the general reflections of such an observer have far more value than his judgment of particulars:

There is no Victorian era at all. I have lived and observed things from William IV, to George V, and, great as the changes have been, both material and spiritual, there has been little spasmodic in it at any time. From 1789 to 1918 there has been a continuous post-revolutionary stream.[6]

That is the kind of reflection that seems to us to be within the special province of old age. It proceeds from a million observations of which the younger generation can have no experience; and Mr Harrison could substantiate it with first-hand knowledge of almost every one in the nineteenth century who shared in the spiritual and material develop-ment of the time. Far from complaining, as Mr Harrison anticipates, of his egotism in dwelling upon what he has seen, heard and felt, we should for our part keenly relish a far more complete record of his experience than we have here. That, we have reason to hope, since Mr Harrison makes mention of a diary, is a pleasure only deferred. In the present volume, though it is for the most part concerned with the events of the moment, there are startling evidences of his extraordinary range over the past. 'I took down that delightful book, *The Crescent and the Cross, 1845*, by Eliot Warburton. Well do I recall the delight it gave us when it first appeared with Kinglake's *Eöthen*.'[7] How, after all, can a memory which holds that retain as truly the impressions of the present moment – how refrain from a slighting comparison between them? And then there are the classics. Aeschylus has taken up some of the room that the moderns would allow to Mr Hardy.[8] Sophocles, Virgil, Horace, Rabelais, Jane Austen, Scott have, not so strangely, closed the doors to their descendants. Perhaps this closing of the doors is one of the necessary results of having convictions and refusing to die, as lyric poets according to Mr Harrison's computation have to die, at the age of fifty-two.[9] Anyhow, part of Mr Harrison's definition of religion is to enjoy 'continuous communion of soul with those of a like mind who are working out their duty in the eye and with the help of Providence'.[10] 'Of a like mind' – there is the stumbling block. The belief that there is one mind about moral and spiritual purposes which is the right one is the mark of Mr Harrison's generation, but no longer of ours.

1 – A review in the *TLS*, 17 July 1919, (Kp C158) of *Obiter Scripta. 1918* (Chapman & Hall, 1919) by Frederic Harrison (1831–1923), writer, and a leading figure in the English positivist movement, whose interest in the writings of Comte was stimulated by Richard Congreve, his tutor at Wadham College, Oxford, where Harrison took a first in classics and was a fellow, 1854–6. He was a friend of Leslie Stephen (1832–1904), who recalled him in his *Mausoleum Book* (OUP, 1977), p. 8: 'I joined the Cosmopolitan, then and I believe still a famous resort for the select intellects of London, and a smaller society on the same plan called the Century. To it belonged many of the clever young writers and barristers, chiefly of the radical persuasion. I chiefly remember Fred. Harrison and some of his positivist friends. We used to meet on Wednesday and Sunday evenings, to smoke and drink in moderation and discuss the Universe and the Reform movement of 1866–7.' Harrison was a prolific author; his works include *Cromwell* (1888), *Studies in Early Victorian Literature* (1895), *William the Silent* (1897), *Ruskin* (1902), and *The German Peril* (1915).
2 – Harrison, 'An Early Victorian', p. 40, which continues: '–Gradgrinds and Pecksniffs, bred up on Darwin, Stuart Mill, Spencer, Comte, and Carlyle. Why, we used to think that Tennyson and Browning were poets; we knew nothing of Cubism in geometry, art, or music; we believed that Evolution opened a new world to science; that marriage vows were meant to be kept – at any rate, were respectable; that the life and the manners of women were not quite those of men-about-town.' The *Fortnightly Review* (in fact a monthly) was originally edited by G. H. Lewes (1817–78), who was succeeded as editor in 1867 by John Morley (1838–1923). Other contributors: Thomas Henry Huxley (1825–95); Walter Bagehot (1826–77); Anthony Trollope (1815–82); George Eliot (1819–80); Lord de Tabley (1835–95);

William Lecky (1838–1903); E. A. Freeman (1823–92); A. C. Swinburne (1837–1909); George Meredith (1828–1909); Walter Pater (1839–94); Herbert Spencer (1820–1903); Mark Pattison (1813–84); Frederick Myers (1843–1901); Arthur J. Balfour (1848–1930).

3 – *Ibid.*, 'The Great Old Books', p. 37, which continues: 'I read patiently the Press for all shades, except the vilest Pacifism . . . For the rest and relief of mind I turn to the great classics . . . How boy or girl in these cruel days can soak themselves in "shockers", short stories, "smart" up-to-date tales of women with a past and men with no future, I cannot understand. Yet such pour out daily with *saugrenu* pictures that could hardly amuse an errand-boy.'

4 – *Ibid.*, 'The Vanity Fair of London', p. 15.

5 – *Ibid.*, 'Mr Asquith's Romanes Lecture', p. 128.

6 – *Ibid.*, 'No Real Victorian Era', p. 145.

7 – *Ibid.*, 'The Crescent and the Cross, 1845', pp. 169–70, which continues: 'and well do I remember the shock of the author's premature death in the burning at sea of the s.s. *Amazon*.' Eliot Warburton (1810–52), miscellaneous writer, had been bound for the Isthmus of Darien aboard the ill-fated *Amazon*, on the vessel's maiden voyage. Alexander Kinglake (1809–91), whose *Eöthen* was first published in 1844.

8 – Thomas Hardy (1840–1928).

9 – *Ibid.*, 'Average Age of Lyric Poets is 52', p. 114.

10 – *Ibid.*, 'Culture is not Religion', p. 141, which begins: 'But, surely, all modern and rational ideas of religion mean the faith and the resolution to do one's work in the world in accordance with the moral and spiritual purposes of a righteous life, and in . . .'

Horace Walpole

One hundred and ten letters by Horace Walpole are here printed by Dr Toynbee for the first time. These, together with twenty-three now printed in full, new matter from hitherto unpublished material, and Dr Toynbee's notes, make up two volumes of rare delight. If the two volumes were ten we should still urge Dr Toynbee to fresh researches; we should still welcome the discovery of a large chest put away in some old country house and stuffed to the brim with Walpole's letters. Although there is nothing in the new letters of surpassing brilliance, nothing that draws a new line on the familiar face, there is once more, and for too short a time, the peculiar and unmistakable pleasure of Walpole's society. He does not need to be brilliant; he does not need to be indiscreet; let him draw up to the table, take the pen in his gouty fingers, and write – anything, everything, so long as he continues to write. These last letters, swept up from many different sources with intervals between them and lacking continuity, are yet neither trivial nor disconnected. We fall into step at once. We take our delightful promenade through the greater part of the eighteenth century. We see in passing many old friends. It is as entertaining as ever. The first solemn chimes of the nineteenth century, which mean that Horace Walpole must retire, are as vexatious to us as the clock that strikes and sends a child complaining up to bed.

Perhaps it is fanciful to detect the charm of the mature Walpole in 'My first letter to my mother', with which the book opens: 'Dear Mama, I hop you are wall and I am very wall and I hop papa is wall . . . and I am very glad to hear by Tom that all my cruataurs ar all wall.'[2] Yet this is an engaging letter, as the dark-eyed little boy in the miniature is a charming little boy; and there can be no doubt that Walpole far sooner than most children knew his own mind and could overcome the difficulties of spelling. There was never a transition stage of awkward immaturity when he said more than he meant, or less than he meant, or what he did not mean. At the age of twenty-three he appears in Rome a complete man of the world, and so much his own master that he can already quiz the great ladies who are seeing the sights, execute commissions for fans and snuff-boxes, exchange compliments with learned men, keep his own mind admirably free from enthusiasm, and end a letter:

Good-night, child, I am in a violent hurry. Oh, Porto Bello, the delightful news! Corradini is certainly to be Pope, and soon. Next post I shall probably be able to tell you he certainly is not.[3]

The author of that sentence is already completely equipped for his part. He has broken the back of the stubborn English tongue; for ever more it is going to run his errands, carry his light burdens, do his behests; he has at his disposal an indefatigable slave. More than that, he has already taken up his position, sees the spectacle from his own angle, and for close on eighty years there will he stand, witty, malicious, observant, detached, the liveliest of gossips, the most alert of friends. The son of a Prime Minister endowed with a handsome sinecure, a position of some sort was assured him had he been both dunce and dullard. But Horace Walpole was not a dullard, and he was much more than the son of a Prime Minister. He stood out against his hereditary doom with a resolution which commands our respect, though it has caused him to be disparaged since, as no doubt it raised a laugh against him at the time. He would not drink; he would not dice; he would not be a country gentleman; he would not be a politician. He would, in short, be nothing save what it pleased him to be.

On the whole it pleased him best to be a gentleman, for there is no reason why a gentleman should not write the wittiest letters in the world, provided that he does it carelessly, and has for correspondents the most exalted and the most accomplished of his time. The chief characteristic of this class he had acquired very young, perhaps at the cost of some labour – even, it is possible, of some renunciation. 'Good-night, child, I am in a violent hurry.' Whatever pains his letter had cost him, it was essential to pass it off as the merest trifle, something dashed down while he waited for the rain to stop – something, as the phrasing shows, spontaneous, careless, but spoken naturally in a tone of the highest breeding. He was careful to repeat the boast that he was in a violent hurry whenever he wrote anything. As for rhapsody of emotion or profundity of learning, those qualities he left to the professional writers who had only their brains to live by. Moreover, it is permissible for the amateur to spend his time over problems which fascinated Walpole, though no man of sense could waste a thought upon them. Since no one, himself least of all, took him seriously, he could devote several pages to the discussion of that difficult and vexed question – the age at which Lady Desmond died. Was she really 163, and could it be possible that she had danced with Richard the Third? For some reason these questions stirred his imagination. His eagerness to know the exact condition of Queen Catherine Parr's corpse, when it was dug up and examined, would seem excessive – save indeed that the lady was of the highest rank.[4] For it is not possible to deny that he was a snob, and of the determined breed whose mothers have been Shorters while their fathers, though not of noble birth, have been exalted by their abilities to familiar converse with the great. Yet once that dart is levelled, no other can find a lodgment. It is not easy to call him dilettante or gossip, poetaster or dandy, when before these charges are out of your mouth the culprit has owned them of his own accord and gone out of his way to pronounce his sentence:

Good God! Sir, what am I that I should be offended at, or above, criticism or correction? I do not know who ought to be – I am sure no author. I am a private man of no consequence, and at best an author of very moderate abilities.[5]

Even in matters of taste, upon which he had spent most of his life and a large part of his fortune, he was open to correction by people possessed of greater learning than he could claim. He was nothing but a private gentleman.

The reader will perceive that the habit of understatement is not only the essence of good breeding, but also a tool of great value in the hand of a writer. An author who knows no more than other people, who has no dignity to keep up, no convictions to enforce, no philosophy to expound, can say what he likes and think what he chooses. No one need attend to him. But if, in addition, by a mere stroke of luck, he possesses the wittiest of pens and the most observant of eyes, if he knows everybody worth knowing and sees everything worth seeing, we shall of course get every word he writes by heart. Since, however, writers should be serious, we shall in revenge allow him very little credit for his performance. It is the fashion to say that Walpole was so amusing because he was so frivolous, so witty because he was so heartless. He was certainly very much put out when old Madame du Deffand fell in love with him, and thought that at her age she could afford to talk about it openly. 'Dès le moment que je cessai d'être jeune, j'ai eu une peur horrible de devenir un vieillard ridicule,' he wrote to her; and she replied, 'Vos craintes sur le ridicule sont des terreurs paniques, mais on ne guérit point de la peur; je n'ai point vu une semblable faiblesse.'[6] He was terribly afraid of ridicule, and yet the old lady, whose passion he had snubbed, showed considerable penetration, when she spoke of 'l'extrême vérité de votre caractère'.[7] Understatement long persisted in, partly from motives of taste and propriety and partly from fear of ridicule, had disciplined Walpole's emotions so that they scarcely dared show themselves above ground; yet what there is of them, as sometimes happens with emotions repressed rather than exploited, rings startlingly true. '. . . he loved me and I did not think he did', he wrote of his quarrel with Gray, when Gray was dead.[8] But as for his heart, let that rest in peace; there is some indecency in prying into it, and he would certainly prefer that we should credit him with none at all than allow him a grain too much. His brain is our affair.

And yet here once more shall we not be guilty of some credulity if we accept him entirely at his own estimate? The affectation of indifference, the pose of amateurishness, were common foibles at that time among men of birth whose brains could not abstain altogether from the ink-pot. But perhaps there were moments when Walpole wished that his father's name had been Shorter as well as his mother's, and that fate had required him to use pen and paper in earnest and not merely provide them, at a handsome salary, for the use of the young men at the Treasury. At any rate his warmest praises in the present volume are not for Lady Di's illustrations in 'Sut water' to The Mysterious Mother, nor even for Mrs Damer's model of 'a shock dog in wax',[9] but for the plays of

Shakespeare. 'Moi, je me ferais brûler pour la primauté de Shakespeare.' Admiring the French and owing much to them, still when it comes to tragedy what are Voltaire and Racine and Corneille,[10] compared with Shakespeare? How did Voltaire dare criticise Shakespeare? 'Grossly ignorant and tasteless'[11] was he not to see that the phrase 'a bare bodkin' is as sublime in one way as the simplicity of Lady Percy's speech is sublime in another? 'I had rather have written the two speeches of Lady Percy in the second part of *Henry IV* than all Voltaire ...[12] But my enthusiasm for Shakespeare runs away with me.'[13] That is, indeed, an unwonted spectacle. But perhaps young Mr Jephson, the playwright, owed all this talk about Shakespeare and the English language 'far more energie, and more sonorous too, than the French', and these interesting speculations about 'a novel diction',[14] 'a very new and peculiar style' which might have amazing effect, 'by fixing on some region of whose language we have little or no idea'[15]—perhaps Mr Jephson drew all this down upon himself because the old dandy and aristocrat did for the time being envy young Mr Jephson, who could set himself seriously to the task of writing and need not, since his name was Jephson, scribble off a tragedy 'in a violent hurry'.

A queer sort of imagination haunted the seemingly prosaic edifice of Walpole's mind. What but imagination gone astray and vagrant over pots and pans instead of firmly held in place was his love of knick-knacks and antiquities, Strawberry hills and decomposing royalties? And once at least Walpole made a little confession to Madame du Deffand. Of all his works he preferred *The Castle of Otranto*, for there he said 'j'ai laissé courir mon imagination; les visions et les passions m'échauffaient'.[16] Vision and passion are not the gifts that we should ascribe offhand to Horace Walpole; and yet as we lose ourselves in the enormous variety and entertainment of his letters we must allow that somehow from his own angle he saw truly, he judged independently. Somehow he was not only the wittiest of men, but the most observant and not the least kindly. And among the writers of English prose he wears forever and with a peculiar grace a coronet of his own earning.

1–A review in the *TLS*, 31 July 1919, (Kp C159) of *The Supplement to the Letters of Horace Walpole, Fourth Earl of Orford*. Chronologically arranged and edited with notes and indices by Paget Toynbee, MA, D Litt, FR Hist.Soc., in two volumes with portraits and facsimiles, vol. i, 1725–1783; vol. ii, 1783–1796 (OUP, 1918). For which VW also read: *The Letters of Horace Walpole, Earl of Orford*. Ed. Peter Cunningham (2 vols, Richard Bentley, 1857); Leslie Stephen, 'Horace Walpole', *Hours in a Library* (1874 etc.); Austin Dobson, *Horace Walpole. A Memoir*

(Osgood, McIlvaine, 1893). Horace Walpole (1717–97), author, antiquarian, and MP, 1741–68, fourth son of Sir Robert Walpole who was premier, 1715–17, 1721–42. In 1747 he acquired the property near Twickenham from which he created his little Gothic castle Strawberry Hill.

On Sunday, 20 July 1919, VW wrote in her diary: 'Perhaps I will finish the account of the peace celebrations. What herd animals we are after all! – even the most disillusioned. At any rate, after sitting through the procession & the peace bells unmoved, I began after dinner to feel that if something was going on, perhaps one had better be in it. I routed up poor L. & threw away my Walpole . . . We went out just before ten. Explosions had for some time promised fireworks'; and on Thursday, 24 July, she remarked: 'Last night we had Forster & the Bussys. It was not the mixture we should have chosen, since Forster would come out better alone. However, such are the penalties of owning a press. I feel something like Horace Walpole who had to limit the visitors to Strawberry Hill to 4 daily –'

See also 'Gothic Romance' below; 'Romance', II VW Essays; 'Two Antiquaries: Walpole and Cole' and 'The Humane Art', VI VW Essays. Reprinted: G&R, CE. Reading Notes (MHP, B2).

2 – For the first quotation, Toynbee, vol. i, p. 1, fn, quoting Walpole's endorsement of his letter; and for the second, ibid., 'Letter A [1725]. Written at the age of 8 to Lady Walpole', p. 1. Lady Walpole, née Catherine Shorter (d.1737), granddaughter of Sir John Shorter, Lord Mayor of London in 1688, married Robert Walpole (who was created Knight of the Bath in May 1725) in 1700.

3 – Ibid., Letter no. 26, to Sir Horace Mann (1701–86), British envoy at Florence, 16 April 1740, pp. 13–14, which has a dash before 'Corradini' and no comma after 'Pope'.

4 – For Lady Desmond, ibid., Letter no. 540*, to C.O. Esq., 17 September 1757, p. 81.

5 – The source of Walpole's protestation has resisted discovery.

6 – For the first quotation, Toynbee, vol. i, to the Marquise du Deffand, 10 October 1766, p. 144; and for the second, from the Marquise, 19 October, ibid., fn2. Marie de Vichy-Chamrond, Marquise du Deffand (1697–1780) whom Walpole first met in 1765.

7 – Ibid., p. 227, fn2.

8 – For the quotations, Dobson, pp. 53–4, quoting Walpole writing to the poet Rev. William Mason (1724–97), 2 March 1773. Walpole had been at Eton with Thomas Gray (1716–71), whose works he published in 1757. Mason was an admiring friend, and as a poet an imitator, of Gray.

9 – For the first quotation, ibid., p. 195, and see pp. 244–5: 'Lady Di Beauclerk (1734–1808), whose illustrations to Dryden's Fables are still a frequent item in second-hand catalogues, has a personal connection with Strawberry through the curious little closet bearing her name, which, with the assistance of Mr Essex, a Gothic architect from Cambridge, Walpole in 1776–8 managed to tuck in between the Cabinet and the Round Tower. It was built on purpose to hold the "seven incomparable drawings" executed in a fortnight, which her Ladyship prepared to illustrate The Mysterious Mother [Walpole's tragedy of incest, published in 1768] . . . They were hung on Indian blue damask, in frames of black and gold, and . . . Miss Pope, the actress, when she dined at Strawberry, was affected by them to such a

degree that she shed tears, although she did not know the story . . .'; and for the second quotation, Toynbee, vol. ii, 'Additions and Corrections to Volumes i–xvi', p. 125.
10–For the quotation, Toynbee, vol. i, Letter no. 1221*, to the Marquise du Deffand, July 1768, p. 170. William Shakespeare (1564–1616); Voltaire (François-Marie Arouet, 1694–1778); Jean Racine (1639–99); Pierre Corneille (1606–84).
11–Ibid., vol. i, Letter no. 16088***, to the dramatist, poet and sometime infantry captain Robert Jephson (1736–1803), February 1775, p. 254.
12–Ibid., p. 253.
13–Ibid., p. 254.
14–For both quotations, ibid., p. 256. Jephson's tragedy Braganza, for which Walpole wrote an epilogue, was produced in February 1775 at Drury Lane and received with great acclaim. His The Count of Narbonne, based upon Walpole's The Castle of Otranto (1764), was performed at Covent Garden in 1781.
15–For both quotations, ibid., Letter no. 1608**, February 1775.
16–Ibid., vol. i, Letter no. 1164**, to the Marquise du Deffand, 13 March 1767, p. 152.

These Are the Plans

Poetry is a much safer refuge than prose. A large number of the young men who left behind them enough verse to fill a little book before they were killed evidently wrote poetry because it allowed them to express their feelings without a sense of irreticence. This rhyme, this metre, these old poetical phrases, serve as a mask behind which the writer dares say something that he would blush to say with the inflection of everyday speech in prose. Poets, of course, come to poetry from quite a different direction, but Mr Donald Johnson does not make us feel that he was by nature a poet. No doubt he would have written poetry, and no doubt he would have burned it. But things being as they were, his friends killed, his life changed, himself ordered from a Cambridge library to the front with the likelihood of death, feelings that would have faded unrecorded, some that would never have been felt at all or without such intensity, were necessarily expressed, and poetry was less of an effort, more of a disguise, than prose. For one reason or another, therefore, there are a number of poems in his book which make an appeal, perhaps not strictly poetic, to the reader's sympathies:

> Look long on the last lilac ere it fade;
> So soon it dies; and when it flowers again

Thy body in the still earth will be laid,
Asleep to memory, and numb to pain;
Deaf to earth's music; and for thee no more
The crocus-shower'd laburnum shall awake,
And to the dawn its dancing tresses shake –
Tresses more radiant than Apollo wore.[2]

The sonnet from which these lines are taken is called 'Spring, 1915'; and in 1916 its writer was dead. So again with 'A Memory', 'The Wish', and 'L'Inconnue'.[3] Our knowledge of his circumstances gives these poems an intensity beyond their poetic merit, though when he wrote directly of what he felt he wrote far better than elsewhere. The longer poems upon classical subjects are such exercises as might well occupy the leisure of a scholar engaged, as Mr Johnson was engaged at the outbreak of war, upon the text of Chaucer; they would teach him to read his text with greater understanding; but, personal feeling being absent and words used much as pieces in a poetic puzzle, these exercises have little independent life of their own.

So far as we can read Charles Sorley's character between the lines of his book, nothing would have annoyed him more than to find himself acclaimed either a poet or a hero. He was far too genuine a writer not to be disgusted by any praise implying that his work, at the stage it had reached, was more than a promise and an experiment. It is indeed largely because Charles Sorley was experimental, here trying his hand at narrative, here at description, always making an effort to shed the conventional style and press more closely to his conception, that one is convinced that he was destined, whether in prose or in verse, to be a writer of considerable power. The writer's problem presented itself very early in his life. Here at Marlborough, where he was at school, the downs showed themselves not, as other poets have seen them, soft, flowery, seductive, but stony, rain-beaten, wind-blown beneath a clay-coloured sky. He tried to put down in verse his delight in that aspect of nature and his corresponding notion of a race of men.

Stern, sterile, senseless, mute, unknown,
But bold, O, bolder far than we![4]

He tried to say how much had been revealed to him when he wandered, as he was fond of doing, alone among the downs:

I who have walked along her downs in dreams,
And known her tenderness, and felt her might,
And sometimes by her meadows and her streams
Have drunk deep-storied secrets of delight,

* * *

> Have had my times, when, though the earth did wear
> Her selfsame trees and grasses, I could see
> The revelation that is always there,
> But somehow is not always clear to me.[5]

Succeeding these schoolboy attempts at landscape comes the natural mood of feeling that beauty is better not expressed, and that his spirit, compared with the spirits of the poets, is dumb. Running alongside of them, also, is his characteristic view – or the view that was characteristic of that stage of his life – of our modern sin of inactivity. The rain beats and the wind blows, but we are sluggish and quiescent –

> We do not see the vital point
> That 'tis the eighth, most deadly, sin
> To wail, "The world is out of joint" –
> And not attempt to put it in.
>
> We question, answer, make defence,
> We sneer, we scoff, we criticize,
> We wail and moan our decadence,
> Enquire, investigate, surmise –[6]

We might of course cap these verses with a stanza to prove that Sorley found satisfaction in the outbreak of war, and died bidding men

> On, marching men, on
> To the gates of death with song.
> Sow your gladness for earth's reaping,
> So you may be glad through sleeping,
> Strew your gladness on earth's bed.
> So be merry, so be dead.[7]

And yet from the evidence of his poetry, and still more from the evidence of his remarkable prose, it is clear that Sorley was as far from trumping up a precocious solution, as ready to upset all his convictions and be off on a fresh track, as any other boy with a mind awakening daily more widely to the complexity of things, and naturally incapable of a dishonest or sentimental conclusion. 'A Call to Action', from which we have quoted, was written when Sorley, at the age of seventeen, was going through a phase of admiration for the work of Mr Masefield. And then came a time, in Germany, of 'setting up and smashing of deities', Masefield and Hardy and Goethe being the gods to suffer, while Ibsen and the Odyssey and Robert Browning inherited the vacant pedestals.[8] Almost at once the war broke out.

I'm sure the German nature is the nicest in the world, as far as it is not warped by the German Empire ⟨he wrote⟩.[9] I regard the war as one between sisters . . . the efficient and intolerant against the casual and sympathetic . . . but I think that tolerance is the larger virtue of the two, and efficiency must be her servant. So I am quite glad to fight against the rebellious servant . . .[10] Now you know what Sorley thinks about it.[11]

'What Sorley thinks about it' appears to us of extreme interest, because, as our quotations have tried to show, Sorley thought for himself, and fate contrived that the young men of his generation should have opportunities for doing the thinking of a lifetime in a very few years. Such opportunities for changing his mind and moving on Sorley used to the full. There was, directly he joined the army, the problem of what he called 'the poorer classes'. 'The public school boy', he said, 'should live among them to learn a little Christianity; for they are so extraordinarily nice to one another'.[12] After that reflection there comes, a page or two later, the remark: 'I have had a conventional education: Oxford would have corked it'.[13] So his dream for next year is to be perhaps in Mexico, selling cloth.

Or in Russia, doing Lord knows what: in Serbia, or the Balkans: in England never. England remains the dream, the background: at once the memory, and the ideal . . . Details can wait – perhaps for ever. These are the plans.[14]

It is upon the plans rather than upon the details that one is inclined to dwell, asking oneself to what goal this generation, captained by men of such vigour and clearsightedness as Sorley, was making its way.

> We know not whom we trust
> Nor whitherward we fare
> But we run because we must
> Through the great wide air,[15]

are lines from an early poem that seem to express a force yet undirected seeking a new channel. But the poems are more than scattered details to be used to illustrate an imaginary career. They have often enough literary merit to stand upon their own feet independently of any personal considerations. They have the still rarer merit of suggesting that the writer is so well aware of his own purpose that he is content to leave a roughness here, a jingle there, for the sake of getting on quickly to the next stage. What the finished work, the final aim, would have been we can only guess, for Charles Sorley at the age of twenty was killed near Hulluch.

1 – A signed review in the *Athenaeum*, 1 August 1919, (Kp C160) of *Poems* . . . with a prefatory note by P. Giles, Litt. D. (Master of Emmanuel College, Cambridge)

(CUP, 1919) by Donald F. Goold Johnson (1890–1916) and of *Marlborough and Other Poems* (CUP, 4th ed., 1919) by Charles Hamilton Sorley (1895–1915).

Johnson had worked as a schoolteacher before becoming a choral scholar at Emmanuel College. He won the Chancellor's Medal for verse in 1914, with a poem on 'The Southern Pole', and after graduating engaged in Chaucer scholarship. With the outbreak of war he enlisted in the Manchester Regiment and in 1915 went to France, where he died in action.

Sorley was educated at Marlborough College, 1908–13, and won, but did not take up, a scholarship to Oxford in 1914. Instead he enlisted, became a captain in the Suffolk Regiment and was killed in action. His book, in less extended form, had first appeared in 1916.

The same issue of the *Athenaeum* also contained articles by: Lytton Strachey, on 'Voltaire'; T. S. Eliot, on 'Was There a Scottish Literature?' (immediately preceding VW's piece); and E. M. Forster on 'Tagore as a Novelist'.

2–Johnson, 'Spring, 1915', p. 3.
3–*Ibid.*, 'A Memory', pp. 38–9; 'A Wish', p. 40; 'L'Inconnue', pp. 22–3.
4–Sorley, 'Stones', dated 14 July 1913, p. 7.
5–*Ibid.*, 'Marlborough', p. 23, fourth and sixth stanzas.
6–'A Call to Action', p. 46 and p. 47, seventh and eleventh stanzas respectively.
7–*Ibid.*, 'All the hills and vales along', p. 72.
8–For the quotation, *ibid.*, 'Illustrations in Prose', no. i, 'Richard Jefferies [1848–87]', p. 94. John Masefield (1878–1967); Thomas Hardy [1840–1928]; Henrik Ibsen (1828–1906); Robert Browning (1812–89).
9–*Ibid.*, 'Illustrations in Prose', no. iv, 'Germany', p. 103.
10–*Ibid.*, p. 105.
11–*Ibid.*, p. 106.
12–For both quotations, *ibid.*, p. 110: 'They [the men] never open their mouths in the barrack-room without the introduction of the unprintable swear-words and epithets: they have absolutely no "morality" (in the narrower, generally accepted sense): yet the public schoolboy should live among them . . .'
13–*Ibid.*, no. vii, 'Eternally to Do', p. 116.
14–*Ibid.*
15–*Ibid.*, 'The Song of the Ungirt Runners', p. 59.

Herman Melville

Somewhere upon the horizon of the mind, not recognisable yet in existence, *Typee* and *Omoo*, together with the name of Herman Melville, float in company. But since Herman Melville is apt to become Whyte Melville or Herman Merivale and *Omoo* for some less obvious reason connects itself with the adventures of an imaginary bushranger who is liable to turn jockey and then play a part in the drama of *Uncle*

Tom's Cabin, it is evident that a mist, due to ignorance or the lapse of time, must have descended upon those far distant regions.[2] Ignorance we do not scruple to admit; the lapse of time, since the first of August marks the centenary of Melville's birth, is undeniable; but this haziness may spring in part from a little seed dropped years ago by the books themselves. Was not some one talking about the South Seas?

Typee, they said, was in their opinion the best account ever written of – something or other. Memory has dropped that half of the sentence, and then, as memory will, has drawn a great blue line and a yellow beach. Waves are breaking; there is a rough white frill of surf; and how to describe it one does not know, but there is, simultaneously, a sense of palm trees, yellow limbs, and coral beneath clear water. This blundering brushwork of memory has been corrected since by Stevenson, Gauguin, Rupert Brooke[3] and many others. Yet, in some important respects, Herman Melville, with his *Typee* and *Omoo* and his ineradicable air of the early forties, has done the business better than the more sophisticated artists of our own day.

He was not sophisticated; perhaps it would be wrong to call him an artist. He came, indeed, to the Marquesas Islands as an ordinary seaman on board a whaling ship in the year 1842. Nor was it a love of the picturesque, but rather a hatred of salt beef, stale water, hard bread, and the cruelty of a captain that led him, in company with another sailor, to try his fortunes inland. They deserted, and, with as much food and calico as they could stow in the front of their frocks, made off into the interior of Nukuheva. But at what point their marvellous adventures in reaching the valley of the Typees cease to be authentic and become, for the sake of an American public, of the heroic order we have no means of saying. The number of days that two strong men, going through incredible exertions meanwhile, can support themselves upon a hunk of bread soaked in sweat and ingrained with shreds of tobacco must be fewer than Melville makes out; and the cliff down which they lowered themselves by swinging from creeper to creeper with horrid gaps between them – was it as steep as he says, and the creepers as far apart? And did they, on another occasion, as he asserts, break a second gigantic fall by pitching on to the topmost branches of a very high palm tree? It matters little; whatever the proportions of art and truth, each obstacle, and that is all we ask of it, seems impassable. There can be no way out of this, one says for the tenth time, a little grimly, for one has come to feel a kind of comradeship for the poor wretches in their struggles; and then, at the last moment, the incredible sagacity of Toby and the manful endurance of Melville find an outlet, as they deserve to do; and we have just drawn breath and judged them warranted in breaking off another precious crumb of the dwindling loaf when Toby, who has run on a little ahead, gives a shout, and behold, the summit on which they stand is not the end of their journey, but a ravine of immense depth and steepness still separates them from the valley of their desire; the bread must be put back uneaten and, with Melville's leg getting more and more painful, and nothing to cheer us but the conviction than it is better to die of starvation here than in the hold of a whaling ship, off again we must start. Even when the valley is reached there is a terrible moment while Melville hesitates whether to reply *Typee* or *Happar*[4] to the demand of the native chief, and only by a fluke saves them from instant death; nor need one be a boy in an Eton jacket to skip half a dozen chapters in a frenzy to make sure that the reason of Toby's disappearance was neither tragic nor in any way to his discredit as a friend.

But, then, when they are settled as the guests, or rather as the idolised prisoners, of the Typees, Melville appears to change his mind, as an artist is not generally supposed to do. Dropping his adventures, at which, as Stevenson said, he has proved himself 'a howling cheese',[5] he becomes engrossed in the lives and customs of the natives. However much the first half of the book owed to his imagination, the second we should guess to be literally true. This random American sailor having done his best to excite our interest in the usual way, now has to confess that what he found when he blundered into the midst of this tribe of South Sea islanders was – a little puzzling. They were savages, they were idolaters, they were inhuman beasts who licked their lips over the tender thighs of their kindred; and at the same time they were crowned with flowers, exquisite in beauty, courteous in manner, and engaged all day long in doing not only what they enjoyed doing but what, so far as he could judge, they had every right to enjoy doing. Of course, he had his suspicions. A dish of meat was not to be tasted until he had ascertained that it was pig slaughtered hospitably for him and not human flesh. The almost universal indolence of the natives was another remarkable and not altogether reassuring characteristic. Save for one old lady who busied herself 'rummaging over bundles of old tappa, or making a prodigious clatter among the calabashes',[6] no one was ever seen to do anything in the way of work. Nature, of course, abetted them in their indolence. The breadfruit tree, with very little effort on their part, would give them all the food they wanted; the cloth tree, with the same gentle solicitation, provided them with tappa for their clothing. But the work needed for these processes was light; the climate divine; and the only intimations of industry were the clear musical sounds of the different mallets, one here, one there, beating out the cloth, which rang charmingly in unison throughout the valley.

Being puzzled, Melville, very naturally, did his best to make a joke of it. He has a good laugh at Marheyo for instance, who accepted a pair of mouldy old boots with profound gratitude, and hung them round his neck for an ornament. The ancient naked women who leapt into the air 'like so many sticks bobbing to the surface, after being pressed perpendicularly into the water',[7] might be widows mourning their husbands slain in battle, but they did not seem to him decorous; he could not take his eyes off them. And then there were no laws, human or divine, except the queer business of the taboo. Yet what puzzled Herman Melville, as it puzzled Lord Pembroke twenty years later,[8] was that this simple, idle, savage existence was after all remarkably pleasant. There must be something wrong about happiness granted on such easy terms. The earl, being the better educated of the two, puzzled out the reason. He had been smothered with flowers and hung with mats until he looked like a cross between a Roman Catholic priest and a youthful Bacchus. He had enjoyed it immensely.

I was so happy there, that I verily believe I should have been content to dream away my life, without care or ambition . . . It could not be, and it was best for me as it was . . . Peace, and quiet, and perfect freedom, are useful medicines, but not wholesome diet. Their charm lies in contrast; there is no spark without the concussion of the flint and steel; there is no fine thought, even no perfect happiness, that is not born of toil, sorrow, and vexation of spirit.[9]

So the earl and the doctor sailed back to Wilton, and Providence saw to it that they were shipwrecked on the way. But Melville only made his escape with the greatest difficulty. He was almost drugged into acquiescence by those useful medicines, peace, quiet and perfect freedom. If there had been no resistance to his going he might have succumbed for ever. Laughter no longer did its office. It is significant that in the preface to his next book he is careful to insist that 'should a little jocoseness be shown upon some curious traits of the Tahitians, it proceeds from no intention to ridicule'.[10] Did his account of some curious traits of European sailors, which directly follows, proceed from no intention to satirise? It is difficult to say, Melville reports very vividly and vigorously, but he seldom allows himself to comment. He found the whaling vessel that took him off in 'a state of the greatest uproar';[11] the food was rotten; the men riotous; rather than land and lose his crew, who would certainly desert and thus cost him a cargo of whale oil, the captain kept them cruising out at sea. Discipline was maintained by a daily allowance of rum and the kicks and cuffs of the chief mate. When at last the sailors laid their case before the English Consul at Tahiti the fountain of justice seemed to them impure. At any rate, Melville and others who had insisted upon their legal rights found themselves given into the charge of an old native who was directed to keep their legs in the stocks. But his notion of discipline was vague, and somehow or other, what with the beauty of the place and the kindness of the natives, Melville began once more, curiously and perhaps dangerously, to feel content. Again there was freedom and indolence; torches brandished in the woods at night; dances under the moon, rainbow fish sparkling in the water, and women stuck about with variegated flowers. But something was wrong. Listening, Melville heard the aged Tahitians singing in a low, sad tone a song which ran: 'The palm trees shall grow, the coral shall spread, but man shall cease';[12] and statistics bore them out. The population had sunk from two hundred thousand to nine thousand in less than a century. The Europeans had brought the diseases of civilisation along with its benefits. The missionaries followed, but Melville did not like the missionaries. 'There is, perhaps, no race on earth,' he wrote, 'less disposed, by nature, to the monitions of Christianity'[13] than the Tahitians, and to teach them any useful trade is an impossibility. Civilisation and savagery blended in the strangest way in the palace of Queen Pomaree. The great leaf-hung hall, with its mats and screens and groups of natives, was furnished with rosewood writing desks, cut-glass decanters, and gilded candelabras. A cocoanut kept open the pages of a volume of Hogarth's prints. And in the evenings the Queen herself would put on a crown which Queen Victoria had good-naturedly sent her from London, and walk up and down the road raising her hand as people passed her to the symbol of majesty in what she thought a military salute. So Marheyo had been profoundly grateful for the present of a pair of old boots. But this time, somehow, Melville did not laugh.

1 – An essay in the *TLS*, 7 August 1919, (KpC161) to mark the centenary of the birth of Herman Melville (1819–91), author of *Typee* (1846), *Omoo* (1847), *Mardi* (1849, an account of life in the valley of Typee), *Moby Dick* (1851), *et al.*

VW noted in her diary on Saturday, 12 July 1919: 'The effect of the war would be worth describing, & one of these days at Monks House – but why do I let myself imagine spaces of leisure at Monks House? I know I shall have books that must be read too, just as here & now I should be reading Herman Melville, & Thomas

Hardy, not to say Sophocles, if I'm to finish the Ajax, as I wager myself to do, before August.'

Her essay is based upon the following works by Melville, in the following editions: *Typee. Life in the South Seas*. Edited with an introduction by W. P. Trent, Professor of English Literature in Columbia University, New York. Illustrated by H. Moore (S.P.C.K., 1903); *Omoo. A narrative of adventures in the South Seas* (Everyman's Library, J. M. Dent & Co., 1908). Reprinted: *B&P*. Reading Notes: MHP, B2 1.

2 – George John Whyte-Melville (1821–78), popular writer, a 28-volume edition of whose works was published by Tauchnitz in 1860–79; and, presumably, Herman (Charles) Merivale (1839–1906), dramatist. The series of connections leading to Harriet Beecher Stowe's *Uncle Tom's Cabin; or, Life among the Lowly* (1851–2) has not been disentangled.

3 – Robert Louis Stevenson (1850–94), who died at Vailima in Samoa, where he had settled in 1890, spent six weeks in the Marquesas Islands in 1888. His experiences in the South Seas inform the stories in *Island Nights' Entertainments* (1893) and *In the South Seas* (1896) and are recorded in his correspondence, from which VW quotes briefly below. Paul Gauguin (1848–1903), as well as being the renowned painter of exotic 'primitive' South Seas pictures (37 of his paintings had been included in the First Post-Impressionist Exhibition, 1910), was also the author of an autobiographical novel *Noa Noa* (1894–1900), set in Tahiti; he died at Atuona in the Marquesas Islands. (A volume of his correspondence had been recently published and was reviewed in the *Athenaeum* by E. M. Forster – see 'Forgotten Benefactors', n1, above.) Rupert Brooke (1887–1915) visited the Pacific from San Francisco in 1913–14, staying some months in Tahiti; a section of poems entitled 'The South Seas' is contained in his *Poems 1911–1914*. See also *Letters from America*, with a preface by Henry James (Sidgwick & Jackson, 1916), on which VW made two brief reading notes in MHP, B2 1.

4 – *Typee*, ch. ix, p. 81: 'After undergoing this scrutiny till I grew absolutely nervous, with a view of diverting it if possible, and conciliating the good opinion of the warrior, I took some tobacco from the bosom of my frock and offered it to him. He quietly rejected the proffered gift, and, without speaking, motioned me to return it to its place. ¶In my previous intercourse with the native of Nukuheva and Tior, I had found that the present of a small piece of tobacco would have rendered any of them devoted to my service. Was this act of the chief a token of his enmity? Typee or Happar? I asked within myself. I started, for at the same moment this identical question was asked by the strange being before me . . . I paused for a second, and I know not by what impulse it was that I answered "Typee". The piece of dusky statuary nodded in approval, and then murmured "Motarkee!" – "Motarkee", said I, without further hesitation – "Typee motarkee".' The word 'typee' in the Marquesian dialect signifies a cannibal.

Toby was Melville's shipmate, Richard Tobias Greene, with whom he had escaped ashore at the Marquesas Islands from the brutal hardships aboard the whaler *Acushnet*.

5 – *The Works of Robert Louis Stevenson* (xxv vols., Chatto & Windus, 1912), vol. xxiv), Stevenson to Charles Baxter, written aboard the yacht *Casco*, 6 September 1888, p. 295: 'Excuse me if I write little: when I am at sea, it gives me a headache; when I am in port, I have my diary crying out "Give, give". I shall have a fine book of

travels, I feel sure; and will tell you more of the South Seas after very few months than any other writer has done – except Herman Melville perhaps, who is a howling cheese.'

6–*Typee*, ch. x, p. 101.

7–*Ibid.*, ch. xii, p. 212: 'I was amused at the appearance of four or five old women, who, in a state of utter nudity, with their arms extended flatly down their sides, and holding themselves perfectly erect, were leaping stiffly into the air, like so many sticks bobbing to the surface, after being pressed perpendicularly into the water. They preserved the utmost gravity of countenance, and continued their extraordinary movements without a single moment's cessation. They did not appear to attract the observation of the crowd around them, but I must candidly confess that, for my own part, I stared at them most pertinaciously.'

8–George Herbert, 13th Earl of Pembroke (1850–95), who served as undersecretary for war, 1874–5, in Disraeli's government, had made, while not yet 21, two Pacific voyages in the company of Dr George Henry Kingsley (1827–92), traveller and author, and together they published *South Sea Bubbles by the Earl and the Doctor* (Richard Bentley & Son, 1872).

9–*South-Sea Bubbles*, ch. i, 'Tahiti', p. 45; the first ellipsis marks the omission of: 'I was Society Islandized, in fact'; and the second, of: 'Perhaps after a time a man's feelings and thoughts would become degraded and numbed by such a life; he would lose that power of enjoyment that made it at first so charming and pleasant to him.'

10–*Omoo*, Preface, p. x: 'Should a little jocoseness be shown upon some curious traits of the Tahitians, it proceeds from no intention to ridicule: things merely described as, from their novelty, they first struck an unbiassed observer.'

11–*Ibid.*, ch. iii, p. 11.

12–*Ibid.*, ch. xlix, p. 197, written in three verses in the original.

13–*Ibid.*, ch. xlv, p. 177, which has: 'In fact, there is, perhaps, no race upon earth, less disposed, by nature, to the monitions of Christianity, than the people of the South Seas. And this assertion is made with full knowledge of what is called the "Great Revival at Sandwich Islands", about the year 1836; when several thousand were, in the course of a few weeks, admitted into the bosom of the Church.'

The Russian Background

Thanks chiefly to the labours of Mrs Garnett[2] we are now not so much at sea when a new translation from the Russian novelists comes our way. Since *The Bishop* is the seventh volume of the tales of Tchehov, this comparative degree of enlightenment does not say much perhaps for our perspicacity. We ought not, as we read, to be still drawing a rough plan, with the left hand, of this strange Russian temperament; we ought not to feel any warmth of self-approbation when the sketch rapidly fills itself in and wears a momentary air of completeness.

Yet the seventh volume finds us not quite so ill-prepared as its predecessors. No one now is going to be so foolish as to complain that the story of 'The Bishop' is not a story at all but only a rather vague and inconclusive account of a bishop who was distressed because his mother treated him with respect, and soon after died of typhoid. We are by this time alive to the fact that inconclusive stories are legitimate; that is to say, though they leave us feeling melancholy and perhaps uncertain, yet somehow or other they provide a resting point for the mind – a solid object[3] casting its shade of reflection and speculation. The fragments of which it is composed may have the air of having come together by chance. Certainly it often seems as if Tchehov made up his stories rather in the way that a hen picks up grain. Why should she pick here and there, from side to side, when, so far as we can see, there is no reason to prefer one grain to another? His choice is strange, and yet there is no longer any doubt that whatever Tchehov chooses he chooses with the finest insight. He is like the peasant in his story 'The Steppe', who could see the fox lying on her back playing like a dog far in the distance, where no one else could see her. Like Vassya, Tchehov's sight is so keen that he has, 'besides the world seen by everyone, another world of his own, accessible to no one else, and probably a very beautiful one'.[4]

All these doubts and false starts are now powerless to disturb our enjoyment of Tchehov. We may, therefore, attempt to press on a step further. Is it possible to adopt with Tchehov the position that comes so easily in the case of writers of one's own tongue? We want to understand the great sum of things which a writer takes for granted, which is the background of his thought; for if we can imagine that, the figures in the foreground, the pattern he has wrought upon it, will be more easily intelligible. Our own background, so far as we can detach ourselves from it, is presumably a very complex and yet very orderly civilisation. The peasant, even in the depths of the country, has his station assigned to him, and is in a thousand ways controlled by London; and there must be very few windows in England from which it is not possible to see the smoke of a town by day or its lamps by night. We become more aware of the detail and of the intricacy of all that we hold in our minds when Tchehov describes 'the things that come back to your mind', 'the things one has seen and treasured'[5] – the things, that is, which form his background.

... of the unfathomable depth and infinity of the sky one can only form a conception at sea and on the steppes by night when the moon is shining. It is terribly lonely and caressing ...[6] Everything looks different from what it is ... You drive on and suddenly see standing before your right in the roadway a dark figure like a monk . . . the figure comes closer, grows bigger; now it is on a level with the chaise, and you see it is not a man, but a solitary bush, or a great stone . . .[7] You drive on for one hour, for a second . . . You meet upon the way a silent old barrow or a stone figure put up God knows when and by whom . . .[8] the soul responds to the call of the lovely austere fatherland, and longs to fly over the steppes with the nightbird.[9]

Tchehov is here describing, very beautifully we can guess even through the coarse mesh of a foreign tongue, the effect of the steppe upon a little company of travellers. The steppe is the background for that particular story. Yet, as the travellers move slowly over the immense space, now stopping at an inn, now overtaking some shepherd or waggon, it seems to be the journey of the Russian soul, and the empty space, so sad and so passionate, becomes the background of his thought. The stories themselves, in their inconclusiveness and intimacy, appear to be the result of a chance meeting on a lonely road. Fate has sent these travellers across our path; whoever they may be, it is natural to stop and talk, and as they will never come our way again it is possible to say all kinds of things that we do not say to friends. The English reader may have had something of the same experience when isolated on board ship on a sea voyage. From the surrounding emptiness, from the knowledge that they will soon be over, these meetings have an intensity, as if shaped by the hand of an artist, which long preserves their significance in memory. 'All this,' says Tchehov, describing a camp by the wayside where the men sit gathered together over the camp fire – 'all this was of itself so marvellous and terrible that the fantastic colours of legend and fairy tale were pale and blended with life.'[10] Take away the orderly civilisation: look from your window upon nothing but the empty steppe, feel towards each human being that he is a traveller who will be seen once and never again, and then life 'of itself' is so terrible and marvellous that no fantastic colouring is necessary. Almost all the stories in the present volume are stories of peasants; and whether or not it is the effect of this solitude and emptiness, each obscure and brutish mind has had rubbed in it a little transparency through which the light of the spirit shines amazingly. Thus the convict Yakov, as he walks in chains, comes by this means to the conviction that 'at last [. . .] he had learned the true faith . . . He knew it all now and understood where God was.' But this is not merely the end of a Tchehov story;[11] it is also the light which, falling fitfully here and there, marks out their conformity and form. Without metaphor, the feelings of his characters are related to something more important and far more remote than personal success or happiness.

1 – A review in the *TLS*, 14 August 1919, (Kp C162) of *The Bishop and Other Stories* ... from the Russian by Constance Garnett (Chatto & Windus, 1919) by Anton Tchehov (1860–1904). See also '*The Cherry Orchard*' below; 'Tchehov's Questions', *II VW Essays*; and see 'The Russian Point of View', *IV VW Essays* and *CR1*. Reprinted: *B&P*.

2 – Constance Garnett, *née* Black (1862–1946), took a first in classics at Newnham College, Cambridge, in 1883, and in the early 1890s began to learn Russian. Her translations of the Russian classics, including virtually all of Chekhov, had an immense influence upon VW (see *II VW Essays*, Intro.). She was the wife of the author and publisher's reader Edward Garnett, and mother of the novelist David Garnett (1892–1981), one of the younger generation in Bloomsbury.

3 – Almost the title of VW's story 'Solid Objects', begun in 1918 and published in the *Athenaeum*, 22 October 1920 (reprinted in *CSF*).

4 – Tchehov, 'The Steppe', p. 235.

5 – For both quotations, *ibid.*, p. 220, for the context of which see n8 below.

6 – *Ibid.*, p. 219, which has 'Of the unfathomable'.

7 – *Ibid.*, p. 218, which has no matter between 'it is' and 'You drive on', where VW has an ellipsis; and which also has 'The figure comes closer'.

8 – *Ibid.*, p. 219. The first ellipsis is Chekhov's. The passage continues: '; a nightbird floats noiselessly over the earth, and little by little those legends of the steppes, the tales of men you have met, the stories of some old nurse from the steppe, and all the things you have managed to see and treasure in your soul, come back to your mind'.

9 – *Ibid.*, p. 220.

10 – *Ibid.*, p. 263.

11 – For the quotation, *ibid.*, 'The Murder', p. 137, which continues: 'and how He was to be served, and the only thing he could not understand was why men's destinies were so diverse, why this simple faith which other men receive from God for nothing and together with their lives, had cost him such a price that his arms and legs trembled like a drunken man's from all the horrors and agonies which as far as he could see would go on without a break to the day of his death' – and which is not literally, but two paragraphs from, the end of the story.

A Real American

American literature is still terribly apt to excite the snobbish elements in an English critic. It is either feeble with an excess of culture, or forcible with a self-conscious virility. In either case it appears to be influenced by the desire to conciliate or flout the European standards; and such deference not only never attains its object, but, perhaps deservedly, brings its own punishment in the shape of patronage and derision. One cannot help, on such occasions, boasting of the English descent from

Shakespeare. At first sight Mr Dreiser appears to be another of those pseudo-Europeans whose productions may pass muster across the Atlantic, but somehow look over here like careful copies from the old masters. There are many stories, we should suppose, neither better nor worse and indeed much resembling 'Free' in the current magazines. But what we should expect an English writer to rattle off with some dash and self-confidence, the American writer produces slowly, languidly, with much fumbling for words and groping for subtleties which seem to escape him. The end is apparent long before it is reached, and we come to it in a listless straggling way which makes the whole expedition seem rather pointless. As there is perhaps no more fatiguing form of mental exercise than the reading of short stories told without zest, the prospect of ten more to come descended like a mist upon the horizon. The cloud lifted, however, against all expectation, as a dull day gets finer and finer without one's seeing exactly where the light comes from. While we were growing more and more conscious that Mr Dreiser lacked all the necessary qualities for a writer of short stories – concentration, penetration, form – unconsciously we were reading on at a great rate and enjoying the book considerably. At a certain point then it was necessary to come to terms with Mr Dreiser and to inform him that, if he would consent to drop his claim to be a writer of short stories, we for our part would renounce our privileges as the lineal descendants of Shakespeare.

And yet what did our pleasure come from? It did not come from the usual sources; it did not come from excitement or shock; it came, as if surreptitiously, from a sense of American fields and American men and women and of America herself, gross, benevolent, and prolific. For some hundreds of years, of course, the existence of America has been a well-known fact; but the lettered classes have kept their country in the background, or presented it in a form suited to European taste. Mr Dreiser, however, appears to be so much of an American that he describes it without being aware that he is doing anything of the kind. In the same way a home-bred child describes the family in which he has been brought up. There is little evidence that Mr Dreiser has been influenced by Europe. He is not perceptibly cultivated. His taste seems to be bad. When he describes an artist, we, on the other hand, see a journalist.

Davies swelled with feeling. The night, the tragedy, the grief, he saw it all. But also with the cruel instinct of the budding artist, that he already was, he was beginning to meditate on the character of story it would make – the colour, the pathos. [. . .] 'I'll get it all in!' he exclaimed, feelingly, if triumphantly, at last. 'I'll get it all in!'[2]

Mr Dreiser gets a great deal too much of it in, but, together with the colour and the pathos, there is another quality which excuses his sins of taste, and perhaps explains them. He has genuine vitality. His interest in life, when not impeded by the restrictions of a definite form, bubbles and boils over and produces *Twelve Men*, a much more interesting work than *Free*.

Whether we are able to recognise the originals or not, these twelve character sketches are extremely readable. And to an English reader they are, besides, rather strange. With superficial differences, each of these men is of a large, opulent, masterful character. Each is, as Mr Dreiser defines it, 'free', with 'the real spiritual freedom where the mind, as it were, stands up and looks at itself, faces Nature unafraid, is aware of its own weaknesses, its strengths ... kicks dogma out of doors, and yet deliberately and of choice holds fast to many, many simple and human things, and rounds out life, or would, in a natural, normal, courageous, healthy way'.[3] One of these men writes songs, another directs companies, a third builds toy engines. They are all busy and engrossed, and in love with life. Yet with all their power they seem childish – childish in their love of fame, in their love of mankind, in their sentimentality and simplicity. One is certain that their songs will be bad ones, their pictures melodramatic, their stories mere journalism. But their animal spirits are superb. Nor are they entirely animal. The abundance of life in their veins overflows into all kinds of fine and friendly relations with their fellows. Mr Dreiser described them with such enthusiasm that his work has a character of its own – an American character. He is not himself by any means a great writer, but he may be the stuff from which, in another hundred years or so, great writers will be born.

1–A review in the *TLS*, 21 August 1919, (Kp C163) of *Free and Other Stories* and of *Twelve Men* (Boni & Liveright, 1918 and 1919) by Theodore Dreiser (1871–1945), whose works at this date included *Sister Carrie* (1900), *The Financier* (1912) and *The Genius* (1915). Reprinted: CW.
2–*Free and Other Stories*, 'Nigger Jeff', p. 111.
3–*Twelve Men*, 'Peter', p. 1.

The Royal Academy

'The motor-cars of Empire – the bodyguard of Europe – the stainless knight of Belgium' – such is our English romance that nine out of ten of those passing from the indiscriminate variety of Piccadilly to the courtyard of Burlington House do homage to the embattled tyres and the kingly presence of Albert on his high-minded charger[2] with some nonsense of this sort. They are, of course, only the motor-cars of the rich grouped round a statue; but whether the quadrangle in which they stand radiates back the significance of everything fourfold, so that King Albert and the motor-cars exude the essence of kingliness and the soul of vehicular traffic, or whether the crowd is the cause of it, or the ceremonious steps leading up, the swing-doors admitting and the flunkeys fawning, it is true that, once you are within the precincts, everything appears symbolic, and the state of mind in which you ascend the broad stairs to the picture galleries is both heated and romantic.

Whatever visions we may have indulged, we find ourselves on entering confronted by a lady in full evening dress. She stands at the top of a staircase, one hand loosely closed round a sheaf of lilies, while the other is about to greet someone of distinction who advances towards her up the stairs. Not a hair is out of place. Her lips are just parted. She is about to say, 'How nice of you to come!'[3] But such is the skill of the artist that one does not willingly cross the range of her cordial and yet condescending eye. One prefers to look at her obliquely. She said, 'How nice of you to come!' so often and so graciously while I stood there that at last my eye wandered off in search of people of sufficient distinction for her to say it to. There was no difficulty in finding them. Here was a nobleman in a kilt, the Duke of R.;[4] here a young officer in khaki, and, to keep him company, the head and shoulders of a young girl, whose upturned eyes and pouting lips appear to be entreating the sky to be bluer, roses to be redder, ices to be sweeter, and men to be manlier for her sake. To do her justice, the gallant youth seemed to respond. As they stepped up the staircase to the lady in foaming white he vowed that come what might – the flag of England – sweet chimes of home – a woman's honour – an Englishman's word – only a scrap of paper[5] – for your sake, Alice – God save the King – and all the rest of it. The range of her vocabulary was more limited. She kept her gaze upon the sky or the ice or whatever it might be with a simple sincerity which was enforced by a single row of

pearls and a little drapery of white tulle about the shoulders. 'How nice
of you to come!' said the hostess once more. But immediately behind
them stumped the Duke, a bluff nobleman, 'more at home on the brae-
side than among these kickshaws and knick-knacks, my lady. Splendid
sport. Twenty antlers and Buck Royal. Clean between the eyes, eh what?
Out all day. Never know when I'm done. Cold bath, hard bed, glass of
whiskey. A mere nothing. Damned foreigners. Post of duty. The Guard
dies, but never surrenders. The ladies of our family – Up, Guards, and at
them! Gentlemen –'[6] and, as he utters the last words in a voice choked
with emotion, the entire company swing round upon their heels,
displaying only a hind view of their perfectly fitting mess-jackets, since
there are some sights that it is not good for man to look upon.

The scene, though not all the phrases, comes from a story by Rudyard
Kipling.[7] But scenes from Rudyard Kipling must take place with
astonishing frequency at these parties in order that the English maidens
and gallant officers may have occasion to insist upon their chastity on
the one hand and protect it on the other, without which, so far as one can
see, there would be no reason for their existence. Therefore it was
natural to look about me, a little shyly, for the sinister person of the
seducer. There is, I can truthfully say, no such cur in the whole of the
Royal Academy; and it was only when I had gone through the rooms
twice and was about to inform the maiden that her apprehensions,
though highly creditable, were in no way necessary that my eye was
caught by the white underside of an excessively fine fish. 'The Duke
caught that!' I exclaimed, being still within the radius of the ducal glory.
But I was wrong. Though fine enough, the fish, as a second glance put it
beyond a doubt, was not ducal; its triangular shape, let alone the fact
that a small urchin in corduroys held it suspended by the tail, was
enough to start me in the right direction. Ah, yes – the harvest of the sea,
toilers of the deep, a fisherman's home, nature's bounty – such phrases
formed themselves with alarming rapidity – but to descend to details.
The picture, No. 306, represents a young woman holding a baby on her
knee.[8] The child is playing with the rough model of a ship; the large fish
is being dangled before his eyes by a brother a year or two older in a pair
of corduroys which have been cut down from those worn by the
fisherman engaged in cleaning cod on the edge of the waves. Judging
from the superb rosiness, fatness, and blueness of every object depicted,
even the sea itself wearing the look of a prize animal tricked out for a
fair, it seemed certain that the artist intended a compliment in a general
way to the island race. But something in the woman's eye arrested me. A

veil of white dimmed the straightforward lustre. It is thus that painters represent the tears that do not fall. But what, we asked, had this great hulk of a matron surrounded by fish, any one of which was worth eighteenpence the pound, to cry for? Look at the little boy's breeches. They are not, if you look closely, of the same pattern as the fisherman's. Once that fact is grasped, the story reels itself out like a line with a salmon on the end of it. Don't the waves break with a sound of mockery on the beach? Don't her eyes cloud with memories at the sight of a toy boat? It is not always summer. The sea has another voice than this; and, since her husband will never want his breeches any more – but the story when written out is painful, and rather obvious into the bargain.

The point of a good Academy picture is that you can search the canvas for ten minutes or so and still be doubtful whether you have extracted the whole meaning. There is, for example, No. 248, 'Cocaine'.[9] A young man in evening dress lies, drugged, with his head upon the pink satin of a woman's knee. The ornamental clock assures us that it is exactly eleven minutes to five. The burning lamp proves that it is dawn. He, then, has come home to find her waiting? She has interrupted his debauch? For my part, I prefer to imagine what in painters' language (a tongue well worth separate study) would be called 'a dreary vigil'. There she has sat since eight-thirty, alone, in pink satin. Once she rose and pressed the photograph in the silver frame to her lips. She might have married that man (unless it is her father, of which one cannot be sure). She was a thoughtless girl, and he left her to meet his death on the field of battle. Through her tears she gazes at the next photograph – presumably that of a baby (again the painter has been content with a suggestion). As she looks a hand fumbles at the door. 'Thank God!' she cries as her husband staggers in and falls helpless across her knees, 'thank God our Teddy died!' So there she sits, staring disillusionment in the eyes, and whether she gives way to temptation, or breathes a vow to the photographs, or gets him to bed before the maid comes down, or sits there for ever, must be left to the imagination of the onlooker.

But the queer thing is that one wants to be her. For a moment one pretends that one sits alone, disillusioned, in pink satin. And then people in the little group of gazers begin to boast that they have known sadder cases themselves. Friends of theirs took cocaine. 'I myself as a boy for a joke –' 'No, George – but how fearfully rash!' Everyone wished to cap that story with a better, save for one lady who, from her expression, was acting the part of consoler, had got the poor thing to bed, undressed her, soothed her, and even spoken with considerable sharpness to that unworthy brute, unfit to be a husband, before she moved on in a pleasant glow of self-satisfaction. Every picture before which one of these little groups had gathered seemed to radiate the strange power to make the beholder more heroic and more romantic; memories of childhood, visions of possibilities, illusions of all kinds poured down upon us from the walls. In a cooler mood one might accuse the painters of some exaggeration. There must be well over ten thousand delphiniums in the Royal Academy, and not one is other than a perfect specimen. The condition of the turf is beyond praise. The sun is exquisitely adapted to the needs of the sundials. The yew hedges are irreproachable; the manor house a miracle of timeworn dignity; and as for the old man with a scythe, the girl at the well, the village donkey, the widow lady, the gipsies' caravan, the boy with a rod, each is not only the saddest, sweetest, quaintest, most picturesque, tenderest, jolliest of its kind, but has a symbolical meaning much to the credit of England. The geese are English geese, and even the polar bears, though they have not that advantage, seem, such is the persuasion of the atmosphere, to be turning to carriage rugs as we look at them.[10]

It is indeed a very powerful atmosphere; so charged with manliness and womanliness, pathos and purity, sunsets and Union Jacks, that the shabbiest and most suburban catch a reflection of the rosy glow. 'This is England! these are the English!' one might explain if a foreigner were at hand. But one need not say that to one's compatriots. They are, perhaps, not quite up to the level of the pictures. Some are meagre; others obese; many have put on what is too obviously the only complete outfit that they possess. But the legend on the catalogue explains any such discrepancy in a convincing manner. 'To give unto them beauty for ashes. Isaiah lxi. 3'[11] – that is the office of this exhibition. Our ashes will be transformed if only we expose them openly enough to the benignant influence of the canvas. So we look again at the Lord Chancellor and Mr Balfour, at the Lady B., at the Duke of R., at Mr Ennever of the Pelman Institute,[12] at officers of all descriptions, architects, surgeons, peers, dentists, doctors, lawyers, archbishops, roses, sundials, battlefields, fish, and Skye terriers. From wall to wall, glowing with colour, glistening with oil, framed in gilt, and protected by glass, they ogle and elevate, inspire and command. But they overdo it. One is not altogether such a bundle of ashes as they suppose, or sometimes the magic fails to work. A large picture by Mr Sargent called 'Gassed'[13] at last pricked some nerve of protest, or perhaps of humanity. In order to emphasise his point that the soldiers wearing bandages round their eyes cannot see, and therefore claim our compassion, he makes one of them raise his leg to the level of his elbow in order to mount a step an inch or two above the ground. This little piece of over-emphasis was the final scratch of the surgeon's knife which is said to hurt more than the whole operation. After all, one had been jabbed and stabbed, slashed and sliced for close on two hours. The lady began it, the Duke continued it; little children had wrung tears; great men extorted veneration. From first to last each canvas had rubbed in some emotion, and what the paint failed to say the catalogue had enforced in words. But Mr Sargent was the last straw. Suddenly the great rooms rang like a parrot-house with the intolerable vociferations of gaudy and brainless birds. How they shrieked and gibbered! How they danced and sidled! Honour, patriotism, chastity, wealth, success, importance, position, patronage, power – their cries rang and echoed from all quarters. 'Anywhere, anywhere, out of this world!' was the only exclamation with which one could stave off the brazen din as one fled downstairs, out of doors, round the motor-cars, beneath the disdain of the horse and its rider, and so out into the comparative sobriety of Piccadilly. No doubt the reaction was excessive; and I must leave it to Mr Roger Fry to decide whether the emotions here recorded are the proper result of one thousand six hundred and seventy-four works of art.[14]

1 – An essay in the *Athenaeum*, 22 August 1919, (Kp C164) on the hundred and fifty-first Exhibition of the Royal Academy of Arts, 5 May–9 August 1919, at Burlington House, Piccadilly. 'I spend a good deal of my time at the Royal Academy,' VW wrote to Vanessa Bell on 17 July 1919 (*II VW Letters*, no. 1068), 'It is a very amusing and spirited place. I get an immense deal of pleasure from working out the pictures. But I mustn't tell you, or you won't read my article. I can't settle down to write it, though, because I always remember pictures that I haven't quite worked out, and I have to go back again. The crowd is such that it is often difficult to get a clear view of a picture. I think Cocaine is one of the best, but there is a marine piece which is also very good [see below for both pictures].'

VW made the following notes for her article (MHP, B 2): 'The brushed up Sunday appearance of Polar bears – they'll certainly become mats. Young women of England preserved in this sanctuary. And then the amount of meaning – see 127 [Landing of 1st Canadian Division at St Nazaire, February 1915. Finished sketch for painting for the Canadian War Memorials, by Edgar Bundy RA]. a little child has run out – an officer looking his feelings – struggling with his feelings. the blueness of the delphiniums. The ladies –. The presentation portraits – everyone at height of success – frowning blond gentlemen – The President [.] Old age dissolving in tears.

¶*Cocaine:* very good: young wife; wedding ring [;] clock 11 min to 5. lamp. burning to show it['s] morning; photograph of man she *might* have married in the background; she has taken off his coat; in a pink silk wrapper, beautifully dressed; his head in her lap – What will happen –? the future. Comments.'

Even with the assistance of *The Royal Academy Illustrated* (Walter Judd Ltd., 1919), which contains prints of a selection of the paintings, it has not always been possible to relate VW's descriptions and some phrases, which may or may not be allusions, to titles in the Royal Academy catalogue. The notes that follow are therefore not exhaustive.

See also 'The private view of the Royal Academy . . .' below, and see the ms of *Jacob's Room,* notebook no. 3, Berg Collection, for an unpublished account of the Royal Academy's hundred and fifty-fifth exhibition, 1 May–7 August 1922. Reprinted: *G&R, CE.*

2–Equestrian statue, no. 1674, Walter Winans and Alexander J. Leslie, 'H.M. The King of the Belgians'.

3–This painting remains unidentified.

4–Oil painting, no. 123, Sir Arthur Cope RA (d.1940), 'His Grace the Duke of Richmond and Gordon, KG, DSO', reproduced in *Royal Academy Illustrated.*

5–Oil painting, no. 321, John Bowie (d.1941), 'The Scrap of Paper: Britain Declares War'.

6–At least two of these phrases are of historic origin: 'La Garde meurt, mais ne se rend pas,' attributed to General Cambronne (1770–1842), when summoned to surrender at Waterloo; and: 'Up Guards and at them again!', the Duke of Wellington at Waterloo.

7–If this scene is indeed from a work by Rudyard Kipling (1865–1936), it is an extremely free pastiche without any identifiable origin in one of his stories.

8–Oil painting, no. 306, John R. Reid (d.1926) [of Osprey Cottage, Polperro, Cornwall], 'The Wonders of the Deep'.

9–Oil painting, no. 248, 'Cocaine' by Alfred Priest, reproduced in *Royal Academy Illustrated.*

10–For the imminent carriage rugs, oil paintings: no. 125, Arthur Wardle, 'Where the Ice King Reigns', reproduced in *Royal Academy Illustrated*; and no. 291, J. Murray Thomson, 'Polar Bears'.

11–The epigraph to the catalogue.

12–Oil paintings: no. 197, Glyn Philpot RA (1884–1937), 'The Rt Hon. Lord Birkenhead, Lord High Chancellor, Treasurer of Gray's Inn, 1917–19. Painted for the Honorary Society of Gray's Inn'; no. 229, George Fiddes Watt (1873–1960), 'The Rt Hon. James Balfour MP'; no. 626, Hugh G. Riviere (d.1956), 'The Lady Betty Trafford', reproduced in *Royal Academy Illustrated*; no. 140, Seymour Lucas RA (d.1923), 'W. J. Ennever Esq. Founder of the Pelman Institute. Presentation Portrait', reproduced in *Royal Academy Illustrated.*

13–Oil painting, no. 120, John Singer Sargent (1856–1925), 'Gassed', lent by the Imperial War Museum.

14–Whether Roger Fry (1866–1934) visited the exhibition and uttered his opinion on the propriety of VW's emotions is not known; but the RA was certainly not a favourite haunt of his.

The exhibition comprised not only oil paintings, of which it contained six hundred and sixty-six, but also included water colours, miniatures, drawings, engravings, architectural drawings and models, and sculptures.

'Sonia Married'

If anyone wishes to take the measure of Mr Stephen McKenna's *Sonia Married* by the rough method of comparison, let him recall the once famous *Dodo* of Mr E. F. Benson.[2] Sonia is another of those irresistible chattering up-to-date ladies who compel the most surly to tolerate and even to forgive by talking at dinner parties at the tops of their voices in the following manner: 'Tell him ⟨her husband⟩ that I shall elope to Sloane Square – I don't believe anyone's ever eloped to Sloane Square, but its the handiest place in the world; even the Hounslow and Barking non-stop train stops there – so sweet of them I always think – I shall go there with Peter and live in his flat and star in *revue* . . .'[3] and so on. Remembering that the female dodo implies a male, it is easy to infer that the husband admires his wife's wit and is a simple-hearted trustful fellow with ideas and aspirations which keep him at home while she dines out. He thinks it very right that other men should admire her, and when the crash comes, he used, if memory serves us, after displaying a gentlemanly toleration, to be killed in the hunting-field. But Mr McKenna is painstakingly modern; and he has done his best to bring his version up to date. David O'Rane has been blinded in the early days of the war, and now believes in social reform, loving one's neighbour, and trusting one's wife. He has a habit of sitting on the floor stroking the head of a Saint Bernard dog, while he talks sometimes with 'cold vibrant passion', and sometimes with boyish eagerness about the future of England. '. . . Its got to stand for a good deal more than it did before the war; we owe it to the fellows who have died and the fellows who are dying now.'[4]

His contribution to the problem is to turn a very large room in his house on the Embankment into what his wife's family and friends call a 'casual ward' or a 'doss house'.[5] By this they mean that the door is unlocked, and anyone who chooses can come in and eat cake in front of a large fire. It is chiefly used by Members of Parliament and a consumptive pacifist in an orange-coloured tie, who, though extremely voluble, seem highly respectable, and in no particular need of a cake. But on one occasion O'Rane, in his unworldly way, brought home a drunken soldier whom he had found in the street. The man was an officer, the visit lasted only one night, but 'it was the last straw for Sonia'.[6] She went off with one of the Members of Parliament; and O'Rane, forgetting that he had said on page 78 that if his wife fell in love with another man and ran away with him he would not want to stop her, forgetting, moreover, his own conduct with a lady secretary, behaves as if he had never read a line of Shelley or professed any love for his neighbour. The deplorable truth is that he chases, or believes that he chases, the consumptive pacifist violently about the room. The real malefactor, Mr Grayle, M.P., is soundly drubbed by another elderly politician, who, in telling the story, remarks, 'His one weak point was the injured knee, and I concentrated my attack on that.'[7]

These unpleasantnesses would no doubt melt into a rose-tinted mist if the boyish charm of O'Rane and the irresistible fascination of Sonia had done their work. Without such an anaesthetic the operation of reading is full of painful little shocks as if one kept on waking up in the middle of having a tooth out. Their conduct, if one looks at it with open eyes, seems alternately frivolous and bestial. But, to do Mr McKenna justice, his concern is not with the conduct of his characters but with their conversation. He manages to keep that going all the time, if not brilliantly, still with remarkable smartness, considering how much they talk and how easily the psychological complexities of the O'Ranes might have been disposed of in half a dozen words. The war is very cleverly rigged up in the background – Mr Asquith resigns; Lord Kitchener is drowned;[8] and the battles of the drawing room are represented with great verisimilitude. One keeps asking oneself 'Who can the Duchess of Ross be meant for?' or 'Which of our peeresses looks like "a lioness that has been rolling in French chalk"?'[9] This amounts to saying that *Sonia Married* runs every chance of great popularity; and if we have omitted to praise the skill, deftness, and smartness of the story it must be that we are perhaps a little shocked to find that the dodo is by no means extinct.

1 – A review in the *TLS*, 28 August 1919, (Kp C165) of *Sonia Married* (Hutchinson & Co., 1919) by Stephen McKenna (1888–1934), whose *Sonia* (1917) had enjoyed great popular success. McKenna was educated at Westminster School and Christ Church, Oxford; he served during the war in the Intelligence Section of the War Trade Department, and later took part in the Balfour Mission to America, a background which informs the novel under review. Reprinted: *CW*.
2 – E. F. Benson (1867–1940) whose immensely successful novel *Dodo* first appeared in 1893.
3 – McKenna, ch. ii, p. 71, which has '*any*one's' and 'trains stop', and does not italicise '*revue*'.

4–For both quotations, *ibid.*, ch. iii, p. 92; the latter is adapted from a longer sentence.

5–For 'casual ward', *ibid.*, ch. ii, p. 51 and ch. iii, p. 91; and for 'doss house', ch. iii, p. 104.

6–*Ibid.*, ch. iii, p. 94, a complete sentence.

7–*Ibid.*, ch. vi, pp. 248–9, which continues: 'before he could reduce the distance between us'.

8–The Hon. Herbert Henry Asquith (1852–1928) resigned as premier on 5 December 1916, in favour of Lloyd George, following the tragic failure of the Somme offensive and his resultant unpopularity. Horatio Herbert Kitchener, 1st Earl Kitchener (1850–1916), Secretary of State for War, was drowned when the cruiser HMS *Hampshire* sank somewhere off the Orkneys in June 1916 having hit a mine; he was bound for consultations in Russia.

9–McKenna, ch. ii, p. 63, describing the character Lady Maitland.

Wilcoxiana

How can one begin? Where can one leave off? There never was a more difficult book to review. If one puts in the Madame de Staël of Milwaukee, there will be no room for the tea-leaves; if one concentrates upon Helen Pitkin, Raley Husted Bell[2] must be done without. Then all the time there are at least three worlds spinning in and out, and as for Ella Wheeler Wilcox – Mrs Wilcox is indeed the chief problem. It would be easy to make fun of her; equally easy to condescend to her; but it is not at all easy to express what one does feel for her. There is a hint of this complexity in her personal appearance. We write with forty photographs of Mrs Wilcox in front of us. If you omit those with the cats in her arms and the crescent moons in her hair, those stretched on a couch with a book, and those seated on a balustrade between Theodosia Garrison and Rhoda Hero Dunn,[3] all primarily a tribute to the Muse, there remain a number which represent a plump, personable, determined young woman, vain, but extremely vivacious, arch, but at the same time sensible, and always in splendid health. She was never a frump at any stage of her career. Rather than look like a bluestocking, she would have forsaken literature altogether. She stuck a rod between her arms to keep her back straight; she galloped over the country on an old farm horse; she defied her mother and bathed naked; at the height of her fame 'a new stroke in swimming or a new high dive gave me more of a thrill than a new style of verse, great as my devotion to the Muses was, and ever has been'.[4] In short, if one had the pleasure of meeting Mrs Wilcox, one would find her a very well-dressed, vivacious, woman of the world. But, alas for the simplicity of the problem! there is not one world but three.

The pre-natal world is indicated rather sketchily. One is given to understand that Mrs Wilcox is appearing for by no means the first time. There have been Ella Wheeler Wilcoxes in Athens and Florence, Rome and Byzantium. She is a recurring, but an improving phenomenon. 'Being an old soul myself,' she says, 'reincarnated many more times than any other member of my family, I knew the truth of spiritual things not revealed to them.'[5] One gift, at least, of supreme importance she brought with her from the shades – 'I was born with unquenchable hope . . . I always expected wonderful things to happen to me.'[6] Without hope, what could she have done? Everything was against her. Her father was an unsuccessful farmer; her mother an embittered woman worn down by a life of child-bearing and hard work; the atmosphere of the home was one of 'discontent and fatigue and irritability'.[7] They lived far out in the country, five miles from a post office, uncomfortably remote even from the dissipations of Milwaukee. Yet Ella Wheeler never lost her belief in an amazing future before her; she was probably never dull for five minutes together. Although acutely aware that her father's taste in hats was distressing, and that the farmhouse walls were without creepers, she had the power within her to transform everything to an object of beauty. The buttercups and daisies of the fields looked to her like rare orchids and hothouse roses. When she was galloping to the post on her farm horse, she expected to be thrown at the feet of a knight, or perhaps the miracle would be reversed and it was into her bosom that the knight would be pitched instead. After a day of domestic drudgery, she would climb a little hill and sit in the sunset and dream. Fame was to come from the East, and love and wealth. (As a matter of fact, she notes, they came from the West.) At any rate something wonderful was bound to happen. 'And I would awaken happy in spite of myself, and put all my previous melancholy into verses – and dollars.'[8] The young woman with the determined mouth never forgot her dollars, and one respects her for saying so. But often Miss Wheeler suggested that in return for what he called her 'heart wails'[9] the editor should send her some object from his prize list – bric-à-brac, tableware, pictures – anything to make the farmhouse more like the house of her dreams. Among the rest came six silver forks, and, judge of her emotion! conceive the immeasurable romance of the world! – years later she discovered that the silver forks were made by the firm in which her husband was employed.

But it is time to say something of the poetic gift which brought silver forks from Milwaukee, and letters and visits from complete strangers, so that she cannot remember 'any period of my existence when I have not been before the public eye'.[10] She was taught very little; there were odd volumes of Shakespeare, Ouida, and Gauthier [sic][11] scattered about the house, but no complete sets. She did not wish to read, however. Her passion for writing seems to have been a natural instinct – a gift handed down mature from Heaven, and manifesting itself whenever it chose, without much control or direction from Mrs Wilcox herself. Sometimes the Muse would rise to meet an emergency. 'Fetch me a pencil and pad!' she would say, and, in the midst of a crowd, to the amazement of the beholders, and to the universal applause, she would dash off precisely the verse required to celebrate the unexpected arrival of General Sherman.[12] Yet sometimes the Muse would obstinately forsake her. What could have been more vexatious than its behaviour in the Hotel Cecil, when Mrs Wilcox wished to write a poem about Queen Victoria's funeral? She had been sent across the Atlantic for that very purpose. Not a word could she write. The newspaperman was coming for her copy at nine the next morning. She had not put pen to paper when she went to bed. She was in despair. And then at the inconvenient hour of three a.m. the Muse relented. Mrs Wilcox woke with four verses running in her head. 'I felt an immense sense of relief. I knew I could write something the editor would like; something England would like.' And, indeed, 'The Queen's Last Ride' was set to music by a friend of King Edward's,[13] and sung in the presence of the entire Royal family, one of whom afterwards graciously sent her a message of thanks.

Capricious and fanciful, nevertheless the Muse has a heart of gold; she never does desert Mrs Wilcox. Every experience turns, almost of its own accord and at the most unexpected moments, to verse. She goes to stay with friends; she sits next a young widow in the omnibus. She forgets all about it. But as she stands before the looking-glass fastening her white dress in the evening, something whispers to her:

> Laugh and the world laughs with you,
> Weep and you weep alone.
> For the sad old earth must borrow its mirth,
> It has trouble enough of its own.

The following morning at the breakfast table I recited the quatrain to the Judge and his wife . . . and the Judge, who was a great Shakespearean scholar, said, 'Ella, if you keep the remainder of the poem up to that epigrammatic standard, you will have a literary gem.'

She did keep the poem up to that standard, and two days later he said,

'Ella, that is one of the biggest things you ever did, and you are mistaken in thinking it uneven in merit, it is all good and up to the mark.'[14] Such is the depravity of mankind, however, that a wretched creature called Joyce, belonging to 'the poison-insect order of humanity', as Mrs Wilcox says, afterwards claimed that he had written 'Solitude' himself – written it, too, upon the head of a whisky barrel in a wine-room.[15]

A poetess also was very trying. Mrs Wilcox, who is generosity itself, detected unusual genius in her verse, and fell in love with the idea of playing Fairy Godmother to the provincial poetess. She invited her to stay at an hotel, and gave a party in her honour. Mrs Croly, Mrs Leslie, Robert Ingersoll, Nym Crinkle, and Harriet Webb all came in person.[16] The carriages extended many blocks down the street. Several of the young woman's poems were recited; 'there was some good music and a tasteful supper'.[17] Moreover, each guest, on leaving, was given a piece of ribbon upon which was printed the verse that Mrs Wilcox so much admired. What more could she have done? And yet the ungrateful creature went off with the barest words of thanks; scarcely answered letters; refused to explain her motives, and stayed in New York with an eminent literary man without letting Mrs Wilcox know.

To this day when I see the occasional gems of beauty which still fall from this poet's pen I feel the old wound ache in my heart . . . Life, however, always supplies a balm after it has wounded us . . . The spring following this experience my husband selected a larger apartment [. . .][18]

For by this time Ella Wheeler was Wilcox.

She first met Mr Wilcox in a jeweller's shop in Milwaukee. He was engaged in the sterling-silver business, and she had run in to ask the time. Ironically enough, she never noticed him. There was Mr Wilcox, a large, handsome man with a Jewish face and a deep bass voice, doing business with the jeweller, and she never noticed his presence. Out she went again, anxious only to be in time for dinner, and thought no more about it. A few days later a very distinguished-looking letter arrived in a blue envelope. Might Mr Wilcox be presented to her? 'I knew it was, according to established ideas, bordering on impropriety, yet I so greatly admired the penmanship and stationery of my would-be acquaintance that I was curious to know more of him.' They corresponded. Mr Wilcox's letters were 'sometimes a bit daring', but never sentimental; and they were always enclosed in envelopes 'of a very beautiful shade', while 'the crest on the paper seemed to lead me away from everything banal and common'.[19] And then the Oriental paper-knife arrived. This had an extraordinary effect upon her such as had hitherto been produced only by reading 'a rare poem, or hearing lovely music, or in the presence of some of Ouida's exotic descriptions'.[20] She went to Chicago and met Mr Wilcox in the flesh. He seemed to her – correctly dressed and very cultured in manner as he was – 'like a man from Mars'.[21] Soon afterwards they were married, and almost immediately Mr Wilcox, to the profound joy of his wife, expressed his belief in the immortality of the soul.

Mrs Wilcox was now established in New York, the admired centre of a circle of 'very worth-while people'.[22] Her dreams in the sunset were very nearly realised. The Bungalow walls were covered with autographs of brilliant writers and the sketches of gifted artists. Universal brotherhood was attempted. It was the rule of the house 'to treat mendicants with sympathy and peddlers with respect'. No one left without 'some little feeling of uplift'.[23] What was wanting? In the first place, 'the highbrows have never had any use for me.'[24] The highbrows could be dispatched with a phrase. 'May you grow at least a sage bush of a heart to embellish your desert of intellect!'[25]

All the same, in her next incarnation she will have nothing to do with genius. 'To be a gifted poet is a glory; to be a worth-while woman is a greater glory.'[26] There are moments when she wishes that the Muse would leave her at peace. To be the involuntary mouthpiece of Songs of Purpose, Passion, and Power, greet the war with *Hello, Boys,* and death with *Sonnets of Sorrow and Triumph,*[27] to feel that at any moment a new gem may form or a fresh cameo compose itself, what fate could be more appalling? Yet such has been the past, and such must be the future, of Ella Wheeler Wilcox.

---

1 – A signed review in the *Athenaeum*, 19 September 1919, (Kp C166) of *The Worlds and I* (Gay & Hancock Ltd., 1918) by Ella Wheeler Wilcox (1850–1919), upon whom see *I VW Diary*, 7 August 1918: 'I'm much impressed by the extreme badness of B[yron]'s poetry – such of it as [Thomas] Moore quotes with almost speechless admiration. Why did they think this Album stuff the finest of fine poetry? It reads hardly better than L.E.L. [Letitia Elizabeth Landon, 1802–38] or Ella Wheeler Wilcox.'

The same issue of the *Athenaeum* carried an article by T. S. Eliot on 'Swinburne and the Elizabethans'. Reprinted: *B&P*.

2 – For Milwaukee's Madame de Staël, see the account of 'Mrs Salon', a schoolteacher and clergyman's wife, in Wilcox, ch. iv, p. 72; for Helen Pitkin, harpist and linguist, of New Orleans – 'a combination of Mesdames Récamier and de Staël' – *ibid.*, ch. x, p. 147; for Ralcy [sic] Husted Bell (1869–1931), poet and

physician, author of *Songs of the Shawangunks* (1891) and *The Philosophy of Painting* (1916), and other works, *ibid.*, ch. xii, p. 175.

3 – For Theodosia Garrison, pen name of Theodosia Pickering of Newark, N.J., who became Mrs Frederic Faulks, and for Rhoda Hero Dunn, pen name of Rhoda Burnham Dunn, *ibid.*, ch. xi, pp. 167, 168.

4 – *Ibid.*, ch. xi, p. 164.

5 – *Ibid.*, ch. iii, p. 67.

6 – *Ibid.*, ch. i, p. 26.

7 – *Ibid.*

8 – *Ibid.*

9 – *Ibid.*, p. 32.

10 – *Ibid.*, ch. xiii, p. 185, adapted.

11 – Ouida (Marie Louise de la Ramée, 1839–1908); Théophile Gautier (1811–72).

12 – For the quotation, Wilcox, ch. iii, p. 61; the general concerned was, in fact, Philip Henry Sheridan (1831–88), who became commanding general of the U.S. Army on the retirement of General W. T. Sherman (1820–91) in 1883.

13 – For the quotation, *ibid.*, ch. xiv, p. 198; and for the poem, commissioned by the editor of the New York *American, ibid.*, pp. 199–200. Queen Victoria (1819–1901); Edward VII (1841–1910), whose talented friend is unidentified.

14 – For the poem, 'Solitude' – of which the first stanza is quoted here – published in the New York *Sun*, 21 February 1883, *ibid.*, ch. v, pp. 88–9; and for the other quotations, p. 89.

15 – For John Joyce of Washington and his claims, *ibid.*, pp. 89–90.

16 – Jane Cunningham Croly (pseud. Jennie June, 1829–1901), newspaperwoman, founder in 1889 of the New York Women's Press Club, Miriam Florence Folline Leslie (c.1836–1914), editor, businesswoman, and ardent feminist, wife of the engraver and publisher Frank Leslie, Robert Green Ingersoll (1833–99), lawyer, orator and author, known as 'the great agnostic', Nym Crinkle, pseudonym of Andrew Carpenter Wheeler (1835–1903), Harriet Webb, elocutionist.

17 – Wilcox, ch. x, p. 140; the young woman is not identified.

18 – *Ibid.*, ch. x, p. 141.

19 – For these quotations, *ibid.*, ch. vi, pp. 95–6.

20 – *Ibid.*, pp. 97–8, which has: 'or in the perusal of Ouida's exotic descriptions'.

21 – *Ibid.*, p. 98.

22 – *Ibid.*, ch. ix, p. 132.

23 – For the first quotation, *ibid.*, ch. xi, p. 158, and for the second, p. 159.

24 – *Ibid.*, ch. xv, p. 227, adapted.

25 – *Ibid.*, p. 230, adapted.

26 – *Ibid.*, ch. xi, p. 169.

27 – *Poems of Purpose* (1916); *Poems of Passion* (1883); *Poems of Power* (1901); *Hello, Boys!* (1918); *Sonnets of Sorrow and Triumph* (1918).

'September'

September is a better book than *Shops and Houses*. It is, indeed, a very
able book. With candour and with sincerity Mr Swinnerton has applied
his brain to a very difficult task. Here is a woman, Marian Forster by
name, aged thirty-eight, no longer in love with her husband, but
affectionate and tolerant of his occasional lapses. By no means for the
first time she discovers that he is in love, but this time it is with a friend of
hers, Cherry Mant, a girl of twenty-two. She takes her husband's
conduct very much for granted; it is the question of the girl that puzzles
her. What is her intention? How far is she culpable? What is the relation
between them as hostess and guest, mature woman and undeveloped
girl, living for the time in the same country house? Later, Nigel Sinclair, a
young man nearer Cherry's age than her own, makes his appearance. He
falls in love with Mrs Forster, she with him, yet at the critical moment
she stops short. She cannot give herself away; something checks her, and
the moment passes. Still in love with him as she is, she realises the
presence of an obstacle, undefined at first, later revealed, and once more
discovered to be the same girl, Cherry Mant. Believing that his rejection
was final, Nigel Sinclair had gone to her and fallen in love with her. But
Nigel Sinclair scarcely counts. The relationship between the two women
is the theme of the book; and as Mr Swinnerton has been at pains to
endow each with character, and to make out from his own insight how
such a relation might shape itself, the development is original enough to
have an unusual air of truth.

Given a woman close on forty, naturally reserved, intelligent enough
to be detached, with an obstinate conviction of the importance of
conduct, neither love nor jealousy has free play. She will always be
taking them up and passing them before the light of other ideals.

It was insight that Marian craved. She incessantly sought it. She may have been a dull
woman, a woman remote from the pursuit of ordinary pleasures; but at least she had
this single ideal . . . She desired nothing but the improvement of the world. She could
accept nothing less than the disinterested pursuit of clear and noble ends.[2]

From this standpoint 'the clear and noble' thing to be aimed at is not, in
the present case, personal happiness. Neither is it the luxury of denunciation. Mrs Forster in pursuing her ideals has to bring about the union of
the man she loves with her rival. She has also so to scrutinise her feelings

that affection predominates over jealousy in her relations with Cherry Mant. Her own spoils from the contest are neither romantic nor showy, and the conclusion is of an autumnal quality. She achieves nothing for herself but courage and the power to sympathise with others; and Mr Swinnerton caps his work with the sentence that 'if it is not the first of gifts, it is among those most rarely bestowed upon poor mortals, and is without price.'[3]

Mrs Forster's figure is finely and logically outlined, because the intellect has had much to do with the shaping of it; and wherever Mr Swinnerton can use his brain he uses it to good effect. But the figure of Cherry Mant is a much more hazardous piece of work. Ideals have no such consistent control over her. The intellect is there, but it is at the mercy of a thousand instincts. Once more we are reminded of the supreme difficulty of transferring the mind of one sex into that of the other. The mental changes which each woman produces in the other are credible for the most part, always interesting and often subtle. Yet it is impossible not to hear, as the close tense narrative proceeds, a sound as of the cutting of steps in ice. Mr Swinnerton is making a little too sure because at heart he is not sure at all. Up we go; firmly we plant our feet, but not without a sense of effort; the atmosphere is dry; the scene a little bare. It is easy enough to mark out the boundaries of Mr Swinnerton's talent – to say that his is a lucid rather than a beautiful mind, intellectual in its scope, rather than imaginative. But praise ought to have the last word and the weightiest. For among modern novelists very few would choose to make the fruit of the contest something so quiet and, until we give it a second look, so ordinary as the power which Marian Forster retrieved from the wreck of brighter hopes. Few would plan their story so consistently with that end in view. We read with the conviction that we are being asked to attend to a problem worth solving – a conviction so rare as by itself to prove that *September* is a novel of exceptional merit.

1 – A review in the *TLS*, 25 September 1919, (Kp C167) of *September* (Methuen & Co., 1919), by Frank Swinnerton (1884–1982). 'I've reviewed Hope [Mirrlees]; Gosse & Swinnerton,' VW noted in her diary on Sunday, 28 September 1919, 'all in the past 10 days so that the great autumn downpour is beginning. It crosses my mind now & then that Night & Day will be one drop of it: but that seems to belong to London – not here [Monks House, Rodmell].' See also 'Honest Fiction', VW's review of Swinnerton's *Shops and Houses* (1918), in *II VW Essays*. Reprinted: *CW*.

2—Swinnerton, bk iii, ch. ii, p. 202, which concludes: 'All else seemed to her to be dust and ashes'.
3—*Ibid.*, bk iii, ch. xi, p. 288, the last sentence of the book.

Mr Gosse and His Friends

It is a frequent and rather a melancholy reflection that most of our criticism is the work of elderly people. Young people, of course, produce it in any quantity, but being ashamed on re-reading of its violence, or repenting their misplaced enthusiasms, instead of collecting they crumple it up in a ball and toss it behind the grate. Therefore the sort of volume which represents English criticism is a book like this of Mr Gosse's – sober, discreet, mellow, judicious, the fruit of love, no doubt, but of love which has been familiar with its object for so many years that it is now respectful rather than passionate. In part, this autumnal quality in Mr Gosse's book is due to the depressing aesthetics of Mr Balfour;[2] and in part to the subjects of which it treats. They tend to be a little snuff-coloured and sedate. It is only natural to approach Catharine Trotter in a mood of modified enthusiasm, since her chief claim to notoriety appears to be that Mr Austin Dobson has never heard of her and that the biographers of Locke have ignored her existence.[3] No one is going to flush and kindle when recording the passage of the Wartons[4] – a pair of staid brethren who heralded incongruously the advent of the romantic movement. The mention of Bulwer-Lytton, again, raises nothing more disturbing than a smile and a vision of embroidered waistcoats, and to be enthusiastic about Lady Dorothy Nevill, or Lord Cromer, or Lord Redesdale would be, undoubtedly, to be foolish.[5]

Nobody wants criticism to be foolish. Cutting capers to attract attention is also tedious in the long run. But now and then one comes across a critic who, with all his learning and discrimination, has yet never lost his youthful capacity for strong and direct emotion. Those are the qualities that make it impossible not to re-read the letters of Edward FitzGerald.[6] How the love of good writing oozes and drips from every page! How fresh and green his pastures remain! But then FitzGerald never took upon himself the office which Mr Gosse is so frequently called upon to discharge. He never delivered an address at the Mansion House.[7] Addresses have to be delivered; centenaries have to be commemorated; and suitable priests have to be appointed for the purpose.

Nor is the art of delivering addresses to be despised. These round, sonorous sentences make very pleasant reading, and, far from signifying nothing, signify quite as much as any audience is likely to require. How successful they must have been at the time can be judged from the sense which they produce in quite different surroundings of a ceremony, of rites duly succeeding one another, and of an audience dispersing in content and complacency. The stone has been raised; the turf has been smoothed, and the great man will sleep all the better for another hundred years.

But there is another side to Mr Gosse's talent which some prefer to his official suavity. The relation between them, perhaps, is closer than appears at first sight, just as a cat's claws owe something of their sharpness to the velvet in which they are for the most part encased. A touch of malice seems to be implied by the comparison; and, if a quick sense of the oddities and vagaries of other human beings, a delight in the foibles rather than in the passions of mankind is proof of malice, then Mr Gosse must be held guilty. It is not malice, however, but a sudden glowing and quickening of the imagination which lights up the face of Tennyson so vividly in the following phrase: – 'A gaunt, black, touzled man, rough in speech, brooding like an old gipsy over his inch of clay pipe stuffed with shag, and sucking in port-wine with gusto.' The lady who pressed Mr Gosse to give her 'one of his portraits'[8] was, indeed, happily inspired. One can see in fancy the pleasure with which Mr Gosse laid aside his rules and measures and squeezed a bright lump of paint on to his palette. Moreover, in demanding a portrait of Lady Dorothy Nevill, the lady in question chose exactly the right subject for Mr Gosse's art. The little old lady is exquisitely set down. 'Her head, slightly sunken into the shoulders, was often poised a little sideways, like a bird's that contemplates a hemp-seed. She had no quick movements, no gestures; she held herself very still.'[9] So it goes on. The manner is admirably courteous and discreet; yet at the least tremor or flicker of character in his subject Mr Gosse is at once on the alert. The mouse never has time to get back to its hole; the mouse positively seems to enjoy being caught. Old ladies and traditions, the charm of high civilisation, and the amenities of aristocracy, would seem at first sight to provide Mr Gosse with his most congenial materials. He is notably ill at ease, or unable to put his sitter at her ease, when he attempts to portray Charlotte Brontë. Yet it is that 'narrowness of vision' which he is 'sometimes tempted to find quite distressing'[10] that alienates Mr Gosse, for genius, in almost any guise save the prudish and the provincial, has the strongest fascination for him. An anecdote in the paper from which we have quoted gives an amusing proof of his breadth of sympathy. At one time he was constantly seeing Verlaine.[11] He was also faithful in his attendance at Charles Street. Lady Dorothy, who liked great men, insisted that he should bring the poet to see her. Naturally, with his habits, this was impossible. 'It was difficult to find a little French eating-house in Soho where he could be at home. She then said: "Why can't you take me to see him in this eating-house?" I had to explain that of the alternatives that was really the least possible. She was not pleased.'[12] Lady Dorothy cannot go to Soho; Verlaine cannot come to Mayfair, but Mr Gosse is equally at home in both. Occasionally there are born such ambassadors between the hostile sections of society, and we cannot be sufficiently thankful when one of them is furnished with a pen.

1 – A review in the TLS, 2 October 1919, (Kp C168) of *Some Diversions of a Man of Letters* (William Heinemann, 1919) by Edmund Gosse (1849–1928). 'I have Gosse to review,' VW noted in her diary on Sunday, 21 September 1919, 'which makes me rig up some fancy scene as I stumble about the fields.'

2 – Gosse, 'Preface: On Fluctuations of Taste', pp. 4–5 and p. 10, on the statesman philosopher Arthur Balfour (1848–1930), author of *Foundations of Belief* (1895), to the 'brilliant second chapter' of which Gosse alludes with particular attention to the question: 'Is there any fixed and permanent element in beauty?'

3 – *Ibid.*, 'Catharine Trotter [1679–1749], the Precursor of the Bluestockings', pp. 39–62; dramatist and philosophical writer, she was a friend of Congreve, and the author of a *Defence of Mr Locke's Essay on the Human Understanding* (1702). For Austin Dobson (1840–1921), poet, man of letters and authority on the 18th century, *ibid.*, p. 62.

4 – *Ibid.*, 'The Message of the Wartons. Two Pioneers of Romanticism: Joseph and Thomas Warton', pp. 65–90, delivered as the Warton Lecture, before the British Academy, 27 October 1915. Joseph Warton (1722–1800), critic, noted for his *Essay on the Genius of Pope* (2 vols., 1756, 1782); Thomas Warton (1728–90), author of a *History of English Poetry from the Close of the Eleventh to the Commencement of the Eighteenth Century* (3 vols., 1774, 1778, 1781).

5 – For Edward Bulwer-Lytton (1803–73), see *ibid.*, 'The Author of "Pelham"', pp. 117–37; Bulwer-Lytton's second novel *Pelham, or the Adventures of a Gentleman*, appeared in 1828. For: Lady Dorothy Nevill (1826–1913), on whom VW was shortly to write for the *Athenaeum* (see Headnote at p. 136 below); Lord Cromer (Evelyn Baring, 1841–1917, statesman and author); and Lord Redesdale (Algernon Bertram Freeman-Mitford, 1837–1916, diplomatist and author), see *ibid.*, 'Three Experiments in Portraiture', pp. 181–230.

6 – Edward Fitzgerald (1809–83), whose letters first appeared in 1889; neither he nor they are referred to by Gosse.

7 – Gosse, 'The Shepherd of the Ocean', p. 15, an address delivered at the Mansion House, 29 October 1918, on the tercentenary of Sir Walter Raleigh's death.

8–For Tennyson, *ibid.*, 'The Agony of the Victorian Age', p. 321, adapted, from a more extensive sentence; the essay deals at length with Lytton Strachey's *Eminent Victorians* (1918). For Lady Burghclere requesting a portrait of Lady Dorothy Nevill, *ibid.*, 'Three Experiments in Portraiture', p. 181.
9–*Ibid.*, p. 183.
10–*Ibid.*, 'The Challenge of the Brontës', p. 149; Charlotte Brontë (1816–55).
11–Paul Verlaine (1844–96).
12–*Ibid.*, 'Three Experiments in Portraiture', p. 194.

'Madeleine'

From her preface to *Madeleine, One of Love's Jansenists*, it is evident that Miss Hope Mirrlees is unusually aware both of the difficulties and of the possibilities of the art of fiction. That is at once something gained; to be aware of a difficulty may not mean that you solve it, but it does imply an intelligent choice. To decide, however, what Miss Mirrlees's choice is, one must, of course, cover the preface with one's hand and read the book.

It is a story of French life in the middle of the seventeenth century. The family of Troqueville, consisting of Monsieur, Madame, and Madeleine, their only child, aged seventeen, has just left Lyons and settled in Paris. M. Troqueville is a humble and, perhaps, rather shady lawyer. It is only through Madame Troqueville, whose father was a judge, that they have access to the higher ranks of Parisian society. But why should they wish to live in Paris, or to dine with coarse old Madame Pilou? It is due to Madeleine. Everything is due to Madeleine. For behind Paris and through the person of Madame Pilou she has a vision. Even as a child in Lyons she had a vision; but at that time it was one that could be compassed satisfactorily by making her schoolfellows believe that her father was a duke. Growing up, the desire, imagination, or whatever it may be, concentrates upon Mademoiselle de Scudéry; to know Mademoiselle de Scudéry, to be her intimate friend, has become an obsession. It is not a thing that can be confessed, shared, or analysed honestly. '... there is something almost indecently intimate in a nervous fear or obsession'.[2] It means internally a thousand times more than it can mean externally.

From this bare statement we can, at any rate, see that Miss Mirrlees has made her choice. It is the inner world that matters. Her analysis is extremely interesting. In the first place we are convinced of the intensity of Madeleine's feeiing; and in the second she is of an unusual temperament, intellectual as well as ardent, instinctive, but also subtle. 'For her most fantastic superstition she always felt the need of a semi-philosophical basis';[3] and there is, therefore, a learned strain in the book, an analysis of religion and philosophy, quotations from the Latin, translations from the Greek. Madeleine, a little laboriously perhaps, is both Précieuse and Jansenist; but the labour is justified, since she remains a human being. Perhaps the other characters are inferior to her in that respect. They interest the writer less vividly, and after giving them the right clothes, which are, of course, picturesque, and an oath or a joke in the spirit of the age, she is inclined to let them go as if her duty were discharged.

When Madeleine at length makes the acquaintance of Mademoiselle de Scudéry one is not disappointed by the poignancy of her disillusionment; one is delighted by the subtlety with which the old dream with new threads in it is spun afresh. But the Hôtel de Rambouillet, one cannot help supposing, would have put up more of a fight than Miss Mirrlees allows. Jacques, the lover who has been rejected in favour of Mademoiselle, would not, perhaps, have marched so tamely to the wars. The balance between the outer and the inner is, after all, a terribly precarious business. They depend upon each other with the utmost closeness. If dreams become too widely divorced from truth they develop into an insanity which in literature is generally an evasion on the part of the artist. He has been forced to drop half his holding. But the success of Madeleine, if not complete, is sufficient to show that Miss Mirrlees has grasped her problem with exceptional firmness. The three visits are paid. The illusion is shattered. The divorce between the reality and the imagination is complete. 'But with hope were cut the cables binding her to reality, and it was out into the void that she danced now.'[4] The little shock of emotion with which one comes to this conclusion is token that one has been led to it rightly. It is a proof that it is well worthwhile to read this difficult and interesting novel.

1—A review in the TLS, 9 October 1919, (Kp C169) of Madeleine. One of Love's Jansenists (W. Collins Sons & Co. Ltd., 1919) by Hope Mirrlees (1887–1978), whose modernist experiment, Paris. A Poem, was among a number of mss. VW listed in her diary on 18 June 1919 as having been submitted or promised to The Hogarth Press; it was published by them in May 1920. Hope Mirrlees had read classics at Newnham College, Cambridge, and studied French in Paris; she was a friend of VW's sister-in-law Karin Stephen.

VW wrote to Clive Bell on Wednesday, 24 September 1919 (*II VW Letters*, no. 1083): 'At this moment Leonard is tortured with eczema ... and I have to review Hope Mirrlees, which is even worse, as every word will be picked over. It's all sapphism so far as I've got – Jane [Harrison] and herself.' On Sunday 28 September, she noted in her dairy: 'We are on war rations, & told to be brave & good [because of the Rail Strike, 27 September–6 October]. Not since coaching days has the village of Rodmell been so isolated as it is at the present moment ... I have given myself a respite from Hope Mirrlees, whose review ought to have been despatched this morning.' And on Sunday, 11 October, she wrote: 'My review, laboured & well meaning as it was, of Hope's book has so far drawn no letter of thanks from her. I'm not sure that she didn't cherish some boundless dream about it. A whole column, in the middle, comparing her with greatness only. Well, I've had my dreams too. At the same time I'm generally rather surprised by the goodness of reality.' VW entered the title and publisher of this work in her reading notebook (MHP, B2i), but made no notes upon it there.

2 – Mirrlees, ch. iii, p. 34, which begins: 'It is wellnigh impossible for any one to be very explicit about their own nerves, for there is . . .' Madeleine de Scudéry (?1607–1701), French novelist, author of the pseudo-historical *Artamène; ou, Le Grand Cyrus* (1649) and *Clélie* (1654–60), and a leading light at the Rambouillet salon.

3 – *Ibid.*, ch. xxi, p. 191, which begins: 'For in Madeleine there was this much of rationalism – perverted and scholastic though it might be – that for her . . .'

4 – *Ibid.*, ch. xxxiv, p. 274.

Landor in Little

The collected works of Walter Savage Landor[2] occupy at least eight volumes. The question begins to be asked whether he will be allowed to take all that luggage with him on the journey to posterity upon which he set out with such unbounded confidence. It seems not. The critics who decide such matters are already making up neat little parcels and consigning the bulk of him to the great lumber room of oblivion. Why, when so greatly praised and so greatly deserving of praise, such should be his fate one can scarcely tell. 'His works are bulky, and in every way rather difficult of approach for the ordinary reader,'[3] says Mr Bailey in his discriminating introduction. Yet Landor's prose, he goes on to say, 'not merely frequently, but almost constantly, sounds the insistent and imperative claim to rank as the work of a master, a claim which has never been seriously disputed'.[4] The fatal thing is that it is never, or seldom, seriously debated. He is a master, but one of those solitary potentates who rule over an almost deserted land.

Partly, no doubt, his isolation is due to the difficulty of reading dialogue. The ascent is a great deal steeper than that which the imagination has to climb in order to attack a play. The transition from life to literature is at its most abrupt. Melanchthon is talking to Calvin; Andrew Marvell to Bishop Parker; Tasso to Cornelia.[5] Unless you have in store an unusual amount of imaginative steam, the task of setting these bare bones in action is too severe to be undertaken frequently. We have done it, however, sometimes for the Greeks and sometimes for the French with inspiriting and encouraging results. But the trouble, or at least one of the troubles, with Landor is the trouble which most writers of dialogue share with him – they are always holding dialogues with themselves. As Mr Bailey says, 'We cannot tell from the style whether it be Southey or Porson, Aesop or Rhodope, who is speaking.'[6] The one voice which is unmistakable and unfaltering is the voice of Landor himself. The masters of English prose do not readily imperil their mastery by speaking out of their proper person. Yet no one can shut the book in the middle of an imaginary conversation without a regret that is not merely formal, or can see the complete works of Landor on a shelf without a tantalising consciousness of all the beauty there embedded. If he were merely a master of prose whose perfect periods begin by delighting and end by satiating, there would no be pang in our desertion. But single passages stand out in memory as some poetry does, but very little prose; they have that 'pure, almost unthinking beauty',[7] as Mr Bailey calls it, which one can neither define nor forget.

There are no fields of amaranth on this side of the grave; there are no voices, O Rhodope, that are not soon mute, however tuneful; there is no name, with whatever emphasis of passionate love repeated, of which the echo is not faint at last.

O my beloved! [...] Sad is the day, and worse must follow, when we hear the blackbird in the garden and do not throb with joy.

Our last excess of this nature was nearer the sea, where, when our conversation paused awhile in the stillness of midnight, we heard the distant waves break heavily. Their sound, you remarked, was such as you could imagine the sound of a giant might be, who, coming back from travel into some smooth and level and still and solitary place, with all his armour and all his spoils about him, casts himself slumberously down to rest.[8]

Those and their like are the passages that we cannot surrender, and yet for the most part fail to find. As, however, Mr Bailey implies by making a Day-book of his selections, Landor not only constantly said beautiful things beautifully, but as constantly things that stand the wear and tear of daily life – things one reads over in a second, apparently forgets, and turns up later in the day with a momentary hope that, instead of having read them, one has thought them.

Communicate your happiness freely; confine your discontent within your own bosom. There chastise it; be sure it deserves its chastisement.

Baronets are prouder than anything we see on this side of the Dardanelles, excepting the proctors of universities and the vergers of cathedrals. . . .

Love always makes us better, Religion sometimes, Power never.[9]

Then, again, it is artfully contrived by Mr Bailey that the subject prescribed for a good many days' meditation is Walter Savage Landor himself – the violent old man who jumps up in some of his portraits with all his white hair on end like an infuriated Jack-in-the-box. 'You, by the favour of a Minister are Marquis of Normanby; I by the grace of God am Walter Savage Landor.'[10] Even, therefore, if you keep to the minute ration of a few lines which Mr Bailey allows for each day in the year it will be clear from Monday's reading that Landor was a wise man; from Tuesday's that he was a man of character; and from Wednesday's that he was a poet. In what measure these rare qualities are combined, and for what reason they are, if they are, ineffective, can only be decided by attacking the Conversations in their entirety. No doubt the blank page at the end of this charming little book is provided to hold a good resolution – namely, whatever else may happen in nineteen twenty-one, to read Landor through.

1 – A review in the *TLS*, 16 October 1919, (Kp, C170) of *A Day-Book of Landor*. Chosen by John Bailey (Clarendon Press, 1919). 'I have no time to fill this page,' VW wrote in her diary on Tuesday, 7 October 1919, 'since I must read my review book, (Landor), read Logan's stories [. . . *from the Old Testament Retold by Logan Pearsall Smith*, published by The Hogarth Press in May 1920], write a letter or two, & I've let the time since tea slip.'

2 – Walter Savage Landor (1775–1864), author, most notably, of *Imaginary Conversations* (1824, 1828, 1829). Leslie Stephen describes him in the *DNB* as 'for nearly ninety years a typical English public schoolboy, full of humours, obstinacy, and Latin verses, and equally full of generous impulses, chivalrous sentiment, and power of enjoyment', the 'peculiar merits' of whose prose 'are recognised as unsurpassable by all the best judges'. An eight-volume edition of Landor's works was published in 1876. See also 'Landor's Imaginary Conversations' in Stephen's *Hours in a Library* (1874 etc).

3 – Landor, intro., p. v.   4 – *Ibid.*, p. vii.

5 – Philip Melanchthon (1497–1560), the Lutheran scholar; John Calvin (1509–64); Andrew Marvell (1621–78); Samuel Parker (1640–88), Bishop of Oxford; Torquato Tasso (1544–95); Cornelia (*fl.* 2nd cent. B.C.), Roman matron, mother of the Gracchi.

6 – Landor, intro., pp. viii–ix; Robert Southey (1774–1843), one of the few men with whom the hot-tempered Landor sustained a lifelong friendship; Richard Porson (1759–1843), classical scholar; Aesop, the fabulist, and Rhodope, Thracian nymph, wife of Haemus and mother of Hebrus, a playmate of Persephone.

7–*Ibid.*, p. vi.

8–The quotations are respectively for: April 20, 'Aesop and Rhodope', *ibid.*, p. 36; February 11, 'Leofric and Godiva', p. 13; and March 9, 'Lord Brooke and Sir Philip Sidney', p. 22.

9–The quotations are respectively for: April 26, 'Epicurus, Leontion, and Ternissa', *ibid.*, p. 38; May 31, 'William Penn and Lord Peterborough', p. 48; April 16, 'Pericles and Aspasia', p. 34.

10–*Ibid.*, May 11, 'Landor to Lord Normanby', p. 42; Constantine Henry Phipps, 1st Marquis of Normanby, 2nd cr. (1797–1863).

Dostoevsky in Cranford

It is amusing sometimes to freshen one's notion of a great, and thus semi-mythical, character by transplanting him in imagination to one's own age, shore, or country village. How, one asks, would Dostoevsky have behaved himself upon the vicarage lawn? In 'Uncle's Dream', the longest story in Mrs Garnett's new volume, he enables one to fancy him in those incongruous surroundings. Mordasov bears at any rate a superficial resemblance to Cranford.[2] All the ladies in that small country town spend their time in drinking tea and talking scandal. A newcomer, such as Prince K., is instantly torn to pieces like a fish tossed to a circle of frenzied and ravenous seagulls. Mordasov cannot be altogether like Cranford, then. No such figure of speech could be used with propriety to describe the demure activities and bright-eyed curiosities of the English circle of ladies. After sending our imaginary Dostoevsky, therefore, pacing up and down the lawn, there can be no doubt that he suddenly stamps his foot, exclaims something unintelligible, and rushes off in despair. 'The instinct of provincial newsmongers sometimes approaches the miraculous . . . They know you by heart, they know even what you don't know about yourself. The provincial ought, one would think, by his very nature to be a psychologist and a specialist in human nature. That is why I have been sometimes genuinely amazed at meeting in the provinces not psychologists and specialists in human nature, but a very great number of asses. But that is aside; that is a superfluous reflection.'[3] His patience is already exhausted; it is idle to expect that he will linger in the High-street or hang in a rapture of observation round the draper's shop. The delightful shades and subtleties of English provincial life are lost upon him.

But Mordasov is a very different place from Cranford. The ladies do not confine themselves to tea, as their condition after dinner sometimes testifies. Their tongues wag with a fury that is rather that of the open marketplace than of the closed drawing room. Though they indulge in petty vices such as listening at keyholes and stealing the sugar when the hostess is out of the room, they act with the brazen boldness of viragoes. One would be alarmed to find oneself left alone with one of them. Nevertheless, in his big rough way, Dostoevsky is neither savagely contemptuous nor sadly compassionate; he is genuinely amused by the spectacle of Mordasov. It roused, as human life so seldom did, his sense of comedy. He tries even to adapt his dialogue to the little humours of a gossiping conversation.

'Call that a dance! I've danced myself, the shawl dance, at the breaking-up party at Madame Jarnis's select boarding-school – and it really was a distinguished perform- ance. I was applauded by senators! The daughters of princes and counts were educated there! . . . Only fancy' (she runs on, as if she were imitating the patter of Miss Bates) 'chocolate was handed round to everyone, but not offered to me, and they did not say a word to me all the time . . . The tub of a woman, I'll pay her out!'[4]

But Dostoevsky cannot keep to that tripping measure for long. The language becomes abusive, and the temper violent. His comedy has far more in common with the comedy of Wycherly[5] than with the comedy of Jane Austen. It rapidly runs to seed, and becomes a helter-skelter, extravagant farce. The restraint and aloofness of the great comic writers are impossible to him. It is probable, for one reason, that he could not allow himself the time. 'Uncle's Dream', 'The Crocodile', and 'An Unpleasant Predicament'[6] read as if they were the improvisations of a gigantic talent reeling off its wild imaginations at breathless speed. They have the diffuseness of a mind too tired to concentrate, and too fully charged to stop short. Slack and ungirt as it is, it tumbles out rubbish and splendour pell-mell.

Yet we are perpetually conscious that, if Dostoevsky fails to keep within the proper limits, it is because the fervour of his genius goads him across the boundary. Because of his sympathy his laughter passes beyond merriment into a strange violent amusement which is not merry at all. He is incapable, even when his story is hampered by the digression, of passing by anything so important and loveable as a man or a woman without stopping to consider their case and explain it. Thus at one moment it occurs to him that there must be a reason why an unfortunate clerk could not afford to pay for a bottle of wine. Immediately, as if recalling a story which is known to him down to its most minute detail, he describes how the clerk had been born and brought up; it is then necessary to bring in the career of his brutal father-in-law, and that leads him to describe the peculiarities of the five unfortunate women whom the father-in-law bullies. In short, once you are alive, there is no end to the complexity of your connections, and sorrow and misery are so rubbed into the texture of life that the more you examine it, the more cloudy and confused it becomes. Perhaps it is because we know so little about the family history of the ladies of Cranford that we can put the book down with a smile. Still, we need not underrate the value of comedy because Dostoevsky makes the perfection of the English product appear to be the result of leaving out all the most important things. It is the old, unnecessary quarrel between the inch of smooth ivory[7] and the six feet of canvas with its strong coarse grains.

1 – A review in the TLS, 23 October 1919, (Kp C171) of An Honest Thief and Other Stories . . . from the Russian by Constance Garnett (William Heinemann, 1919) by Fyodor Dostoevsky (1821–81). For Constance Garnett (1862–1946) – who translated the whole of Dostoevsky's oeuvre – see 'The Russian Background' above, n. 2.
    See also 'Dostoevsky the Father' below; 'More Dostoevsky' and 'A Minor Dostoevsky', II VW Essays. Reprinted: B&P.
2 – The story 'Uncle's Dream' is subtitled as being 'From the Annals of Mordasov'. Cranford: the eponymous location of Elizabeth Gaskell's novel published 1851–3.
3 – Dostoevsky, 'Uncle's Dream', ch. vii, p. 67–8, which has 'specialists on human nature' in both instances.
4 – Ibid., ch. vi, p. 59. Miss Bates, character in Jane Austen's Emma (1816).
5 – William Wycherley (1640–1716).
6 – The other stories in An Honest Thief not otherwise referred to are: 'A Novel in Nine Letters', 'Another Man's Wife', 'The Heavenly Christmas Tree', 'The Peasant Marey', 'Bobok', 'The Dream of a Ridiculous Man'.
7 – See William Austen-Leigh, Jane Austen. Her Life and Letters (Smith, Elder & Co., 1913), ch. xx, p. 378, Jane Austen writing to her nephew Edward Austen, 16 December 1816, on the subject of two last chapters of his novel: 'How could I possibly join them on to the little bit (two inches wide) of ivory on which I work with so fine a brush, as produces little effect after much labour?' (quoted in 'Jane Austen', II VW Essays).

Winged Phrases

No one, perhaps, has ever spent a pleasant evening talking about books without wondering why it is that the things that are said are so much better than the things that are written. One reason will occur to most people; enthusiasm, which is the life-blood of criticism, tells in tone and manner, for or against, rightly or wrongly, with a conviction and sincerity which are unmistakable yet scarcely to be preserved, save by the rare masters of expression, in print. And where there is warmth of feeling, everything else, it seems, easily follows – the nicest discriminations, the most daring conjectures, illuminations and felicities clustering one on top of another like blue and purple soap bubbles at the end of a pipe, and, like bubbles, breaking and vanishing. Mr Moore has a much better phrase for the ardours of conversation when he speaks of Banville 'throwing winged phrases into the air that, rising with rapid wing-beats, floated, wheeled, and chased each other like birds whose pastime is flying'.[2] But to cut the matter short, here is Mr George Moore talking about books, and giving us the most delightful example of printed talk that we can remember to have met with in English – if, indeed, it be in English. One chapter is actually written in French; the others, as Henry James said of one of Mr Moore's novels, seem to be translated from that language.[3] Not, of course, that Mr Moore is anything but a master of his own tongue, which is presumably the Irish. It is the thinking, or, more obscurely, the atmosphere, that seems to be in French; and had we not express evidence to the contrary we should imagine that these conversations took place in a Parisian café, at a little round table, with a glass of his favourite chocolate in front of him, rather than in the 'long narrow slum' of Ebury Street, or in the Georgian solidity of Regent's Park.[4]

For the first two conversations are with Mr Gosse, and Mr Moore's theme is that 'English prose narrative is the weakest part of our literature.'[4] A casual remark made somewhere by Mr Gosse that 'English genius had gone into poetry'[5] had started Mr Moore upon the toils of composition; when, the door opening and the maid announcing Mr Gosse, he threw himself into the far more congenial task of conversation. Such is the setting. But if anyone will momentarily recall the course of a conversation when both the talkers have the theme by heart, can toss the ball where they like, and return the lightest or wildest flick of the other's racquet, he will agree that any report by a third person is valueless. Besides, one of the great merits of such conversation is that it proves nothing. Whether Mr Moore proved his case against prose fiction we do not remember. Our impression is that he danced round that stout matron with elfish vivacity, assuring her that her place was at the wash-tub and her demeanour of a plebeian stolidity out of all keeping with the incorrigible triviality of her mind; when, having made her look both flustered and foolish, he suddenly transformed her into a slim and shapely goddess and fell at her feet in an ecstasy of adoration. This is neither a full nor an accurate report. In the course of an undulating dialogue which meanders in and out, round and round the feet of Fielding, Thackeray, Dickens and Trollope,[7] they are all, for one reason or another, found wanting, lacking in breeding, in depth, in seriousness, in sensibility; but suddenly he stops himself short; there is one English novelist whose wine is of the purest – Jane Austen. There is one scene in one of her books where 'we find the burning human heart in English prose narrative for the first and, alas, for the last time'. The book is *Sense and Sensibility*;[8] the scene we will not specify, for most people will like nothing better than to find it for themselves, and enjoy nothing more than to hear Mr Moore praise it for them.

Then we rush on, it matters not how, to the question of names, and if you reflect what our novelists are called you will no longer be surprised by the mediocrity of what they have written.

Trollope! Did ever anybody bear a name that predicted a style more trollopy. Anthony, too, in front of it, to make matters worse. And Walter Scott is a jog-trot name, a round-faced name, a snub-nosed, spectacled, pot-bellied name, a placid, beneficent, worthy old bachelor name; a name that evokes all conventional ideas and formulas, a Grub Street name, [. . .] an old oak and Abbotsford name; a name to improvise novels to buy farms with. And Thackeray is a name for a footman, for the syllables clatter like plates, and when we hear it we say, We shall want the carriage at half-past 2, Thackeray.[9]

We have broken a vow which we made not to quote from Mr Moore, and we are now punished; for to interrupt Mr Moore is as barbarous as to silence the nightingale. Mr Gosse alone is able to do it. From time to time Mr Gosse recalls him to the matter in hand, or suggests that the drawing-room window, in front of which they are sitting, had better be closed. But Mr Gosse has his place in the composition. He serves to define Mr Moore. He brings out the fact that we are hearing the voice of a fallible, frivolous, occasionally aggravating, elderly gentleman who will not refrain from poking fun at the Athenaeum Club,[10] or at any other object that takes his fancy. And is it not because the fallible human being is absent in most books of criticism that we learn so little from them? Such is human imperfection that to love one thing you are almost constrained to hate another. Far from suppressing this natural lopsidedness, Mr Moore indulges it, avows it, and carries us away on the breath of his preference. We have not listened long to the brilliant and often beautiful denunciation of English prose narrative before we perceive that our companion, if we may call him so, is heading for some favourite landmark. One scans the horizon for the first sight of it. Can it be in Germany? In France much more probably. But surely he cannot altogether ignore Russia! One tries to remember the date of Mr Moore's birth. It was *Esther Waters*,[11] one reflects, that first made one look up and down the bookshelves for another book with the name of George Moore on the back of it. We were always, perhaps, a little disappointed after *Esther Waters*. The language was abundant and flexible, the rhythm of the most musical fluidity; what was wanting? Concentration or intensity was it? Some power, perhaps, of getting outside himself, or forgetting all about himself? And then George Moore is not a good name for a novelist; and now we recollect that it is above all things a philosophical name. Whatever the reason, nothing came up to *Esther Waters*, until the autobiographies began; and still they seem to us the very best autobiographies in the Irish language, for the soft cadence in which they are written is Irish and has nothing whatever to do with English. But while we are thus musing, Mr Moore has reached his goal; he is prostrate before his idol; and it is of course, Turgenev. But we must not call him Turgenev.

Ivan Tourguéneff. Hearken, reader, to the musical syllables – Ivan Tourguéneff; repeat them again and again, and before long the Fates coiled in their elusive draperies in the British Museum will begin to rise up before your eyes; the tales of the great Scythian tale-teller are as harmonious as they, and we ask in vain why the Gods should have placed the light of Greece in the hands of a Scythian.[12]

These words are the prelude to a hymn of praise so sincere and so inspiring that, whatever our own view of Turgenev, we feel that we know him better because we have seen him through the eyes of someone who loves him. Yet love which springs from so profound a source almost necessarily brings with it an instinctive jealousy: for unconsciously so much of ourselves is in whatever we love. So Mr Moore, believing that since the world began there have been only two tale-tellers, Balzac and Turgenev, and that Turgenev is the greater of the two, is necessarily and sincerely unjust.

Tolstoy writes with a mind as clear as an electric lamp, a sizzling white light, crude and disagreeable, and Flaubert's writing is as beautiful as marquetry, or was thought to be so once. Be this as it may, he is no tale-teller; his best books are not novels, but satires. There is Huysmans with *En Route*, and the Goncourts have written interesting pages, which some future generation may glance at curiously. There have been men of genius who wrote novels, Dostoieffsky, for instance; but vapours and tumult do not make tales, and before we can admire them modern life must wring all the Greek out of us. His farrago is wonderful, but I am not won. Maupassant wrote perfect tales, but they are so very little.[13]

We must find another word than the word 'unjust' to describe a judgment which one may think jealous or capricious, but which we cannot deny, urged as it is by a fervid conviction, to be both penetrating and true. Let us read on a little farther in the conversation with Mr Balderston:

I admire Tolstoy; but if I only dared – I beg of you, he interrupted. Well, I continued, Gautier used to boast that the visible world was visible to him, but to no one was it ever so visible as it is to Tolstoy. His eyesight exceeds all eyesight before or since. At this point I paused, and my visitor and I sat looking at each other, myself very much abashed . . . What is your conclusion? That Tolstoy is not a great psychologist, I answered tremblingly, for when he comes to speak of the soul he is no longer certain; he doesn't know. But I'm saying something that no one will agree with, that no one has ever said.[14]

That is memorable and stimulating criticism because, even if one had not read the praises of Turgenev which precede and partly inspire it, one would know that it is the fruit not of coldness, but of love. The love of art which is the light that Mr Moore carries with him through all the libraries in the world wavers and flickers, gutters and splutters, but never goes out. The pages, the faces, of Pater and Mallarmé, of Rudyard Kipling and Henry James,[15] are alike lit up – partially, of course, leaving great tracts of them in shadow, but so warmly and brightly that we know that if we cannot see what Mr Moore sees for ourselves, it exists somewhere for him. The faces crowd and cluster, but among them all we see most vividly the engrossed and ardent countenance of the writer himself, hanging absorbed over the pages of others, weaving with infinite delicacy and toil a new page of his own. Truly, we can conjure up no more exhilarating and encouraging spectacle than the spectacle of Mr George Moore, who declares himself an Ishmael and an outcast in England, determining that he will live to the age of ninety in order that he may be able to write English prose 'nearly as well as I should like to be able to write it.'[16]

1 – A review in the TLS, 30 October 1919, (Kp C172) of Avowals (Privately printed, 1919) by George Moore (1852–1933). 'I've been reading one book you'd like,' VW wrote to Roger Fry, 2 November 1919 (II VW Letters, no. 1089), 'George Moore, Avowals – partly memories, partly criticism and very amusing though when I said in a review that I felt strong affection for him, the Times went and cut it out.' See also 'A Born Writer' below, and 'George Moore', IV VW Essays, Reprinted: CW.
2 – Moore, ch. xv, p. 280: 'After a slight pause [Victor] Hugo answered: I'd like to hear, Banville, what argument you would find to support your extravagant theory, and Banville, finding himself in the midst of a company who could appreciate his

humour, spoke for twenty minutes, throwing winged phrases into the air that, rising with rapid wing-beats, floated, wheeled and chased each other like birds whose pastime is flying, while we, almost breathless, watched their hazardous evolutions, glad at last at seeing them perch with a flutter of wings on a full stop – verb, noun, adjective, adverb, always in the right place; note of interrogation, note of exclamation, comma, semicolon, colon, and every clause fitting perfectly in that improvisation on the theme that it is absurd to be in love after seventeen and three months.' Théodore de Banville (1823–91), Parnassian poet.

3–Ch. xiii, pp. 224–51, is written in French, and takes the form of a lecture on Honoré de Balzac (1799–1850) and Shakespeare. The source of this remark by Henry James (1843–1916) has not been discovered.

4–For the 'long narrow slum', Moore, ch. iv, p. 124. Moore lived at No. 121 Ebury Street; he visited Edmund Gosse (1849–1928) at No. 17 Hanover Terrace, Regent's Park.

5–*Ibid.*, ch. i, p. 5. Moore's opinion here is echoed in VW's account of him some years later in her diary, 9 March 1926: 'But my good friend (to me – half hesitating to call me this) what have you to say for Hardy? You cannot find anything to say. English fiction is the worst part of English literature. Compare it with the French – with the Russians.'

6–*Ibid.*

7–Henry Fielding (1707–54); W. M. Thackeray (1811–63); Charles Dickens (1812–70); Anthony Trollope (1815–82).

8–For the quotation, Moore, ch. i, p. 42; Jane Austen's *Sense and Sensibility* was published in 1811.

9–*Ibid.*, ch. iv, p. 127, which has: 'Did anybody ever', and, where VW omits the ellipsis: 'a nerveless name, an arm-chair name'.

10–'. . . that august abode of prelacy and literature' (*ibid.*, p. 3), to which he mistakenly believed Gosse belonged.

11–*Esther Waters* (1894), discussed by VW in 'A Born Writer', below.

12–Moore, ch. iv, p. 128: Ivan Turgenev (1818–83).

13–*Ibid.*, pp. 130–1.

14–*Ibid.*, ch. v, pp. 138–9. The conversation is, in fact, with 'one of Tolstoy's critics, and one of Tourgéneff's translators' (p. 137), not otherwise identified. His conversations with Balderston, 'a young American . . . writer' (*ibid.*, p. 101), are recorded in chapters iii and xvi.

15–Walter Pater (1839–94); Stéphane Mallarmé (1842–98); Rudyard Kipling (1865–1936); Henry James (1843–1916).

16–Moore, ch. xv, p. 282, which has: 'nearly as well as I should like to write it.'

Real Letters

How, in writing of Miss Eden's letters, is one to avoid the old common-place about the penny post and the death of letter writing? From Miss Eden herself, the witty and distinguished lady who wrote *The Semi-Detached House* and *The Semi-Attached Couple* one would have expected witty letters. But Pamela FitzGerald,[2] in no way distinguished save as the daughter of Lord Edward and the mother of a very large family, in our opinion surpasses her. She is, perhaps, the more spontaneous and the richer natured of the two. Be this as it may, the memorable thing is that both ladies have the art of letter writing by nature – by which we mean to express our conviction that if either of them saw a large sheet of paper and a quill pen she said, with a smile, 'Now I'll write a letter!' and sat down and filled her paper with the greatest pleasure in the world. Nothing, it seems, could be easier; in our time nothing is more rare. How, one wonders, did these young ladies of little education, though high breeding, hit off, while still in their teens, this happy spirited manner of conveying to each other the amusements, the pleasures, the annoyances of life? There were, it is impossible to doubt, rules well known to them and scrupulously observed. You will not find them rashly confiding, or introspective; their sense of humour is their standby; they would rather laugh than cry; and whatever they think proper for a letter they know how to put into words. But we will let Miss Eden, aged twenty two, speak for herself.

My dearest Sister, – I am going to write you a long letter, and I shall be like a ginger-beer bottle now, if once the cork is drawn. I shall spirtle you all over – not that I have anything to say, but just a few remarks to make. In the first place I am eternally obliged to you for your just and proper appreciation of autumn . . . I tried some cool admiration of it upon Louisa, but she said she did not like it, as it led to winter and the children wanted new coats, and she must write to Grimes, of Ludgate-hill, for patterns of cloth, &c. However, London is a very pretty check to enthusiasm; there are no trees to look brown and yellow, and the autumn air only blows against poor Lord Glengall's hatchment, and the few people that wander about the streets seem to think it cold and uncomfortable . . . I enclose you some Fleur d'Orange because it is so genteel. Pray remark, when it is going down, whether your sensations are not remarkably ladylike.[3]

So it runs on, easy, witty, controlled, the young lady knowing how to turn a sentence as, presumably, she knew how to run her needle in and out of the pattern of her embroidery. The pattern of the letters was a gay and variegated one. The young ladies paid their round of country visits to all the great houses, and exchanged their impressions of Longleat and Chatsworth and Bowood. Pamela now takes up the pen. She has been staying with Lord and Lady Bute at Mount Stuart, and sketches their portraits.

My mind is grown much more easy since I have clearly ascertained, weighed, and measured that I don't like Lord Bute . . . He is not purse-proud nor personally proud of his looks; but the sheer genuine article, pride, which nowadays one seldom meets with barefaced. He is proud of his ancestors, proud of the red puddle that runs in his veins, proud of being a Stuart, a Bute, and a Dumfries. He apes humility and talks of the honour people do him in a way that sounds like 'down on your knees' . . . She is pleasant enough in a middling way, no particular colour in her ideas. She never moots, or shocks, or pushes one back, but she don't go any further, content to dwell in decencies for ever. She likes a joke when it is printed and published for her, but I suppose a manuscript joke never occurred to her.[4]

Neither Miss Eden nor Miss FitzGerald, one is refreshed to find, dwells in decencies for ever; they are surprisingly open in their speech. Both of them, too, have a passion for the country, even in its more horrid aspects. 'One is a better human creature,' wrote Pamela, 'when one has seen a mountain, and it does one good.' 'I only wish I could see a mountain with you,'[5] she added, for their devotion was warm and founded upon distinct differences of opinion. Miss Eden, as became Lord Auckland's sister,[6] was apt to include a little gossip about Ministers and policies in her letters, and was therefore all the better pleased to hear of nothing but children from Lady Campbell. 'Other people or papers tell public news. What a pleasure it is to have a letter!'[7]

But we cannot give in extracts the more delightful quality which the volume possesses as a whole. It is a story, a drama; the characters marry and change and grow up, and we watch them changing beneath our eyes. The judgment of Miss Dickinson's selections and the unusual excellence of her materials give the book what we so seldom find in biographies – construction and artistic purpose. Of the figures who make up this amusing and vivacious early nineteenth-century group, none appears to us a more happy conception than Lady Sarah Robinson, as she is bandied to and fro between Emily and Pamela and Lady Theresa Lewis – eccentric, valetudinarian, despotic, the wife of the gentleman who was Prime Minister for five months and then resigned 'stating that his wife's health would no longer allow him to remain in office.'[8] Here we have the family version of her vagaries, as she drives out with the apothecary beside her to feel her pulse, or complains, when the doctor fails to call before two, 'Physicians, I believe, always neglect their dying patients,'[9] or forces Mr Robinson to dine in her dressing room that she may check his appetite, or forbids him to visit the stables –

'Sarah, I wish I might go to the stables?' 'No, dearest, I told you before not to go.' 'Yes; but I want to see my horses. Mayn't I go?' 'No, darling, you said you would not ask it if I let you out.' 'Yes, but one of my horses is sick, and I want to see it.' 'Well, then, if Mama will go with you, you may.'[10]

The story of Lady Sarah and Mr Robinson should have been written by Jane Austen. Indeed, Jane Austen seems all the time to be round the corner, nor is she altogether out of sight. Mrs Elton is a household word as early as 1825; already in 1826 Mr Collins is 'the immortal Collins'.[11] For Miss Eden was as good a judge of books as people who call themselves uneducated and know Boswell by heart generally are;[12] and if Pamela had not had quite so many children or Sir Guy Campbell had ever got that comfortable appointment which was his due – but we must break off upon the verge of reflections which would carry us too far. For, like all good letters, Miss Eden's letters bring so much of life into view, and hint at so much more than we can see, that far from falling asleep over her pages, as Miss Dickinson predicts, we feel that we have been completely woken up and set gossiping.

---

1 – A review in the *TLS*, 6 November 1919, (Kp C173) of *Miss Eden's Letters*. Edited by her great-niece Violet Dickinson (Macmillan & Co. Ltd., 1919).

Emily Eden (1797–1869), novelist and traveller, author of two novels, *The Semi-Detached House* (1859) and *The Semi-Attached Couple* (1860), and of accounts of India, was the daughter of William Eden, 1st Baron Auckland, and Eleanor, *née* Elliot, sister of the 1st Earl of Minto. Her great-niece Violet Dickinson (1865–1948), for many years VW's most intimate friend, had been working on the Eden papers in 1916. VW wrote to her on 26 May that year: 'O and by the way, I'm told that you produced your life of your Aunt or grandmother, and made a tremendous success. *Please lend me a copy* – nothing is quite so nice as old family letters.' (*II VW Letters*, no. 759; see also no. 822).

On 4 November 1919 (*ibid.*, no. 1090), VW wrote to say she had also just read *Miss Eden's Letters*: 'I think it is one of the best collections for ever so long. But why not more from your own pen? Surely, the style is identical with hers. I was kept happy for hours with them, and only wished they'd go on and on and on. Are there no more? I've written a review, but had to keep it so short that I couldn't say half I wanted to. ¶Lytton Strachey has just written to me to say that he's reading them too, and finds them far superior to anything of the present day. He had read some years ago in Lord Clarendon's Life, and always hoped for more. Also, he finds that he's your cousin – through the Colviles [Lady Colvile was Strachey's aunt and a niece by marriage of Miss Eden].' In 1922 VW asked Violet Dickinson whether The Hogarth

Press might publish a further collection of Miss Eden's letters (*ibid.*, no. 1226), but nothing came of the idea.

2 – Pamela FitzGerald (1796–1869) was the daughter of the Irish rebel Lord Edward FitzGerald (1763–98) and his wife Pamela. In 1820 she married Sir Guy Campbell (1786–1849), a soldier, eventually promoted to Major-General. They had eleven children.

3 – *Letters*, Miss Eden to her sister Eleanor, Countess of Buckinghamshire, 7 October 1819, pp. 41–2.

4 – *Ibid.*, Lady Campbell (Pamela FitzGerald) to Miss Eden, 3 March 1821, pp. 66–7, which has 'the genuine article pride which' and 'published and printed'. Lady Campbell's hosts were the 2nd Marquess of Bute and his wife Maria, daughter of the 3rd Earl of Guildford.

5 – *Ibid.*, Lady Campbell to Miss Eden, 28 February 1821, p. 66, slightly adapted.

6 – George Eden, Earl of Auckland (1784–1849), statesman and governor-general of India, second son of William Eden.

7 – *Letters*, Miss Eden to Lady Campbell, from Government House, Calcutta, 16 August 1836, p. 270.

8 – *Ibid.*, editorial note, p. 114. Lady Sarah Robinson, daughter of Robert, 4th Earl of Buckinghamshire, and wife of Frederick John Robinson, who, in 1827, succeeded Canning as Prime Minister. He was ineffectual in office and resigned in January 1828. Lady (Maria) Theresa Lewis, *née* Villiers (d. 1865), had married the novelist and dramatist Thomas Henry Lister (1800–42) in 1830, and in 1844 married Sir George Cornewall Lewis (1806–63), statesman and author. She edited Emily Eden's novel *The Semi-Detached House* (1859).

9 – *Ibid.*, Miss Eden to Miss Villiers, Novemberr 1827, p. 154.

10 – *Ibid.*, 15 December 1826, p. 122; each unit of the dialogue in the original is divided from the next by a dash.

11 – For Mrs Elton, Jane Austen's *Emma* (1816), *ibid.*, Miss Eden to Miss Villiers, 1825, p. 89: 'My sister Louisa [Colville] and four of her children passed a fortnight here at the end of last month, and our whole time was spent in "exploring in the barouche landau", as Mrs Elton observes.' And for Mr Collins – 'not the Professor Collins, but the far greater *Pride & Prejudice* Collins' – *ibid.*, Miss Eden to Miss Villiers, 1826, p. 104.

12 – See *ibid.*, intro., p. ix: 'She had read Boswell's *Life of Johnson* [1791], the *Memoires du Cardinal de Retz* [1717; Eng. tr. 4 vols. 1723], Shakespeare, and knew a great part of the Bible almost by heart before she was eleven.'

The Limits of Perfection

If Mr Beerbohm had never written another word, the reviewer's task would be simple. Here, he would say, laying down *Seven Men* with a deep sigh of contentment, is a little masterpiece; so perfect in itself that one need scarcely take account of what it promises. But when a book is not the first, but apparently the seventh,[2] one's conscience, or it may be one's vanity, is more exacting. One takes for granted what one can only call Mr Beerbohm's perfection, and then, as if one could swallow perfection and still keep one's critical capacity unsated, one looks about for something more.

The truth is perhaps that here and there in *Seven Men* Mr Beerbohm himself looks about – stands on tiptoe and peeps over the palisade which he has erected round his exquisite plot. Little airs blow in from outside for which Mr Beerbohm is not responsible, which he has not invited, and has not subdued. We admit that we find it difficult to give an example of what we mean. But in the story of James Pethel,[3] the man who lived for the sake of taking risks, one is sorry for his wife; and one feels that one ought either not to be sorry at all or to be much sorrier than one is. She has not accommodated herself to Mr Beerbohm's world; she remains too much like the women outside. Then there is the brilliant description of the weekend party at Keeb,[4] when the ghost of the author who was not invited haunts the author who was. Again we feel that life has insisted upon breaking in; it is fantastic, it is brilliant, but somehow it is too much like the real thing that real novelists describe. Casting about for some explanation, one hazards this: among the books that Mr Beerbohm has written there ought to be one that is very large and very dull. Of course there is no such thing. He has always done the things that he does best. Yet sometimes, one figures, literature refuses to be pampered and cockered any longer; life comes trickling through some unguarded chink, and the writer who has not run all the risks and broken his pen upon every kind of enterprise is, for once and for a second, at a loss.

If this explanation has any truth in it, we admit that we think it much to Mr Beerbohm's credit. His mastery over his own method is such that he could, if he chose, keep exactly within its limits. He is not forced to go beyond them; it is the demon of human sympathy that now and then compels him into the outer air. For a second he makes his own perfection look a little small. Quickly he draws back again. Instantly, like some cuttlefish dispersing a silver and crepuscular fluid instead of a dense and a dark, he emits his perfect little disk of fantasy, wit, and satire. The *Seven Men* here depicted stand almost precisely in the centre of it. They are brilliantly displayed. The silvery yet searching light falls with the utmost exactitude into every crease and wrinkle of their faces. There is a background, too, in due harmony with the figure. The whole of the artistic niceties of the *Yellow Book*[5] and of the Café Royal are con-

centrated in the first few pages of Enoch Soames. Soames was a writer.
His first book was called 'Negations': –

He wore a soft black hat of clerical kind but of Bohemian intention, and a grey
waterproof cape which, perhaps, because it was waterproof, failed to be romantic. I
decided that 'dim' was the *mot juste* for him. I had already essayed to write, and was
immensely keen on the *mot juste*, that Holy Grail of the period . . .[6] Seated, he was
more self-assertive. He flung back the wings of his cape with a gesture which – had
not those wings been waterproof – might have seemed to hurl defiance at things in
general. And he ordered an absinthe. 'Je me tiens toujours fidèle,' he told Rothen-
stein, 'à la sorcière glauque.'[7]

Once you can do that – and Mr Beerbohm goes on doing it till the last
line of the 'Savonarola'[8] with a subtlety, a precision, a sense of humour
which do not disguise the fact that his eye is unwinkingly fastened on a
definite object – why, one may ask, do anything else? Why demand that
Charles Lamb shall be Charles Dickens?[9] But a critic must be exacting; it
is not the doing it that he objects to; it is the going on doing it.

1–A review in the TLS, 6 November 1919, (Kp C174) of *Seven Men* (Heinemann,
1919) by Max Beerbohm (1872–1956), writer and caricaturist, a friend much
admired in Bloomsbury, particularly by VW and Lytton Strachey, whose collection
of essays *Portraits in Miniature* (1931) was dedicated to Beerbohm. See 'A Flying
Lesson', below. See also 'The Modern Essay', in *IV VW Essays* and CR1.
2–Apart from several volumes of caricatures, Beerbohm had by this date published
The Works of Max Beerbohm (1896), *The Happy Hypocrite* (1897), *More* (1899),
Yet Again (1909), *Zuleika Dobson* (1911), *A Christmas Garland* (1912).
3–Beerbohm, 'James Pethel', pp. 107–35.
4–Keeb Hall, home of the Duke and Duchess of Hertfordshire, in the story 'Hilary
Maltby and Stephen Braxton', pp. 51–104.
5–The *Yellow Book*, an illustrated quarterly published in the period 1894–7, to
which Beerbohm was a contributor.
6–Beerbohm, 'Enoch Soames', p. 6.
7–*Ibid.*, p. 8.
8–'"Savonarola" Brown', pp. 175–219.
9–Charles Lamb (1775–1834); Charles Dickens (1812–70).

George Eliot

VW's essay in the TLS, 20 November 1919, (Kp C175) on the occasion
of the centenary of George Eliot's birth was later revised for inclusion in
The Common Reader: 1st series (1925). The reader is referred to *IV VW*

Essays, where the revised version, together with variants in the form of footnotes, is reprinted in its place as part of *The Common Reader*.

Maturity and Immaturity

On his mother's side a Wyndham, but on his father's a Tennant, there is no reason, either in eulogy or in excuse, to call Wyndham Tennant an aristocrat. Yet one finds oneself thinking of him as an aristocrat, and judging that the chief interest of his memoir lies in its revelation of the aristocratic point of view. Perhaps the best answer to the question as to what that may mean is to quote one or two stories:

> When his Mother visited among the poorer streets of Westminster, he could only be prevailed on to cross those darkened thresholds by being given a large tin of sweets that he might distribute largesse as he went. He left the children in little throngs and clusters smiling in his wake.... Finally he went no more with her, for his heart suffered and he was too wise to think that either toys, sweets, clothes, kindly interest, or money, would ever gloss over such surroundings.[2]

Again, when he rode a motor-bicycle he was uneasy at the amount of dust that he raised. He wrote therefore, in very large letters, 'Apologies for the Dust', tied the placard to the tail of his machine, and then 'went sweeping through the Southern counties in unparalleled speed'.[3] The impulsiveness, the lack of self-consciousness, the desire that slum children and agitated pedestrians shall smile in his wake, with all that this implies of good fortune, good temper, and the most innocent belief in the goodness of life, are the attractive virtues of an aristocrat. But one has to reflect that it is possible presumably to ride a motor-bicycle slowly, in which case apologies are unnecessary; and that you need not give up the problem of poverty because the sorrows of the poor are not altogether appeased by feeding them on sweets out of a large tin. In a middle-class family certainly the apology, and probably the sweets, would have been judged rather childish than admirable. This is not due to a superior morality, but rather to the fact that middle-class surroundings are not such as to prompt a perpetual effervescence of gratitude and joy. The middle-class attitude is one of reticence and even of suspicion; whereas the bounty and pleasantness of the aristocratic environment produce a natural desire to make other people happy. Wyndham Tennant was always spending his pocket-money upon buying guns for the village boys and silk ties for the housemaids. At the age of three his manners were so good and his self-possession such that he delighted a lady by asking, with his little bow, how her peacocks' tails were growing. No more demonstrative schoolboy can ever have existed. Most children secretly think their mother the most beautiful of women, and even their uncle the most brilliant of men. But Edward Tennant always thought so, and he thought nothing secretly. He gloried in uttering his beliefs aloud. He would kiss a tree under which he had spent a pleasant afternoon, he would kiss his bed for having taken care of him every night of the term. 'I am longing for the blessed joy of seeing darling You, and darling Everybody Else. I love them all.'[4] Those, incredible as it seems, are the words of a schoolboy of eleven. Again, he went to an Advent service:

The sermon was preached by the Bishop of Dorking, who is shortly going to Japan as a missionary. He *is* a dear man. He was *so, so* kind to me. He said he is a cousin of Aunt Annie's. His words were 'Then we are relations; so shake hands.'[5]

Clearly, no one has ever laughed at him, or snubbed him, and the whole world seems to him, as he journeys from Wiltshire to Scotland and back again to Queen Anne's Gate, a cordial, appreciative family circle entirely populated by the cousins of Aunt Annie advancing with outstretched hands. He writes a charming little poem, and his uncle George Wyndham at once says 'in all seriousness that Gray and Tennyson alone give the model for that "tour de force" in solemn verse'.[6]

From his natural confidence spring all those demonstrative ways which are at once so charming and (to be honest) so strangely disconcerting when published in a book. For if, as is likely, one is neither related to Aunt Annie nor has ever heard of her existence, there is something indecent, though childish and disarming, in the amazing aristocratic irreticence which is displayed – the assumption that everybody must know you, and be interested in hearing all about you. One is reminded of the old village woman who insists upon showing one her bad toe. No doubt it is better to display one's bad toe than to follow the middle-class habit of denying that one has any legs at all. It is better even as a preparation for writing poetry. One must learn to speak of one's feelings; one must learn to do it beautifully. But the aristocrat appears never to learn anything. He seems condemned to remain a gifted and instinctive child. The delightful talents never mature; the park is mistaken for the world, the family for the human race; and the smiles of the Muse are solicited with a pocket full of sweets. But none of this applies to 'The Mad Soldier', a poem suddenly conceived in the vein of

Mr Sassoon;[7] and to say what would have been the course of a writer who died at the age of nineteen is obviously out of the question.

Perhaps, if one had not read the memoir of Wyndham Tennant first, one would not have thought of saying that Joyce Kilmer was mature. One would have taken it for granted that a young man who has to earn his living and support a wife and child before he is of age must possess that particular quality or perish. Joyce Kilmer, the American poet, seems to have flourished in every possible way until a shell put an end to him in France. He was a highly successful journalist. He was rapidly increasing in weight. He enjoyed an enormous appetite. When he came down to breakfast he usually asked what there was going to be for dinner. He had a profound admiration for Mr Belloc and for Mr Chesterton.[8] He turned out between four and five thousand words an hour, and spent those hours by choice in walking up and down the family sitting room with the youngest baby screaming on his shoulder. He possessed, in short, that alarming combination which the worst writers always seem to possess – a superb vitality attached to an inferior brain. But, if human beings were divided into the separate sections of a Neapolitan ice, life would be less interesting, though a great deal simpler than it is. It is true that Kilmer's poetry appears to us exactly the right stuff for the world to cut out and paste in its hat, which, according to Mr Holliday, is what the world has done; but he had the invaluable gift which makes its possessor at once important, though we can only define it vaguely as the gift of maturity. He was interested in a great many things beside himself. He enjoyed almost everything. He was justly proud of the fact that he could use every idea that came to him three times over. He kept a special tail-coat in which to lecture to 'blue-nosed salons' upon 'certain aspects of Victorian verse';[9] but he knew, one feels, exactly when he put it on, and when he took it off. Thus, though thousands of words issued from his mouth every day, they never seem to have impaired his belief in literature. He believed in Walter Pater, Gerard Hopkins, Scott and Charles Lamb. On the battlefield he read Gray's 'Elegy'.[10] And, when the war came, with a vigour that reminds one of a large dog shaking the drops from his coat he shook himself free from his thousands of words and refused to write a line.

To tell the truth. I am not at all interested in writing nowadays ⟨he said⟩.[11] The only sort of book I care to write about the world war is the sort people will read after the war is over – a century after it is over! . . . It will be episodic – chaotic, perhaps – no glib tale, no newspaper man's work, but, with God's help, a work of art.[12]

For, unexpected though it may seem, Joyce Kilmer had become a fervent Catholic, and God's help played a very large and a very mysterious part in his affairs. The Catholic faith, he said, 'is more important, more beautiful, more necessary than anything else in life'.[13] One must write to the glory of the Catholic faith.

But into all this there is no space to plunge. Unwillingly, one must break off, for, as so frequently happens in reading a memoir written in good faith, one is interested in the man out of all proportion to what one is told about him. Little facts have a significance which one cannot justify. Why should it seem so characteristic, for example, that he should beg his wife not to call their children by nicknames, and not to say that *Carnival* was a fine book?[14] Turning over the thought of Joyce Kilmer, one lets him go reluctantly as if one had come to know him much better than one could account for. Does that amount to saying that he was, among other things, remarkably mature?

1–A signed review in the *Athenaeum*, 21 November 1919, (Kp C176) of *Edward Wyndham Tennant: A Memoir* (John Lane, 1919) by his mother Pamela Glenconner, and of *Joyce Kilmer*, ed. with a memoir by Robert Cortes Holliday (2 vols., Hodder & Stoughton, 1917).

Edward Wyndham Tennant (1897–1916) was educated at Winchester; he joined the Grenadier Guards in 1914 and was killed in the Battle of the Somme on 22 September 1916, in which year his *Worple Flit and Other Poems* was published. His mother, Pamela Adelaide Genevieve, *née* Wyndham (d.1928), was the widow of Edward Priaulx Tennant, 1st Lord Glenconner; in 1922 she married Viscount Grey of Fallodon.

(Alfred) Joyce Kilmer (1886–1918), American poet, journalist, and, in 1913, Roman Catholic convert, is best known for his collection *Trees and Other Poems* (1914). He was a sergeant in the intelligence section of the 165th U.S. Infantry and died in action in France on 30 July 1918, near the Ourcq river.

VW noted in her diary on Sunday, 19 October 1919: 'Tuesday I had to read through 2 volumes of an American scribbler sent me by [J. Middleton] Murry [editor of the *Athenaeum*].' On Thursday, 4 December 1919, she wrote to Molly MacCarthy (*II VW Letters*, no. 1104): 'I've been meeting your friends, the Bibesco's: Elizabeth [*née* Asquith] seemed to be an admirable but almost timorous matron . . . I said all the most impossible things in a very loud voice; abused Lady Glenconner, and then attacked Rupert Brooke.' Which may be glossed from her diary, Saturday 6 December: 'Elizabeth was nicer, & less brilliant than I expected . . . Again, its a help to write things down; but there's a gulf between writing & publishing. This was said, I remember, owing to my rash abuse of Lady Glenconner & Wyndham Tennant. – her Aunt of course. She turned round, a little uneasily, to disclaim all admiration for Lady G. I suppose she wishes to stand well with the intellectuals.'

The same issue of the *Athenaeum* carried articles by: Katherine Mansfield, 'A Ship Comes Into the Harbour', on VW's *Night and Day* (see *I VW Diary*, 28 November

1919); Leonard Woolf on 'Far Eastern Politics'; Sydney Waterlow on 'George Eliot 1819–80'; Wyndham Lewis on 'Prevalent Design' (pt i).

2 – Glenconner, ch. ii, p. 12.

3 – *Ibid.*, ch. xi, p. 116.

4 – *Ibid.*, ch. iv, p. 55, written from his preparatory school, West Downs, in 1908.

5 – *Ibid.*, p. 58, which has 'hands!'.

6 – *Ibid.*, ch. iii, p. 23, George Wyndham (1863–1913), Tory statesman and man of letters, writing to his sister, Pamela Glenconner, from the Hotel Burlington, Dover, in 1906.

7 – *Ibid.*, 'Poems', pp. 292–3. Tennant's poem, dated 13 June 1916, appeared that year in the Sitwells' anthology *Wheels*. Siegfried Sassoon (1886–1967), who was still to publish his first collection of poems, had earned the nickname 'Mad Jack' for deeds of bravery while serving at the Front in the Royal Welch Fusiliers.

8 – Kilmer, vol. i, 'Memoir', p. 55.

9 – For the blue noses and for the Victorian verse, *ibid.*, p. 57 and p. 58 respectively.

9 – *Ibid.*, vol. ii, 'Letters', Kilmer to his wife, 24 May 1918, p. 211: 'Whiles we smoked and gazed at the lovely valley miles below us – whiles we took turns in reading aloud from – what do you suppose? The Oxford Book of English Verse! We read Gray's Elegy [in a Country Churchyard], the first chorus from Atalanta in Calydon, "They told me, Heraclitus", that witch poem of William Bell Scott, "Love in the Valley", "Lake Isle of Innisfree", "Keith of Ravelston", and half a dozen other poems, all of which brought you most poignantly and beautifully before me.' Walter Pater (1839–94), Gerard Manley Hopkins (1844–89), William Bell Scott (1811–90), Charles Lamb (1775–1834).

11 – *Ibid.*, to Robert Cortes Holilday, 7 May 1918, p. 115.

12 – *Ibid.*, to his wife, 14 March 1918, p. 186.

13 – *Ibid.*, to the same, 21 April 1918, p. 197.

14 – *Ibid.*, to the same, 18 May 1918, pp. 217–18. *Carnival* (1912) by Compton Mackenzie.

Watts-Dunton's Dilemma

If Mr Kernahan does not make us feel that he knew Swinburne intimately, that, perhaps, is a contribution to our knowledge of Swinburne.[2] The stories that are told of him are never intimate; they always remain the stories that are told about a poet. No doubt the reason is that his human relations during the later part of his life were limited to such an extent that the greater number of the notes in his scale remained dumb. One or two, such as his passion for Victor Hugo[3] and his passion for Elizabethan plays, are struck over and over again. But the one human relation which survived his conversion to temperance – for Mr Kernahan thinks that we may now allude to the brandy bottle – was that with

Watts-Dunton;[4] and the interest of Mr Kernahan's little book lies in the fact not that he knew Swinburne but that he knew Swinburne's friend.

What he knew of Watts-Dunton is a little at variance with what we have hitherto been told. There were ups and downs, it appears, even in the smooth surface of life at Putney. Swinburne sometimes made fun of his friend. He was occasionally bored. Watts-Dunton, according to Mr Kernahan, was well aware that certain of Swinburne's friends were inclined to say unkind things:

They accuse me of jealously seeking to keep him away from them. It is true that I do so keep them away – one dear soul especially, whom he loves, whom I love, and who I am sure loves him. . . . When that dear soul, whom I love and honour – but who thinks, I fear, unkindly of me – is gone, I have the very deuce of a time in trying to soothe and to quiet him.[5]

Whether this and other of the conversations printed within inverted commas bear any close resemblance to what was actually said, we do not know. The padded and portly style, which Philip Marston[6] shares equally with Swinburne and Watts-Dunton, may have been current in the circle. But the words certainly convey the dilemma in which the sedulous little man, whose leanings, he said, 'were strongly Noncon-formist', and who, though fond of posing as a gipsy, 'was in heart in the suburbs with Mrs Grundy',[7] was placed. He had rescued his poet; there could be no doubt of his devotion; but it becomes apparent that the main instrument of redemption was a benevolent system of falsehood. When he first knew Swinburne the brandy bottle stood by the poet's bedside. Watts-Dunton induced him to substitute port, on the ground that Tennyson drank port; then Burgundy, for the reason that it was beloved of the Three Musketeers; next claret, on some equally plausible pretext; and, finally, 'the wine of the country, Shakespeare's brown October'[8] – in other words, the comparatively harmless bottled beer. Thus his body was rescued; and the stratagem was surely justifiable. But when it came to his mind, Watts-Dunton adopted the same tactics; and that, perhaps, is more questionable. In order to renew Swinburne's self-confidence, he assured him that the first poem written after convalescence was the best he had ever done. The same thing, for the same reason, had to be repeated next time:

And so, to my shame – I must throw myself on the mercy of my friends and his friends – I got into the way of praising . . . and, so far as I can see, not until death comes to call the one or the other of us away, and so to deliver me out of the coils into which I have got myself, shall I be set free.[9]

That was Watts-Dunton's dilemma. A comedy might be written to fit the title; but in the comedy there should be a thread of tragedy. Swinburne, thus lulled and beguiled, was kept prisoner, as if by a spell, at Putney. Evil spirits from the outer world now and again almost succeeded in awaking him. They came and talked. He became 'extraordinarily excited';[10] his eyes glittered; his limbs twitched; he spoke faster and faster, more and more brilliantly and beautifully, and also more and more loudly. Up rushed Watts-Dunton in a state of terror. His captive was waking and escaping:

'For God's sake, don't say another word ... He must be got to lie down and if possible to sleep, or I shall have him half out of his mind to-night.'[11]

At this apparition the enchanted bird folded his feathers and huddled in a corner of his cage. Sleep descended: he lived to a ripe old age; he preserved his sanity; he became a Conservative; Queen Victoria had no more loyal subject. But undoubtedly, what with the lies, what with the genius, what with the brandy, and what with the friends, Watts-Dunton did have the 'very deuce of a time'.

1 – A review in the TLS, 11 December 1919, (Kp C177) of *Swinburne As I Knew Him*. With some unpublished letters from the poet to his cousin the Hon. Lady Henniker Heaton (John Lane, 1919) by Coulson Kernahan (1858–1943), author of *God and the Ant* (1895) and numerous other works. See also 'In Good Company' (a large extract from which is quoted at the back of the book under review among 'Some Opinions' of Kernahan's previous volume) and 'Swinburne Letters', *II VW Essays*.
2 – Algernon Charles Swinburne (1837–1909).
3 – Victor-Marie Hugo (1802–85).
4 – Theodore Watts-Dunton (1832–1914), critic, novelist, poet, friend and protector of Swinburne, with whom he shared his home at The Pines, Putney, from 1879 until Swinburne's death.
5 – Kernahan, ch. ii, pp. 20–1.
6 – Philip Bourke Marston (1850–87), the blind poet, on whom Swinburne wrote an elegy (*Fortnightly Review*, January 1891); an anecdote of his concerning Swinburne is the subject of Kernahan, ch. iv.
7 – For the first quotation, *ibid.*, ch. viii, p. 81; and for the second, ch. iii, p. 35: 'While Watts-Dunton was indulging in Borrow and "Children of the Open Air" at receptions, he was in heart in the suburbs with Mrs Grundy [from Thomas Morton's *Speed the Plough* (1798)] and worshipping propriety as personified in Tennyson.'
8 – For the favourite tipple of Alfred, Lord Tennyson (1809–92), *ibid.*, ch. i, p. 9; for that of Dumas's Musketeers, pp. 12–13; and for Shakespeare's beer, pp. 15–16.
9 – *Ibid.*, ch. viii, pp. 78–9.
10 – *Ibid.*, ch. ii, p. 17.
11 – *Ibid.*, ch. ii, p. 19.

The Intellectual Imagination

'Is not life both a dream and an awakening?'[2] Mr de la Mare asks in his study of Rupert Brooke. The greatest poets, having both the visionary imagination and the intellectual imagination, deal with both sides of life; in the lesser poets either the one kind of imagination or the other predominates. Blake and Shelley are obvious instances of the visionary; Donne and Meredith of the intellectual.[3] The distinction is finely and subtly elaborated by Mr de la Mare; and when he affirms that Rupert Brooke possessed the intellectual imagination in a rare degree we assent with a conviction which shows that the problem of Rupert Brooke's poetry has, for us, come nearer solution.

A poet of one's own time and acquaintance is inevitably much of a problem. We hear so many strains in his voice that will be silent in a hundred years' time. Nor do we know what allowance to make for our personal attachment, nor what for old arguments and theories once taken in such good part and such high spirit by an unknown and eager boy. There is in existence a copy of his first volume, in which a pencil has underlined each adjective judged wrong or unnecessary. The lines still stand, though the poet is dead and famous. He would not have had it otherwise. But, do what we will, it is idle to read 'The Fish',[4] where a great number of those marks occur, without finding them the signposts of memories and dreams. Rupert Brooke was certainly fond of adjectives. But was not his passion for loading his lines, like the fingers of some South American beauty, with gem after gem, part of his boldness and brilliancy and strength? So he went to the South Seas, turned Socialist, made friend after friend, and passed from one extreme to another of dress and diet – better preparation, surely, for the choice of the right adjective than to sit dreaming over the fire with a book. But all this time one is not reading 'The Fish'; one is thinking of Rupert Brooke, one is dreaming of what he would have done. When we turn again to Mr de la Mare, he helps us to define what was, and still is, our case against the adjectives. Magic, he says, 'is all but absent from his verse'.[5] The words remain separate, however well assorted. Though he has described most of the English country sights, it has never happened to us, walking the woods, to hum over a line or two and, waking, to find them his. The test is personal and, of course, imperfect. Yet perhaps the same is generally true of those poets in whom the intellectual imagination predominates. The supreme felicities of Keats[6] or Shelley seem to come when the engine of the brain is shut off and the mind glides serene but unconscious, or, more truly, perhaps, is exalted to a different sphere of consciousness. Like Meredith and like Donne, Rupert Brooke was never for a second unconscious. The brain was always there, working steadily, strenuously, and without stopping.

There can be no question that his brain was both a fine instrument and a strong one; but there are other questions, for is it not true that the intellectual poet, unlike the visionary poet, improves and develops with age? Though Keats died younger, and Shelley only a year or two older, than Rupert Brooke, both left behind them unmistakable proof not merely that they were great poets, but that their greatness was of a particular character. If we cannot call Rupert Brooke a great poet, that is to some extent the result of feeling that, compared with the others, he has left us only sketches and premonitions of what was to come. He was of the type that reacts sharply to experience, and life would have taught him much, perhaps changed him greatly. Like Dryden, like Meredith, like Donne himself, as Mr Pearsall Smith has lately shown us, it might have been in prose and not in poetry that he achieved his best.[7] It might have been in scholarship; it might have been in action. But if we seem to disparage what he left, there again we trace the effect of friendship. We do not want our friend rapt away into the circle of the good and the great. We want still to cherish the illusion that the poems will be bettered, the adjectives discussed, the arguments resumed, the convictions altered. The actual achievement must always have for those who knew him a ghostly rival in the greatness which he did not live to achieve. But he was of the few who seem to exist in themselves, apart from what they accomplish, apart from length of life. Again and again Mr de la Mare turns from the poetry, greatly though he admires it, to bathe and warm himself in the memory of the man. One sort of magic may have been absent from his verse but 'above all Brooke's poems are charged with and surrender the magic of what we call personality. . .'[8] What, if he had lived, he would have *done* in this world is a fascinating but an unanswerable question. This only can be said: that he would have gone on being his wonderful self.'[9] One might add that he still goes on being his self, since none of those who knew him can forget him; and it must be a wonderful self when no two people remember the same thing, but all are agreed that he was wonderful.

1 – A review in the *TLS*, 11 December 1919, (Kp C178) of *Rupert Brooke and the*

Intellectual Imagination. A Lecture (Sidgwick & Jackson, 1919) by Walter de la Mare (1873–1956), who delivered his lecture on 27 March 1919 before Rugby School, at which Rupert Brooke (1887–1915) was a pupil and where Brooke's father, William Parker Brooke (d.1910), was a master.

VW wrote to Molly MacCarthy (4 December 1919, *II VW Letters*, no. 1104) that she had 'said all the most impossible things in a very loud voice' to Elizabeth Bibesco, *née* Asquith, 'abused Lady Glenconner, and then attacked Rupert Brooke ...'

See also 'The New Crusade', 'Rupert Brooke', and, for de la Mare, 'Dreams and Realities', *II VW Essays*. Reprinted: *B&P*.

2–de la Mare, p. 13.

3–William Blake (1757–1827); Percy Bysshe Shelley (1792–1822); John Donne (1573–1631); George Meredith (1828–1909).

4–Written at Munich in March 1911 and published in *Poems 1905–1911* (1911).

5–de la Mare, p. 27: 'Though "magic" in the accepted sense is all but absent from his verse – the magic that transports the imagination clean into another reality, that drenches a word, a phrase, with the light that was never strangely cast even on the Spice Islands or Cathay, he has that other poetic magic that can in a line or two present a portrait, a philosophy, and fill the instant with a changeless grace and truth.'

6–John Keats (1795–1821).

7–John Dryden (1631–1700). See Logan Pearsall Smith, intro., *Donne's Sermons. Selected Passages* (OUP, 1919).

8–de la Mare, p. 29.

9–*Ibid.*, p. 39.

Behind the Bars

VW's review in the *Athenaeum*, 12 December 1919, (Kp C179) of *The Life and Letters of Lady Dorothy Nevill* (Methuen, 1919) by Ralph Nevill, was later minimally revised and included, under the title 'Lady Dorothy Nevill', in *The Common Reader*: 1st series (1925). The reader is referred to *IV VW Essays*, where the revised version, together with variants in the form of footnotes, is reprinted in its place as part of *The Common Reader*.

Memories of Meredith

Whether we are well advised in pulling our watches to pieces to see how they are made we do not know. Here is George Meredith, a wonderfully complex and sensitive mechanism, as his books bear witness; and here are we for the twentieth time, perhaps, eagerly searching in Lady Butcher's book to learn how the machine that produced the novels was constructed. Although her Memories are wholly personal, with scarcely a word of literary criticism, our eagerness is, as usual, partly gratified and partly defeated. We always learn something even from the simplest of observers; but the danger is that we may learn things that are out of the picture. Some little saying or incident jumps at us with its life and veracity, but upon the mind's picture of Meredith it lies incongruously, as an authentic fragment of his necktie stuck upon the oil paint of Watts's portrait.[2]

Lady Butcher, born Miss Brandreth, can look back with satisfaction to the most appropriate introduction to Meredith that fate could bestow. As a child of thirteen she was induced by a cousin to throw pebbles upon his bed-room window at dawn, and then to invite him to go with them to the top of Box Hill to see the sunrise. On arrival at the top, fate devised a delightful variation upon the expected theme by prompting her to recite a hymn from Keble's *Christian Year*.[3] Meredith 'gravely listened to the birds singing around us', and then 'poured forth the most wonderful prose hymn to Nature, Life, and what he called *obligation*, by which I understood he meant Duty'.[4] We can assimilate that scene with the greatest ease; and to know that Meredith said that he had trained himself when he walked 'to observe and not to feel', is a valuable note to set down in the margin of the 'Woods of Westermain'.[5] It is less easy to reconcile oneself to the inordinate cracking of stiff little jokes which seem to imply audience and stage and actor arrayed in tights and silk stockings. An elderly professor, for instance, went to a fancy dress ball, and Meredith rejoiced in describing the spectacle. 'He trips forth as a cavalier of the time of Charles II! His form – his form, dear! is clad in pale mauve satin and lace ruffles!'[6] Mr Meredith, convulsed with mirth till the tears ran down his cheeks, kept exclaiming between shouts of laughter, 'His form! Pale mauve satin and lace ruffles! His form!'[7] But if the satire and the censure seem a little forced in private life, they have their more spiritual counterpart in the novels. From the novels, however, we should scarcely have guessed that he cherished an almost prudish respect for the ceremonies and the conventions. To the women of the novels he granted unusual liberty; but in practice he would not allow a girl to travel a short distance alone, nor walk in the country without a maid beside her. The presence of young women at a French play – 'very funny, but replete with the *esprit Gaulois*' – spoilt all his pleasure. 'How can the mothers allow their daughters to remain?'[8] he kept on murmuring. When someone praised Maupassant's stories in Miss Brandreth's presence, he said 'They are really improper. You had better not read them.' Then added, '*I could be funny* if I neglected the proprieties as he does!'[9] The stringency and the puritanism are no doubt also latent in the novels, but the shock of them in actual life affects us, for the moment disagreeably.

But if the sense of the writer stepping out from behind his books and delivering his message in person is abrupt and disturbing in some instances, it is singularly refreshing in others. Compared with most of his contemporaries Meredith left little record of his artistic methods and but few literary judgements. Lady Butcher has preserved one or two examples of both kinds, slight enough, scribbled carelessly in a girl's diary, but falling freshly from his lips. He picked up one of Charlotte Yonge's novels and, admiring her control of dialogue, went on 'to point out his difficulties in making conversation in books natural, and the banal "she said" and "he said"'.[10] One could have guessed at his dilemma, and one would have given much to press him further, for dialogue is one of the crucial problems in fiction, and Meredith provided an original solution; but as it is, that is an excellent lead. That he thought his poems would outlive his novels is, perhaps, well known, but that among his poems he preferred the verse in *Vittoria*,

> Our life is but a little holding, lent
> To do a mighty labour,[11]

is characteristic. Characteristic, too, and so far as we know as yet unrecorded, is his disparagement of Jane Austen –

I could not induce him to share, or even tolerate, my eulogies upon her style and presentment of character. Indeed, one day he declared that the heroines of her book were wanting in refinement. . . . Jane Austen's heroes he frankly detested, and made us laugh heartily with speeches caricaturing her style, made by priggish young gentlemen to the maidens of their choice.[12]

After reading Lady Butcher one needs to draw back a little with half-closed eyes to fit the various fragments together; but in a moment or two it will be seen that they merge quite rightly into the figure of the great man.

1–A review in the *TLS*, 18 December 1919, (Kp C180) of *Memories of George Meredith* [1828–1909] O.M. (Constable & Co., 1919) by Lady Butcher, Alice Mary. See also 'Small Talk About Meredith', above; 'On re-reading Meredith', *II VW Essays*; and 'The Novels of George Meredith', *IV VW Essays*.
2–The portrait of Meredith by G. F. Watts (1817–1904) – half-length, profile to right – painted in 1893, was donated to the National Portrait Gallery (no. 1543) in 1909 at the wish of the artist.
3–John Keble (1792–1866), *The Christian Year* (1827), a poetical work based on the Book of Common Prayer.
4–Butcher, ch. i, p. 3.
5–For the quotations, *ibid.*, ch. i, p. 4. Meredith's poem 'The Woods of Westermain', appeared in the volume *Poems and Lyrics of the Joy of Earth* (1883).
6–*Ibid.*, ch. iii, pp. 35–6, which has 'ruffles!!'. The professor is not identified.
7–*Ibid.*, p. 36.
8–For both quotations, *ibid.*, ch. vii, p. 78.
9–*Ibid.*, pp. 82–3. Guy de Maupassant (1850–93).
10–*Ibid.*, ch. i, p. 16. Charlotte M. Yonge (1823–1901).
11–*Ibid.*, ch. iv, p. 53. Meredith's novel *Vittoria* was published in 1867. The verse reads:

> 'Our life is but a little holding, lent
> To do a mighty labour: we are one
> With Heaven and the stars, when it is spent,
> To serve God's aim.'

12–*Ibid.*, ch. ix, p. 95. Jane Austen (1775–1817).

'Gold and Iron'

In developing a photograph first one black patch appears on the greyish film and then another. By degrees the square of the picture defines itself; here is the edge of a wall; here, isolated but unmistakable, the outline of a croquet hoop. One rocks the fluid from side to side, and watches anxiously for an increasing thickening and intricacy, or the film will certainly prove either under exposed or over. Thus with the books of Mr Joseph Hergesheimer, now appearing with such frequency, one watches anxiously to see whether the undoubted eminence of his talent in this respect and that will be supported all round by other gifts until the picture covers the whole surface of the film and we are in possession of a complete work of art.

'Wild Oranges', the first story in the present book, *Gold and Iron*, suggests that Mr Hergesheimer is still in process of development. There is no doubt at all that he is mature in certain respects. He wants to describe a ship, a shore, a deserted house, an orange tree, and he does it directly, succinctly, with the assurance of maturity. He gets the essential background with little effort and considerable mastery. But, remembering *Java Head*, it is with some anxiety that we see a woman's shape emerging upon the film. For women will talk, and that is where Mr Hergesheimer hitherto has come to grief. Millie Stopes, who has been marooned on the coast of Georgia in company with a homicidal lunatic and a father who fled from Virginia forty years ago because in the Civil War women hung an apron on his door, has every reason to be, like the wild oranges that grew round the house, thick of rind and bitter of flavour. But set her, as she stoops catching fish in her solitude, by the side of some girl in Mr Conrad's[2] pages, and you feel that here Mr Hergesheimer's talent ebbs and deserts him. She is a silhouette posed a trifle melodramatically against the sunset; and, as usual, the sunset is more vivid than the woman. There is something set and sterile about her. But just as we are making this point another speck on the film catches our eyes and, developing, changes the picture once more. John Woolfolk, the sailor who has dropped anchor opposite the ruined house, takes Millie for a sail. She is terrified by the open sea. He has to put back to shore again. The yacht anchors in the bay and Millie sits brooding on the deck. '"What is it," she demanded of John Woolfolk, "that lives in our own hearts and betrays our utmost convictions and efforts, and destroys us against all knowledge and desire?" "It may be called heredity," he replied.'[3] That perhaps derives from Ibsen,[4] but at any rate we feel a new force blowing through the stiff, still pages. Mr Hergesheimer makes for the open sea with a theme behind him.

The two stories that follow are better composed, but not so interesting as the first. For one thing Mr Hergesheimer goes back to his iron masters and his seaport life of a hundred years ago; and, though the stories display his good qualities, they seem, to recur to the photographic figure, to be arrested in their development. In the act of asserting their passion his figures are stricken with frost; and yet the gesture is always a fine one. Our conclusion, then, must be – but happily we do not feel impelled to come to a conclusion. 'Wild Oranges' justifies us in holding our judgement in suspense. Mr Hergesheimer is still in process of development.

1 – A review in the *TLS*, 25 December 1919, (Kp C181) of *Gold and Iron* (William Heinemann, 1919) by Joseph Hergesheimer (1880–1954); for biographical note, see '*Java Head*', n.1, above. See also 'The Pursuit of Beauty', 'Pleasant Stories', below, and '*The Three Black Pennys*', II *VW Essays*. Reprinted: *CW*.
2 – Joseph Conrad (1857–1924).
3 – Hergesheimer, 'Wild Oranges', pp. 37–8, which continues: 'he replied; "that is its simplest phase. The others extend into the realms of the fantastic."'
4 – Henrik Ibsen (1828–1906).

·

Reading

Why did they choose this particular spot to build the house on? For the sake of the view perhaps. Not, I suppose, that they looked at views as we look at them, but rather as an incentive to ambition, as a proof of power. For in time they were lords of that valley, green with trees, and owned at least all that part of the moor that lies on the right-hand side of the road. At any rate the house was built here, here a stop was put to trees and ferns; here one room was laid upon another, and down some feet into the earth foundations were thrust and deep cool cellars hollowed out.

The house had its library; a long low room, lined with little burnished books, folios, and stout blocks of divinity. The cases were carved with birds pecking at clusters of wooden fruit. A sallow priest tended them, dusting the books and the carved birds at the same time. Here they all are; Homer and Euripides; Chaucer; then Shakespeare; and the Elizabethans, and following come the plays of the Restoration, more handled these, and greased as if from midnight reading, and so down to our time or very near it, Cowper, Burns, Scott, Wordsworth[2] and the rest. I liked that room. I liked the view across country that one had from the window, and the blue line between the gap of the trees on the moor was the North Sea. I liked to read there. One drew the pale armchair to the window, and so the light fell over the shoulder upon the page. The shadow of the gardener mowing the lawn sometimes crossed it, as he led his pony in rubber shoes up and down, the machine giving a little creak, which seemed the very voice of summer, as it turned and drew another broad belt of green by the side of the one just cut. Like the wake of ships I used to think them, especially when they curved round the flower beds for islands, and the fuchsias might be lighthouses, and the geraniums, by some freak of fancy, were Gibraltar; there were the red coats of the invincible British soldiers upon the rock.

Then tall ladies used to come out of the house and go down the grass drives to be met by the gentlemen of those days, carrying racquets and white balls which I could just see, through the bushes that hid the tennis lawn, bounding over the net, and the figures of the players passed to and fro. But they did not distract me from my book; any more than the butterflies visiting the flowers, or the bees doing their more serious business on the same blossoms, or the thrushes hopping lightly from the low branches of the sycamore to the turf, taking two steps in the direction of some slug or fly, and then hopping, with light decision, back to the low branch again. None of these things distracted me in those days; and somehow or another, the windows being open, and the book held so that it rested upon a background of escallonia hedges and distant blue, instead of being a book it seemed as if what I read was laid upon the landscape not printed, bound, or sewn up, but somehow the product of trees and fields and the hot summer sky, like the air which swam, on fine mornings, round the outlines of things.

These were circumstances, perhaps, to turn one's mind to the past. Always behind the voice, the figure, the fountain there seemed to stretch an immeasurable avenue, that ran to a point of other voices, figures, fountains which tapered out indistinguishably upon the furthest horizon. If I looked down at my book I could see Keats and Pope behind him, and then Dryden and Sir Thomas Browne[3] – hosts of them merging in the mass of Shakespeare, behind whom, if one peered long enough, some shapes of men in pilgrims' dress emerged, Chaucer perhaps, and again – who was it? some uncouth poet scarcely able to syllable his words; and so they died away.

But, as I say, even the gardener leading his pony was part of the book, and, straying from the actual page, the eye rested upon his face, as if one reached it through a great depth of time. That accounted for the soft swarthy tint of the cheeks, and the lines of his body, scarcely disguised by the coarse brown stuff of his coat, might have belonged to any labouring man in any age, for the clothing of the field labourer has changed little since Saxon days, and a half-shut eye can people a field much as it was before the Norman conquest. This man took his place naturally by the side of those dead poets. He ploughed; he sowed; he drank; he marched in battle sometimes; he sang his song; he came courting and went underground raising only a green wave in the turf of the churchyard, but leaving boys and girls behind him to continue his name and lead the pony across the lawn, these hot summer mornings.

Through that same layer of time one could see, with equal clearness, the more splendid figures of knights and ladies. One could see them; that is true. The ripe apricot of the ladies' dress, the gilt crimson of the knights set floating coloured images in the dark ripples of the lake water. In the church too you see them laid out as if in triumphant repose, their hands folded, their eyes shut, their favourite hounds at their feet, and all the shields of their ancestors, faintly touched still with blue and red, supporting them. Thus garnished and made ready they seem to await, to expect, in confidence. The day of judgement dawns. His eyes open, his hand seeks hers, he leads her forth through the opened doors and the lines of angels with their trumpets, to some smoother lawn, more regal residence and mansions of white masonry. Meanwhile, the silence is scarcely broken by a word. It is, after all, a question of seeing them.

For the art of speech came late to England. These Fanshawes and Leghs, Verneys, Pastons, and Hutchinsons,[4] all well endowed by birth and nature and leaving behind them such a treasure of inlaid wood and old furniture, things curiously made, and delicately figured, left with it only a very broken message or one so stiff that the ink seems to have dried as it traced the words. Did they, then, enjoy these possessions in silence, or was the business of life transacted in a stately way to match these stiff polysyllables and branching periods? Or, like children on a Sunday, did they compose themselves and cease their chatter when they sat down to write what would pass from hand to hand, serve for winter gossip round a dozen firesides, and be laid up at length with other documents of importance in the dry room above the kitchen fireplace?

'In October, as I told you,' wrote Lady Fanshawe some time about the year 1601, 'my husband and I went into France by way of Portsmouth where, walking by the seaside . . . two ships of the Dutch shot bullets at us, so near that we heard them whiz by us: at which I called my husband to make haste back, and began to run. But he altered not his pace, saying, if we must be killed, it were as good to be killed walking as running.'[5] There, surely, it is the spirit of dignity that controls her. The bullets whiz across the sand, but Sir Richard walks no faster, and summons up his idea of death – death visible, tangible, an enemy, but an enemy of flesh and blood to be met courageously with drawn sword like a gentleman – which temper she (poor woman) admires, though she cannot, on the beach at Portsmouth, altogether imitate. Dignity, loyalty, magnanimity – such are the virtues she would commend, and frame her speech to, checking it from its natural slips and trifles, and making believe that life for people of gentle birth and high morality was thus decorous and sublime. The pen, too, when the small shot of daily life came whizzing about her – eighteen children in twenty-one years she bore and buried the greater part – must curb itself to walk slowly, not to run. Writing is with them, as it can no longer be with us, making; making something that will endure and wear a brave face in the eyes of posterity. For posterity is the judge of these ideals, and it is for that distant and impartial public that Lady Fanshawe writes and Lucy Hutchinson, and not for John in London or Elizabeth married and gone to live in Sussex; there is no daily post for children and friends bringing to the breakfast table not only news of crops and servants, visitors and bad weather, but the subtler narrative of love and coldness, affection waning or carried on secure; there is no language it seems for that frail burden. Horace Walpole, Jane Carlyle, Edward FitzGerald[6] are ghosts on the very outskirts of time. Thus these ancestors of ours, though stately and fair to look upon, are silent; they move through galleries and parks in the midst of a little oasis of silence which holds the intruding modern spirit at bay. Here, again, are the Leghs; generations upon generations of them, all red haired, all living at Lyme, which has been building these three centuries and more, all men of education, character, and opportunity, and all, by modern standards, dumb. They will write of a fox hunt and how afterward 'a Bowle of Hott Punch with ye Fox's foot stew'd in it' was drunk, and how 'Sir Willm drunk pretty plentifully, and just at last perceiv'd he should be fuddled, "but", quoth he, "I care not if I am, I have kill'd a fox today".'[7] But having killed their fox, drunk their punch, raced their horses, fought their cocks, and toasted, discreetly, the King over the water, or, more openly, 'A Fresh Earth and High Metaled Terrier,'[8] their lips shut, their eyes close; they have nothing more to say to us. Taciturn or crass as we may think them, dull men inheriting their red hair and very little brain beneath it, nevertheless more business was discharged by them, more of life took its mould from them than we can measure, or, indeed, dispense with. If Lyme had been blotted out and the thousand other houses of equal importance which lay about England like little fortresses of civilisation, where you could read books, act plays, make laws, meet your neighbours, and talk with strangers from abroad, if these spaces won from the encroaching barbarity had not persisted till the foothold was firm and the swamp withheld, how would our more delicate spirits have fared – our writers, thinkers, musicians, artists – without a wall to shelter under, or flowers upon which to sun their wings? Waging war year after year upon winter and rough weather, needing all their faculties to keep the roof sound, the larder full, the children taught and clothed, dependants cared for, naturally our ancestors appear in their spare time rather surly and silent – as plough-boys after a long day's work scrape the mud from their boots, stretch the cramped muscles of their backs, and stumble off to bed without thought of book or pen or evening paper. The little language of affection and intimacy which we seek in vain necessitates soft pillows, easy chairs, silver forks, private rooms; it must have at its command a store of little words, nimble and domesticated, coming at the call of the lightest occasion, refining themselves to the faintest shadow. Above all perhaps, good roads and carriages, frequent meetings, partings, festivities, alliances, and ruptures are needed to break up the splendid sentences; easy chairs it may be were the death of English prose. The annals of an old and obscure family like the Leghs show clearly enough how the slow process of furnishing the bare rooms and taking coach for London, as a matter of course, abolish its isolation, merge the dialect of the district into the common speech of the land, and teach, by degrees, a uniform method of spelling. One can see in fancy the face itself changing, and the manner of father to son, mother to daughter, losing what must have been their tremendous formality, their unquestioned authority. But what dignity, what beauty broods over it all!

It's a hot summer morning. The sun has browned the outermost leaves of the elm trees, and already, since the gale, one or two lie on the grass, having completed the whole range of existence from bud to withered fibre and become nothing but leaves to be swept up for the autumn bonfires. Through the green arches the eye with a curious desire seeks the blue which it knows to be the blue of the sea; and knowing it can somehow set the mind off upon a voyage, can somehow encircle all this substantial earth with the flowing and the unpossessed. The sea – the sea – I must drop my book, the pious Mrs Hutchinson, and leave her to make what terms she can with Margaret, Duchess of Newcastle.[9] There's a sweeter air outside – how spicy, even on a still day, after the house! – and bushes of verbena and southernwood yield a leaf as one passes to be crushed and smelt. If we could see also what we can smell – if, at this moment crushing the southernwood, I could go back through the long corridor of sunny mornings, boring my way through hundreds of Augusts, I should come in the end, passing a host of less-important figures, to no less a person than Queen Elizabeth herself. Whether some tinted wax-work is the foundation of my view, I do not know; but she always appears very distinctly in the same guise. She flaunts across the terrace superbly and a little stiffly like the peacock spreading its tail. She seems slightly infirm, so that one is half inclined to smile; and then she raps out her favourite oath as Lord Herbert of Cherbury[10] heard it, as he bowed his knee among the courtiers, when, far from being infirm, she shows a masculine and rather repulsive vigour. Perhaps, under all that stiff brocade, she has not washed her shrivelled old body? She breakfasts off beer and meat and handles the bones with fingers rough with rubies. It may be so, yet Elizabeth, of all our kings and queens, seems most fit for that gesture which bids the great sailors farewell, or welcomes them home to her presence again, her imagination still lusting for the strange tales they bring her, her imagination still young in its wrinkled and fantastic casket. It is their youth; it is their immense fund of credulity; their minds still unwritten over and capable of such enormous designs as the American forests cast upon them, or the Spanish ships, or the savages, or the soul of man – this is what makes it impossible, walking the terrace, not to look upon the blue sea line, and think of their ships. The ships, Froude says, were no bigger than a modern English yacht.[11] As they shrink and assume the romantic proportions of the Elizabethan ship, so the sea runs enormously larger and freer and with bigger waves upon it than the sea of our time. The summons to explore, to bring back dyes and roots and oil, and find a market for wool and iron and cloth has been heard in the villages of the West. The little company gathers together somewhere off Greenwich. The courtiers come running to the palace windows; the Privy Councillors press their faces to the panes. The guns are shot off in salute, and then, as the ships swing down the tide, one sailor after another walks the hatches, climbs the shrouds, stands upon the mainyards to wave his friends a last farewell. For directly England and the coast of France are beneath the horizon, the ships swim into the unfamiliar, the air has its voices, the sea its lions and serpents, evaporations of fire and tumultuous whirlpools. The clouds but sparely hide the Divinity; the limbs of Satan are almost visible. Riding in company through the storm, suddenly one light disappears; Sir Humfrey Gilbert has gone beneath the waves: when morning comes they seek his ship in vain. Sir Hugh Willoughby[12] sails to discover the North-West passage, and makes no return. Sometimes, a ragged and worn-out man comes knocking at the door, and claims to be the boy who went years ago to sea and is now come back to his father's house. 'Sir William his father and my lady his mother knew him not to be their son, until they found a secret mark, which was a wart upon one of his knees.'[13] But he brings with him a black stone, veined with gold, or an ivory tusk, or a lump of silver, and stories of how such stones are strewn about to be picked up off the ground as you will. What if the passage to the fabled land of uncounted riches lay only a little further up the coast? What if the known world was only the prelude to some more splendid panorama? When, after the long voyage, the ships dropped anchor in the great river of the Plate and the men went exploring through the undulating lands, startling the grazing herds of deer and glimpsing between the trees the dusky limbs of savages, they filled their pockets with pebbles that might be emeralds, or rubies, or sand that might be gold. Sometimes, rounding a headland, they saw far off a string of savages slowly descending to the beach bearing on their heads and linking their shoulders together with heavy burdens for the Spanish king.

These are the fine stories, used effectively all through the West Country to decoy the strong men lounging by the harbour side to leave their nets and fish for gold. Less glorious but more urgent, considering the state of the country, was the summons of the more serious-minded to set on foot some intercourse between the merchants of England and the merchants of the East. For lack of work, this staid observer wrote, the poor of England were driven to crime and 'daily consumed with the gallows'.[14] Wool they had in plenty, fine, soft, strong, and durable; but no market for it and few dyes. Gradually owing to the boldness of private travellers, the native stock had been improved and embellished. Beasts and plants had been imported; and along with them the seeds of all our roses. Gradually little groups of merchant men settled here and there on the borders of the unexplored, and through their fingers the precious stream of coloured and rare and curious things begins slowly and precariously to flow towards London; our fields are sown with new flowers. In the south and west, in America and the East Indies, the life was pleasanter and success more splendid; yet in the land of long winters and squat-faced savages the very darkness and strangeness draw the imagination. Here they are, three or four men from the west of England set down in the white landscape with only the huts of savages near them, and left to make what bargains they can and pick up what knowledge they can, until the little ships, no bigger than yachts, appear at the mouth of the bay next summer. Strange must have been their thoughts; strange the sense of the unknown; and of themselves, the isolated English, burning on the very rim of the dark, and the dark full of unseen splendours. One of them, carrying a charter from his company in London, went inland as far as Moscow, and there saw the Emperor, 'sitting in his chair of estate, with his crown on his head, and a staff of goldsmith work in his left hand'.[15] All the ceremony that he saw is carefully written out, and the sight upon which the English merchant, the vanguard of civilisation, first set eyes has the brilliancy still of a Roman vase or other shining ornament dug up and stood for a moment in the sun before, exposed to the air, seen by millions of eyes, it dulls and crumbles away. There, all these centuries, the glories of Moscow, the glories of Constantinople, have flowered unseen. Many are preserved as if under shades of glass. The Englishman, however, is bravely dressed for the occasion, leads in his hand, perhaps, 'three fair mastiffs in coats of red cloth' and carries a letter from Elizabeth 'the paper whereof did smell most fragrantly of camphor and ambergris, and the ink of perfect musk'.[16]

Yet if by means of these old records, courts and palaces and Sultans' presence chambers are once more displayed, stranger still are the little disks of light calling out of obscurity for a second some unadorned savage, falling like lantern light upon moving figures. Here is a story of the savage caught somewhere off the coast of Labrador, taken to England and shown about like a wild beast. Next year they bring him back and fetch a woman savage on board to keep him company. When they see each other they blush; they blush profoundly; the sailor notices it but knows not why it is. And later the two savages set up house together on board ship, she attending to his wants, he nursing her in sickness, but living, as the sailors note, in perfect chastity. The erratic searchlight cast by these records falling for a second upon those blushing cheeks three hundred years ago among the snow, sets up that sense of communication which we are apt to get only from fiction. We seem able to guess why they blushed; the Elizabethans would notice it, but it has waited over three hundred years for us to interpret it.

There are not perhaps enough blushes to keep the attention fixed upon the broad yellow-tinged pages of Hakluyt's book. The attention wanders. Still if it wanders, it wanders in the green shade of forests. It floats far out at sea. It is soothed almost to sleep by the sweet-toned voices of pious men talking the melodious language, much broader and more sonorous sounding than our own, of the Elizabethan age. They are men of fine limbs, arched brows, beneath which the oval eyes are full and luminous, and thin golden rings are in their ears. What need have they of blushes? What meeting would rouse such emotions in them? Why should they whittle down feelings and thoughts so as to cause embarrassment and bring lines between the eyes and perplex them, so that it is no longer a ship or a man that comes before them, but some thing doubtful as a phantom, and more of a symbol than a fact? If one tires of the long dangerous and memorable voyages of M. Ralph Fitch, M.

Roger Bodenham, M. Anthony Jenkinson, M. John Lok, the Earl of Cumberland[17] and others, to Pegu and Siam, Candia and Chio, Aleppo and Muscovy, it is for the perhaps unsatisfactory reason that they make no mention of oneself; seem altogether oblivious of such an organism; and manage to exist in comfort and opulence nevertheless. For simplicity of speech by no means implies rudeness or emptiness. Indeed this free-flowing, equable narrative, though now occupied merely with the toils and adventures of ordinary ships' companies, has its own true balance, owing to the poise of brain and body arrived at by the union of adventure and physical exertion with minds still tranquil and unstirred as the summer sea.

In all this there is no doubt much exaggeration, much misunderstanding. One is tempted to impute to the dead the qualities we find lacking in ourselves. There is balm for our restlessness in conjuring up visions of Elizabethan magnanimity; the very flow and fall of the sentences lulls us asleep, or carries us along as upon the back of a large, smooth-paced cart horse, through green pastures. It is the pleasantest atmosphere on a hot summer's day. They talk of their commodities and there you see them; more clearly and separately in bulk, colour, and variety than the goods brought by steamer and piled upon docks; they talk of fruit; the red and yellow globes hang unpicked on virgin trees; so with the lands they sight; the morning mist is only just now lifting and not a flower has been plucked. The grass has long whitened tracks upon it for the first time. With the towns too discovered for the first time it is the same thing. And so, as you read on across the broad pages with as many slips and somnolences as you like, the illusion rises and holds you of banks slipping by on either side, of glades opening out, of white towers revealed, of gilt domes and ivory minarets. It is, indeed, an atmosphere, not only soft and fine, but rich, too, with more than one can grasp at any single reading.

So that, if at last I shut the book, it was only that my mind was sated, not the treasure exhausted. Moreover, what with reading and ceasing to read, taking a few steps this way and then pausing to look at the view, that same view had lost its colours, and the yellow page was almost too dim to decipher. So the book must be stood in its place, to deepen the brown line of shadow which the folios made on the wall. The books gently swelled neath my hands as I drew it across them in the dark. Travels, histories, memoirs, the fruit of innumerable lives. The dusk was brown with them. Even the hand thus sliding seemed to feel beneath its palm fulness and ripeness. Standing at the window and looking out into the garden, the lives of all these books filled the room behind with a soft murmur. Truly, a deep sea, the past, a tide which will overtake and overflow us. Yes, the tennis players looked half-transparent already, as they came up the grass lawn to the house, the game being over. The tall lady stooped and picked a pallid rose; and the balls which the gentleman kept dancing up and down upon his racquet, as he walked beside her, were dim little spheres against the deep green hedge. Then, as they passed inside, the moths came out, the swift grey moths of the dusk, that only visit flowers for a second, never settling, but hanging an inch or two above the yellow of the Evening Primroses, vibrating to a blur. It was, I supposed, nearly time to go into the woods.

About an hour previously, several pieces of flannel soaked in rum and sugar had been pinned to a number of trees. The business of dinner now engrossing the grown-up people we made ready our lantern, our poison jar, and took our butterfly nets in our hands. The road that skirted the wood was so pale that its hardness grated upon our boots unexpectedly. It was the last strip of reality, however, off which we stepped into the gloom of the unknown. The lantern shoved its wedge of light through the dark, as though the air were a fine black snow piling itself up in banks on either side of the yellow beam. The direction of the trees was known to the leader of the party, who walked ahead, and seemed to draw us, unheeding darkness or fear, further and further into the unknown world. Not only has the dark the power to extinguish light, but it also buries under it a great part of the human spirit. We hardly spoke, and then only in low voices which made little headway against the thoughts that filled us. The little irregular beam of light seemed the only thing that kept us together, and like a rope prevented us from falling asunder and being engulfed. It went on indefatigably all the time, making tree and bush stand forth, in their strange night-dress of paler green. Then we were told to halt while the leader went forward to ascertain which of the trees had been prepared, since it was necessary to approach gradually lest the moths should be startled by the light and fly off. We waited in a group, and the little circle of forest where we stood became as if we saw it through the lens of a very powerful magnifying glass. Every blade of grass looked larger than by day, and the crevices in the bark much more sharply cut. Our faces showed pale and as if detached in a circle. The lantern had not stood upon the ground for ten seconds before we heard (the sense of hearing too was much more acute) little crackling sounds which seemed connected with a slight waving and bending in the surrounding grass. Then there emerged here a grasshopper, there a beetle, and here again a daddy longlegs, awkwardly making his way from blade to blade. Their movements were all so awkward that they made one think of sea creatures crawling on the floor of the sea. They went straight, as if by common consent, to the lantern, and were beginning to slide or clamber up the glass panes when a shout from the leader told us to advance. The light was turned very cautiously towards the tree; first it rested upon the grass at the foot; then it mounted a few inches of the trunk; as it mounted our excitement became more and more intense; then it gradually enveloped the flannel and the cataracts of falling treacle. As it did so, several wings flitted round us. The light was covered. Once more it was cautiously turned on. There were no whirring wings this time, but here and there, dotted about on the veins of sweet stuff, were soft brown lumps. These lumps seemed unspeakably precious, too deeply attached to the liquid to be disturbed. Their probosces were deep plunged, and as they drew in the sweetness, their wings quivered slightly as if in ecstasy. Even when the light was full upon them they could not tear themselves away, but sat there, quivering a little more uneasily perhaps, but allowing us to examine the tracery on the upperwing, those stains, spots, and veinings by which we decided their fate. Now and again a large moth dashed through the light. This served to increase our excitement. After taking those we wanted and gently tapping the unneeded on the nose so that they dropped off and began crawling through the grass in the direction of their sugar, we went on to the next tree. Cautiously shielding the light, we saw from far off the glow of two red lamps which faded as the light turned upon them; and there emerged the splendid body which wore those two red lamps at its head. Great underwings of glowing crimson were displayed. He was almost still, as if he had alighted with his wing open and had fallen into a trance of pleasure. He seemed to stretch across the tree, and beside him other moths looked only like little lumps and knobs on the bark. He was so splendid to look upon and so immobile that perhaps we were reluctant to end him; and yet when, as if guessing our intention and resuming a flight that had been temporarily interrupted, he roamed away, it seemed as if we had lost a possession of infinite value. Somebody cried out sharply. The lantern bearer flashed his light in the direction which the moth had taken. The space surrounding us seemed vast. Then we stood the light upon the ground, and once more after a few seconds, the grass bent, and the insects came scrambling from all quarters, greedy and yet awkward in their desire to partake of the light. Just as the eyes grow used to dimness and make out shapes where none were visible before, so sitting on the ground we felt we were surrounded by life, innumerable creatures were stirring among the trees; some creeping through the grass, others roaming through the air. It was a very still night, and the leaves intercepted any light from the young moon. Now and again a deep sigh seemed to breathe from somewhere near us, succeeded by sighs less deep, more wavering and in rapid succession, after which there was profound stillness. Perhaps it was alarming to have these evidences of unseen lives. It needed great resolution and the fear of appearing a coward to take up the light and penetrate still further into the depths of the wood. Somehow this world of night seemed hostile to us. Cold, alien, and unyielding, as if preoccupied with matters in which human beings could have no part. But the most distant tree still remained to be visited. The leader advanced unrelentingly. The white strip of road upon which our boots had grated now seemed for ever lost. We had left that world of lights and homes hours ago. So we pressed on to this remote tree in the most dense part of the forest. It stood there as if upon the very verge of the world. No moth could have come as far as this. Yet as the trunk was revealed, what did we see? The scarlet underwing was already there, immobile as before, astride a vein of sweetness, drinking deep. Without waiting a second this time the poison pot was uncovered and adroitly manoeuvred so that as he sat there the moth was covered and escape cut off. There was a flash of scarlet within the glass. Then he composed himself with folded wings. He did not move again.

The glory of the moment was great. Our boldness in coming so far was rewarded, and at the same time it seemed as though we had proved our skill against the hostile and alien force. Now we could go back to bed and to the safe house. And then, standing there with the moth safely in our hands, suddenly a volley of shot rang out, a hollow rattle of sound in the deep silence of the wood which had I know not what of mournful and ominous about it. It waned and spread through the forest: it died away, then another of those deep sighs arose. An enormous silence succeeded. 'A tree,' we said at last. A tree had fallen.[18]

What is it that happens between the hour of midnight and dawn, the little shock, the queer uneasy moment, as of eyes half open to the light, after which sleep is never so sound again? Is it experience, perhaps – repeated shocks, each unfelt at the time, suddenly loosening the fabric? breaking something away? Only this image suggests collapse and distintegration, whereas the process I have in mind is just the opposite. It is not destructive whatever it may be, one might say that it was rather of a creative character.

Something definitely happens. The garden, the butterflies, the morning sounds, trees, apples, human voices have emerged, stated themselves. As with a rod of light order has been imposed upon tumult; form
upon chaos. Perhaps it would be simpler to say that one wakes, after
Heaven knows what internal process, with a sense of mastery. Familiar
people approach all sharply outlined in morning light. Through the
tremor and vibration of daily custom one discerns bone and form,
endurance and permanence. Sorrow will have the power to effect this
sudden arrest of the fluidity of life, and joy will have the same power. Or
it may come without apparent cause, imperceptibly, much as some bud
feels a sudden release in the night and is found in the morning with all its
petals shaken free. At any rate the voyages and memoirs, all the lumber
and wreckage and accumulation of time which has deposited itself so
thickly upon our shelves and grows like a moss at the foot of literature, is
no longer definite enough for our needs. Another sort of reading matches
better with the morning hours. This is not the time for foraging and
rummaging, for half-closed eyes and gliding voyages. We want something that has been shaped and clarified, cut to catch the light, hard as
gem or rock with the seal of human experience in it, and yet sheltering as
in a clear gem the flame which burns now so high and now sinks so low
in our own hearts. We want what is timeless and contemporary. But one
might exhaust all images, and run words through one's fingers like water
and yet not say why it is that on such a morning one wakes with a desire
for poetry.

There is no difficulty in finding poetry in England. Every English home
is full of it. Even the Russians have not a deeper fountain of spiritual life.
With us it is, of course, sunk very deep; hidden beneath the heaviest and
dampest deposit of hymn books and ledgers. Yet equally familiar, and
strangely persistent in the most diverse conditions of travel and climate,
is the loveliness of the hurrying clouds, of the sun-stained green, of the
rapid watery atmosphere, in which clouds have been crumbled with
colour until the ocean of air is at once confused and profound. There will
certainly be a copy of Shakespeare in such a house, another *Paradise
Lost*, and a little volume of George Herbert. There may be almost as
probably, though perhaps more strangely, *Vulgar Errors* and the *Religio
Medici*.[19] For some reason the folios of Sir Thomas Browne are to be
found on the lowest shelf of libraries in other respects entirely humdrum
and utilitarian. His popularity in the small country house rests perhaps
chiefly upon the fact that the *Vulgar Errors* treats largely of animals.
Books with pictures of malformed elephants, baboons of grotesque and

indecent appearance, tigers, deer, and so on, all distorted and with a queer facial likeness to human beings, are always popular among people who care nothing for literature. The text of *Vulgar Errors* has something of the same fascination as these woodcuts. And then it may not be fanciful to suppose that even in the year nineteen hundred and nineteen a great number of minds are still only partially lit up by the cold light of knowledge. It is the most capricious illuminant. They are still apt to ruminate, without an overpowering bias to the truth, whether a kingfisher's body shows which way the wind blows; whether an ostrich digests iron; whether owls and ravens herald ill-fortune; and the spilling of salt bad luck; what the tingling of ears forebodes, and even to toy pleasantly with more curious speculations as to the joints of elephants and the politics of storks, which came within the province of the more fertile and better-informed brain of the author. The English mind is naturally prone to take its ease and pleasure in the loosest whimsies and humours. Sir Thomas ministers to the kind of wisdom that farmers talk over their ale, and housewives over their tea cups, proving himself much more sagacious and better informed than the rest of the company, but still with the door of his mind wide open for any curious thing that chooses to enter in. For all his learning, the doctor will consider what we have to say seriously and in good faith. He will perhaps give our modest question a turn that sends it spinning among the stars. How charming, for example, to have found a flower on a walk, or a chip of pottery or a stone, that might equally well have been thunderbolt, or cannon ball, and to have gone straightway to knock upon the doctor's door with a question. No business would have had precedence over such a matter as this, unless indeed someone had been dying or coming into the world. For the doctor was evidently a humane man, and one good to have at the bedside, imperturbable, yet sympathetic. His consolations must have been sublime; his presence full of composure; and then, if something took his fancy, what enlivening speculations he must have poured forth, talking, one guesses, mostly in soliloquy, with the strangest sequences, in a rapt pondering manner, as if not expecting an answer, and more to himself than to a second person.

What second person, indeed, could answer him? At Montpellier and Padua he had learnt, but learning, instead of settling his questions, had, it seems, greatly increased his capacity for asking them. The door of his mind opened more and more widely. In comparison with other men he was indeed learned; he knew six languages; he knew the laws, customs, and policies of several states, the names of all the constellations, and most of the plants of his country; and yet – must one not always break off thus? – 'yet methinks, I do not know so many as when I did but know a hundred, and had scarcely ever simpled further than Cheapside'.[20] Suppose indeed that certainty had been attainable; it had been proved to be so, and so it must be; nothing would have been more intolerable to him. His imagination was made to carry pyramids. 'Methinks there be not impossibilities enough in religion for an active faith.'[21] But then the grain of dust was a pyramid. There was nothing plain in a world of mystery. Consider the body. Some men are surprised by sickness. Sir Thomas can only 'wonder that we are not always so'; he sees the thousand doors that lead to death; and in addition – so he likes to speculate and fantastically accumulate considerations – 'it is in the power of every hand to destroy us, and we are beholden unto everyone we meet, he doth not kill us.'[22] What, one asks, as considerations accumulate, is ever to stop the course of such a mind, unroofed and open to the sky? Unfortunately, there was the Deity. His faith shut in his horizon. Sir Thomas himself resolutely drew that blind. His desire for knowledge, his eager ingenuity, his anticipations of truth, must submit, shut their eyes, and go to sleep. Doubts he calls them. 'More of these no man hath known than myself; which I confess I conquered, not in a martial posture, but on my knees.'[23] So lively a curiosity deserved a better fate. It would have delighted us to feed what Sir Thomas calls his doubts upon a liberal diet of modern certainties, but not if by so doing we had changed him, but that is the tribute of our gratitude. For is he not, among a variety of other things, one of the first of our writers to be definitely himself? His appearance has been recorded – his height moderate, his eyes large and luminous, his skin dark, and constantly suffused with blushes. But it is the more splendid picture of his soul that we feast upon. In that dark world, he was one of the explorers; the first to talk of himself, he broaches the subject with an immense gusto. He returns to it again and again, as if the soul were a wondrous disease and its symptoms not yet recorded. 'The world that I regard is myself; it is the microcosm of my own frame that I cast mine eye on: for the other I use it but like my globe, and turn it round sometimes for my recreation.'[24] Sometimes, he notes, and he seems to take a pride in the strange gloomy confession, he has wished for death. 'I feel sometimes a hell within myself; Lucifer keeps his court in my breast; Legion is revived in me.'[25] The strangest ideas and emotions have play in him, as he goes about his work, outwardly the most sober of mankind, and esteemed the greatest physician in Norwich. Yet, if his friends could see into his mind! But they cannot. 'I am in the dark to all the world, and my nearest friends behold me but in a cloud.'[26] Strange beyond belief are the capacities that he detects in himself, profound the meditation into which the commonest sight will plunge him, while the rest of the world passes by and sees nothing to wonder at. The tavern music, the Ave Mary Bell, the broken pot that the workman has dug out of the field – at the sight and sound of them he stops dead, as if transfixed by the astonishing vista. 'And surely it is not a melancholy conceit to think we are all asleep in this world, and that the conceits of this life are as mere dreams –'[27] No one so raises the vault of the mind, and, admitting conjecture after conjecture, positively makes us stand still in amazement, unable to bring ourselves to move on.

With such a conviction of the mystery and miracle of things, he is unable to reject, disposed to tolerate and contemplate without end. In the grossest superstition there is something of devotion; in tavern music something of divinity: in the little world of man something 'that was before the elements and owes no homage unto the sun'.[28] He is hospitable to everything and tastes freely of whatever is set before him. For upon this sublime prospect of time and eternity the cloudy vapours which his imagination conjures up, there is cast the figure of the author. It is not merely life in general that fills him with amazement, but his own life in particular, 'which to relate were not a history, but a piece of poetry, and would sound to common ears like a fable'.[29] The littleness of egotism has not as yet attacked the health of his interest in himself. I am charitable, I am brave, I am averse from nothing, I am full of feeling for others, I am merciless upon myself, 'For my conversation, it is like the sun's, with all men, and with a friendly aspect to good and bad';[30] I, I, I – how we have lost the secret of saying that!

In short Sir Thomas Browne brings in the whole question, which is afterwards to become of such importance, of knowing one's author. Somewhere, everywhere, now hidden, now apparent in whatever is written down is the form of a human being. If we seek to know him, are we idly occupied, as when, listening to a speaker, we begin to speculate about his age and habits, whether he is married, has children, and lives in Hampstead? It is a question to be asked, and not one to be answered. It will be answered, that is to say, in an instinctive and irrational manner, as our disposition inclines us. Only one must note that Sir Thomas is the first English writer to rouse this particular confusion with any briskness. Chaucer – but Chaucer's spelling is against him. Marlowe then, Spenser, Webster, Ben Jonson?[31] The truth is the question never presents itself quite so acutely in the case of a poet. It scarcely presents at all in the case of the Greeks and Latins. The poet gives us his essence, but prose takes the mould of the body and mind entire.

Could one not deduce from reading his books that Sir Thomas Browne, humane and tolerant in almost every respect, was nevertheless capable of a mood of dark superstition in which he would pronounce that two old women were witches and must be put to death? Some of his pedantries have the very clink of the thumbscrew: the heartless ingenuity of a spirit still cramped and fettered by the bonds of the Middle Ages. There were impulses of cruelty in him as in all people forced by their ignorance or weakness to live in a state of servility to man or nature. There were moments, brief but intense, in which his serene and magnanimous mind contracted in a spasm of terror. More often by far he is, as all great men are, a little dull. Yet the dullness of the great is distinct from the dullness of the little. It is perhaps more profound. We enter into their shades acquiescent and hopeful, convinced that if light is lacking the fault is ours. A sense of guilt, as the horror increases, mingles itself with our protest and increases the gloom. Surely, we must have missed the way? If one stitched together the passages in Wordsworth, Shakespeare, Milton, every great writer in short who has left more than a song or two behind him, where the light has failed us, and we have only gone on because of the habit of obedience, they would make a formidable volume – the dullest book in the world.

Don Quixote[32] is very dull too. But his dullness, instead of having that lethargy as of a somnolent beast which is characteristic of great people's dullness – 'After my enormous labours, I'm asleep and intend to snore if I like,' they seem to say – instead of this dullness Don Quixote has another variety. He is telling stories to children. There they sit round the fire on a winter's night, grown-up children, women at their spinning, men relaxed and sleepy after the day's sport, 'Tell us a story – something to make us laugh – something gallant, too – about people like ourselves only more unhappy and a great deal happier.' Obedient to this demand, Cervantes, a kind accommodating man, spun them stories, about princesses lost and amorous knights, much to their taste, very tedious to ours. Let him but get back to Don Quixote and Sancho Panza and all is well, for him, we cannot help thinking, as for us. Yet what with our natural reverence and inevitable servility, we seldom make our position, as modern readers of old writers, plain. Undoubtedly all writers are immensely influenced by the people who read them. Thus, take Cervantes and his audience – we, coming four centuries later, have a sense of breaking into a happy family party. Compare that group with the group (only there are no groups now since we have become educated and isolated and read our books by our own firesides in our own copies) but compare the readers of Cervantes with the readers of Thomas Hardy.[33] Hardy whiles away no firelit hour with talks of lost princesses and amorous knights – refuses more and more sternly to make things up for our entertainment. As we read him separately so he speaks to us separately, as if we were individual men and women, rather than groups sharing the same tastes. That, too, must be taken into account. The reader of today, accustomed to find himself in direct communication with the writer, is constantly out of touch with Cervantes. How far did he himself know what he was about – how far again do we over-interpret, misinterpret, read into Don Quixote a meaning compounded of our own experience, as an elder person might read a meaning into a child's story and doubt whether the child himself was aware of it? If Cervantes had felt the tragedy and the satire as we feel them, could he have forborne as he does to stress them – could he have been as callous as he seems? Yet Shakespeare dismissed Falstaff callously enough. The great writers have this large way with them, nature's way; which we who are further from nature call cruel, since we suffer more from the effects of cruelty, or at any rate judge our suffering of greater importance, than they did. None of this, however, impairs the main pleasure of the jolly, delightful, plain-spoken book built up, foaming up, round the magnificent conception of the Knight and the world which, however people may change, must remain for ever an unassailable statement of man and the world. That will always be in existence. And as for knowing himself what he was about – perhaps great writers never do. Perhaps that is why later ages find what they seek.

But to return to the dullest book in the world. To this volume Sir Thomas has added certainly one or two pages. Yet should one desire a loophole to escape it is always possible to find one in the chance that the book is difficult, not dull. Accustomed as we are to strip a whole page of its sentences and crush their meaning out in one grasp, the obstinate resistance which a page of Urn Burial offers at first trips us and blinds us. 'Though if Adam were made out of an extract of the Earth, all parts might challenge a restitution, yet few have returned their bones farre lower than they might receive them'[34] – We must stop, go back, try out this way and that, and proceed at a foot's pace. Reading has been made so easy in our days that to go back to these crabbed sentences is like mounting only a solemn and obstinate donkey instead of going up to town by an electric train. Dilatory, capricious, governed by no consideration save his own wish, Sir Thomas seems scarcely to be writing in the sense that Froude wrote or Matthew Arnold.[35] A page of print now fulfills a different office. Is it not almost servile in the assiduity with which it helps us on our way, making only the standard charge on our attention and in return for that giving us the full measure, but not an ounce over or under our due? In Sir Thomas Browne's days weights and measures were in a primitive condition, if they had any existence at all. One is conscious all the time that Sir Thomas was never paid a penny for his prose. He is free since it is the offering of his own bounty to give us as little or as much as he chooses. He is an amateur; it is the work of his leisure and pleasure; he makes no bargain with us. Therefore, as Sir Thomas has no call to conciliate his reader, these short books of his are dull if he chooses, difficult if he likes, beautiful beyond measure if he has a mind that way. Here we approach the doubtful region – the region of beauty. Are we not already lost or sunk or enticed with the very first words? 'When the Funeral pyre was out, and the last valediction over, men took a lasting adieu to their interred Friends.'[36] But why beauty should have the effect upon us that it does, the strange serene confidence that it inspires in us, none can say. Most people have tried and perhaps one of the invariable properties of beauty is that it leaves in the mind a desire to impart. Some offering we must make; some act we must dedicate, if only to move across the room and turn the rose in the jar, which, by the way, has dropped its petals.

1 – An essay first published posthumously in *CDB* and almost certainly written in 1919. See Editorial Note pp. xxiii–xxiv. Reprinted: *CE*.

2 – Geoffrey Chaucer (1340?–1400); William Shakespeare (1564–1616); William Cowper (1731–1800); Robert Burns (1759–96); Sir Walter Scott (1771–1832); William Wordsworth (1770–1850).

3 – John Keats (1795–1821); Alexander Pope (1688–1744); John Dryden (1631–1700); Sir Thomas Browne (1605–82).

4 – The Fanshawes are documented in: *The Memoirs of Ann Lady Fanshawe. Wife of the Honble Sir Richard Fanshawe, Bart, 1600–72* (John Lane, 1907), upon which VW wrote in 'Lady Fanshawe's Memoirs', *I VW Essays*; the Leghs in: *The House of Lyme. From its Foundation to the End of the Eighteenth Century* (William Heinemann, 1917) by Lady Newton, upon which VW wrote in '*The House of Lyme*', *II VW Essays*.

For the Verneys, to whom VW alludes again in 'The Elizabethan Lumber Room' (see *IV VW Essays* and *CR1*), see *Memoirs of the Verney Family During the Seventeenth Century* (1892, 1899). For VW on the Paston family see 'The Pastons and Chaucer', *IV VW Essays* and *CR1*. For the Hutchinsons see *Memoirs of the Life of Colonel Hutchinson . . . to which is Prefixed the Life of Mrs Hutchinson, written by Herself* (1806).

5 – Fanshawe, p. 47, quoted in *I VW Essays*, p. 145.

6 – Horace Walpole (1717–97); Jane Welsh Carlyle (1801–66); Edward Fitzgerald (1809–83).

7 – Newton, ch. xxv, p. 357, quoted in *II VW Essays*, p. 100.

8 – *Ibid.*, ch. xxvii, p. 369, quoted in *II VW Essays*, p. 99.

9 – Lucy Hutchinson, *née* Apsley (b.1620), wife of the regicide Colonel John Hutchinson (1615–64); Margaret Cavendish, Duchess of Newcastle (1624?–74), upon whom VW wrote in 'The Duke and Duchess of Newcastle-upon-Tyne', *I VW Essays*, and 'The Duchess of Newcastle', *IV VW Essays* and *CR1*.

10 – Elizabeth I (1533–1603); Edward, Lord Herbert of Cherbury (1583–1648), philosopher, poet, diplomatist, author of a celebrated *Autobiography* (1764, 1886), and of a *Life of Henry VIII* (1649). See also 'The Poems, English and Latin, of Edward, Lord Herbert of Cherbury' below.

11 – J. A. Froude, *English Seamen in the 16th century* (Longmans, Green & Co., 1895), 'Drake's Voyage Around the World', p. 107, where the vessels are described as being no bigger than 'a second-rate yacht of a modern noble lord,' which VW quotes in 'Trafficks and Discoveries', *II VW Essays*, p. 331.

12 – Sir Humphrey Gilbert (1539–83); Sir Hugh Willoughby (d.1554).

13 – *Hakluyt's Collection of the Early Voyages, Travels and Discoveries of the English Nation* (5 vols, R. H. Evans, 1809–12), vol. iii, p. 169, concerning Thomas Buts, which VW quotes in 'Trafficks and Discoveries', *II VW Essays*, p. 332.

14 – *Ibid.*, vol. iii, p. 45, quoted in *II VW Essays*, p. 330.

15 – *Ibid.*, vol. i, p. 352, quoted in *II VW Essays*, p. 333.

16 – For the first quotation, *ibid.*, vol. ii, p. 291, and for the second, *ibid.*, p. 453, both quoted in *II VW Essays*, p. 332.

17 – Ralph Fitch (1550?–1611), traveller in India, one of the first Englishmen to travel overland to India via the Euphrates valley. Roger Bodenham captain of the *Aucher*, who in 1551 set out on a voyage to the islands of Candia and Chio in the Levant. Anthony Jenkinson (d.1611), captain general of the Muscovy Company's expeditions to Russia in 1557 and 1566. John Lok, captain of the second voyage to Guinea in 1554. George Clifford, 3rd Earl of Cumberland (1558–1605), naval commander.

18 – Cf., *Jacob's Room* (1922), ch. ii (3rd ed., The Hogarth Press, 1945, pp. 21–2): 'The upper wings of the moth which Jacob held were undoubtedly marked with kidney-shaped spots of a fulvous hue. But there was no crescent upon the underwing. The tree had fallen the night he caught it. There had been a volley of pistol-shots suddenly in the depths of the wood. And his mother had taken him for a burglar when he came home late. The only one of her sons who never obeyed her, she said . . . The tree had fallen, though it was a windless night, and the lantern, stood upon the ground, had lit up the still green leaves and the dead beech leaves. It was a dry place. A toad was there. And the red underwing had circled round the light and flashed and gone. The red underwing had never come back, though Jacob had waited. It was after twelve when he crossed the lawn and saw his mother in the bright room, playing patience, sitting up.' And see *MoB*, p. 104, for a brief account of the operations of the Stephen children's Entomological Society.

19 – John Milton, *Paradise Lost* (1667); George Herbert (1593–1633), author of *The Temple* (1633). For VW on Sir Thomas Browne (1605–82), author of

Pseudodoxia Epidemica or Enquiries into . . . Vulgar and Common Errors (1646), *Religio Medici* (1642) and *Hydrotaphia. Urn Burial; or a discourse of the sepulchral urns lately found in Norfolk* (1658), see 'Sir Thomas Browne' below, and see 'The Elizabethan Lumber Room', *IV VW Essays* and *CR1*.

20–Browne, *Religio Medici*, pt ii, sect. viii (*The Works of Sir Thomas Browne*, ed. Simon Wilkin, 4 vols, Henry G. Bohn, 1846; vol. ii, p. 104).

21–*Ibid.*, pt i, sect. viii, p. 13, which continues: ':the deepest mysteries ours contains have not only been illustrated, but maintained, by syllogism and the rule of reason. I love to lose myself in a mystery; to pursue my reason to an *O altitudo!*'

22–For both quotations, *ibid.*, sect. xliv, p. 63.

23–*Ibid.*, sect. xix, p. 27.

24–*Ibid.*, pt ii, sect. xi, p. 110.

25–*Ibid.*, pt i, sect. li, p. 75, which begins: 'The heart of man is the place the devils dwell in;'.

26–*Ibid.*, pt ii, sect. iv, p. 95, which begins: 'This I perceive in myself; for'.

27–*Ibid.*, sect. xi, p. 111, which continues: 'dreams, to those of the next, as the phantasms of the night, to the conceit of the day.'

28–*Ibid.*: 'There is surely a piece of divinity in us; something that was before the elements, and . . .'

29–*Ibid.*, sect. xi, p. 110: 'Now for my life, it is a miracle of thirty years, which to relate . . .'

30–*Ibid.*, sect. x, p. 109.

31–Christopher Marlowe (1564–93); Edmund Spenser (1552?–99); John Webster (1580?–1625?); Ben Jonson (1572–1637).

32–Miguel de Cervantes (1547–1616), *Don Quixote de la Mancha* (1605).

33–Thomas Hardy (1840–1928).

34–Browne, *Hydrotaphia. Urn Burial* (1658), ch. i (*Works*, vol. iii, p. 455), which continues: '; not affecting the graves of giants, under hilly and heavy coverings, but content with less than their own depth, have wished their bones might lie soft, and the earth be light upon them.'

35–J. A. Froude (1818–94); Matthew Arnold (1822–88).

36–Browne, *Hydrotaphia. Urn Burial*, 'The Epistle Dedicatory. To my worthy and honoured Friend, Thomas Le Gros, of Crostwick, Esquire', p. 451, which continues: ', little expecting curiosity of future ages should comment upon their ashes; and, having no old experience of the duration of their relicks, held no opinion of such after-considerations.'

1920

Pictures and Portraits

There are two buildings on the same promontory of pavement, washed by the same incessant tide – the National Gallery and the National Portrait Gallery. In order to enter either it is only necessary to pass through a turnstile, and, on some days of the week, to part with a sixpenny bit. But always, on the paving stone at the doorway, it seems as if the pressure of humanity glued you to its side. As easily might a pilchard leap from the shoal and join the free sport of dolphins as a single individual ascend those steps and enter those doors. The current of the crowd, so swift and deep, the omnibuses swimming bravely on the surface, here a little string of soldiers caught in an eddy, there a hearse, next a pantechnicon van, then the discreet coach of royalty, followed by a black cell upon wheels with a warder at the grating, – all this, floated along in a stream of sound at once continuous and broken up into a kind of rough music, makes it vain to think of pictures. They are too still, too silent.

It would never occur to anyone with a highly developed plastic sense to think of painting as the silent art. Yet that perhaps is at the root of the ordinary English repugnance to pictures. There they hang as if the passage of centuries had left them indifferent. In private stress or public disaster we can wring no message from them. What they see across the room I am not sure: perhaps some gondola in Venice hundreds of years ago. But let who can and will indulge his fancy thus; the little token, the penny bunch of violets brought in from the street, is silently rejected. Our loves, our desires, the moment's eagerness, the passing problem,

163

receive no sort of sympathy or solution. Under the solemn stare we fade and dwindle and dissolve. Yet it cannot be denied that our resurrection, should it come to pass, is singularly august. We rise, purged and purified; deprived, it is true, of a tongue, but free from the impertinences and solicitations of that too animated and active member. The silence is hollow and vast as that of a cathedral dome. After the first shock and chill those used to deal in words seek out the pictures with the least of language about them – canvases taciturn and congealed like emerald or aquamarine – landscapes hollowed from transparent stone, green hill-sides, skies in which the clouds are eternally at rest. Let us wash the roofs of our eyes in colour; let us dive till the deep seas close above our heads. That these sensations are not aesthetic becomes evident soon enough, for, after a prolonged dumb gaze, the very paint on the canvas begins to distil itself into words – sluggish, slow-dropping words that would, if they could, stain the page with colour; not writers' words. But it is not here our business to define what sort of words they are; we are only concerned to prove our unfitness to review the caricatures of Mr Kapp. His critics are all agreed that he combines the gifts of the artist with those of the caricaturist. We have nothing to say of the artist, but having the National Portrait Gallery in mind, perhaps it may not be presumptuous to approach him from that point of view.

It needs an effort, but scarcely a great one, to enter the National Portrait Gallery. Sometimes indeed an urgent desire to identify one among the dead sends us post haste to its portals. The case we have in mind is that of Mrs John Stuart Mill.[2] Never was there such a paragon among women. Noble, magnanimous, inspired, thinker, reformer, saint, she possessed every gift and every virtue. One thing alone she lacked, and that, no doubt, the National Portrait Gallery could supply. She had no face. But the National Portrait Gallery, interrogated, wished to be satisfied that the inquirer was dependent upon a soldier; pensions they provided, not portraits; and thus set adrift in Trafalgar Square once more the student might reflect upon the paramount importance of faces.[3] Without a face Mrs John Stuart Mill was without a soul. Had her husband spared three lines of eulogy to describe her personal appearance we should hold her in memory. Without eyes or hair, cheeks or lips, her stupendous genius, her consummate virtue, availed her nothing. She is a mist, a wraith, a miasma of anonymous merit. The face is the thing. Therefore we turn eagerly, though we have paused too long about it, to see what faces Mr Kapp provides for the twenty-three gentlemen and the one old lady whom he calls *Personalities*.

There is very little of the anonymous about any of the twenty-four. There is scarcely a personality, from Mr Bernard Shaw to Mrs Grundy,[4] whom we have not seen in the flesh. We turn the pages, therefore, to see not what their bodies look like, but whether Mr Kapp can add anything to our estimate of their souls. We look, in particular, at the portraits of Lord Morley[5] and of Mr Bernard Shaw. Years ago Lord Morley shook the hand that writes these words. Whether he was Chief Secretary for Ireland or Prime Minister of England was a matter of complete indifference to a child; a child, presumably, was less than nothing whatever to him. But his manner – cordial, genial, quick as if stepping forward from a genuine impulse of friendliness – has never ceased to shed lustre upon every mention of his name. Where is the handshake in Mr Kapp's portrait? The lean, smoke-dried pedant's face looks as if scored upon paper by a pen clogged and corroded, as pens are in advertisements, with old ink. It may be so; to Mr Kapp it must be so; the handshake, perhaps, could only be rendered by a wash of sepia, which would have spoiled the picture as a work of art. Then there is Mr Bernard Shaw. Gazing from the gallery of some dismal gas-lit hall, one has seen him, often enough, alert, slight, erect, as if combating in his solitary person the forces of inertia and stupidity massed in a sea upon the floor. On a nearer glance, he appeared much of a knight-errant, candid, indeed innocent of aspect; a Don Quixote born in the Northern mists – shrewd, that is to say, rather than romantic. Mr Kapp has the legendary version – the diabolic. Moustache and eyebrows are twisted into points. The fingers are contorted into stamping hooves. There is no hint of blue in the eye. But again one must remember the limitations of black and white. It is a question of design, texture, handwriting, the relation of this with that, of art in short, which we pass by with our eyes shut. When we know little or nothing about the subject, and thus have no human or literary susceptibilities to placate, the effect is far more satisfactory. That 'The Politician' (Mr Masterman)[6] has the long body cut into segments and the round face marked with alarming black bars of the Oak Eggar caterpillar, we find it easy and illuminating to believe. There is something sinister about him; he swarms rapidly across roads; he smudges when crushed; he devours leaf after leaf. 'The Bishop' (the Bishop of Norwich)[7] is equally symbolical. His is emitting something sonorous through an oblong slit of a mouth; you can almost hear the heavy particle descending through the upper stories of the elongated countenance until it pops with a hollow click out of the orifice. The Duke of Devonshire[8] for all the world resembles a seal sleek from the sea, his mouth pursed to a button signifying a desire for mackerel. But the mackerel he is offered is not fresh, and, tossing himself wearily backwards, he flops with a yawn into the depths. By what sleight of hand Mr Kapp has conveyed the fact that the golden thread extracted by Sir Henry Wood[9] from the sound of the Queen's Hall Orchestra is really a hair from his soup we do not know. The truth of the suggestion, however unpleasant, is undeniable. But words, words! How inadequate you are! How weary one gets of you! How you will always be saying too much or too little! Oh to be silent! Oh to be a painter! Oh (in short) to be Mr Kapp!

1 – A signed review in the *Athenaeum*, 9 January 1920, (Kp C182) of *Personalities. Twenty-four drawings* (Martin Secker, 1919) by Edmond X. Kapp (1890–1978), draughtsman and painter, an exhibition of whose drawings had been shown at the Little Art Rooms, Duke Street, Adelphi, May–June 1919.
2 – Formerly Mrs Harriet Taylor, who married J. S. Mill (whose own portrait by Watts *is* in the NPG, no. 1009, dated 1873) in 1851, and whose unparalleled excellences he celebrated in his *Autobiography* (1867).
3 – The National Portrait Gallery, re-interrogated, have been unable to shed any light on the matter of soldiers and pensions.
4 – Kapp, no. 3, dated 1914, and no. 24, undated, respectively. George Bernard Shaw (1856–1950). Mrs Grundy, the character epitomising propriety created by the playwright Thomas Morton (1764?–1838).
5 – *Ibid.*, no. 2, undated. John Morley, 1st Viscount Morley of Blackburn (1838–1923), statesman, man of letters, friend of Leslie Stephen, had been Chief Secretary for Ireland (1886, 1892–5), Secretary of State for India (1905–10), and Lord President of the Council (1910–14).
6 – *Ibid.*, no. 5, dated 1914. Rt Hon. C. F. G. Masterman (1874–1927).
7 – *Ibid.*, no. 17, dated 1914.
8 – *Ibid.*, no. 21, dated 1914.
9 – *Ibid.*, no. 11, 'The Golden Thread' (Sir Henry Wood [1869–1944]), undated.

An American Poet

In his introduction to *General William Booth*, Mr Nichols devotes a good deal of space to a portrait of the poet. He is tall, broad shouldered, has a ruddy complexion, straw-golden hair, eyes of 'piercing sky-blue' that shut and re-open with 'the effect of a blind abruptly shot up in a sunward room'; he hands you his thought 'struggling and kicking like a puppy with an extraordinary animation of watchfulness as to what you will make of it'.[2] It is a good description; it makes you see not only Mr

Lindsay, but also Mr Nichols. You see that Mr Nichols is much impressed by the size, the sunburn, the vitality; this man writes poetry, yet he is much like a farm labourer to look at. The Englishman is disposed to think well of Mr Lindsay's poems on that account. Then he finds that Mr Lindsay tours the country reciting his poetry for a living, and that has proved to Mr Nichols 'once and for all that poetry has too long been manufactured and read in the study; that the enmity between poetry and the populace has its origin in *print*; whereby poetry has lost its "springiness"; has become a thing too much of the eye; a cult of solitude ... the refuge of preciosity in those folk who have made of poetry a retreat from life and not an explanation and justification in beauty of life'.[3] There you have the Englishman doing what it is so fatally easy for the English of the present day to do – worshipping vitality, divesting himself of culture, trying to get away, to get back, to forget, to renew.

But we can be generous without being obsequious. There is every reason to believe that America can bring something new to literature; it is high time, we may add, that America did. Nobody is so certain of an enthusiastic welcome in England as a true American poet; directly the figure or the shadow of one appears above the horizon all eyes are shaded and turned in his direction. What hopes are there then, of Nicholas Vachel Lindsay? Naturally, inevitably perhaps, the answer is not a single jubilant hail! but one that takes time and thought to deliver; one of the qualified kind. In the first place, *General William Booth* does not contain Mr Lindsay's best work. His best work, according to his own account, is the yet unpublished *Golden Book of Springfield*; in Mr Nichols's opinion *The Congo* is a better book than *General William Booth*; and of the books we know we prefer *The Chinese Nightingale*.[4] Nevertheless, both in its goodness and in its badness, *General Booth* is full of interest. Should you have the habit, to which the reviewer must confess, of reading introductions last, you will have noticed certain qualities in Mr Lindsay's work before you find them confirmed by what is said of him in the Introduction. The atmosphere is not at all that of the study: it is much more that of the street corner. As you read or recite you imagine a little crowd gathered round a Salvation Army officer, who, mounted on a tub, gesticulates and vociferates, not, perhaps, to the solace of your soul. There is in many of Mr Lindsay's poems the same earnest insistence upon the obvious which in these street crowds always makes it appear that the message of the preacher is addressed not to you, but to your neighbour. Mr Lindsay is charged with several messages to deliver about Beauty and Temperance and the future of Illinois. One feels that he would sacrifice his poetry rather than his message; and that the fusion of one with the other is not complete. Poetry may run clear for a moment; at the next the gospel clouds it. That the combination is not repulsive – as from our description it certainly should be – is due in the first place to the preacher's simple-mindedness; and in the second to the poet's indisputable though debatable gift. You walk on with the tune running in your head. It comes back of its own accord later in the day. Has it not somehow addressed itself to you also? Here are three verses from a short sermon of four:

> The dew, the rain, and moonlight
> All prove our Father's mind.
> The dew, the rain, and moonlight
> Descend to bless mankind.
> Come, let us see that all men
> Have land to catch the rain,
> Have grass to snare the spheres of dew,
> And fields spread for the grain.
>
> *   *   *   *
>
> A net to snare the moonlight,
> A sod spread to the sun,
> A place of toil by daytime,
> Of dreams when toil is done.[5]

Or, again, he will beat out his message with incredible pertinacity and simplicity:

> The moral,
> The conclusion,
> The verdict now you know; –
> 'The saloon must go,
> The saloon must go,
> The saloon,
> The saloon,
> The saloon
> Must go.'[6]

A fragment separated from the whole gives little idea of the cumulative power which the whole possesses. His gift is rhythmical, one suspects, rather than verbal, until further discoveries make it wise to suspend that judgement for a time. With the rhythm goes, in many of the poems, a queer suggestion of instrumental music. Here, one feels, the cymbals should clash; here sounds the brass; here the tambourines; and here and here should be dancing and swaying in time. The audience should take their measure from the poet, who, as he recites, stands in the centre of a circle with his feet wide apart, so that he may turn on his heel, speaking rapidly, his hands moving, his voice 'changing in pace, rhythm and volume, but never in tone'.[7] There would be no disrespect in some rhythmical response as Mr Lindsay recites the following:

> [Bass drum beaten loudly.]
> Booth led boldly with his big bass drum –
> (Are you washed in the blood of the Lamb?)
> The Saints smiled gravely and they said: 'He's come.'
> (Are you washed in the blood of the Lamb?)
> Walking lepers followed, rank on rank,
> Lurching bravoes from the ditches dank,
> Drabs from the alleyways and drug-fiends pale –
> Minds still passion-ridden, soul-powers frail –
> Vermin-eaten saints with mouldy breath,
> Unwashed legions with the ways of Death –
> (Are you washed in the blood of the Lamb?)[8]

But since we in England do our reading, for reasons of climate, indoors, in solitude generally, and for the most part in silence, we apply other tests to Mr Lindsay's poetry than those enforced by the open air. The test of language is one of them, and it seems doubtful whether Mr Lindsay is aware that there is such a test. The language is generally too large and loose for the thought; it is often even more banal than the thought – pompous, careless, slack, and conventional. No beating of drums, dancing, or gesture could make the following stanza anything but rhetoric of the feeblest kind:

> Too many weary men shed honest tears,
> Ground by machines that give the Senate ease.
> Too many little babes with bleeding hands
> Have heaped the fruits of empire on your knees.[9]

It is indeed difficult, as one copies the above lines, to account for the fact that a book so waterlogged with mediocrity should yet remain buoyant and seaworthy. Much must be attributed to Mr Lindsay's sincerity. That a poet should be capable of such staring commonplace is disarming. Only youth could be so innocent; only youth could suppose that such truisms are true. Perhaps the undoubted effectiveness of his rhythms is also the result of youth. A sophisticated ear would fight shy of them. They swing and rock and balance, carry you over acres of ploughed field, sweep you, now and then, off your feet. No great strain is laid upon the intellect; the strain is on the emotions. If you stop to examine the

lines separately none is specially memorable. But the whole moral of Mr
Lindsay's work, as we understand it, is that single lines should not be
memorable. He is the poet of the whole and not of the detail. For this
reason it is difficult to represent him fairly in short quotations. Read at
length and read aloud, the quality which Mr Nichols calls 'springiness' is
apparent. If there is none of the minute felicity and none of the intensity
of modern English verse, there is a freshness which we could not match
among ourselves. The words, careless, gross, or violent as they may be,
seem to be leaving the lips of a living man; they have not been dug from a
cold mine of thought and laid in minute glittering particles upon the
page. Perhaps the reader may see what we mean in the following little
poem:

> Look you, I'll go pray,
> My shame is crying,
> My soul is gray and faint,
> My faith is dying.
> Look you, I'll go pray –
> 'Sweet Mary make me clean,
> Thou rainstorm of the soul,
> Thou wine from worlds unseen.'[10]

That may be taken to prove that his moods are not always strenuous and
didactic.

But however we rate Mr Lindsay's worth as a poet, it is impossible,
though it may well be unfair, not to seize upon those strains in him which
appear to us, rightly or wrongly, the proof of his American birth – his
simplicity; his moral earnestness; his primitive love of rhythm; his
faculty for using the common speech so that it seems not common but
enviably fresh and even exquisite at moments. There are the strains
which, in their odd combinations, give him his newness in our eyes.
Perhaps we relish his newness too highly; perhaps it distracts us from
other qualities that lie more deeply hid. A critic writing of the *Chinese
Nightingale* would have less to say about the American quality of Mr
Lindsay's work. But in writing of *General William Booth* one can
scarcely avoid laying stress upon its rousing nature, its alternate beauty
and commonplaceness, and its simply emotional appeal. We look into
the bubbling cauldron from which something shapely of a new kind may
one of these days emerge.

1–A review in the *TLS*, 29 January 1920, (Kp C182.1) of *General William Booth
Enters into Heaven and Other Poems*. With an introduction by Robert Nichols

(Chatto & Windus, 1919) by Nicholas Vachel Lindsay (1879–1931). The work originally appeared in 1913 and was its author's first published volume. Lindsay's writings were much admired by his friend and biographer Edgar Lee Masters, upon whom VW wrote in 'A Talker', *II VW Essays*.

VW noted in her diary on Saturday, 10 January 1920: 'I also think (as Lotty [Hope, domestic servant] won't come in – my evening wasting – Lindsay to read – oh dear) that my charms are beneath the horizon; Mary [Hutchinson]'s about level with the eye; & Nessa's rising resplendent like the harvest moon.'

2–For all three quotations, Lindsay, intro., p. vi.

3–*Ibid.*, p. xi, which has 'study, that'. The ellipsis marks the omission of ', only too often morose, and of solicitude for the things of the soul that it is only too often'.

4–For Mr Nichols's opinion, *ibid.*, p. xiii. *The Golden Book of Springfield* (1920), of which Lindsay wrote (*ibid.*, p. x) 'the real me 1908–1919 is all hid in this', was a mystic utopia based on ideas also expounded in his prose autobiography *Adventures While Preaching the Gospel of Beauty* (1914). *The Congo and Other Poems* (1914); *The Chinese Nightingale and Other Poems* (1917).

5–*Ibid.*, 'A Net to Snare the Moonlight', p. 106, first, second and last stanzas.

6–Lindsay, *The Chinese Nightingale and Other Poems* (Macmillan Co., 1917), 'The Drunkard's Funeral', p. 69.

7–Lindsay, *General William Booth*, intro., p. xii: 'In reciting the communal hymns ... Vachel Lindsay stands in the centre of a circle of auditors with his feet wide apart that he may turn on either heel while chanting, and with his hands and elbows in the first position of that exercise known to youth as "Arms outward – FLING!"' The head is slightly tilted back, the nostrils expanded, the eyes closed. During the delivery – which is rapid and even, changing in pace, rhythm and volume, but never in tone – his arms, especially the hands, gesture slightly, and his face, at least to my observation, becomes a trifle pale.'

8–*Ibid.*, 'General William Booth Enters into Heaven [To be sung to the tune of *The Blood of the Lamb*, with indicated instrument]', p. 1, opening lines.

9–*Ibid.*, 'To the United States Senate', p. 50.

10–*Ibid.*, 'Look you, I'll go pray', p. 38.

English Prose

If it should be proposed to appoint Mr Pearsall Smith Anthologist Royal to the English-speaking races, I, for one, would willingly contribute rather more than I can afford to his stipend. For three hundred years and more a dead preacher called John Donne[2] has cumbered our shelves. The other day Mr Pearsall Smith touched him with his wand, and behold! – the folios quake, the pages shiver, out steps the passionate preacher; the fibres of our secular hearts are bent and bowed beneath the unaccustomed tempest. But no figure could be more misleading than this of the wand and the wizard. Conceive, rather, a table piled with books; folio pages turned and turned again; collations, annotations, emendations, expurgations; voyages in omnibuses; hours of disillusionment – for who reads prose? life wasting under the rays of a green lamp; the prize of months one solitary paragraph – truly if Mr Pearsall Smith is a wizard he has learned his craft where none but the bold and the faithful dare follow him. Therefore if I go on to say that in one respect I am his superior, it will be understood that it is not to his learning that I refer. I refer to his taste. In reading the *Treasury of English Prose* I became aware that my taste is far better than Mr Pearsall Smith's; it is in fact impeccable. But I need scarcely hasten to add what everyone knows for himself; in matters of taste each man, woman and child in the British Isles is impeccable; so are the quadrupeds. A dog who did not rate his own taste better than his master's would be a dog not worth drowning.

This being said, let us waste no more time but proceed at once to Stevenson. I had hoped, not very confidently, to look for Stevenson in vain. I had hoped that the habit of cutting out passages from Stevenson about being good and being brave and being happy was now confined to schoolmasters and people at the head of public institutions. I had hoped that private individuals were beginning to say, 'What is the point of Stevenson? Why did they call him a master of prose? What did our fathers mean by comparing this thin-blooded mummery with Scott or Defoe?'[3] – but I had hoped in vain. Here is Stevenson occupying one of two hundred and fifteen pages with reflections upon Happiness – reflections addressed in a private letter to a friend. It begins all right. Nobody can deny that it needs every sort of good quality to step along so briskly, with such apparent ease, such a nice imitation of talk running down the pen and flowing over the paper. Nor do I shiver when the pen steps more circumspectly. A writer's letters should be as literary as his printed works. But all my spines erect themselves, all my prejudices are confirmed when I come to this: 'But I know pleasure still; pleasure with a thousand faces, and none perfect, a thousand tongues all broken, a thousand hands and all of them with scratching nails. High among these I place this delight of weeding out here alone by the garrulous water, under the silence of the high wood, broken by incongruous sounds of birds.'[4] Then I know why I cannot read the novels; then I know why I should never allow him within a mile of the anthologies.

Skipping (for no one reads an anthology through), we next alight upon Walter Pater[5] – nervously, prepared for disappointment. Can he possibly be what he once seemed? – the writer who from words made blue and gold and green; marble, brick, the wax petals of flowers; warmth too and scent; all things that the hand delighted to touch and the nostrils to smell, while the mind traced subtle winding paths and surprised recondite secrets. This, and much more than this, comes back to me with renewed delight in Mr Pearsall Smith's quotations. The famous one still seems to me to deserve all its fame; the less famous, about a red hawthorn tree in full flower – 'a plumage of tender crimson fire out of the heart of the dry wood'[6] – revives the old joys and makes the nerve of the eye vibrate again; but if one cannot praise fitly it is better to be silent and only say that there can be no doubt – from the quotations at least – about Walter Pater.

About Emerson[7] there is I think considerable doubt; or rather there is no doubt at all that he must be altogether different from what we supposed to deserve eleven full pages where there is no room for a single line of Dryden, Cowper, Peacock, Hardy, the Brontës, Jane Austen, Meredith[8] (to take the obvious omissions); only two scraps of Sterne and a page and a bit of Conrad.[9] Yet one sees what Mr Pearsall Smith means. Emerson wrote for anthologies. Passages seem to break off in one's hands like ripe fruit without damage to the tree. The first passage reads beautifully; the second almost as well. But then – what is it? Something bald and bare and glittering – something light and brittle – something which suggests that if this precious fruit were dropped it would shiver into particles of silvery dust like one of those balls that were plucked from the boughs of ancient Christmas trees, and slipped and fell – is Emerson's fruit *that* kind of fruit? Of course the lustre is admirable – the dust, the dust of the stars.

But if Mr Pearsall Smith puts in and leaves out according to a rule of his own, that is an indispensable merit in an anthologist. He puts in, for example, Jeremy Taylor,[10] and so reveals a great English writer who, to my shame, had been no more than an obscure clerical shade among the folios. For that I could forgive him – I was going to say the neglect of Mr Hardy; but Mr Pearsall Smith can hardly have neglected all, or almost all, the great English novelists. He has rejected them, and that is another matter, that leads one to consider what may be his reasons. I suppose there are at least twenty of them, and all so profound and lying at the roots of things that to lay bare a single one would need more columns than I have words. Lightly then will I run over a few suggestions and leave them to wither or perhaps fall on fertile soil. To begin with, every novelist would, I suppose, suspect a critic who complimented him on the beauty of his writing. 'But that's not what I'm after,' he would say, and add, a moment later, with the susceptibility of his kind, 'You mean, I'm dull.' And as a matter of fact the great novelists very seldom stop in the middle or in the beginning of their great scenes to write anything that one could cut out with a pair of scissors or loop round with a line of red ink. The greatest of novelists – Dostoevsky – always, so Russian scholars say, writes badly. Turgenev,[11] the least great of the Russian trinity, always, they say, writes exquisitely. That Dostoevsky would have been a greater novelist had he written beautifully into the bargain no one will deny. But the novelist's task lays such a load upon every nerve, muscle, and fibre that to demand beautiful prose in addition is, in view of human limitations, to demand what can only be given at the cost of a sacrifice. Let us choose two instances from among the writers of our own tongue. There is no novel by Mr Conrad which has not passages of such beauty that one hangs over them like a humming-bird moth at the mouth of a flower. Yet I believe that one pays for such beauty in a novel. To achieve it the writer has had to shut off his energy in other directions. Hence, I think, so many pages of Mr Conrad's novels are slack and slumberous, monotonous like the summer sea. Mr Hardy, on the other hand, has not in the course of some twenty volumes written a single passage fit to be included in a treasury of English prose. Impossible! Yet I could not, at a moment's notice, lay my hand on one. The greater number of our novelists are in the same boat with him. But what, then, can we be talking about? What is this 'beautiful English prose'?

Surely the most beautiful of all things! the reader of Mr Pearsall Smith's selection will exclaim – the most subtle, the most profound, the most moving and imaginative. And who are the people who keep it alive, extend its powers, and increase its triumphs? The novelists. Only we must not go to them for perfect passages, descriptions, perorations, reflections so highly wrought that they can stand alone without their context. We must go to them for chapters, not for sentences; for beauty, not tranquil and contained, but wild and fleeting like the light on rough waters. We must seek it particularly where the narrative breaks and gives way to dialogue. But it must be conceded that the novelists put their English to the most menial tasks. She has to do all the work of the house; to make the beds, dust the china, boil the kettle, sweep the floors. In return she has the priceless privilege of living with human beings. When she has warmed to her task, when the fire is burning, the cat here, the dog there, the smoke rising from the chimney, the men and women feasting or love-making, dreaming or speculating, the trees blowing, the moon rising, the autumn sun gold upon the corn – then read Mr Hardy and see whether the common prose of English fiction does not carry herself like the Queen she is – the old Queen, wise in the secrets of our hearts; the young Queen with all her life before her. For though English poetry was a fine old potentate – but no, I dare not breathe a word against English poetry. All I will venture is a sigh of wonder and amazement that when there is prose before us with its capacities and possibilities, its power to say new things, make new shapes, express new passions, young people should still be dancing to a barrel organ and choosing words because they rhyme.

1 – A signed review in the *Athenaeum*, 30 January 1920, (Kp C183) of *A Treasury of English Prose* (Constable & Co. Ltd., 1919) ed. Logan Pearsall Smith (1865–1946), American-born man of letters, educated at Harvard and Oxford, and from 1913 a British citizen. The Hogarth Press published his *Stories from the Old Testament* in May 1920. 'I wrote my article on English prose for Murry,' VW noted in her diary on Wednesday, 7 January 1920, '& now finish Rossetti, taking leave still from the Times [*Literary Supplement*].'
See also 'Moments of Vision', *II VW Essays*. Reprinted: *B&P*.
2 – John Donne (1573–1631), forty-five extracts from whose sermons are reproduced in Smith.
3 – Robert Louis Stevenson (1850–94). Neither Sir Walter Scott (1771–1832) nor Daniel Defoe (1660?–1731) is represented in Smith.
4 – Smith, p. 203, an extract from Stevenson's *Vailima Letters* (1895).
5 – Walter Pater (1839–94).
6 – Smith, p. 195, an extract entitled 'The Red Hawthorn', from Pater's 'Imaginary Portrait. The Child in the House', *Macmillan's Magazine*, August 1878: 'I have remarked how, in the process of our brain-building, as the house of thought in which we live gets itself together like some airy bird's nest of floating thistle-down and chance straws, compact at last, little accidents have their consequence; and thus it happened that, as he walked one evening, a garden gate, usually closed, stood open; and lo! within, a great red hawthorn, in full flower, embossing heavily the bleached and twisted trunk and branches, so aged that there were but few green leaves thereon – a plumage of tender, crimson fire out of the heart of the dry wood . . . Was it some periodic moment in the expansion of soul within him, or mere trick of heat in the heavily-laden summer air?'
7 – Ralph Waldo Emerson (1803–82), upon whom, incidentally, VW had written in 'Emerson's Journals', *I VW Essays*.
8 – John Dryden (1631–1700); William Cowper (1731–1800); Thomas Love Peacock (1785–1866); Thomas Hardy (1840–1928); Charlotte Brontë (1816–55), Emily Brontë (1818–48), Anne Brontë (1820–49); Jane Austen (1775–1817); George Meredith (1828–1909).
9 – Smith, pp. 113–14, reproduces 'A Fragment' from Sterne's *A Sentimental Journey* (1768) and 'Death of Le Fevre' from *Tristram Shandy* (1760–7); and *ibid.*, pp. 208–9, an extract from Conrad's 'Youth' (1902) and a passage on 'The English Speech' from *Some Reminiscences* (1912).

10–Jeremy Taylor (1613–67), of whose work Smith reproduces twenty-nine extracts.
11–Fyodor Dostoevsky (1821–81); Ivan Turgenev (1818–83).

Cleverness and Youth

We know for ourselves that Mr Huxley is very clever; and his publisher informs us that he is young. For both these reasons his reviewers may pay him the compliment, and give themselves the pleasure, of taking him seriously. Instead, that is, of saying that there are seven short stories in *Limbo* which are all clever, amusing, and well written, and recommending the public to read them, as we can conscientiously do, we are tempted to state, what it is so seldom necessary to state, that short stories can be a great deal more than clever, amusing, and well written. There is another adjective – 'interesting'; that is the adjective we should like to bestow upon Mr Huxley's short stories, for it is the best worth having.

The difficulty is that in order to be interesting, as we define the word, Mr Huxley would have to forgo, or go beyond, many of the gifts which nature and fortune have put in his way. Merely to skim the quotations in 'Richard Greenow'[2] and the rest is to perceive that Mr Huxley is extemely well-read; then he has evidently first-hand knowledge of a great public school, which he calls Aesop; and of an Oxford college, which he calls Canteloup; moreover, whatever the intellectual fad of the metropolis, he is fated to know both its professors and its disciples. His eyes have opened perforce upon the follies of the upper middle classes and the unfortunate physical infirmities of the *intelligentsia*. This is none of Mr Huxley's fault, but it is a little his misfortune, and it is better worth attention since so many of the young and the clever of our country are inevitably in the same case. To have named the reading of books as an obstacle to the writing of stories needs some explanation. We hold no brief for the simple peasant. Yet we cannot help thinking that it is well to leave a mind under a counterpane of moderate ignorance; it grows more slowly, but being more slowly exposed it avoids that excessive surface sensibility which wastes the strength of the precocious. Again, to be aware too soon of sophisticated society makes it tempting for a young writer to use his first darts in attack and derision. If he is as dexterous and as straightforward as Mr Huxley the attack is an inspiriting spectacle. Humbug seems to collapse, pretension to be pricked. Here is the portrait of a fellow of Canteloup,

who had had the most dazzling academic career of his generation ...[3] Mr Glottenham did not prepossess at a first glance; the furrows of his face were covered with a short grey sordid stubble; his clothes were disgusting with the spilth of many years of dirty feeding; he had the shoulders and long hanging arms of an ape – an ape with a horribly human look about it. When he spoke it was like the sound of a man breaking coke; he spoke incessantly and on every subject. His knowledge was enormous; but he possessed the secret of a strange inverted alchemy – he knew how to turn the richest gold to lead, could make the most interesting topic so intolerably tedious that it was impossible, when he talked, not to loathe it.[4]

There is an equally amusing description of a dinner with the Head-master of Aesop and Mrs Cravister, a lady of 'swelling port' and unexpected utterance, who talks to the bewildered boys now about eschatology, now about Manx cats ('No tails, no tails, like men. How symbolical everything is!'),[5] now about the unhappy fate of the carrion crow, who mates for life. It is amusing; it is perhaps true; and yet as one reads one cannot help exclaiming that English society is making it impossible to produce English literature. Write about boots, one is inclined to say, about coins, sea anemones, crayfish – but, as you value your life, steer clear of the English upper middle classes. They lie, apparently, so open to attack, they are undoubtedly such an obstacle to vision; but their openness is the openness of the tiger's jaw which ends by swallowing you whole and leaving no trace. 'Happily Ever After' is but another proof of their rapacity. Mr Huxley sets out to kill a great many despicable conventions, and to attack a large and disgusting school-master. But having laughed at the conventions and the schoolmaster, they suddenly turn the tables on him. Now, they seem to say, talk about something that you do believe in – and behold, Mr Huxley can only stammer. Love and death, like damp fireworks, refuse to flare up in such an atmosphere, and as usual the upper middle classes escape unhurt.

But with Mr Huxley it is only necessary to wait a little longer; and we can wait without anxiety. He is not merely clever, well-read, and honest, but when he forgets himself he discovers very charming things. The best story – barring 'Happy Families', a play, which, after two readings, we understand insufficiently to pronounce upon – is not a story at all, but a description of an interview in a bookshop. He opens a book of fashion plates.

Beauties in crinolines swam with the amplitude of pavilioned ships across the pages. Their feet were represented as thin and flat and black, like tea-leaves shyly protruding from under their petticoats ... And it occurred to me then that if I wanted an emblem to picture the sacredness of marriage and the influence of the home, I could not do better than choose two little black feet like tea-leaves peeping out decorously from under the hem of wide, disguising petticoats. While heels and thoroughbred insteps should figure – oh well, the reverse.[6]

And then he sees a piano – 'the yellow keys grinned at me in the darkness like the teeth of an ancient horse'.[7] Emboldened by our pleasure in such good writing as this, we would admonish Mr Huxley to leave social satire alone, to delete the word 'incredibly'[8] from his pages, and to write about interesting things that he likes. Nobody ever takes advice; even so, we hazard the opinion that Mr Huxley's next book will be not only clever, amusing, and well-written, but interesting into the bargain.

1–A review in the *TLS*, 5 February 1920, (Kp C184) of *Limbo* (Chatto & Windus, 1920) by Aldous Huxley (1894–1963), who, after taking a first in English at Balliol College, Oxford, in 1916, served on the land during the last years of the war at Garsington Manor, home of Lady Ottoline and Philip Morrell. He then taught at Repton and Eton before marrying Maria Nys in 1919; thereafter he devoted himself to writing, his first novel, *Crome Yellow*, appearing in 1921. VW had met him for the first time in 1917.
   On 23 June 1920, VW reflected in her diary: 'Haven't I lately dismissed [John Middleton] Murry's play, & exactly appraised K[atherine Mansfield]'s story, & summed up Aldous Huxley, & doesn't it somehow wound my sense of fitness to hear Roger [Fry] mangling these exact values?'
   See also 'Adventurers All', *II VW Essays*. Reprinted: *CW*.
2–Huxley, 'Farcical History of Richard Greenow', pp. 1–115.
3–*Ibid.*, pt iv, p. 41.
4–*Ibid.*, pp. 40–1.
5–For the first quotation, *ibid.*, pt i, p. 14, and for the second p. 18.
6–*Ibid.*, 'The Bookshop', pp. 261–2.
7–*Ibid.*, p. 263.
8–For instances of which, *ibid.*, 'Happily Ever After', p. 133 ('incredibly absurd and incongruous'), p. 155 ('so incredibly bad'), p. 160 ('How incredibly remote'); 'Cynthia', p. 257 ('seeming incredibly close at hand'); 'The Death of Lully', p. 269 ('effortless and incredibly swift').

Mr Norris's Method

After writing novels for forty years, Mr Norris has given us not merely, as we may guess, forty novels, but an additional volume which has upon the back of it for title W. E. Norris. Although we admit to finding this supernumerary volume always among the best of any author's works, we will at present only extract from it the information that Mr Norris is likely to deprecate enthusiasm as an unnecessary expense of spirit on the part of a reviewer. If we were to offer him incense, he would probably only complain of the smoke. He would point out that above all things he values clearness of sight. It is not due to his fine stock of this commodity that, after forty years of writing, *The Triumphs of Sara* issues in its turn, firm, competent and kindly, extremely readable, a little cool, and entirely self-possessed?

But clearness of sight is not so common that we can afford to rate its products cheaply. Indeed, we have to own that even with Mr Norris himself dissuading us there was an impulse, half way through this forty-first novel, of dangerous enthusiasm. Lincolnshire; ratting; the Leppingtons of Storr; Uncle Tom asking questions; Jimmy in the Guards; Peggy playing cricket; Aunt Matilda playing patience; Lady Leppington playing the piano; the pleasant country home; the good breeding, the good temper, the good judgment of everyone concerned, did at last produce that warm appreciative mood in the critic which in the kettle precedes, by some five minutes, the hiss and hubbub of boiling over. How this calamity was averted is only to be explained by remarking that an heiress from Manchester called Sara comes upon the scene, and, at her first appearance among the Leppingtons, is convicted by Mr Norris of killing her rat by a fluke. It is an anxious predicament; for a young woman in a novel by Mr Norris must kill something, and if she kills rats by a fluke the presumption is that she kills men by profession. 'From beneath her long lashes she shot at him one of those glances which she knew by experience found their mark every time she had recourse to them.'[2] That is Sara's form of sport, and, as our quotation shows, Mr Norris is not altogether at his ease in describing it. Yet it is amazing and even instructive to observe how seldom we are allowed to feel any awkwardness. The clear-sighted and unsentimental relationship between Sara and Euan Leppington, who, through marriage and separation and reconciliation, remain good friends, is not only a clever and truthful performance, but a nice example of a novelist's economy. Mr Norris is not going to waste his time over the impossible. He is not going to be rushed off his own neat strip of indisputable territory. If his characters suffer for it, suffer they must. No one can complain that they are not sensible; and Englishwomen are notoriously cold-hearted. The chief damage that this caution inflicts upon us is that we can rely so implicitly upon a life-belt when the liner is torpedoed that, should the kettle boil in the middle of the chapter, there is no reason to postpone tea. The nuisance of being torpedoed, as Mr Norris points out, is not that you are drowned, but that you are rescued 'without other belongings than the clothes on your back'.[3] Why we should complain of feeling safe when Mr Norris is so much better fitted to deal with safety than with disaster is puzzling, until, in the crucial scene of the book, we find a reason which justifies our dissatisfaction. Sara Leppington surprises her husband alone with Mrs Furness in a Brighton hotel. Now Mrs Furness loved Euan, and, we submit, had only to say so rather forcibly in order to send the legitimate wife who did not love him skulking home in disgrace. As it is, Mrs Furness is driven off as a small terrier is driven from a large dog's bone by a horrid outburst of loud meaningless barking. But though a happy ending is assured, and presumably the desired heir to the Leppington estates, the feeling of safety rests upon such false foundations that we are more uneasy than if the whole fabric had been blown sky-high before our eyes.

This conclusion, however, need only be reached if you wish to come to a conclusion, if, that is to say, you stray off Mr Norris's land on to debatable territory where he makes no pretence to rule. Stay within his precincts and you are still perfectly safe.

1–A review in the TLS, 4 March 1920, (Kp C185) of The Triumphs of Sara (Hutchinson & Co., 1920) by W. E. (William Edward) Norris (1847–1925). See also 'The Obstinate Lady' above, 'Mr Norris's Standard' below, and 'Barham of Beltana' and 'Lone Marie', I VW Essays. Reading Notes (Berg, xxv). Reprinted: CW.
2–Norris, ch. vi, p. 72.
3–Ibid., ch. xix, p. 222: 'To have been snatched from the jaws of death is a matter for due and devout gratitude to Providence; yet to have been so snatched without other belongings than the clothes on your back is an experience which may well damp down the first flames of thankfulness in the human breast . . .'

A Talk About Memoirs

Judith: I wonder – shall I give my bird a real beak or an orange one? Whatever they may say, silks have been ruined by the war. But what are you looking behind the curtain for? Ann: There is no gentleman present? Judith: None, unless you count the oil portrait of Uncle John. Ann: Oh, then, we can talk about the Greeks! There is not a single memoir in the whole of Greek literature. There! You can't contradict me; and so we go on to wonder how the ladies of the race spent the morning when it was wet and the hours between tea and dinner when it was dark. *Judith:* The mornings never are wet in Athens. Then they don't drink tea. They drink a red sweet stuff out of glasses, and eat lumps of Turkish delight with it. *Ann:* Ah, that explains! A dry, hot climate, no twilight, wine, and blue sky. In England the atmosphere is naturally aqueous, and as if there weren't enough outside, we drench ourselves with tea and coffee at least four times a day. It's atmosphere that makes English literature unlike any other – clouds, sunsets, fogs, exhalations, miasmas. And I believe that the element of water is supplied chiefly by the memoir writers. Look what great swollen books they are! (She lifts five volumes in her hands, one after another.) Dropsical. Still, there are times – I suppose it's the lack of wine in my blood – when the mere thought of a classic is repulsive. *Judith:* I agree with you. The classics – oh dear, what was I going to say? – something very wise, I know. But I can't embroider a parrot and talk about Milton in the same breath. *Ann:* Whereas you could embroider a parrot and talk about Lady Georgiana Peel?[2] *Judith:* Precisely. Do tell me about Lady Georgiana Peel and the rest. Those are the books I love. *Ann:* I do more than love them; I reverence them as the parents and begetters of our race. And if I knew Mr Lytton Strachey,[3] I'd tell him what I think of him for behaving disrespectfully to the great English art of biography. My dear Judith, I had a vision last night of a widow with a taper setting fire to a basketful of memoirs – half a million words – two volumes – stout – blue – with a crest – genealogical trees – family portraits – all complete. 'Art be damned!' I cried, and woke in a frenzy. *Judith:* Well, I fancy she heard you. But let's begin on Lady Georgiana Peel. *Ann:* Lady Georgiana Peel was born in the year 1836, and was the daughter of Lord John Russell. The Russells are said to be descended from Thor, the God of Thunder; their more direct ancestor being one Henri de Rozel, who, in the eleventh century[4] – *Judith:* We'll take their word for it. *Ann:* Very well. But don't forget it. The Russells are cold in temperament, contradictious by nature. Ahem! Lord and Lady John were resting under an oak tree in Richmond Park when Lord John remarked how pleasant it would be to live in that white house behind the palings for the rest of their lives. No sooner said than the owner falls ill and dies. The Queen, with that unfailing insight, etc., sends for Lord John, etc., and offers him the lodge for life, etc., etc., etc. I mean they lived happily ever after, though as time went by, a factory chimney somewhat spoilt the view.[5] *Judith:* And Lady Georgiana? *Ann:*

Well, there's not much about Lady Georgiana. She saw the Queen having her hair brushed, and she went to stay at Woburn. And what d'you think they did there? They threw mutton chops out of the window 'for whoever cared to pick them up.' And each guest had a piece of paper by his plate 'in which to wrap up an eatable for the people waiting outside'.[6] *Judith:* Mutton chops! people waiting outside! *Ann:* Ah, now the charm begins to work. A snowy Christmas – imagine a fair-haired little girl at the window – early in the forties the scene is – frost on the ground – a mutton chop descending. Don't you see all the arms going up and the poor wretches trampling the flower-beds in their struggles? But, 'I think,' she says, 'the custom died out.'[7] And then she married, and her husband's riding was the pride of the county; and when he won a race he gave something to the village church. But I don't know that there's much more to be said. *Judith:* Please go on. The charm is working; I'm not asleep; I'm in the drawing room at Woburn in the forties. *Ann:* Lady Georgiana being, as I told you, descended from the God of Thunder, is not one to take liberties with life. The scene is a little empty. There's Charles Dickens[8] wearing a pink shirt front embroidered with white; the Russell mausoleum in the background; sailors with icicles hanging from their whiskers; the Grosvenor boys shooting snipe in Belgrave Square;[9] Lord John handing the Queen down to dinner – and so forth. Let's consult Mr Bridges. He may help us to fill it in. 'Our mothers were modelled as closely as might be on the example of the Great Queen . . . If they were not always either beautiful or wise they gained love and respect everywhere without being either . . . But, whatever happens, women will still be women and men men.'[10] Shall I go on skipping? *Judith:* I seem to gather that the wallpapers were dark and the sideboards substantial. *Ann:* Yes, but we've too much furniture already. Life is what we want. (She turns over the pages of several volumes without saying anything.) *Judith:* Oh, Ann; it's fearfully dull at Woburn in the forties. Moreover, my parrot is turning into a sacred fowl. I shall be presenting him to the village church next. Is no one coming to call? *Ann:* Wait a moment. I fancy I see Miss Dempster approaching. *Judith:* Quick; let me look at her picture. A devout, confidential lady – Bedchamber woman to Queen Victoria, I should guess.[11] I can fancy her murmuring: 'Poor, poor Princess'; or, 'Dearest Lady Charlotte has had a sad loss in the death of her favourite gillie,' as she extracts from the Royal Head a sleek tortoiseshell pin and lays it reverently in the golden tray. By the way, can you imagine Queen Victoria's hair? I can't. *Ann:* Lady Georgiana says it was 'long and fair'.[12] Be that as it may, Miss

Dempster had nothing to do with her hair-pins — save that, I think it likely her daydreams took that direction. She was a penniless lass with a long pedigree; Scotch, of course, moving in the best society — 'one of the Shropshire Corbets who (through the Leycesters) is a cousin of Dean Stanley'[13] – that's her way of describing people; and for my part I find it very descriptive. But wait — here's a scene that promises well. Imagine the terrace of the Blythswoods' villa at Cannes. An eclipse of the moon is taking place; the Emperor Dom Pedro of Portugal[14] has his eye fixed to the telescope; it is chilly, and a copper-coloured haze suffuses the sky. Meanwhile, Miss Dempster and the Prince of Hohenzollern walk up and down talking. What d'ye think they talk about? . . . 'we agreed that it had never occurred to us before that *somewhere* our Earth's shadow must be ever falling . . . Speaking of the dark and shadowed days of human life I quoted Mrs Browning's lines: "Think, the passing of a trial, To the nature most undone, Like the shadow on the dial, *Proves* the presence of the *sun*."'[15] You don't want to hear about the death of the Duke of Albany and his appearance in his coffin or the Emperor of Germany and his cancer? *Judith:* For Heaven's sake, no! *Ann:* Well, then, we must shut up Miss Dempster. But isn't it queer how Lady Georgiana and the rest have made us feel like naughty, dirty, mischievous children? I don't altogether enjoy the feeling, and yet there is something august in their unyielding authority. They have fronts of brass; not a doubt or a desire disturbs them outwardly; and so they proceed over a world which for us is alternately a desert or a flowering wilderness stuck about with burning bushes and mocking macaws, as if it were Piccadilly or the Cromwell Road at three o'clock in the afternoon, I detect passions and pieties and convictions all dumb and deep sunk which serve them for a kind of spiritual petrol. What, my dear Judith, have we got in its place? *Judith:* If, like me, you'd been sitting in the drawing room at Woburn for the past fifty years, you would be feeling a little stiff. Did they never amuse themselves? Was death their only amusement, and rank their sole romance? *Ann:* There were horses. I see your eyes turned with longing to Dorothea Conyers and John Porter. Now you can get up and come to the stables. Now, I assure you, things are going to hum a little. In both these books we get what I own was somewhat disguised in the others — a passion for life. I confess that I like John Porter's view of life better than Dorothea Conyers', though, from the lips of a novelist, there is charm in her reflection: 'Unfortunately, I shall never be a popular short-story writer: I do something just wrong';[16] one feels inclined to tell her to shorten her stirrups or have her fetlocks fired and see whether *that* wouldn't do the trick. But this cherry-cheeked elderly gentleman, this quintessence of all good coachmen and trusty servants, this lean old trainer with his shrewd little eyes, and the horseshoe tiepin and the look of integrity and service honestly performed, of devotion given and returned – I can't help feeling that he is the pick of the bunch. I like his assumption that the whole world exists for racing, or, as he is careful to put it, for 'the amelioration of the thoroughbred'.[17] I like the warmth with which he praises his horses for holding their own on the course and begetting fine children at the stud. 'I thought the world of him,' he says of Isonomy, 'and his achievements as a sire strengthened my regard and admiration.'[18] 'That the horse I almost worshipped was afflicted with wind infirmity,' he says in another place, nearly killed him; and when Ormonde,[19] for he it was, proved incurable and went to Australia, John Porter plucked a few hairs from tail and mane to keep, doubtless in some inner pocket, 'as a memento of a great and noble creature'.[20] What character he detects in them, and how humanely he respects it! Madam Eglantyne must be humoured in her fancy to be delivered of her children under a tree in the park. Sir Joseph Hawley – not a racehorse, but the owner of racehorses – what a character – what a fine fellow he was! – 'a really great man . . . a noble friend to me and my family . . . stern, straight and fearless';[21] so John Porter writes of him, and when the Baronet for the last time left his cigar to waste on the mantelpiece, John Porter pocketed the ashes and has them now 'put carefully away'[22] in memory of his master. Then I like to read how Ormonde was born at half-past six on a Sunday evening, as the stable boys were going to Church, with a mane three inches long, and how always at the critical moment Fred Archer made a little movement in the saddle and 'lengthening his stride, Ormonde shot ahead, to win in a canter';[23] and how he was not only a giant among giants, but, like all magnanimous heroes, had the disposition of a lamb, and would eat cakes and carnations out of a Queen's hand. How splendid we should think it if it were written in Greek! Indeed, how Greek it all is! *Judith:* Are you sure there is nothing about the village church? *Ann:* Well, yes. John Porter did in token of gratitude add 'some suitable embellishments to the village church';[24] but, then (as there are no gentlemen present) so did the Greeks, and we think no worse of them for doing so. *Judith:* Perhaps. Anyhow, John Porter is the pick of the bunch. He enjoyed life; that's what the Victorians – but, go on – tell me how Orme was poisoned.[25]

1 – A signed review in the *New Statesman*, 6 March 1920, (Kp C186) of *Recollections of Lady Georgiana Peel*. Compiled by her daughter Ethel Peel (John Lane, 1920); *Victorian Recollections* (G. Bell & Sons Ltd. 1919) by J. A. Bridges; *The Manners of My Time* (Grant Richards Ltd, 1920) by C. L. Hawkins Dempster; *Sporting Reminiscences* (Methuen & Co. Ltd, 1920) by Dorothea Conyers; *John Porter of Kingsclere: An Autobiography* ... written in collaboration with Edward Moorhouse, author of 'The History and Romance of the Derby' (Grant Richards, 1919). Reprinted: *G&R, CE*.

2 – Lady Georgiana Adelaide Peel, daughter of Lord John Russell, 1st Earl Russell (1792–1878), statesman, Prime Minister, and Adelaide, *née* Lister (d. 1838), widow of the second Lord Ribblesdale. Lady Georgiana married Archibald Peel, son of Jonathan Peel (1799–1879), politician and patron of the turf. She was an aunt of the philosopher Bertrand Russell.

3 – (Giles) Lytton Strachey (1880–1932) whose *Eminent Victorians* had appeared in 1918 and whose *Queen Victoria* was to be published in 1921.

4 – For Thor and for Henri de Rozel – 'who in the eleventh century left his native village ... in Normandy, to follow the fortunes of William the Conqueror' – Peel, pt i, p. 1.

5 – The Russells' grace-and-favour house was Pembroke Lodge, Richmond Park.

6 – Peel, pt i, p. 20.

7 – *Ibid.*, which has: 'that custom'.

8 – Charles Dickens (1812–70).

9 – Peel, pt ii, p. 110.

10 – Bridges, ch. i, p. 13.

11 – C. L. Hawkins Dempster (1835–1913), author of *The Maritime Alps and their Seaboard* (1885) and a number of popular novels, including *Véra; or, The Russian Princess and the English Earl* (1871). Indeed, her photograph in the preliminary pages of *Manners* does bear some resemblance to Queen Victoria.

12 – Peel, pt i, p. 19; which has 'long fair hair'.

13 – Dempster, ch. xi, p. 142.

14 – *Ibid.*, ch. xv, p. 226, which has 'Emperor Dom Pedro of Brazil'.

15 – *Ibid.*, ch. xv, p. 227, quoting a letter, 11 February 1888, from Villa Rey, Cannes, to the author's uncle.

16 – Conyers, ch. iii, p. 57.

17 – Porter, 'Blue Gown's Derby', p. 125.

18 – *Ibid.*, 'Pageant and Isonomy', p. 187.

19 – For the quotation, 'The Career of Ormonde', p. 268: 'The idea that the horse I almost worshipped was afflicted with wind infirmity distressed me in a way I cannot describe. I hardly slept at all the following night.' Ormonde was sold to a party in Argentina, not Australia.

20 – *Ibid.*, p. 283.

21 – *Ibid.*, 'Turf Reform', p. 163 and p. 164; Sir Joseph Hawley, 3rd Bart (1813–75).

22 – *Ibid.*, p. 162, slightly adapted.

23 – *Ibid.*, 'The Career of Ormonde', p. 262.

24 – *Ibid.*, 'The Removal to Kingsclere', p. 109, adapted.

25 – For the poisoning episode, *ibid.*, 'Orme and la Flèche', pp. 339–42. Orme was about to be entered in the 1892 Two Thousand Guineas when he fell ill from what

was suspected to be mercurial poisoning. He recovered in time to win the Eclipse Stakes two or three months later.

Money and Love

Steep though the ascent may be, the reward is ours when we stand on the top of the hill; stout though the biography undoubtedly is, the prospect falls into shape directly we have found the connecting word. The diligent reader of memoirs seeks it on every page – never rests until he has found it. Is it love or ambition, commerce, religion, or sport? It may be none of these, but something deep sunk beneath the surface, scattered in fragments, disguised behind frippery. Whatever it be, wherever it be, once found there is no biography without its form, no figure without its force. Stumbling and blundering in the first volume of Mr Coleridge's life of Thomas Coutts, we laid hands at length upon two words which between them licked rather a portly subject into shape, doing their work, as might be expected from their opposite natures, first this side, then that, until what with a blow here and a blow there poor Thomas Coutts was almost buffeted to death. Yet the friction kept him alive; he lived, in an emaciated condition, to the age of eighty-six. And of the two words one is money and the other is love.

Love in the first place had it all its own way. He married his brother's servant, Susannah Starkie, a woman older than himself. If he had been a poor man the marriage would have been thought sensible enough and the wife, one may be sure, would have come in for a word of praise from the biographers. But as he was always a rich man, and became eventually the richest man in the whole of England, it was incumbent on Thomas Coutts to prove that the Starkies, though now declined, were descended from the ancient family of the Starkies of Leigh and Pennington, and it is inevitable that we should inquire whether Mrs Coutts broke her heart and lost her wits 'beneath the burden of an honour to which she was not born'.[2] There is no doubt that she lost her wits. Her heart, one must suppose, since no sound of its breakage has escaped, was smothered to death. She is scarcely mentioned. Perhaps she dropped her aitches. Perhaps it was as much as she could do to stand upright at the top of the staircase in Stratton Street and shake hands with the Royal Dukes without displaying her origin. She contrived never to give offence and never to attract attention; and, from a housemaid, what more could be expected? Save for one sinister gleam when she speaks a whole sentence in her proper person, it is all dark and dim and decorous. She had her children, it is true; of whom three daughters survived. But the children were heiresses, and must be sent to fashionable schools, where Mr Coutts, more ambitious for them than for himself, hinted his wish that they should make friends with the daughters of Lord George Sutton, 'as I should like them to be acquainted with honest people'.[3] They had a French Countess of the old nobility for their governess. From their birth onwards they were swathed and swaddled in money.

In his office in the Strand, year in, year out, Thomas Coutts made his fortune by methods which will be plain enough to some readers and must remain a matter of mystery to others. He was a hard-headed man of business; he was indefatigable; he 'knew how to be complaisant and how and when to assert his independence';[4] he was judicious in the floating of Government loans; and he lived within his means. We may accept Mr Coleridge's summary of his business career, and take his word for it that the rolling up of money went forward uneventfully enough. To the outsider there is a certain grimness in the spectacle. Who is master and who is slave? The two seem mixed in bitter conflict of some sort – such groans escape him now and then, and the lean, wire-drawn face, with the tight-closed lips and the anxious eyes, wears such an expression of nervous apprehension. Once, when he was driving with his old friend Colonel Crawfurd, he sat silent hour after hour, and the Colonel, reaching home, wrote in a fury to demand an explanation of 'this silent contempt', which in another would have demanded sword or pistol. 'It is too, too foolish', exclaimed poor Coutts; the truth was merely that 'my spirit's gone, and my mind worn and harras'd', and 'I am now rather an object of pity than resentment'.[5]

But whatever secret anguish compelled the richest man in England to drive hour after hour in silence, there were also amenities and privileges attached to his state which lightened the office gloom and tinged the ledgers with radiance. The reader becomes aware of a curious note in the tone in which his correspondents address him. There is an intimate, agonised strain in all their voices. His correspondents were some of the greatest people in the land; yet they wrote generally with their own hands, and often added the injunction: 'Burn this Letter the moment it is read' ⟨...⟩ 'Name it not to my Lord,' this particular document continues, 'or to any creature on earth.'[6] For royal as they were, beautiful, highly gifted, they were all in straits for money; all came to Thomas Coutts; all approached him as suppliants and sinners beseeching his help and confessing their follies as if he were something between doctor and priest. He heard from Lady Chatham the story of her distress when the payment of Chatham's pension was delayed; he bestowed £10,000 upon Charles James Fox, and earned his effusive gratitude; the Royal Dukes laid their sad circumstances before him; Georgiana, Duchess of Devonshire, confessed her gambling losses, called him her dear friend and died in his debt. Lady Hester Stanhope thundered and growled melodiously enough from the top of Mount Lebanon.[7] Naturally, then, Thomas Coutts had only to say what he wanted, and some very powerful people bestirred themselves to get it for him. He wanted introductions for his daughters among the French nobility; he wanted George the Fourth to bank with him;[8] he wanted the King's leave to drive his carriage through St James's Park. But he wanted some things that not even the Duchess of Devonshire could procure. He wanted health; he wanted a son-in-law.

There was, Mr Coleridge says, 'a singular dearth of suitors for his daughters and his ducats'.[9] Was it that Mrs Coutts had in her housemaid days thrown soapsuds over Lord Dundonald?[10] Or was it that the presence of madness in the Coutts family showed itself unmistakably in the frequent 'nervous complaints'[11] of the three sisters? At any rate, Sophia, the youngest, was nineteen when she became engaged to Francis Burdett;[12] and heiresses presumably should be wearing their coronets years before that. Then her two elder sisters pledged their affections suitably enough. But love always came among the Couttses wearing the mask of tragedy or comedy, or both together in grotesque combination. The two young men, thus singled out, against all advice and entreaty rushed the Falls of Schaffhausen in an open punt. Both were drowned.[13] Two years later Susan recovered sufficiently to marry Lord Guilford; and after mourning for seven years Fanny accepted Lord Bute; but Lord Bute was a widower of fifty-six with nine children, and Lord Guilford fell from his horse 'when in the act of presenting a basket of fruit to Miss Coutts',[14] and so injured his spine that he languished in bodily suffering for years before, prematurely, he died.

But from all those impressions and turns of phrase which, more than any statement of facts, shape life in biographies as they do in reality, we are convinced that Thomas Coutts loved his daughters intensely and sincerely, pitying their sufferings, devising pleasures and comforts for them, and sometimes, perhaps, wishing to be assured that when all was said and done they were happy, which, upon the same evidence, it is easy to guess that they were not. Even in these days Sir Francis Burdett caused his father-in-law some anxiety. The following extract hints the reason of it:

Going to Piccadilly yesterday at two o'clock, I met Mr Burdett. . . . I asked him where he was going . . . I asked him if he had been under any engagement to Mr Whitefoord, upon which, to do him justice, he blushed – and, with great signs of astonishment, confessed that he had entirely forgot it, though he had particularly remembered it the day before . . . To us, *exact people*, these things seem strange.[15]

Probably Mr Coutts was not altogether surprised to find that a man who was capable of forgetting an engagement could defy the House of Commons, stand a siege in his house, be taken forth by Life Guards through a crowd shouting 'Burdett for ever!' and suffer imprisonment in the Tower.[16] Later, Coutts had to insist that his son-in-law should leave his house; but on that occasion our sympathies are with the banker. Like most people, Sir Francis lost his temper, his manners, his humanity, and everything decent about him when he was in danger of losing a legacy. But for the present the legacies were secure, and the surface of life was splendid and serene. Mr and Mrs Coutts lived in the great house in Stratton Street; they travelled from one fine country seat to another, the guests of a Duke here, of an Earl there; their wealth increased and increased, and Thomas Coutts was consulted upon delicate matters by Prime Ministers and Kings. He acted as ambassador between the House of Hanover and the House of Stuart – almost equally to his delight, he transmitted winter petticoats from Paris to Devonshire House.

But the splendid surface had deep cracks in it, and when William the Fourth dined with the Couttses, Mrs Coutts – so he declared, would always whisper to him on the way downstairs, "'Sir, are you not George the Third's *father*? "I always answered in the affirmative," ⟨said the King⟩, "there's no use contradicting, women, young or old, eh?"'[17] She was losing her wits. For the last ten years of her life she was out of her mind. But old Coutts would have her lead the King down to dinner, and would tend her faithfully himself when doctors and daughters besought him to put her under control. He was a devoted husband.

At the same time he was a devoted lover. During the ten years that Mrs Coutts was going from bad to worse and being tenderly cared for by her husband, he was lavishing horses, carriages, villas, sums in the 'Long Annuities', upon a young actress in Little Russell Street.[18] The paradox has disturbed his biographers. Leaving to others the task of determining how far the relation between the old banker and the young woman was immoral, we must admit that we like him all the better for it; more, it seems to prove that he loved his wife. For the first time he hears the birds at dawn and notices the spring leaves. Like his Harriot, birds and leaves seem to him innocent and fresh.

You who can look to Heaven with so much pleasure and so pure a heart must have great pleasure in viewing such beautiful skies . . .[19] eat light nourishing food – mutton roast and broiled is the best – [. . .] porter is not good for you . . .[20] I kiss the paper you are to look upon and beg you to kiss it just here. Your dear lips will then have touched what mine touch just now . . . The estate of Otham, you see, I have enquired about. Your 3 p. ct. Consol and Long Annuity . . .[21]

So it goes on from birds to flannel night-caps, from eternal devotion to profitable investments; but the strain that links together all these diverse notes is his recurring and constant adoration for Harriot's 'pure, innocent, honest, kind, affectionate heart'.[22] It was a terrible blow to his daughters and sons-in-law to find that at his age he was capable of entertaining such illusions. When it came out that, four days after Mrs Coutts was buried, the old gentleman of seventy-nine had hurried off to St Pancras Church and married himself (illegally, as it turned out, by one of those misadventures which always beset the Coutts family when they were in love) to an actress of no birth and robust physique, the lamentations that rent the family in twain were bitter in the extreme. What would become of his money? As they could not ask this openly, they took the more roundabout way of 'imputing to the servants'[23] at Stratton Street that Mrs Coutts was poisoning her husband and was in the habit of receiving men in her bedroom when half-undressed. Coutts replied to his daughters and his sons-in-law in bitter, agitated letters which make painful, though spirited, reading after a hundred years. How they tortured him! How they grudged him his happiness! How grateful he would have been for a word of sympathy! Still, he had his Harriot, and though she was only gone into the next room, he must write her a letter to say how he loves her and trusts her and begs her not to mind the spiteful things that his family say about her. 'Your constant, happy, and most affectionate husband' he signs himself, and she invokes 'My beloved Tom!'[24] Indeed, Harriot deserved every penny she got, and we rejoice to think that she got them all. She was a generous woman. She was bountiful to her stepdaughters; she was always burying broken-down actors in luxury, and putting up marble tablets to their memories; and she married a Duke.[25] But every year of her life she drove down to Little Russell Street, got out of her carriage, dismissed her servants, and walked along the dirty lane to have a look at the house where she had begun life as 'a poor little player child'.[26] And once, long after Tom was dead, she dreamed of Tom, and noted on the flyleaf of her prayer-book how he had come to her looking 'well, tranquil, and divine. He anxiously desired me to change my shoes', which was, no doubt, true to the life; but in the dream it was 'for fear of taking cold, as I had walked through waters to him',[27] which somehow touches us as if Tom and Harriot had walked through bitter waters to rescue their little fragment of love from all that money.

1 – A signed review in the *Athenaeum*, 12 March 1920, (Kp C187) of *The Life of Thomas Coutts* [1735–1822]. *Banker. With numerous illustrations* (2 vols, John Lane, 1920) by Ernest Hartley Coleridge. Reprinted: *G&R, CE*.

2 – Coleridge, vol. i, ch. ii, p. 33, an unattributed quotation.

3 – *Ibid.*, ch. vii, letter xiii, Coutts to Colonel John Walkinshaw Crawfurd (1721–93), 7 August 1779, p. 121, which has: 'as they are a good race and I should'.

4 – *Ibid.*, vol. ii, ch. xxxii, p. 395, which has: 'by knowing how'.

5 – For Colonel Crawfurd's complaint, *ibid.*, vol. i, ch. xi, letter xxvi, to Coutts, 30 December 1786, p. 206: 'The silent contempt with which you treated me from yesterday morning, till you got into the coach in the afternoon, gives me more uneasiness than ever I felt in the course of a long life. The lie or a blow given, brings the affair to a speedy issue; and if it had been any person to whom I am under fewer obligations than to you, Sir, I should have demanded an immediate explanation.' For Coutts's reply, *ibid.*, letter xxvii, 31 December 1786, p. 207: 'My spirits gone, and my mind worn and harras'd by many vexations and "sick of many griefs", as Shakespeare makes Brutus say to Cassius, ¶ "with itself at war ¶ Forgets the due of rights to other men". ¶ I was, yesterday, and am now rather an object of pity than of resentment. I wished you as to coming here or staying in town, to do as you found it most agreeable to yourself. As it is now I should rather, I confess, wish to see you here – but not with sword and pistol. What can I say more! *It is too foolish.*'

6 – *Ibid.*, ch. ix, letter x, from Lady Mountstuart, 16 November 1782, pp. 153–4.

7 – For the correspondence between Coutts and Lady Chatham, *née* Lady Hester Grenville (d.1803), wife of William Pitt, 1st Earl Chatham (1708–78), see *ibid.*, vol. i, ch. vi, pp. 92–101. For Coutts's relations with Charles James Fox (1749–1806), to whom he advanced £10,000 in two instalments, in 1787 and 1788, with whom he was unacquainted and whose politics he did not share, *ibid.*, ch. xii. For his involvement with Georgiana, Duchess of Devonshire, *née* Spencer (1757–1806), *ibid.*, vol. ii, ch. xxiii; and for Lady Hester Stanhope (1776–1839), *ibid.*, ch. xxx.

8 – Which he did, as his father had done before him. George IV (1762–1830), reigned from 1820.

9 – Coleridge, vol. ii, ch. xvi, p. 2, which has: 'the singular'; Coutts's daughters: Susan (b.1771), Frances (b.1773), Sophia (b.1775).

10 – *Ibid.*, vol. i, ch. ii, p. 27: 'Nor is there any doubt that Susannah Starkie was servant to James Coutts . . . there is Lord Dundonald's statement in a letter to the *Morning Post* (25 March 1822), that in his youthful days he occasionally saw her in the nursery "washing some of the young lady's clothes", and that his "boyish tricks may have aggravated her to throw some of the soapsuds at him"'. Archibald, 9th Lord Dundonald (1749–1831).

11 – E.g., *ibid.*, vol. ii, ch. xvi, p. 9.

12—Sophia married Sir Francis Burdett in 1793 — see also n. 16 below.

13—The two young men concerned were George Samuel Browne, 8th Viscount Montague, and Charles Sedley Burdett, second son of Francis Burdett. See Coleridge, vol. ii, ch. xvi, pp. 32–3, quoting the *Gentleman's Magazine*, October 1793.

14—*Ibid.*, ch. xviii, p. 76, quoting the *Gentleman's Magazine*, April 1802, which has: 'when he was in the act'. Susan Coutts married George Augustus, 3rd Earl of Guilford, in 1796; Frances married John, 1st Marquis of Bute, in 1800.

15—*Ibid.*, ch. xix, letter xiii, Coutts to Caleb Whitefoord (1734–1810), wit and diplomatist, 1797, p. 100, which has: 'Mr Whitefoord!', 'and with great signs of astonishment confessed' and 'strange!'

16—For the quotation, *ibid.*, ch. xxvi, p. 266. Sir Francis Burdett (1770–1844), politician, friend of Horne Tooke and of Jeremy Bentham, an ardent and radical champion of reform, was, in 1820, fined £2,000 and imprisoned for three months, following certain unsubstantiated condemnations of the authorities he made in connection with the Peterloo Massacre of 16 August 1819.

17—*Ibid.*, ch. xxii, p. 183. This was when William IV (1765–1837), who reigned from 1830, was still Duke of Clarence; he was George III's third son.

18—Harriot Mellon (1777–1837), a comic actress discovered by Sheridan in a strolling company at Stratford in 1795 and engaged by him for Drury Lane, where she stayed until her marriage to Coutts in 1815 and subsequent retirement.

19—Coleridge, vol. ii, ch. xxvii, letter xiv, 25 June 1813, p. 301.

20—*Ibid.*, ch. xxiv, letter iv, 13 September 1807, p. 254.

21—*Ibid.*, letter iii, 31 August 1807, p. 252, which continues: 'if sold at present, would about buy it'.

22—*Ibid.*, letter iv, p. 254.

23—*Ibid.*, ch. xxix, p. 331: 'In an undated letter (1876 or 1877) Coutts accuses Lady Guilford of "imputing to the servants" (of Holly Lodge or Stratton Street) that their mistress was poisoning her father in bed, and that but half-dressed herself, she had brought two men with her to the bedroom.'

24—For the first quotation, *ibid.*, p. 342, slightly adapted, and for the second, *ibid.*, p. 340.

25—She married in June 1827 William Aubrey de Vere, 9th Duke of St Albans.

26—Coleridge, vol. ii, ch. xxxii, p. 398.

27—*Ibid.*, ch. xxxi, p. 366, which has 'through water'.

Men and Women

If you look at a large subject through the medium of a little book you see for the most part something of such vague and wavering outline that, though it may be a Greek gem, it may almost equally be a mountain or a bathing machine. But though Mlle Villard's book is small and her subject vast, her focus is so exact and her glass so clear that the outline

woman of the middle class has now some leisure, some education, and
some liberty to investigate the world in which she lives, it will not be in
this generation or in the next that she will have adjusted her position or
given a clear account of her powers. 'I have the feelings of a woman,'
says Bathsheba in Far from the Madding Crowd, 'but I have only the
language of men.'[6] From that dilemma arise infinite confusions and
complications. Energy has been liberated, but into what forms is it to
flow? To try the accepted forms, to discard the unfit, to create others
which are more fitting, is a task that must be accomplished before there
is freedom or achievement. Further, it is well to remember that woman
was not created for the first time in the year 1860. A large part of her
energy is already fully employed and highly developed. To pour such
surplus energy as there may be into new forms without wasting a drop is
the difficult problem which can only be solved by the simultaneous
evolution and emancipation of man.

1–A review in the TLS, 18 March 1920, (Kp C188) of La Femme Anglaise Au xix[e]
siècle et son Évolution d'après le roman anglais contemporain (Henri Didier, 1920)
by Léonie Villard. Reprinted: B&P.
2–Villard does not refer to the Shakespearean characters, or to Dora Spenlow, the
'child-wife' in Charles Dickens's David Copperfield (1849–50); she does make
repeated reference to Samuel Richardson's Clarissa Harlowe (and to Pamela
Andrews), to George Meredith's Diana Warwick, and to W. M. Thackeray's Helen
Pendennis.
3–The hero of Charlotte Brontë's Jane Eyre (1847).
4–Villard makes repeated reference to Jane Eyre (also to Shirley Keeldar) and to
George Borrow's Isopel Berners, heroine of Lavengro (1851) and The Romany Rye
(1858).
5–Villard, pt ii, 'La Libération de L'Energie Feminine', ch. i, p. 118; the ellipsis
marks the omission of: ', toutes les besognes domestiques, que, à la fin du xviii[e]
siècle, une maitresse de maison devait au moins diriger et surveiller,'.
6–Thomas Hardy, Far From the Madding Crowd (1874), ch. li (Macmillan, 1974,
p. 303): 'I don't know – at least, I cannot tell you. It is difficult for a woman to define
her feelings in language which is chiefly made by men to express theirs.' Villard
makes no reference to Hardy.

Freudian Fiction

Mr Beresford is always a conscientious writer, but in An Imperfect
Mother one cannot help feeling that conscience can at best play a
stepmother's part in the art of fiction. She can keep things neat and

orderly, see that no lies are told, and bring up her stepchildren to lead strenuous and self-respecting lives. But the joys of intimacy are not hers; there is something perfunctory in the relationship. In this case we hazard the opinion that, from the highest motives, Mr Beresford has acted the part of stepfather to some of the very numerous progeny of Dr Freud.[2] The chief characters, Cecilia, Stephen, and Margaret Weatherley, are his children and not Mr Beresford's. On page 12 there is certain proof of it:

Something within him had inarticulately protested against his conscientious endeavours to submit himself to the idea of this new ambition ... He had been harassed, too, by a persistent nightmare, quite new in his experience – a nightmare of being confined in some intolerably dark and restricted place from which he struggled desperately to break out. Sometimes he had succeeded, and waked with a beautiful sense of relief.[3]

After that one expects to find that Stephen is beginning, unconsciously, to fall in love with the schoolmaster's daughter; nor is one surprised to discover that he is the victim of an unacknowledged passion for his mother. It follows that she returns his affection in the inarticulate manner of those who lived before Freud, and, finding herself supplanted by Margaret Weatherley, decided to run away with Threlfall the organist. This is strictly in accordance with the new psychology, which in the sphere of medicine claims to have achieved positive results of great beneficence. A patient who has never heard a canary sing without falling down in a fit can now walk through an avenue of cages without a twinge of emotion since he has faced the fact that his mother kissed him in his cradle. The triumphs of science are beautifully positive. But for novelists the matter is much more complex; and should they, like Mr Beresford, possess a conscience, the question how far they should allow themselves to be influenced by the discoveries of the psychologists is by no means simple. Happily, that is their affair; our task in reviewing is comparatively easy, although we, too, are conscious of a division of mind which twenty or even ten years ago could hardly have afflicted our predecessors. Stated briefly, our dilemma resolves itself into this. Judged as an essay in morbid psychology, *An Imperfect Mother* is an interesting document; judged as a novel, it is a failure. All this talk, we find ourselves protesting when Mr Beresford in his able way describes Medboro', or the building of a factory, is irrelevant to the case. We cannot help adopting the professional manner of a doctor intent upon his diagnosis. A love scene interests us because something bearing significantly upon our patient's state of mind may emerge. Our attention is rewarded.

She laughed at his deliberation. 'You *are* a funny boy,' she chided him. 'One might think I was your mother' . . . The reference used as a simile finished Stephen. The obscure resistance that he had been fighting to overcome was no longer physical inertia; it had become a positive impulse.[4]

Yes, says the scientific side of the brain, that is interesting; that explains a great deal. No, says the artistic side of the brain, that is dull and has no human significance whatever. Snubbed and discouraged, the artist retreats; and before the end of the book the medical man is left in possession of the field; all the characters have become cases; and our diagnosis is now so assured that a boy of six has scarcely opened his lips before we detect in him unmistakable symptoms of the prevailing disease.

There remains the question whether we are not pandering to some obsolete superstition when we thus decree that certain revelations are of medical significance, others of human; that some are only fit for the columns of the *Lancet*, others for the pages of fiction. If it is true that our conduct in crucial moments is immensely influenced, if not decided, by some forgotten incident in childhood, then surely it is cowardice on the part of the novelist to persist in ascribing our behaviour to untrue causes. We must protest that we do not wish to debar Mr Beresford from making use of any key that seems to him to fit the human mind. Our complaint is rather that in *An Imperfect Mother* the new key is a patent key that opens every door. It simplifies rather than complicates, detracts rather than enriches. The door swings open briskly enough, but the apartment to which we are admitted is a bare little room with no outlook whatever. Partly, no doubt, this is to be attributed to the difficulty of adapting ourselves to any new interpretation of human character; but partly, we think, to the fact that, in the ardours of discovery, Mr Beresford has unduly stinted his people of flesh and blood. In becoming cases they have ceased to be individuals.

1 – A review in the *TLS*, 25 March 1920, (Kp C189) of *An Imperfect Mother* (W. Collins Sons & Co. Ltd, 1920) by J. D. [John Davys] Beresford (1873–1947), son of a Northamptonshire clergyman; he started his career in an architect's office and began in 1907 to write for the *Westminster Gazette*. As well as several novels, he also wrote a study of *H. G. Wells* (1915).

See also '*Revolution*' and 'Mr Bennett and Mrs Brown', n1, below. Reprinted: CW.

2 – Sigmund Freud (1856–1939), whose works The Hogarth Press began to publish in 1922.

3 – Beresford, ch. i, p. 12, which has 'experience, a nightmare' and 'succeeded and waked'.
4 – *Ibid.*, ch. iii, p. 135, which has: 'One might think I was your mother. I'm not quite old enough for that, you know. I'm only just twenty-eight'; and 'That reference'.

'The Letters of Henry James'

Who, on stepping from the cathedral dusk, the growl and boom of the organ still in the ears, and the eyes still shaded to observe better whatever intricacy of carving or richness of marble may there be concealed, can breast the stir of the street and instantly and briskly sum up and deliver his impressions? How discriminate, how formulate? How, Henry James may be heard grimly asking, dare you pronounce any opinion whatever upon me? In the first place only by taking cover under some such figure as implies that, still dazed and well-nigh drowned, our gesture at the finish is more one of exclamation than of interpretation. To soothe and to inspirit there comes, a moment later, the consciousness that, although in the eyes of Henry James our attempt is foredoomed to failure, nevertheless his blessing is upon it. A renewal of life, on such terms as we can grant it, upon lips, in minds, here in London, here among English men and women, would receive from him the most generous acknowledgement; and with a royal complacency, he would admit that our activities could hardly be better employed. Nor are we left to grope without a guide. It would not be easy to find a difficult task better fulfilled than by Mr Percy Lubbock in his Introduction and connecting paragraphs. It seems to us, and this not only before reading the letters but more emphatically afterwards, that the lines of interpretation he lays down are the true ones. They end – as he is the first to declare – in the heart of darkness; but any understanding that we may have won of a difficult problem is at every point fortified and corrected by the help of his singularly thoughtful and intimate essay. His intervention is always illuminating.

It must be admitted that these remarks scarcely seem called for by anything specially abstruse in the first few chapters. If ever a young American proved himself capable of giving a clear and composed account of his experiences in Europe during the seventies of the last century that young American was Henry James. He recounts his seeings and doings, his dinings out and meetings, his country-house visits, like a guest too well-bred to show surprise even if he feels it. A 'cos-mopolitanised American', as he calls himself, was far more likely, it appears, to find things flat than to find them surprising;[2] to sink into the depths of English civilisation as if it were a soft feather bed inducing sleep and warmth and security rather than shocks and sensations. Henry James, of course, was much too busy recording impressions to fall asleep; it only appears that he never did anything, and never met anyone, in those early days, capable of rousing him beyond the gay and sprightly mood so easily and amusingly sustained in his letters home. Yet he went everywhere; he met everyone, as the sprinkling of famous names and great occasions abundantly testify. Let one fair specimen suffice:

Yesterday I dined with Lord Houghton – with Gladstone, Tennyson, Dr Schliemann (the excavator of old Mycenæ, &c.), and half a dozen other men of 'high culture'. I sat next but one to the Bard and heard most of his talk, which was all about port wine and tobacco; he seems to know much about them, and can drink a whole bottle of port at a sitting with no incommodity. He is very swarthy and scraggy, and strikes one at first as much less handsome than his photos: but gradually you see that it's a face of genius. He had I know not what simplicity, speaks with a strange rustic accent and seemed altogether like a creature of some primordial English stock, a thousand miles away from American manufacture. Behold me after dinner conversing affably with Mr Gladstone – not by my own seeking, but by the almost importunate affection of Lord H. But I was glad of a chance to feel the 'personality' of a great political leader – or as G. is now thought here even, I think, by his partisans, ex-leader. That of Gladstone is very fascinating – his urbanity extreme – his eye that of a man of genius – and his apparent self-surrender to what he is talking of, without a flaw. He made a great impression on me – greater than anyone I have seen here: though 'tis perhaps owing to my *naïveté*, and unfamiliarity with statesmen . . .[3]

And so to the Oxford and Cambridge boat race. The impression is well and brightly conveyed; what we miss, perhaps, is any body of resistance to the impression – any warrant for thinking – that the receiving mind is other than a stretched white sheet. The best comment upon that comes in his own words a few pages later. 'It is something to have learned how to write.'[4] If we look upon many of these early pages as experiments in the art of writing by one whose standard of taste exacts that small things must be done perfectly before big things are even attempted, we shall understand that their perfection is of the inexpressive kind that often precedes a late maturity. He is saying all that his means allow him to say. Moreover, he is saying it already, as most good letter writers learn to say it, not to an individual but to a chosen assembly. 'It is, indeed, I think, the very essence of a good letter to be shown,' he wrote; 'it is wasted if it is kept for *one* . . . I give you full leave to read mine aloud at your soirées!'[5]

Therefore, if we refrain from quotation, it is not that passages of the necessary quality are lacking. It is, rather, that while he writes charmingly, intelligently and adequately of this, that and the other, we begin by guessing and end by resenting the fact that his mind is elsewhere. It is not the dinner parties – a hundred and seven in one season – nor the ladies and gentlemen, nor even the Tennysons and the Gladstones that interest him primarily; the pageant passes before him: the impressions ceaselessly descend; and yet as we watch we also wait for the clue, the secret of it all. It is, indeed, clear that if he discharged the duties of his position with every appearance of equanimity the choice of the position itself was one of momentous importance, constantly requiring examination, and, with its promise of different possibilities, harassing his peace till the end of time. On what spot of the civilised globe was he to settle? His vibrations and vacillations in front of that problem suffer much in our report of them, but in the early days the case against America was simply that '. . . it takes an old civilisation to set a novelist in motion'.[6]

Next, Italy presented herself; but the seductions of 'the golden climate'[7] were fatal to work. Paris had obvious advantages, but the drawbacks were equally positive – 'I have seen almost nothing of the literary fraternity, and there are fifty reasons why I should not become intimate with them. I don't like their wares, and they don't like any others; and, besides, they are not *accueillants*'.[8] London exercised a continuous double pressure of attraction and repulsion to which finally he succumbed, to the extent of making his headquarters in the metropolis without shutting his eyes to her faults. 'I am attracted to London in spite of the long list of reasons why I should not be; I think it, on the whole, the best point of view in the world . . . But the question is interminable.'[9] When he wrote that he was thirty-seven; a mature age; an age at which the native growing confidently in his own soil is already putting forth whatever flower fate ordains and natural conditions allow. But Henry James had neither roots nor soil; he was of the tribe of wanderers and aliens; a winged visitant, ceaselessly circling and seeking, unattached, uncommitted, ranging hither and thither at his own free will, and only at length precariously settling and delicately inserting his proboscis in the thickset lusty blossoms of the old garden beds.

Here, then, we distinguish one of the strains, always to some extent present in the letters before us, from which they draw their unlikeness to any others in the language, and, indeed, bring us at times to doubt whether they are 'in the language' at all. If London is primarily a point of view, if the whole field of human activity is only a prospect and a pageant, then we cannot help asking, as the store of impressions heaps itself up, what is the aim of the spectator, what is the purpose of his hoard? A spectator, alert, aloof, endlessly interested, endlessly observant, Henry James undoubtedly was; but as obviously, though not so simply, the long drawn process of adjustment and preparation was from first to last controlled and manipulated by a purpose which, as the years went by, only dealt more powerfully and completely with the treasures of a more complex sensibility. Yet, when we look to find the purpose expressed, to see the material in the act of transmutation, we are met by silence, we are blindly waved outside. 'To write a series of good little tales I deem ample work for a life time [. . .] It's at least a relief to have arranged one's life time.'[10] The words are youthful, perhaps intentionally light; but few and frail as they are, they have almost alone to bear the burden built upon them, to answer the questions and quiet the suspicions of those who insist that a writer must have a mission and proclaim it aloud. Scarcely for a moment does Henry James talk of his writing; never for an instant is the thought of it absent from his mind. Thus, in the letters to Stevenson[11] abroad we hear behind everything else a brooding murmur of amazement and horror at the notion of living with savages. How, he seems to be asking himself, while on the surface all is admiration and affection, can he endure it – how could I write my books if I lived in Samoa with savages? All refers to his writing; all points in to that preoccupation. But so far as actual statement goes the books might have sprung as silently and spontaneously as daffodils in spring. No notice is taken of their birth. Nor does it matter to him what people say. Their remarks are probably wide of the point, or if they have a passing truth they are uttered in unavoidable ignorance of the fact that each book is a step onward in a gradual process of evolution, the plan of which is known only to the author himself. He remains inscrutable, silent, and assured.

How, then, are we to explain the apparent inconsistency of his disappointment when, some years later, the failure of *The Bostonians* and *Princess Casamassima* brought him face to face with the fact that he was not destined to be a popular novelist –

. . . I am still staggering ⟨he wrote⟩ a good deal under the mysterious and to me inexplicable injury wrought – apparently – upon my situation by my two last novels, the *Bostonians* and the *Princess*, from which I expected so much and derived so little. They have reduced the desire, and the demand, for my productions to zero – as I judge from the fact that though I have for a good while past been writing a number of good short things, I remain irremediably unpublished.[12]

Compensations at once suggested themselves; he was 'really in better form than ever' and found himself 'holding the "critical world" at large in singular contempt';[13] but we have Mr Lubbock's authority for supposing that it was chiefly a desire to retrieve the failure of the novels that led him to strive so strenuously, and in the end so disastrously, for success upon the stage. Success and failure upon the lips of a man who never for a moment doubted the authenticity of his genius or for a second lowered his standard of the artist's duty have not their ordinary meaning. Perhaps we may hold that failure in the sense that Henry James used it meant, more than anything, failure on the part of the public to receive. That was the public's fault, but that did not lessen the catastrophe or make less desirable the vision of an order of things where the public gratefully and with understanding accepts at the artists' hands what is, after all, the finest essence, transmuted and returned, of the public itself. When *Guy Domville* failed, and Henry James for one 'abominable quarter of an hour' faced the 'yelling barbarians' and 'learned what could be the savagery of their disappointment that one wasn't perfectly the *same* as everything else they had ever seen'[14] he had no doubts of his genius, but he went home to reflect:

I have felt for a long time past that I have fallen upon evil days – every sign and symbol of one's being in the least wanted, anywhere or by anyone, having so utterly failed. A new generation, that I know not, and mainly prize not, has taken universal possession.[15]

The public henceforward appeared to him, so far as it appeared at all, a barbarian crowd incapable of taking in their rude paws the beauty and delicacy that he had to offer. More and more was he confirmed in his conviction that an artist can neither live with the public, write for it, nor seek his material in the midst of it. A select group, representative of civilisation, had at the same time protested its devotion, but how far can one write for a select group? Is not genius itself restricted, or at least influenced in its very essence by the consciousness that its gifts are to the few, its concern with the few, and its revelation apparent only to scattered enthusiasts who may be the advance guard of the future or only a little band strayed from the high road and doomed to extinction while civilisation marches irresistibly elsewhere? All this Henry James poised, pondered, and held in debate. No doubt the influence upon the direction of his work was profound. But for all that he went serenely forward; bought a house, bought a typewriter, shut himself up, surrounded himself with furniture of the right period, and was able at the critical moment by the timely, though rash, expenditure of a little capital to ensure that certain hideous new cottages did not deface his point of view. One admits to a momentary malice. The seclusion is so deliberate; the exclusion so complete. All within the sanctuary is so prosperous and smooth. No private responsibilities harassed him; no public duties claimed him; his health was excellent and his income, in spite of his protests to the contrary, more than adequate to his needs. The voice that issued from the hermitage might well speak calmly, subtly, of exquisite emotions, and yet now and then we are warned by something exacting and even acid in its tone that the effects of seclusion are not altogether benign. 'Yes. Ibsen is ugly, common, hard, prosaic, bottomlessly bourgeois . . .'[16] 'But, oh yes, dear Louis, ⟨Tess of the D'Urbervilles⟩ is vile. The pretence of "sexuality" is only equalled by the absence of it, and the abomination of the language by the author's reputation for style.'[17] The lack of 'æsthetic curiosity' in Meredith and his circle was highly to be deplored. The artist in him 'was nothing to the good citizen and liberalized bourgeois'.[18] The works of Tolstoy and Dostoevsky are 'fluid puddings', and 'when you ask me if I don't feel Dostoevsky's "mad jumble, that flings things down in a heap", nearer truth and beauty than the picking up and composing that you instance in Stevenson, I reply with emphasis that I feel nothing of the sort.'[19] It is true that in order to keep these points at their sharpest one has had to brush aside a mass of qualification and explanation which make each the apex of a formidable body of criticism. It is only for a moment that the seclusion seems cloistered, and the feelings of an artist confounded with those of a dilettante.

Yet as that second flits across the mind, with the chill of a shadow brushing the waves, we realise what a catastrophe for all of us it would have been if the prolonged experiment, the struggle and the solitude of Henry James's life had ended in failure. Excuses could have been found both for him and for us. It is impossible, one might have said, for the artist not to compromise, or, if he persists in his allegiance, then, almost inevitably, he must live apart, for ever alien, slowly perishing in his isolation. The history of literature is strewn with examples of both disasters. When, therefore, almost perceptibly at a given moment, late in the story, something yields, something is overcome, something dark and dense glows in splendour, it is as if the beacon flamed bright on the hilltop; as if before our eyes the crown of long deferred completion and culmination swung slowly into place. Not columns but pages, and not pages but chapters, might be filled with comment and attempted analysis of this late and mighty flowering, this vindication, this crowded gathering together and superb welding into shape of all the separate strands, alien instincts, irreconcilable desires of the twofold nature. For, as we dimly perceive, here at last two warring forces have coalesced; here, by a prodigious effort of concentration, the field of human activity is brought into fresh focus, revealing new horizons, new landmarks, and new lights upon it of right and wrong.

But it is for the reader at leisure to delve in the rich material of the later letters and build up from it the complex figure of the artist in his completeness. If we choose two passages – one upon conduct, the other upon the gift of a leather dressing case – to represent Henry James in his later mood we purposely brush aside a thousand others which have innumerable good claims to be put in their place.

If there be a wisdom in not feeling – to the last throb – the great things that happen to us, it is a wisdom that I shall never either know or esteem. Let your soul live – it's the only life that isn't on the whole a sell ⟨. . .⟩[20]
That ⟨the dressing case⟩ is the grand fact of the situation – that is the tawny lion, portentous creature in my path. I can't get past him, I can't get round him, and on the other hand he stands glaring at me, refusing to give way and practically blocking all my future. I can't live with him, you see; because I can't live *up* to him. His claims, his pretensions, his dimensions, his assumptions and consumptions, above all the manner in which he causes every surrounding object (on my poor premises or within my poor range) to tell a dingy or deplorable tale – all this makes him the very scourge of my life, the very blot on my scutcheon. He doesn't regild that rusty metal – he simply takes up an attitude of gorgeous swagger, straight in front of all the rust and the rubbish, which makes me look as if I had stolen *somebody else's* (regarnished *blason*) and were trying to palm it off as my own . . . *He is out of the picture* – out of *mine*; and behold me condemned to live for ever with that canvas turned to the wall. Do you know what that means?[21]

And so on and so on. There, portentous and prodigious, we hear unmistakably the voice of Henry James. There, to our thinking, we have exploded in our ears the report of his enormous, sustained, increasing, and overwhelming love of life. It issues from whatever tortuous channels and dark tunnels like a flood at its fullest. There is nothing too little, too large, too remote, too queer for it not to flow round, float off and make its own. Nothing in the end has chilled or repressed him; everything has fed and filled him; the saturation is complete. The labours of the morning might be elaborate and austere. There remained an irrepressible fund of vitality which the flying hand at midnight addressed fully and affectionately to friend after friend, each sentence, from the whole fling of his person to the last snap of his fingers, firmly fashioned and throwing out at its swiftest well nigh incredible felicities of phrase.

The only difficulty, perhaps, was to find an envelope that would contain the bulky product, or any reason, when two sheets were blackened, for not filling a third. Truly, Lamb House was no sanctuary, but rather a 'small, crammed and wholly unlucrative hotel',[22] and the hermit no meagre solitary but a tough and even stoical man of the world, English in his humour, Johnsonian in his sanity, who lived every second with insatiable gusto and in the flux and fury of his impressions obeyed his own injunction to remain 'as solid and fixed and dense as you can'.[23] For to be as subtle as Henry James one must also be as robust; to enjoy his power of exquisite selection one must have 'lived and loved and cursed and floundered and enjoyed and suffered',[24] and, with the appetite of a giant, have swallowed the whole.

Yet, if he shared with magnanimity, if he enjoyed hugely, there remained something incommunicable, something reserved, as if, in the last resort, it was not to us that he turned, nor from us that he received, nor into our hands that he placed his offerings. There they stand, the many books, products of 'an inexhaustible sensibility',[25] all with the final seal upon them of artistic form, which, as it imposes its stamp, sets apart the object thus consecrated and makes it no longer part of ourselves. In this impersonality the maker himself desired to share – 'to take it,' as he said, 'wholly, exclusively with the pen (the style, the genius) and absolutely not at all with the person,' to be 'the mask without the face',[26] the alien in our midst, the worker who when his work is done turns even from that and reserves his confidence for the solitary hour, like that at midnight when, alone on the threshold of creation, Henry James speaks aloud to himself 'and the prospect clears and flushes, and my poor blest old genius pats me so admirably and lovingly on the back that I turn, I screw round, and bend my lips to passionately, in my gratitude, kiss its hands.'[27] So that is why, perhaps, as life swings and clangs, booms and reverberates, we have the sense of an altar of service, of sacrifice, to which, as we pass out, we bend the knee.

1–A review in the TLS, 8 April 1920, (Kp C190) of The Letters of Henry James [1843–1916] Selected and edited by Percy Lubbock (2 vols, Macmillan & Co. Ltd, 1920). See II VW Letters, nos. 1107 and 1126, and II VW Diary, 10 April 1920.

See also 'Within the Rim' above, and 'Henry James's Ghost Stories' (also 'On Rereading Novels') below; 'Mr Henry James's Latest Novel', I VW Essays; 'The Old

Order', '*The Method of Henry James*', *II VW Essays*. Reprinted: *DoM, CE*. Reading Notes (MHP, B 2).

2—*Letters*, vol. i, to Alice James, 15 September 1878, p. 64: 'But don't envy me too much; for the British country-house has at moments, for a cosmopolitanised American, an insuperable flatness.'

3—*Ibid.*, to William James, 29 March 1877, p. 53, which has: 'talking of, without a flaw'. Richard Monckton Milnes, 1st Baron Houghton (1809–85); W. E. Gladstone (1809–98); Alfred, Lord Tennyson (1809–92); Heinrich Schliemann (1822–90).

4—*Ibid.*, to the same, 14 November 1878, p. 66: 'I hold to this, strongly; and if I don't as yet seem to proceed upon it more, it is because, being "very artistic", I have a constant impulse to try experiments of form, in which I wish not to run the risk of wasting or gratuitously using big situations. But to these I am coming now. It is something to have learned how to write, and when I look round me and see how few people (doing my sort of work) know how (to my sense), I don't regret my step-by-step evolution.'

5—For the first quotation and the second up to the ellipsis, *ibid.*, to Grace Norton, 17 October 1882, p. 94, which has: 'of the very essence,' and for the remainder, *ibid.*, p. 95, which has 'read them aloud'.

6—*Ibid.*, to W. D. Howells, 31 January 1880, p. 72: 'I sympathize even less with your protest against the idea that it takes an old civilization to set a novelist in motion – a proposition that seems to me so true as to be a truism.'

7—*Ibid.*, to Grace Norton, 15 December 1877, p. 57, which has: 'that golden'.

8—*Ibid.*, to W. D. Howells, 28 May 1876, p. 49, which continues: 'Turgenev is worth the whole heap of them, and yet he himself swallows them down in a manner that excites my extreme wonder. But he is the most loveable of men and takes all things easily. He is so pure and strong a genius, that he doesn't need to be on the defensive as regards his opinions and enjoyments.'

9—For the quotation up to the ellipsis, *ibid.*, to Charles Eliot Norton, 13 November 1880, p. 74, which has: 'attached to London', and for the remainder, *ibid.*, p. 75, which continues: ', and idle into the bargain.'

10—*Ibid.*, to the same, 16 January 1871, p. 31; the ellipsis marks the omission of: 'I dream that my life-time shall have done it.'

11—Robert Louis Stevenson (1850–94).

12—*Letters*, vol. i, to W. D. Howells, 2 January 1888, p. 136, which has: 'and (to me) inexplicable'. *The Bostonians* and *The Princess Casamassima* were both published in 1886.

13—For the first quotation, *ibid.*, which has: 'than I have ever been'; and for the second, *ibid.*, p. 137, which has 'a singular'.

14—For the first two quotations, *ibid.*, to William James, 9 January 1895, p. 233, and for the last, *ibid.*, to the same, 2 February 1895. James's play *Guy Domville* had been produced at the St James's Theatre in January 1895, with George Alexander and Marion Terry in the leading roles.

15—*Ibid.*, to W. D. Howells, 22 January 1895, pp. 236–7, which has: 'I have felt, for a long time past, that' and 'in the least wanted'.

16—*Ibid.*, to Julian R. Sturgis, 1893, p. 217. Henrik Ibsen (1828–1906).

17—*Ibid.*, to Robert Louis Stevenson, 17 February 1893, p. 205. Thomas Hardy, *Tess of the D'Urbervilles, A Pure Woman* (1891).

18 – For the first quotation regarding George Meredith (1828–1909), *ibid.*, vol. ii, to Edmond Gosse, 13 October 1912, p. 263, and for the second, *ibid.*, to the same, 15 October 1912, p. 266.

19 – For the first quotation, *ibid.*, to Hugh Walpole, 19 May 1912, p. 246, and for the second, *ibid.*, p. 245. L. N. Tolstoy (1828–1910); Fyodor Dostoevsky (1821–81).

20 – *Ibid.*, vol. i, to A. C. Benson, 28 December 1896, p. 259.

21 – *Ibid.*, vol. ii, to Walter V. R. Berry, 8 February 1912, pp. 226–7, which continues: '– to have to give up going about at all, lest complications (of the most incalculable order) should ensue from its being seen what I go about with.'

22 – *Ibid.*, vol. i, to W. E. Norris, 17 September 1903, p. 434. James acquired the lease of Lamb House, Sussex, in 1897.

23 – *Ibid.*, to Grace Norton, 28 July 1883, p. 101: 'Only don't, I beseech you, *generalize* too much in these sympathies and tendernesses – remember that every life is a special problem which is not yours but another's, and content yourself with the terrible algebra of your own. Don't melt too much into the universe, but be as solid . . .'

24 – *Ibid.*, vol. ii, to Hugh Walpole, 21 August 1913, p. 335: 'We must know, as much as possible, in our beautiful art, yours and mine, what we are talking about – and the only way to know is to have lived . . .'

25 – *Ibid.*, to Henry Adams, 21 March 1914, p. 374: 'It's, I suppose because I am that queer monster, the artist, an obstinate finality, an inexhaustible sensibility.'

26 – For both quotations, the subject of which is Walter Pater (1839–94), *ibid.*, vol. i, to Edmund Gosse, 13 December 1894, p. 228, which has: 'i.e. to have taken it out all, wholly, exclusively' and: 'He is the mask without the face, and there isn't in his total superficies a tiny point of vantage for the newspaper to flap his wings on.'

27 – *Ibid.*, intro., p. xxi, Lubbock quoting James, source unidentified.

'The Higher Court'

Pioneers – a subscription performance – Sunday evening – the very name of the play – all conspire to colour one's preconceptions. We are not going to enjoy ourselves comfortably all over (that is the shade of it); we are going to be wrought into a sharp nervous point. How queer the Strand will look when we come out; how sharp and strange will be our contact with our fellows for the whole of Monday morning and a considerable part of the afternoon! In short, we are going to be scraped and harrowed and precipitated into some surprising outburst of bitterness against – probably the Divorce Laws. On the other hand, there is the new Bastardy Bill, and Dr Freud may very well have discovered something entirely new and completely devastating about children's toys.[2] What, when you come to think of it, is a Teddy bear?

These remarks are made to explain and to excuse the avidity with which, when the curtain went up upon a family breakfast table in West Kensington, we seized upon the fact that Idalia Pryce-Green was a Roman Catholic. Dr Foster's visit before breakfast, his proposal to Polly Pryce-Green, Polly's departure for Paris, the poverty, simplicity, pluck, and unworldliness of the Pryce-Green family were strewn, we felt, lightly upon a sinister concealment. Polly hints at it. 'Not in the whole of West Kensington could you find a nicer girl than my sister –' such, or nearly such, are her words. 'She saves us the price of a general servant and gives you the blouse off her back for the asking. But' – here she winks one eye and her brother Ethelbert whistles in a peculiar manner – 'strike her religion and you strike a stone.' The door opens and a policeman brings in a stretcher. A man has been run over by a motor-car. He is probably dead, looks like a tramp, is a stranger to all of them, but, as he gave the address of their flat before losing consciousness, will they allow him to stay? Of course, the Pryce-Greens do that. He is a stranger. It is Idalia who dwells upon that word symbolically, and as she does so the scales fall from our eyes. A play where the word 'stranger' is rolled upon the tongue with relish is not a play of intellect; it is a play of sentiment, as indeed we might have guessed directly Miss Mary Jerrold stepped upon the stage. There is no sinister concealment about her. In her paper bag she carries hot rolls for her sister's breakfast, and though we are told that she has been to early Mass, we have only to look at her to see that early Mass is a habit (perhaps the only habit this unselfish little creature allows herself) – a Spartan habit, like having a cold bath every morning all through the year. Inconvenient, perhaps a little ridiculous, but we are not going to be scraped and harrowed by Idalia's habits. Let her go to her Mass by all means.

Once this is realised, we settle down with some relief to enjoy the story, for a play of sentiment must provide something for people to feel about, and thus, in addition to feelings, which are always interesting, we have a plot which is invariably exciting, so that, though we have not the space to say it, there is much to be said in favour of the play of sentiment.

It is true that the plot was unravelled in the stalls before the first act was over. It was bruited abroad that the stranger was a millionaire, and it was added that the crisis would hinge upon the conflict between love and religion. But then the stalls, presumably, know more about million-aires than West Kensington does, and the Pryce-Greens, one cannot help thinking, were innocent even for West Kensington. 'Why, you don't mean to say that you've been in a taxi!' was one of Idalia's exclamations, and as for a cheque-book – what is a cheque-book? But then the millionaire was also an extreme case of Park Lane. He was, perhaps plausibly, ignorant of the existence of weekly bills, but his sight had been so deranged by his mansion that the bare, dingy flat never ceased, when he limped in from his bedroom, to look to him 'somehow beautiful'. 'You see, I have never had a home.' At this point, and it was made fairly often, he would suppress manly emotion by means of that odd catch in the throat which no woman can hear without wishing that it were still the fashion to carry fans. Need one write it all out? If we refrain it is partly that it went better on the stage than it can possibly do in print. It was not merely the efficiency of the acting. (Both Miss Jerrold and Mr Randle Ayrton gave the impression that they are in the habit of carrying far heavier burdens than these.) Nor was it solely that Miss Young, when she took her eyes off her plot, gave a shrewd glance at her characters which promised better things in future. What shone forth from all the obvious and the inane was that it is impossible to be bored by a play as one is bored by a novel. One saw what was coming, one could not altogether approve of the way it came, but one did not wish to leave the theatre until it was certain that Idalia Pryce-Green had married her millionaire. The only obstacle ahead was the religious obstacle, and that, on our theory, would be overcome when Idalia realised that the habit of taking a cold bath before breakfast was nothing more than a habit. She realised it, if anything, too easily. She gave way. She agreed to a mixed marriage with the millionaire, and in the same breath or the very next, she wanted to know for certain that he had eaten a good dinner. Was that all? Well, at any rate, Idalia was happy, and one does not expect the intellect to put up much resistance in the fourth act of a play of sentiment. But wait – they were still talking. 'She's *divorced* – not dead,' said the millionaire. 'Surely you understood that?' But Idalia had not understood it, and from her expression it was evident that it would take her at least five minutes to understand it. She would, of course, win through, and the curtain would come down rather more conclusively than we had expected upon the defeat of Roman Catholicism by love. But the curtain wavered. The millionaire wavered. We all wavered. Could it be possible? Could she be going to haggle over this? She could. The door slammed – not tragically, but with irritation. He was gone. 'Good heavens! So you do care more for your cold baths than for millionaires. Well, one had hoped better things of you.' That is what we said as we trooped into the Strand, irritated and baffled, and feeling that, though it were to save our lives, nothing would have induced Idalia Pryce-Green to walk under a ladder.

1 – A signed dramatic review in the *NS*, 17 April 1920, (Kp C191) of *The Higher Court* by M. E. M. Young in a production by the Pioneer Players at the Strand Theatre, on the evening of Sunday, 11 April 1920. M. E. M. Young was also the author of *A War Pilgrimage* (1917), reprinted from the *Month*, in *Collected Publications of the Catholic Truth Society*. Her play was published in 1931, with no reference to its having been performed. VW's precise quotations are not to be found in the published version, which may or may not have been revised, and are apparently, and if so, understandably, summary in nature. No cast list has been traced.

2 – A motion to reform the Divorce Law was defeated in the House of Commons by 134 votes to 91 on 14 April 1920. The provisions of the Illegitimate Children Bill were reported in *The Times*, 10 April 1920. The allusion to Sigmund Freud (1856–1939) remains unelucidated.

An Imperfect Lady

Little is known of Sappho, and that little is not wholly to her credit. Lady Jane Grey has merit, but is undeniably obscure. Of George Sand the more we know the less we approve. George Eliot was led into evil ways which not all her philosophy can excuse. The Brontës, however highly we rate their genius, lacked that indefinable something which marks the lady; Harriet Martineau was an atheist; Mrs Browning was a married woman; Jane Austen, Fanny Burney, and Maria Edgeworth have been done already;[2] so that, what with one thing and another, Mary Russell Mitford is the only woman left. This is no vain parade of erudition; we are trying to find out what considerations had weight with Miss Hill when she decided to write *Mary Russell Mitford and Her Surroundings*. Two emerge from the rest and may be held of paramount importance. In the first place, Miss Mitford was a lady; in the second, she was born in the year 1787.

There is no need to labour the extreme importance of the date when we see the word 'surroundings' on the back of a book. Surroundings, as they are called, are invariably eighteenth-century surroundings. When we come, as of course we do, to that phrase which relates how 'as we looked upon the steps leading down from the upper room, we fancied we saw the tiny figure jumping from step to step',[3] it would be the grossest outrage upon our sensibilities to be told that those steps were Athenian, Elizabethan, or Parisian. They were, of course, eighteenth-century steps, leading down from the old panelled room into the shady garden, where, tradition has it, William Pitt played marbles,[4] or, if we like to be bold, where on still summer days we can almost fancy that we hear the drums of Bonaparte on the coast of France. Bonaparte is the limit of the imagination on one side, as Monmouth[5] is on the other; it would be fatal if the imagination took to toying with Prince Albert or sporting with King John. But fancy knows her place, and there is no need to labour the point that her place is the eighteenth century. The other point is more obscure. One must be a lady. Yet what that means, and whether we like what it means, may both be doubtful. If we say that Jane Austen was a lady and that Charlotte Brontë was not one, we do as much as need be done in the way of definition, and commit ourselves to neither side.

It is undoubtedly because of their reticence that Miss Hill is on the side of the ladies. They sigh things off and they smile things off, but they never seize the silver table by the legs or dash the teacups on the floor. It is in many ways a great convenience to have a subject who can be trusted to live a long life without once raising her voice. Sixteen years is a considerable stretch of time, but of a lady it is enough to say, 'Here Mary Mitford passed sixteen years of her life and here she got to know and love not only their own beautiful grounds but also every turn of the surrounding shady lanes.'[6] Her loves were vegetable, and her lanes were shady. Then, of course, she was educated at the school where Jane Austen and Mrs Sherwood[7] had been educated. She visited Lyme Regis, and there is mention of the Cobb. She saw London from the top of St Paul's, and London was much smaller then than it is now. She changed from one charming house to another, and several distinguished literary gentlemen paid her compliments and came to tea. When the dining-room ceiling fell down it did not fall on her head, and when she took a ticket in a lottery she did win the prize. If in the foregoing sentences there are any words of more than two syllables, it is our fault and not Miss Hill's; and to do that writer justice there are not many whole sentences in the book which are neither quoted from Miss Mitford nor supported by the authority of Mr Crissy.[8]

But how dangerous a thing is life! Can one be sure that anything not wholly made of mahogany will to the very end stand empty in the sun? Even cupboards have their secret springs, and when, inadvertently we are sure, Miss Hill touches this one, out, terrible to relate, topples a stout old gentleman. In plain English, Miss Mitford had a father. There is nothing actually improper in that. Many women have had fathers. But Miss Mitford's father was kept in a cupboard: that is to say, he was not a nice father. Miss Hill even goes so far as to conjecture that when 'an imposing procession of neighbours and friends' followed him to the grave, 'we cannot help thinking that this was more to show sympathy and respect for Miss Mitford than from special respect for him'.[9] Severe as the judgement is, the gluttonous, bibulous, amorous old man did something to deserve it. The less said about him the better. Only, if from your earliest childhood your father has gambled and speculated, first with your mother's fortune, then with your own, spent your earnings, driven you to earn more, and spent that too; if in old age he has lain upon a sofa and insisted that fresh air is bad for daughters, if, dying at length, he has left debts that can only be paid by selling everything you have or sponging upon the charity of friends – then even a lady sometimes raises her voice. Miss Mitford herself spoke out once. 'It was grief to go; there I had toiled and striven and tasted as deeply of bitter anxiety, of fear, and of hope as often falls to the lot of woman.'[10] What language for a lady to use! for a lady, too, who owns a teapot. There is a drawing of the teapot at the bottom of the page. But it is now of no avail; Miss Mitford has smashed it to smithereens. That is the worst of writing about ladies; they have fathers as well as teapots. On the other hand, some pieces of Dr Mitford's Wedgwood dinner service are still in existence, and a copy of Adam's Geography, which Mary won as a prize at school, is 'in our temporary possession'.[11] If there is nothing improper in the suggestion, might not the next book be devoted entirely to them?

1–A review in the TLS, 6 May 1920, (Kp C192) of Mary Russell Mitford [1787–1855] and Her Surroundings. With illustrations by Ellen G. Hill and reproductions of portraits (John Lane, 1920) by Constance Hill, incorporated in 'Miss Mitford', CR I. VW noted in her diary on Saturday, 8 May 1920; 'Massingham has postponed seeing L. [regarding the literary editorship of the Nation, see Appendix IV] which may mean that there's some obstacle. Thinking it over, I shouldn't be sorry if it fell through; for I cant help suspecting that work of this kind means more of a tie than any money – all the gold of Peru poured into my lap as Miss Mitford says – could repay. Besides, why should I slip the collar round his neck & myself spring free? Partly owing to Lytton, partly to the horror of writing 1, 2, 3, 4, reviews on end, 3 concerning Mitford too, I've been groaning & grumbling, & seeing myself caged, & all my desired ends – Jacob's Room that is – vanishing down avenues. But 1 review weekly won't hurt.'

See also 'A Good Daughter' and 'The Wrong Way of Reading' below; 'The Letters of Mary Russell Mitford', IV VW Essays; and 'Miss Mitford', IV VW Essays and CR I.

2–Sappho (born c. 612 BC), lyric poet, of Eresus and Mytilene in Lesbos, daughter of Scamandronymus and Cleis, author of nine books of poetry, of whose work only fragments survive. Lady Jane Grey (1637–54), daughter of the Earl of Dorset and Frances Brandon, a niece of Henry VIII, was nominally and reluctantly for nine days queen of England. George Sand (1804–76). George Eliot (1819–80). Charlotte (1816–55), Emily (1818–48) and Anne Brontë (1820–49). Harriet Martineau (1802–76). Elizabeth Barrett Browning (1806–61). Jane Austen (1775–1817). Fanny Burney (1752–1840). Maria Edgeworth (1767–1849).
3–Hill, ch. v, p. 37.
4–*Ibid.*, p. 30: 'This old porch had its special historical association, for here William Pitt [1759–1806] as a child used to play marbles when his father the great Lord Chatham [1708–78] rented the Great House [at Lyme Regis].'
5–*Ibid.*, p. 33: 'The Great House is full of traditions of past history, and its gloomy vaults and passages below ground must have witnessed many a tragic scene at the time of the Monmouth Rebellion [1685]' etc etc.
6–*Ibid.*, ch. xii, pp. 99–100, which continues: 'where the first violets and primroses were to be found, and delighted in the wide expanse of its neighbouring common gay with gorse and broom.'
7–*Ibid.*, ch. viii, p. 64, concerning the Abbey School 'for young ladies' at Reading, which in 1798 removed to London where it was attended by Miss Mitford. Mrs Mary Martha Sherwood, *née* Butt (1775–1851), author of popular books for children and young people.
8–J. Crissy published *The Works of M. R. Mitford, Prose and Verse* (1840).
9–Hill, ch. xxxvi, pp. 341–2, which has: 'We cannot'. Dr George Mitford (d. 1842) – 'clever, selfish, unprincipled, and extravagant, with an unhappy love of speculation and whist' (*DNB*) – who married an heiress, is estimated to have frittered away some £70,000 before finally becoming totally dependent upon his literary daughter.
10–*Ibid.*, ch. xxxvii, p. 358, which has: '"It was grief to go," she writes; "there I had toiled"'.
11–*Ibid.*, ch. ix, p. 72. Alexander Adam, *A Summary of Geography and History Both Ancient and Modern* (1794).

A Good Daughter

Chiefly by means of quotations Miss Hill here presents us with the portrait of an amiable and distinguished lady, who wrote *Rienzi* and *Our Village*, won £20,000 in a lottery, supported a spendthrift father, thought him 'the handsomest and cheerfullest of men',[2] and had presumably an infinity of feelings which are now only to be guessed at. We can scarcely go wrong if we suppose them to refer in about equal proportions to her father and to her money.

Dr Mitford[3] was one of those splendid and imaginative men who dominate plain daughters, believe themselves to be descended from one of William the Conqueror's knights, and muddle away their wives' fortunes and their daughters' earnings upon buying china, building mansions, and financing the schemes of French marquises. Mary, too, was romantic. If she had had her way she would have deserted the bluebells and the cowslips and written nothing but high tragedy. *Rienzi*, was a great success; but her father was her prime romance, and tragedy failed to support her father. It is amusing to reflect that the florid gentleman who spreads prosperously across the canvas was maintained for a number of years upon the loves of milkmaids and the frolics of greyhounds.[4]

Miss Mitford was kept hard at work describing *Our Village*. To be a popular writer in the year 1850 it was necessary to write well. The women writers, in particular, wrote very well. Presumably the ordeal of appearing in print was then so severe that no lady went through it without taking pains with her deportment. Jane Austen, moreover, had set the fashion. 'Of course, I shall copy as closely as I can Nature and Jane Austen,'[5] wrote Miss Mitford. The result is that Miss Mitford is still readable – well-preserved, as we say of some trim, hale, old spinster who has never been ravaged by passion or lost her figure in bearing children. That is her public appearance. In private she was evidently a sentimental, conservative, impulsive English lady with a deep respect for conventions, property, the classics, and the Church. '. . . as an establishment, the Church ought to remain; for to say nothing of the frightful precedent of sweeping away property, which would not stop there, the country would be overrun with fanatics.'[6] Even that is only her drawing-room appearance. For she had a little room to herself up in the roof, and there, alone – for Mrs Mitford was dead[7] and the doctor often engaged at cards – she did her accounts, waited for the door to slam, wrote about her greyhounds, and sighed pretty frequently. 'There I have toiled and striven and tasted as deeply of bitter anxiety, of fear, and of hope as often falls to the lot of woman.'[8]

When Lord Melbourne gave her a pension of £100 she exclaimed: 'Is not this very honourable to the kind feelings of our aristocracy?'[9] and thanked God that there would be a cushion for her father's white hairs so long as he lived. He lived to the year 1842. She survived him 13 years. But what is the use of scolding her now? It was none of his fault, she said; had all the gold of Peru been poured into her lap she would not have exchanged him for another. Life had been very pleasant; poetry very beautiful, and, as she lay dying, she observed that it is the small things that matter – sparrows, robins, and fine weather.

1 – A signed review in the *Daily Herald*, 26 May 1920, (Kp C192.1) of *Mary Russell Mitford* [1787–1855] *and Her Surroundings. With illustrations by Ellen G. Hill and reproductions of portraits* (John Lane, 1920) by Constance Hill. See also 'An Imperfect Lady' above, 'The Wrong Way of Reading' below; '*The Letters of Mary Russell Mitford*', *IV VW Essays*; and 'Miss Mitford', *IV VW Essays* and *CR 1*.
2 – Mitford, *Recollections of a Literary Life* (3 vols., Richard Bentley, 1852), vol. i, ch. i, p. 4, which omits 'the'. Mitford's poetical tragedy *Rienzi*, first produced at Drury Lane on 11 October 1828, was an immediate success; her similarly popular rural sketches, *Our Village* (1824–32), were originally serialised, from 1819, in the *Lady's Magazine*.
3 – For details of Miss Mitford's father George, see n9, 'A Perfect Lady', above.
4 – Followed in the *Daily Herald* by the sub-heading 'Nature and Jane Austen'.
5 – Hill, ch. xxiii, p. 207, writing to Sir William Elford, 19 February 1825; Jane Austen (1775–1817).
6 – *Ibid.*, ch. xxxvi, p. 340, writing to Rev. William Harness, 2 May 1834.
7 – Mrs Mary Mitford, *née* Russell (d.1830).
8 – Hill, ch. xxxvii, p. 358, which has: 'There I had'.
9 – *Ibid.*, ch. xxxvi, p. 336, to Emily Jephson, 31 May 1837; William Lamb, 2nd Viscount Melbourne (1779–1848), Whig prime minister, 1834, 1835–41.

An Old Novel

In the year 1854 Miss Charlotte Ogle, calling herself Ashford Owen, published her first novel, *A Lost Love*, which she wrote at the age of twenty-two, and which is now offered again to a later generation. Whether she ever wrote a second novel, as, considering that she died only two years ago at the age of eighty-six, she may well have done, we are unable to say. From internal evidence we should guess that *A Lost Love* was not only a first novel, but a solitary novel. If after sixty-six years we can still listen with sympathy to its frail melancholy note like that of some plaintive old organ in a back street, it is because it is saying with such unmistakable sincerity, 'I am unhappy.' When first novels say that and nothing more, they are often very interesting books, but they leave no successors. The stress of feeling which for the time shaped the world into a story dies out; and next year the world is merely a helter-skelter of daily life, and the girl who scribbled on half-sheets of notepaper her passionate version of it now declares that there is nothing left to write about.

One can fancy that Miss Ogle was a little surprised at herself about the year 1856. Wonder mingled with her surprise, for famous people sought her friendship and great men proclaimed her immortality. Yet all she had done had been to steal from the family party in the Northumberland parsonage and write a story about herself. It is not a very good story. Directly her characters step beyond the range of her little bull's-eye lantern of egotism they became queer and distorted, or faint and awkward. But this egotism, by which we mean being young and unhappy and bewildered and honest, is a startling illuminant, and may well have led Sir Henry Taylor, Mr Lecky, Sir Mountstuart Grant Duff,[2] and other distinguished gentlemen to say that they would have given all their tragedies, histories, and leading articles to have written the scene where Georgy Sandon says farewell for the last time to James Erskine. Whatever scene they may have chosen (and we have no authority for saying that they chose any), what they meant was that Miss Charlotte Ogle had a capacity for feeling that left them a little envious; and drew their tears. But where the Victorians cried in 1854 what do we do in 1920? That is one of the questions that we keep asking as we read, and perhaps the pleasure which is still to be had from *A Lost Love* largely consists in asking such questions, and taking the liberty to supply the answers.

Sir Henry Taylor, who admired the book greatly, probably saw nothing fantastic in James Erskine, and could understand perfectly why Georgy Sandon loved him so passionately. The fascinations of the charming Mrs Everett exercised some sway over him. He thought that there was no alternative for a girl who had lost her lover but to marry the man she had already rejected. When she died in childbed he was profoundly moved, but could not doubt that she had done the right thing. If it is only by imagining Sir Henry Taylor's pleasure that we get any pleasure, it can scarcely be said that our pleasure is pure. On the other hand, where Sir Henry read on without raising his eyebrows, we not only read but re-read, and yield at times to the temptation of reading aloud. 'Georgy was on a sofa, in the corner, busily working at a large parrot . . .[3] Her tears fell fast, and still she did not cease her playing . . . She knew his footstep without turning her head, and she stopped. "Do you keep your beautiful playing a secret, dear lady?" he asked, and leaned over the pianoforte. There was a sense of mastery somehow expressed in those low, quiet words that could not have been felt better if he had called her by her name.'[4] Sentences like these, with all that they conjure up of chandeliers and fire-screens, give us much the same fanciful pleasure as Georgy's embroidered parrot would give us if we saw it in a curiosity shop today. But since in such unmistakable accents *A Lost Love* says 'I am unhappy,' these dusty draperies have not altogether smothered the wearer. Georgy Sandon was unhappy because she discovered that James Erskine loved Constance Everett. Miss Ogle was unhappy because she was young. Being young and unhappy, she felt and can make us feel that the world is not commonplace. It is, rather, shocking and terrible. Things that are said casually in the drawing room make her go upstairs, lean her head against the window-pane, and ask herself, 'What can be the meaning of this?' And as she looks out of the window the 'fine sycamore trees'[5] in the darkness and the sound of the waves on the beach not far off mix with her thoughts and are there to this day in her writing. But when she had written it all down it did not seem to represent her feelings in the least, as Georgy Sandon explained to James Erskine when they talked about first novels. 'Writing is very pleasant, but no one can say all they think and feel through it ... not even in that wondrous bit of aspiring egotism – a first book.' James Erskine kindly reassured her, and said, 'If we know everything we should see, I dare say, that some books are costly to their writers.'[6] *A Lost Love* has that quality – it was costly to its writer. We know that this clergyman's daughter had read all the books in her father's study. Through the frail body of *A Lost Love* we see distinctly, to our amusement and even instruction, the skeleton of the traditional form. We should not see it so distinctly in a work of genius, and that is why it is much more easy to trace the course of literature in the little books than in the great.

1–A review in the *TLS*, 27 May 1920, (Kp C193) of *A Lost Love* ... With a Foreword by the author and a Personal Note by Frances M. Charlton (1855; 3rd ed., John Murray, 1920) by Ashford Owen, pseudonym for Charlotte Ogle (1832–1918), eldest daughter of Rev. Edward Ogle and his wife and cousin, Sophia, daughter of Sir Charles Ogle, Bart.
2–Owen, 'Personal Note', p. xiv. Sir Henry Taylor (1800–86), verse dramatist. William Edward Hartpole Lecky (1838–1903), historian and essayist. Sir Mountstuart Elphinstone Grant Duff (1829–1906), statesman and author.
3–*Ibid.*, ch. iv, p. 20.
4–*Ibid.*, ch. v, p. 29.
5–Neither quotation occurs in Owen, although the book contains several references to sycamore trees.

6–For the first quotation, *ibid.*, ch. xiii, p. 118, and for the second, p. 119, both slightly adapted.

The Wrong Way of Reading

Speaking truthfully, *Mary Russell Mitford and Her Surroundings* is not a good book. It neither enlarges the mind nor purifies the heart. There is nothing in it about Prime Ministers and not very much about Miss Mitford. Yet, as one is setting out to speak the truth, one must own that there are certain books which can be read without the mind and without the heart, but still with considerable enjoyment. To come to the point, the great merit of these scrapbooks, for they can scarcely be called biographies, is that they license mendacity. One cannot believe what Miss Hill says about Miss Mitford, and thus one is free to invent Miss Mitford for oneself. Not for a second do we accuse Miss Hill of telling lies. That infirmity is entirely ours. For example: 'Alresford was the birthplace of one who loved nature as few have loved her, and whose writings "breathe the air of the hayfields and the scent of the hawthorn boughs", and seem to waft to us "the sweet breezes that blow over ripened cornfields and daisied meadows".'[2] It is perfectly true that Miss Mitford was born at Alresford, and yet, when it is put like that, we doubt whether she was ever born at all. Indeed she was, says Miss Hill; she was born 'on the 16th December, 1787'. 'A pleasant house in truth it was', Miss Mitford writes. 'The breakfast-room . . . was a lofty and spacious apartment'.[3] So Miss Mitford was born in the breakfast room about eight-thirty on a snowy morning between the Doctor's second and third cups of tea. 'Pardon me,' said Mrs Mitford,[4] turning a little pale, but not omitting to add the right quantity of cream to her husband's tea, 'I feel . . .' That is the way in which Mendacity begins. There is something plausible and even ingenious in her approaches. The touch about the cream, for instance, might be called historical, for it is well known that when Mary won £20,000 in the Irish lottery, the Doctor spent it all upon Wedgwood china, the winning number being stamped upon the soup plates in the middle of an Irish harp, the whole being surmounted by the Mitford arms, and encircled by the motto of Sir John Bertram, one of William the Conqueror's knights, from whom the Mitfords claimed descent. 'Observe,' says Mendacity, 'with what an air the Doctor drinks his tea, and how she, poor lady, contrives to curtsey as she leaves the room.' Tea? I inquire, for the Doctor, though a fine figure of a man, is already purple and profuse, and foams like a crimson cock over the frill of his fine laced shirt. 'Since the ladies have left the room,' Mendacity begins, and goes on to make up a pack of lies with the sole object of proving that Dr Mitford kept a mistress in the purlieus of Reading and paid her money on the pretence that he was investing it in a new method of lighting and heating houses invented by the Marquis de Chavannes.[5] It came to the same thing in the end – to the King's Bench Prison, that is to say; but instead of allowing us to recall the literary and historical associations of the place, Mendacity wanders off to the window and distracts us again by the platitudinous remark that it is still snowing. There is something very charming in an ancient snowstorm. The weather has varied almost as much in the course of generations as mankind. The snow of those days was more formally shaped and a good deal softer than the snow of ours, just as an eighteenth-century cow was no more like our cows than she was like the florid and fiery cows of Elizabethan pastures. Sufficient attention has scarcely been paid to this aspect of literature, which, it cannot be denied, has its importance. The snow falls heavily. The Portsmouth mail coach has already lost its way; several ships have foundered, and Margate pier has been totally destroyed. At Hatfield Peverel twenty sheep have been buried, and though one supports itself by gnawing wurzels which it has found near it, there is grave reason to fear the French King's coach has been blocked on the road to Colchester. It is now the 16th of February, 1808.

Poor Mrs Mitford! Twenty-one years ago she left the breakfast-room, and no news has yet been received of her child. Even Mendacity is a little ashamed of itself, and, picking up *Mary Russell Mitford and Her Surroundings*, announces that everything will come all right if we possess ourselves in patience. The French King's coach was on its way to Bocking; at Bocking lived Lord and Lady Charles Murray-Aynsley; and Lord Charles was shy. Lord Charles had always been shy. Once, when Mary Mitford was five years old – sixteen years, that is, before the sheep were lost and the French King went to Bocking – Mary 'threw him into an agony of blushing by running up to his chair in mistake for my papa'. He had indeed to leave the room. Miss Hill, who, somewhat strangely, finds the society of Lord and Lady Charles pleasant, does not wish to quit it without 'introducing an incident in connection with them which took place in the month of February, 1808'.[6] But is Miss Mitford concerned in it? To some extent; that is to say, Lady Charles was a cousin of the Mitfords; and Lord Charles was shy. Mendacity is quite ready to deal with the 'incident' even on these terms, but we have had enough of trifling. Miss Mitford may not be a great woman; for all we know she was not even a good one; but we have certain responsibilities as a reviewer which we are not going to evade.

A sense of the beauty of nature has never been altogether absent from English literature; yet no one can deny that the difference between Pope and Wordsworth in this respect is very considerable. *Lyrical Ballads* was published in 1798; Miss Mitford's *Our Village* first saw the light in 1824.[7] One being in verse and the other in prose, it is not necessary to labour a comparison which contains, however, elements of justice. Like her great predecessor, Miss Mitford much preferred the country to the town; and thus perhaps it may not be inopportune to dwell for a moment upon the King of Saxony, Mary Anning, and the ichthyosaurus. Let alone the fact that Mary Anning and Mary Mitford had a Christian name in common, they are further connected by what can scarcely be called a fact, but may without hazard be called a probability. Mary Mitford was looking for fossils at Lyme Regis only fifteen years before Mary Anning found one. The King of Saxony visited Lyme in 1844, and, seeing the head of an ichthyosaurus in Mary Anning's window, asked her to drive to Pinny, and explore the rocks. While they were looking for fossils, an old woman seated herself in the King's coach – was she Mary Mitford? Truth compels us to say that she was not;[8] but there is no doubt that Mary Mitford often expressed a wish that she had known Mary Anning, and it is singularly unfortunate to have to state that she never did. In the year 1844 Mary Mitford was fifty-seven years of age, and so far what we know of her is curiously negative; she had not known Mary Anning, she had not found an ichthyosaurus, she had not been out in the snowstorm, and she had not seen the King of France.

But then, in justice to Miss Hill and her fellow-biographers, what do we know of people? Even in the case of our friends the deposit of certainty is all spun over by a myriad changing shades; what they are depends upon what we are; then there are marriage, separation, the taking of office, and the birth of children; in short, when we come to say what anyone is like we often find ourselves in Miss Hill's predicament without her excuse and merely reply that an anonymous old woman once sat in the King of Saxony's coach. If this is so with the living, what can we know about the dead? Surely we can only invent them, and the best biographers are those who have most inventive power, along with an affinity of temperament which easily transmits shocks of love and hatred. Therefore poor Miss Mitford – but how 'poor' Miss Mitford if we know nothing about her? The truth is, however vain, trifling, or insipid a biography may be, so long as it makes mention of man or woman, it never fails to stir vibrations of sympathy – account for it how one can. A phrase in a letter, a glance from a portrait, an old name on a tomb, and the mischief is done – we love or we hate. Admitting that the adjective is probably wrong, we go on: Poor Miss Mitford was poor from a variety of reasons. In the first place she was consumed by a passion for her father. Squat, broad, beetle-browed herself, she could never see him in his blue coat and buff waistcoat without feeling that she scarcely deserved to be his daughter. Mrs Mitford was entirely of the same way of thinking, only, as she was wont to say when the two women took counsel together, her case was worse than Mary's, for she had £3,000 which the Rev. William Harness[9] would not allow her to touch, and besides, Mary was so clever with her pen. 'If only we had a pony carriage,' she sighed, for they were now in a small cottage on the Reading Road, and all the china was sold or broken, 'I could take him for a drive and it might distract his mind'[10] – from dwelling upon schemes for lighting houses, she meant. Mary looked out of the window. As it happened, two dogs were fighting, a beggar-woman was sauntering down the road, and a tinker's cart stood in front of the wheelwright's shop. Seizing her pen, she dashed off a description of the scene, and once more won the prize. *Our Village* went into three editions immediately. 'My dear father and mother have been out in the pony cart three or four times already, to my great delight,' she wrote.[11] A pony cart seems a handsome return for looking out of the window, and yet if we consider what it must be like to sit at the same window, year in, year out, hoping that a dog may trip up an old woman, or that the cobbler's little girl may break the jug in which she is carrying him his beer in order that the Americans may rejoice in the simplicity of rural England, one feels that to smash the window, strangle the doctor, and hamstring all the ponies in Berkshire would, as they say in novels, be the work of a moment. Even Miss Mitford has been known to curse the leveret. Her own taste was for tragedy and the drama. She wanted to write about Rienzi, the friend of Petrarch; about Charles I, and Inez de Castro; but how write plays when your father is 'addicted to games of chance'?[12] Back to the sitting room went poor Miss Mitford. 'Not for all the gold of Peru would I exchange him for another!'[13] she exclaimed, however. For people had a way of pitying her; and that she could not stand.

So one word is by no means enough for Miss Mitford. There are thousands craving to be used of her. Again, consider all the scenes of which she is the centre. Which are we to choose? Her father lay decaying on the sofa. He would not let her leave the room. He slept at last. Putting her fingers to her lips, and undoing the latch without disturbing him, she stepped out on to the common. Her heart rose within her. So safe, so good, so holy it all seemed to her, and the air so sweet. There was a cuckoo and the church bell ringing for service. She thanked God for England. Then old Dr Mitford died. How kind people were – coming to the funeral from miles away! Then she made the acquaintance of Mr James Payn.[14] Then Keren-Happuch found a glow-worm in her bedroom. She was extremely fond of glow-worms. 'K. said that "now I could not go to them they came to me".'[15] Had they come in with the wild woodbine? She liked writing all this in a letter to a literary young man, and he liked to hear her talk of 'Keats, Wordsworth and myself'[16] all in the same breath. It was a little awkward when she got upon her father, as she was apt to do, and kindling and quivering said what a patriot, what a martyr he had been, when all the world knew – or did the world know? One never can tell. Anyhow, it was easy to lead her back to her books. Her walls were packed with them. They were strewn on the floor. She would denounce a bad book 'as though it were a thing of life'.[17] All sorts of books, all sorts of men she would discuss with vehemence, yet with sobriety. 'But then I suppose I am the least romantic person that ever wrote plays. Do write good English, Mr Payn, and for Heaven's sake, don't go and marry for love!'[18] That was one of the queer things about her, and her cottage was such a commonplace villa, too, standing right on the high road without a creeper to its face. Then, again, though she was undoubtedly dressed, no one could tell what she was dressed in; or know from looking at her as she lay on two chairs which was tiny Miss Mitford and which was rug, quilt, skirt, or dressing-gown. There was no mistaking her face, however – immensely broad, with a 'deep globular brow' and two such eyes as Charles Kingsley had never seen in an Englishwoman's head – glowing and glittering and yet 'perfectly honest the while'.[19] But now we must stop making up stories about Miss Mitford.

1 – A signed review in the *Athenaeum*, 28 May 1920, (Kp C194) of *Mary Russell Mitford* [1787–1855] *and Her Surroundings. With illustrations by Ellen G. Hill and reproductions of portraits* (John Lane, 1920) by Constance Hill, partially incorporated in 'Miss Mitford', *CR1* (see *IV VW Essays*). See also 'An Imperfect Lady' and 'A Good Daughter', above; and '*The Letters of Mary Russell Mitford*', *IV VW Essays*.

2 – Hill, ch. i, pp. 1–2; the source of the matter quoted by Hill has not been traced.

3 – For the first quotation, *ibid.*, p. 2, and for the remainder, *ibid.*, p. 3.

4 – Dr George Mitford (d.1842) and his wife Mary, *née* Russell (d.1830).

5 – For Dr Mitford and the Marquis, a French refugee, in whose scheme the doctor invested and lost £5,000, plus the cost of a subsequent, protracted lawsuit, Hill, ch. xvii, pp. 140–1.

6 – Louis XVIII (1755–1824), reigned from 1814–15. Lord Charles Murray Aynsley, Dean of Bocking, was a son of John Murray, 3rd Duke of Athol (1729–74) and Lady Charlotte; his wife was a first cousin of Dr Mitford. For the first quotation, *ibid.*, ch. iv, p. 28, and for the second, *ibid.*, ch. xiv, p. 110, which has: 'we should like to introduce'.

7 – Alexander Pope (1688–1744); William Wordsworth (1770–1850). Mitford's *Our Village* (1824–32) was originally serialised, from 1819, in the *Lady's Magazine*.

8 – Cf. Hill, ch. vi, pp. 44–6.

9 – For Rev. William Harness (1790–1869), editor and biographer of Shakespeare, and 'the only remnant' of the Mitford family property, of which he was a trustee, *ibid.*, ch. xix, pp. 158–9.

10 – This passage does not occur in Hill and its origin has not been discovered.

11 – Hill, ch. xxiii, adapted.

12 – *Ibid.*, ch. iv, p. 22; Mitford's poetical tragedy *Rienzi* (1828) was based on the life of Cola di Rienzi (1313?–54), the republican who briefly ruled Rome and was murdered in a popular uprising. Rienzi had met the poet Petrarch (1304–74) while visiting Avignon in 1343. For Mitford's other dramatic projects, *ibid.*, ch. xxvi, p. 238: 'Her play of Charles I, the subject of which was suggested to her by Macready, was condemned by the Licenser . . . *Inez de Castro*, was still more unfortunate, for after having been rehearsed three times at the Lyceum Theatre . . . it was suddenly withdrawn for some unknown reason'. Inez de Castro (d.1355), famous for her romantic love affair with Dom Pedro, heir to the Portuguese throne.

13 – *Ibid.*, ch. xvii, p. 140, letter to Dr Mitford, 5 July 1811, which has: 'I would not exchange my father, even though we toiled together for our daily bread, for any man on earth, though he could pour the gold of Peru into my lap'.

14 – James Payn (1830–98), novelist, whose *Some Literary Recollections* (Smith, Elder, & Co., 1884) is dedicated to Leslie Stephen, 'a critic blind to no literary merit save his own'.

15 – Payn, ch. iii, 'Miss Mitford', pp. 84–5, adapted; Mrs Karenhappuch Swetman was Mitford's maid.

16 – *Ibid.*, p. 86, quoting Mitford on the painter Benjamin Haydon (1786–1846): '"When I and Wordsworth and Keats [1795–1821], and many others my betters, first knew him, and were writing, as if in concert, sonnets to him", &c'.

17 – *Ibid.*, p. 82: 'There is hardly any work of merit of that time . . . which she does not discuss in these letters, and always with a vehemence of feeling and expression as though it were a thing of life'.

18 – For the first sentence, *ibid.*, p. 80; the second sentence appears to be VW's invention.

19 – For both quotations, *ibid.*, p. 79 n1; Charles Kingsley (1819–75).

Body and Brain

One might read the lives of all the Cabinet Ministers since the accession of Queen Victoria without realising that they had a body between them. To imagine any of the statues in Parliament Square running, climbing, or even in a state of nudity is not only impossible but also unseemly. The life, dignity, character of statesmen is centred in the head; the body is merely a stalk, smooth, black and inexpressive, whether attenuated or obese, at the end of which flowers a Gladstone, a Campbell-Bannerman, or a Chamberlain.[2] But you have only to look at a photograph of Theodore Roosevelt to see that he and his body are identical. The little round pugnacious head with the eyes screwed up as if charging an enemy is as much part of his body as a bull's head is part of his body. Decency requires that a man's body shall be cut off from his head by collar, frock coat and trousers, but even under that disguise we still see, without any sense of unseemliness, bones, muscles, and flesh.

As Mr Thayer remarks in the course of his witty and sensible biography, very little is yet known of the interaction between mind and body. The mind in biography as in sculpture is treated as a separate and superior organ attached to an instrument which is, happily, becoming obsolete. If Cabinet Ministers exercise their bodies for a few hours it is only in order to clarify their brains. But Roosevelt, though given by nature a sickly and asthmatic body which might have claimed the pampered life of a slave, always treated his body as a companion and equal. Indeed, his education until he left college was more the education of the body than of the mind. It was not until he had wrought a light weak frame into a tough thick body capable of immense endurance that his brain came into partnership. If he used his brain at all it was not to think about books but about animals. He was taken on a tour through Europe as a small boy, but what did he see? Only that there are flocks of aquatic birds on the banks of the Nile, and that in Cairo there is a book by an English clergyman that tells you a great deal about them. In Venice he wrote in his diary, 'We saw a palace of the doges. It looks like a palace you could be comfortable and snug in (which is not usual).' 'The poor boys have been dragged off to the orful picture galery'[3] wrote his little sister. Roosevelt had no artistic sense either as a boy or man, so that we are not able to consider the effect upon an artist of owning a body. But directly the body and mind came into partnership it was plain that for political purposes no combination is more powerful.

American politics in the 'eighties appear to an English reader as a rough-and-tumble shindy of public-house loafers in which the only serviceable weapon is a strong right arm. When Roosevelt said on leaving college 'I am going to try to help the cause of better government in New York; I don't exactly know how,' his ambition seemed to his friends 'almost comic'. Politics were not for 'gentlemen'.[4] Jake Hess, the Republican Boss, and his heelers were equally amused. What business had a youth of the 'kid glove and silk stocking set' among such as them? After a little experience of him they owned that he was 'a good fellow' – 'a good mixer'.[5] Both friends and enemies were wont to expatiate upon his luck. Directly Roosevelt was safely shelved for life as Vice-President, President McKinley was shot dead.[6] The greatest prize in the United States fell into his hands without an effort. That was the sort of thing that always happened to Roosevelt. But it is impossible to feel that his progress had anything accidental about it. Fortune, indeed, showed herself quite ready to suppress him had he been made of suppressible material. The year 1883 found him out of politics, alienated from many of his best friends, and bereaved of his wife. Intellectually and emotionally he was disillusioned and disheartened. Then flooded in to his rescue that strange passion for using muscles and breathing fresh air and throwing oneself naked upon nature and seeing what happens next which cannot be called intellectual but which is certainly not merely animal. He became a ranchman. His companions were uncivilised; his duties were those of a primitive man. He lived with horses and cattle and at any moment might have to shoot or be shot. The same thing happened with the desperadoes of Little Missouri as had happened with Boss Hess and his heelers. They began by despising his spectacles and ended by thinking him the same kind of man as themselves. When he was President of the United States a cowboy came up to him and said, '"Mr President, I have been in jail a year for killing a gentleman." "How did you do it?" asked the President, meaning to inquire as to the circumstances. "Thirty-eight on a forty-five frame," replied the man, thinking that the only interest the President had was that of a comrade who wanted to know with what kind of tool the trick was done.'[7] No other President, it is said, from Washington to Wilson would have drawn that answer.

Undoubtedly, it was not his fight against Trusts, or his action in ending the Russo-Japanese war,[8] or any other political faith of his that gave him his popularity so much as the fact that his development was not limited to the organs of the brain. He was a good mixer. We have seen the effect upon bosses and cowboys. Now let us go to the other extreme and see how the President affected a highly cultivated Frenchman, the ambassador, M. Jusserand. Desired by his government to sketch some account of the President's temperament, M. Jusserand sent a dispatch describing 'a promenade' in Washington. 'I arrived at the White House punctually in afternoon dress and silk hat . . . The President wore knickerbockers, thick boots and soft felt hat, much worn . . . On reaching the country, the President went pell-mell over the fields, following neither road nor path, always on, on, straight ahead! I was much winded, but I would not give in, nor ask him to slow up, because I had the honour of La Belle France at heart. At last we came to the bank of a stream, rather wide and too deep to be forded. I sighed relief . . . But judge of my horror when I saw the President unbutton his clothes and heard him say, "We had better strip, so as not to wet our things in the creek." Then I, too, for the honour of France, removed my apparel, everything except my lavender kid gloves. The President cast an inquiring look at these [. . .] but I quickly forestalled any remark by saying, "With your permission, Mr President, I will keep these on, otherwise it would be embarrassing if we should meet ladies."[9] And so we jumped into the water and swam across.' They came out on the other side firm friends. That is the result of taking off everything except one's lavender kid gloves.

It was the combination of brain and body that was remarkable – for neither, separately, excelled immensely those of other men. Was it not the essence of his teaching that almost any man can achieve great things by getting the utmost use out of 'the ordinary qualities that he shares with his fellows'?[10] Put an ordinary man under a microscope and you see President Roosevelt. Unfortunately, many shadows are needed even in the crudest snapshot. Directly you are conscious of being ordinary you cease to be ordinary. And, after all, can we call the President a perfect example of a successful man? Are we not conscious towards the end of his life of a lack of balance which destroys his value as a magnified specimen of the human race? The slaughter of animals played too large a part in his life. And why start exploring the Brazilian River of Doubt at the age of fifty-five?[11] Nature, outraged, sent him back with a fever in his bones from which he died years before his time. So difficult is it at this late stage of civilisation for one and the same person to have both body and brain.

1 – A review in the *NS*, 5 June 1920, (Kp C195) of *Theodore Roosevelt. An Intimate Biography* ... with illustrations (Constable & Co., 1919) by William Roscoe Thayer. VW had earlier written on Theodore Roosevelt (1858–1919), 25th President of the USA, 1901–9, in *'A Week in the White House'*, I *VW Essays*. Reprinted: *B&P*.

2 – W. E. Gladstone (1809–98), Liberal Prime Minister, 1868–74, 1880–5, 1886, 1892–4. Sir Henry Campbell-Bannerman (1836–1908), Liberal Prime Minister, 1905–8. Joseph Chamberlain (1836–1914), leader of the Liberal Unionists, 1891–1903.

3 – For the first quotation, Thayer, ch. i, p. 10, and for the second, *ibid.*, p. 9, which begins: 'I am so glad Mama has let me stay in the butiful hotel parlor while the poor boys ...'

4 – For the first quotation, *ibid.*, p. 21; for the second and third, *ibid.*, ch. ii, p. 27.

5 – Jacob Hess, Republican 'boss' of the 21st district of New York City. For the first two quotations, *ibid.*, p. 29: 'They probably marveled to see him so unlike what they believed a youth of the "kid-glove" and "silk-stocking" set would be, and they accepted him as a "good fellow"'; and for the last quotation, *ibid.*, p. 28, which has: 'a good "mixer"'.

6 – William McKinley (1843–1901), elected President in 1897, was shot on 6 September 1891 by Leon Czolgosz, an anarchist, and died some days later.

7 – *Ibid.*, ch. xvii, p. 278, quoting an anecdote of Roosevelt's Harvard classmate, Charles G. Washburn.

8 – Roosevelt had been an ardent champion of Trust Law reform and prosecuted abuses under the Sherman Anti-Trust Act of 1890. He played a mediating role in the Russo-Japanese War, 1904–5, and brought about its end with the Treaty of Portsmouth.

9 – Thayer, ch. xvii, pp. 262–3, which has: 'To my surprise, the President soon joined me in a tramping suit with knickerbockers ...' and 'honor of *La Belle France* in my heart'. Jean Jules Jusserand (1855–1932), ambassador to Washington (1902–15), befriended successive American presidents and considerably influenced Franco-American relations. He was a literary scholar and the author of several works, including a *Literary History of the English People* (1895) and *Shakespeare in France* (1898).

10 – *Ibid.*, ch. xx, p. 328: 'The average man who is successful – the average statesman, the average public servant, the average soldier, who wins what we call great success – is not a genius. He is a man who has merely the ordinary qualities that he shares with his fellows, but who has developed those ordinary qualities to a more than ordinary degree.'

11 – In 1914, Roosevelt and a party of twenty, including his son Kermit, undertook an expedition to central Brazil, intending to find and then to descend the Rio da Duvido to its juncture with the Madeira river, and thence on to the Amazon. The party succeeded, but not without Roosevelt and the others coming very close to death from starvation and disease.

'The Mills of the Gods'

Miss Elizabeth Robins must be used by this time to being told that she writes like a man. What the reviewers mean is that a page of her writing has the kind of bare brevity which marks the talk even of undergraduates. The idea may be commonplace, the knowledge superficial, but it stands unpalliated by superfluous phrases. For this aspect of her art there can be nothing but praise. If you miss a sentence you will not find that a slight variety of the same thing offers you another chance of understanding. You must read even the first story, which is the worst in the book, *The Mills of the Gods*, with attention. You will find yourself stopping to have another look at the fine hard fabric before passing on.

Therefore, one pays Miss Robins the compliment of formulating one's case against her; and what is our case against her? Only that she is a pre-war writer. At the end of each of the seven series one can pencil a date – any date between 1895 and 1910 will do; the date that is quite out of the question is the date 1920. It was between those years that old English houses were so very old; that strong men went gold digging in the Yukon, and Italian counts of satanic disposition lived upon the tops of mountains with beautiful wives. In those days there were suffrage raids, and butlers, and haunted houses.[2] Houses, indeed, played a very large part in life; and life itself was a great deal more at the mercy of coincidence and mystery than it is now. Life, in short, was somehow different. But that is not true. Life is precisely the same; and our charge against Miss Robins amounts simply to this – that, misled largely by her strong dramatic sense, she has backed certain human qualities which dropped out of the race and neglected others which are still running. So, at least, we define the queer sense we have after being impressed and interested – that all this happened a very long time ago. If there had not been a war we should not have felt this with anything like the same force. The war withered a generation before its time. Yet among the pre-war writers we do not know many who do their job with Miss Robins's efficiency, or give us the assurance, at all times so comfortable, that, although the story may be of no great concern, the mind behind it is exceptionally robust.

1–A review in the *TLS*, 17 June 1920, (Kp C196) of *The Mills of the Gods and Other Stories* (Thornton Butterworth Ltd, 1920) by Elizabeth Robins (1862–1952),

American actress and feminist, pioneer of Ibsen on the London stage, a friend of Leslie and Julia Stephen and, later, of the Woolfs themselves, who published her essay *Ibsen and the Actress* in 1928. Among her works are *The Magnetic North* (1904), *The Convert* (1907), *My Little Sister* (1913), and the autobiographical *Both Sides of the Curtain* (1940). See 'A Dark Lantern', *I VW Essays*.
2 – For the Yukon – whither Elizabeth Robins' brother once went (see *Raymond and I*, The Hogarth Press, 1956) –, Robins, 'Monica's Village', pp. 127–65. For the Italian Count – Renzo Bellucci, known as 'Satanuccio' – *ibid.*, the title story, pp. 195–280. For suffrage raids, *ibid.*, 'Under His Roof. A story of military suffrage', pp. 95–124. For the butler – old Massing – *ibid.*, 'The Derrington Ghost', pp. 51–91.

A Disillusioned Romantic

As it is impossible for any writer to remain stationary, a new book always sets the reader a new problem. When the new book comes late in the list of its author's works we must be ready to grasp some new development wrought out of the stuff of his old achievement. The worst compliment we could pay Mr Conrad would be to talk of *The Rescue* as if it were an attempt to rewrite *Lord Jim*[2] twenty years later. But in what direction can we expect Mr Conrad to develop? So we may ask with our finger upon the cover of the new book. It is a difficult question to answer. For Mr Conrad is a romantic writer. Romantic writers die young. It seems at least harder to preserve the romantic attitude to life against the pressure of continued experience than any other. The romantic writer will either cease to write, or his writing will undergo some violent change. It is true that Mr Conrad by the greatness of his talent and the good fortune that kept him on the high seas long after most men are tethered to two or three miles of pavement preserved his youthful beliefs far into maturity. By its artistic completeness Mr Conrad's work satisfied us of his unbroken good faith. Then, as one novel succeeded another, there were signs that the inevitable changes were taking place. He did not relinquish; there were no signs of disillusionment; but it seemed as if what had been before sufficient were now inadequate; and the perfection of the earlier books became broken and confused. There might be something in this to bewilder, but there was nothing to regret; and it could easily be held that in *Chance* and *Victory*[3] Mr Conrad was advancing, not in the sense of improving, but in the sense of attacking a problem that was different from those magnificently solved before. If Mr Conrad was ceasing to be romantic, was it not that he surveyed a wider range of human life and therefore attempted to express in his novels a more complicated philosophy? And now we have *The Rescue*.

The first part of the book is called by a name that might stand for much of Mr Conrad's work – 'The Man and the Brig'. The man and the brig – together they represent a noble and romantic conception of the passions and duties of mankind. The brig lies becalmed off one of the islands of the Eastern Archipelago. Her captain, Tom Lingard, a man of about thirty-five, is at once her master and her lover. 'To him she was always precious – like old love; always desirable – like a strange woman; always tender – like a mother; always faithful – like a favourite daughter of a man's heart.' Her qualities, 'speed, obedience, trustworthiness, endurance, beauty, capacity to do and to suffer',[4] inspire corresponding qualities in the man. You accept the fact of them lying there alone at sea with complete satisfaction as if apart from the external beauty there was a deep internal harmony which, however strained, must ultimately result in that concord with which a work of art dies upon the ear whether the event is tragic or joyous. Nowhere has Mr Conrad indicated more finely than in these opening chapters the outlines of what we have come to accept as his belief. The world rests upon a few very simple ideas, 'so simple that they must be as old as the hills'.[5] Lingard is another of those men of simple nature possessed by the greatness of an idea – a man 'ready for the obvious, no matter how startling, how terrible or menacing, yet defenceless as a child before the shadowy impulses of his own heart'.[6] He was romantic. It matters not how often Mr Conrad tells the story of the man and the brig. Out of the million stories that life offers the novelist, this one is founded upon truth. And it is only Mr Conrad who is able to tell it us.

But if the statement of the theme is extremely fine, we have to admit that the working out of the theme is puzzling; we cannot deny that we are left with a feeling of disappointment. Lingard has committed himself and his brig to espouse the cause of the Rajah Hassim and his sister Immada, to reinstate whom he has come in secret supplied with arms. But, before he is able to land, a rowing boat brings word that an English yacht has gone ashore on a sandbank nearby. Reluctantly he goes to her help. There, sitting on the deck, toying with a fan, he sees the beautiful Mrs Travers, the wife of a distinguished English politician travelling in pursuit of useful information. By her stands d'Alcacer, a man of the same world. Their world is altogether the opposite of Lingard's world. Nor could the men of that world have deflected him from his purpose for a moment. But the woman, beautiful, schooled in the training of civilisation, is at heart as passionate as Lingard himself. Unlike him, she has as yet found no object worthy of her passion. Her husband, 'enthusiastically devoted to the nursing of his own career', has ceased to inspire any feeling whatever; and her days went by 'without a glimpse of sincerity or true passion, without a single true emotion – not even that of a great sorrow'.[7] Lingard appeared to her as a revelation not only of manhood, but of life itself. In him almost from the first moment she wakes the same ardour; she is the apotheosis of all that he has felt for his ship, for the natives who trust in him, and for their cause. What could be more romantic, one asks, than the encounter and union of two such natures? Yet here, at the moment when she wakes, when he tells her what he has told no one else, hesitation possesses us. Is it not beautifully told? Of course it is. Is there anything in man or woman, scene or setting, unworthy or jarring upon our senses? If anything, the setting is too flawless in its perfection and the characters too fixed in their nobility. Mr Conrad has never striven harder to heap up beauty of scene and romance of circumstance until the slightest movement tells like that of an actor upon the stage. Perhaps the reason of our hesitation is to be found in that sentence. In the earlier part of the book beauty has sprung naturally from the rightness of the central conception. Now beauty seems to be sought with effort, as though to bolster up some deficiency in the central idea. It is as if Mr Conrad's belief in romance had suddenly flagged and he had tried to revive it by artificial stimulants. Mrs Travers is clothed in beauty from head to foot. Sea, sky, and ship all emphasise the tremendous impressiveness of the spectacle. Mr Conrad describes her with phrase after phrase of noble and stately eloquence, yet as they accumulate it becomes more and more difficult to refer them to the feelings of a living person. The air is thick with romance like a thunderous sky, and we await almost with fear the lightning flash of passion which is to cleave the dark asunder. And then as the long story winds through the involutions of a complicated plot we give up expecting the lightning. Our disappointment centres in the relationship between Lingard and Mrs Travers. In him Mrs Travers was to have found 'the naked truth of life and passion buried under the growth of centuries'.[8] The moment comes, but they cannot take advantage of it. It seems as if they had lived too long to believe implicitly in romance, and can only act their parts with dignity and do their best to conceal the disillusionment which is in their hearts. We are disillusioned also.

The story is both long and elaborate. It need scarcely be said that Mr Conrad provides out of his great riches all sorts of compensation for what we have called the central deficiency. If he were not Mr Conrad we should sink all cavil in wonder at the bounty of his gift. Here are scenes of the sea and of the land, portraits of savage chiefs and of English sailors, such as no one else can paint. But with Mr Conrad, as with all writers of first-rate power, we seek that which connects the beauty and brilliancy of detail – that central idea which, gathering the multiplicity of incidents together, produces upon our minds a final effect of unity. When Lingard parts from Mrs Travers and is left upon the sandbank alone by the grave of the faithful Jaffir, we should upon our showing be left with a conviction that admits no doubt. As it is, our frame of mind is uncomfortably ambiguous. True, the strength of Mrs Travers's instincts was impaired by civilisation. True, Lingard was drawn from the sphere where his virtues could have their full effect. And if it is tragedy that we demand what could be more tragic than that a man like Lingard should be betrayed and that a woman like Mrs Travers should have betrayed him? Simplicity has been undone by sophistication, and fidelity and endurance have not availed. The elements of tragedy are present in abundance. If they fail to strike one unmistakable impression upon us, it is, we think, because Mr Conrad has attempted a romantic theme and in the middle his belief in romance has failed him.

1–A review in the *TLS*, 1 July 1920, (Kp C197) of *The Rescue. A Romance of the Shallows* (J. M. Dent & Sons Ltd, 1920) by Joseph Conrad (1857–1924).
   'I was struggling, at this time [during a visit from the philosopher G. E. Moore]', VW confided in her diary on Wednesday, 23 June 1920, 'to say honestly that I don't think Conrad's last book a good one. I have said it. It is painful (a little) to find fault there, where almost solely, one respects. I cant help suspecting the truth to be that he never sees anyone who knows good writing from bad, & then being a foreigner, talking broken English, married to a lump of a wife, he withdraws more & more into what he once did well, only piles it on higher & higher, until what can one call it but stiff melodrama. I would not like to find The Rescue signed Virginia Woolf. But will anyone agree with this? – anyhow nothing shakes my opinion of a book – nothing – nothing. Only perhaps if its the book of a young person – or of a friend – no, even so, I think myself infallible.' On Tuesday, 6 July, she returned to her theme, but upon a slightly less confident note: 'And am I a critic? Take Conrad's book. We were at the first Athenaeum lunch – a long single file of insignificant brain workers eating bad courses. Katherine [Mansfield] was opposite, & I heard her enthusiastically praising this very book. At last, appealed to, I confessed my perversity, whereupon she hedged – so did I. But which is right? I still maintain that I'm the true seer, the one independent voice in a chorus of obedient sheep, since they praise unanimously.'
2–*Lord Jim* (1900).
3–*Chance* (1914); *Victory* (1915).

4 – For the first quotation, *The Rescue*, pt i, 'The Man and the Brig' p. 17, which has: 'the favourite daughter'; and for the second, p. 18, which concludes: '–all but life.'
5 – Conrad, *Some Reminiscences* (Eveleigh Nash, 1912), 'A Familiar Preface', p. 20.
6 – *The Rescue*, pt i, p. 17, which continues: '; what could have been the thoughts of such a man, when once surrendered to a dreamy mood, it is difficult to say.'
7 – For both quotations, *ibid.*, pt iii 'The Capture', p. 139.
8 – *Ibid.*, p. 152, which has: 'Mrs Travers found that Lingard was touching, because he could be understood. How simple was life, she reflected. She was frank with herself. She considered him apart from social organisation. She discovered he had no place in it. How delightful! Here was a human being and the naked truth of things was not so very far from her notwithstanding the growth of centuries.'

The Pursuit of Beauty

Among the advantages of having been born three or four centuries ago one cannot help including, perhaps wrongly, the advantage of having no past. The consciousness then was not impeded at every point by the knowledge of what had been said in that book, or painted on that canvas. In particular, writers like Mr Hergesheimer, whose sense of beauty is exceptionally lusty, would have gratified it more simply and fully than is likely to be possible again. Writing now with beauty as one's theme, how can one avoid taking as symbols of two different ideals two statues, both of extreme antiquity, one the grayish-green image of a squat Chinese god, the other the white figure of the Greek Victory? One would wish to avoid it, because symbols are, unfortunately, apt to impose themselves. Linda Condon and Dodge Pleydon both show signs of the mould. They would not have taken this shape, one feels, unless their maker had been deeply versed in book learning. But then, again, it is largely because Mr Hergesheimer is a sophisticated writer that he is an interesting writer. Let us never discourage the novelist from finding strange elements in the composition of modern life. And after all, though Queen Elizabeth was a model of vigour she was also a dirty old woman, dabbling her fingers in the gravy, and amenable, one supposes, to pains and pleasures only of the most direct kind.

The first years of Linda Condon's life were presided over by the green Chinese image with the expression of placid and sneering lust. Stella Condon, her mother, had long lived upon the benefactions of anonymous gentlemen in hotels – a sumptuous life, stuffed with eating and drinking and finery and debauchery. Mr Hergesheimer has no prudery about ugliness. It is the complement of his love of beauty. Plush bedrooms, cosmetics, strewn toilet tables and tumbled underlinen, all that makes the iridescence of decay, is truthfully rendered. More remarkable is his success in making us feel that Stella Condon was alive, even sensitive and warm-hearted, in the midst of the garbage. 'Always remember mamma telling you that the most expensive corsets are the cheapest in the end.'[2] Such was her life's philosophy, delivered in rather a thick voice, for she was 'mussed'[3] with drink, to her daughter of ten. But, nevertheless, she is the most sympathetic and most imaginative figure in the book. Linda, the daughter of this mother and of a vanished father, the son of old tradition and culture, is, rightly no doubt, denied the directness of her mother's appeal. She is anything but direct. Considering the variety and strangeness of the qualities that have been shredded into her, it would have been a rare triumph had she glowed with life.

But life, in the usual sense, is the quality purposely denied her, for is she not, mysteriously, beauty rather than life, the spirit rather than the body, at every turn inhibited from the common responses of the usual woman? It is her function to live in the statue and not in the children of her body. Her soul is preserved by the sculptor, Dodge Pleydon, in bronze, for it is through the man that she exists. When, in a belated attempt to feel the ordinary passions of humanity, she comes to live with him she realises that it is not her in the flesh but her in the spirit that he desires. Therefore she leaves him to cherish the beautiful body which, at any rate in the expression that he has given to it, is ultimately enough for her, too.

The story lends itself to fantastic treatment, for the freedom of which we find ourselves occasionally hungering. But Mr Hergesheimer keeps to the solid and the actual. The difficult experiment is hardly successful, though the failure is more marked in Dodge Pleydon than in Linda herself. One would have guessed him, were it not for the name on the title page, a woman's hero – large, brutal, brilliant, cherishing in a lacquer box a lost glove. The icy finger of theory has chilled him, so that one feels him not fantastic but unreal. That charge might be levelled against Linda herself also, but in a different sense. She is like one of those watches that are made too elaborately to be able to go. Yet, though we hold it the supreme merit of watches to be able to go, as Stella Condon goes, there is great pleasure to be had in these delicate mechanisms. They are well worth picking to pieces.

1 – A review in the *TLS*, 8 July 1920, (Kp C198) of *Linda Condon* (William Heinemann, 1920) by Joseph Hergesheimer (1880–1954); for biographical note see '*Java Head*', n1, above. See also '*Gold and Iron*' above, 'Pleasant Stories' below, and '*The Three Black Pennys*', II *VW Essays*. Reprinted: *CW*.
2 – Hergesheimer, ch. iii, p. 29.
3 – *Ibid.*, ch. xxi, p. 142: 'The insinuations of women, the bareness of their revelations, her mother returning unsteady and mussed from dinner, were unutterably disgusting.'

Pure English

Although readers seldom admit it, an irrational element enters into their liking and disliking for books as certainly as it enters their feelings for people. It would never do for a professional aesthete to leave it at that. It scarcely does for a private person. No sooner have we recovered from the shock of feeling anything than we find good reasons for having felt it. Nevertheless, at any rate where the ordinary reader is concerned, it is his feeling, and not the reasons he gives for his feeling, that is of interest. That is genuine; that is the root and motive of the greater part of our reading, the sap which causes books to go on budding from the tree.

Save for the introduction and appearance, both of high excellence, one due to Mr Brett-Smith the other to Mr Blackwell, *Gammer Gurton's Needle* [sic] had for us little preliminary charm. We will not deny that some old books are better than any new ones, but we will also confess that curled in the heart of the world's greatest masterpieces we have come upon cankers of the most repulsive description. Age alone is no guarantee of excellence. Indeed, when one considers how much of our pleasure in literature springs, probably wrongly, from our instant identification of our own feelings with those expressed, and how seldom it is that a sixteenth-century poet says much to the point about the soul of a twentieth-century journalist it will be agreed that one source of pleasure is almost certainly dried up. Then again one is probably justified in assuming that what is 'held to be the first comedy in our language'[2] owes its perpetuation to curiosity rather than to sensibility. It is a mummy and not a living being, a footprint which has somehow escaped the natural obliteration of time. For such reasons, or prejudices, our greeting to Gammer Gurton may have been respectful, but was certainly lacking in warmth.

But who shall trace how it is that coldness yields to curiosity, and curiosity to warmth, or satisfactorily define what constitutes that relationship between book and reader? For the essence of it is instinctive rather than rational. It is personal, complex, as much composed of the reader's temperament perhaps as of the writer's. To make a clean breast of it, hour and season and mood, the day's brightness or the moment's despondency, all weigh down the scales. With such impressionable instruments are we provided; of such unstable elements are our judgements compounded. No wonder that a second reading often reverses the verdict of a first. One particular reader then, upon a particular occasion, read *Gammer Gurton's Needle* with pleasure. Perhaps one had better say no more about it. After, however, receiving that impression, which momentarily overlays all others, the unplaiting process automatically begins. One wishes to explain to oneself this warm, jovial, contented emotion; to justify it by proving it well founded. 'Warm, jovial, contented' – these three adjectives after a moment's reflection prompt the idea that we enjoy *Gammer Gurton's Needle* because it is typically English. A Frenchman could only enjoy such a play by an effort. To us it comes straightforwardly, like thinking to oneself.

> Many a myle haue I walked, diuers and sundry waies
> And many a good mãs house haue I bin at in my daies
> Many a gossip's cup in my time haue I tasted,
> And many a broche and spyt haue I both turned and basted.[3]

Not by reading but by nature one understands Diccon, the rascally tramp who never knows where he will sleep the night, and filches the bacon and sets the good women by the ears. When one says that one understands him one means that he is thoroughly congenial. This approbation, which may well be a subtle form of self-approbation, applies to Hodge and the Gammer, to Dame Chat and Dr Rat. It applies, more vaguely, to the old village and the muddy fields. The scene is rude enough; the humour of the characters simple, but what an energy there is in it! With what a swing and directness it goes! The spelling trips us now and then, but that is the only obstacle, and a trifling one, to our enjoyment. The story rattles itself off without a hitch. As Gammer Gurton sits mending Hodge's breeches she saw [sic] Gyb the cat half inside the milk pan.

> Ah hore, out thefe, she cryed aloud, and swapt the breches downe,
> Up went her staffe, and out leapt gyb, at doors into the towne.[4]

In the flurry the precious needle 'my fayre longe strayght neele that was myne onely treasure'[5] is lost. Diccon hints that neighbour Chat has stolen it. The two women have at each other in such fashion that the four centuries between us are thin as a paper wall. Every word rings out sharp and clear. The case is tried before the baily; and in the end, owing to a well directed blow of Diccon's fist, the needle is found sticking in the hinder parts of Hodge. It is a simple tale. Whoever the writer may have been he stuck to his story, and save for the irrepressible outburst of the splendid drinking song –

> I can not eat but lytle meate,
> My stomacke is not good.[6]

sought no embellishment. But, to return to our analysis of pleasure, his straightforward method serves to release a deep current, first of joy in the English qualities, and then of relish for the plain language, the free manners, to which we have grown so little used. His characters can scarcely open their mouths without saying something which, upon reflection, we must call coarse. But this is an afterthought imposing itself upon a direct judgement that not only is indecency of this kind enjoyable, but it is also wholesome and natural. What, we ask regretfully, has clipped our language and tied our pens? Why should expression be now either so strictly limited or so thickly veiled? Presumably because women are now equally with men readers of the printed page and actors of the drama. There are not wanting signs that education is already bringing a change to pass; but meanwhile for certain kinds of pleasure one must resort to the old writers. Hard upon that, however, comes the reflection that though plain speaking and free acting have an irresistible charm, *Gammer Gurton* palls before the end through excess of horseplay. The characters are by no means without such rude shaping as befits their parts, but William Stevenson, if we credit him with the work,[7] was no poet. He sang his song in praise of ale with splendid vigour, but for the majority of human pleasures, for the look of things, for love and for death he had no sense at all. At any rate, he makes no explicit mention of them. But when the story is told with such spirit, when so clear before us comes the cottage, with the end of the candle hid in the shoe behind the old brass pan, the cat's gleaming eyes, the game of cards, poor Hodge's drudgery in the fields and his desire to appear decently before his mistress on Sunday, the voice of poetry, though still dumb, seems about to burst into song. Here and there one pauses as if to listen for it. No, it is too early; the petals are furled in the buds; the birds hopping among leafless twigs. Of all these things, and of many besides, is our pleasure composed.

1 – A review in the *TLS*, 15 July 1920, (Kp C199) of *Gammer Gvrtons Nedle* by Mr S. Mr of Art, ed. H. F. B. Brett-Smith, no. 2 in the Percy Reprints series (Basil Blackwell, 1920). The work was first published in 1575.

2 – This is not stated in Brett-Smith.

3 – Brett-Smith, act i, sc. i, p. 4, opening lines spoken by Diccon.

4 – *Ibid.,* sc. iii, p. 9, ll. 35–6, spoken by Tyb, Gammer Gurton's maid, which has no punctuation at the end of either line.

5 – *Ibid.,* sc. iv, p. 10, l. 5, spoken by Gammer Gurton.

6 – *Ibid.,* act ii, p. 16, opening song.

7 – William Stevenson (d.1575), Fellow of Christ's College, Cambridge, to whom authorship is attributed by Brett-Smith, following Henry Bradley, in preference to the traditional candidate, John Still (1543–1608).

Mr Kipling's Notebook

Between the ages of sixteen and twenty-one, speaking roughly, every writer keeps a large notebook devoted entirely to landscape. Words must be found for a moon-lit sky, for a stream, for plane trees after rain. They 'must' be found. For the plane tree dries very quickly, and if the look as of a sea-lion sleek from a plunge is gone, and nothing found to record it better than those words, the wet plane tree does not properly exist. Nothing can exist unless it is properly described. Therefore the young writer is perpetually on the stretch to get the things expressed before it is over and the end of the day finds him with a larder full of maimed objects – half-realised trees, streams that are paralytic in their flow, and leaves that obstinately refuse to have that particular – what was the look of them against the sky, or, more difficult still to express, how did the tree erect its tent of green layers above you as you lay flat on the ground beneath? Early in the twenties this incessant matching and scrutiny of nature is relaxed, perhaps in despair, more probably because the attention has been captured by the usual thing – the human being. He wanders into the maze. When once more he can look at a tree it seems to him quite unnecessary to consider whether the bark is like a wet seal, or the leaves are jagged emeralds. The truth of the tree is not in that kind of precision at all. Indeed the old notebooks, with their trees, streams, sunsets, Piccadilly at dawn, Thames at midday, waves on the beach, are quite unreadable. And for the same reason so is much of Mr Kipling – quite unreadable.

A fat carp in a pond sucks at a fallen leaf with just the sound of a wicked little worldly kiss. Then the earth steams and steams in silence, and a gorgeous butterfly, full six inches from wing to wing, cuts through the steam in a zigzag of colour and flickers up to the forehead of the god.[2]

That is a perfect note. Every word of it has been matched with the object with such amazing skill that no one could be expected to bury it in a notebook. But when it is printed in a book meant to be read consecutively, and on to it are stitched all the notes that Mr Kipling has made with unfaltering eye, and even increasing skill, it becomes, literally, unreadable. One has to shut the eyes, shut the book, and do the writing over again. Mr Kipling has given us the raw material; but where is this to go, and where that, and what about the distance, and who, after all, is seeing this temple, or God, or desert? All notebook literature produces the same effect of fatigue and obstacle, as if there dropped across the path of the mind some block of alien matter which must be removed or assimilated before one can go on with the true process of reading. The more vivid the note the greater the obstruction. The malady can be traced to Lord Tennyson, who brought the art of taking notes to the highest perfection, and displayed the utmost skill in letting them, almost imperceptibly, into the texture of his poetry. Here is an example:

> Crisp foam-flakes scud along the level sand,
> Torn from the fringe of spray.[3]

That must have been seen one day on the beach at Freshwater,[4] and preserved for future use; and when we come upon it we detect its bottled origin, and say, 'Yes, that is exactly like a foam-flake, and I wonder whether Tennysons's foam-flakes were yellowish, and had that porous look which I myself have thought of comparing to the texture of cork? "Crisp" he calls it. But surely cork . . .' and so on through all the old business of word-matching, while the 'Dream of Fair Women' wastes in air. But when Keats wanted to describe autumn, he said that he had seen her 'sitting careless on a granary floor';[5] which does all the work for us, whether innumerable notes were the basis of it or none at all. Indeed, if we want to describe a summer evening, the way to do it is to set people talking in a room with their backs to the window, and then, as they talk about something else, let someone half turn her head and say, 'A fine evening,' when (if they have been talking about the right things) the summer evening is visible to anyone who reads the page, and is for ever remembered as of quite exceptional beauty.

To return to Mr Kipling. Is he then directing us to nothing, and are these brilliant scenes merely pages torn from the copy-book of a prodigy among pupils? No; it is not so simple as that. Just as the railway companies have a motive in hanging their stations with seductive pictures of Ilfracombe and Blackpool Bay, so Mr Kipling's pictures of places are painted to display the splendours of Empire and to induce young men to lay down their lives on her behalf. And again, it is not so simple as that. It is true that Mr Kipling shouts, 'Hurrah for the Empire!' and puts out his tongue at her enemies. But praise as crude as this, abuse as shallow, can be nothing but a disguise rigged up to justify some passion or other of which Mr Kipling is a little ashamed. He has a feeling, perhaps, that a grown man should not enjoy making bridges, and using tools, and camping out as much as he does. But if these activities are pursued in the service of Empire, they are not only licensed, but glorified. Hence the excuse. Yet it is the passion that gives his writing its merit, and the excuse that vitiates it:

I wonder sometimes whether any eminent novelist, philosopher, dramatist, or divine of to-day has to exercise half the imagination, not to mention insight, endurance, and self-restraint, which is accepted without comment in what is called 'the material exploitation' of a new country ... The mere drama of it, the play of the human virtues, would fill a book.[6]

It has, indeed, filled many books, from the travels of Hakluyt to the novels of Mr Conrad,[7] and if Mr Kipling would concentrate upon 'the mere drama of it, the play of the human virtues', there would be no fault to find with him. Even as it is, there are pages in the *Letters of Travel* in the contemplation of which the most lily-livered Socialist forgets to brand the labouring and adventuring men with the curse of Empire. There is, for example, an account of a bank failure in Japan. All Mr Kipling's sympathy with men who work is there displayed, and there, too, much more vividly than by means of direct description, is expressed the excitement and strangeness of the East. Up to a point that is perfectly true; Mr Kipling is a man of sympathy and imagination. But the more closely you watch the more puzzled you become. Why do these men, in the first shock of loss, step there, turn their backs just there, and say precisely that? There is something mechanical about it, as if they were acting; or is it that they are carefully observing the rules of a game?

A man passed stiffly, and some one of a group turned to ask lightly, 'Hit, old man?' 'Like Hell,' he said, and went on biting his unlit cigar ... 'We're doing ourselves well this year,' said a wit grimly. 'One free-shooting case, one thundering libel case, and a bank smash. Showing off pretty before the globe trotters, aren't we?'[8]

It is as if they were afraid to be natural. But Mr Kipling ought to have insisted that with him at least they should drop this pose, instead of which the effect of his presence is to make them talk more by rule than ever. Whether grown-up people really play this game, or whether, as we suspect, Mr Kipling makes up the whole British Empire to amuse the solitude of his nursery, the result is curiously sterile and depressing.

1 – A signed review in the *Athenaeum*, 16 July 1920, (Kp C200) of *Letters of Travel, 1892–1913* (Macmillan & Co. Ltd, 1920) by Rudyard Kipling (1865–1936).
  The same issue of the *Athenaeum* also contained an article by E. M. Forster, 'Big Stick and Green Leaf', reviewing *Recreation. An Address* by Viscount Fallodon. Reprinted: *B&P*.
2 – Kipling, 'The Edge of the East', p. 45.
3 – Alfred, Lord Tennyson, 'A Dream of Fair Women' (originally published in *Poems*, 1833), stanza 10, ll. 39–40.
4 – Tennyson did not take his house, Farringford, at Freshwater in the Isle of Wight, until 1853.
5 – John Keats, 'To Autumn' (1819), stanza 2, l. 14.
6 – Kipling, 'A People at Home', p. 135.
7 – Richard Hakluyt (1552?–1616); Joseph Conrad (1857–1924).
8 – Kipling, 'Some Earthquakes', p. 66.

The Plumage Bill

If I had the money and the time I should, after reading 'Wayfarer', in the *Nation* of 10 July, go to Regent Street, buy an egret plume, and stick it – is it in the back or the front of the hat? – and this in spite of a vow taken in childhood and hitherto religiously observed. The Plumage Bill has been smothered; millions of birds are doomed not only to extinction but to torture; and 'Wayfarer's' comment is, 'What does one expect? They have to be shot in parenthood for child-bearing women to flaunt the symbols of it, and, as Mr Hudson says, one bird shot for its plumage means ten other deadly wounds and the starvation of the young. But what do women care? Look at Regent Street this morning!'[2] One can look at Regent Street without leaving one's room. The lower half of the houses is composed of plate glass. One might string substantives and adjectives together for an hour without naming a tenth part of the dressing bags, silver baskets, boots, guns, flowers, dresses, bracelets and fur coats arrayed behind the glass. Men and women pass incessantly this way and that. Many loiter and perhaps desire, but few are in a position to enter the doors. Most of them merely steal a look and hurry on. And then there comes on foot, so that we may have a good look at her, a lady of a different class altogether. A silver bag swings from her wrist. Her gloves are white. Her shoes lustrous. She holds herself upright. As an object of beauty her figure is incomparably more delightful than any other object in street or window. It is her face that one must discount, for, though discreetly tinted and powdered, it is a stupid face, and the look she sweeps over the shop windows has something of the greedy petulance of a pug-dog's face at tea-time. When she comes to the display of egret plumes, artfully arranged and centrally placed, she pauses. So do many women. For, after all, what can be more etherially and fantastically lovely? The plumes seem to be the natural adornment of spirited and fastidious life, the very symbols of pride and distinction. The lady of the stupid face and beautiful figure is going tonight to the opera; Clara Butt is singing Orpheus; Princess Mary will be present;[3] a lemon-coloured egret is precisely what she wants to complete her toilet. In she goes; the silver bag disgorges I know not how many notes; and the fashion writers next day say that Lady So-and-So was 'looking lovely with a lemon-coloured egret in her hair'.

But since we are looking at pictures let us look at another which has the advantage of filling in certain blank spaces in our rough sketch of Regent Street in the morning. Let us imagine a blazing South American landscape. In the foreground a bird with a beautiful plume circles round and round as if lost or giddy. There are red holes in its head where there should be eyes. Another bird, tied to a stake, writhes incessantly, for red ants devour it. Both are decoys. The fact is that before 'the child-bearing woman can flaunt the symbols of parenthood' certain acts have to be devised, done, and paid for. It is in the nesting season that the plumes are brightest. So, if we wish to go on making pictures, we must imagine innumerable mouths opening and shutting, opening and shutting, until – as no parent bird comes to feed them – the young birds rot where they sit. Then there are the wounded birds, trailing leg or wing, as they flutter off to droop and falter in the dust. But perhaps the most unpleasant sight that we must make ourselves imagine is the sight of the bird tightly held in one hand while another hand pierces the eyeballs with a feather. But these hands – are they the hands of men or of women? The Plumage Bill supporters say that the hunters 'are the very scum of mankind'. We may assume that the newspapers would have let us know if any of the other sex had been concerned in it. We may fairly suppose then that the birds are killed by men, starved by men, and tortured by men – not vicariously, but with their own hands. 'A small band of East End profiteers' supports the trade; and East End profiteers are apt also to be of the male sex. But now, as 'Wayfarer' says, the birds 'have to be shot in parenthood for child-bearing women to flaunt the symbols of it'.

But what is the nature of this compulsion? Well, men must make their livings, must earn their profits, and must beget children. For though some people say that they can control their passions, the majority maintain that they should be protected from them rather than condemned for them. In other words, it is one thing to desire a woman; quite another to desire an egret plume.

There remains, however, a body of honourable and disinterested men who are neither plume hunters, profiteers, nor women. It is their duty, as it is within their power, to end the murder and torture of the birds, and to make it impossible for a single egret to be robbed of a single plume. The House of Commons took the matter up. The Plumage Bill was sent to Standing Committee C. With one exception each of its sixty-seven members was a man. And on five occasions it was impossible to get a quorum of twenty to attend. The Plumage Bill is for all practical purposes dead. But what do men care? Look wherever you like this morning! Still, one cannot imagine 'Wayfarer' putting it like that. 'They have to be shot for child-begetting men to flaunt the symbols of it . . . But what do men care? Look at Regent Street this morning!' Such an outburst about a fishing-rod would be deemed sentimental in the extreme. Yet I suppose that salmon have their feelings.

So far as I know, the above, though much embittered by sex antagonism, is a perfectly true statement. But the interesting point is that in my ardour to confute 'Wayfarer', a journalist of admitted humanity, I have said more about his injustice to women than about the sufferings of birds. Can it be that it is a graver sin to be unjust to women than to torture birds?[4]

1–A signed article in the Woman's Leader, 23 July 1920, (Kp C200.1) on a parliamentary bill to prohibit the importation of plumage. After a successful initial passage through both houses, the bill, a subject of considerable press controversy, was repeatedly balked in committee by the failure to secure a quorum. VW wrote in her diary on Tuesday, 13 July 1920: 'Now for oh Reviewing! – Three weeks I think have passed without a word added to Jacob['s Room]. How is one to bring it through at this rate. Yet its all my fault – why should I do the Cherry Orchard & Tolstoy for Desmond [MacCarthy], why take up the Plumage Bill for Ray [Strachey, editor of the Woman's Leader]? But after this week I do no more.'
2–'Wayfarer' was H. W. Massingham (1860–1924), editor of the Nation, 1907–23, and a highly active member of the Plumage Bill Group. In his column of 10 July

1920 he had written: 'Now that the Plumage Bill has been smothered the massacre of the innocents will continue. Nature puts an end to birds and the trade together. Her veto will be final, and as science declares that six years without birds means the end of her animate system, the end of the Plumage Trade may possibly coincide with the end of *us*' and follows this with details of the decline in various species, culminating in the quotation given here.

3–On 1 July 1920, Dame Clara Butt (1872–1936), concert singer, made her first professional appearance in opera in Gluck's *Orfeo* under Sir Thomas Beecham at Covent Garden. According to *The Times* of the following day: 'Princess Mary, wearing blue and white, with a fillet of diamonds, and Princess Victoria were present . . .'

4–Massingham replied to VW's article in a letter to the editor which appeared in the *Woman's Leader* for 30 July, and she responded in a letter published in the issue for 6 August. Massingham argued that her point of view was wrong and that by adopting it she played into the hands of the bill's opponents, and continued: 'Personally, I cannot judge from Mrs Woolf's ambiguous article, whether she is for or against the plumage trade. As a writer of great distinction, she should have made herself clearer, for she undoubtedly leaves the impression that she was converted by the passage in the *Nation* she refers to from a mild dislike of the trade to a warm support of it. She has in fact fallen a victim to a mental confusion – confounding a statement of fact with its moral implications. The facts are precisely as the *Nation* stated . . . I would again remind Mrs Woolf that I am not assessing moral values or attempting an ethical Roland to her Oliver. I would not have written a reply to her at all did I not feel that articles of the kind she has written . . . do a great deal more harm than the trade can do by its propaganda in its own defence, because they obscure the issue and encourage women (without whose help as voters the Bill can never be passed) and men alike to become party adherents and to turn their eyes away from their real and profoundly important common duty of preserving the heritage and continuity of evolution and raising the moral currency of civilised nations . . . Mrs Woolf's article, in short, is not the way of truth, which it is the business of men and women equally to seek, the more so if the party, sect, community or sex to which one or other of them belong is involved in the issue. And women are unquestionably involved in the plumage trade (as men, of course, in other iniquities), since if, as a body, they would refuse to indulge in a form of adornment as vile in taste as in the method of procuring it, no Plumage Bill would be necessary.'

Here is VW's response: 'Madam, There is little use, I am afraid, in writing articles; still less in answering those who disagree with them. To Mr Massingham my meaning is ambiguous, and my ways untruthful; to me, his meaning is plain enough but almost, if not entirely, off the point. Let me clear up some at least of my ambiguities. Not for an instant did I accuse Mr Massingham of bias or partiality. I am wholly against the plumage trade. At the age of ten or thereabouts I signed a pledge never to wear one of the condemned feathers, and have kept the vow so implicitly that I cannot distinguish osprey from egret. Cocks, hens, parrots, and ostriches are the only birds whose feathers I recognise or wear. The huge majority of women are as ignorant and as innocent as I am. With this in my mind, I picked up the *Nation* and read the half sentimental and wholly contemptuous phrases about 'What do women care?' and 'Look at Regent Street this morning!"' which I quoted in my article. I have no reason to suppose that Mr Massingham either wrote the sentences of which I complain, or approved the tone of them. But it was against them that my article, with sufficient plainness as I thought, was directed. Had I wished to attack the plumage trade I should not have lumbered my space with the statement, in that case utterly irrelevant, that men are more to be blamed for it than women. I should have stuck simply to the fact that the trade is abominable and the cruelty repulsive. But to make such a denunciation in your columns seemed to me superfluous. To denounce as forcibly as I could the injustice of Wayfarer's remark seemed, on the contrary, an odious but obvious necessity. It was with that end in view that I endeavoured to prove that in this instance men, rather than women, are to be charged with cruelty and indifference. I did not confound a statement of fact with its moral implications. To torture birds is one thing, and to be unjust to women is another, and it was, I hope, plain to some of my readers that I was attacking the second of these crimes and not the first. Thus, when Mrs [Meta] Bradley [*Woman's Leader,* 30 July] asks "Does it matter in the least to the birds so foully slain whether the blame rests most with men or women?" I reply that I am not writing as a bird, or even a champion of birds; but as a woman. At the risk of losing such little reputation for humanity as I may still possess I hereby confess that it seems to me more necessary to resent such an insult to women as Wayfarer casually lets fall than to protect egrets from extinction. That is my way of "raising the moral currency of civilised nations". But that does not mean that I have not the highest respect for Mr Massingham's way also. ¶ Had you placed six columns of your paper at my disposal, instead of a thousand words, I might have given some of my reasons for attaching so great, some will say excessive, an importance to a phrase in a newspaper. On some future occasion you will, perhaps, allow me to explain why it is that such phrases, common as they are, serve not merely to produce an outburst of sex antagonism, but seem to me for the more serious harm they do to deserve trouncing and denial until either they are forced down their writers' throats or justified up to the hilt. But what the effect of them is, and why the damage is so disastrous not merely to women's relations with men but to her art and her conduct are questions far too broad and too complex to broach at the tail end of a letter. ¶ In conclusion, as I have lost my temper, caused Mr Massingham to waste his time, and in his opinion (though I think he overrates the power of my pen) done more harm to the cause than "a round score of Miss Yateses [E. Florence Yates, a prominent campaigner on the part of the plumage trade]", I should like to make whatever reparation I can. Plainly with this example of my own ambiguity as a writer before me, it would never do to write another article solely from the birds' point of view. But I will give myself the pleasure of spending whatever sum I receive for my article, not upon an egret plume, but upon a subscription to the Plumage Bill Group. With prayers to you therefore to make it as handsome as possible.'

'The Cherry Orchard'

Although every member of the audience at the Art [sic] Theatre last week had probably read Tchekhov's The Cherry Orchard several times, a large number of them had, perhaps, never seen it acted before. It was no doubt on this account that as the first act proceeded the readers, now transformed into seers, felt themselves shocked and outraged. The beautiful, mad drama which I had staged often enough in the dim recesses of my mind was now hung within a few feet of me, hard, crude, and over-emphatic, like a cheap coloured print of the real thing. But what right had I to call it the real thing? What did I mean by that? Perhaps something like this.

There is nothing in English literature in the least like The Cherry Orchard. It may be that we are more advanced, less advanced, or have advanced in an entirely different direction. At any rate, the English person who finds himself at dawn in the nursery of Madame Ranevskaia feels out of place, like a foreigner brought up with entirely different traditions. But the traditions are not (this, of course, is a transcript of individual experience) so ingrained in one as to prevent one from shedding them not only without pain but with actual relief and abandonment. True, at the end of a long railway journey one is accustomed to say goodnight and go to bed. Yet on this occasion, since everything is so strange, the dawn rising and the birds beginning to sing in the cherry trees, let us gather round the coffee-cups; let us talk about everything in the whole world. We are all in that queer emotional state when thought seems to bubble into words without being spoken. The journey is over and we have reached the end of everything where space seems illimitable and time everlasting. Quite wrongly (since in the production approved by Tchekhov the birds actually sing and the cherries are visible on the trees) I had, on my imaginary stage, tried to give effect to my sense that the human soul is free from all trappings and crossed incessantly by thoughts and emotions which wing their way from here, from there, from the furthest horizons – I had tried to express this by imagining an airy view from the window with ethereal pink cherries and perhaps snow mountains and blue mist behind them. In the room the characters spoke suddenly whatever came into their heads, and yet always vaguely, as if thinking aloud. There was no 'comedy of manners'; one thought scarcely grazed, let alone struck sparks from, another; there was no conflict of individual wills. At the same time the characters were entirely concrete and without sentimentality. Not for an instant did one suppose that Madame Ranevskaia was wrapping up a mystic allusion to something else when she spoke. Her own emotions were quite enough for her. If what was said seemed symbolical, that was because it was profound enough to illumine much more than an incident in the life of one individual. And, finally, though the leap from one thought to another was so wide as to produce a sense of dangerous dislocation, all the separate speeches and characters combined to create a single impression of an overwhelming kind.

The actors at the Art Theatre destroyed this conception, first, by the unnatural emphasis with which they spoke; next by their determination to make points which brought them into touch with the audience but destroyed their harmony with each other; and, finally, by the consciousness which hung about them of being well-traind English men and women ill at ease in an absurd situation, but determined to make the best of a bad business. One instance of irrepressible British humour struck me with considerable force. It occurred in the middle of Charlotte's strange speech in the beginning of the second act. 'I have no proper passport. I don't know how old I am; I always feel I am still young,' she begins. She goes on, 'When I grew up I became a governess. But where I come from and who I am, I haven't a notion. Who my parents were – *very likely they weren't married* – I don't know.'[2] At the words I have italicised, Dunyasha bounced away from her to the other end of the bench, with an arch humour which drew the laugh it deserved. Miss Helena Millais seemed to be delighted to have this chance of assuring us that she did not believe a word of this morbid nonsense, and that the old jokes still held good in the world of sanity round the corner. But it was Miss Ethel Irving who showed the steadiest sense of what decency requires of a British matron in extremity. How she did it, since she spoke her part accurately, it is difficult to say, but her mere presence upon the stage was enough to suggest that all the comforts and all the decencies of English upper-class life were at hand, so that at any moment her vigil upon the bench might have been appropriately interrupted by a manservant bearing a silver tray. 'The Bishop is in the drawing-room, m'lady.' 'Thank you, Parker. Tell his Lordship I will come at once.'[3] In that sort of play, by which I mean a play by Sheridan or Oscar Wilde, both Miss Irving and Miss Millais would charm by their wit, spirit and competent intellectual outfit. Nor, though the quotation I have made scarcely proves it, have we any cause to sneer at English comedy or at the tradition of acting which prevails upon our stage. The only question is whether the same methods are as applicable to *The Cherry Orchard* as they are to *The School for Scandal*.[4]

But there are four acts in *The Cherry Orchard*. How it may have been with the other readers I do not know, but before the second act was over some sort of compromise had been reached between my reader's version and the actor's one. Perhaps in reading one had got the whole too vague, too mad, too mystical. Perhaps as they went on the actors forgot how absurd such behaviour would be thought in England. Or perhaps the play itself triumphed over the deficiencies of both parties. At any rate, I felt less and less desire to cavil at the acting in general and more and more appreciation of the acting of Mr Chancellor, Mr Dodd, Mr Pearson and Miss Edith Evans in particular. With every word that Mr Felix Aylmer spoke as Pishchick, one's own conception of that part plumped itself out like a shrivelled skin miraculously revived. But the play itself – that was what overwhelmed all obstacles, so that though the walls rocked from floor to ceiling when the door was shut, though the sun sank and rose with the energetic decision of the stage carpenter's fist, though the scenery suggested an advertisement of the Surrey Hills rather than Russia in her wildness, the atmosphere of the play wrapped us round and shut out everything alien to itself. It is, as a rule, when a critic does not wish to commit himself or to trouble himself that he refers to atmosphere. And, given time, something might be said in greater detail of the causes which produced this atmosphere – the strange dislocated sentences, each so erratic and yet cutting out the shape so firmly, of the realism, of the humour, of the artistic unity. But let the word atmosphere be taken literally to mean that Tchekhov has contrived to shed over us a luminous vapour in which life appears as it is, without veils, transparent and visible to the depths. Long before the play was over we seemed to have sunk below the surface of things and to be feeling our way among submerged but recognisable emotions. 'I have no proper passport. I don't know how old I am; I always feel I am still young' – how the words go sounding on in one's mind – how the whole play resounds with such sentences, which reverberate, melt into each other, and pass far away out beyond everything! In short, if it is permissible to use such vague language, I do not know how better to describe the sensation at the end of *The Cherry Orchard*, than by saying that it sends one into the street feeling like a piano played upon at last, not in the middle only but all over the keyboard and with the lid left open so that the sound goes on.

This being so, and having felt nothing comparable to it from reading the play, one feels inclined to strike out every word of criticism and to implore Madame Donnet[5] to give us the chance of seeing play after play, until to sit at home and read plays is an occupation for the afflicted only, and one to be viewed with pity, as we pity blind men spelling out their Shakespeare with their fingers upon sheets of cardboard.

1–A signed dramatic review in the NS, 24 July 1920, (Kp C201) of The Cherry Orchard (1904) by Anton Chekhov (1860–1904), in a production by the Arts Theatre at St Martin's Theatre, on 11 and 12 July 1920. According to The Times,1 July 1920, the company used Constance Garnett's translation, which was later published in The Cherry Orchard and Other Plays (Chatto & Windus, 1923), to which source reference is made in the notes below.

VW noted in her diary on Tuesday, 13 July 1920: 'Now for oh Reviewing! – Three weeks I think have passed without a word added to Jacob['s Room]. How is one to bring it through at this rate. Yet its all my fault – why should I do the Cherry Orchard & Tolstoy for Desmond [MacCarthy, literary editor of the NS], why take up the Plumage Bill for Ray [Strachey]? But after this week I do no more'. See also II VW Letters, no. 1137, to David Garnett.

Cast list: Madame Ranevskaia, Ethel Irving; Anya, Irene Rathbone; Varya, Margery Bryce; Leonid Andreevitch, Leyton Chancellor; Lopakhin, Joseph A. Dodd; Petya Trofimov, Hesketh Pearson; Simeonov-Pishchik, Felix Aylmer; Charlotta Ivanovna, Edith Evans; Epikhodov, William Armstrong; Dunyasha, Helena Millais; Fiers, Ernest Paterson; Yasha, J. M. Roberts; Tramp, Matthew Forsyth. See also 'The Russian Background' above; 'Tchehov's Questions', II VW Essays; and see 'The Russian Point of View', IV VW Essays and CR 1.

2–The Cherry Orchard, act ii, pp. 28–9, which has: 'Charlotta (musingly). I haven't a real passport of my own, and I don't know how old I am, and I always feel that I'm a young thing. When I was a little girl, my father and mother used to travel about to fairs and give performances – very good ones. And I used to dance salto-mortale and all sorts of things. And when papa and mamma died, a German lady took me and had me educated. And so I grew up and became a governess. But where I came from, and who I am, I don't know ... Who my parents were, very likely they weren't married ... I don't know (takes a cucumber out of her pocket and eats). I know nothing at all (a pause). One wants to talk and has no one to talk to ... I have nobody.'

3–Parker is the name of the Butler in Lady Windermere's Fan (1892) by Oscar Wilde (1854–1900), but the lines are not in the play.

4–Richard Brinsley Sheridan (1751–1816), The School for Scandal (1777).

5–Madame Donnet, otherwise unidentified, directed the production.

A Born Writer

After many years *Esther Waters* appears again, entirely revised, and with an introduction which, to our disappointment, has more to say about Irish politics than about English fiction. Whether any critic of those days predicted a long life for the book we know not. At what date it was written and what views the author had in mind we are not told. At any rate in the summer of 1920 it sets out again; and whether for a long voyage and by reason of what qualities it has survived so far the critics of today must make up their minds. That is not easy. For it is a quiet book, and an old-fashioned rather than an old book. About a century ago it was the habit of novelists to produce masterpieces which were known for such from the moment of birth. *Waverley, Pickwick,* and *Jane Eyre*[2] are all cases in point. The public applauded and the critics clapped hands with them unanimously. Later, for reasons which it would lead us astray to discuss, the process of recognition was much more gradual and difficult, and far from acclaiming at the outset the public had to be coaxed and even coerced before it would tolerate. But *Esther Waters* belongs neither to one class nor to the other. It was neither admitted a classic from the start nor has it fought a battle, won a victory, and founded a school. Somehow it has come through the press of the struggle by qualities which are not so easy to define.

Leaving aside such obvious merits as the story, which is varied and interesting, and the style, which, with occasional spaces of melody and charm, is invariably lucid and effortless, it seems as if the book's virtue lay in a shapeliness which is at once admirable and disconcerting. The novel begins with the sentence, 'She stood on the platform watching the receding train.' A few pages before the end the sentence recurs.[3] Esther Waters stands once more on the platform watching the receding train. Once more a servant's oblong box, painted a reddish brown, is on the seat beside her. Between these two appearances eighteen years have passed,

eighteen years of labour, suffering, and disappointment. A great deal had happened, so much that she could not remember it all. The situations she had been in; her life with that dear, good soul, Miss Rice; then Fred Parsons; then William again! her marriage, the life in the public-house, money lost and money won, heartbreakings, death, everything that could happen had happened to her.'[4]

But the recurring scene is not a formal device to reduce the varied incidents of her life to symmetry. All through Mr Moore has curbed himself to this particular ending, renouncing this, insisting upon that, allowing himself few or none of the licences and redundances in which English novelists luxuriate. The life of a servant girl is a long series of sordid drudgeries scattered with scant pleasures; and thus he has presented it, without taking refuge in sentiment or in romance. Throughout the names are insignificant; the places (with the exception of Woodview, and there we are limited to the kitchen and the pantry) without charm; while the fates above preserve blank faces in the discharge of their duties. No one is allowed either sensational reprieve or sensational disaster. A number of writers have outdone Mr Moore in the force with which they depict poverty and misery, but they have failed to penetrate beyond their day because they have always dashed the picture from their hands in an access of indignation or clouded it with tears. They have rarely had his power of maintaining that in art life needs neither condemnation nor justification. The story owes much of its buoyancy and permanency to the fact that we can examine it dispassionately. There it hangs, complete, apart. Yet by this we do not mean that there is no morality to be found in it; for when Mr Moore calls *Esther Waters* 'as characteristically English as *Don Quixote* is Spanish',[5] he means perhaps that in the person of Esther he has laid bare honesty, fidelity, courage, and has made these, the Saxon virtues, rather than the charms and subtleties of the Latins, the leading qualities in the drama. But he himself remains invisible.

Vivid, truthful, so lightly and yet so firmly constructed as it is, what then prevents us from talking of immortality and greatness? In one word, the quality of the emotion. Although in retrospect there is not a single scene that lacks animation, or a single character clumsily or conventionally portrayed, both scenes and characters are nevertheless curiously flat. The dialogue is always toneless and monotonous. The conception springs from no deep original source, and the execution has that sort of evenness which we see in the work of a highly sensitive student copying on to his canvas the picture of some great master. If that is the reason why *Esther Waters* does not affect us directly as a more imperfect but more original work is capable of doing, we cannot deny that it holds a very distinguished place in English fiction. Moreover, though the public will always prefer both Shakespeare and Mrs Henry Wood,[6] *Esther Waters* will go on being read and re-read with peculiar interest by those who attempt the art of novel writing themselves. For, when all is said and done, Mr Moore is a born writer; and, though great novelists are rare, of how many people in a generation can one say truthfully that?

1—A review in the *TLS*, 29 July 1920, (Kp C202) of *Esther Waters* (1894; William Heinemann Ltd, 1920) by George Moore (1852–1933). See also 'Winged Phrases', above, and 'George Moore', *IV VW Essays*. Reprinted: *CW*.
2—Sir Walter Scott, *Waverley* (1814); Charles Dickens, *The Pickwick Papers* (1836–7); Charlotte Brontë, *Jane Eyre* (1847).
3—Moore, ch. xliv, p. 395, repeats, in fact, the entire opening paragraph: 'She stood on the platform watching the receding train. The white steam curled above the few bushes that hid the curve of the line, evaporating in the pale evening. A moment more and the last carriage would pass out of sight, the white gates at the crossing swinging slowly forward to let through the impatient passengers'; and part of the opening of the ensuing paragraph: 'An oblong box painted reddish brown . . .'
4—*Ibid.*, p. 396.
5—*Ibid.*, 'Epistle Dedicatory', p. v: 'It is quite in accordance with the humour of the great Aristophanes above us, beneath us, within us, without us, that an Irishman should write a book as characteristically English as *Don Quixote* is Spanish, and when the author of *Esther Waters* dedicates his work to another Irishman, it must be plain to all that he is holding the mirror up to Nature. But there is another reason why I should dedicate this book to you. You are an Irish Protestant like myself, and you could always love Ireland without hating England and . . .' Moore's dedicatee was Thomas William Rolleston (1857–1920), man of letters.
6—Mrs Henry (Ellen) Wood (1814–87), best-known as the author of *East Lynne* (1861).

Gorky on Tolstoy

Sometimes by accident an untouched amateur photograph of a great personage will drop out of an album or of an old drawer, and instantly the etchings, the engravings, the portraits by Watts and Millais[2] seem insipid and lifeless. Such is the effect of Gorky's Notes upon Tolstoy. However we had come by our portrait of him it now appears conventionalised and dead. And since Gorky is not a photographer but a writer of great penetration and sincerity this untouched picture is not of the body but of the mind, and makes us wish to go straight to the 'Kreutzer Sonata' or *War and Peace*[3] to see whether even our conception of Tolstoy's books has not been changed by the light shed upon him.

Our imaginary snapshot often gives us a shock at first, because the little figure is so unmistakably like that of other men. It appears that his legs were short, or that he showed a curious lack of taste in his neck-ties, or that the hands clutching the stick were thick and clumsy. So Gorky shocks us at first by showing us that Tolstoy was no different from other men in being sometimes conceited, intolerant, insincere, and in allowing his private fortunes to make him vindictive in his judgements.

I always disliked what he said about women – it was unspeakably 'vulgar', and there was in his words something artificial, insincere, and at the same time very personal. It seemed as if he had once been hurt and could neither forget nor forgive.[4]

Beyond everything else Gorky conveys a sense of Tolstoy's power. He brings us so much nearer to him than before that we feel his force as if it were uncovered. And there is something frightening in contact with such a power when it is malevolent.

In Leo Nicolayevitch there is much which at times roused in me a feeling very like hatred, and this hatred fell upon my soul with crushing weight. His disproportionately overgrown individuality is a monstrous phenomenon, almost ugly, and there is in him, something of Sviatogor, the bogatir, whom the earth can't hold. Yes, he is great.[5]

But his greatness was a greatness of the whole, in which his special greatness as a writer appears as an accident of no particular importance. Before his eyes, and very close to them, he seems always to be holding human life, scrutinising it, trying to penetrate into it, and accidentally throwing off profound, coarse, wise sayings, as if they were sparks struck out by his mind in collision with some reality which existed only for him.

'Man survives earthquakes, epidemics, the horrors of disease and all the agonies of the soul, but for all time his most tormenting tragedy has been, is, and will be – the tragedy of the bedroom!' Saying this he smiled triumphantly: at times he has the broad, calm smile of a man who has overcome something extremely difficult or from whom some sharp, long-gnawing pain has lifted suddenly.[6]

At such times, of course, there was not a pebble on the road or a leaf upon a tree, a drunken woman, a hawk, or two guardsmen walking down the street, whom he did not see once and for all, so that we see them and feel the disgust, delight, excitement or whatever it was that the sight roused in him. But Gorky also conveys very remarkably the sense of the man who lived apart from his sayings, silent, vast and lonely, like someone who has never got caught up in the ordinary round of existence, but appears to others like a pilgrim 'terribly homeless and alien to all men and things',[7] or like a person 'just arrived from some distant country, where people think and feel differently and their relations and language are different'.[8] 'Though he speaks a great deal and as a duty upon certain subjects his silence is felt to be still greater. Certain things one cannot tell to anyone. Surely he has some thoughts of which he is afraid.'[9] In that last sentence we have perhaps a clue to very much of Tolstoy.

But even as we choose this and that sentence to show the fascination of Gorky's book we understand why it is that he writes in his preface to it, 'And I do not finish it, for somehow or other that is not possible.'[10] For we have scarcely said that Tolstoy was lonely and withdrawn when we remember how he charmed a room full of different people as if he were 'a man orchestra'[11] playing all the different instruments of which he was composed by turn. He seldom talked of literature, and yet we should have to add that he spoke of all writers as though they were his children, and to say that not only his passionate interest in art, but his triumph in his own achievements, sprang out now and again like a flame that has found an outlet. Then our picture of him, small, shrivelled and grey, wearing a peasant's blouse, must be succeeded by another in which he appears like a creature of the purest blood, noble, dignified, speaking with exquisite point and reserve.

The life of Tolstoy cannot be finished. But Gorky's picture comes nearer than the others to completeness, because he makes no attempt to include everything, to explain everything, or to sum up all in one consistent whole. Here there is a very bright light, here darkness and emptiness. And perhaps this is the way in which we see people in reality.

1 – A review in the New Statesman, 7 August 1920, (Kp C204) of Reminiscences of Leo Nicolayevitch Tolstoi [1828–1910] by Maxim Gorky [1868–1936] (The Hogarth Press, 1920). Authorised translation . . . by S. S. Koteliansky [1881–1955, a Ukrainian Jew who came to England in 1910] and Leonard Woolf.

'We worked at Kot's book . . .', VW noted in her diary on 5 May 1920, 'We are publishing Gorki, & perhaps this marks some step over a precipice – I don't know.' See also II VW Letters, no. 1130; and see 'Tolstoy's "The Cossacks"', II VW Essays.

2 – G. F. Watts (1817–1904); Sir John Everett Millais (1829–96).

3 – 'The Kreutzer Sonata' (1889), War and Peace (1865–9).

4 – Gorky, 'A Letter', p. 58.

5 – Ibid., p. 39, which has 'is great'; 'bogatir' is annotated earlier in Gorky (p. 23): 'A hero in Russian legend, brave, but wild and self-willed like a child.'

6 – Ibid., xxi, p. 19.

7 – Ibid., ix, p. 11.

8 – Ibid., xxxv, p. 32.

9 – Ibid., xiii, p. 13.

10 – Ibid., Pref., p. 5.

11 – Ibid., 'A Letter', p. 51: 'He explains to them ['a company of people of all kinds'] the teaching of Lao-Tse, and he seems to me an extraordinary man-orchestra,

possessing the faculty of playing several instruments at the same time, a brass trumpet, a drum, a harmonium, and flute.'

A Character Sketch

The respectable union between us and British biography is now dissolved. The golden ring is thrown away and the marriage lines consumed. Our affections are bestowed upon *Frederick Locker-Lampson, A Character Sketch*, by the Right Honourable Augustine Birrell. Never again shall we take to bed with us the life of Thomas Henry Huxley in two volumes; or Alfred Tennyson by his son; or Coleridge by James Dykes Campbell; or Samuel Barnett by his widow.[2] Mr Birrell has seduced us. The metaphor is of course in the worst of taste. We make use of it only because it happens to express the sense of illicit freedom, of unhoped-for adventure, which this witty quarto volume produces upon a mind long habituated to decorous wedlock with the portly great. One feels that there must be something wrong. Who was Frederick Locker? one asks. And what a relief it is to find that Mr Birrell occasionally writes bad grammar and at least once misquotes a poet! Let us dismiss them both. One is insignificant; the other inaccurate. Where is the life of Lord Kitchener by Sir George Arthur? Where is the fifth, sixth, or seventh volume of Lord Beaconsfield by Mr Moneypenny [*sic*] and Mr Buckle in conjunction?[3] Where, where, where is anything dark, solid, vouched for, and respectable to protect one from this lapse into biographic immorality? They were all within reach, and yet ... and yet ...

Mr Birrell's biography reads so queerly because it brings before us a real human being. It is not that he is more profound than others, or that he has a story to tell to which we cannot fail to listen. The secret is one of those obvious secrets, which, so they say, are always the best kept. We all know it – life would be intolerable else. Yet by what name are we to call it? It is that the values of life are quite different from those of biography. There is such a thing as living. We are enmeshed in a texture of incredible fineness. It is character that enchants and colours. Achievement has nothing to do with it – but after all it is not so easy to say what the secret is. Let us ask Mr Birrell to try his hand at a definition:

Life, which in this respect, as indeed in many others, is quite unlike biography, is not a series of episodes, or of sentimental adventures, or of descriptive scenes, or even the drudgery of daily existence, but consists in the *passage of Time*; of perpetually stepping towards the westering sun. To describe this passage of time, to record the changes wrought by the chiming hours, is beyond the reach of the artist in words . . .[4]

That may be so, but it is, we maintain, the duty of the biographer to try.

The first necessity is to throw overboard a great deal of ballast. 'Mr Locker has left his mark for ever upon the annals of the British Admiralty.' 'He combined the intellectual vigour of a man with the tenderness of a woman.' 'Frugal and even austere to himself, he was generous to a fault where others were concerned. The extent of his benefactions will never be known' – we have looked in vain for these statements in Mr Birrell's book. Oddly naked, a little indecent, it appears without them. The suspicion gains upon us that Mr Locker was not – is it conceivable? – a great success. He sat in Whitehall and wrote rhymes; he travelled in Italy and bought blue china; occasionally he produced a little poem. By degrees he collected enough books to be worth keeping in a strong-room. He was dyspeptic and moody and inclined to melancholy. Indeed, he thought 'all he had done, however well done, was contemptible and all he was insignificant'.[5] Even so he kept on the hither side of melancholia. He was never converted on the one hand, or suicidal on the other. He was kindly, it is true, but his kindliness took such fantastic shapes that it is difficult to perorate satisfactorily about that. A bust of Voltaire and a live tortoise – such were the gifts he lugged about with him on a hot summer's day, thinking to please his friends.[6] As likely as not, half of them laughed at him – such a dandy, such a coxcomb, such a tiny attenuated figure of a man when peeled of his great fur coat; and the rest, much more than the half, though our grammar is spoiled by it, were inordinately fond of him. In short, putting one thing with another, it is abundantly clear that Mr Locker was a character. He would have filled two pages in one of the essays of Elia[7] to perfection. It seems to us a genuine tribute to Mr Birrell's perspicacity and humanity to find ourselves constantly reminded of that great storehouse of biography. When we observe that Mr Locker was born in 1821 and died in 1895, and thus lived through the heat of the Victorian midday, the feat on both their parts is the more miraculous. How did Mr Locker survive? How did Mr Birrell dare to tell the truth about him?

One of the chief merits of Mr Birrell's method, which is a peculiar compound of wit and sanity, is that it reduces these nineteenth-century phantoms to human scale. At the end of the book he prints a selection of letters from some of the most mythical – Tennyson and Thackeray,

Browning and Ruskin, George Eliot and Matthew Arnold.[8] They wrote much better letters than we do, but otherwise there is nothing to complain of. The monsters were not for ever propagating books and children, and desisting from their labours only to heave a grampus groan and then descend to the yeasty depths again. They were clear, sportive, even graceful and affectionate – to Frederick Locker that is. Thackeray, in particular, inspires the fancy that one could have talked to him as to a human being. Such is the effect of falling into the hands of a chronicler who will not be put upon by airs and graces. Naturally half the credit belongs to Mr Locker himself. It would, one guesses, have been very difficult to impose upon him. When a rare book presented itself he had a measuring rod with which he tested its pretensions to the fraction of an inch. Such was his method with poets and their poetry. His appetite was small, his taste fastidious; he rejected much, modestly blaming his own debility; but the famous people of his day rated the verdict of his rod very highly. It is impossible to mistake the tone in which they write to him. After such flattery as it was their wont to batten on, there was a sharpness in Mr Locker's judgements that pleased the palate. One after another wrote something affectionate in the first editions of their works which he was apt to produce from his pockets at propitious moments. He did not obtrude his own books unduly (there were only five little volumes), and yet the most unlikely people admired them sincerely. If we wished to ingratiate Mr Locker with the younger generation we should quote not only what Mr Hardy said of his 'perfect literary taste', but his praise of Mr Locker's poetry.[9] We forbear because it strikes us that perhaps Mr Locker would not wish to be ingratiated with the younger generation. He was a man of peculiar temperament – whimsical, indolent, worldly, honest. How it may be with other readers we know not, but with us the test of a good biography is that it leaves us with the impulse to write it all over again. 'Who can know him,' we cry out, 'half so intimately as we do?' On this occasion echo, with disconcerting rapidity, answers back, 'Nonsense. Nonsense. Read Mr Birrell. There is no more to be said.'

1 – A signed review in the *Athenaeum*, 13 August 1920, (Kp C205) of *Frederick Locker-Lampson. A Character Sketch*. With a small selection from letters addressed to him and bibliographical notes on a few of the books formerly in the Rowfant Library (Constable & Co., 1920). Composed and edited by his son-in-law the Rt Hon. Augustine Birrell [1850–1933], Honorary Fellow of Trinity Hall and one of the benchers of the Inner Temple.

Frederick Locker (1821–95), poet, sometime Admiralty clerk, had married first, in 1849, Lady Charlotte Bruce (d.1872), a daughter of the 7th Earl of Elgin (of marble fame), and then in 1874, Jane Lampson (d.1915), daughter of Sir Curtis Lampson, of Rowfant, Sussex. His works include: *London Lyrics* (1887); the anthology *Lyra Elegantiarum* (1867); *Patchwork* (1879), a collection of miscellaneous writings; and *My Confidences. An Autobiographical Sketch* (1896).

Essayist and Liberal statesman – he was Chief Secretary for Ireland, 1907–16, under Asquith – Augustine Birrell had married in 1888 Eleanor Tennyson, *née* Locker (d.1915), widow of Lionel Tennyson, younger son of the poet. Francis ('Frankie') Birrell, his son, was one of the younger generation associated with Bloomsbury.

See also 'Augustine Birrell', *V VW Essays*.

The same issue of the *Athenaeum* also contained an article by Roger Fry on 'Bolshevik Art'.

2 – Leonard Huxley, *Life and Letters of Huxley* (2 vols. 1900); Hallam Tennyson, *Alfred Lord Tennyson: A Memoir* (1897); James Dykes Campbell, *Coleridge: A Narrative of the Events of his Life* (1894); Dame Henrietta Octavia Weston Barnett, *Canon Barnett. His Life, Work and Friends* (2 vols. 1918).

3 – Sir George Arthur, *Life of Lord Kitchener* (3 vols, 1920); William F. Monypenny and George Earle Buckle, *The Life of Disraeli* (6 vols, 1910–20).

4 – Birrell, p. 67.

5 – *Ibid.*, p. 69.

6 – *Ibid.*, p. 81: '. . . a bust of Voltaire and an unusually lively tortoise, generally half way out of a paper bag.'

7 – Charles Lamb, *Elia* (1823 and 1828) and *The Last Essays of Elia* (1833).

8 – Alfred, Lord Tennyson (1809–92); W. M. Thackeray (1811–63); Robert Browning (1812–89); John Ruskin (1819–1900); George Eliot (1819–80); Matthew Arnold (1822–88). Birrell also printed (on p. 136) a letter from Leslie Stephen, dated 30 March 1877: 'I am afraid I have done a dreadfully stupid thing. I took your poem out of my pocket as I walked across the park, read it once or twice, mentally accepted it with thanks and put it back (as I thought), in my pocket. Now I cannot find it! I have looked and am looking everywhere but so far in vain. I write at once hoping that you have another copy at home and then I shall only give you or your daughter the trouble of copying it out again. I am grievously ashamed of myself for I never did such a thing before (except once when the loss was no loss) and blush at my stupidity. As I did not read often enough to know your verses by heart I must bother you. Please set my mind at rest as soon as you can. Yours (in sack cloth and ashes) . . .

I don't think that Hutton [then editing the literary pages of the *Spectator*] can have picked my pocket and I saw no other Editor about.'

9 – Birrell, p. 139; Thomas Hardy (1840–1928).

John Evelyn

Should you wish to make sure that your birthday will be celebrated three hundred years hence, your best course is, undoubtedly, to keep a diary. Yet most of us prefer to put our trust in poems, plays, novels, and histories. One in a generation, perhaps, has the courage to lock his genius in a private book and the humour to gloat over a fame which will be his only in the grave. There can be no doubt that the good diarists are those who write either for themselves or for a posterity so distant that it can safely hear every secret and justly weigh every motive. For such an audience there is no need either of affectation or of restraint. But a diary written to be published in the author's lifetime is no better than a private version of the newspaper, and often worse. The good opinion of our contemporaries means so much to us that it is well worthwhile to tell them lies.

But though these considerations may be just they are not on this occasion much to the point. Whatever else John Evelyn may have been he was neither introspective nor vindictive. The diary, for whose sake we are remembering his three-hundredth birthday, is sometimes composed like a memoir, sometimes jotted down like a calendar. But he never used its pages to reveal the secrets of his heart, and all he wrote might have been read aloud in the evening to his children. If we wonder, then, why we still trouble to read what we must consider the uninspired work of a good man, we have to confess what everybody knows — that it is impossible to read works of genius all day long. We have to confess that this reading, about which so many fine things have been said, is for the most part mere dreaming and idling; lying in a chair with a book; watching the butterflies on the dahlias; a profitless occupation which no critic has taken the trouble to investigate, and on whose behalf only the moralist can find a good word to say. For he will allow it to be an innocent employment, and happiness, though derived from trivial sources, has probably done more to prevent human beings from changing their religions and killing their kings than either philosophy or the pulpit.

It is indeed well, before reading much further in Evelyn's books, to decide where it is that our modern view of happiness differs from his. Undoubtedly ignorance is at the bottom of it. No one can read the story of Evelyn's foreign travels without envying in the first place his sim-

plicity of mind, in the second his activity. To take a simple example of
the difference between us. A butterfly will sit motionless on a flower
while a wheelbarrow is trundled past it. But touch the tip of its wing with
shadow and it is instantly up in the air. Presumably, then, a butterfly has
either small sense of sound or none. Here, no doubt, we are much on a
par with Evelyn. But as for going into the house to fetch a knife with
which to dissect a Red Admiral's head, no sane person in the twentieth
century would entertain such a notion for a second. Individually we may
know as little as Evelyn, but collectively we know so much that there is
little incentive to make private discoveries. We seek the encyclopædia,
not the scissors; and know in ten minutes not only more than was known
to Evelyn in his lifetime, but that the mass of knowledge is so vast that it
is scarcely worthwhile to possess a crumb. Ignorant, yet justly confident
that with his own hands he might advance not merely his private
knowledge but the knowledge of mankind, Evelyn dabbled in all the arts
and sciences, ran about the Continent for ten years, gazed with unflag-
ging gusto upon hairy women and elephants, magic stones and rational
dogs, and drew inferences and framed speculations which are now only
to be matched by listening to the talk of old women round the village
pump. The moon, they say, is so much larger than usual this autumn that
no mushrooms will grow and the carpenter's wife will be brought to bed
of twins. So Evelyn, Fellow of the Royal Society, a gentleman of the
highest culture and intelligence, carefully noted all comets and portents,
and thought it a sinister omen when a whale came up the Thames. Once
before this happened, in the year 1658. 'That year died Cromwell.'[2]
Nature certainly stimulated the devotion of her seventeenth-century
admirers by displays of violence and eccentricity from which she now
refrains. There were storms, floods, and droughts; the Thames frozen
hard; comets flaring in the sky. If a cat so much as kittened in Evelyn's
bed the kitten was inevitably gifted with eight legs, six ears, two bodies,
and two tails.

But to return to happiness. It sometimes appears that if there is an
insoluble difference between our ancestors and ourselves it is that we
draw our happiness from different sources. We rate the same things at
different values. Something of this we may ascribe to their ignorance and
our knowledge. But are we to suppose that ignorance alters the nerves
and the affections? Are we to believe that it would have been an
intolerable penance for us to live familiarly with the Elizabethans?
Should we have found it necessary to leave the room because of
Shakespeare's habits, and to have refused Queen Elizabeth's invitation

to dine? Perhaps so. For Evelyn was a sober man of unusual refinement, and yet he pressed into a torture chamber as we crowd to see the lions fed.

. . . they first bound his wrists with a strong rope or small cable, and one end of it to an iron ring made fast to the wall about four feet from the floor, and then his feet with another cable, fastened about five feet farther than his utmost length to another ring on the floor of the room. Thus suspended, and yet lying but aslant, they slid a horse of wood under the rope which bound his feet, which so exceedingly stiffened it, as severed the fellow's joints in miserable sort, drawing him out at length in an extraordinary manner, he having only a pair of linen drawers upon his naked body.[3]

And so on. Evelyn watched this to the end, and then remarked that 'the spectacle was so uncomfortable that I was not able to stay the sight of another',[4] as we might say that the lions growl so loud and the sight of raw meat is so unpleasant that we will now visit the penguins. Allowing for his discomfort, there is enough discrepancy between his view of pain and ours to make us wonder whether we see any fact with the same eyes, marry any woman from the same motives, or judge any conduct by the same standards. To sit passive when muscles tore and bones cracked, not to flinch when the wooden horse was raised higher and the executioner fetched a horn and poured two buckets of water down the man's throat, to suffer this iniquity on a suspicion of robbery which the man denied – all this seems to put Evelyn in one of those cages where we still mentally seclude the riff-raff of Whitechapel. Only it is obvious that we have somehow got it wrong. If we could maintain that our susceptibility to suffering and love of justice were proof that all our humane instincts were as highly developed as these, then we could say that the world improves and we with it. But let us get on with the diary.

In 1652, when it seemed that things had settled down unhappily enough, 'all being entirely in the rebels' hands', Evelyn returned to England with his wife of twelve, his Tables of Veins and Arteries,[5] his Venetian glass and the rest of his curiosities, to lead the life of a country gentleman of strong Royalist sympathies at Deptford. What with going to church and going to town, settling his accounts and planting his garden – 'I planted the orchard at Sayes Court; new moon, wind west.'[6] – his time was spent much as ours is. But there was one difference which it is difficult to illustrate by a single quotation because the evidence is scattered all about in little insignificant phrases. The general effect of them is that he used his eyes. The visible world was always close to him. The visible world has receded so far from us that to hear all this talk of buildings and gardens, statues and carving, as if the look of things assailed one out of doors as well as in, and were not confined to a few small canvases hung upon the wall, seems strange. No doubt there are a thousand excuses for us; but hitherto we have been finding excuses for him. Wherever there was a picture to be seen by Julio Romano, Polydore, Guido, Raphael, or Tintoretto,[7] a finely built house, a prospect, or a garden nobly designed, Evelyn stopped his coach to look at it, and opened his diary to record his opinion. On August 27 Evelyn, with Dr Wren and others, was in St Paul's surveying 'the general decay of that ancient and venerable church'; held with Dr Wren another judgement from the rest; and had a mind to build it with 'a noble cupola, a form of church building not as yet known in England but of wonderful grace' in which Dr Wren concurred. Six days later the Fire of London altered their plans.[8] It was Evelyn again who, walking by himself, chanced to look in at the window of 'a poor solitary thatched house in a field in our parish', there saw a young man carving at a crucifix, was overcome with an enthusiasm which does him the utmost credit, and carried Grinling Gibbons and his carving to Court.[9]

Indeed, it is all very well to be scrupulous about the sufferings of worms and sensitive to the dues of servant girls, but how pleasant also if, with shut eyes, one could call up street after street of beautiful houses. A flower is red; the apples rosy-gilt in the afternoon sun; a picture has charm, especially as it displays the character of a grandfather and dignifies a family descended from such a scowl; but these are scattered fragments – little relics of beauty in a world that has grown indescribably drab. To our charge of cruelty Evelyn might well reply by pointing to Bayswater and the purlieus of Clapham; and if he should assert that nothing now has character or conviction, that no farmer in England sleeps with an open coffin at his bedside to remind him of death, we could not retort effectually offhand. True, we like the country. Evelyn never looked at the sky.

But to return. After the Restoration Evelyn emerged in full possession of a variety of accomplishments which in our time of specialists seems remarkable enough. He was employed on public business; he was Secretary to the Royal Society;[10] he wrote plays and poems; he was the first authority upon trees and gardens in England; he submitted a design for the rebuilding of London; he went into the question of smoke and its abatement – the lime trees in St James's Park being, it is said, the result of his cogitations; he was commissioned to write a history of the Dutch war – in short, he completely outdid the Squire of *The Princess*, whom in many respects he anticipated –

A lord of fat prize oxen and of sheep,
A raiser of huge melons and of pine,
A patron of some thirty charities,
A pamphleteer on guano and on grain,
A quarter sessions chairman abler none.[11]

All that he was, and perhaps shared with Sir Walter another characteristic which Tennyson does not mention. He was, we cannot help suspecting, something of a bore. Or what is this quality, or absence of quality, which checks our sympathy? It is partly that he was better than his neighbours; partly that, though he deplored the vices of his age, he could never keep away from the centre of them. The 'luxurious dallying and profaneness' of the Court, the sight of 'Mrs Nelly' looking over her garden wall and holding 'very familiar discourse' with King Charles[12] on the green walk below, caused him acute disgust; but he could never make up his mind to break with the Court and retire to 'my poor, but quiet villa',[13] which was, of course, one of the show places of England. Then, though he loved his daughter Mary, his grief at her death did not prevent him from counting the number of empty coaches drawn by six horses apiece that attended her funeral. His women friends combined virtue with beauty to such an extent that we can hardly credit them with wit into the bargain. Poor Mrs Godolphin, at least, whom he celebrated in a sincere and touching biography, 'loved to be at the funerals' and chose habitually the 'dryest and leanest morsels of meat',[14] which may be the habits of an angel but do not present her friendship with Evelyn in an alluring light. The whole of our case against Evelyn, however, is summed up in the account of a visit which Pepys paid him on 6 November 1665. First Evelyn showed him some 'painting in little; then in distemper, in Indian ink, water-colour, graving and, above all, the whole secret of mezzo-tint and the manner of it'. He then read his discourse 'about gardenage, which will be a most pleasant piece'. Then a play or two of his making, 'very good, but not as he conceits them I think to be'; then he displayed his Hortus Hyemalis; and finally read aloud, 'though with too much gusto, some little poems of his own that were not transcendent . . . among others, one of a lady looking in at a gate and being pecked at by an eagle that was there'. 'In fine,' Pepys concluded at the end of the long morning's entertainment, 'a most excellent person he is, and must be allowed a little for a little conceitedness; but he may well be so, being a man so much above others.'[15]

Evelyn, as we are bound to remark after dipping into Pepys, was no genius. His writing is opaque rather than transparent. We see no depths through it, nor any very secret movements of mind and heart. He can neither make us hate a regicide nor love Mrs Godolphin beyond reason. But even as we drowse, somehow or other the bygone gentleman sets up, through three centuries, a perceptible tingle of communication, so that without laying stress upon anything in particular we are taking notice all the time. His hypocritical modesty about his own garden is no less evident than his acidity about the gardens of others. The hens at Sayes Court, we may be sure, laid the best eggs in England. When the Tsar drove a wheelbarrow through his holly hedge his cry is that of a man in agony.[16] Editors who wonder at the non-appearance of Mrs Evelyn should reflect that she was chiefly occupied in dusting china and cleaning ink-stains from the carpets. He was constantly asked to act as trustee; discharged his duties punctiliously, and yet grumbled at the waste of his time. Still he had a heart. Though a formal he was a very affectionate man. If paternal egotism probably hastened the death of the little prodigy Richard, he carried the memory of him throughout his life, and sighed deeply, not effusively – for the man with the long-drawn sensitive face was never effusive – when, 'after evening prayers was my child buried near the rest of his brothers – my very dear children.'[17] He was not an artist, perhaps; yet as an artistic method this of going on with the day's story circumstantially, bringing in people who will never be mentioned again, leading up to crises which never take place, has an undoubted merit. On one page we are agog to hear that Evelyn has a mind to visit Sir Thomas Browne.[18] The journey to Norwich in the flying chariot with six horses is precisely described, with the talk by the way. But when at length Evelyn meets Sir Thomas all he has to say of him is that he owns many curiosities; thinks Norfolk a good county for birds; and states that the people of Norwich have lost the art of squaring flints, which, of course, sets Evelyn off upon buildings and flower gardens and Sir Thomas Browne is never mentioned again.

Never to mention people again is a piece of advice that psychological novelists might well lay to heart. All through Evelyn's pages people are coming into the room and going out. The greater number we scarcely notice; the door shuts upon them and they disappear. But now and then the sight of a vanishing coat tail suggests more than a whole figure sitting still in a full light. Perhaps it is that we catch them unawares. Little they think that for three hundred years and more they will be looked at in the act of jumping a gate, or observing, like the old Marquis of Argyle, that the turtle doves in the aviary are owls.[19] There is a certain hot-tempered Captain Wray, for instance, upon whom we linger with unsatisfied affection. We are only told that he was choleric; that he had a dog who killed a goat; that he was for shooting the goat's owner; that when his horse fell down a precipice he was for shooting the horse; and, finally, that, coming to Geneva, he 'fell so mightily in love with one of Monsieur Saladine's daughters that, with much persuasion, he could not be prevailed on to think on his journey into France, the season now coming on extremely hot'. 'Yet,' says Evelyn, 'the ladies of Geneva are not beautiful.' They have 'something full throats'.[20] That is all there is about Captain Wray, but it is enough to start us upon speculations too numerous and too little authentic to be given here. And though the dusk has long closed upon Captain Wray and his bride – who, since the captain was choleric, the season hot, and the goitre prevalent, may never have become his bride after all – we are still curious, as is not usual at the end of psychological novels, to know what became of them. Mr Maynard Smith, had he reached that point, might have told us. For his commentary upon the early life and education of John Evelyn is the very book that an idle reader, reading as much with his eye off the page as on, must rejoice in not only because so much of its information is necessary but because so much of it is superfluous. The reason why Evelyn's father refused a knighthood is illuminating;[21] but it is difficult to see in what respect our knowledge of Evelyn's father's beard is improved by knowing that the Tudors wore beards, that Shakespeare mentioned them, and that the Puritans slept with theirs enclosed in cardboard boxes.

Indeed, had we to give an excuse for wasting our time first over Evelyn, then over Mr Smith's commentary upon Evelyn, which promises and will, we hope, fulfil its promise of exceeding Evelyn himself in length, we could only vaguely and falteringly explain that, whether alive or dead, good or bad, human beings have a hold upon our sympathies. That Evelyn had his faults is true; that we could not have spent an hour in his company without grave disagreement is also probable – though to have been shown over Wotton by the master in his old age when his gardens were flourishing, his grandson doing him credit, his sorrows smoothed out, and the Latin quotations falling pat from his lips, would have been a thing to stick in the memory; but, faults and limitations notwithstanding, he lived for 84 years and kept a record of 55 of them. That is enough for us. For without saying in the old language that he has taught us a lesson or provided an example, we cannot deny that the spectacle of human life on such a scale is full of delight. First we have the oddity of it; then the difference; then as the years go by the sense of coming to know the man better and better. When that is established, the circle in which he moves becomes plain; we see his friends and their doings; so that by degrees it is not one person but a whole society of people whom we watch at their concerns. Fate shepherded them all very straitly. There was no getting out of death or age; nor, though Evelyn protested, could he escape burial in the stone chancel of a church instead of lying in earth with flowers growing over him. All this provokes thought – idle thought, it is true, but of the kind that fills the mind with Evelyn's presence and brings him back, in the sunshine, to walk among the trees.[22]

1–A commemorative essay in the *TLS*, 28 October 1920, (Kp C208) also reviewing *The Early Life and Education of John Evelyn 1620–1641*. With a commentary by H. Maynard Smith (OUP, 1920), and largely based on a reading of *The Diary of John Evelyn* [1620–1706] (1818), probably in the two-volume edition published by J. M. Dent in 1911. For brief allusions to the approaching need to write on Evelyn see *II VW Diary*, 26 September and 1 October 1920. The essay was revised and included as 'Rambling Round Evelyn' in *CR1*; see *IV VW Essays*.

2–Diary, 26 March 1699 (J. M. Dent, 1911, vol. ii, p. 353). Oliver Cromwell (1599–1658).

3–*Ibid.*, 11 March 1651, vol. i, pp. 264–5. This was in Paris, at the Grand Châtelet, seat of the city's criminal and civil judiciary.

4–*Ibid.*

5–For the quotation, *ibid.*, 9 March 1652, vol. i, p. 276. Evelyn attended anatomy lectures at Padua and there obtained his tables, *ibid.*, 16 January 1646, vol. i, p. 214. On his way home he visited Paris where he met and on 27 June 1647 married Mary Browne (c.1635–1709), daughter of the King's Ambassador.

6–*Ibid.*, 19 February 1653, vol. i, p. 285. Evelyn lived at Sayes Court, Deptford, from 1652 until 1694, when he removed to Wotton House in the parish of Wotton or Blackheath, Surrey.

7–Giulio Romano (c.1492–1546); Polidoro Caldara da Caravaggio (c.1500–43); Guido Reni (1575–1642); Raphael (1483–1520); Tintoretto (1518–94).

8–For both quotations, Diary, 27 August 1666, vol. ii, pp. 9–10. The thirteenth-century cathedral restored by Inigo Jones in the mid seventeenth century was almost destroyed by the great fire, 2–7 September 1666. Sir Christopher Wren (1632–1723) was commissioned to design and build the new cathedral in 1668.

9–For both quotations, *ibid.*, 18 January 1671, vol. ii, pp. 56–8. Grinling Gibbons (1648–1721).

10–Evelyn, who became a Fellow of the Royal Society in 1661, was three times its Secretary: 1672–3, 1682, 1691.

11–Tennyson, *The Princess* (1847), 'Conclusion', ll. 86–90.

12–For the Court, Diary, 25 January 1685, vol. ii, p. 207; and for Nell Gwyn (1650–87), who bore Charles II (1630–85) two sons, *ibid.*, 1 March 1671, vol. ii, p. 60.

13–*Ibid.*, 4 October 1683, vol. ii, p. 192.

14–For the first quotation, Evelyn, *The Life of Margaret Godolphin* [1652–78] Ed. Bishop Wilberforce (William Pickering, 1847), p. 14, and for the second, *ibid.*, p. 175, which does not have 'of meat'.

15–For all the quotations, *The Diary of Samuel Pepys*, 5 November 1665 (ed. Latham and Matthews, G. Bell, 1972, pp. 289–90).

16–Evelyn let Sayes Court and in the summer of 1698 it was sublet to Peter the Great (1672–1725).

17–Diary, 29 March 1664, vol. i p. 386. This was Richard (b. and d. 1664), not the prodigy Richard (1652–8).

18–For Evelyn's visit to Sir Thomas Browne (1605–82), *ibid.*, 17 October 1671, vol. ii, pp. 69–70.

19–For Archibald Campbell (c.1607–61), Marquis of Argyll, and the owl-like doves, *ibid.*, 28 June 1656, vol. i, p. 318.

20–For the quotations, *ibid.*, c.July 1646, vol. i, p. 240. Sir William Wray (c.1625–69), believed to have been the Captain Wray who was Governor of Beaumaris Castle during the Protectorate. M. Saladine, unidentified.

21–Maynard Smith, ch. i, p. 2, Evelyn on his father Richard Evelyn (1588–1640): 'He was a studious decliner of honours and titles; being already in that esteem with his country, that they have added little to him besides their burden.' Which is annotated at length, p. 6, n9, explaining how a feudal law revived by Charles I in 1629 put a tax on knighthoods and made knighthoods compulsory for those owning above a certain amount of land, unless they opted out and paid a composition fee. Richard Evelyn declined to appear before the King's commissioners in this connection (as did Cromwell) and was fined accordingly.

22–The next issue of the *TLS*, 4 November, published two letters concerning VW's essay. One was from H. Maynard Smith, cataloguing errors of fact, and concluding that it is 'a waste of time to write on a subject in which you are not interested and about which you know very little'. The other came from Wm. Herbert W. Bliss, a Pepys fan, who thanked the author 'with both hands'. VW – as 'Your Reviewer' – replied to Maynard Smith's complaints in the issue for 11 November: 'Mr Maynard Smith's letter appears to be intended to accuse me of inaccuracies and of misinterpretation in my review of his book on John Evelyn. He has, I admit, succeeded in discovering three slips in four columns, and for these I am willing to offer him and you my apologies. It is true, as Mr Smith points out, that Evelyn lived 85 and not 84 years, and my inaccuracy was due to my taking the date of his death in 1705 old style instead of 1706 new style. It is true that by a slip I wrote 55 instead of 65 years as the number of years for which Evelyn kept his diary, and that, apparently in order to make the most of my slip Mr Smith states that Evelyn kept a diary for 75 years. But for Mr Smith to say that the diary begins in 1731 seems to me as pedantic as it was inaccurate for me to imply that it began in 1751. It is also, I regret to say, true that I said that Mr Evelyn met Mr Pepys on November 6, 1665, when, as Mr Smith rightly points out, it was really on November 5, 1665. ¶ But while I plead guilty to these chronological errors, I maintain my interpretation of Evelyn's character as against Mr Smith's – though I cannot swear that there was a carpet in Mr Evelyn's study. As for the occupations of Mr Evelyn's wife, let Mr Evelyn speak to them for himself: ". . . now within doors, never was any matron more busy than my wife, disposing of our plain country furniture for a naked old extravagant house, suitable to our employments. She has a diary and distaffs, for *lac, linum, et lanam,* and is become a very Sabine".'

Jane Austen and the Geese

Of all writers Jane Austen is the one, so we should have thought, who has had the least cause to complain of her critics. Her chief admirers have always been those who write novels themselves, and from the time of Sir Walter Scott to the time of George Moore[2] she has been praised with unusual discrimination.

So we should have thought. But Miss Austen-Leigh's book shows that we were far too sanguine. Never have we had before us such certain proof of the incorrigible stupidity of reviewers. Ever since Jane Austen became famous they have been hissing inanities in chorus. She did not like dogs; she was not fond of children; she did not care for England; she was indifferent to public affairs; she had no book learning; she was irreligious; she was alternately cold and coarse; she knew no one outside her family circle; she derived her pessimistic view of family life from observing the differences between her father and mother. Miss Austen-Leigh, whose piety is natural but whose concern we cannot help thinking excessive, is persuaded that there is some 'misapprehension'[3] about Jane Austen, and is determined to right it by taking each of the geese separately and wringing his neck. Someone, properly anonymous and we can scarcely help thinking fabulous, has expressed his opinion that Jane Austen was not qualified to write about the English gentry. The fact is, says Miss Austen-Leigh, that she was descended on her father's side from the Austens, who sprang, 'like other county families, from the powerful Clan of the Clothiers';[4] on her mother's from the Leighs of Addlestrop, who entertained King Charles. Moreover, she went to dances. She moved in good society. 'Jane Austen was in every way well fitted to write of the lives and feelings of English gentle people.'[5] In that conclusion we entirely concur. Still, the fact that you are well fitted to write about one set of people may be taken to prove that you are not well fitted to write about another. That profound observation is to the credit of a second anonymous fowl. Nor, to be candid, does Miss Austen-Leigh altogether succeed in silencing him. Jane Austen had, she assures us, opportunities for a wider knowledge of life than falls to the lot of most clergymen's daughters. An uncle by marriage lived in India and was a friend of Warren Hastings. He must have written home about the trial and the climate. A cousin married a French nobleman whose head was cut off in the Revolution. She must have had something to say about Paris and the guillotine. One of her brothers made the grand tour, and two were in the Navy.[6] It is, therefore, undeniable that Jane Austen might have 'indulged in romantic flights of fancy with India or France for a background',[7] but it is equally undeniable that Jane Austen never did. Yet it is difficult to deny that had she been not only Jane Austen but Lord Byron and Captain Marryat[8] into the bargain her works might have possessed merits which, as it is, we cannot truthfully say that we find in them.

Leaving these exalted regions of literary criticism the reviewers now attack her character. She was cold they say, and 'turned away from whatever was sad, unpleasant, or painful'. That is easily disposed of. The family archives contain proof that she nursed a cousin through the measles, and 'attended her brother Henry, in London, in an illness of which he nearly died'.[9] It is as easy from the same source to dispose of the malevolent assertion that she was the illiterate daughter of an illiterate father. When the Rev. George Austen left Steventon he sold five hundred books.[10] The number that he must have kept is quite enough to prove that Jane Austen was a well-read woman. As for the slander that her family life was unhappy, it is sufficient to quote the words of a cousin who was in the habit of staying with the Austens. 'When among this Liberal Society, the simplicity, hospitality, and taste which commonly prevail in different families among the delightful vallies [sic] of Switzerland ever occurs to my memory.'[11] The malignant and persistent critic still remains who says that Jane Austen was without morality. Indeed, it is a difficult charge to meet. It is not enough to quote her own statement, 'I am very fond of Sherlock's sermons.' The testimony of Archbishop Whately[12] does not convince us. Nor can we personally subscribe to Miss Austen-Leigh's opinion that in all her works 'one line of thought, one grace, or quality, or necessity ... is apparent. Its name is – Repentance'.[13] The truth appears to us to be much more complicated than that.

If Miss Austen-Leigh does not throw much light upon that problem, she does one thing for which we are grateful to her. She prints some notes made by Jane at the age of twelve or thirteen upon the margin of Goldsmith's *History of England*. They are slight and childish, useless, we should have thought, to confute the critics who hold that she was unemotional, unsentimental and passionless. 'My dear Mr G——, I have lived long enough in the world to know that it is always so,' she corrects her author amusingly. 'Oh! Oh! The wretches!' she exclaims against the Puritans. 'Dear Balmerino I cannot express what I feel for you!' she cries when Balmerino is executed.[14] There is nothing more in them than that. Only to hear Jane Austen saying nothing in her natural voice when the critics have been debating whether she was a lady, whether she told the truth, whether she could read, and whether she had personal experience of hunting a fox is positively upsetting. We remember that Jane Austen wrote novels. It might be worthwhile for her critics to read them.

1–A review in the TLS, 28 October 1920, (Kp C209) of *Personal Aspects of Jane Austen* [1775–1817] . . . with illustrations (John Murray, 1920) by Mary Augusta Austen-Leigh.

See also 'Jane Austen Practising', 'Jane Austen at Sixty' (headnote), below; '*Jane Austen*', *II VW Essays*; and 'Jane Austen', *II VW Essays*, and *CR* 1.
2–Sir Walter Scott (1771–1832); George Moore (1852–1933).
3–Austen-Leigh, ch. i, p. 9.
4–*Ibid.*, ch. ii, p. 10.
5–*Ibid.*, p. 20.
6–For the uncle by marriage, Saul Tysoe Hancock, husband of Philadelphia Austen, and friend of Warren Hastings (1732–1818), *ibid.*, ch. iv, p. 42; for the cousin, Elizabeth Hancock, who married in 1781 Jean Capotte, Comte de Feuillide, *ibid.*, ch. iii, p. 35; for the brother, Edward, who made the grand tour, *ibid.*, ch. iv, p. 43, and for the naval connection, p. 44.
7–*Ibid.*, ch. iv, p. 59.
8–Lord Byron (1788–1824); Frederick Marryat (1792–1848), upon whom VW later wrote in 'The Captain's Death Bed', *VI VW Essays*.
9–For the first quotation, Austen-Leigh, ch. iii, pp. 33–4, and for the second, p. 34.
10–For Jane Austen's father and his library, *ibid.*, ch. iv, p. 52.
11–*Ibid.*, ch. iii, p. 40, quoting 'An Old Family History' by the Hon. Agnes Leigh, *National Review*, April, 1907, and which has 'valleys'.
12–For the quotation concerning Jane Austen's liking for the *Sermons* (2 vols., 1755) of William Sherlock, DD (1641?–1707), dean of St Paul's, *ibid.*, ch. v, p. 94; and for the testimony of Richard Whately (1787–1863), Archbishop of Dublin, *ibid.*, p. 97, quoting the *Quarterly Review*, January, 1821: 'Miss Austen introduces very little of what is technically called religion into her books, yet that must be a blinded soul which does not recognise the vital essence, everywhere present in her pages, of a deep and enlightened piety.'
13–*Ibid.*, ch. v, p. 68: 'There is one line of thought, one grace, or quality, or necessity, whichever title we like to know it by, apparent in all her works.'
14–For Jane Austen's juvenile commentary upon the *History of England in a Series of Letters* (1764) by Oliver Goldsmith (1730–74), *ibid.*, ch. iii, pp. 26–8, which has 'Wretches' and 'Dear Balmerino!' The first quotation was in response to Goldsmith's

condemnation of those who were 'stunning mankind with a cry of Freedom'. Arthur Elphinstone, 6th Baron Balmerino (1688–1746), the Jacobite leader, executed after the Battle of Culloden.

Postscript or Prelude?

Perhaps the verdicts of critics would read less preposterously and their opinions would carry greater weight if, in the first place, they bound themselves to declare the standard which they had in mind, and, in the second, confessed the course, bound, in the case of a book read for the first time, to be erratic, by which they reached their final decision. Our standard for Mr Lawrence, then, is a high one. Taking into account the fact, which is so constantly forgotten, that never in the course of the world will there be a second Meredith or a second Hardy,[2] for the sufficient reason that there have already been a Meredith and a Hardy, why, we sometimes asked, should there not be a D. H. Lawrence? By that we meant that we might have to allow him the praise, than which there is none higher, of being himself an original; for such of his work as came our way was disquieting, as the original work of a contemporary writer always is.

This was the standard which we had in mind when we opened *The Lost Girl*. We now go on to trace the strayings and stumblings of that mind as it came to the conclusion that *The Lost Girl* is not an original, or a book which touches the high standard which we have named. Together with our belief in Mr Lawrence's originality went, of course, some sort of forecast as to the direction which that originality was likely to take. We conceived him to be a writer, with an extraordinary sense of the physical world, of the colour and texture and shape of things, for whom the body was alive and the problem of the body insistent and important. It was plain that sex had for him a meaning which it was disquieting to think that we, too, might have to explore. Sex, indeed, was the first red-herring that crossed our path in the new volume. The story is the story of Alvina Houghton, the daughter of a draper in Woodhouse, a mining town in the Midlands. It is all built up of solid fabric. If you want a truthful description of a draper's shop, evident knowledge of his stock, and a faithful and keen yet not satiric or sentimental description of James Houghton, Mrs Houghton, Miss Frost and Miss Pinnegar, here you have it. Nor does this summary do any kind of justice to the variety of the cast and the number of events in which they play their parts. But, distracted by our preconception of what Mr Lawrence was to give us, we turned many pages of very able writing in search for something else which must be there. Alvina seemed the most likely instrument to transmit Mr Lawrence's electric shock through the calicos, prints, and miners' shirts by which she stood surrounded. We watched for signs of her development nervously, for we always dread originality, yet with the sense that once the shock was received we should rise braced and purified. The signs we looked for were not lacking. For example, 'Married or unmarried, it was the same – the same anguish, realized in all its pain after the age of fifty – the loss in never having been able to relax, to submit.'³ Again, 'She was returning to Woodhouse virgin as she had left it. In a measure she felt herself beaten. Why? Who knows ... Fate had been too strong for her and her desires. Fate which was not an external association of forces, but which was integral in her own nature.'⁴ Such phrases taken in conjunction with the fact that Alvina, having refused her first suitor, wilted and pined, and becoming a midwife mysteriously revived in the atmosphere of the Islington Road, confirmed us in our belief that sex was the magnet to which the myriad of separate details would adhere. We were wrong. Details accumulated; the picture of life in Woodhouse was built up; and sex disappeared. This detail, then this realism, must have another meaning that we had given them. Relieved, yet a trifle disappointed, for we want originality as much as we dread it, we adopted a fresh attitude, and read Mr Lawrence as one reads Mr Bennett⁵ – for the facts, and for the story. Mr Lawrence shows indeed something of Mr Bennett's power of displaying by means of immense industry and great ability a section of the hive beneath glass. Like all the other insects, Alvina runs in and out of other people's lives, and it is the pattern of the whole that interests us rather than the fate of one of the individuals. And then, as we have long ceased to find in reading Mr Bennett, suddenly the method seems to justify itself by a single phrase which we may liken to a glow or to a transparency, since to quote one apart from the context would give no idea of our meaning. In other words, Mr Lawrence occasionally and momentarily achieves that concentration which Tolstoy⁶ preserves sometimes for a chapter or more. And then again the laborious process continues of building up a model of life from saying how d'you do, and cutting the loaf, and knocking the cigarette ash into the ash tray, and standing the yellow bicycle against the wall. Little by little Alvina disappears beneath the heap of facts recorded about her, and the only sense in which we feel her to be lost is that we can no longer believe in her existence.

So, though the novel is probably better than any that will appear for the next six months, we are disappointed, and would write Mr Lawrence off as one of the people who have determined to produce seaworthy books were it not for those momentary phrases and for a strong suspicion that the proper way to look at *The Lost Girl* is as a stepping stone in a writer's progress. It is either a postscript or a prelude.

1 – A review in the *TLS*, 2 December 1920, (Kp C210) of *The Lost Girl* (Martin Secker, 1920) by D. H. Lawrence (1885–1930).

VW noted in her diary on Wednesday, 8 September 1920, that the editor of the *TLS* had 'suggested a list of victims, Murry & Lawrence among them, at the thought of which I shivered & shuddered, & finally decided to run the risk'; see also *II VW Diary*, Tuesday, 23 November and 'Notes on D. H. Lawrence', *VI VW Essays*. Reprinted: *CW*.

2 – George Meredith (1828–1909); Thomas Hardy (1840–1928).

3 – Lawrence, ch. ii, pp. 33–4.

4 – *Ibid.*, ch. iii, p. 47: 'She was returning to Woodhouse . . . Why? Who knows. But so it was, she felt herself beaten, condemned to go back to what she was before. Fate . . . Her own inscrutable nature was her fate: sore against her will.'

5 – Arnold Bennett (1867–1931).

6 – L. N. Tolstoy (1828–1910).

Pleasant Stories

When Mr Hergesheimer says, 'These stories have but one purpose – to give pleasure,'[2] every reviewer will wish himself a novelist. It is more blessed, that is to say, to give simply and freely than to receive cautiously and questioningly. Of course Mr Hergesheimer gives us pleasure, but so do bright fires, oysters, and clean sheets. It is the dismal office of the reviewer to splinter pleasure into separate pieces which he examines, compares, and judges to be good, better, or best. Excitement, for example – is that the right kind of pleasure or the wrong? About two pages before the end of each of Mr Hergesheimer's seven stories the hand slips out and lies across the print in order to bar the eye from leaping and galloping to the end. Reviewers are epicures. If we read too quick we know that we shall miss the niceties of this careful, economical, and well-trained craftsman. 'Below, the water was invisible in the wrap of night. Naples shone like a pale gold net drawn about the sweep of its hills. A glow like a thumb print hung over Vesuvius; the hidden column of smoke smudged the stars.'[3] The wrap, the net, the thumb-print smudging the stars will each, if you spare the time, yield a little drop of pleasure. Mr Hergesheimer's pages are always strewn with such felicities. He has a fine sense of matter. Still, even the great masters of material description, as Keats was in 'The Eve of St Agnes',[4] always seem to be doing the easy thing when they are doing that. Must we suspect that our pleasure in the 'gowns by Verlat'[5] and the pink pearl necklace is a little gross and indolent? That is putting it too harshly. For, as we say, we have to read on. The stories are far too well contrived to smother us in old lace or hypnotise us with pink pearls while down below the bullfighter is challenging the banker to a duel. Indeed, the main source of our pleasure is that so many things happen and happen so quickly, and seem to be happening to such solid people. For though the space is small and the movements to be gone through in that space many and violent, Mr Hergesheimer gives his figures considerable body. They are forcibly cut out with strong, clean strokes. Perhaps the heaviest meal we have ever eaten in fiction occurs in 'Bread'.[6] As we sit munching solidly through the courses with August Turnbull, we begin to feel that our pleasure is really respectable. The clams, the turtle soup, the thick crimson slices of beef, the ice, the coffee, the long dark roll of oily tobacco, are the right symbols for the man and his life. He will not escape his fate, and his fate will be fitting and satisfactory; and we shall feel that we have been let into a secret about life, which is perhaps the most pleasurable sensation there is. Judge, then, of our disappointment when a melodramatic boat drifts, as if towed invisibly by a cinema man in a tug, ashore at Turnbull's feet, containing a crew of starved, lead-coloured corpses on top of whom Turnbull of course falls dead, solely, as we feel, to give us an extra dollop of pleasure.

In short, if you look back over these seven stories, you will find that your pleasure has come from things that happen and not from the people to whom they happen. Adequate and lifelike as they are, they are obedient dolls to be disposed of, and will fold their limbs and fit into the box when the play is over. We say this with regret, because many of them have acted their parts vigorously and well. Mr Hergesheimer might rightly urge that, if he had let them dawdle about and get ideas into their heads, nothing would have happened. No box would have held them. Very likely we should have been bored. And are we sure that we should not have sacrificed a certain pleasure for one that is not merely uncertain, but also extremely mixed, compounded of all sorts of sighs, hints, hesitations, nebulous and yet startling, full of horror and illumi-nation? Why think of Tchehov[7] when one is reading Mr Hergesheimer? Why spoil what we have by imagining what we have not? Only because it is, in our opinion, a good thing to take writers seriously; for then perhaps they will think it worth their while to give us not simply pleasure, but a good kind of pleasure – for which our appetite is unbounded.

1 – A review in the TLS, 16 December 1920, (Kp C211) of The Happy End (William Heinemann, 1920) by Joseph Hergesheimer (1880–1954); for biographical note see 'Java Head', n1 above. See also 'Gold and Iron', 'The Pursuit of Beauty' above, and 'The Three Black Pennys', II VW Essays. Reprinted: CW.
2 – Hergesheimer, 'Dedication', p. v.
3 – Ibid., 'The Flower of Spain', p. 135.
4 – John Keats, 'The Eve of St Agnes' (1819).
5 – Hergesheimer, 'The Flower of Spain', p. 115: 'Verlat, a celebrated dressmaker, was typical of the Viennese spirit – the gown Lavinia wore resembled, in all its implications, an orchid.'; pp. 121 and 122 have: 'Verlat gown'.
6 – Ibid., 'Bread', pp. 185–219.
7 – Anton Chekhov (1860–1904).

A Flying Lesson

Are there still to be found reviewers who review Mr Beerbohm – conscientious people who make marks in the margin, note numbers on the flyleaf, and propose to themselves to look up Addison, Lamb, and Hazlitt before they go to bed?[2] Perhaps they still exist, in the remoter wilds of England, and for our part we think of them gratefully, grudge them none of their pleasure, and wish them luck. May they bring him to book! Better is it to play even at being a Judge than to abdicate as we do in London when Mr Beerbohm comes before us, and trail our robes in the gutter, and beg the criminal to have a drink, for which we insist upon paying. No, it is high time to stop this foolery. In this review, at any rate, there shall be no mention of the 'incomparable Max'.[3]

Must we then look up Addison, Hazlitt, and Lamb before we go to bed, and sharpen a pencil, and wonder which of the sentences on page a hundred and fifty one deserves to have a loop round it, and why, and what it all comes to? Someone on the marches of Wales or on the borders of Scotland is already doing that; his brow is severe, his pencil sharp.

Ours has rolled beneath the coal-scuttle. We have an overpowering desire to let it lie. Pencils are in the habit of writing. Ours is capable of saying 'B writes like a gentleman' or 'B – poor B – is a Victorian at heart'. And suppose that Mr Beerbohm should read what the pencil has to say about B? There! The cat is out of the bag; the pencil at the opposite side of the room. The truth is plain. Mr Beerbohm is reviewing us.

No longer attempting to write, and abandoning whatever remains of authority, we proceed then to consider why so strange a thing should have happened. What does it mean? A moment's thought assures us that any anxiety on our part as to what Mr Beerbohm may think of this sentence or of that is totally uncalled for. Nothing we may say will penetrate to Rapallo (where the preface is written) on the far Riviera di Levante,[4] or if it did, however vigorously it was launched, bitterly envenomed, or charged with sweetness, against his armour it would flutter and fall softly as a feather. It is a curious combination – to be invulnerable oneself and yet to have the power of influencing others. It is not conferred by the Italian climate, nor indeed by the power of writing well. One gains it only by hovering on the borderland of immortality. Mr Beerbohm is neither one thing nor the other – neither alive and struggling nor dead and enskied. There is all the difference in the world between him and a writer like Addison. Addison, so we say as we read him, wrote superbly. But then he had no choice. Some genius draped in white, with the chiselled features of an Abbey statue held his pen and directed it unfalteringly. He could do not other than he did. Not a word could be placed differently – even by him; our efforts to deflect them are wholly vain. But Mr Beerbohm's page is not yet by any means of the consistency of marble. No classical goddess holds his pen in her white fingers; often we seem to see him mortal, fallible, and striving even as ourselves. That is why we read him almost as if we had written him. Speaking for ourselves (for the presumption may well be personal), the only writers whom we catch ourselves not imitating, or re-writing, but writing, are those ambiguous spirits hovering between the living and the dead. Addison has gone over. Mr Beerbohm hovers between the fields of Asphodel and the flags of Fleet Street. The titles of his essays might well have been the titles of ours. We too might have sat down to luncheon between Swinburne and Watts-Dunton at No. 2, The Pines.[5] But fate this time has called upon Mr Beerbohm. He acquits himself to admiration. Applause is universal as he sits down. But, to be candid, there were several narrow shaves. 'B. only saved by the skin of his teeth,' said the pencil. And again, 'Ice precious thin'; and again, 'Thank God!' We have indeed been almost as nervous during the performance as if it had been our own. Never was there a more beautiful subject, and none therefore exposed to a greater variety of disasters. They come flocking to mind even as Mr Beerbohm takes his way smiling through their midst. Reason tempts him to follow her austere maze. The spirit of English prose begs him to turn his sentences smoother and smoother still. Vanity hints that the first person singular would sound nicely here. Sarcasm proffers her sword. Sentiment has her basket of rose-leaves. Common sense pleads that she can cover a bald patch as well as another. Convention and good manners smile and show false teeth. All these temptations are offered; all are put aside, not violently but gently, as if conscious of their wiles and unafraid to look them in the face. At last we come within sight of the end; and who can approach the last hundred words without a leap of the heart? Consider how much is at stake. Swinburne, Watts-Dunton, Mr Beerbohm himself. All these have been brought through the jaws of death into animation and proportion and being. Yet such is the art of writing that a hundred words, particularly if they come at the end, can obliterate five thousand. Would it not be better simply to refrain? The pencil will say with some show of justice, 'B.'s shirked it', but far better to shirk it than to shriek or to shout or to stamp, or to sit down suddenly upon nothing at all. But even as we shrink Mr Beerbohm has unfurled his wings, skimmed his abyss, and landed, literally, in Elysium. How was it done? We were not looking. Let him do it again. He does it obligingly twenty times over, and each time it seems that one of these days we too shall fly, not very far, not out of sight, but just over the roofs of the houses. Courage then! Let us try. But the houses are higher than they seem.

1–A review in the TLS, 3 December 1920, (Kp C212) of And Even Now (William Heinemann, 1920) by Max Beerbohm (1872–1956). See also 'The Limits of Perfection' above, and see 'The Modern Essay', IV VW Essays and CR1.
2–Joseph Addison (1672–1719); Charles Lamb (1775–1834); William Hazlitt (1778–1830).
3–George Bernard Shaw (1856–1950), in the Saturday Review, 21 May 1898, on relinquishing to Beerbohm his post as the paper's drama critic: 'The younger generation is knocking at the door; and as I open it there steps spritely in the incomparable Max.'
4–Beerbohm had lived at Rapallo, with periodic visits to England, since his marriage in 1910 to the American actress Florence Kahn.
5–Beerbohm, 'No. 2 The Pines' (1914), pp. 57–88; Algernon Charles Swinburn (1837–1909); Theodore Watts-Dunton (1832–1914).

1921

'Revolution'

If the reader finds something amiss with Mr Beresford's *Revolution* he will probably blame the subject. He will say that revolutions are not a fit subject for fiction. And there he will be wrong. But, as we should probably allow if we had him in the armchair opposite, we can see what he means. He means that to write a book about what is going to happen in England when Isaac Perry proclaims a general strike and the Army refuses to obey its officers is not a novelist's business. He feels, and here we agree with him, a little defrauded when a writer like Mr Beresford, who can make you interested in his characters, chooses instead to make you interested in the failure of the Communal milk-cart to arrive at Winston at half-past nine. Yet the fault cannot lie with revolutions. As Tolstoy and Hardy have proved, revolutions are fine things to write about if only they have happened sufficiently long ago.[2] But if you are impelled to invent your own revolution, half your energy will be needed to make sure that it works. A large part of Mr Beresford's labour in writing *Revolution* has been spent, we should guess, upon calculations, of which we invent the following example. If the N.U.R.[3] came out on Thursday is it probable that the Transport Workers would follow suit on Monday morning, and, if so, what would be the effect on the Stock Exchange, and how much would the pound sterling have fallen in New York by the following Friday? The calculation is difficult. Moreover, we have observed that when such arguments are seriously discussed the disputants simplify their labours by using letters of the alphabet instead of proper names. It would be untrue to say that the young soldier

Paul Leaming, his father the merchant, his sister the woman at home, Isaac Perry the trade union leader, Lord Fynemore the aristocrat, are merely letters of the alphabet, but they are far more alphabetical than we like.

We go back, in a digression which the eminence of Mr Beresford's name perhaps sanctions, to wonder what has happened to the author of *Jacob Stahl*, the *House in Demetrius Road* and *These Lynnekers*,[4] to name three very memorable novels out of a total now amounting to fourteen. We say offhand that he is becoming increasingly intellectual and add, by way of explanation, that we find him more and more inclined to think about life and less and less inclined to feel about it. He now seems impelled to write a new novel by the desire to see whether a theory which works correctly in the study will set human legs and arms in motion and even affect the action of the human heart. He is immune, we feel, from all sorts of distractions and beguilements and grows increasingly accurate, methodical and explicit. Thus in *Revolution* it is the intellectual efficiency of the work that we admire. Given certain conditions it appears highly probable that events will happen much as Mr Beresford supposes. The interest is very great. Some of the scenes are highly exciting, nor does Mr Beresford's trained grasp upon the mechanism of behaviour slip or fumble. We feel convinced that a merchant of old Mr Leaming's calibre would continue to mow the field imperturbably under the jeers of the mob. It is he, too, who would be the first to lose his temper at the village council and provoke the leading rebel to shoot him through the head. So far as it goes the psychology is sound and each group of the community is adequately represented by a man or woman of sufficient vitality. But, to tell the truth, the psychology might have been more sketchy than it is without making us uncomfortable. For we are alert to challenge, not the feelings, but the facts. And facts are always disputable. They set one arguing. We find ourselves tempted to suggest alternatives, and seriously wish to draw Mr Beresford's attention to the importance of the cooperative movement which he appears to overlook. Feelings, on the other hand, admit, or should admit, of no dispute. When Mr Beresford introduces Lady Angela and sets her playing Chopin by the light of the last candle we should be convinced that it is Lady Angela who matters, and not the cooperative movement. If our attention wanders it annoys us, because we feel that human beings are too important to be disregarded, and yet, as Lady Angela plays, we cannot help thinking about a possible policy for the left wing of the Labour Party. We want Mr Beresford to turn his mind to that problem, directly the Chopin is over. In short, we want him to give us facts, not fiction.

1 – A review in the *TLS*, 27 January 1921, (Kp C213) of *Revolution* (W. Collins Sons & Co. Ltd., 1921) by J. D. [John Davys] Beresford (1873–1947). VW wrote in her diary on Sunday, 19 December 1920: 'I ought to say how happy I am, since one of these pages said how unhappy I was. I can't see any reason in it. My only guess is that it has something to do with working steadily; writing things out of my head; & never having a compartment empty . . . No doubt I like getting letters from publishers: even to be asked to preside over Mr Beresford slightly kindles me.'

    See also 'Freudian Fiction' above, where there is a more extensive biographical note, and see 'Mr Bennett and Mrs Brown', n1, below. Reprinted: CW.

2 – L. N. Tolstoy (1828–1910); Thomas Hardy (1840–1928), gave fictional treatment to the Napoleonic wars in both *The Trumpet-Major* (1880) and, that more ambitious 'Iliad of Europe from 1789 to 1815', his dramatic verse epic *The Dynasts* (1903, 1906, 1908).

3 – National Union of Railwaymen.

4 – *The Early History of Jacob Stahl* (1911; part of a trilogy including *A Candidate for Truth*, 1912; and *The Invisible Event*, 1915); *The House in Demetrius Road* (1914); *These Lynnekers* (1916).

Mr Norris's Standard

Mr Norris has now been writing novels, his publishers tell us, for forty years, and *Tony the Exceptional* is, we believe, the youngest of a family of fifty, or it may be sixty, for we shall not perjure ourselves by pretending that we have kept strict count, or pretend that we could recite a large proportion of their names offhand. For all that, whenever we meet with one of the short, safe, amiably patronising reviews with which Mr Norris is annually saluted, we want to tell him that we feel, and would, if we could, explain, that he is somehow different from the rest. We may treat him like an old established firm of grocers. We may open the familiar parcel and sniff the contents and say that it is up to sample, a trifle paler, pinker, smaller or rounder than last year's product, but that is only because the reviewers of novels are the laziest and most perfunctory of mortals, and because, to tell the truth, the task of analysing what we mean when we say that Mr Norris is different from the rest is difficult. One has, in the first place, to strike the right pitch. One must resist the temptation to make a discovery of Mr Norris. He is not so great an artist as Flaubert nor so fine a psychologist as Henry James.[2] No; but having shut off the high-lights with one hand one must be equally quick to shut off the shadows with the other. He has no sort of truck with the obscene creatures of the underworld – the mere manufacturers of stuffing. His station, preserved so long with what has come to appear such patient modesty, is precisely in that mid-region between the obscure and the illustrious, where it is most difficult to distinguish clearly. Let us see what we can make out by the light of *Tony the Exceptional*.

The publishers having said that the book is 'well up to Mr Norris's standard – he tells a fascinating story in a straightforward style', we feel impelled to say that far too much attention is paid to Mr Norris's fascinating stories and far too little to the art with which he tells them. The story as it happens is a good one; it mystifies, interests, and works out; but the style is not straightforward if simple, common, or easy to come by is meant by that. Indeed, when one says that Mr Norris is different from the rest, one means largely that he has a gift unfortunately rare among us – a sense of form. No one acquires that sense because he happens to hit upon a good anecdote, or the police-court records would make the best reading in the world. The 280 pages of *Tony* are the result of innumerable acts of selection; the hand that shaped them was inspired by a definite artistic aim. For purely aesthetic reasons which have nothing to do with the story, now this has been left out, now that has been put in. If we ask what Mr Norris has left out, it is easy to reply hurriedly, 'Oh, everything interesting.' He has left out passion, tragedy, philosophy, psychology, and so on. And what has he put in? Again the answer would be hasty – 'Oh, ladies and gentlemen,' meaning by that manners, the manners of good society.

Tony the Exceptional does, on the face of it, lend some support to this view, inasmuch as everyone concerned in it is either a lady or a gentleman, and therefore of good manners, or an ex-shop assistant, and therefore of bad. Never were heights and contours more plainly marked upon a survey map than are the shades of good and bad breeding in a novel by Mr Norris. The serious charge against a novelist of manners is, of course, that he allows himself to be put off by surface tricks which human beings have adopted to decorate or facilitate the rub of daily life. In another hundred years, one might argue, the code will have changed, and where then will be the point of Mr Norris's ladies and gentlemen? Have they not already rather the look of Orientals going through mysterious devotions, prostrating themselves before dusty top hats, obsolete dress clothes, and ancient packs of visiting cards? Doris, for example, will not marry the man she loves because he has told her a lie. She does not consider that lies differ, that liars may be pitiable, that characters are complex. No lady marries a liar; that is her code; and to that she adheres. But she has somehow evolved for herself a dispensation which decrees that if a lady has scratched her initials upon a sixpenny-bit she may, upon delivery of the coin at the critical moment, revoke her decision without compromising her honour. Was there ever an idol made more palpably of wood?

But we have overshot the mark by a long way, as it is not difficult to do, indeed, where the marks are so lightly scored. The situation which we have just declared to be absurd is, as a matter of fact, the most interesting in the book, and the one we should certainly select for analysis if we wished to explain our belief that Mr Norris is not a time-serving, mechanical writer, but a writer of art and intuition. Doris and her code and her sixpence are, we say, absurd. Without disputing the matter Mr Norris quietly goes on to persuade us that Doris is much more pitiable than ridiculous. She knows that she is absurd; she is afraid of her own absurdity. She is a self-contained and rigid character. It is not in her nature to talk and analyse. A sixpence with initials scratched upon it is as near as she can come to self-expression. We are not asked to admire her. Why, even her mother, who adores her, says a little later that she herself cannot influence Doris. 'I don't say that she's right, I only say that she's like that.'[3] It drips out, as if by chance, that mother and daughter never have much to say to each other. Indeed, the mother is a little afraid of her daughter. Thus we are brought to see that Doris is 'like that'. But only a true novelist does it in this way – one scene suggesting and confirming another spontaneously, as bubbles froth at the end of a pipe. And each has sprung not from observation of manners but from insight into the human heart.

A skilful critic might from this point go on to determine why it is that Mr Norris never persists but always draws back with a smile from exploring these moments of intuition. It is difficult not to speak as though his discretion were due to that social tact which he finds so admirable in his characters. To know people intimately one must pursue them into the privacy of their rooms. But Mr Norris is never alone with themselves. There is always a dog upon the hearth-rug. Yet we are inclined to think that it is not a modest estimate of his own powers that restrains him. He obeys a mysterious law which, without knowing exactly what we mean, we call the law of form. The demands of a good story probably help to guide his steps. A love of clean language forbids riot or indiscretion in that department. A moderate, or even slightly cynical, view of human nature checks exuberance of another kind. In short, we would as soon read Mr Norris on a railway journey as a good French novelist, and for much the same reasons. But pending the decisions of the skilful critic we may let Mr Norris, in a characteristic sentence, sum up what we feel to be the supporting backbone of all his fiction – '. . . when you have a standard you have a standard, and there is no use in arguing about it'.[4]

1–A review in the TLS, 10 February 1921, (Kp C214) of Tony the Exceptional (Hutchinson & Co., 1921) by W. E. (William Edward) Norris (1847–1925). See also 'The Obstinate Lady', 'Mr Norris's Method', above, and 'Barham of Beltana', 'Lone Marie', I VW Essays. Reprinted: CW.
2–Gustave Flaubert (1821–80); Henry James (1843–1916).
3–Norris, ch. xix, p. 208.
4–Ibid., ch. v, p. 54.

Henley's Criticism

Five of the essays in the present volume – those on Fielding, Smollett, Hazlitt, and Byron's world – were written to introduce editions of those writers' works, and they appeared from nineteen to twenty-five years ago.[2] Separated from the body of the text, and issued to an age which is more distant in temper than in time, they read not quite perhaps as they read in their own place and season. If we were about to read Tom Jones[3] for the first time and wished before beginning to tune ourselves up to the right pitch, undoubtedly Henley's essay upon Fielding would serve us admirably. We are told who he was, and whom he married, and how he suffered, and what he wrote. More than that we are stirred by the vibration of Henley's sympathy to feel that, if Fielding himself were to step into the room directly Henley had done talking about him, we should spring up and grasp him warmly by the hand. But Fielding does not step into the room. It is Tobias Smollett[4] who comes next. All our preparations for understanding and discriminating fall therefore a little flat. For though Henley has prepared us admirably to welcome Fielding, he has, somehow, given us little to think about in his absence. He takes it that we are about to read him; not that we wish to sift and consider what we have read. Does he not remark upon the last page but one of an essay packed with various information:

I shall say nothing about the four great books, for the very simple reason that everything there is to say about them has been said . . . 'Tis enough, that, as I think, Harry Fielding was a great and good man; who also, by premeditation and design, laboriously created an art, and created it in such terms, and to such a purpose, that none has practised it since his time but must have worked and written differently if this immortal Master had not written and worked before him.[5]

'Tis enough, according to Henley, to prove that a man is great and good. The labour, meditation, and design, the art which these have produced, and the effect of the art upon all who come later need no mention or can be compared with St Paul's Cathedral – 'which I esteem the piece of architecture the nearest to perfection these eyes of mine have seen' – or can be found admirably summed up by Gibbon, Gray, Scott, Coleridge, Byron, Thackeray, George Eliot, Leslie Stephen, and Austin Dobson[6] – to name a few who have held opinions, and held different opinions, upon Fielding's art. As the other essays are influenced to some, though not to the same, extent by this conception of a critic's duty, it may be worth while to consider for a moment what it amounts to.

Henley was not the only one to hold it. Nor is it the result of complete editions requiring introductions by celebrated hands. Life is to blame for decreeing that immortal works shall proceed from mortal bodies. If Fielding had been a man of property, if Burns had been a faithful husband, if Mrs Byron had not been possessed by sentiments of false delicacy at Byron's birth,[7] English literature would be very different from what it is. The truth of that is undeniable; and if we are out to unravel the secret of the artist's achievement, how can we afford to neglect such valuable clues? Critics of Henley's persuasion are, indeed, inspired by a colossal ambition. First they will know the facts; next they will elicit from them whatever is relevant to their purpose; finally, having created the man, set him in his proper surroundings, supplied him with aunts and uncles, followed his wanderings, named his lodgings, and indicated precisely how far and at what points wine, women, heredity, poverty, disease, and a taste for opium have laid hands upon his art, they will then from this elevation soar above the accidental and the temporal and exhibit his work as it appears in the eye of eternity. They are biographers, psychologists, novelists, and moralists; to crown all they can do the critic's business – analyse the work to its elements and rate them at their proper worth. Such being the aim it is natural that few live to achieve it.

The essay upon Fielding is an example of the kind of success and of the kind of failure which are apt to attend upon such attempts. Biography, psychology, and criticism are all squeezed together, and it is much to Henley's credit that they contrive to give off between them so strong an impression that Fielding was a very great man and that St Paul's is a very fine church. Where so much detail has to be compressed it would be idle to look for some recognition of the fact that literature exists independently of writers, or that life is a much larger affair than the lives of the individuals who live it. The essay upon Burns is more elaborate and of more permanent interest. Indeed, it would be difficult to say what fault we have to find with it, or why, when it is done, we still seek something more or something different. Here is criticism, and here are facts. Dutifully Henley has found space for the names of schoolmasters and the dates of departures. He has sifted evidence and weighed judgements. He is well on his guard against the temptation, to which he says Stevenson succumbed when the material prompted, to write 'like a novelist'.[8] Yet the writing is picturesque and often brilliant, Henley being, if anything, always a little too much in love with the crisp and the curled. Every page will stand whatever wear and tear you choose to give it. What, then, is lacking? Perhaps that he has failed to present Burns as a whole. He has not found the key-word, the mysterious clue which, once discovered, draws out, smoothly and inevitably, all the rest. The brilliant fragments refuse to coalesce. He lacks the peculiar power which men like Carlyle and Macaulay[9] possess of so absorbing their subject that it grows again outside of them, a real character; utterly different perhaps from the original, but no more to be ignored. You may turn to Henley's Burns for information, for exact and witty statement, but the figure remains scattered all in little bits within the covers of the book. Yet how persistently we must do battle with Carlyle's Boswell or with Macaulay's Warren Hastings[10] before they will let us come by an opinion of our own! True or false, faithfully or malignantly set down, there they stand before us like living men.

Nothing, when the desire is strong upon you to know a writer, comes amiss – facts, fiction, a scrap of manuscript, a cutting from an Inn ledger. But there are times when we would sweep aside all biography and all psychology for the sake of a single song or a single page expounded and analysed phrase by phrase. When Henley uses this method to establish his claim that T. E. Brown was the superior of Browning[11] as a poet, or, even more blasphemously, the equal of Byron as a letter writer, the facts, as we interpret them, seem to throw dust upon his skill. Once more the freakishness of contemporary criticism is proved. Once more we see how powerless taste and learning and insight are against the tug of personal affection and the prejudice of personal predilections. Brown, like Fielding, like Burns, like Byron, was a man after Henley's heart. And here, perhaps, we come within sight of the true nature of Henley's gift. It is shown most plainly, we think, in the brilliant biographical sketches which he wrote for an edition of Byron's letters. The little canvas precisely suits him. His likings and dislikings are there all to the point. He has scope for his vivacity, his wit, his discernment, but he is not called upon for a breadth of view or a sweep of emotion that were denied him. They are full of amusement, full of curiosity, and full to the brim of vitality. That, perhaps, is the quality that Henley admires most in others and possessed most markedly himself. He loved the brisk, the manly – the pugnacious, the athletes, and the prize-fighters. We should find ourselves treading the maze of psychological criticism if we were to try to guess why it was that this admirable virtue of loving life became to the men of Henley's generation, or rather set, an obsession to which they must testify in season and out. The times perhaps were oppressive. England was at peace. It was more necessary then than now to run no risk of being mistaken for 'a smug, decent, late Victorian journalist!'[12] The two foremost apostles of the creed – Stevenson and Henley – were physically incapable of violence. Whatever all this may imply, Henley's work, as we look back upon it after twenty years, is marked by the vehemence of his belief in virility, by his downright personal preferences, and by something bold and yet restricted in his temper which puts us in mind of a brilliant schoolboy. For, with all a schoolboy's high spirits, he has also something of a schoolboy's natural insensibility.

1–A review in the TLS, 24 February 1921, (Kp C215) of Essays (Macmillan & Co. Ltd., 1920) by William Ernest Henley (1849–1903).
2–Henley, 'Henry Fielding', pp. 1–46, originally published in an edition of Fielding (William Heinemann, 1903); 'Smollett', pp. 47–95, originally published in an edition of Smollett (Constable & Co., 1899); 'William Hazlitt', pp. 96–122, originally published in an edition of Hazlitt (J. M. Dent, 1902–4); 'Byron's World', originally published as notes to a volume of Byron's letters (William Heinemann, 1897). The fifth essay concerned was 'Robert Burns', ibid., pp. 123–229, originally published in the centenary edition of Burns's work (T. C. & E. C. Jack, 1896).
3–Henry Fielding (1707–54), The History of Tom Jones (1749).
4–Tobias Smollett (1721–71).
5–Henley, 'Henry Fielding', p. 45, which has 'an Art'.
6–For the quotation, ibid.: Edward Gibbon (1737–94); Thomas Gray (1716–71); Sir Walter Scott (1771–1832); S. T. Coleridge (1772–1834); Lord Byron (1788–

1824); W. M. Thackeray (1811–63); George Eliot (1819–80); Leslie Stephen (1832–1904), see *Hours in a Library* (1874 etc) and *DNB*; Austin Dobson (1840–1921).

7 – Robert Burns (1759–96) was the unfaithful husband of Jean Armour, with whom he underwent a form of marriage in 1786, legalised in 1788. George Gordon, 6th Lord Byron, was the son of John Byron and his second wife Catherine Gordon; he was born with malformed feet, a condition aggravated and made permanent, according to Byron, by his mother's 'false delicacy' in neglecting to treat them as prescribed.

8 – *Ibid.*, 'Robert Burns', p. 178: 'Stevenson was an acute and delicate critic at many points: but he wrote like a novelist – like Thackeray, say, of Fielding and Sterne – when he wrote of Armour as a "facile and empty-headed gin", and insisted, still possessed of Chambers's vain imaginings, that she was first and last in love with another man'.

9 – Thomas Carlyle (1795–1881); Lord Macaulay (1800–59).

10 – Carlyle, 'Boswell's Life of Johnson', *Fraser's Magazine*, May 1832; Macaulay, 'Warren Hastings', *Edinburgh Review*, October 1841.

11 – Henley, 'T.E.B.', pp. 377–97; Thomas Edward Brown (1830–97), Manx poet, author of *Betsy Lee, a Foc's'le Yarn* (1873) and *Foc's'le Yarns* (1881). Robert Browning (1812–89).

12 – *Ibid.*, 'Robert Burns', pp. 187–8, n1: 'Burns, in any case, was a man of the later Eighteenth Century . . . and to take him out of it, and essay to make him a smug, decent, Late-Victorian journalist is, as I think, to essay a task at once discreditable in aim and impossible of execution.'

A Prince of Prose

What is it that one finds oneself thinking at the end of the first few pages of Mr Conrad's book? That he is a great writer, a master of prose, a prophet, a man of genius? No. That he is a very sensible man. Let us define our meaning further by asking the reader to imagine himself come out of a hot theatre into the open air. He looks at the sky, and it appears to him refreshingly sensible – almost commonplace indeed; sober, neutral tinted, extremely natural. Something like that is the effect upon us of meeting with what we call literature. At last – why have they kept us waiting so long? – someone begins to talk sense in a natural voice. By the power of his own ease and sincerity he breaks the spell which has held us strained and cramped, and makes us aware that there is nothing in the world we wish more passionately than to uncurl our legs and talk sense. Simply to say straight out what comes into our heads is the most heavenly pleasure of all. To be with those who speak their minds is to be in the only company worth having.

Yet we have scarcely set this down as our first impression upon reading Mr Conrad's book than it appears to us so inappropriate as to call for instant qualification. Is Mr Conrad simple? Only with the simplicity which comes of great concentration. If he seems to speak straight out, it is because long previous labour and scrupulous sincerity have eliminated the unessential. And he does not say the first thing that comes into his head, but the last, which is the result of all that have come before it. Neither is it easy to read him, and some words that Mr Conrad lets fall in his preface explain partly why this is so. The papers in this book are occasional articles extracted by editors from time to time, rather, it appears, against his will. They conform to editorial standards of length. They were handed in at the right place and at the right moment. Nevertheless he tells us: '. . . I may say that whenever the various periodicals mentioned in this book called on me to come out and blow the trumpet of personal opinions, or strike the pensive lute that speaks of the past, I always tried to pull on my boots first'.[2] He has merely to review a book, and the book is, as books are apt to be, a bad one. Yet he takes his place at the table, dressed, equipped, ready, as it proves, for quite a long journey.

Some of these ephemeral pages have lasted already twenty-three years; and why should they not last as many more, since they have about them the gravity, the finality, of literature? Mr Conrad makes another remark which helps us to qualify them still further. 'The only thing that will not be found amongst those Figures and Things that have passed away will be Conrad *en pantouffles*. It is a constitutional inability. *Schlafrock und pantoffeln*! Not that! Never!'[3] That expresses precisely something of what we feel when we read Mr Conrad. He is constitution-ally unable to appear in undress. He is hampered in the attempt – if he ever tried to make it – by the fact that he is a foreigner by birth. He is using a language which is not his own. That is why, perhaps, he uses it with such respect, handling the words as if they were precious things lent him by the owner who is away. He is always a stranger among us, a prince (to use his own phrase about Anatole France)[4] who has chosen to make his stay with us, and treats us and our belongings with a courtesy which is the perfection of breeding. But he is always reserved. 'This volume,' he says, 'is as near as I shall ever come to *déshabillé* in public.'[5] It is our own guilty conscience perhaps that makes us fancy some rebuke to our slipshod manners, our voluble confidences, in this quiet decorum.

Seldom sarcastic, and never violent, we are aware that he watches us with the tolerant irony of a man who has given up expecting the impossible. 'Every gift,' he says of Turgenev, 'has been heaped upon his cradle.' And, after enumerating them, he adds, 'There's enough there to ruin the prospects of any writer.'[6] When our civic magistrates declare their views upon literature, when the censor exercises his rights upon the drama, Mr Conrad watches patiently, even compassionately. And it is only at the very last, when he can bear the sight of our stupidity no longer, that he allows himself to wince – that is to say, he smiles.

But the rebuke is conveyed. Behind his utterance, with all its suavity and courtesy, we feel the weight of profound conviction. The waves heave ever so slightly on the surface, but the waters beneath are unfathomably deep. Happily, Mr Conrad is not always engaged in making us perceive our own deficiencies. The conviction which gives his blame its momentum lends also the same massive weight to his praise. The second essay in the book is devoted to Henry James. It is very short, filling accurately, perhaps, its two columns in the pages of the *North American Review*.[7] Yet it seems to us that at last something fundamental has been said, something that has always evaded being said, about Henry James. Seeing that many fine minds have applied themselves to the task, and have filled not many columns but many volumes with their observations, it is at first difficult to perceive how it is that Mr Conrad so easily outdistances them. Perhaps the starting point is different. While all the rest have remained industriously picking up scraps and totting up totals on the outside, Mr Conrad has somehow raised the curtain and gone within. What he says is fragmentary; it is capable of infinite development; but it refers not to what is external and accidental, but to what is fundamental and lasting. 'Mr Henry James is the historian of fine consciences . . . Nobody has rendered better, perhaps, the tenacity of temper, or known how to drape the robe of spiritual honour about the drooping form of a victor in barren strife.'[8] These are strokes which lay bare the foundations.

It is, of course, the novelist and not the critic who is speaking. It is the man who has done the thing himself, and who will, therefore, see more into the plan within the writer's mind and less, perhaps, into the details of achievement. But although Mr Conrad as a novelist must speak with authority, we have still to reckon with the peculiar tone of that authority, with the conviction which is always to be heard in his voice. If the short essays upon Henry James, Maupassant, Turgenev, Anatole France have the weight and unity which belong to literature and not to journalism, it is primarily that they are founded upon certain large and enduring ideas which apply to all fiction and not only to the particular volumes under consideration.

That a sacrifice must be made, that something has to be given up, is the truth engraved in the innermost recesses of the fair temple built for our edification by the masters of fiction. There is no other secret behind the curtain. All adventure, all love, every success is resumed in the supreme energy of an act of renunciation.[9]

This sentence occurs in the paper on Henry James. We turn the page and find that the consummate simplicity of Maupassant's technique is based, 'like all the great virtues',[10] primarily upon self-denial. His conspicuous merit is that he is compassionate, courageous and just. In Anatole France, again, we are bidden to admire a 'profound and unalterable compassion'.[11] It would be almost true to say that Mr Conrad looks, first, for such qualities of character in a writer as would fit him to become a good sea captain – for courage, compassion, self-denial, fidelity to an ideal; and that he regards the purely literary gifts as temptations and seductions which will 'pass between the writer and his probity on the blank sheet of paper'.[12] It would be almost, but it would not be quite true. It is easy and satisfactory, especially in a swift survey, to fit together a rigid framework of Mr Conrad's faith, and if we err in this direction it is he partly who is responsible. He will stress his morality so that the outlines are plain enough, but he will not unveil the secrets of his art or will say disparagingly that 'to have the gift of words is no such great matter'.[13] The few sentences we quote are enough to remind the reader how splendid and yet how difficult to analyse is the gift at Mr Conrad's service whenever he takes a pen in hand. It is not from ignorance of the lusts and delights of literature that Mr Conrad judges them so austerely. He, if any man, has been exposed to temptation, and nobly he has conquered his temptations. But he is not altogether victorious. He has won his composure at the cost of something that was precious too.

If we look for light upon a problem which faced us, we remember, after reading *The Rescue*, we shall find it perhaps in the essay upon Alphonse Daudet.[14] *The Rescue* we felt was full of splendour, and yet we had never before realised so plainly the marked boundaries within which Mr Conrad practises his art. He flies his standard, we felt, with complete sovereignty over certain territories, but beyond them there is chaos. He never risks himself outside. Our vague figure is expressed more precisely by Mr Conrad himself when he draws a distinction between those emotions which, as an artist, one should take with a grain

of salt and those which deserve our most serious homage, if indeed they
are not altogether beyond our range. Daudet, he says, was content to

remain below, on the plain, amongst his creations, and take an eager part in those
disasters, weaknesses, and joys which are tragic enough in their droll way, but are by
no means so momentous and profound as some writers – probably for the sake of
Art – would like to make us believe.[15]

The victims 'struggle drowning in an insignificant pool'. One may,
unwittingly, distort his meaning. But as he puts it it appears that the
emotions of the sophisticated are of little moment compared with what
goes on within the hearts of 'simple and unknown men' travelling 'a path
of toilsome silence . . . with closed lips, or, maybe, whispering their pain
softly – only to themselves'.[16] But it is because we are looking through
Mr Conrad's eyes that we see the prospect drawn to this scale. Look
through Donne's eyes, through Racine's, Molière's, Jane Austen's,[17]
and the insignificant pool is a deep ocean and the struggles of the victims
of enthralling importance. The writer, of course, does not choose what
he sees; he only fortifies himself in his belief, and with age, if he is of a
certain temperament, comes to hold his belief more rigidly. Mr Conrad,
no doubt, would be a greater writer if, besides honouring the quiet deeps
of the heart, he felt also its storms and transiencies, if he were dramatic
as well as static, instant and direct as well as composed and compassionate. But it is of the essence of his genius that the draught he offers us
should have been stood for a moment in the cool. It is the nature of those
convictions for which we honour him that they tend to still the unquiet
blood.

1 – A review in the *TLS*, 3 March 1921, (Kp C216) of *Notes on Life and Letters*
(J. M. Dent & Sons Ltd, 1921) by Joseph Conrad (1857–1924). See also 'A
Disillusioned Romantic' above, 'Mr Conrad: A Conversation', below; 'Lord Jim',
'Mr Conrad's "Youth"', *II VW Essays*; and 'Joseph Conrad', *IV VW Essays* and
CR1.
2 – Conrad, 'Author's Note', p. vi, which begins: 'I don't know whether I dare boast
like a certain South American general who used to say that no emergency of war or
peace had ever found him "with his boots off"; but . . .'
3 – *Ibid.*
4 – *Ibid.*, 'Anatole France. 1904', i 'Crainquebille', p. 45: 'He is a good and politic
prince'; and *ibid.*, p. 50: 'M. Anatole France, a good prince and a good Republican,
will succeed no doubt in being a good Socialist.' The collection of tales *Crainquebille*
by Anatole France (1844–1924) was published in 1904; Conrad's second piece here
deals with France's satirical novel *L'Île des pingouins* (1908).
5 – *Ibid.*, 'Author's Note', p. vii.
6 – *Ibid.*, 'Turgenev', p. 65; the piece consists of a letter to Edward Garnett, upon the

forthcoming publication of his *Turgenev. A Study* (1917). Ivan Turgenev (1818–83).

7–*Ibid.,* 'Henry James [1843–1916]. An Appreciation', pp. 13–23, originally published in the *North American Review,* January 1905.

8–For the quotation up to the ellipsis, *ibid.,* p. 21, which begins: 'As is meet for a man of his descent and tradition'; and for the remainder, *ibid.,* p. 18, which has 'a barren strife'.

9–*Ibid.,* p. 19.

10–*Ibid.,* 'Guy de Maupassant [1850–93]', p. 33, originally an introduction to *Yvette and Other Stories* (1885), translated by Ada Galsworthy and published in 1904.

11–*Ibid.,* 'Anatole France', p. 44.

12–*Ibid.,* 'Guy de Maupassant', p. 35: 'The inherent greatness of the man consists in this, that he will let none of the fascinations that beset a writer working in loneliness turn him away from the straight path, from the vouchsafed vision of excellence. He will not be led into perdition by the seductions of sentiment, of eloquence, of humour, of pathos; of all that splendid pageant of faults that pass between the writer and his probity on the blank sheet of paper, like the glittering cortège of deadly sins before the austere anchorite in the desert air of Thebaïde.'

13–*Ibid.,* 'Books', p. 11, a complete sentence.

14–For VW on Conrad's *The Rescue* (1920), see 'A Disillusioned Romantic' above. 'Alphonse Daudet [1840–97]', *ibid.,* pp. 25–31.

15–*Ibid.,* p. 27.

16–For Daudet's victims, and his simple unknowns, *ibid.,* p. 28.

17–John Donne (1573–1631); Jean Racine (1639–99); Molière (Jean-Baptiste Poquelin, 1622–73); Jane Austen (1775–1817).

George Eliot (1819–1880)

George Eliot was the granddaughter of a carpenter. She made herself, by sheer determination, one of the most learned women – or men – of her time; and at the age of thirty-five became the companion – she could not become the wife – of George Henry Lewes.[2] The facts are notable because they had much influence upon her writing. She had inherited a wide knowledge of farmers, labourers, and country life. She had acquired a mass of book learning. Owing to the prudery of the Victorian age, she lived, after her alliance with Lewes, much cut off from the world.

Her first books – *Scenes of Clerical Life, Adam Bede, Mill on the Floss* – deal with what she has seen with her own eyes, or heard described by her father. As an artist she is at her best in *Silas Marner*,[3] the first part of

The Mill on the Floss, and *Scenes of Clerical Life*. Her genius shows itself in broad views of the Midlands, where rat-catchers, business men and farmers have leisure to drink together; and the tragedies and comedies of love, death, and bankruptcy happen as incidents in a large scheme of things.

She is at her richest and freest when she is bringing to life a Mrs Poyser, or a group at the bar of the Rainbow Inn.[4] But those who wish to confine her to village life and lament the book-learned period which produced *Middlemarch* and *Romola*[5] neglect a very important aspect of her genius. She was one of the first English novelists to discover that men and women think as well as feel, and the discovery was of great artistic moment. Briefly, it meant that the novel ceased to be solely a love story, an autobiography, or a story of adventure. It became, as it had already become with the Russians, of much wider scope. Because it attempts to include more, *Middlemarch*, though inferior to *Silas Marner* in artistic perfection, is one of the most interesting of English novels.

Living much alone and towards the end in an atmosphere of artificial adulation, George Eliot, as *Daniel Deronda*[6] goes to prove, lost much of her vigour and directness. But it seems likely that she will come through the cloud which obscured her after the publication of her life – a dismal soliloquy –[7] and hold her place permanently among the great English novelists. Anyone who wishes to read her will do well to begin with *Scenes of Clerical Life*, to go on with *The Mill on the Floss*, and to end with *Middlemarch*. An edition of her books was published by Messrs. Blackwood in 1913, at the cost of a shilling a volume. The same publishers now issue the complete works of George Eliot in 17 volumes at 2s. per volume.

1–A signed article in the 'Great Names' series in the *Daily Herald*, 9 March 1921, (Kp C216.1). 'I shall be glad to do the article on George Eliot,' VW wrote on 18 January 1921 to the *Daily Herald's* literary editor W. J. Turner, 'and will let you have it some time next week. | My husband asks me to say that he will do the article on Mill [untraced].' (*II VW Letters*, no. 1163).

For 'George Eliot' (*TLS*, 20 November 1919), see headnote above and see *IV VW Essays* and *CR1*; for 'George Eliot' (*N&A*, 30 October 1926), see *IV VW Essays*.

The same page of the paper, entitled 'Books of Today and Tomorrow', carried reviews by: Leonard Woolf (on *Coal, Iron, and War* by Edwin C. Eckel), Siegfried Sassoon and Osbert Sitwell; a story, 'The Spy', by Upton Sinclair; 'Literary Notes' by W. J. Turner; and a picture story, in the 'Children's Corner', of the adventures of 'Bobby Bear in Egypt'.

2–George Henry Lewes (1817–78), writer and editor, author of a *Biographical History of Philosophy* (1845, 1846) and of *Comte's Philosophy of the Sciences*

(1853), had married in 1840; he first met George Eliot in 1851, by which date his marriage had effectively foundered, and, from 1854, although there was no legal divorce, she and Lewes lived together as man and wife.
3 – *Scenes of Clerical Life* (1857), *Adam Bede* (1859), *The Mill on the Floss* (1860), *Silas Marner* (1861).
4 – Mrs Poyser, character in *Adam Bede*; the Rainbow Inn, scene of revelry in *Silas Marner*.
5 – *Middlemarch* (1871–2), *Romola* (1862–3).
6 – *Daniel Deronda* (1874–6).
7 – J. W. Cross, *George Eliot's Life. As Related in her Letters and Journals*. Arranged and edited by her husband (1884).

Congreve

I suppose it must happen that gentlemen with cellars come to fight shy of the old bottles in the corner. The labels slung round their necks testify to their age and to their ancestry. But the dust is thick, the wax all cracked, and Heaven knows whether the fluid within is not by this time gone sour and cloudy. So it is with the old books with famous names. The occasion comes for tasting them. We make all ready, poke the fire, adjust the light, rub the glasses, and then gingerly open *Love for Love, a Comedy*, written by Mr Congreve and first produced on April 30th, 1695, at the New Theatre, in Little Lincoln's Inn Fields. But it has kept uncommonly well. Try a sip with me. 'Well, if he be but as great a sea-beast as she is a land-monster, we shall have a most amphibious breed – the progeny will be all otters.' 'To your element, fish; be mute, fish, and to sea . . .'[2] Don't you agree that this is infinitely better stuff than they make nowadays? In God's name, why does one ever read anything else? – so pleasant is it to shake out a good, wholesome laugh now and again. Yet *Love for Love* is not a jolly play; nor is it a profound play; nor a poetical play; there is nothing that disturbs the social conscience or sends us stumbling up to bed thinking of the sorrows of the world. The nearest we can come to a description of our state at the finish is that we have drunk good wine. We are slightly tipsy. We are about to say something very witty. The maid who brings in the cocoa is about to do something very coarse. Write a letter to make an appointment with the dentist and the sentence, with its two or three round oaths, will be (or will momentarily appear) as beautifully turned as the legs of a Sheraton table.

The truth is that *Love for Love* is much simpler than the kind of play we write nowadays. That is part of the reason why we seem to breathe sea air and look for miles and miles into the distance. There were then two fit topics for conversation – love and money. Both are frankly talked about with the natural relish of people who are not distracted by other concerns, but have kept a sort of virgin energy for the two prime objects of life. They take them much too seriously to muffle them up in decent ambiguity. Further, it is a very small society, acquainted with each other's language so that the pellets of repartee which they are for ever discharging fly straight, hit hard, and yet have about them an extraordinary distinction. They have been at this game for so long that they talk as well as noblemen now shoot peasants. Whether this is not better perceived in reading than in acting is, I think, an open question. At the Lyric Theatre, Hammersmith, last week there were a good many words dropped or fumbled, and Congreve never wrote a speech that did not balance with a kind of tremulous vitality. Knock out a word and the sentence tumbles like a house of cards.

But at the Lyric Theatre things happened rather against expectation. Reading, relishing the wit, getting the effect of the give-and-take of repartee, tend to make for hardness and concentration. It was natural to expect that the same words spoken by living men and women would warm and blossom, and that there would be drawn to the surface other subtleties of character which scarcely come to the top in reading. Yet as the play went on one came to wonder whether the life which was so capably and admirably breathed into figure after figure was the life of the period.

Miss Vivian Rees, for example, acting Angelica, the mother of Peacock's women, the grandmother of Meredith's, was charming to look at, charming to hear, but when it came to flaunting Angelica's philosophy – 'Uncertainty and expectation are the joys of life. Security is an insipid thing; and the overtaking and possessing of a wish discovers the folly of the chase. Never let us know one another better; for the pleasure of a masquerade is done, when we come to shew our faces'[3] – when it came to the wildness and rashness and rakishness of this, Miss Vivian Rees was altogether too demure. If we had been fancying that Scandal somehow represents a kind of chorus, a point of view from which all this heartlessness and brazen morality could be seen shaded and in perspective, Mr Holloway scarcely supported our venture. Indeed the character who came out best was Sir Sampson Legend. To begin with, Mr Roy Byford is a superb figure of a man. To go on with, it seems likely that our natural taste for the burly humour and the florid figures of the past has been nourished, and is even now kept alive by the humour of the music-halls. For the rest, we are too good-hearted or too full-hearted to be witty. Give us wit, and we broaden it into farce.

1 – A signed dramatic review in the *NS*, 2 April 1921, (Kp C217) of *Love for Love* (1695) by William Congreve (1670–1729) in a production by the Phoenix Society at the Lyric Theatre, Hammersmith, on the evening of Sunday, 20 March 1921. VW wrote in her diary on Tuesday, 22 March: 'We had [*T.S.*] Eliot to dinner on Sunday & went to Love for Love, he & I in the Pit; L[eonard] upstairs, with a ticket from the New Statesman. Eliot & I had to drive into Hammersmith in a taxi, having missed our train ... He had the advantage of me in laughing out. He laughed at Love for Love: but thinking I must write about it I was a little on the stretch ... Adrian [Stephen] came in to tell me that Desmond [MacCarthy, literary editor of the *NS*] wanted me, to demand my article instantly.' Cast list: Sir Sampson Legend, Roy Byford; Valentine, Murray Carrington; Scandal, Baliol Holloway; Tattle, Ernest Thesiger; Ben, Tristan Rawson; Foresight, Ben Field; Jeremy, Miles Malleson; Trapland, Eugene Leahy; Buckram, Oswald Roberts; Angelica, Joan Vivian Rees; Mrs Foresight, Helen Haye; Mrs Frail, Athene Seyler; Miss Prue, Catherine Willard; Nurse, Alice Mansfield; Jenny, Clare Harris. See also 'Restoration Comedy' below; 'Congreve', *IV VW Essays*; 'Congreve's Comedies: Speed, Stillness and Meaning', *VI VW Essays*.
2 – For the first quotation, *Love for Love*, act i, sc. xiv (*The Comedies of William Congreve*, 2 vols, Methuen & Co., 1895, vol. ii, p. 31), Mrs Frail to Scandal, Tattle and Valentine; and for the second, *ibid.*, act v, sc. x, p. 113, Sir Sampson Legend to Ben, which continues: ', rule your helm, sirrah, don't direct me'.
3 – Thomas Love Peacock (1785–1866); George Meredith (1828–1909). *Ibid.*, act iv, sc. xx, p. 99, Angelica to Valentine, which continues: '; but I'll tell you two things before I leave you: I am not the fool you take me for; and you are mad and don't know it'.

Ethel Smyth

The orthodox way to review Miss Smyth would be to cut out a sufficient number of good stories about the Kaiser, Queen Victoria, and the Empress Eugénie,[2] and to stitch them together with a thread of admiring comment. But this would give the reader very little idea of the true interest of Miss Smyth's book, which consists not in isolated anecdotes but in the current of the narrative – not in what the Kaiser said to Miss Smyth at Count Bülow's[3] dinner-party, but in the fact that Miss Smyth had been playing golf till 7.15 that evening, had taken the precaution to have her hair done by an expert hairdresser before setting out, had been struggling with obstinate opera singers for hours in the morning: was, in short, Ethel Smyth, a lady of remarkable and original personality and not merely a person to whom things chanced to happen. When we say this we are distinguishing Miss Smyth's book from the ruck of memoirs and placing it with those which, however they vary in merit, have the lasting and fascinating virtue of bringing us into touch with a living man or woman. When, less than two years ago, *Impressions that Remained*[4] made its appearance, a figure hitherto almost unknown, or seen for an instant vigorously waving acknowledgements from a concert platform, became one of those whom we carry about in the mind to think of at odd seasons. It was not that Miss Smyth possessed extraordinary literary power, or that she analysed her soul to its essence. Her method appeared to consist of extreme courage and extreme candour. No doubt there were reticences innumerable, but whatever she chose to describe she described wholly, as it appeared to her, without disguise or titivation. This same directness, coupled as it was with an astonishing vitality, had led her into relationships and situations of such variety and intensity that the truthful account of them was of absorbing interest. The present book is less connected, for 'dealing with modern times, continuity is imposs-ible unless you are prepared either to hurt feelings or to dip your pen in purest solution of rose-coloured amiability'.[5] But it is autobiography; there appears in it again, unmistakably, the figure of the writer. Let us see whether we can put down our impression, drawn from these two sources, of Ethel Smyth.

Miss Smyth may be said to have flourished (so far as these pages are concerned) in the 'nineties of the last century or in the early years of this. The portrait which appears on the cover of the book breathes of that age. Dressed in coat and skirt, tie and collar, Miss Smyth looks the militant, working, professional woman – the woman who had shocked the county by jumping fences both of the field and of the drawing-room, had written operas, was commonly called 'quite mad', and had friends among the Empresses and the charwomen.[6] We remember that it was the age of Charles Furse and Sargent and Henley and Stevenson and the Boer War.[7] We are inclined to risk a theory that the prominent artistic figures of that time were racy, slangy, outspoken men and women; very patriotic, very combative, and very warm-hearted: differing in all these respects, not necessarily for the worse, from those who now occupy the stage. But it would be easy to strain the theory and to impute to an age what is, as a matter of fact, true only of one individual. We may guess that wherever Miss Smyth stood, there a circle formed, and the circle took its colour and its speed from her. For the prevailing quality in Miss Smyth is surely her vitality. One might have expected in the chapter which describes life in a country cottage alone with a maid and a dog some vegetable notes and a good many profound reflections. Instead we seem to hear a terrific bombardment of the piano (she was writing an opera); while at any moment the door bursts open, and is it Ford, the wild Devonshire maid, who comes in, or Faulkner, apologetic and sedate, or Marko, the St Bernard, lately banged about the head by the butcher's boy? – for all these characters have been plainly made known to us. Meals are announced on a sweet-toned hunting-horn. Sometimes she drives off to lunch and talks politics with the Empress Eugénie. Then there are little suppers to celebrate successful concerts to which the Furses come and H. B.,[8] the wine being cooled in a well which, at the last moment before dinner, is discovered to be dug next, and slightly beneath, the cesspool. If vitality is the quality which makes the most peaceful stretches of life pelt past and the humblest people stand out prominent, we must hasten to credit Miss Smyth with a more important gift. She is impressionable, but she is very discriminating. In an enthusiastic temperament we are generally ready to pardon a certain amount of gush. But though Miss Smyth can be strident, she is never sentimental. Indeed, she possesses the combination of enthusiasm and shrewdness which fitted her for what, after her music, appears to be the great pursuit of her life – the pursuit of friendship. Carried by her unthinking directness right to the verge of Queen Victoria's sacred hearthrug, she was not too much abashed to observe, a little later, the astonishing interchange of civilities which took place between Victoria and Eugénie at the open door. Devoted to the Empress as she was, she sets down with complete candour all the contradictions and limitations of a character which for the first time, perhaps, becomes interesting and credible to the reader. Still, it is her tremendous capacity for personal relations that impresses one in the second volume as in the first. How many people, for instance, so value friendship that they would trouble to go 'home by Copenhagen' in order to make acquaintance with the friends of a friend?[9] Of course, she was justified, and one of the most valued relations of her life began there. She was always justified in the sense that her fervour took her hither and thither into every sort of surrounding and into intimacies of extreme intensity and interest. Whether it is the enkindling effect of the past, or whether we should praise Miss Smyth's vivid pen or her warm heart, the men and women of those times appear about five inches taller than those of the present day.

One of the pleasures which makes the thought of our own descent into the abyss of age tolerable is that we may read an account of this very year 1921 from the pen of Miss Smyth. Is it even now going on in our midst – this brave, bustling, important, romantic society?

1 – A review in the *NS*, 23 April 1921, (Kp C218) of *Streaks of Life* (Longmans, Green, & Co., 1921) by Ethel Smyth (1858–1944), composer, author and feminist, cr. DBE in 1922. VW had seen the first performance of Smyth's opera *The Wreckers* at His Majesty's Theatre in 1909, but the two women were not to meet until 1930, when a fond but uneven friendship, pursued with characteristic energy by Ethel, grew between them.

2 – Wilhelm II (1859–1941), German Emperor and King of Prussia, 1888–1918, grandson of Queen Victoria (1819–1901). Eugénie (1826–1920), Empress of the French, 1853–70, consort of Napoleon III.

3 – For Smyth's 'duet' with the Kaiser, at the home of Bernhard Heinrich Martin, Fürst von Bülow (1849–1929), German chancellor, 1900–9, see 'A Winter Storm', pp. 196–202; p. 201: 'At last I so far forgot myself as to wheel round and say: "But the chancellor knows *nothing whatever* about England!" ... "You hear what she says, Bernhard? That you know *nothing whatever* about England!" and then he added, turning to me: "but you know the poor fellow has never been there!"'

4 – *Impressions That Remained* (2 vols., Longmans, Green & Co., 1921). See *I VW Diary*, 28 November 1919: 'I'm reading Ethel Smyth. I wish it were better – (odd that I wrote that genuinely meaning it; but I couldn't have done so with the novels [which she had previously been discussing]). What a subject! That one should see it as a superb subject is a tribute to her, but of course, not knowing how to write, she's muffed it. The interest remains, because she has ridden straight at her recollections, never swerving & getting through honestly, capably, but without power to still & shape the past so that one will wish to read it again. Honesty is her quality; & the fact that she made a great rush at life; friendships with women interest me.' And see *II VW Letters*, no. 1100, to Lytton Strachey, 30 November 1919: 'I'm in the 2nd vol. of Ethel Smyth. I think she shows up triumphantly, through sheer force of honesty. It's a pity she can't write; for I don't suppose one could read it again. But it fascinates me all the same. I saw her at a concert two days ago – striding up the gangway in coat and skirt and spats and talking at the top of her voice. Near at hand one sees that she's all wrinkled and fallen in, and eyes running blue on to the cheeks; but she keeps up the figure of the nineties to perfection. Of course the book is the soul of the nineties. Did you ever know Sue Lushington? Much the same type. Then Ethel's passion for the W.C. (it occurs in every chapter) is of the highest merit.'

5 – Smyth, 'Concerning this Book', p. 1, a complete sentence, which has: 'feelings, or'.

6 – No dust jacket has been traced but the description of the portrait is reminiscent of the photograph of Ethel Smyth taken in 1916 by Olive Edis and reproduced in the preliminary pages of *Impressions That Remained*, vol. ii. The source of the quotation, possibly from the dust jacket, has not been found.

7 – Charles Furse (1868–1904), painter, who had married Katharine, daughter of John Addington Symonds and sister of Madge Vaughan, VW's friend and sometime

passion. John Singer Sargent (1856–1925). W. E. Henley (1849–1903). R. L. Stevenson (1850–94). The South African, or Boer War, 1899–1902.

8–Henry Brewster (1859–1908), Anglo-American poet-philosopher, librettist of *The Wreckers* and an adored friend of Ethel Smyth.

9–Smyth, 'A Winter Storm', p. 158: 'I went home by Copenhagen in order to make the acquaintance of the Benckendorffs [Count Alexander Benckendorff (1849–1917), Russian Ambassador in London from 1903], new and great friends of a friend of mine, Maurice Baring, then attached to the British Legation at Copenhagen.'

Scott's Character

The reader will do well not to be put off by the cocksureness of Mr Stalker's manner or by the singularity of his literary judgements, for his book is shrewd and amusing, outspoken enough to exercise our wits, though not profound enough to convince them. He claims that he has given a new presentation of Scott, a twentieth-century portrait which 'may be unsatisfactory in the eyes of 2020',[2] but is certainly different from that which was current in the nineteenth century. In the nineteenth century the Waverley Novels were still taken seriously. Nowadays Scott's verse is forgotten, and there are two – perhaps more – living novelists who surpass his fiction. These are Mr Stalker's opinions, for we must avow ourselves either much behind the times or much ahead of them in rating the Scottish novels, however the game of placing may be played, among the permanently great, which are none the less great because they have ceased to influence the living. Still, if you hold that his force as a writer is spent, there remains that elusive thing – his personality; and certainly Mr Stalker has Scott's own authority for holding that his life was a great deal more important than his books. It is probably true that Scott's history is known to many who have never read his writings. Like Johnson,[3] or like Socrates, he is a symbol of a type of human nature. Both his gifts and his sufferings are written in huge letters for everyone to read. The inevitable result of this monumental quality is that, like other monuments, he has become, as time goes by, a little weather-beaten, blurred, and sentimentalised. The real Scott, no doubt, was far more sharply featured than the legendary. When we turn to Mr Stalker, then, we do so in the hope that some of the myths may be dissolved and some of the outlines recovered. But our hope is only partially fulfilled. True, the monument is scraped and cleaned, but the jolly Scottish gentleman who stands forth, prosperous and portly, with his horses and his dogs, who practised a little automatic writing before breakfast, is no more the Scott of the novels and the diaries than our weather-worn colossus supporting huge burdens.

The work of restoration is necessarily carried on under difficulties and half in darkness. We have to decide such delicate questions as the question of his heart – was it tough or tender? – which are practically insoluble in the case of our next-door neighbour, and here the evidence is contained in legends and letters more than a hundred years old. No letters remain – none at least have been published – to light up the first and most momentous of Sir Walter's love affairs. He was gay enough less than a year after Williamina[4] refused him. Thirty-five years later he sat upon a tombstone and was agitated to remember how he had cut the lady's initials upon the turf. And later he married Charlotte Charpentier, and neither of them pretended to much fine feeling for the other. Still, when the husband writes of his marriage, 'it was something short of love in all its forms, which I suspect people only feel once in their lives; folk who have been nearly drowned in bathing rarely venturing a second time out of their depths',[5] one may, if one chooses, credit him with first-hand knowledge of the depths and the dangers. But we will not quarrel with Mr Stalker if he likes to be sure that 'there was nothing romantic about Scott, except his iron will, his passion for planting, and his healthy story-telling life',[6] and that if Williamina had been poor and nameless he would not have cared for her at all. With all respect for the divine passion, probably men of great vitality get over the worst attacks, and smother the most prosperous under a hurly-burly of other interests.

But the interest that dominated the immense variety of Scott's interests was, surely, in one form or another, his passion for literature. If you reduce Scott's writing to a mechanical scribbling for money, you reduce him to a level of a hearty and manly but entirely normal Scottish gentleman of orthodox conservative views. To take his own words at their face value appears to us a mistake. Many writers, of whom Carlyle is one and Stevenson[7] another, turn against literature now and then and cry out for a life of action, just as the man of action would rather have written the poem than have done the deed which it describes. Scott, no doubt, rated literature very low, as one is apt to rate one's own possessions, but that is no proof that he was not a confirmed writer, with a prodigious gift for the calling. Anyone who wants to come near the character of Scott, or to analyse the nature of his charm, must give full eight to the fact that he spent hours every day during the greater part of his life with the creatures of his imagination. The temperament which naturally indulges itself thus is quite distinct from that which has no such bent. Long before it was a question of earning money Scott was living with the kings and barons and ballad-makers of the past. When it came to writing he had merely to turn on the tap and the accumulated resources rushed out. That this is not the way in which the works of Flaubert[8] were produced is certain; but it is also probable that genius of a certain type must work unconsciously, like a natural force which issues unchanged, almost unnoticed by its possessor. To read Scott's life and not to see that he was perpetually under the sway of this power is to miss the flavour and proportion of the whole. He had no say in the matter. Whether he wrote well or ill, for money or for pleasure, Scott was as much the slave of his imagination as a drunkard is the slave of his dram. What was Abbotsford but the realisation of some romantic dream? Scott presumably never once in his life saw it as it appears to the tourist today – a large, ugly building, stuffed with sham armour, plaster casts, and pompous heraldry. But the tourist must have the soul of a furniture dealer if he cannot at the same time see how to Scott it was all mixed up with Scotland, and the past, and chivalry. It is true – and Mr Stalker puts the case with undeniable force – that scarcely anything can be said in favour of Scott's politics. He was servile to dukes and hostile to working-men. But again the pitch is queered by his excessive indulgence in the pleasures of the imagination. The Duke of Buccleugh appeared before him all rayed round with the colours of the past – the living representative of the 'old Knights of Branxholm'.[9] The weaver who wanted his wages raised was a dangerous vermin nibbling at the fabric of romance. But to do him justice Scott was thoroughly inconsistent in putting his views into practice. Some of his best friends were working-men; his imagination is never so happy as when it lights up the lives of peasants; and if Mr Stalker seeks proof that Scott could withstand the aristocracy, he should ponder the scene one night at Abbotsford when the vulgar Mrs Coutts had arrived and some ladies of title were rude to her. The 'lovely marchioness'[10] was beckoned into the armorial hall by Scott, and there talked to, she said, as if she had been his daughter. At any rate, there was no more laughing at Mrs Coutts. And a few days later Lockhart found Sir Walter alone over his whisky and cigar and told him the rumour of Constable's failure. And Sir Walter took it all very calmly and lit another cigar. And Lockhart found him early next morning helping his little grandson to feed a fleet of ducklings outside Lockhart's house, for he had been more alarmed than he had let on, had driven all night to see

Constable, had proved the rumours false, and after breakfast walked home through his woods 'leaning on my shoulder all the way, which he seldom as yet did, except with Tom Purdie . . .'[11] So it goes on, and each epithet and scene and incident serves to make us more and more sure that we know Sir Walter and are not to be argued out of our knowledge.

1—A review in the TLS, 28 April 1921, (Kp C219) of The Intimate Life of Sir Walter Scott [1771–1832] (A. & C. Black Ltd, 1921) by Archibald Stalker. See 'The Antiquary' below, and 'Gas at Abbotsford', VI VW Essays. See also 'Across the Border', II VW Essays; and see V VW Diary, pp. 151–2; VI VW Letters, p. 247; 'Sir Walter Scott' by Leslie Stephen in Hours in a Library (1874 etc), and the DNB entry on Scott, also by Stephen.

2—Stalker, ch. i, p. 2.

3—Dr Samuel Johnson (1709–84).

4—Williamina (1776–1810), daughter of Sir John and Lady Belsches, who in 1797 married Sir William Forbes, Bart.

5—Stalker, ch. v, p. 39, quoting Scott writing to Lady Abercorn, 21 January 1810, which has 'depth'. Scott met Charlotte Mary Charpentier (d.1826), the daughter of a French refugee, in 1797 while on a visit to the Lake District, where the Charpentier family, having been befriended by the Marquis of Downshire, lived at Gilsland. The couple were married that year, on 24 December, at St Mary's Church, Carlisle.

6—Ibid., p. 36, a complete sentence.

7—Thomas Carlyle (1795–1881); Robert Louis Stevenson (1850–94).

8—Gustave Flaubert (1821–80).

9—The source of this allusion has not been traced.

10—For Mrs Coutts and the 'lovely Marchioness', J. G. Lockhart, Life of Sir Walter Scott (10 vols, Robert Cadell, 1839), vol. viii, pp. 73–4. See also 'Money and Love', above.

11—Cf. ibid., vol. x, pp. 122–3. Thomas Purdie, a contrite poacher, whom Scott employed first as his shepherd, next as his bailiff, and who became a lifelong friend.

Gothic Romance

It says much for Miss Birkhead's natural good sense that she has been able to keep her head where many people would have lost theirs. She has read a great many books without being suffocated. She has analysed a great many plots without being nauseated. Her sense of literature has not been extinguished by the waste-paper baskets full of old novels so courageously heaped on top of it. For her 'attempt to trace in outline the origin of the Gothic romance and the tale of terror'[2] has necessarily led her to grope in basements and attics where the light is dim and the dust is thick. To trace the course of one strand in the thick skein of our literature is well worth doing. But perhaps Miss Birkhead would have increased the interest of her work if she had enlarged her scope to include some critical discussion of the aesthetic value of shock and terror, and had ventured some analysis of the taste which demands this particular stimulus. But her narrative is quite readable enough to supply the student with material for pushing the enquiry a little further.

Since it is held that Gothic romance was introduced by Horace Walpole's *Castle of Otranto*, in the year 1764, there is no need to confound it with the romance of Spenser or of Shakespeare. It is a parasite, an artificial commodity, produced half in joke in reaction against the current style, or in relief from it. If we run over the names of the most famous of the Gothic romancers – Clara Reeve, Mrs Radcliffe, Monk Lewis, Charles Maturin, Sarah Wilkinson[3] – we shall smile at the absurdity of the visions which they conjure up. We shall, perhaps, congratulate ourselves upon our improvements. Yet since our ancestors bought two thousand copies of Mrs Bennett's *Beggar Girl and Her Benefactors*,[4] on the day of publication, at a cost of thirty-six shillings for the seven volumes, there must have been something in the trash that was appetising, or something in the appetites that was coarse. It is only polite to give our ancestors the benefit of the doubt. Let us try to put ourselves in their places. The books that formed part of the ordinary library in the year 1764 were, presumably, Johnson's *Vanity of Human Wishes*, Gray's Poems, Richardson's *Clarissa*, Addison's *Cato*, Pope's *Essay on Man*.[5] No one could wish for a more distinguished company. At the same time, as literary critics are too little aware, a love of literature is often roused and for the first years nourished not by the good books, but by the bad. It will be an ill day when all the reading is done in libraries and none of it in tubes. In the eighteenth century there must have been a very large public which found no delight in the peculiar literary merits of the age; and if we reflect how long the days were and how empty of distraction, we need not be surprised to find a school of writers grown up in flat defiance of the prevailing masters. Horace Walpole, Clara Reeve, and Mrs Radcliffe all turned their backs upon their time and plunged into the delightful obscurity of the Middle Ages, which were so much richer than the eighteenth century in castles, barons, moats, and murders.

What Horace Walpole began half in fun was continued seriously and with considerable power by Mrs Radcliffe. That she had a conscience in the matter is evident from the pains she is at to explain her mysteries when they have done their work. The human body 'decayed and disfigured by worms, which were visible in the features and hands',[6] turns out to be a waxen image credibly placed there in fulfilment of a vow. But there is little wonder that a novelist perpetually on the stretch first to invent mysteries and then to explain them had no leisure for the refinements of the art. 'Mrs Radcliffe's heroines', says Miss Birkhead, 'resemble nothing more than a composite photograph in which all distinctive traits are merged into an expressionless type'.[7] The same fault can be found with most books of sensation and adventure, and is, after all, inherent in the subject; for it is unlikely that a lady confronted by a male body stark naked, wreathed in worms, where she had looked, maybe, for a pleasant landscape in oils, should do more than give a loud cry and drop senseless. And women who give loud cries and drop senseless do it in much the same way. That is one of the reasons why it is extremely difficult to write a tale of terror which continues to shock and does not first become insipid and later ridiculous. Even Miss Wilkinson, who wrote that 'Adeline Barnett was fair as a lily, tall as the pine, her fine dark eyes sparkling as diamonds, and she moved with the majestic air of a goddess,'[8] had to ridicule her own favourite style before she had done. Scott, Jane Austen, and Peacock[9] stooped from their heights to laugh at the absurdity of the convention and drove it, at any rate, to take refuge underground. For it flourished subterraneously all through the nineteenth century, and for sixpence you can buy today at the bookstall the recognisable descendant of The Mysteries of Udolpho. Nor is Adeline Barnett by any means defunct. She is probably an earl's daughter at the present moment; vicious, painted; in society. But if you call her Miss Wilkinson's Adeline she will have to answer none the less.

It would be a fine exercise in discrimination to decide the precise point at which romance becomes Gothic and imagination moonshine. Coleridge's lines in 'Kubla Khan' about the woman wailing for her demon lover are a perfect example of the successful use of emotion.[10] The difficulty, as Miss Birkhead shows, is to know where to stop. Humour is comparatively easy to control; psychology is too toilsome to be frequently overdone; but a gift for romance easily escapes control and cruelly plunges its possessor into disrepute. Maturin and Monk Lewis heaped up horrors until Mrs Radcliffe herself appeared calm and composed. And they have paid the penalty. The skull-headed lady, the vampire gentleman, the whole troop of monks and monsters who once froze and terrified now gibber in some dark cupboard of the servants' hall. In our day we flatter ourselves the effect is produced by subtler means. It is at the ghosts within us that we shudder, and not at the decaying bodies of barons or the subterranean activities of ghouls. Yet the desire to widen our boundaries, to feel excitement without danger, and to escape as far as possible from the facts of life drives us perpetually to trifle with the risky ingredients of the mysterious and the unknown. Science, as Miss Birkhead suggests, will modify the Gothic romance of the future with the aeroplane and the telephone. Already the bolder of our novelists have made use of psychoanalysis to startle and dismay. And already such perils attend the use of the abnormal in fiction – the younger generation has been heard to complain that the horror of *The Turn of the Screw*[11] is altogether too tame and conventional to lift a hair of their heads. But can we possibly say that Henry James was a Goth?

1–A review in the *TLS*, 5 May 1921, (Kp C220) of *The Tale of Terror. A Study of the Gothic Romance* (Constable & Co. Ltd, 1921) by Edith Birkhead, M.A., assistant lecturer in English literature in the University of Bristol, formerly Noble Fellow in the University of Liverpool.

See also 'Henry James's Ghost Stories' below; 'Romance' and 'Across the Border', *II VW Essays*. Reprinted: *G&R, CE*.

2–Birkhead, ch. xii, p. 221, which has: 'origin and development'.

3–Horace Walpole (1717–97); Edmund Spenser (1552?–99); William Shakespeare (1564–1616); Clara Reeve (1729–1807), author of *The Champion of Virtue, a Gothic Story* (1777) and *The Progress of Romance, through Times, Centuries, and Manners* (1785); Mrs Ann Radcliffe (1764–1823), author of *The Mysteries of Udolpho* (1794) etc.; Matthew Lewis (1775–1818), author of *The Monk* (1796); Charles Maturin (1782–1824), author of *Melmoth the Wanderer* (1820), etc; Sarah Scudgell Wilkinson, author of numerous romances, published between 1803 and 1828, among them *Adeline; or The Victim of Seduction* (1828).

4–Agnes Maria Bennett, *The Beggar Girl and Her Benefactors* (1797).

5–Samuel Johnson, *The Vanity of Human Wishes* (1749); Thomas Gray's odes were published by Horace Walpole in 1757, his collected poems appeared in 1768; Samuel Richardson, *Clarissa Harlowe* (1747–8); Joseph Addison, *Cato* (1713); Alexander Pope, *An Essay on Man* (1733–4).

6–Birkhead, ch. iii, p. 50, quoting *The Mysteries of Udolpho* (1794).

7–*Ibid.*, p. 45, which has '"type"'.

8–*Ibid.*, ch. iv, p. 78.

9–Sir Walter Scott (1771–1832); Jane Austen (1775–1817); Thomas Love Peacock (1785–1866).

10–S. T. Coleridge, 'Kubla Khan; or, A Vision in a Dream' (1816), 11 12ff:
> 'But oh! that deep romantic chasm which slanted
> Down the green hill athwart a cedarn cover!
> A savage place! as holy and enchanted
> As e'er beneath a waning moon was haunted
> By woman wailing for her demon-lover!'

11–Henry James, *The Turn of the Screw* (1898).

Patmore's Criticism

Books of collected essays are always the hardest to read, because, collected though they may be, it is often only the binding that joins them together. And when the author was a man whose main work in life was to write poetry, it is more than likely that his essays will be mere interjections and exclamations uttered spasmodically in the intervals of his proper pursuits. The list of contents makes us suspect the sort of thing we are to find. One day Coventry Patmore will write upon Mr Gladstone; another upon December in Garden and Field; again upon Coleridge; next upon dreams; and finally it will strike him to set down his views upon Liverpool Cathedral and Japanese houses.[2] But our foreboding that we shall be jerked from topic to topic and set down in the end with a litter of broken pieces is in this case quite unfounded. For one thing, these thirty-seven papers were written within the compass of eleven years. Next, as Mr Page points out, Coventry Patmore's criticism was based upon considered principles. 'The book is a book of doctrine, and is "original" only in that it goes back to origins; the doctrines are those of Aristotle, of Goethe, of Coleridge, indeed, as one can imagine Patmore's saying, "of all sensible men". The style only that holds them together is his own.'[3]

The style which holds so many separate parts so firmly is undoubtedly a good one. One would perhaps feel some discomfort, some unfitness in finding a column of such solid construction among the blurred print of an evening newspaper. Clearly one must look not among ephemeral scribblers but among established worthies if one is to find a writer against whom to test the merits and defects of Patmore's style. It is much in the eighteenth-century manner – concise, plain, with little imagery, extravagance, adventure, or inequality. Placed directly after one of Johnson's Lives of the Poets[4] one of Patmore's essays can be read, so far as the diction goes, without any of that gradual loosening of the attention which attacks us as prose weakens under the adulteration of unnecessary words, slack cadences, and worn out metaphors. But thus read we shall somehow gather the impression that while Johnson is constantly outrageous and Patmore almost invariably civilised, Johnson's papers are the small visible fragment of a monster, Mr Patmore's essays have about them no such suggestion of unexpressed magnitude. A few pages seem to hold quite comfortably all that he has to say. He is small and wiry, rather than large and loose.

But the chief distinction of Mr Patmore's criticism is that to which Mr Page draws attention. He had a great dislike for the impressionist criticism which is 'little more than an attempt to describe the feelings produced in the writers by the works they profess to judge'[5] and tried consistently to base his own judgements upon doctrines set beyond the reach of accident and temperament. His pages provide many examples of the successful practice of this form of criticism, and some also of the defects which, though not inherent in the method, seem most apt to attack those who pursue it.

In the essay upon out-of-door poetry, for instance, instead of dallying with roses and cabbages and all the other topics which so pleasantly suggest themselves, he makes straight for the aesthetic problem. The quality which distinguishes good descriptive poetry from bad descriptive poetry is, he says, that the poet in the first case has seen things 'in their living relationships'.

The heather is not much, and the rock is not much; but the heather and the rock, discerned in their living expressional relationship by the poetic eye, are very much indeed – a beauty which is living with the life of man, and therefore inexhaustible ... but true poets and artists know that this power of visual synthesis can only be exercised, in the present state of our faculties, in a very limited way; hence there is generally, in the landscapes and descriptions of real genius, a great simplicity in and apparent jealousy of their subjects, strikingly in contrast with the works of those who fancy that they are describing when they are only cataloguing.[6]

This is fruitful criticism because it helps us to define our own vaguer conceptions. Much of Wordsworth (here Mr Patmore would not agree) is oppressive because the poet has not seen nature with intensity either in relation to his poem, to himself, or to other human beings; but has accepted her as something in herself so desirable that description can be used in flat stretches without concentration. Tennyson[7] is of course the master of those Victorian poets who carried descriptive writing to such a pitch that if their words had been visible the blackbirds would certainly have descended upon their garden plots to feed upon the apples and the plums. Yet we do not feel that this is poetry so much as something fabricated by an ingenious craftsman for our delight. Of the moderns, Mr Hardy[8] is without rival in his power to make nature do his will, so that she neither satiates nor serves as a curious toy, but appears at the right moment to heighten, charm, or terrify, because the necessary fusion has already taken place. The first step towards this absorption is to see things with your own eyes, in which faculty Patmore held the English poets to be easily supreme.

Then, from poetry we turn to the little essay which is, of course, quite insufficient to deal with Sir Thomas Browne; but here again Patmore speaks to the point, drawing attention not to his own qualities, but to those which are in the work itself. 'The prose of the pre-revolutionary period was a fine art. In proportion to the greatness of its writers, it was a continually varying flow of music, which aimed at convincing the feelings as the words themselves the understanding. The best post-revolutionary prose appeals to the understanding alone.'[9] The prose of the *Religio Medici* (oddly enough Patmore values neither *Urn Burial* nor *Christian Morals*) is certainly fine art. Yet in reading it again one is struck as much by the easy colloquial phrases as by the famous passages. There is an intensity of the modern sort as well as the poetic sonority of the ancient. The art of the deliberate passages is evident; but in addition to that Sir Thomas has something impulsive, something we may call, in default of a better word, amateurish about him as if he wrote for his own pleasure with language not yet solidified, while the best modern prose writers seem to remember, unwillingly no doubt, that prose writing is a profession.

Whether or not we agree with what Patmore says on these points, it is good criticism because it makes us turn to think about the book under consideration. But the criticism which is based upon the 'doctrines of Aristotle, of Goethe, and of Coleridge', especially when practised in the columns of a newspaper,[10] is apt to have the opposite effect. It is apt to be sweeping and sterile. The laws of art can be stated in a little essay only in so compressed a form that unless we are prepared to think them out for ourselves, and apply them to the poem or novel in question, they remain barren, and we accept them without thinking. 'There is no true poem or novel without a moral; least of all such as, being all beauty (that is to say, all order), are all moral.'[11] A statement of that kind applied with little elaboration to the *Vicar of Wakefield* does not illumine the book, but, especially when coupled with an uncalled for fling at Blake, 'who seems to have been little better than an idiot'[12] withdraws attention from the *Vicar of Wakefield* and concentrates it upon Coventry Patmore. For it is evident that though the manner remains oracular this is the voice of a private person – of a person, moreover, who has written poetry himself, has been attacked by the critics, and has evolved a highly individual philosophy, into which Goldsmith and Coventry Patmore fit precisely as they are, but Blake, Shelley, and Miss

Austen[13] can only be made to fit by taking a knife to their edges. Blake was little better than an idiot; *Pride and Prejudice* was inferior to *Barchester Towers*;[14] Shelley was an immoral writer; and by the side of Thomas Hardy, not indeed his equal but worthy of comparison and of the highest eulogy, appears the author of *The Mischief of Monica*, a lady, it is now perhaps necessary to say, called Mrs Walford.[15] For these freaks and oddities it is, of course, unnecessary to make Aristotle responsible. *The Angel in the House* is the undoubted parent. In an impressionist critic of the school which Patmore condemned you will meet precisely the same freaks of prejudice and partisanship, but with the difference that as no attempt is made to relate them to doctrines and principles they pass for what they are, and, the door being left wide open, interesting ideas may take the opportunity to enter in. But Patmore was content to state his principle and shut the door.

But if Patmore was an imperfect critic the very imperfections which make it sometimes useless to argue further about literature prove that he was a man of great courage and conviction, much out of harmony with his age, intolerant of the railway, a little strident we may think in his conservatism, and over punctilious in his manner, but never restrained by sloth or cowardice from coming out into the open and testifying to his faith like a bright little bantam (if we may use the figure without disrespect) who objects to express trains, and says so twice a day, flying to the top of the farmyard wall and flapping his wings.

1 – A review in the *TLS*, 26 May 1921, (Kp C221) of *Courage in Politics and Other Essays 1885–1896*. [With a preface by F. Page] (OUP, 1921) by Coventry Patmore (1823–96), poet and critic, whose works include the eulogy to married love *The Angel in the House* (1854–62), and two collections of criticism, *Principle in Art* (1889) and *Religio Poetae* (1893).

On Monday, 21 May 1921, VW wrote in her diary: 'I was up in the Strand with 12 copies of *Monday or Tuesday* [Hogarth Press, March 1921]; so that sells a little; & 2 goslings, to be sent to Lewes; & my review of Patmore for the Times; & then caught a train home, put my great lupins & peonies in water, & should now settle with concentration to my book. But which book? I've a notion of reading masterpieces only; for I've read literature in bulk so long. Now I think's the time to read like an expert. Then I'm wondering how to shape my Reading book; the more I read of other peoples criticism the more I trifle; can't decide; or need I just yet. But how I enjoy the exercise of my wits upon literature – reading it as literature. And I think I can do this the better for having read through such a lot of lives, criticisms, every sort of thing.' See also *II VW Letters*, no. 1177, to Lady Robert Cecil.

Reprinted: *B&P*. See Editorial Note, p. xxv.

2 – For discussion of Gladstone, Patmore, 'Manifest Destiny', pp. 9–11, and the title

essay, pp. 11–17. The other essays referred to: 'December in Garden and Field', pp. 37–40; '"Great Talkers" I "Coleridge"', pp. 70–4, and 'Coleridge', pp. 84–92; 'Dreams', pp. 97–101; 'Liverpool Cathedral', pp. 194–9.

3 – *Ibid.*, Pref., p. 4, which has: 'origins: the' and 'Patmore saying'.

4 – Samuel Johnson, *The Lives of the Poets* (1779–81).

5 – Patmore, 'Hegel', p. 108, and Pref., p. 3: 'He deprecated the merely subjective appreciation . . .'

6 – *Ibid.*, 'Out-of-Door Poetry', p. 35, which continues: 'This power of seeing things in their living relationships, which constitutes genius, is rather a virtue than a talent; and the general intuition that it is so is perhaps the reason why so many departures from the common code are condoned in men of great genius – much being pardoned to those who have much loved.'

7 – William Wordsworth (1770–1850); Alfred, Lord Tennyson (1809–92), of whom Patmore was a friend.

8 – Patmore, 'Hardy's Novels', pp. 132–7; Thomas Hardy (1840–1928).

9 – *Ibid.*, 'Sir Thomas Browne [1605–82]', p. 55; *Religio Medici* (1643), *Urn Burial* (1658), *Christian Morals* (1716). For VW on 'Sir Thomas Browne' see below.

10 – For the quotation see n3 above. The majority of Patmore's essays collected here originally appeared in the *St James's Gazette*.

11 – Patmore, 'Goldsmith', p. 61. Oliver Goldsmith (1730–74), whose *Vicar of Wakefield* appeared in 1766.

12 – *Ibid.*; William Blake (1752–1827).

13 – For Patmore on Percy Bysshe Shelley (1792–1822), 'The Morality of "Epipsychidion"', *ibid.*, pp. 110–14. Jane Austen (1775–1827).

14 – *Ibid.*, 'Goldsmith', p. 69, which has: 'Now compare Miss Austen's stories with *Tom Jones* [Henry Fielding, 1749], or *Vanity Fair* [W. M. Thackeray, 1847–8], or *Barchester Towers* [Anthony Trollope, 1857] . . . the truth is, that *Tom Jones, Vanity Fair* and *Barchester Towers* are works of more value than *Emma* [1816], *Northanger Abbey* [1818], and *Sense and Sensibility* [1811] because the former are masculine and the latter feminine.' Patmore does not mention *Pride and Prejudice* (1813).

15 – *Ibid.*, 'Hardy's Novels', p. 134: 'Among living writers there are two – one well and one at present comparatively little known – whose work in this kind can scarcely be surpassed; namely, Thomas Hardy and L. B. Walford [1845–1915. *The Mischief of Monica*, 3 vols, 1891].' And see 'Mrs Walford's Novels', pp. 137–40.

Trousers

If the readers of the *New Statesman* will buy Mr Edwards' book they will hear of something to their advantage. They will learn that though they have always been accustomed to think themselves average men they are, by reason of that very fact, the only judges of art. Not only are they the only judges; they are the only creators. For the average man can cultivate his appearance, and that is the first of the arts; he can behave like a gentleman, and that is the second; he can dress well, and that is the third. The architect, the painter and the sculptor, though admitted among the minor artists, cannot compete with the man or woman who, divinely beautiful, exquisitely tactful, and superbly attired, practises the three major arts to perfection.

But our proficiency in the art of being beautiful is much determined by the accidents of birth. At this point we find Mr Edwards consoling, if not entirely convincing. 'Noses straight, aquiline or retroussé may so harmoniously be set upon the face that they are neither insignificant nor yet obtrusive . . . One man may have rather thin legs, and another man rather thick legs, and both may be possessed of a good figure.' There is only one physical defect which is completely damning, and that is bow legs. 'Bow legs are an abomination. The reason is that, being arranged in two equal and opposite curves enclosing a space, they create at about the level of the knees where the space is widest a marked focal centre'[2] – in short, the bow-legged are inevitably ill-bred; no one can help looking at their legs, and discord and rebellion result. The parents of the bow-legged, Mr Edwards is of opinion, 'ought to be visited with a severe penalty'.

Nevertheless, however scurvily Nature may have behaved, you can temper her severity (short of bow legs) by attention to the art of manners. Much can be done by grace of posture. You should be careful not to open the jaws widely, smack the lips, or expose the contents of the mouth in eating. Unless it is to amuse a baby, do not pretend to be a horse, for to walk on all fours 'without humorous intent' is to display 'the ultimate degree of bad manners to which it is possible to attain'.[3]

But the shortest survey of Mr Edwards' book must not fail to point out that besides laying down the law the author is at great pains to ascertain what that law is. Owing to native obtuseness, no doubt, we have been unable to grasp the grammar of design, although Mr Edwards has been to nature herself to discover it, and is confident that our assent will be complete and instantaneous 'because the law of mind has an intimate connection with the law of nature, and it is impossible to acknowledge the one without paying an equal deference to the other'.[4] In spite of diagrams of feet, hands, eyes, noses, ships and houses, many of his statements seem to us controversial, and some highly obscure. We will only mention the principle of resolved duality. 'Nature,' says Mr Edwards, 'does not tolerate duality.'[5] The hands differ; so do the eyes. But when Mr Edwards goes on to assert that trousers, owing to 'the irremediable effect of duality', seem 'to invite disrespect',[6] we entirely dissent. We go further. We have conceived them in isolation from the jacket, as advised, and still see nothing to laugh at in trousers. As for the final and most striking example of duality resolved, to wit, the Holy Trinity, the questions which Mr Edwards decides are too grave to be touched on in a review. We need only say that the origin of the Holy Ghost, long a subject of dispute among theologians, is now accounted for – quite simply, too.[7]

1–A review in the NS, 4 June 1921, (Kp C222) of *The Things Which Are Seen* (Philip Allan & Co., 1921) by A. Trystan Edwards, MA, formerly Scholar of Hertford College, Oxford. Associate of the Royal Institute of British Architects, and Associate Member of the Town Planning Institute.

2–For the quotations, Edwards, Pt i, 'The Hierarchy of the Arts', ch. iii, p. 62, which has: 'But bow legs'; and *ibid.*, p. 63.

3–*Ibid.*, p. 60.

4–*Ibid.*, Pt ii, 'Form and Subject', ch. i, p. 136.

5–*Ibid.*, ch. ii, p. 138: 'If we study examples of animal and vegetable life, we find that organic nature deals most freely in the singular and plural numbers, but it does not tolerate duality, unless this duality has been so modified as to partake of the character of unity.'

6–*Ibid.*, p. 51: 'Of course there are certain garments, such as a pair of trousers, which, however designed, must violate the canon. Thus it comes about that while coats, jackets, tunics, skirts and kilts all have a certain dignity, and can with propriety be mentioned even in poetry of the highest rank, a pair of trousers seems to invite disrespect, for it suffers from the irremediable defect of duality. Trousers when seen in conjunction with the rest of the costume of which they form a part are quite tolerable and may even appear elegant, but conceived in isolation they become a subject of ridicule.'

7–*Ibid.*, pp. 171–2: 'It is common knowledge that when once the divinity of Jesus had been declared and accepted, the nature of the Godhead presented a very difficult problem to the Christian theologians ... If both the divinity and the separate personality of Jesus were to be retained, it was necessary to postulate a third person in the deity which, in addition to the other two, would form a group, a unity. When once the divinity of Jesus is accepted, the existence of the Holy Ghost becomes an aesthetic necessity.'

A Glance at Turgenev

If this were not the sixteenth volume of a classic – if it were the first volume by an unknown writer – what should we find to say? To begin with we should say that M. Turgenev is an observant young man, who, if he can restrain his faculty for observing detail may in time have something to offer us. 'She had the habit of turning her head to the right while she lifted a morsel to her mouth with the left hand, as if she were playing with it.'[2] '. . . They pacified the infuriated curs, but a maid-servant was obliged to drag one of them . . . into a bedroom, getting bitten on her right hand in the process.'[3] In themselves both those facts are admirably noted; but we should not fail to point out that it is dangerous to observe like that – dangerous to stress little facts because one happens to have a store of them in readiness. All round us are strewn the melancholy relics of those who have insisted upon telling us that she was bitten on the right hand, but raised her fork with the left. And then, even as we are making this observation, the details dissolve and disappear. There is nothing left but the scene itself. It lives unsupported, unvouched for. The father and mother; the two girls; the visitors; the very sheep dogs and the food on the table are all contributing spon-taneously to the final impression which makes us positive, when the door shuts and the two young men drive off, that nothing will induce Boris Andreyitch to marry Emerentsiya. That is the principal thing we know; but we also know, as the house recedes in the distance, that in the drawing-room Emerentsiya is simpering over her conquest; while the plain sister Polinka has run upstairs and is crying to the maid that she hates visitors; they will talk to her about music; and then her mother scolds her.

That scene is not the work of a prentice hand. It is not the result of keen eyesight and notebooks crammed with facts. But it would be impossible if we had only that scene before us to say that we detect a master's hand and are already certain that this unknown Russian writer is the famous novelist Turgenev. The story goes on, however. Greatly to the surprise of his friend, Boris marries a simple country girl. They settle down; life is perfect, but perhaps a trifle dull. Boris travels. He goes to Paris, and there drifting vaguely into an affair with a young woman he is challenged by her lover and killed. Far away in Russia his widow mourns for him sincerely. But after all Boris did not 'belong to the number of people who are irreplaceable. (And indeed are there such people?)' Nor was his widow 'capable of devoting herself forever to one feeling. (And indeed are there such feelings?)'[4] So she marries her husband's old friend, and they live peacefully in the country, and have children and are happy, 'for there is no other happiness on earth'.[5] Thus, that first scene which was so lively and suggestive has led to other scenes; they add themselves to it; they bring in contrast, distance, solidity. In the end everything seems to be there. Here is a world able to exist by itself. Now perhaps we can talk with some certainty of a master; for now we have not a single brilliant episode which is gone the moment after, but a succession of scenes attached one to another by the feelings which are common to humanity. Space forbids us to inquire more minutely by what means this is achieved. Besides, there are other books by Turgenev which illustrate his powers more clearly. The stories in this volume[6] are not equal to his best work. But they have this characteristic of greatness – they exist by themselves. We can judge from them what sort of world Turgenev created. We can see in what respects his vision was different from other people's.

Like most Russian writers, he was melancholy. Beyond the circle of his scene seems to lie a great space, which flows in at the window, presses upon people, isolates them, makes them incapable of action, indifferent to effect, sincere, and open-minded. Some background of that sort is common to much of Russian literature. But Turgenev adds to this scene a quality which we find nowhere else. They are sitting as usual talking round the samovar, talking gently, sadly, charmingly, as Turgenev's people always do talk, when one of them ceases, gets up, and looks out of the window. 'But the moon must have risen,' she says, 'that's moonlight on the tops of the poplars.'[7] And we look up and there it is – the moonlight on the poplars. Or take, as an example of the same power, the description of the garden in 'Three Meetings':

Everything was slumbering. The air, warm and fragrant, did not stir; only from time to time it quivered as water quivers at the fall of a twig. There was a feeling of languor, of yearning in it. . . . I bent over the fence; a red field poppy lifted its stalk above the rank grass . . .[8]

and so on. Then the woman sings, and her voice sounds straight into an atmosphere which has been prepared to wrap it up, to enhance it, and float it away. No quotation can convey the impression, for the description is part of the story as a whole. What is more, we feel again and again that Turgenev evades his translator. It is not Mrs Garnett's fault. The English language is not the Russian. But the original description of the garden in the moonlight must be written, not with this inevitable careful exactness, but flowingly; there must be melody, variety, transparency. But the general effect is there even if we miss the beauty with which it is rendered. Turgenev, then, has a remarkable emotional power; he draws together the moon and the group round the samovar, the voice and the flowers and the warmth of the garden – he fuses them in one moment of great intensity, though all round are the silent spaces, and he turns away, in the end, with a little shrug of his shoulders.

1 – A review in the TLS, 8 December 1921, (Kp C223) of *Two Friends and Other Stories*... Translated from the Russian by Constance Garnett [1862–1946, see 'The Russian Background', above, n2] (William Heinemann, 1921) by Ivan Turgenev (1818–83).
2 – Turgenev, 'The Two Friends', pp. 49–50, which concludes: '; and Boris Andreyitch very much disliked this habit.'
3 – *Ibid.*, p. 38, adapted.
4 – For both quotations, *ibid.*, p. 121.
5 – *Ibid.*, p. 122.
6 – In addition to the stories discussed by VW, the collection also includes 'Father Alexey's Story'.
7 – Turgenev, 'A Quiet Backwater', p. 267.
8 – *Ibid.*, 'Three Meetings', p. 159; the first ellipsis is Turgenev's; the passage continues: 'before me, and a great round drop of night dew glittered with a dark light in its open cup. Everything was slumbering, everything lay luxuriously and seemed to be gazing upwards, waiting without stirring ... What was this warm, not yet sleeping night awaiting?'

Fantasy

When one reads that very amusing book, *Candide*, certain sentences strike one's attention as if the weight behind them had suddenly become prodigious. 'Travaillons sans raisonner, dit Martin; c'est le seul moyen de rendre la vie supportable.'[2] The reason appears to be that Voltaire knew his own meaning and shaped it so skilfully that we receive the impact instantly, indelibly, at one blow like the stroke of an unerring swordsman. We drag in Voltaire in the hope that he may help us out of a difficulty. We have to define Mr Jacks' new book *Legends of Smokeover*. Perhaps we shall shorten our task if we begin by saying that while Voltaire and Mr Jacks are both satirists, Voltaire was a Frenchman and Mr Jacks is an Englishman; while Voltaire is scathing, wild and witty, Mr Jacks is emotional, fantastic and decorous; while Voltaire writes 100 little pages which we shall remember for the rest of our lives, Professor Jacks writes 300 large ones which we shall have forgotten the day after tomorrow. That is true, as it is true, perhaps, of every book destined to appear this month of December, 1921. But in this case one is sorry that it should be so; it seems more than usually a waste, a pity.

Legends of Smokeover begins by being a satire. The vast smoky town, its wealth, its profiteers, its complete ignorance of ideal or direction, fall under the lash of a sharp intelligent brain endowed with a delightful capacity for speaking its meaning. If Mr Jacks next proceeds to be fantastic, grotesque, and extravagant that is all to the good. The subject demands it. The satirist is a man who judges the prevailing opinions of mankind to be absurd, and brings this home to us by setting up somehow or other his own version of the truth. There are many ways in which he may do this, and one of the most effective is that which Mr Jacks attempts, when he creates in contrast with the prosperous industrial city five eccentric human beings who by the standards of Smokeover are judged to be insane. But the satirist, however he may pile absurdity upon absurdity, must make us feel, by a single phrase, by a single word, that his eye is all the time fixed upon the truth. He must be concentrated and passionate inwardly, however freakish he may appear on the surface. But Professor Jacks is freakish without being passionate. He sees things not as they are but as the symbols and veils of a hidden reality. The veil of Smokeover rolls up; and behind it we see beauty and truth, courage and virtue. He calls them legends.

Now it is an invariable rule in the growth of literature that legends originate at the places of transit where ideal things pass over into actualities. They haunt the bridges between the visible world and its heavenly counterpart; they gather at the fords and ferries which carry the traffic of the eternal values across the River of Forgetfulness into the scene of their temporal manifestations. Two or three of these bridges, all in the very heart of Smokeover, the author was able to find.[3]

After reading that we own that we cannot remember why we dragged in Voltaire. There are so many other people, it seems as one goes on reading, whom one might drag in with greater fitness – Peacock, Mr E. M. Forster and Mrs Hemans, Queen Victoria, Martin Tupper and Samuel Butler.[4] Perhaps it would be simpler to call this queer composite personality, at once so clear and so cloudy, so shrewd and so sentimental, so advanced and so Victorian, Mr Jacks and have done with it.

As we have said there are five figures whose strange adventures are related in the book, Rumbelow the betting man, Hooker the profiteer, Miss Wolfstone the adventuress, Ripplemark the Professor of Virtue, and Mrs Rumbelow, generally called 'My Lady'. But if we are asked what they stand for, what the gambling establishment signifies, or how we expound the fable of the transfigured mouse, we do not know where to begin. The meanings are so many; the allegories so prolific, the symbolism so incessant that at last we give up looking for a meaning and let the entertainment proceed. All we can vouch for is that everything has a meaning; that significant phrases, witty phrases, suggestive phrases are sprinkled so thick that it is a thousand pities that we should get tired before we have picked them all up. 'So live that by affirming your own personality you may help others to affirm theirs.' 'Throw away the broken umbrella and get a firm grasp on the woman's arm.' 'Finance the moral ideal.'[5] Why should we get tired of picking up phrases like these? Perhaps because they seem to refer to nothing in particular; there is nothing hard for them to ring against; the real and the unreal have melted together into one many coloured mist. 'Il faut cultiver notre jardin'[6] said Voltaire; and the sentence endures, like a diamond.

1 – A review in the *TLS*, 15 December 1921, (Kp C224) of *Legends of Smokeover* (Hodder & Stoughton, 1921) by L. P. [Lawrence Pearsall] Jacks (1860–1955), Unitarian divine, Principal of Manchester College, Oxford, 1915–31.
2 – Voltaire (1694–1778), *Candide, ou l'optimisme* (1759; *Les Oeuvres Complètes de Voltaire*, Voltaire Foundation, 1980, vol. xlviii, ch. xxx, p. 260, ll. 130–1).
3 – Jacks, 'Smokeover and Its Smoke', pp. 18–19.
4 – Thomas Love Peacock (1785–1866); E. M. Forster (1879–1970); Mrs Felicia Dorothea Hemans, *née* Browne (1793–1835), author of 'The boy stood on the burning deck'; Queen Victoria (1837–1901); Martin Farquhar Tupper (1810–89), author of *Proverbial Philosophy* (1838–42); Samuel Butler (1835–1902).
5 – For the first quotation, Jacks, 'Miss Wolfstone becomes Clairvoyant', p. 188; for the second, *ibid.*, 'The Mad Millionaire Has a Near Shave', p. 120, which has: 'He must throw away his broken umbrella'; and for the third, *ibid.*, p. 110; 'I said that I meant to Finance the Moral Ideal'.
6 – Voltaire, ch. xxx, p. 260, ll. 146–7: 'Cela est bien dit, répondit Candide, mais il faut cultiver notre jardin.'

Henry James's Ghost Stories

It is plain that Henry James was a good deal attracted by the ghost story, or, to speak more accurately, by the story of the supernatural. He wrote at least eight of them, and if we wish to see what led him to do so, and what opinion he had of his success, nothing is simpler than to read his own account in the preface to the volume containing 'The Altar of the Dead'.[2] Yet perhaps we shall keep our own view more distinct if we neglect the preface. As the years go by certain qualities appear, and others disappear. We shall only muddle our own estimate if we try, dutifully, to make it square with the verdict which the author at the time passed on his own work. For example, what did Henry James say of 'The Great Good Place?

There remains 'The Great Good Place' (1900) – to the spirit of which, however, it strikes me that any gloss or comment would be a tactless challenge. It embodies a calculated effect, and to plunge into it, I find, even for a beguiled glance – a course I indeed recommend – is to have left all else outside.[3]

And to us, in 1921, 'The Great Good Place' is a failure. It is another example of the fact that when a writer is completely and even ecstatically conscious of success he has, as likely as not, written his worst. We ought, we feel, to be inside, and we remain coldly outside. Something has failed to work, and we are inclined to accuse the supernatural. The challenge may be tactless, but challenge it we must.

That 'The Great Good Place' begins admirably, no one will deny. Without the waste of a word we find ourselves at once in the heart of a situation. The harassed celebrity, George Dane, is surrounded by unopened letters and unread books; telegrams arrive; invitations accumulate; and the things of value lie hopelessly buried beneath the litter. Meanwhile, Brown the man-servant announces that a strange young man has arrived to breakfast. Dane touches the young man's hand, and, at this culminating point of annoyance, lapses into a trance or wakes up in another world. He finds himself in a celestial rest-cure establishment. Far bells toll; flowers are fragrant; and after a time the inner life revives. But directly the change is accomplished we are aware that something is wrong with the story. The movement flags; the emotion is monotonous. The enchanter waves his wand and the cows go on grazing. All the characteristic phrases are there in waiting – the silver bowls, the melted hours – but there is no work for them to do. The story dwindles to a sweet soliloquy. Dane and the Brothers become angelic allegorical figures pacing a world that is like ours but smoother and emptier. As if he felt the need of something hard and objective the author invokes the name of the city of Bradford; but it is vain. 'The Great Good Place' is an example of the sentimental use of the supernatural and for that reason no doubt Henry James would be likely to feel that he had been more than usually intimate and expressive.

The other stories will presently prove that the supernatural offers great prizes as well as great risks; but let us for a moment dwell upon the risks. The first is undoubtedly that it removes the shocks and buffetings of experience. In the breakfast room with Brown and the telegram Henry James was forced to keep moving by the pressure of reality; the door must open; the hour must strike. Directly he sank through the solid ground he gained possession of a world which he could fashion to his liking. In the dream world the door need not open; the clock need not strike; beauty is to be had for the asking. But beauty is the most perverse of spirits; it seems as if she must pass through ugliness or lie down with disorder before she can rise in her own person. The ready-made beauty of the dream world produces only an anaemic and conventionalised version of the world we know. And Henry James was much too fond of the world we know to create one that we do not know. The visionary imagination was by no means his. His genius was dramatic, not lyric. Even his characters wilt in the thin atmosphere he provides for them, and we are presented with a Brother when we would much rather grasp the substantial person of Brown.

We have been piling the risks, rather unfairly, upon one story in particular. The truth is perhaps that we have become fundamentally sceptical. Mrs Radcliffe[4] amused our ancestors because they were our ancestors; because they lived with very few books, an occasional post, a newspaper superannuated before it reached them, in the depths of the country or in a town which resembled the more modest of our villages, with long hours to spend sitting over the fire drinking wine by the light of half a dozen candles. Nowadays we breakfast upon a richer feast of horror than served them for a twelvemonth. We are tired of violence; we suspect mystery. Surely, we might say to a writer set upon the supernatural, there are facts enough in the world to go round; surely it is safer to stay in the breakfast room with Brown. Moreover, we are impervious to fear. Your ghosts will only make us laugh, and if you try to express some tender and intimate vision of a world stripped of its hide we shall be forced (and there is nothing more uncomfortable) to look the other way. But writers, if they are worth their salt, never take advice. They always run risks. To admit that the supernatural was used for the last time by Mrs Radcliffe and that modern nerves are immune from the wonder and terror which ghosts have always inspired would be to throw up the sponge too easily. If the old methods are obsolete, it is the business of a writer to discover new ones. The public can feel again what it has once felt – there can be no doubt about that; only from time to time the point of attack must be changed.

How consciously Henry James set himself to look for the weak place in our armour of insensibility it is not necessary to decide. Let us turn to another story, 'The Friends of the Friends',[5] and judge whether he succeeded. This is the story of a man and woman who have been trying for years to meet but only accomplish their meeting on the night of the woman's death. After her death the meetings are continued, and when this is divined by the woman he is engaged to marry she refuses to go on with the marriage. The relationship is altered. Another person, she says, has come between them. 'You see her – you see her; you see her every night!'[6] It is what we have come to call a typically Henry James situation. It is the same theme that was treated with enormous elaboration in *The Wings of the Dove*.[7] Only there, when Milly has come between Kate and Densher and altered their relationship for ever, she has ceased to exist; here the anonymous lady goes on with her work after death. And yet – does it make very much difference? Henry James has only to take the smallest of steps and he is over the border. His characters with their extreme fineness of perception are already half-way out of the body. There is nothing violent in their release. They seem rather to have achieved at last what they have long been attempting – communication without obstacle. But Henry James, after all, kept his ghosts for his ghost stories. Obstacles are essential to *The Wings of the Dove*. When he removed them by supernatural means as he did in 'The Friends of the Friends' he did so in order to produce a particular effect. The story is very short; there is no time to elaborate the relationship; but the point can be pressed home by a shock. The supernatural is brought in to provide that shock. It is the queerest of shocks – tranquil, beautiful, like the closing of chords in harmony; and yet, somehow obscene. The living and the dead by virtue of their superior sensibility have reached across the gulf; that is beautiful. The live man and the dead woman have met alone at night. They have their relationship. The spiritual and the carnal meeting together produce a strange emotion – not exactly fear, nor yet excitement. It is a feeling that we do not immediately recognise. There is a weak spot in our armour somewhere. Perhaps Henry James will penetrate by methods such as these.

Next, however, we turn to 'Owen Wingrave'[8] and the enticing game of pinning your author to the board by detecting once more traces of his fineness, his subtlety, whatever his prevailing characteristics may be, is rudely interrupted. Pinioned, tied down, to all appearance lifeless, up he jumps and walks away. Somehow one has forgotten to account for the genius, for the driving power which is so incalculable and so essential. With Henry James in particular we tend, in wonder at his prodigious dexterity, to forget that he had a crude and simple passion for telling stories. The preface to 'Owen Wingrave' throws light upon that fact, and incidentally suggests why it is that 'Owen Wingrave' as a ghost story misses its mark. One summer's afternoon, many years ago, he tells us, he sat on a penny chair under a great tree in Kensington Gardens. A slim young man sat down upon another chair near by and began to read a book.

Did the young man then, on the spot, just *become* Owen Wingrave, establishing by the mere magic of type the situation, creating at a stroke all the implications and filling out all the pictures? ... my poor point is only that at the beginning of my session in the penny chair the seedless fable hadn't a claim to make or an excuse to give, and that, the very next thing, the penny-worth still partly unconsumed, it was fairly bristling with pretexts. 'Dramatize it, dramatize it!' would seem to have rung with sudden intensity in my ears.[9]

So the theory of a conscious artist taking out his little grain of matter and working it into the finished fabric is another of our critical fables. The truth appears to be that he sat on a chair, saw a young man, and fell asleep. At any rate, once the group, the man, or perhaps only the sky and the trees become significant, the rest is there inevitably. Given Owen Wingrave, then Spencer Coyle, Mrs Coyle, Kate Julian, the old house, the season, the atmosphere must be in existence. Owen Wingrave implies all that. The artist has simply to see that the relations between these places and people are the right ones. When we say that Henry James had a passion for story-telling we mean that when his significant moment came to him the accessories were ready to flock in.

In this instance they flocked in almost too readily. There they are on the spot with all the stir and importance that belong to living people. Miss Wingrave seated in her Baker Street lodging with 'a fat catalogue of the Army and Navy Stores, which reposed on a vast desolate table-cover of false blue'; Mrs Coyle, 'a fair fresh slow woman', who admitted and indeed gloried in the fact that she was in love with her husband's pupils, 'Which shows that the subject between them was treated in a liberal spirit';[10] Spencer Coyle himself, and the boy Lechmere – all bear, of course, upon the question of Owen's temperament and situation, and yet they bear on so many other things besides. We seem to be settling in for a long absorbing narrative; and then, rudely, incongruously, a shriek rings out; poor Owen is found stretched on the threshold of the haunted room; the supernatural has cut the book in two. It is violent; it is sensational; but if Henry James himself were to ask us: 'Now, have I frightened you?' we should be forced to reply: 'Not a bit.' The catastrophe has not the right relations to what has gone before. The vision in Kensington Gardens did not, perhaps, embrace the whole. Out of sheer bounty the author has given us a scene rich in possibilities – a young man whose problem (he detests war and is condemned to be a soldier) has a deep psychological interest; a girl whose subtlety and oddity are purposely defined as if in readiness for future use. Yet what use is made of them? Kate Julian has merely to dare a young man to sleep in a haunted room; a plump Miss from a parsonage would have done as well. What use is made of the supernatural? Poor Owen Wingrave is knocked on the head by the ghost of an ancestor; a stable bucket in a dark passage would have done it better.

The stories in which Henry James uses the supernatural effectively are, then, those where some quality in a character or in a situation can only be given its fullest meaning by being cut free from facts. Its progress in the unseen world must be closely related to what goes on in this. We must be made to feel that the apparition fits the crisis of passion or of conscience which sent it forth so exactly that the ghost story, besides its virtues as a ghost story, has the additional charm of being also symbolical. Thus the ghost of Sir Edmund Orme appears to the lady who jilted him long ago whenever her daughter shows signs of becoming engaged. The apparition is the result of her guilty conscience, but it is more than that. It is the guardian of the rights of lovers. It fits what has gone before; it completes. The use of the supernatural draws out a harmony which would otherwise be inaudible. We hear the first note close at hand, and then, a moment after, the second chimes far away.

Henry James's ghosts have nothing in common with the violent old ghosts – the blood-stained sea captains, the white horses, the headless ladies of dark lanes and windy commons. They have their origin within us. They are present whenever the significant overflows our powers of expressing it; whenever the ordinary appears ringed by the strange. The baffling things that are left over, the frightening ones that persist – these are the emotions that he takes, embodies, makes consoling and companionable. But how can we be afraid? As the gentleman says when he has seen the ghost of Sir Edmund Orme for the first time: 'I was ready to answer for it to all and sundry that ghosts are much less alarming and more amusing than was commonly supposed.'[11] The beautiful urbane spirits are only not of this world because they are too fine for it. They have taken with them across the border their clothes, their manners, their breeding, their band-boxes, and valets and ladies' maids. They remain always a little worldly. We may feel clumsy in their presence, but we cannot feel afraid. What does it matter, then, if we do pick up *The Turn of the Screw*[12] an hour or so before bedtime? After an exquisite entertainment we shall, if the other stories are to be trusted, end with this fine music in our ears, and sleep the sounder.

Perhaps it is the silence that first impresses us. Everything at Bly is so profoundly quiet. The twitter of birds at dawn, the far-away cries of children, faint footsteps in the distance stir it but leave it unbroken. It accumulates; it weighs us down; it makes us strangely apprehensive of noise. At last the house and garden die out beneath it. 'I can hear again, as I write, the intense hush in which the sounds of evening dropped. The rooks stopped cawing in the golden sky, and the friendly hour lost for the unspeakable minute all its voice.'[13] It is unspeakable. We know that the man who stands on the tower staring down at the governess beneath is evil. Some unutterable obscenity has come to the surface. It tries to get in; it tries to get at something. The exquisite little beings who lie innocently asleep must at all costs be protected. But the horror grows. Is it possible that the little girl, as she turns back from the window, has seen the woman outside? Has she been with Miss Jessel? Has Quint visited the boy? It is Quint who hangs about us in the dark; who is there in that corner and again there in that. It is Quint who must be reasoned away, and for all our reasoning returns. Can it be that we are afraid? But it is not a man with red hair and a white face whom we fear. We are afraid of something, unnamed, of something, perhaps, in ourselves. In short, we turn on the light. If by its beams we examine the story in safety, note how masterly the telling is, how each sentence is stretched, each image filled, how the inner world gains from the robustness of the outer, how beauty and obscenity twined together worm their way to the depths – still we must own that something remains unaccounted for. We must admit that Henry James has conquered. That courtly, worldly, sentimental old gentleman can still make us afraid of the dark.

1 – An essay in the *TLS*, 22 December 1921, (Kp C225). 'I am struggling with Henry James' ghost stories for The Times;' VW noted in her diary on Tuesday, 15 November 1921, 'have I not just laid them down in a mood of satiety?' On Sunday, 18 December, she remarked how she had 'had to put in semicolons to my Hen James article while talking to Ralph [Partridge] over my shoulder & then to rush to catch a train to Hampstead to dine with [Dorothy] Brett & [Mark] Gertler.' Then, on Monday, 19 December, she added 'a postscript . . . on the nature of reviewing' in response to queries from the editor of the *TLS*, Bruce Richmond: '"Mrs Woolf? I want to ask you one or two questions about your Henry James article – ¶ First (only about the right name of one of the stories.) And now you use the word "lewd". Of course, I dont wish you to change it, but surely that is rather a strong expression to apply to anything by Henry James. I haven't read the story lately of course – but still my impression is – ¶ Well, I thought that when I read it: one has to go by one's

impressions at the time. ¶ But you know the usual meaning of the word? It is – ah – *dirty* – Now poor dear old Henry James – At anyrate, think it over, & ring me up in 20 minutes. ¶ So I thought it over & came to the required conclusion in twelve minutes & a half. ¶ But what is one to do about it? He made it sufficiently clear not only that he wouldn't stand "lewd", but that he didn't much like anything else. I feel that this becomes more often the case, & I wonder whether to break off, with an explanation, or to pander, or to go on writing against the current. This last is probably right, but somehow the consciousness of doing that cramps one. One writes stiffly, without spontaneity. Anyhow, for the present I shall let it be, & meet my castigation with resignation. People will complain I'm sure; & poor Bruce fondling his paper like an only child dreads public criticism, & is stern with me, not so much for disrespect to poor old Henry, but for bringing blame on the Supplement.' The word 'lewd' does not occur in VW's Reading Notes (Berg, xxvi) but her note, on 'The Way It Came' (1896), is perhaps of interest: '"Another person has come between us". A touch of the sensual wh. under the circs. is obscene'.

See also 'Within the Rim', 'The Letters of Henry James' above; 'Mr Henry James's Latest Novel', *I VW Essays*; 'The Old Order', 'The Method of Henry James', *II VW Essays*; and see 'Gothic Romance' above and 'Across the Border', *II VW Essays*. Henry James (1843–1916). Reprinted: *G&R, CE*.

2 – The Altar of the Dead' originally published in *Terminations* (1895) and collected in the 'New York Edition' of *Novels and Tales* (24 vols, Macmillan, 1908–09), vol. xvii, Pref., pp. v–xxix.

3 – *Novels and Tales*, vol. xvi, Pref., pp. ix–x, which has: 'it strikes me, any gloss'; 'The Great Good Place' was originally collected in *The Soft Side* (1900).

4 – Mrs Ann Radcliffe, *née* Ward (1764–1823), author of *The Mysteries of Udolpho* (1794) etc.

5 – Originally entitled 'The Way It Came' and collected in *Embarrassments* (1896), upon which VW's reading notes are based; it was collected under the new title in *Novels and Tales*, vol. xvii.

6 – *Embarrassments*, 'The Way It Came', ch. vii, p. 260, which has a colon, not a semi-colon.

7 – Published in 1902.

8 – 'Owen Wingrave' (1893), collected in *Novels and Tales*, vol. xvii.

9 – *Novels and Tales*, vol. xvii, Pref., pp. xxii–xxiii, which has: 'filling out all the picture?'.

10 – For the first quotation, *ibid.*, 'Owen Wingrave', p. 281; for the second, *ibid.*, p. 290; and for the third, *ibid.*, p. 291.

11 – *Ibid.*, 'Sir Edmund Orme', p. 390; the story was originally published in 1891.

12 – Published in 1898.

13 – *The Turn of the Screw* (Wm Heinemann, 1898), p. 31, which has: 'lost, for the minute, all its voice'.

1922

Dostoevsky the Father

It would be a mistake to read this book as if it were a biography. Mlle Dostoevsky expressly calls it a study, and to this the reader must add that it is a study by a daughter. The letters, the facts, the testimonies of friends, even to a great extent the dates which support the orthodox biography are here absent or are introduced as they happen to suit the writer's purpose. And what is a daughter's purpose in writing a study of her father? We need not judge her very severely if she wishes us to see him as she saw him – upright, affectionate, infallible, or, if he had his failings, she is to be excused if she represents them as the foibles of greatness. He was extravagant perhaps. He gambled sometimes. There were seasons when, misled by the wiles of women, he strayed from the paths of virtue. We can make allowance for these filial euphemisms; and if we come to feel, as this book makes us feel, that the daughter was fond as well as proud of her father, that is a real addition to our knowledge. At the same time, we should have listened more sympathetically if Mlle Dostoevsky had suppressed her version of the quarrel between Dostoevsky and Turgenev. To make out that your father is a hero is one thing; to insist that his enemies are villains is another. Yet she must have it that all the blame was on Turgenev's side; that he was jealous, a snob, 'even more cruel and malicious than the others'.[2] She neglects the testimony supplied by Turgenev's own works, and, what is more serious, makes no mention of the evidence on the other side which must be known to her. The effect is naturally to make the reader scrutinise Dostoevsky's character more closely than he would otherwise have

327

done. He asks himself inevitably what there was in the man to cause this shrill and excited partisanship on the part of his daughter. The search for an answer among the baffling yet illuminating materials which Mlle Dostoevsky supplies is the true interest of this book.

If we were to be guided by her we should base our inquiry upon the fact that Dostoevsky was of Lithuanian descent on his father's side. Mlle Dostoevsky has read Gobineau,[3] and shows a perverse ingenuity and considerable industry in attributing almost every mental and moral characteristic to race heredity. Dostoevsky was a Lithuanian and thus loved purity; he was a Lithuanian and thus paid his brother's debts; he was a Lithuanian and thus wrote bad Russian; he was a Lithuanian and thus a devout Catholic. When he complained that he had a strange and evil character he did not realise that it was neither strange nor evil, but simply Lithuanian. As Dostoevsky himself never attached much import- ance to his descent, we may be allowed to follow his example. We shall not come much closer to him by pursuing that track. But Mlle Dostoevsky increases our knowledge by more indirect methods. A clever little girl cannot run about her father's house without picking up many things which she is not expected to know. She knows whether the cook is grumbling; which of the guests bores her parents; whether her father is in a good temper, or whether there has been some mysterious grown-up catastrophe. Considering that Aimée was very young when her father died, she could scarcely be expected to observe anything of much greater importance than this. But then she is a Russian. She has that apparently involuntary candour which must make family life so disconcerting in Russia. Her father's greatness subdues her to a dutiful attitude, which, if reverent, is also a little colourless. But no one else has that power over her. 'Her self-esteem was always excessive, almost morbid; a trifle would offend her, and she easily fell a victim to those who flattered her.'[4] Thus she describes her mother, and her mother is still alive. As for her uncles and aunts, her step-brother, her father's first wife, his mistress, she is completely outspoken about them all and – were it not that she qualifies her blame by detecting strains of Slav, Norman, Ukrainian, Negro, Mongol, and Swedish blood – equally severe. That, indeed, is her contribution to our knowledge of Dostoevsky. No doubt she exagger- ates; but there can also be no doubt that her bitterness is the legacy of old family quarrels – sordid, degrading, patched-up, but bursting out afresh and pursuing Dostoevsky to the verge of his death-chamber. The pages seem to ring with scoldings and complainings and recriminations; with demands for more money and with replies that all the money has been spent. Such, or something like it, we conclude, was the atmosphere in which Dostoevsky wrote his books.

His father was a doctor who had to resign his appointment owing to drunkenness; and it was on account of his drunken savagery that his serfs smothered him one day beneath the cushions of his carriage as he was driving on his estate. Two of Dostoevsky's brothers were drunkards; his sister was miserly to the verge of insanity, and was also murdered, for her money. Her son was 'so stupid that his folly verged on idiocy. My uncle Andrey's son, a young and brilliant savant, died of creeping paralysis. The whole Dostoevsky family suffered from neurasthenia.'[5] And to the family eccentricity one must add what appears to the English reader the national eccentricity – the likelihood, that is to say, that if Dostoevsky escapes death on the scaffold and survives imprisonment in Siberia he will marry a wife who has a handsome young tutor for her lover, and will take for his mistress a girl who arrives at his bedside at seven in the morning brandishing an enormous knife with which she proposes to kill a Frenchman. Dostoevsky dissuades her, and off they go to Wiesbaden where 'my father played roulette with passionate absorption, was delighted when he won, and experienced a despair hardly less delicious when he lost'.[6] It is all violent and extreme. Later, even, when Dostoevsky was happily married, there was still a worthless stepson who expected to be supported; still the brothers' debts to pay; still the sisters trying to make mischief between him and his wife; and then the rich aunt Kumanin must needs die and leave her property to stir up the last flames of hatred among the embittered relations. 'Dostoyevsky lost patience and, refusing to continue the painful discussion, left the table before the meal was finished.'[7] Three days later he was dead. One thinks of Farringford flourishing not so very far away. One wonders what Matthew Arnold, who deplored the irregularities of the Shelley set, would have said to this one.[8]

And yet, has it anything to do with Dostoevsky? One feels rather as if one had been admitted to the kitchen where the cook is smashing the china, or to the drawing room where the relations are gossiping in corners, while Dostoevsky sits upstairs alone in his study. He had, it is clear, an extraordinary power of absenting his mind from his body. The money troubles alone, one would think, were enough to drive him distracted. On the contrary, it was his wife who worried, and it was Dostoevsky, says his daughter, who remained serene, saying, 'in tones of conviction, "We shall never be without money."'[9] We catch sight of his body plainly enough, but it is rather as if we passed him taking his afternoon walk, always at four o'clock, always along the same road, so absorbed in his own thoughts that 'he never recognised the acquaintance he met on the way'.[10] They travelled in Italy, visited the galleries, strolled in the Boboli gardens, and 'the roses blooming there struck their Northern imaginations'.[11] But after working at *The Idiot* all the morning how much did he see of the roses in the afternoon? It is the waste of his day that is gathered up and given us in place of his life. But now and then, when Mlle Dostoevsky forgets the political rancours of the moment and the complex effect of the Norman strain upon the Lithuanian temperament, she opens the study door and lets us see her father as she saw him. He could not write if he had a spot of candle-grease on his coat. He liked dried figs and kept a box of them in a cupboard from which he helped his children. He liked eau-de-Cologne to wash with. He liked little girls to wear pale green. He would dance with them and read aloud Dickens and Scott.[12] But he never spoke to them about his own childhood. She thinks that he dreaded discovering signs of his father's vices in himself; and she believes that he 'wished intensely to be like others'.[13] At any rate, it was the greatest pleasure of her day to be allowed to breakfast with him and to talk to him about books. And then it is all over. There is her father laid out in his evening dress in his coffin; a painter is sketching him; grand dukes and peasants crowd the staircase; while she and her brother distribute flowers to unknown people and enjoy very much the drive to the cemetery.

1–A review in the *TLS*, 12 January 1922, (Kp C226), of *Fyodor Dostoyevsky* [1821–81]: *A Study* (Heinemann, 1921) by Aimée [Lubov] Dostoyevsky – Dostoevsky's daughter by his second wife and former secretary Anna Grigorevna Snitkina, whom he had married in 1867.

VW wrote in her diary on Saturday, 26 November 1921: 'Kot[eliansky] just gone after hearing Leonard his Russian; & so I have an odd half hour to fill up, & reach for this book. I have been cross examining Kot upon the quarrel between Dostoevsky & Turgenev, & find him stuffed with facts, & of course passionate severe & uncompromising. For once in a way I shall have some truth to put in my article. We have spent the day mostly indoors . . . A yellow, prickly kind of day, with the quiet which comes of fog, & is accentuated, as it happens, by the road being up. It is said we are to have wood pavement.'

See also 'Dostoevsky in Cranford' above; 'More Dostoevsky' and 'A Minor Dostoevsky', *II VW Essays*. Reprinted: *B&P*.

2–Dostoyevsky, ch. xxiv, p. 213: 'Russian coarseness amazed Dostoyevsky . . . It astonished him still more when he encountered it in the literary salons of the period . . . But when the unexpected success of his first novel excited the jealousy of the younger writers, they avenged themselves by calumnies and insults . . . Losing his self-control, Dostoyevsky said absurd things, and excited the laughter of his

unfeeling companions. Turgenev [1818–85] in particular delighted in tormenting him. He was of Tatar origin, and showed himself to be even more cruel and malicious than the others.'
3–Joseph Arthur, Comte de Gobineau (1816–82), man of letters, diplomat, whose anti-semitism and belief in the supremacy of the Nordic race found expression in *Essai sur l'inégalité des races humaines* (1853–5) – published in English translation as *The Inequality of the Human Races* (1915).
4–Dostoyevsky, ch. xiii, p. 133.
5–*Ibid.*, ch. iii, p. 37.
6–*Ibid.*, ch. x, pp. 108–9.
7–*Ibid.*, ch. xxx, p. 272.
8–Farringford: the home of Tennyson at Freshwater on the Isle of Wight. For Matthew Arnold on the Shelley set, see his 'Byron' in *Essays in Criticism. Second Series* (1888).
9–Dostoyevsky, ch. ix, p. 172.
10–*Ibid.*, ch. xxii, p. 194, slightly adapted.
11–*Ibid.*, ch. xvii, p. 158: 'My father was busily occupied in Florence; he was writing his novel, *The Idiot* [1866], which he had begun at Geneva ... In fine weather they would stroll in the Cascine or the Boboli Gardens. The roses blooming there in the month of January struck their northern imaginations.'
12–Charles Dickens (1812–70); Sir Walter Scott (1771–1832).
13–Dostoyevsky, ch. xx, p. 177: 'This eternal dreaminess, so characteristic of writers and men of science, was a great annoyance to my father, who considered it humiliating and ridiculous. He wished intensely to be like others. But great minds cannot manifest themselves after the fashion of commonplace men.'

Jane Austen Practising

The summer of 1922, remarkable for public reasons in many ways, was privately remarkable for the extreme coldness of its nights. Six blankets and a quilt? A rug and a hot water bottle? All over England men and women went up to bed with such words upon their lips. And then, between two and three in the morning, they woke with a start. Something serious had happened. It was stifling. It was portentous. Steps must be taken immediately. But what a frightful effort it needs in the early hours of the morning to throw off all one's clothes!

All over England for the past ten or twenty years the reputation of Jane Austen has been accumulating on top of us like these same quilts and blankets. The voices of the elderly and distinguished, of the clergy and the squirearchy, have droned in unison praising and petting, capping quotations, telling little anecdotes, raking up little facts. She is

the most perfect artist in English literature. And one of her cousins had
his head cut off in the French Revolution. Did she ever go fox hunting?
No, but she nursed Miss Gibson through the measles. Her knowledge of
the upper middle classes was unrivalled. One of her ancestors
entertained King Charles. Macaulay, of course, compared her with
Shakespeare.[2] And where is Mansfield Park? So they pile up the quilts
and counterpanes until the comfort becomes oppressive. Something
must be done about it. But what a frightful effort it needs at this time of
day to shake off all these clothes!

Now opportunely, in the nick of time, comes *Love and Freindship* to
give us the very chance we want. Here is a little book written by Jane
Austen long before she was the great Jane Austen of mythology. The
Jane Austen of *Love and Freindship* was a girl of seventeen scribbling
stories to amuse the schoolroom. One is dedicated with mock solemnity
to her brother. Another is neatly illustrated with water colour heads by
her sister. Nobody (for we may leave Mr Chesterton to the end) has been
here before us, and so we may really read Jane Austen by ourselves for
the first time.

She is a girl of seventeen writing in a country parsonage. And on page
two, without turning a hair, out she raps 'natural daughter'.[3] Yet her
mother might have come in at that very moment. The eighteenth
century, of course, still persisted. The little Austens had the freedom of
the house as no other children were to have it for a century at least.
Money and marriage would no doubt be jokes in the nursery as they
were, much more coarsely, jokes upon the stage. And clever children,
beginning to laugh at their elders, would in the year 1790 pick up the last
new novel and make fun of its heroine. 'Ah! what could we do but what
we did? We sighed and fainted on the sofa.'[4] When Jane Austen read that
aloud, no doubt her brothers and sisters took the reference to Adeline
Barrett,[5] or whoever was the fashionable heroine of the moment. And as
the Austens were a large family, and Mrs Austen stitched and darned
and lay an invalid on the sofa, her daughters, while still very young, were
well aware that life in a country parsonage has little in common with life
in Mrs Radcliffe's novels.[6] This is all plausible enough, and much more
might be written in the same strain. But it has nothing whatever to do
with *Love and Freindship*. For this girl of seventeen is not writing to
amuse the schoolroom. She is not writing to draw a laugh from sister and
brothers. She is writing for everybody, for nobody, for our age, for her
own; she, in short, is writing. 'A sensibility too tremblingly alive to every
affliction of my Friends, my Acquaintance, and particularly to every

affliction of my own, was my only fault, if a fault it could be called. Alas! how altered now! Tho' indeed my own Misfortunes do not make less impression on me than they ever did, yet now I never feel for those of an other.'[7] The authoress of those lines had, if not a whole sitting room to herself, some private corner of the common parlour where she was allowed to write without interruption. But now and then, as the writing of *Love and Freindship* proceeded, a brother or a sister must have asked what she was laughing at. And then Jane Austen read aloud, 'I die a martyr to my grief for the loss of Augustus. One fatal swoon has cost me my life. Beware of Swoons, Dear Laura . . . Run mad as often as you chuse, but do not faint . . .'[8] And taking up her pen again she wrote, it is clear, as fast as she could write, and faster than she could spell, for the incredible adventures of Laura and Sophia popped into her head as quick as lightning. She was in the enviable position of having one page to fill and a bubbling fancy capable of filling half a dozen. So if she wants to dispose of the husband of Phillipa she decrees that he shall have one talent, driving, and one possession, a coach, and he shall drive for ever between Edinburgh and Stirling, or, for Jane Austen does not exaggerate, shall drive to Stirling every other day. And Philander and Gustavus – what shall we do with them? Oh, their mothers (and, by the way, no one knew who their fathers were – perhaps Philip Jones the bricklayer, and Gregory Staves the staymaker) – their mothers kept their fortune of nine hundred pounds in the table drawer. So they stole it, and wrapped it in nine parcels, and spent it in seven weeks and a day, and came home and found their mothers starved, and went upon the stage and acted Macbeth. Spirited, easy, full of fun, verging with freedom upon sheer nonsense, there can be no doubt that *Love and Freindship* makes excellent reading. But what is this note which never merges in the rest, which sounds distinctly and penetratingly all through the volume? It is the sound of laughter. The girl of seventeen is laughing, in her corner, at the world.

Girls of seventeen are always laughing. They laugh when Mr Binney helps himself to salt instead of sugar. They almost die of laughing when old Mrs Tomkins sits down upon the cat. But they are crying the moment after. They have no fixed point from which they see that there is something eternally laughable in human nature. They do not know that wherever they go and however long they live they will always find Lady Grevilles snubbing poor Marias at a dance. But Jane Austen knew it. That is one reason why she is so impersonal and remains for ever so inscrutable. One of those fairies who are said to attend with their gifts upon cradles must have taken her on a flight through the air directly she was born. And when she was laid in her cradle again she knew what the world looked like. She had chosen her kingdom. She had agreed that if she might rule over that territory she would covet no other. Thus at seventeen she had few illusions about other people and none about herself. Whatever she writes is finished and turned and set in its relation to the universe like a work of art. When Jane Austen, the writer, wrote down, in the most remarkable sketch in the book, a little of Lady Greville's conversation,[9] there is no trace of anger at the snub which Jane Austen, the clergyman's daughter, no doubt once received. Her gaze passes straight to the mark, and somehow we know precisely where, upon the map of human nature, that mark is. We know because Jane Austen kept to her compact; she never trespassed beyond her boundaries. Never, even at the emotional age of seventeen, did she round upon herself in shame, and obliterate a sarcasm in a spasm of compassion, or blur an outline in a mist of rhapsody. Spasms and rhapsodies, she seems to have said, end here. And the boundary line is perfectly distinct. But she does not deny that moons and mountains and castles exist – on the other side. She has even one romance of her own. It is for the Queen of Scots. She really admired her very much. 'One of the first characters in the World', she called her, 'a bewitching Princess whose only freind was then the Duke of Norfolk, and whose only ones now Mr Whitaker, Mrs Lefroy, Mrs Knight and myself.'[10] With these words the passion is neatly circumscribed, and rounded with a laugh. It is amusing to remember how the young Brontës wrote, not so very much later, about the Duke of Wellington.[11]

It may be that we are reading too much into these scraps and scribbles. We are still under the influence of the quilts and counterpanes. But just as we determine to shake ourselves free – and, after all, she was a limited, tart, rather conventional woman for all her genius – we hear a snatch of music. 'Yet truth being I think very excusable in an historian.' And again, 'She was nothing more than a mere good tempered, civil, and obliging young woman; as such we could scarcely dislike her – she was only an object of contempt.' And yet again, '. . . for what could be expected from a man who possessed not the smallest atom of sensibility, who scarcely knew the meaning of simpathy, and who actually snored.'[12] She is only humming a tune beneath her breath, trying over a few bars of the music for *Pride and Prejudice* and *Emma*. But we know that there is no one else who can sing like that. She need not raise her voice. Every syllable comes quite distinctly through the gates of time.

And whatever they may say about her genius and her cousins and *Mansfield Park*[13] we are content to listen all day long to Jane Austen practising.

1–A signed review in the *NS*, 15 July 1922, (Kp C227) of *Love & Freindship and Other Early Works* now first printed from the original Ms... with a preface by G. K. Chesterton [1874–1936] (Chatto & Windus, 1922) by Jane Austen (1775–1817). See also 'Jane Austen and the Geese' above, 'Jane Austen at Sixty' below; *'Jane Austen', II VW Essays*; and 'Jane Austen', *IV VW Essays* and *CR 1*. Reading Notes (MHP, B 2q).

2–For Lord Macaulay's comparison, *Critical and Historical Essays* (1843) 'Madame D'Arblay' (2 vols, J. M. Dent, 1907, vol. ii, p. 603): 'Shakespeare has had neither equal nor second. But among the writers who, in the point which we have noticed, have approached nearest to the manner of the great master, we have no hesitation in placing Jane Austen, a woman of whom England is justly proud. She has given us a multitude of characters, all, in a certain sense, commonplace, all such as we meet every day. Yet they are all as perfectly discriminated from each other as if they were the most eccentric of human beings.'

3–Austen, 'Love and 'Freindship', Letter 3rd, Laura to Marianne, p. 6: 'My Father was a native of Ireland and an inhabitant of Wales; my Mother was the natural Daughter of a Scotch Peer by an Italian Opera-girl – I was born in Spain and received my Education at a Convent in France.'

4–*Ibid.*, Letter 9th, from the same to the same, p. 18, which has 'but what we did!'

5–Or, possibly, Adeline Barnett; see 'Gothic Romance', p. 306.

6–Mrs Ann Radcliffe, *née* Ward (1764–1823), author of *The Mysteries of Udolpho* (1794) etc.

7–Austen, 'Letter 3rd', p. 6, which has: 'Freinds, my Acquaintance and'.

8–*Ibid.*, 'Letter the 14th', Laura to Marianne, p. 34, which has ellipses after 'Augustus' and 'Life', and: 'chuse; but'.

9–*Ibid.*, 'A Collection of Letters', 'Letter the Third, from a Young Lady in distressed Circumstances to her freind', pp. 109–14.

10–For the first quotation, *ibid.*, 'The History of England', 'Henry the 7th', p. 88, slightly adapted; and for the second, *ibid.*, 'Elizabeth', p. 92, which has: 'this bewitching Princess'.

11–For the Brontës and the 1st Duke of Wellington (1769–1852) see, for example, the Rev. Patrick Brontë quoted in Elizabeth Gaskell, *The Life of Charlotte Brontë* (1857; Penguin, 1975, pp. 93–4).

12–For the first quotation Austen, 'The History of England', 'James the 1st', p. 94: 'As I am myself partial to the roman catholic religion, it is with infinite regret that I am obliged to blame the Behaviour of any Member of it: yet Truth being I think very excusable in an Historian, I am necessitated to say that in this reign the roman Catholics of England 'did not behave like Gentlemen to the protestants'; for the second, *ibid.*, 'Love and Freindship', pp. 32–3, which has: 'Object of Contempt'; and for the third, *ibid.*, p. 38, which has: 'Sensibility'.

13–*Pride and Prejudice* (1813), *Emma* (1816), *Mansfield Park* (1814).

On Re-reading Novels

So there are to be new editions of Jane Austen and the Brontës and George Meredith. Left in trains, forgotten in lodging-houses, thumbed and tattered to destruction, the old ones have served their day, and for the new-comers in their new houses there are to be new editions and new readings and new friends. It speaks very well for the Georgians. It is still more to the credit of the Victorians. In spite of the mischief-makers, the grandchildren, it seems, get along very nicely with the grandparents; and the sight of their concord points inevitably to the later breach between the generations, a breach more complete than the other, and perhaps more momentous. The failure of the Edwardians, comparative yet disastrous – that is a question which waits to be discussed. How the year 1860 was a year of empty cradles; how the reign of Edward the Seventh[2] was barren of poet, novelist, or critic; how it followed that the Georgians read Russian novels in translations; how they benefited and suffered; how different a story we might have told today had there been living heroes to worship and destroy – all this we find significant in view of the new editions of the old books. The Georgians, it seems, are in the odd predicament of turning for solace and guidance not to their parents who are alive, but to their grandparents who are dead. And so, as likely as not, we shall be faced one of these days by a young man reading Meredith for the first time.

He has bought *Harry Richmond*[3] and he is in the middle of it, and he is obviously annoyed when they come and ask him for his ticket. Is he not enviable? And what was it like, reading *Harry Richmond* for the first time? Let us try to remember. The book begins with a statue who turns out be a man, and there is a preposterous adventurer, somehow descended from the Royal family, and there is a scene at a dinner-party, and a fire, and a dashing, impetuous girl, and a handsome manly boy, and England in June at night, and stars and rivers and love-making and gallantry. In short, the young man ought to be enjoying himself, and one of these days we will read *Harry Richmond* again. But there are difficulties to be faced. We do not mean that Meredith is said (perhaps not so truly) to be under a cloud. In our climate that is inevitable. But we mean that to read a novel for the second time is far more of an undertaking than to read it for the first. To rush it breathlessly through does very well for a beginning. But that is not the way to read finally; and somehow or other these fat Victorian volumes, these *Vanity Fairs*, *Copperfields*, *Richmonds*, and *Adam Bedes* must be read finally, if we are to do them justice – must be read as one reads *Hamlet*, as a whole.[4] But, then, one reads *Hamlet* in the four hours between dinner and bedtime. It is not beyond human endurance to read it from first to last, in and out, and, so far as our faculties permit, as a whole, *Hamlet* may change; we know, indeed, that *Hamlet* will change; but tonight *Hamlet* is ours. And for that reason, too, we hesitate before reading *Harry Richmond* again. Tonight *Harry Richmond* will not be ours. We shall have broken off a tantalising fragment; days may pass before we can add to it. Meanwhile the plan is lost; the book pours to waste; we blame ourselves; we abuse the author; nothing is more exasperating and dispiriting. Better leave the Victorian novelists to crumble on the shelves and be bolted whole by schoolboys. Let us confine ourselves to apt quotations from Mrs Gamp,[5] and find Hartfield on the map. Let us call Jane Austen 'Jane', and debate for ever which curate Emily Brontë loved. But the business of reading novels is beyond us, and there is nothing more melancholy than the sight of so many fine brains irrevocably expressed in the one form which makes them for ever inaccessible. So, instead of reading *Harry Richmond*, we will envy the young man opposite and wish Defoe and Fanny Burney[6] at the bottom of the sea. They were the parents of the modern novel, and their burden is heavy.

Some such mood of exasperation and bewilderment, of violence, yet of remorse, is abroad at present among those common readers whom Dr Johnson respected, for it is by them, he said, that 'must be finally decided all claim to poetical honours'.[7] It bodes ill for fiction if the commons of letters vote against it, so let us lay bare our dilemma without caring overmuch if we say some foolish things and many vague ones. To begin with, we have obviously got it into our heads that there is a right way to read, and that is to read straight through and grasp the book entire. The national habit has been formed by the drama, and the drama has always recognised the fact that human beings cannot sit for more than five hours at a stretch in front of a stage. And on top of that we are by temperament and tradition poetic. There still lingers among us the belief that poetry is the senior branch of the service. If we have an hour to spend we feel that we lay it out to better advantage with Keats than with Macaulay.[8] And so perhaps we come to novels neither knowing the right way to read them nor very much caring to acquire it. We ask one thing and they give us another. They are so long, so dull, so badly written; and, after all, one has life enough on one's hands already without living it all over again between dinner and bedtime in prose. Such are the stock complaints, and they lose nothing of their acrimony if with the same breath we have to admit that we owe more to Tolstoy, Dostoevsky, and Hardy than we can measure; that if we wish to recall our happier hours they would be those Conrad has given us and Henry James;[9] and that to have seen a young man bolting Meredith whole recalls the pleasure of so many first readings that we are even ready to venture a second. Only with these contrary impulses at work it will be a hazardous affair. Not again shall we be floated over on the tide of careless rapture. The pleasure we shall now look for will lie not so obviously on the surface; and we shall find ourselves hard pressed to make out what is the lasting quality, if such there be, which justifies these long books about modern life in prose. The collective reading of generations which has set us at the right angle for reading plays has not yet shaped our attitude to fiction. That *Hamlet* is a work of art goes without saying; but that *Harry Richmond* is a work of art has to be said for the first time.

Some months ago Mr Percy Lubbock applied himself to answer some of these questions in *The Craft of Fiction*, a book which is likely to have much influence upon readers, and may perhaps eventually reach the critics and writers. To say that it is the best book on the subject is probably true; but it is more to the point to say that it is the only one. He has attempted a task which has never been properly attempted, and has tentatively explored a field of inquiry which it is astonishing to find almost untilled. The subject is vast and the book short, but it will be our fault, not Mr Lubbock's, if we talk as vaguely about novels in the future as we have done in the past. For example, do we say that we cannot read *Harry Richmond* twice? We are led by Mr Lubbock to suspect that it was our first reading that was to blame. A strong but vague emotion, two or three characters, half a dozen scattered scenes – if that is all that Harry Richmond means to us, the fault lies, perhaps, not with Meredith, but with ourselves. Did we read the book as he meant it to be read, or did we not reduce it to chaos through our own incompetency? Novels, above all other books, we are reminded, bristle with temptations. We identify ourselves with this person or with that. We fasten upon the character or scene which is congenial. We swing our imaginations capriciously from spot to spot. We compare the world of fiction with the real world and judge it by the same standards. Undoubtedly we do all this, and easily find excuses for so doing. 'But meanwhile the book, the thing he made, lies imprisoned in the volume, and our glimpse of it was too fleeting, it seems, to leave us with a lasting knowledge of its form.'[10] That is the point. There is something lasting that we can lay hands on. There is, Mr Lubbock argues, such a thing as the book itself. We should read at arm's length from the distractions we have named. We must receive impressions, but we must relate them to each other as the author intended; and we can only do his bidding by making ourselves acquainted with his method. When we have shaped our impressions, as the author would have us, we are then in a position to perceive the form itself, and it is this which endures, however mood or fashion may change. In Mr Lubbock's own words:

But with the book in this condition of a defined shape, firm of outline, its form shows for what it is indeed – not an attribute, one of many and possibly not the most important, but the book itself, as the form of the statue is the statue itelf.[11]

Now, as Mr Lubbock laments, the criticism of fiction is in its infancy, and its language, though not all of one syllable, is baby language. This word 'form', of course, comes from the visual arts, and for our part we wish that he could have seen his way to do without it. It is confusing. The form of the novel differs from the dramatic form – that is true; we can, if we choose, say that we see the difference in our mind's eyes. But can we see that the form of The Egoist[12] differs from the form of Vanity Fair? We do not raise the question in order to stickle for accuracy where most words are provisional, many metaphorical, and some on trial for the first time. The question is not one of words only. It goes deeper than that, into the very process of reading itself. Here we have Mr Lubbock telling us that the book itself is equivalent to its form, and seeking with admirable subtlety and lucidity to trace out those methods by which novelists build up the final and enduring structure of their books. The very patness with which the image comes to the pen makes us suspect that it fits a little loosely. And in these circumstances it is best to shake oneself free from images and start afresh with a definite subject to work upon. Let us read a story and set down our impressions as we go along, and so perhaps discover what it is that bothers us in Mr Lubbock's use of the word form. For this purpose there is no more appropriate author than Flaubert; and, not to strain our space, let us choose a short story, 'Un Cœur Simple',[13] for example, for, as it happens, it is one that we have practically forgotten.

The title gives us our bearings, and the first words direct our attention to Madame Aubain's faithful servant Félicité. And now the impressions begin to arrive. Madame's character; the look of her house; Félicité's appearance; her love affair with Théodore; Madame's children; her visitors; the angry bull. We accept them, but we do not use them. We lay them aside in reserve. Our attention flickers this way and that, from one to another. Still the impressions accumulate, and still, almost ignoring their individual quality, we read on, noting the pity, the irony, hastily observing certain relations and contrasts, but stressing nothing; always awaiting the final signal. Suddenly we have it. The mistress and the maid are turning over the dead child's clothes. 'Et des papillons s'envolèrent de l'armoire.'[14] The mistress kisses the servant for the first time. 'Félicité lui en fut reconnaissante comme d'un bienfait, et désormais la chérit avec un dévouement bestial et une vénération religieuse.'[15] A sudden intensity of phrase, something which for good reasons or for bad we feel to be emphatic, startles us into a flash of understanding. We see now why the story was written. Later in the same way we are roused by a sentence with a very different intention: 'Et Félicité priait en regardant l'image, mais de temps à autre se tournait un peu vers l'oiseau.'[16] Again we have the same conviction that we know why the story was written. And then it is finished. All the observations which we have put aside now come out and range themselves according to the directions we have received. Some are relevant; others we can find no place for. On a second reading we are able to use our observations from the start, and they are much more precise; but they are still controlled by these moments of understanding.

Therefore the 'book itself' is not form which you see, but emotion which you feel, and the more intense the writer's feeling the more exact without slip or chink its expressions in words. And whenever Mr Lubbock talks of form it is as if something were interposed between us and the book as we know it. We feel the presence of an alien substance which requires to be visualised imposing itself upon emotions which we feel naturally, and name simply, and range in final order by feeling their right relations to each other. Thus we have reached our conception of 'Un Cœur Simple' by working from the emotion outwards, and, the reading over, there is nothing to be seen; there is everything to be felt. And only when the emotion is feeble and the workmanship excellent can we separate what is felt from the expression and remark, for example, what excellence of form *Esther Waters* possesses in comparison with *Jane Eyre*. But consider the *Princesse de Clèves*.[17] There is vision and there is expression. The two blend so perfectly that when Mr Lubbock asks us to test the form with our eyes we see nothing at all. But we feel with singular satisfaction, and since all our feelings are in keeping, they form a whole which remains in our minds as the book itelf. The point is worth labouring, not simply to substitute one word for another, but to insist, among all this talk of methods, that both in writing and in reading it is the emotion that must come first.[18]

Still, we have only made a beginning, and a very dangerous one at that. To snatch an emotion and luxuriate in it and tire of it and throw it away is as dissipating in literature as in life. Yet, if we wring this pleasure from Flaubert, the most austere of writers, there is no limit to be put upon the intoxicating effects of Meredith and Dickens and Dostoevsky, of Scott[19] and Charlotte Brontë. Or, rather, there is a limit, and we have found it over and over again in the extremes of satiety and distrust. If we are to read them a second time, we must somehow discriminate. Emotion is our material; but what do we mean by emotion? How many different kinds of emotion are there not in one short story, of how many qualities, and composed of how many different elements? And, therefore, to get our emotion directly, and for ourselves, is only the first step. We must go on to test it and riddle it with questions. If nothing survives, well and good; if something remains, all the better. The resolution is admirable; the only difficulty is how to enforce it. Did we thus wish to examine our impressions of some new play or poem, there are many dead, and five or six living, critics at whose command we cheerfully revise our views. But when it is fiction, and fiction hot from the press, far from accepting the judgement of any living critic or the applause or neglect of the public, we are forced, after comparing half a dozen judgements, each based on a different conception of the art or on no conception at all, either to do the work for ourselves or to conclude that for some mysterious reason the work cannot be done. There may be something so emotional in fiction that the critics inevitably lose their heads. There may be something so unamenable to discipline in the art itself that it is hopeless either to judge it by the old standards or to devise new ones afresh. But now – at last – Mr Lubbock applies his Röntgen rays. The voluminous lady submits to examination. The flesh, the finery, even the smile and witchery, together with the umbrellas and brown paper parcels which she has collected on her long and toilsome journey, dissolve and disappear; the skeleton alone remains. It is surprising. It is even momentarily shocking. Our old familiar friend has vanished. But, after all, there is something satisfactory in bone – one can grasp it.

In other words, by concentrating on the novelist's method Mr Lubbock draws our attention to the solid and enduring thing to which we can hold fast when we attack a novel for the second time. Here is something to which we can turn and turn again, and with each clearer view of it our understanding of the whole becomes more definite. Here is something removed (as far as may be) from the influence of our fluctuating and private emotions. The novelist's method is simply his device for expressing his emotion; but if we discover how that effect is produced we shall undoubtedly deepen the impression. Let us put it to the proof, since words are misleading. It is essential in 'Un Cœur Simple' that we should feel the lapse of time; the incidents are significant because they are scattered so sparsely over so long a stretch of years, and the effect must be given in a few short pages. So Flaubert introduces a number of people for no purpose, as we think; but later we hear that they are now all dead, and we realise then for how long Félicité herself has lived. To realise that is to enforce the effect. It fastens our attention upon the story as a work of art, and gives us such a prise on it as we have already, thanks to their more rigid technique, upon drama and poetry, but have to contrive for fiction, afresh, each time we open a book.

But that is one detail in a short story. Can we sharpen our impressions of a long and crowded novel in the same way? Can we make out that the masters – Tolstoy and Flaubert, and Dickens, and Henry James, and Meredith – expressed by methods which we can trace and understand the enormous mass and the myriad detail of their books? If so the novel, the voluminous Victorian novel, is capable of being read, as we read *Hamlet*, as a whole. And the novelists, children of instinct, purveyors of illusion and distraction at the cheapest rates quoted in literature, are of the blood royal all the same. That is the conclusion to which Mr Lubbock certainly brings us by means of an argument which is at once fascinating and strangely unfamiliar. We have been along the road so often and have wasted so many matches looking for sign-posts in dark corners. We must have been aware that a novelist, before he can persuade us that his world is real and his people alive, must solve certain questions and acquire certain skill. But until Mr Lubbock pierced through the flesh and made us look at the skeleton we were almost ready to believe that nothing was needed but genius and ink. The novelists themselves have done little to open our eyes. They have praised the genius and blamed the ink, but they have never, with two famous exceptions, invited us in to see the process at work. Yet obviously there must be a process, and it is at work always and in every novel. The simplest story begins more often than not, as Mr Lubbock points out, by the use of three different methods: the scene, the retrospect, the summary. And our innocence is gauged by the fact that though we swallow them daily it is with our eyes tight shut. Names have to be found and methods defined now for the first time.

No writer, indeed, has so many methods at his disposal as a novelist. He can put himself at any point of view; he can to some extent combine several different views. He can appear in person, like Thackeray; or disappear (never perhaps completely), like Flaubert. He can state the facts, like Defoe, or give the thought without the fact, like Henry James. He can sweep the widest horizons, like Tolstoy, or seize upon one old apple-woman and her basket, like Tolstoy again. Where there is every freedom there is every licence; and the novel, open-armed, free to all comers, claims more victims than the other forms of literature all put together. But let us look at the victors. We are tempted, indeed, to look at them a great deal more closely than space allows. For they too look different if you watch them at work. There is Thackeray always taking measures to avoid a scene, and Dickens (save in *David Copperfield*) invariably seeking one. There is Tolstoy dashing into the midst of his story without staying to lay foundations, and Balzac[20] laying foundations so deep that the story itself seems never to begin. But we must check the desire to see where Mr Lubbock's criticism would lead us in reading particular books. The general view is more striking, and a general view is to be had.

Let us look not at each story separately, but at the method of story-telling – the use, that is, of each of these processes – which runs through them all. Let us look at it in Richardson's hands, and watch it changing and developing as Thackeray applies it, and Dickens and Tolstoy and Meredith and Flaubert and the rest. Then let us see how in the end Henry James, endowed not with greater genius but with greater knowledge and craftsmanship, surmounts in *The Ambassadors* problems which baffled Richardson in *Clarissa*.[21] The view is difficult; the light is bad. At every angle some one rises to protest that novels are the outburst of spontaneous inspiration, and that Henry James lost as much by his devotion to art as he gained. We will not silence that protest, for it is the voice of an immediate joy in reading without which second readings would be impossible, for there would be no first. And yet the conclusion seems to us undeniable. Henry James achieved what Richardson attempted. 'The only real *scholar* in the art'[22] beats the amateurs. The late-comer improves upon the pioneers. More is implied than we can even attempt to state.

For from that vantage ground the art of fiction can be seen, not clearly indeed, but in a new proportion. We may speak of infancy, of youth, and of maturity. We may say that Scott is childish and Flaubert by comparison a grown man. We may go on to say that the vigour and splendour of youth almost outweigh the more deliberate virtues of maturity. And then we may pause upon the significance of 'almost', and wonder whether, perhaps, it has not some bearing upon our reluctance to read the Victorians twice. The gigantic, sprawling books still seem to reverberate the yawns and lamentations of their makers. To build a castle, sketch a profile, fire off a poem, reform a workhouse, or pull down a prison were occupations more congenial to the writers, or more befitting their manhood, than to sit chained at a desk scribbling novels for a simple-minded public. The genius of Victorian fiction seems to be making its magnificent best of an essentially bad job. But it is never possible to say of Henry James that he is making the best of a bad job. In all the long stretch of The Wings of the Dove[23] and The Ambassadors there is not a hint of a yawn, not a sign of condescension. The novel is his job. It is the appropriate form for what he has to say. It wins a beauty from that fact – a fine and noble beauty – which it has never worn before. And now at last (so we seem to see) the novel is a form distinct from any other. It will not burden itself with other people's relics. It will choose to say whatever it says best. Flaubert will take for his subject an old maid and a stuffed parrot. Henry James will find all he needs round a tea-table in a drawing room. The nightingales and roses are banished – or at least the nightingale sounds strange against the traffic, and the roses in the light of the arc lamps are not quite so red. There are new combinations of old material, and the novel, when it is used for the sake of its qualities and not for the sake of its defects, enforces fresh aspects of the perennial story.

Mr Lubbock prudently carries his survey no farther than the novels of Henry James. But already the years have mounted up. We may expect the novel to change and develop as it is explored by the most vigorous minds of a very complex age. What have we not, indeed, to expect from M. Proust alone?[24] But if he will listen to Mr Lubbock, the common reader will refuse to sit any longer open-mouthed in passive expectation. That is to encourage the charlatan to shock us and the conjuror to play us tricks. We must press close on his heels, and so bring to bear upon the novelist who spins his books in solitude the pressure of an audience. The pressure of an audience will not reduce the novel to a play which we can read through in the four hours between dinner and bedtime. But it will encourage the novelist to find out – and that is all we ask of him – what it is that he means and how best to show it us.

1–An essay in the TLS, 20 July 1922, (Kp C228) – 'very laborious, yet rather gifted' (II VW Diary, 23 June 1922) – occasioned by the publication of new editions of The

Novels of Jane Austen [1775–1817] (5 vols, J. M. Dent, 1922); *The Novels of Charlotte* [1816–55], *Emily* [1818–48] and *Anne* [1820–49] *Brontë* (6 vols, J. M. Dent, 1922); *The Works of George Meredith* [1828–1909] (19 vols, Constable, 1922); and drawing considerably upon VW's reading of *The Craft of Fiction* (Jonathan Cape, 1921) by Percy Lubbock (1879–1965), critic, author, friend and editor of Henry James (see 'The Letters of Henry James' above), whose arguments – 'I agree he has his merits' (*II VW Letters*,. no. 1205, 2 December 1921, to Katherine Arnold-Forster) – were to continue to attract VW's critical attention for several years.

On Wednesday, 15 February 1922, she remarked in her diary that she and Lytton Strachey had 'disagreed violently about Lubbock's book' and on 1 June she wrote to Janet Case that she 'must settle down to think about Mr Percy Lubbock and the Craft of Fiction, about which I have to write tomorrow, and every idea has gone under water. They were swarming last week, when I wanted to write a story.' (*II VW Letters*, no. 1254.) Her thoughts returned to Lubbock in the following October, see note 18 below. (See also *III VW Letters*, no. 1498, to Roger Fry; no. 1832, to E. M. Forster).

See 'Modern Novels' above, 'Mr Bennett and Mrs Brown' and 'Character in Fiction' below; 'On Re-reading Meredith', *II VW Essays*; 'What is a Novel?', *IV VW Essays*; and see *VI VW Essays* for VW's revised version of the present essay (see Editorial Note, p. xxiv). Reprinted: *Mom, CE*. Reading Notes (Berg, xxvi) (MHP, B 2q).

2–Edward VII reigned 1901–10.

3–George Meredith, *The Adventures of Harry Richmond* (1870–71).

4–W. M. Thackeray, *Vanity Fair* (1847–8); Charles Dickens, *David Copperfield* (1849–50); George Eliot, *Adam Bede* (1859); William Shakespeare, *Hamlet*, 1603–4.

5–Sarah Gamp, character in Dickens's *The Life and Adventures of Martin Chuzzlewit* (1843–4).

6–Daniel Defoe (1660?–1731); Fanny Burney (1752–1840).

7–Dr Johnson (1709–84), *Lives of the Poets* (1779–81), 'Gray', opening of the final paragraph: 'In the character of his *Elegy [Written in a Country Churchyard*, 1750] I rejoice to concur with the common reader; for by the common sense of readers uncorrupted with literary prejudices, after all the refinements of subtilty and the dogmatism of learning, must be finally decided all claim to poetical honours' – from which VW was to quote in her prefatory note 'The Common Reader' in *CR 1*.

8–John Keats (1795–1821); Lord Macaulay (1800–59).

9–L. N. Tolstoy (1828–1910); Fyodor Dostoevsky (1821–81); Thomas Hardy (1840–1928); Joseph Conrad (1857–1924); Henry James (1843–1916).

10–Lubbock, ch. i, p. 15.

11–*Ibid.*, ch. ii, p. 24.

12–George Meredith, *The Egoist* (1879).

13–Published in *Trois Contes* (1877) by Gustave Flaubert (1821–80).

14–Flaubert, *Trois Contes*, (Paris, Bibliothèque Charpentier, 1900), 'Un Coeur Simple', pt iii, p. 58: 'Toutes ses petites affaires occupaient un placard dans la chambre à deux lits. Mme Aubain les inspectait le moins souvent possible. Un jour d'été, elle se résigna; et des papillons s'envolèrent de l'armoire.'

15—*Ibid.*, p. 59.

16—*Ibid.*, pt iv, p. 76.

17—George Moore, *Esther Waters* (1894), upon which VW wrote in 'A Born Writer' above; Charlotte Brontë, *Jane Eyre* (1847); Marie Madeleine Motier, Countess de La Fayette, *La Princesse de Clèves* (1678).

18—Cf, *II VW Diary*, 15 October 1923: 'It took me a year's groping to discover what I call my tunnelling process, by which I tell the past by instalments, as I have need of it. This is my prime discovery so far; & the fact that I've been so long finding it, proves, I think, how false Percy Lubbock's doctrine is—that you can do this sort of thing consciously. One feels about in a state of misery—indeed I made up my mind one night to abandon the book [*Mrs Dalloway*, 1925]—& then one touches the hidden spring.'

19—Sir Walter Scott (1771–1832).

20—Honoré de Balzac (1799–1850).

21—Henry James, *The Ambassadors* (1903); Samuel Richardson, *Clarissa Harlowe* (1747–8).

22—Lubbock, ch. xii, p. 187: 'And thus it happens that the novelist who carried his research into the theory of the art further than any other—the only real scholar in the art—is the novelist whose methods are most likely to be overlooked or mistaken, regarded as simply a part of his own original quiddity.'

23—*The Wings of the Dove* (1902).

24—Marcel Proust (1871–1922) whose *A la recherche du temps perdu* was published 1913–27.

Modern Essays

VW's essay in the *TLS*, 30 November 1922 (Kp C229), was later revised for inclusion, under the same title, in *The Common Reader*: 1st series (1925). The reader is referred to *IV VW Essays*, where the revised version, together with variants in the form of footnotes, is printed in its place as part of *The Common Reader*.

Eliza and Sterne

Of the many difficulties which afflict the biographer, the moral difficulty must surely be the greatest. By what standard, that is to say, is he to judge the morals of the dead? By that of their day, or that of his own?

Or should he, before putting pen to paper, arrive at some absolute standard of right and wrong by which he can try Socrates and Shelley and Byron and Queen Victoria and Mr Lloyd George? The problem, though it lies at the root of biography and affects it in every fibre, is for the most part solved or shelved by taking it for granted that the truth was revealed about the year 1850 to the fortunate natives of the British Isles, who need only in future take into account circumstances of date, country, and sex in order to come to a satisfactory conclusion upon all cases of moral eccentricity submitted to their judgement. If we write the life of Elizabeth Draper,[2] for instance, we must lay great stress upon the question of the morality or immorality of her relations with Sterne. We must ransack the evidence and profess relief or censure as the balance sways for her or against. We must attach more importance to her conduct in this respect than in any other. Mr Wright and Mr Sclater go through the ceremony with rigid consistency. Her 'moral culpability'[3] is debated at every point, and we are invited to assist at a trial which, as it proceeds, comes to have less and less reality either for us or for anybody else. But in saying that we admit no levity. We are only saying what every reader of biography knows but few writers care to confess – that times are changed; that in 1850 Eliza would not have been invited to Court, but that in 1922 we should all be delighted to sit next her at dinner.

Yet morality, though it may be the crucial difficulty, is by no means the only difficulty that the biographer has to face. There are the white ants of Anjengo – 'a peculiarly voracious breed', who, not satisfied with devouring the 'bulk of the old archives'[4] of a town which is at once the birthplace of Eliza and the seat of the pepper industry, have eaten away a much more precious material – the life of Eliza herself. Again and again her conscientious biographers have to admit that the facts are lost. 'History ... is often most tantalisingly silent upon points of real interest.'[5] The chief actor leaves the stage, often at the crisis of her fate, and in her absence our attention is directed to the antiseptic quality of wood ashes in the treatment of smallpox; to the different natures of the Hooka, the Calloon, and the Kerim Can; to the method, still in vogue, of hunting deer with cheetahs; and to the fact that one of Eliza's uncles was killed by a sack of caraway seeds falling on his head as he walked up St Mary-at-Hill in the year 1778. These familiar diversions, which do not perhaps advance the cause of biography, are excusable when the subject is, as Eliza Draper was, an obscure woman, dead almost a century and a half, whose thirty-five years would have been utterly forgotten were it not that for three months in one of them she was loved by Laurence Sterne.

She was loved, but the depredations of time and the white ants leave us in little doubt that the love was on his side, not on hers. If she was anybody's Eliza (which is by no means certain) she was Thomas Limbrey Sclater's Eliza.[6] To him she wrote affectionately all her life; to him she sent one of Sterne's love-letters; and it was of him she thought when the ship was carrying her back to India and away from Sterne for ever. She should have had more sense of the becoming. She should have realized the predicament in which she places posterity. But Eliza was a woman of impulse rather than of reflection. 'Committing matrimony',[7] as her sister called it, with Daniel Draper of Bombay at the age of fourteen she ruined her chances for ever. He was thirty-four, had several illegitimate children, was afflicted with the writer's cramp, and possessed all those virtues which lead officials to the highest promotion and make their wives jump into the arms of Commodore Clarke.[8]

'. . . By nature cool, Phlegmatic, and not adorned by Education with any of those pleasing Acquirements which help to fill up the Vacuums of time agreeably, if not usefully, added to which, Methodically formed, in the Extreme, by long habit, and not easily roused into active measures by any Motive Unconnected with his sense of duty.'[9]

Such a man (Eliza wrote of her husband in words which, since her emotions were strong and her grammar weak, we take the liberty of paraphrasing) is quite unfitted to be the husband of a lady entitled to 'the Appellation of Belle Indian'; who loved society much but solitude more; who read Montaigne and the *Spectator*;[10] who was fourth if not third upon the Governor's invitation list; who wrote letters which some thought worthy of publication; who had been told finally by a friend that nature designed her for the wife of

'a very feeling Poet and Philosopher, rather than to a Gentleman of Independance and General Talents, and the reason he was pleased to assign to it was, the natural and supposed qualities of my heart, together with an expressive Countenance and a manner capable of doing justice to the tender Passions'.[11]

This 'acknowledged Judge of Physiognomy'[12] was, we may guess, no less a person than the great Mr Sterne. Eliza met him at the house of Mrs James in Gerrard Street in the year 1767. Draper's increasing cramp had the somewhat incongruous effect of bringing them together. Having tried the English spas without success, Draper returned to Bombay and Eliza was left in London to continue the conversation with Sterne. From the Journal to Eliza[13] we can judge fairly accurately what they talked about. Eliza was the most charming of women, Sterne the most passionate of men. Life was cruel, Mrs Sterne intolerable, early marriages deplorable, Bombay distant, and husbands exacting. The only happiness was to mingle thoughts and tears, to share ecstasies and exchange portraits, and pray for some miracle, such as the simultaneous deaths of Elizabeth Sterne and Daniel Draper, which might unite them eternally in the future. But though this was undoubtedly what they said, it is no such easy matter to be certain what they meant. Sterne was fifty-four, and Eliza twenty-two. Sterne was at the height of his fame, and Eliza at the height not of her beauty, which was little, but of her charm, which was great. But Sterne was engaged in writing the *Sentimental Journey*,[14] and Eliza must sometimes have felt that though it was most wonderful and flattering to have a celebrated author sitting by her bedside when she fell ill, and reading her letters aloud to the ladies and gentlemen of the highest rank, and displaying her picture, and buying ten handsome brass screws for her cabin, and running her errands round London, still he was fifty-four, had a dreadful cough, and sometimes, she noticed, looked out of the window in a very curious way. No doubt he was thinking about his writing. He assured her that he found her of the very greatest help. And he told her that he had brought her name and picture into his work, 'where,' he said, 'they will remain when you and I are at rest';[15] and he went on to write an elegy upon her, and no doubt worked himself up into one of those accesses of emotion which any woman would have given her eyes to inspire, yet lying ill in bed Eliza found them a little fatiguing, and could not help thinking that Thomas Limbrey Sclater, who was not in the least likely to become immortal, was a great deal more to her taste than Laurence Sterne. Thus, if we must censure Eliza, it is not for being in love with Sterne, but for not being in love with him. She let him write her the letters of a lover and propose to her the rights of a husband. But when she reached India she had almost forgotten him, and his death recalled only 'the mild generous good Yorick'[16] whose picture hung, not above her heart, but over her writing-table.

Arrived in India with eleven years of life before her, the provoking creature proceeded to live them as if she did not care a straw for those 'Annotators and Explainers'[17] who would, Sterne said, busy themselves in after ages with their names. She gave herself up to trivial interests and nameless captains; to sitting till three in the morning upon a 'cool Terrasse';[18] to hunting antelopes with leopards; to driving down the streets of Tellicherry with an escort of armed Sepoys; to playing with her children and pouring out her soul in long, long letters to Mr Sclater and Mrs James, to that petty process of living, in short, which is of such inexplicable interest to others engaged in the same pursuit. It is all very obscure and highly conjectural. She was very happy at Tellicherry in the year 1769 and very unhappy in the year 1770. She was always being happy and then unhappy and blaming herself and hoping that her daughter would be a better woman than her mother. Yet Eliza did not think altogether badly of herself. It was her complexion that was to blame, and the 'happy flexibility'[19] of her temper. Vain, charming, gifted, sympathetic, her relations with her husband grew steadily more and more desperate. At last, when it was quite certain that Draper loved Leeds, her maid, and neither on Tuesday nor on Wednesday did he say that word 'sympathetick of regret' which 'would have saved me the perilous adventure',[20] Eliza either jumped from her window into a boat or was otherwise conveyed to the flagship of Sir John Clarke and thence to her uncle's house at Masulipatam. This time, without a doubt, her biographers regretfully conclude, 'Eliza was "lost"'.[21] But Eliza was not in the least of that opinion herself. She turned up imperturbably in Queen Anne Street, Cavendish Square, 'which shows that she had considerable social resources';[22] but there, alas, proceeded to fall in love with the Abbé Raynal.[23] Was she incorrigible or was he, perhaps like others of his countrymen, apt to exaggerate? The terms in which he addressed Anjengo[24] would lead one to suspect the latter. But death, with infinite discretion, spares us the inquiry. Eliza died at the age of thirty-five, and some unknown friend raised a monument to her memory in Bristol Cathedral with the figures of Genius and Benevolence on either side and a bird in the act of feeding its young. So after all somebody liked Eliza, and it is as certain as anything can be that a woman with such a tombstone was moving in the highest circles of Bristol society at the time of her death.

1–A review in the TLS, 14 December 1922, (Kp C230) of Sterne's Eliza. Some Account of her Life in India: with her Letters written between 1757 and 1774 (William Heinemann, 1922) by Arnold Wright and William Lutley Sclater. See also 'Sterne', I VW Essays; 'Sterne's Ghost' and 'A Sentimental Journey', IV VW Essays. Reprinted: G&R, CE. Reading Notes (MHP, B 2q).
2–Elizabeth 'Eliza' Draper, née Sclater (1744–78), married in July 1758 Daniel Draper, then with the East India Company but shortly to enter government service.
3–Wright/Sclater, intro., p. v.
4–Ibid., ch. i, p. 4.
5–Ibid., ch. xi, p. 148.

6–Thomas Limbrey Sclater (1742–1809), Eliza's cousin.

7–Wright/Sclater, ch. ii, p. 21, Mary Sclater on her marriage to the future Governor of Bombay, Rawson Hart Boddam, in a letter, dated 18 November 1760, to her uncle Rev. Thomas Pickering, which has: 'having followed my sister Draper's example by comitting [sic] Matrimony'.

8–Commodore Sir John Clarke, under whose protection Eliza lived immediately upon leaving her husband in January 1773.

9–Wright/Sclater, ch. x, p. 131, Eliza writing to Thomas Limbrey Sclater on 4 March 1772, which begins: 'Not that I think I should have any aversion to the Idea of being secluded from the World, if my Husband had those Companionable Virtues which are requisite, to banish the Dull severe, in a very retired situation; but He has not – this my dear friend, your own knowledge of him must have convinced you of, – by Nature cool . . .'

10–For the quotation, *ibid.*, ch. x, p. 139, Eliza writing to Mrs James (later Lady; wife of Commodore Sir William James), on 15 April 1772: 'I am a good deal altered in my Appearance, James, since you used to view me with the Eyes of Kindness, due only, to a second self – but my Head, and Heart, itself Love does not mislead me are both, much improved, and the Qualities of Reflexion and tenderness, are no bad Substitutes for that clearness of Complexion, and Je-ne-scai-quoi-dire which my flatterers used to say entitled me to the Apellation of Belle Indian.' The *Spectator* was produced by Sir Richard Steele and Joseph Addison, 1711–12, and revived by Addison for a short period in 1714.

11–*Ibid.*, ch. vi, p. 82, Eliza writing to Thomas Limbrey Sclater, 10 April 1769.

12–*Ibid.*

13–*Journal to Eliza*, which was first published in 1904.

14–*A Sentimental Journey through France and Italy* (1768).

15–Wright/Sclater, ch. iv, p. 57: 'I have brought your name, Eliza, and picture into my work – where they will remain when you and I are at rest for ever. – Some annotator or explainer of my works in this place will take occasion to speak of the friendship which subsisted so long and faithfully betwixt Yorick and the Lady he speaks of – her name he will tell the world – was Draper – a native of India – married to a gentleman in the India service of that name . . .'

16–*Ibid.*, ch. x, p. 138, Eliza writing to Mrs James, 15 April 1772: 'You had told me that Sterne was no more – I had heard it before but this confirmation afflicted me; for I was almost an idolater of his work, while I fancied him the mild, generous good Yorick we had so often thought him to be.'

17–See n15 above.

18–*Ibid.*, ch. ix, p. 118, Eliza writing to Thomas Limbrey Sclater, on her birthday, 5 April 1771.

19–*Ibid.*, ch. vii, p. 98, Eliza writing to the same, May 1769: 'You must not think me vain my dear Cousin, if I tell you I've that happy flexibility about me that easily makes me accommodate myself to a necessary or present situation, and I flatter myself I'm beloved by such of the Malabars as are within reach of my notice.'

20–*Ibid.*, ch. xi, p. 151, Eliza writing to her husband, on 14 January 1773, the night she fled his house.

21–*Ibid.*, ch. xi, p. 154: 'She tells Horsley, the intimate friend of her happier hours, that she "is lost, for ever lost" to every claim which could entitle her to his esteem . . .

Eliza was "lost", not merely in the sense that by her flight she had compromised herself irretrievably, but that she had sacrificed to the fullest extent her honour.'
22—*Ibid.*, ch. xiii, p. 173.
23—Guillaume Thomas François, Abbé Raynal (1713–96), historian, philosopher and priest dismissed from his parish in Paris, where the condemnation of his *Histoire philosophique et politique des établissements et du commerce des Européens dans les deux Indes* (1770) led to his temporary exile in England.
24—Wright/Sclater, ch. i, p. 1, epigraph, quotes from Raynal's *Histoire*: 'Territory of Anjengo, you are nothing, but you have given birth to Eliza . . .'

1923

How It Strikes a Contemporary

In the first place a contemporary can scarcely fail to be struck by the fact that two critics at the same table at the same moment will pronounce completely different opinions about the same book. Here, on the right, it is declared a masterpiece of English prose; on the left, simultaneously, a mere mass of waste paper which, if the fire could survive it, should be thrown upon the flames. Yet both critics are in agreement about Milton and about Keats.[2] They display an exquisite sensibility and have undoubtedly a genuine enthusiasm. It is only when they discuss the work of contemporary writers that they inevitably come to blows. The book in question, which is at once a lasting contribution to English literature and a mere farrago of pretentious mediocrity, was published about two months ago. That is the explanation; that is why they differ.

The explanation is a strange one. It is equally disconcerting to the reader who wishes to take his bearings in the chaos of contemporary literature and to the writer who has a natural desire to know whether his own work, produced with infinite pains and in almost utter darkness, is likely to burn for ever among the fixed luminaries of English letters or, on the contrary, to put out the fire. But if we identify ourselves with the reader and explore his dilemma first, our bewilderment is short-lived enough. The same thing has happened so often before. We have heard the doctors disagreeing about the new and agreeing about the old twice a year on the average, in spring and autumn, ever since Robert Elsmere, or was it Stephen Phillips,[3] somehow pervaded the atmosphere, and there was the disagreement among grown-up people about them. It would be

353

much more marvellous, and indeed much more upsetting, if, for a wonder, both gentlemen agreed, pronounced Blank's book an undoubted masterpiece, and thus faced us with the necessity of deciding whether we should back their judgement to the extent of ten and sixpence. Both are critics of reputation; the opinions tumbled out so spontaneously here will be starched and stiffened into columns of sober prose which will uphold the dignity of letters in England and America.

It must be some innate cynicism, then, some ungenerous distrust of contemporary genius, which determines us automatically as the talk goes on that, were they to agree – which they show no signs of doing – half a guinea is altogether too large a sum to squander upon contemporary enthusiasms, and the case will be met quite adequately by a card to the library. Still the question remains, and let us put it boldly to the critics themselves. Is there no guidance nowadays for a reader who yields to none in reverence for the dead, but is tormented by the suspicion that reverence for the dead is vitally connected with understanding of the living? After a rapid survey both critics are agreed that there is unfortunately no such person. For what is their own judgement worth where new books are concerned? Certainly not ten and sixpence. And from the stores of their experience they proceed to bring forth terrible examples of past blunders; crimes of criticism which, if they had been committed against the dead and not against the living, would have lost them their jobs and imperilled their reputations. The only advice they can offer is to respect one's own instincts, to follow them fearlessly and, rather than submit them to the control of any critic or reviewer alive, to check them by reading and reading again the masterpieces of the past.

Thanking them humbly, we cannot help reflecting that it was not always so. Once upon a time, we must believe, there was a rule, a discipline, which controlled the great republic of readers in a way which is now unknown. That is not to say that the great critic – the Dryden, the Johnson, the Coleridge, the Arnold[4] – was an impeccable judge of contemporary work, whose verdicts stamped the book indelibly and saved the reader the trouble of reckoning the value for himself. The mistakes of these great men about their own contemporaries are too notorious to be worth recording. But the mere fact of their existence had a centralising influence. That alone, it is not fantastic to suppose, would have controlled the disagreements of the dinner-table and given to random chatter about some book just out an authority now entirely to seek. The diverse schools would have debated as hotly as ever, but at the back of every reader's mind would have been the consciousness that there was at least one man who kept the main principles of literature closely in view: who, if you had taken to him some eccentricity of the moment, would have brought it into touch with permanence and tethered it by his own authority in the contrary blasts of praise and blame. But when it comes to the making of a critic, Nature must be generous and Society ripe. The scattered dinner-tables of the modern world, the chase and eddy of the various currents which compose the Society of our time, could only be dominated by a giant of fabulous dimensions. And where is even the very tall man whom we have the right to expect? Critics, of course, abound. But the too frequent result of their able and industrious pens is a desiccation of the living tissues of literature into a network of little bones Nowhere shall we find the downright vigour of Dryden, or Keats with his fine and natural bearing, or Flaubert[5] and his fanaticism, or Coleridge, above all, brewing in his head the whole of poetry and letting issue now and then one of those profound general statements which are caught up by the mind when hot with the friction of reading as if they were of the soul of the book itself.

And to all this, too, the critics, generously, agree. A great critic, they say, is the rarest of beings. But should one miraculously appear, how should we maintain him, on what should we feed him? Great critics, if they are not themselves great poets, are bred from the profusion of the age. And our age is meagre to the verge of destitution. There is no name which dominates the rest, no master in whose workshop the young are proud to serve apprenticeship. Mr Hardy has long since withdrawn from the arena, and there is something exotic about the genius of Mr Conrad[6] which makes him not so much an influence as an idol, honoured and admired, but aloof and apart. As for the rest, though they are many and vigorous and in the full flood of creative activity, there is none whose influence can seriously affect his contemporaries, or penetrate beyond our day to that not very distant future which it pleases us to call immortality. If we make a century our test, and ask how much of the work produced in these days in England will be in existence then, we shall have to answer not merely that we cannot agree upon the same book, but that we are more than doubtful whether such a book there is. It is an age of fragments. A few stanzas, a few pages, a chapter here and there, the beginning of this novel, the end of that, are equal to the best of any age or author. But can we go to posterity with a sheaf of loose pages, or ask the readers of those days, with the whole of literature before them, to sift our enormous rubbish heaps for our tiny pearls? To such questions it is fitting that a writer should reply; yet with what conviction?

At first the weight of pessimism seems sufficient to bear down all opposition. It is a lean age, we repeat, with much to justify its poverty; but, frankly, if we pit one century against another the comparison seems overwhelmingly against us.

Waverley, the *Excursion*, 'Kubla Khan', *Don Juan*, Hazlitt's Essays, *Pride and Prejudice*, 'Hyperion' and *Prometheus Unbound* were all published between 1800 and 1821.[7] Our century has not lacked industry; but if we ask for masterpieces it appears on the face of it that the pessimists are right. It seems as if an age of genius must be succeeded by an age of endeavour; riot and extravagance by cleanliness and hard work. All honour, of course, to those who have sacrificed their immortality to set the house in order. But if we ask for masterpieces, where are we to look? A little poetry, we may feel sure, will survive; a few poems by Mr Yeats, by Mr Davies, by Mr de la Mare. Mr Lawrence, of course, has moments of greatness. Mr Beerbohm in his way is perfect. Mr Strachey paints portraits. Mr Eliot makes phrases. Passages in *Far Away and Long Ago* will undoubtedly go to posterity entire. *Ulysses* was a memorable catastrophe – immense in daring, terrific in disaster.[8] And so, picking and choosing, we select now this, now that, hold it up for display, hear it defended or derided, and finally have to meet the objection that even so we are only agreeing with the critics that it is an age incapable of sustained effort, littered with fragments, and not seriously to be compared with the age that went before.

But it is just when opinions universally prevail and we have added lip service to their authority that we become sometimes most keenly conscious that we do not believe a word that we are saying. It is a barren and exhausted age, we repeat; we must look back with envy to the past. Meanwhile it is one of the first fine days of spring. Life is not altogether lacking in colour. The telephone, which interrupts the most serious conversations, has a romance of its own. And the random talk of people who have no chance of immortality and thus can speak their minds out has a setting, often, of lights, streets, houses, human beings, beautiful or grotesque, which will weave itself into the moment for ever. But this is life; the talk is about literature. We must try to disentangle the two, and justify the rash revolt of optimism against the superior plausibility, the finer distinction, of pessimism. In one sense, of course, optimism is universal. No one would seriously choose to go back a hundred years. There is something about the present with all its trivialities which we would not exchange for the past, however august – just as an instinct, blind but essential to the conduct of life, makes every tramp prefer to be himself rather than any king, or hero, or millionaire of them all. And modern literature in spite of its imperfections has the same hold on us, the same endearing quality of being part of ourselves, of being the globe in which we are and not the globe which we look upon respectfully from outside. Nor has any generation more need than ours to cherish its contemporaries. We are sharply cut off from our predecessors. A shift in the scale – the war, the sudden slip of masses held in position for ages – has shaken the fabric from top to bottom, alienated us from the past and made us perhaps too vividly conscious of the present. Every day we find ourselves doing, saying, or thinking things that would have been impossible to our fathers. And we feel the differences which have not been noted far more keenly than the resemblances which have been very perfectly expressed. New books lure us to read them partly in the hope that they will reflect this re-arrangement of our attitude – these scenes, thoughts, and apparently fortuitous groupings of incongruous things which impinge upon us with so keen a sense of novelty – and, as literature does, give it back into our keeping, whole and comprehended. Here indeed there is every reason for optimism. No age can have been more rich than ours in writers determined to give expression to the differences which separate them from the past and not to the resem- blances which connect them with it. It would be invidious to mention names, but the most casual reader dipping into poetry, into fiction, into biography can hardly fail to be impressed by the courage, the sincerity, in a word by the widespread originality of our time. But our exhilaration is strangely curtailed. Book after book leaves us with the same sense of promise unachieved, of intellectual poverty, of brilliance which has been snatched from life but not transmuted into literature. Much of what is best in contemporary work has the appearance of being noted under pressure, taken down in a bleak shorthand which preserves with astonishing brilliance the movements and expressions of the figures as they pass across the screen. But the flash is soon over, and there remains with us a profound dissatisfaction. The irritation is as acute as the pleasure was intense.

Now, of course, is the time to correct these extremes of opinion by consulting, as the critics advise, the masterpieces of the past. We feel ourselves indeed driven to them, impelled not by calm judgement but by some imperious need to anchor our instability upon their security. But, honestly, the shock of the comparison between past and present is at first disconcerting. Undoubtedly there is a dullness in great books. There is an unabashed tranquillity in page after page of Wordsworth and Scott and Miss Austen which is sedative to the verge of somnolence. Opportunities occur and they neglect them. Shades and subtleties accumulate and they ignore them. They seem deliberately to refuse to gratify those senses which are stimulated so briskly by the moderns; the senses of sight, of sound, of touch – above all, the sense of personality vibrating with perceptions which, since they are not generalised, but have their centre in some particular person at some precise moment, serve to make that person and that moment vivid to the utmost extreme. There is little of all this in the works of Wordsworth and Scott and Jane Austen. From what, then, arises that sense of security which gradually, delightfully, and completely overcomes us? It is the power of their belief – their conviction, that imposes itself upon us. In Wordsworth, the philosophic poet, this is obvious enough. But it is equally true of the careless Scott, who scribbled masterpieces to build castles before breakfast, and of the modest maiden lady who wrote furtively and quietly simply to give pleasure. In both there is the same natural conviction that life is of a certain quality. They have their judgement of conduct. They know the relations of human beings towards each other and towards the universe. Neither of them probably has a word to say about the matter outright. But everything depends on it. Only believe, we find ourselves saying, and all the rest will come of itself. Only believe, to take a very simple instance which the recent publication of *The Watsons*[9] brings to mind, that a nice girl will instinctively try to soothe the feelings of a boy who has been snubbed at a dance, and then, if you believe it implicitly and unquestioningly, you will not only make people a hundred years later feel the same thing, but you will make them feel it as literature. For certainty of that kind is the condition which makes it possible to write. To believe that your impressions hold good for others is to be released from the cramp and confinement of personality. It is to be free, as Scott was free, to explore with a vigour which still holds us spell-bound the whole world of adventure and romance. It is also the first step in that mysterious process in which Jane Austen was so great an adept. The little grain of experience being selected, believed in, and set outside herself, could be put precisely in its place, and she was then free to make it, by a process which never yields its secret to the analyst, into that complete statement which is literature.

So, then, our contemporaries afflict us because they have ceased to believe. The most sincere of them will only tell us what it is that happens to himself. They cannot make a world, because they are not free of other human beings. They cannot tell stories, because they do not believe that stories are true. They cannot generalise. They depend on their senses and emotions, whose testimony is trustworthy, rather than on their intellects, whose message is obscure. And they have perforce to deny themselves the use of some of the most powerful and some of the most exquisite of the weapons of their craft. Set down at a fresh angle of the eternal prospect, they can only whip out their notebooks and record with agonised intensity the flying gleams, which light on what? and the transitory splendours, which may perhaps compose nothing whatever. The critics may well declare that if the age is indeed like this – and our vision is determined, of course, by our place at the table – then the risks of judging contemporary work are greater than ever before. There is every excuse for them if they are wide of the mark; and no doubt it would be better to retreat, as Matthew Arnold advised, from the burning ground of the present, 'of which the estimates are so often not only personal, but personal with passion',[10] to the safe tranquillity of the past. But the note of pessimism jars. It is true that the writer of the present day must renounce his hope of making that complete statement which we call a masterpiece. He must be content to be a taker of notes. But if notebooks are perishable volumes, he may reflect that they are, after all, the stuff from which the masterpieces of the future are made. Truth, again, to speak in the manner of the myth-makers, has always been thus volatile, sometimes coming quietly into the open and suffering herself to be looked at, at others flying averted and obscured. But if she is the truth then we do well to watch for her most brief apparitions; and the sight of her will convince us that she is always the same, from Chaucer even to Mr Conrad. The difference is on the surface; the continuity in the depths.

As for the critic, whose task it is to pass judgement on the books of the moment, let him think of them as the anonymous activities of free craftsmen working under the lash of no master, but obscurely, with ardour, and in the interest of a greater writer who is not yet born. Let him therefore be generous of encouragement, but chary of bestowing wreaths which fade and coronets which fall off. Let him see the present in relation to the future. Let him, in short, slam the door upon the cosy company where butter is plentiful and sugar cheap, and emulate rather that gaunt aristocrat, Lady Hester Stanhope,[11] who kept a milk-white horse in her stable in readiness for the Messiah, and was forever scanning the mountain tops, impatiently, but with confidence, for the first signs of His approach.

1—An essay in the *TLS*, 5 April 1923, (Kp C231) later revised for inclusion in *CR 1* (see Editorial Note, p. xxv). 'And tomorrow I must get on with How It Strikes a Contemporary,' VW recorded in her diary on Saturday, 17 March 1923, 'Alas, for the break in my scheme of work – but we must make money, just when I don't want to; & so the novels get shelved, & Reading, which I had tackled afresh, must be put away, & I must accept Desmond [MacCarthy]'s reviewing, & Maynard [Keynes]'s too, if offered; still I haven't any good cause to complain.'

See also *III VW Diary*, Sunday, 23 June 1929: 'At Rodmell I read through the Common Reader; & this is very important – I must learn to write more succinctly. Especially in the general idea essays like the last, How It strikes a Contemporary, I am horrified by my own looseness. This is partly that I dont think things out first; partly that I stretch my style to take in crumbs of meaning. But the result is a wobble & diffusity & breathlessness which I detest.' The essay's title derives from that of Browning's poem in *Men and Women* (1855).

See also *IV VW Essays*. Reading Notes (Berg, xix).

2—John Milton (1608–74); John Keats (1795–1821).

3—Mrs Humphry Ward, *Robert Elsmere* (1888), an immensely popular best-seller, promulgating its author's view 'that Christianity could be revitalized by discarding its miraculous element and emphasizing its social mission' (*DNB*); Stephen Phillips (1864–1915), dramatic poet, who, upon the performance of his *Paolo and Francesca* (1900) in 1902, was 'greeted as the successor of Sophocles and Shakespeare' (*ibid.*).

4—John Dryden (1631–1700); Samuel Johnson (1709–84); S. T. Coleridge (1772–1834); Matthew Arnold (1822–88).

5—Gustave Flaubert (1821–80).

6—Thomas Hardy (1840–1928); Joseph Conrad (1857–1924).

7—Sir Walter Scott, *Waverley* (1814); William Wordsworth, *The Excursion* (1814); S. T. Coleridge, 'Kubla Khan' (1816); George Gordon, Lord Byron, *Don Juan* (1819–24); William Hazlitt's career as an essayist reached its peak in the period 1817–25 – it began in 1805 with the publication of *On the Principles of Human Action*; Jane Austen, *Pride and Prejudice* (1813); John Keats, 'Hyperion' (1820); Percy Bysshe Shelley, *Prometheus Unbound* (1820).

8—W. B. Yeats (1865–1939); W. H. Davies (1871–1940); Walter de la Mare (1873–1956); D. H. Lawrence (1885–1930); Max Beerbohm (1872–1956); Lytton Strachey (1880–1932); T. S. Eliot (1888–1963); W. H. Hudson, *Far Away and Long Ago* (1918); James Joyce, *Ulysses* (1922).

9—Jane Austen, *The Watsons* (1871), republished, with an introduction by A. B. Walkley (Leonard Parsons, 1923).

10—T. H. Ward, ed., *The English Poets* (OUP, 1880), vol. i, Matthew Arnold, 'General Introduction', p. xlvi: 'But we enter on burning ground as we approach the poetry of times so near us, poetry like that of Byron, Shelley, and Wordsworth, of which . . .'

11—Lady Hester Lucy Stanhope (1776–1839), indefatigable eccentric, upon whom VW wrote in 'Lady Hester Stanhope', *I VW Essays*; see also 'The Eccentrics' above.

To Spain

You, who cross the Channel yearly, probably no longer see the house at Dieppe, no longer feel, as the train moves slowly down the street, one civilisation fall, another rise – from the ruin and chaos of British stucco this incredible pink and blue phœnix, four stories high, with its flower-pots, its balconies, its servant girl leaning on the window-sill, indolently looking out. Quite unmoved you sit reading – Thomas Hardy, perhaps – bridging abysses, preserving continuity, a little contemptuous of the excitement which is moving those who feel themselves liberated from one civilisation, launched upon another to such odd gestures, such strange irreticences. But reflect how much they have already gone through. Try to recall the look of London streets seen very early, perhaps very young, from a cab window on the way to Victoria. Everywhere there is the same intensity, as if the moment, instead of moving, lay suddenly still, became suddenly solemn, fixed the passers-by in their most transient aspects eternally. They do not know how important they have become. If they did, perhaps they would cease to buy newspapers and scrub door-steps. But we who are about to leave them feel all the more moved that they should continue to do these homely things on the brink of that precipice – our departure. Therefore it is natural that those who have survived the crossing, with its last scrutiny of passing faces so like a little rehearsal of death, should be shaken; should move handbags; start conversations; and tremble for one intoxicating moment upon the brink of that ideal society where everyone without fear or hesitation reveals the depths of his soul.

But it is only for a moment. Next, the disembodied spirit fluttering at the window desires above all things to be admitted to the new society where the houses are painted in lozenges of pale pink and blue; women wear shawls; trousers are baggy; there are crucifixes on hilltops; yellow mongrel dogs; chairs in the street; cobbles – gaiety, frivolity, drama, in short. 'I'm awfully sorry for Agnes, because now they can't be married till he gets a job in London. It's too far to get back from the works for midday dinner. I should have thought the father would have done something for them.' These detached sentences, spoken a little brokenly (for they are frowning into tiny mirrors and drawing combs intently through fair bobbed hair) by two English girls, fall like the bars of a prison-house heavily across the mind. It is from them that we must escape; the hours, the works, the divisions, rigid and straight, of the old British week. Already, as the train moved out of Dieppe, these obstructions seemed bubbling and boiling in the cauldron of a more congenial civilisation. The days of the week diminished; the hours disappeared. It was five o'clock, but no banks had simultaneously shut their doors, nor from innumerable lifts had millions of citizens emerged in time for dinner, or in the poorer suburbs for slices of cold meat and Swiss roll laid orderly in shallow glass dishes. There must be divisions, even for the French, but where they fall we cannot tell, and the lady in the corner, so pale, so plump, so compact, seemed as she sat smiling to be riding life over ditches and boundaries smoothed out by the genius of the Latin race.

She rose to go to the dining car. As she sat down she took a small frying-pan from her handbag and hid it discreetly beneath a tent made from a copy of *Le Temps*. Deftly, as each dish was served, she secreted a portion in the absence of the waiter. Her husband smiled. Her husband approved. We only knew that she was brave. They might be poor. The helpings were large. The French have mothers. To redress perpetually the extravagances of life, and make the covering fit the fact instead of bulging in ostentatious emptiness, was part, no doubt, of the French genius for living. Still, when it comes to the thick, yellow rind of a not fresh cheese – Ironically smiling, she condescended, in that exquisite tongue which twinkles like diamonds with all its accents, to explain that she kept a dog. But she might have kept – anything. 'Life is so simple,' she seemed to say.

'Life is so simple – life is so simple,' said the wheels of the Sud Express all night long in that idiotic or ironic way they have, for any message less appropriate to the uneasy darkness, the clank of chains, the anguished cries of railwaymen, and, in the dawn, the misery of the unrested body could scarcely be imagined. But travellers are much at the mercy of phrases. Taken from home, which, like a shell, has made them hard, separate, individual, vast generalisations formulate in their exposed brains; the stress of wheel or window-blind beats into rhythm idiotic sayings of false profundity about life, repeats to distraction fragments of prose, and makes them stare with ferocious melancholy at the land-scape, which, in the middle of France, is dull enough. The French are methodical; but life is simple; the French are prosaic; the French have roads. Yes, they have roads which strike from that lean poplar there to Vienna, to Moscow; pass Tolstoy's house, climb mountains, then march, all shop decorated, down the middle of famous cities. But in

England the road runs out on to a cliff; wavers into sand at the edge of the sea. It begins to seem dangerous to live in England. Here actually one could build a house and have no neighbours; go for a walk along this eternal white road for two, three, four miles, and meet only one black dog and one old woman who, depressed perhaps by the immensity of the landscape and the futility of locomotion, has sat herself down on a bank, attached her cow to her by a rope, and there sits, unmoved, incurious, monumental. Could our English poets for a moment share her seat and think her thoughts, forget the parish, the pansy, and the sparrow's egg, and concentrate (as she appears to do) upon the fate of man!

But as the country grows larger and larger outside Bordeaux the concentration which is needed to produce even the simplest of little thoughts is rent as a glove is torn by the thrust of a large hand. Blessed are painters with their brushes, paints, and canvases. But words are flimsy things. They turn tail at the first approach of visual beauty. They let one down in the most literal sense into a chaotic, an alarming chasm, filled – for the eye pours it all in – with white towns, with mules in single file, with solitary farms, with enormous churches, with vast fields crumbling at evening into pallor, with fruit trees blazing askew like blown matches, and trees burning with oranges, and clouds and storms. Beauty seems to have closed overhead, and one washes this way and that in her waters. It is always on the shoulders of a human being that one climbs out; a profile in the corridor; a lady in deep mourning who steps into a motor-car and drives across an arid plain – where and why? a child in Madrid throwing confetti effusively upon the figure of Christ; an Englishman discussing, while his hat obscures half the Sierra Nevada, Mr Churchill's last article in *The Times*. 'No,' one says to beauty – as one rebukes an importunate dog – 'down, down; let me look at you through the eyes of human beings.'

But the Englishman's hat is no measure of the Sierra Nevada. Setting out next day upon foot and mule-back, this wrinkled red and white screen, this background for hats, this queer comment (especially at sunset) upon Mr Churchill's article in *The Times*, is found to consist of stones, olive trees, goats, asphodels, irises, bushes, ridges, shelves, clumps, tufts, and hollows innumerable, indescribable, unthinkable. The mind's contents break into short sentences. It is hot; the old man; the frying pan; it is hot; the image of the Virgin; the bottle of wine; it is time for lunch; it is only half-past twelve; it is hot. And then over and over again come all those objects – stones, olives, goats, asphodels, dragon-flies, irises, until by some trick of the imagination they run into

363

phrases of command, exhortation, and encouragement such as befit soldiers marching, sentinels on lonely nights, and leaders of great battalions. But must one give up the struggle? Must one relinquish the game? Yes, for the clouds are drifting across the pass; mules mind not what they carry; mules never stumble; they know the way. Why not leave everything to them?

Riders, as night comes on (and the pass was very misty), seem to be riding out of life towards some very enticing prospect, while the four legs of their beasts carry on all necessary transactions with the earth. Riders are at rest; on they go, and on and on. And, they muse, what does it all matter; and what harm can come to a good man (behold two priests stepping out of the drizzle, bowing and disappearing) in life or after death? And then, since a fox has crossed the path, which is on turf and must be nearly at the top of the mountain, how strangely it seems as if they were riding in England, a long day's journey, hundreds of years ago, and the danger is over, and they see the lights of the inn, and the hostess comes into the courtyard and bids them sit round the fire while she cooks dinner, which they do, half-dreaming, while clumsy boys and girls with red flowers pass and repass in the background, and the mother suckles her baby, and the old man, who never speaks, breaks tufts from the brushwood and throws them on the fire, which blazes up, and the whole company stares.

But, good heavens! One never knows what days follow what nights. Good heavens again! 'Don Fernando had a passion for pigeon pie, and so kept pigeons up here' – on his roof, that is, from which one has this astonishing, this strange, this disturbing view of the Alpujarras. 'He died last summer in Granada.' Did he, indeed? It is the light, of course; a million razor-blades have shaved off the bark and the dust, and out pours pure colour; whiteness from fig trees; red and green and again white from the enormous, the humped, the everlasting landscape. But listen to the sounds on the roof – first the fluttering pigeons; then water rushing; then an old man crying chickens for sale; then a donkey braying in the valley far below. Listen; and as one listens this random life begins to be issued from the heart of a village which has faced the African coast with a timeless and aristocratic endurance for a thousand years. But how say this (as one descends from the blaze) to the Spanish peasant woman who bids one enter her room, with its lilies and its washing, and smiles and looks out of the window as if she too had looked for a thousand years?

1–A signed essay in the N&A, 5 May 1923, (Kp C233) reprinted in the NR, 6 June 1923. The Woolfs had set out for Spain, crossing the Channel from Newhaven to Dieppe, on 27 March 1923. They travelled via Paris, Madrid and Granada, to Yegen in the Sierra Nevada and the hospitality of the writer Gerald Brenan (introduced to Bloomsbury by Ralph Partridge, friend of Lytton Strachey) with whom they stayed 5–13 April. Brenan accompanied them on their homeward journey as far as Alicante, after which, via Valencia, Perpignan and Montauban, the Woolfs made their way back to Paris, where they arrived on the 22nd. LW returned to London on the 24th, to take up his new post as literary editor of the N&A (see Appendix IV), and VW followed on the 27th.

VW noted in her diary, on Friday 11 May: 'Have I not with infinite labour, written for the first number of the Nation To Spain? Am I not sitting waiting for L. to "come back from the office" like other wives . . . As I say, I cannot go into the journey . . . I stayed in Paris by way of facing life.'

From Carmen de los Fosos, Generalife, Granada she wrote to her sister Vanessa Bell, on 1 April (III VW Letters, no. 1376): 'It's an awful long journey – and we still have 2 days on mules and in diligences before we reach Gerald's house, up in the Sierra Nevada – mountains, I may tell you, always with snow on them. Nevertheless I am determined never to live long in England again. The rapture of getting into warmth and colour and good sense and general congeniality of temper is so great. I was overcome by the beauty of Dieppe – don't you think we might share a Chateau so large that we never met? . . . I shall learn French at once.'

On 16 April she waxed lyrical to Roger Fry, from Murcia (ibid., no. 1380): 'It has been the greatest success so far. I am amazed that we should live in England and order dinner every morning and edit the Nation and catch trains when we might roll in bliss every moment of the day and sit and drink coffee on a balcony overlooking lemon trees and orange trees with mountains behind and every sort of colour and shade perpetually changing which I do now: then a delicious lunch off rice and bacon and olive oil and onions and figs and sugar mixed, then off to a place where cypresses and palm trees grow together.' (See also ibid., nos., 1374–5, 1377–9, 1381–2, 1388.)

The same issue of the N&A contained LW's 'World of Books' column, on a new edition of Men of Letters (1916) by Dixon Scott, with an introduction by Max Beerbohm; and articles by: J. M. Keynes, on 'British Policy in Europe'; and Lytton Strachey, on 'Sarah Bernhardt'.

See also 'An Andalusian Inn', I VW Essays. Reprinted: Mom.

Romance and the Heart

Both Miss Wilson and Miss Richardson are serious novelists, and we must therefore put our minds at their service with the consciousness that, though criticise them we must, something of positive value, which that criticism should reveal, remains. And in trying to make out what this gift of theirs amounts to it is not necessary to go with great detail into the particular examples before us. Each writer is mature; each has written many books, and here, again, each is doing her own work in her own way.

Miss Wilson is a romantic. That is the first impression which her vigour and freedom make upon us. While other novelists sit studying the skeleton of humanity and painfully tracing the relations of tiny fibres, Miss Wilson hurls a sponge at the blackboard, takes her way into the forest, flings herself on a couch of amaranth, and revels in the thunder. For her not only the sky, but the soul too, is always thundering and lightening. There are no mouse-coloured virtues; no gradual transitions; all is genius, violence, and rhapsody, and her thick crowded utterance, often eloquent and sometimes exquisite, recalls the stammer of a bird enraptured with life in June. Yet she is not, as this description might imply, sentimentally lyrical, and frequently, if pardonably, absurd. One of the remarkable qualities of her work is that she handles the great explosives with complete good faith. She believes in thunder, violence, genius, and rhapsody. Therefore, no one is going to sneer at her for saying so. Moreover, she constantly renews her sense of the marvellous by touching the earth, if only with the tip of her toe. She can be sardonic and caustic; she can mention the stomach.

Why is it, then, that she fails to convince us of the reality of her romance? It is because her sense of it is more conventional than original. She has taken it from poetry rather than from life, and from minor poetry more frequently than from major. She has not, like Meredith,[2] used her freedom from the ties of realism to reveal something new in the emotions of human beings when they are most roused to excitement. Nor has she gone the other way to work. She has not taken the usual and made it blossom into the extraordinary. When we begin a play by Ibsen[3] we say that there can be nothing romantic about a room with bookcases and upholstered furniture. But in the end we feel that all the forests and nightingales in the world cannot be so romantic as a room with bookcases and upholstered furniture. That is an exaggeration, however; we have overshot the mark. Nightingales and forests are forever romantic, and it is merely cowardice to be afraid of saying so. But writers are afraid, and very naturally afraid, lest their own feeling for such famous things may not be strong enough to persist against the multitude of other people's feelings. Miss Wilson has no such fear. And thus she has the romantic power of making us feel the stir and tumult of life as a whole. She gives us a general, not a particular, sense of excitement. When at the end of the book Marichaud exclaims: 'Life is the thing, Paul. Life is to be the thing,'[4] we feel that at last someone has put into words what we have been feeling for two hundred and fifty pages. And to have made us feel that life is the thing for two hundred and fifty pages is a real achievement.

There is no one word, such as romance or realism, to cover, even roughly, the works of Miss Dorothy Richardson. Their chief characteristic, if an intermittent student be qualified to speak, is one for which we still seek a name. She has invented, or, if she has not invented, developed and applied to her own uses, a sentence which we might call the psychological sentence of the feminine gender. It is of a more elastic fibre than the old, capable of stretching to the extreme, of suspending the frailest particles, of enveloping the vaguest shapes. Other writers of the opposite sex have used sentences of this description and stretched them to the extreme. But there is a difference. Miss Richardson has fashioned her sentence consciously, in order that it may descend to the depths and investigate the crannies of Miriam Henderson's consciousness. It is a woman's sentence, but only in the sense that it is used to describe a woman's mind by a writer who is neither proud nor afraid of anything that she may discover in the psychology of her sex. And therefore we feel that the trophies that Miss Richardson brings to the surface, however we may dispute their size, are undoubtedly genuine. Her discoveries are concerned with states of being and not with states of doing. Miriam is aware of 'life itself'; of the atmosphere of the table rather than of the table; of the silence rather than of the sound. Therefore she adds an element to her perception of things which has not been noticed before, or, if noticed, has been guiltily suppressed. A man might fall dead at her feet (it is not likely), and Miriam might feel that a violet-coloured ray of light was an important element in her consciousness of the tragedy. If she felt it, she would say it. Therefore, in reading *Revolving Lights* we are often made uncomfortable by feeling that the accent upon the emotions has shifted. What was emphatic is smoothed away. What was important to Maggie Tulliver[5] no longer matters to Miriam Henderson. At first, we are ready to say that nothing is important to Miriam Henderson. That is the way we generally retaliate when an artist tells us that the heart is not, as we should like it to be, a stationary body, but a body which moves perpetually, and is thus always standing in a new relation to the emotions which are its sun. Chaucer, Donne, Dickens – each if you read him, shows this change of the heart. That is what Miss Richardson is doing on an infinitely smaller scale. Miriam Henderson is pointing to her heart and saying she feels a pain on her right, and not on her left. She points too didactically. Her pain, compared with Maggie Tulliver's, is a very little pain. But, be that as it may, here we have both Miss Wilson and Miss Richardson proving that the novel is not hung upon a nail and festooned with glory, but, on the contrary, walks the high road, alive and alert, and brushes shoulders with real men and women.

1 – A review in the N&A, 19 May 1923, (Kp C234) of *The Grand Tour* (Methuen & Co. Ltd, 1923) by Romer Wilson and of *Revolving Lights* (Duckworth & Co., 1923) by Dorothy M. Richardson.
    Florence Roma Muir Wilson (1891–1930) had studied law at Girton College, Cambridge, and worked as a civil servant. Her third novel *The Death of Society* (1921) won the Hawthornden prize.
    For an account of VW's interest in and reactions to the writings of Dorothy Miller Richardson (1873–1957) see '*The Tunnel*', n1, above. *Revolving Lights* was the seventh volume in Richardson's novel cycle *Pilgrimage*. '. . . I must read Miss Dorothy Richardson,' VW wrote to Janet Case on 4 May 1923 (*III VW Letters*, no. 1386), 'having been bribed by very large sums of money to do what of all things I have come to detest – write reviews for the Nation. All I say is commonplace: reading the books is sheer agony: it is warm and seductive; apples are out, and bees are busy, but in order to make large sums of money here I must sit at my books. As a matter of fact, she interests me rather.' Reprinted: *CW*.
2 – George Meredith (1828–1909).
3 – Henrik Ibsen (1828–1906).
4 – Wilson, 'The Future', iii, p. 251, which has 'Thing' in both instances.
5 – George Eliot's character in *The Mill on the Floss* (1860).

Sir Thomas Browne

The only exception which can be taken to the beautiful Golden Cockerel edition of the works of Sir Thomas Browne is a thick black leaf which spots the page too obtrusively for the comfort of the eye and too affectedly for the repose of the spirit. Otherwise the dignity and chastity of the volumes is unmarred. A very occasional misprint reminds us that even at Waltham St Lawrence printers are human, but that, in the circumstances, has its ingratiating side. The 'great revival of interest in the work of Sir Thomas Browne',[2] which the publishers discover would, one might have hoped, have justified a less limited edition and a lower price. But why fly in the face of facts? Few people love the writings of Sir Thomas Browne, but those who do are of the salt of the earth.

For the desire to read, like all the other desires which distract our unhappy souls, is capable of analysis. It may be for good books, for bad books, or for indifferent books. But it is always despotic in its demands, and when it appears, at whatever hour of day or night, we must rise and slink off at its heels, only allowing ourselves to ask, as we desert the responsibilities and privileges of active life, one very important question – Why? Why, that is, this sudden passion for Pepys or Rimbaud? Why turn the house upside down to discover Macaulay's *Life and Letters*? Why will nothing do except Beckford's *Thoughts on Hunting*? Why demand first Disraeli's novels and then Dr Bentley's biography?[3] The answer to all these questions, were they forthcoming, would be valuable, for it is when thus beckoned and compelled by the force of a book's character as a whole that the reader is most capable of speaking the truth about it if he has the mind. What then is the desire that makes us turn instinctively to Sir Thomas Browne? It is the desire to be steeped in imagination. But that is only a snapshot outline of a state of mind which, even as we stand fumbling at the bookcase, can be developed a little more clearly. Locked up in *Urn Burial* there is a quality of imagination which distinguishes it completely from its companions – as chance has it – *The Old Wives' Tale* and *A Man of Property*.[4] In them the imagination is always occupying itself with particular facts; in him with universal ideas. Their turn will come when we want to look a little more sharply at the passing moment; his when the passing moment is a vanity and a weariness. Then while most fiction, the nine volumes of M. Proust[5] for example, makes us more aware of ourselves as individuals, *Urn Burial* is a temple which we can only enter by leaving our muddy boots on the threshold. Here it is all a question not of you and me, or him and her, but of human fate and death, of the immensity of the past, of the strangeness which surrounds us on every side. Here, as in no other English prose except the Bible the reader is not left to read alone in his armchair but is made one of a congregation. But here, too, there is a difference; for while the Bible has a gospel to impart, who can be quite sure what Sir Thomas Browne himself believed? The last chapters of *Urn Burial* beat up on wings of extraordinary sweep and power, yet towards what goal?

But the iniquity of oblivion blindly scattereth her poppy, and deals with the memory of men without distinction to merit of perpetuity ... Darkness and light divide the course of time, and oblivion shares with memory a great part even of our living beings; we slightly remember our felicities and the smartest strokes of affliction leave but short smart upon us ... The Egyptian mummies, which Cambyses or time hath spared, avarice now consumeth. Mummy is become merchandise, Mizraim cures wounds, and Pharaoh is sold for balsams.[6]

Decidedly that is the voice of a strange preacher, of a man filled with

doubts and subtleties and suddenly swept away by surprising imaginations. But it is not for the asperities of dogma that we go to Sir Thomas
Browne. The words quoted above will revive the old amazement. It is as
if from the street we stepped into a cathedral where the organ goes
plunging and soaring and indulging in vast and elephantine gambols of
awful yet grotesque sublimity. The sound booms and quivers and dies
away. But splendour of sound is only one of his attributes. There is, too,
his power of bringing the remote and incongruous astonishingly
together. A piece of an old boat is cheek by jowl with the funeral pyre of
Patroclus. Vast inquiries sweeping in immense circles of ambiguity and
doubt are clenched by short sentences rapped out with solemn authority.
'Life is a pure flame, and we live by an invisible sun within us.'[7] The great
names of antiquity march in astonishing procession; flowers and trees,
spices and gems load the pages with all kinds of colour and substance.
The whole is kept fresh by a perpetual movement of rhythm which gives
each sentence its relation to the next and yet is of huge and cumulative
effect. A bold and prodigious appetite for the drums and tramplings of
language is balanced by the most exquisite sense of mysterious affinities
between ghosts and roses. But these dissections are futile enough, and
indeed by drawing attention to the technical side of Sir Thomas's art do
him some disservice. In books as in people, graces and charms are
delightful for the moment but become insipid unless they are felt to be
part of some general energy or quality of character. To grasp that is to
know them well, but to dally with charms and graces, to appraise them
more and more exquisitely, is to be always at the first stage of acquaintance, superficial, polite, and ultimately bored. It is easy to detach the
fine passages from their context, but in *Urn Burial* this character, this
quality of the whole, though it expresses itself with all the charm of all
the Muses, is yet of a very exalted kind. It is a difficult book to read, it is a
book not always to be read with pleasure, and those who get most from
it are the well-born souls.

But then, unfortunately, we are not all made entirely of salt. We
cannot breathe in these exalted regions for long. We have to admit that
we have bodies as well as minds, and the books which cater for both and
let one relieve the fatigues of the other are the books that have the longest
lease of life. The soul may be exalted in *Urn Burial*; the body is refreshed
in *Religio Medici*. There we can take our ease and trifle and laugh. There
we can indulge in the delicious amusement of feeling, like some psychological spider, from phrase to phrase over the mind and person of Sir
Thomas Browne. For the first to talk of himself broaches the subject with

immense gusto. I am charitable; I am brave; I am averse from nothing; I am full of feeling for others; I am merciless upon myself; I know six languages, the names of all the constellations, and most of the plants of my country. 'For my conversation, it is like the sun's, with all men, and with a friendly aspect to good and bad.'[8] Elsewhere we learn that his height was moderate, his eyes large and luminous, his skin dark and constantly suffused with blushes. He dressed very plainly. He seldom laughed. He collected coins, kept maggots in boxes, dissected the lungs of frogs, and combined a scientific and sceptical attitude towards most things with a profound piety, and indeed with an unfortunate vein of superstition. 'I have ever believed, and do now know, that there are witches,'[9] wrote the most humane of doctors, who in his pursuit of knowledge braved the stench of the spermaceti whale, could tolerate Jews, and had a good word for the deformity of the toad. He was, in short, as we say when we cannot help laughing at the oddities of the people we admire most, a character. We smile in the midst of the solemnities of *Urn Burial* when he remarks, 'Afflictions induce callosities'.[10] The smile broadens to laughter as we mouth out the splendid pomposities, the astonishing conjectures, of *Religio Medici*. Yet it is from the crest of some grotesque flight of fancy that he launches himself upon one of those sentences which yawn like a chasm cut in the earth at our feet. 'We carry with us the wonders we seek without us: there is all Africa and her prodigies in us.'[11] For the imagination which has gone such strange journeys among the dead is still exalted when it swings its lantern over the obscurities of the soul. He is in the dark to all the world; he has longed for death; there is a hell within him; who knows whether we may not be asleep in this world, and the conceits of life be but dreams? Steeped in such glooms, his imagination falls with a peculiar tenderness upon the common facts of human life. He turns it gradually upon the flowers and insects and grasses at his feet, so as to disturb nothing in the mysterious processes of their existence. There is a halo of wonder round everything that he sees. He that considers the thicket in the head of a teazle 'in the house of the solitary maggot may find the Seraglio of Solomon'.[12] The tavern music, the Ave Mary bell, the broken urn that the workman has dug out of the field plunge him into the depths of wonder and lead him, as he stands fixed in amazement, to extraordinary flights of speculation as to what we are, where we go, and the meaning of all things. To read Sir Thomas Browne again is always to be filled with astonishment, to remember the surprises, the despondences, the unlimited curiosities of youth.

1 – A review in the *TLS*, 28 June 1923, (Kp C235) of *Religio Medici* [1642]; *Hydrotaphia. Urn Burial: or a discourse of the sepulchral urns lately found in Norfolk* [1658]; and of *The Garden of Cyrus. Or the Quincuncial lozenge, or network plantation of the ancients artificially, naturally, mystically consider'd* [1658] (Printed and sold at the Golden Cockerel Press, Waltham St Lawrence, Berkshire, 1923) by Sir Thomas Browne [1605–82] physician of Norwich.

See also 'The Elizabethan Lumber Room', *IV VW Essays* and *CR 1*. Reading Notes (Berg, xxv).

2 – See Reading Notes, where the quotation is recorded as being 'from Golden Cock prospectus'.

3 – Samuel Pepys (1633–1703); Arthur Rimbaud (1854–91); George Otto Trevelyan, *Life and Letters of Lord Macaulay* (1876); Peter Beckford, *Thoughts on Hunting* (1781), upon which VW made reading notes in Berg, xxv; Benjamin Disraeli (1804–81); Thomas De Quincey, 'Richard Bentley', in *Studies on Secret Records, Personal and Historic* (vol. vii, *Selections Grave and Gay*, James Hogg, 1857), upon which VW made reading notes in Berg, xxv, and James Henry Monk, *The Life of Richard Bentley, D.D.* (1830).

4 – Arnold Bennett, *The Old Wives' Tale* (1908); John Galsworthy, *The Man of Property* (1906).

5 – Marcel Proust (1871–1922), *A la recherche du temps perdu* (1913–27).

6 – For the matter up to the first ellipsis, Browne, *Urn Burial*, ch. v, p. 44; for the matter up to the second ellipsis, *ibid.*, p. 45; and for the final passage, *ibid.*, p. 46, which has: 'mummies which' and 'spared avarice'.

7 – *Ibid.*, p. 46.

8 – *Religio Medici*, ch. ii, pp. 75–6, which has: 'Sun's – with'.

9 – *Ibid.*, ch. i, p. 34, which begins: 'For my part, I have ever', and continues: '; they that doubt of these do not only deny them but spirits; and are obliquely and upon consequence a sort not of infidels but atheists'.

10 – *Urn Burial*, ch. v, p. 45: 'Afflictions induce callosities; miseries are slippery, or fall like snow upon us, which notwithstanding is no unhappy stupidity.'

11 – *Religio Medici*, ch. i, p. 20, which continues: '; we are that bold and adventurous piece of nature which he that studies wisely learns in a compendium what others labour at in a divided piece and endless volume.'

12 – *The Garden of Cyrus*, ch. iii, p. 25: 'The arbustetum or thicket on the head of the teazil may be observed in this order: and he that considereth that fabrick so regularly palisado'd and stemmed with flowers of the royal colour, in the house of the solitary maggot may find the seraglio of Solomon; and contemplating the calicular shafts & uncous disposure of their extremities, so accommodable unto the office of abstersion, not condemn as wholly improbable the conceit of those who accept it for the herb borith.'

An Impression of Gissing

Gissing's work leaves the reader with an impression of incorruptible honesty, strangely combined with something shrinking and fastidious which would have liked to look the other way if Gissing had not sharply jerked its head back into position. Thus Gissing was an imperfect realist. He had been forced by circumstances to pitch his tent in Grub Streets and Nether Worlds,[2] which were far from his native land. Honesty forced him to describe what he saw there, but it is a shrinking, an embittered honesty which glares and stares and is thus not of the finest quality for the purposes of a novelist. Miss Yates (a very conscientious critic) acutely points out the effect of this alien element upon his work. 'Gissing rarely identifies himself with the suffering he is describing; he is always a little aloof, a little detached from the actual life of the workers. ... His attitude shows a curious mixture of pity and contempt.'[3] Dickens, she proceeds, was not aloof, and therefore of course he gives us a better lighted, a better proportioned world. But Gissing – it is one of the attributes of these imperfect novelists – gives us what of course is not so important as a world, but has its interest, and certainly its intensity – a single figure seen against the world, himself that is. Nor should the admirers of Gissing repudiate this statement as if it were a serious slight upon him. Be yourself with vigour and honesty and uncompromisingly, and it is surprising how you tell upon the landscape. It is arguable that you live almost as long in the manner of Dr Johnson and Samuel Butler[4] as in the other way, which is Shakespeare's way and Jane Austen's. A few people domesticate you very intimately in their minds, and break out at odd intervals into articles and dinners and memoirs. Gissing's fame will be continued largely by posthumous friendship of this sort, because he was to the last fibre of him Gissing, and made a world by virtue of character rather than of creative power.

For all these reasons then it will be well worthwhile one of these days to read *New Grub Street* or *Born in Exile*[5] again. But it will be a melancholy experience. The sufferings of the intellectual of 1890 and thereabouts were appalling. Not only was Gissing poor, intelligent, sensitive and pigheaded, but he was cursed with a passion for literature, a craving for fat, and an irresistible desire to marry the first woman he met in the Marylebone Road.[6] The days of the treadmill began on the honeymoon. The intolerable grind was trodden out in Hoxton, and

Islington and Lambeth and Camberwell. Children were born; health
failed; boilers leaked; doors banged; nerves were exasperated, and,
painfully and desperately, in a perpetual effort to pay doctors' bills and
butchers' bills, pages of the eternal book were wrung from the exhausted
but still conscientious brain. Sufferings more sordid and less normal
than might have been foretold for a man of his calibre fell to Gissing's lot
and are revealed in the *Private Life of Henry Maitland* (now reprinted
with an appendix). It is not a pleasant book for those who like to believe
that the intellect protects people from the meaner miseries and absolves
them from the more ignoble temptations of life. Henry Maitland stole an
overcoat, complained bitterly of the cooking, and feebly collapsed into
marriages which had not even the lure of passion to recommend them.
But memory, who can range hither and thither at her will, sets the
records of Henry Ryecroft[7] beside this dismal one of Henry Maitland.
She recalls the shelf of classics, Greek, Latin, and English, bought with
saved sixpences and lugged home volume by volume to a basement off
the Tottenham Court Road. Then she remembers how he would start up
from stirring the pot with its deep deposits of mutton to extol the
wonders of Greek literature. 'Why, my dear fellow, do you know there
are actually miserable men who do not know – who have never even
heard of – the minuter differences between Dochmiacs and Antispasts!'[8]
He travelled, she bids us remark; he had his years of respite in
Devonshire. And then she concludes, there is a quality in the books as a
whole which, though it may be true that he was a novelist against the
grain and a scholar with it, must have been a source of enduring self-
respect and gratification to its possessor. They are solid books, always of
scrupulous workmanship, and often, as the dreary story tells itself, it
wraps itself about in a glory of sober prose. One will read the books
again partly to recover certain descriptions of Camberwell streets and
suburban cemeteries. And finally memory is of opinion that the works of
Gissing issued between 1880 and 1906 will live longer than many of
their more celebrated contemporaries. For though the angle was sharp
and the vision narrow, Gissing beheld with his own eyes the perpetual
struggles and sufferings of human beings. You may open his books even
now and find yourself figuratively speaking (memory deals much in
figures) in the front parlour of a prosaic lodging house. But there is an
incongruous flower upon the sideboard; and people actually live here.
You will not (and here she glances with obvious malice at these
'celebrated contemporaries') find yourself in a public hall, littered with
pamphlets, strewn with chairs, decorated with banners, while the

badges and umbrellas on the floor testify to the fact that here a great battle of words was fought out and the burning questions of the day decided, which way now scarcely seems to matter.

1–A review in the NS, 30 June 1923, (Kp C236) of *George Gissing* [1857–1903]: *An Appreciation* (Manchester University Press, 1922) by May Yates, M.A., Senior Lecturer in English Language and Literature, Normal College, Bangor, sometime Fellow of the University of Liverpool; and of *The Private Life of Henry Maitland. A record dictated by J.H.* Revised and edited by Morley Roberts (Nash & Grayson, 1923), a work originally published in 1912. (The review is signed 'V'.)

VW worked at her review while staying at the Hôtel de Londres in Paris. 'Here I am,' she wrote to LW on Tuesday, 25 April 1923 (*III VW Letters*, no. 1382), 'already in bed at 10.30, and I shall be asleep within the half hour. I've had quite a successful though a lonely day. I wrote – found nothing to do to my Nation article [unidentified – possibly 'To Spain', above], so began Gissing; lunched at a new place; good; 3 courses . . . Now I've dined at our usual place . . . then chocolate, very good, at the orchestra café, but the music was such that even I could dream no dreams, so came away, got straight into bed, and finished reading my Gissing book; which brings me to the present moment . . . Here I am on Wednesday morning, having had a very good night, no aspirin – slept till 7.45. | I have written at Gissing, and now I'm going to dress and go about my business.' See also 'The Private Papers of Henry Ryecroft', 'The Novels of George Gissing', *I VW Essays*; 'George Gissing', *V VW Essays* and CR2.

2–Gissing, *New Grub Street* (1891), *The Nether World* (1889).
3–Charles Dickens (1812–70). For the quotation, Yates, ch. ii, p. 36; the ellipsis marks the omission of: 'He was incapable of such a passionate exhortation to rebellion as Shelley's *Song to the Men of England*, 1819'.
4–Samuel Butler (1835–1902).
5–*Born in Exile* (1892).
6–Gissing married, in 1879, Helen Harrison (d.1888), from whom he subsequently separated. In 1891 he married again, Edith Underwood; and from 1898 he lived with Gabrielle Fleury.
7–*The Private Papers of Henry Ryecroft* (1903).
8–Roberts, ch. iii (Eveleigh Nash, 1912, p. 77).

Laetitia Pilkington

VW's essay in the *N&A*, 30 June 1923, (Kp C237) was later incorporated with minor revisions into the essay of the same title in *The Common Reader*: 1st series (1925). The reader is referred to *IV VW Essays*, where the later version, together with variants in the form of footnotes, is printed in its place as part of *The Common Reader*.

Mr Conrad: A Conversation

The Otways, perhaps, inherited their love of reading from the ancient dramatist[2] whose name they share, whether they descend from him (as they like to think) or not. Penelope, the oldest unmarried daughter, a small dark woman turned forty, her complexion a little roughened by country life, her eyes brown and bright, yet subject to strange long stares of meditation or vacancy, had always, since the age of seven, been engaged in reading the classics. Her father's library, though strong chiefly in the literature of the East, had its Popes, its Drydens, its Shakespeares, in various stages of splendour and decay; and if his daughters chose to amuse themselves by reading what they liked, certainly it was a method of education which, since it spared his purse, deserved his benediction.

That education it could be called, no one nowadays would admit. All that can be said in its favour was that Penelope Otway was never dull, gallantly ambitious of surmounting small hillocks of learning, and of an enthusiasm which greater knowledge might perhaps have stinted or have diverted less fortunately into the creation of books of her own. As it was, she was content to read and to talk, reading in the intervals of household business, and talking when she could find company, on Sundays for the most part, when visitors came down, and sat, on fine summer days, under the splendid yew tree on the lawn.

On this occasion, a hot morning in August, her old friend David Lowe was distressed but hardly surprised to find five magnificent volumes lying on the grass by her chair, while Penelope acknowledged his presence by putting her fingers between the pages of a sixth and looking at the sky.

'Joseph Conrad,' he said, lifting the admirable books – solid, stately, good-looking, yet meant for a long life-time of repeated re-reading – on to his knee. 'So I see you have made up your mind. Mr Conrad is a classic.'

'Not in your opinion,' she replied; 'I remember the bitter letters you wrote me when you read *The Arrow of Gold* and *The Rescue*.[3] You compared him to an elderly and disillusioned nightingale singing over and over, but hopelessly out of tune, the one song he had learnt in his youth.' 'I had forgotten,' said David, 'but it is true. The books puzzled me after those early novels, *Youth, Lord Jim, The Nigger of the*

'Certainly he was a strange apparition to descend upon these shores in the last part of the nineteenth century – an artist, an aristocrat, a Pole,' said David. 'For after all these years I cannot think of him as an English writer. He is too formal, too courteous, too scrupulous in the use of a language which is not his own. Then, of course, he is an aristocrat to the backbone. His humour is aristocratic – ironic, sardonic, never broad and free like the common English humour which descends from Falstaff. He is infinitely reserved. And the lack of intimacy which I complain of may perhaps be due not merely to those "August abstractions" as you call them, but to the fact that there are no women in his books.' 'There are the ships, the beautiful ships,' said Penelope. 'They are more feminine than his women, who are either mountains of marble or the dreams of a charming boy over the photograph of an actress. But surely a great novel can be made out of a man and a ship, a man and a storm, a man and death and dishonour?' 'Ah, we are back at the question of greatness,' said David. 'Which, then, is the great book, where, as you say, the complex vision becomes simple, and Marlow and the sea captain combine to produce a world at once exquisitely subtle, psychologically profound, yet based upon a very few simple ideas "so simple that they must be as old as the hills"?' 'I have just read *Chance*,'[13] said Penelope. 'It is a great book, I think. But now you will have to read it yourself, for you are not going to accept my word, especially when it is a word which I cannot define. It is a great book, a great book,' she repeated.

1–A signed review in the *N&A*, 1 September 1923, (Kp C239) of *Almayer's Folly, Tales of Unrest, An Outcast of the Islands, The Nigger of the Narcissus, Typhoon, Lord Jim, Youth*, and *Romance* (*Works*, uniform ed., J. M. Dent, 1923) by Joseph Conrad (1857–1924).

'For plans,' VW noted in her diary on Friday, 28 July 1923, 'I have immediately to write a dialogue on Conrad: so must read for that too.' On 3 August following, she wrote to Pernel Strachey: 'But I am engulphed in the works of Conrad, who is a much better writer than all of us put together, don't you agree? Will you sacrifice a brother if I sacrifice myself, Clive Bell, Morgan Forster, Tom Eliot, and anyone else I can think of? Why is there much more difference between 1st rate and 2nd rate than between 3rd rate and 2nd rate, or any other rate?' (*III VW Letters*, no. 1415).

'And I'm slightly dashed by the reception of my Conrad conversation,' she wrote in her diary on Wednesday, 5 September 1923, 'which has been purely negative – No one has mentioned it. I dont think [Raymond] M[ortimer] or [Francis] B[irrell] quite approved. Never mind; to be dashed is always the most bracing treatment for me. A cold douche should be taken (& generally is) before beginning a book. It invigorates; makes one say "Oh all right. I write to please myself," & so go ahead. It also has had the effect of making me more definite & outspoken in my style, which I imagine all to the good. At any rate, I began for the 5th but last time, I swear, what is now to be called The Common Reader . . . To curtail, I shall really investigate literature with a view to answering certain questions about ourselves – Characters are to be merely views: personality must be avoided at all costs. I'm sure my Conrad adventure taught me this. Directly you specify hair, age, &c something frivolous, or irrelevant, gets into the book – Dinner!'

The same issue of the *N&A* also contained: LW's 'World of Books' column, on 'Herman Melville'; the first instalment of Mary MacCarthy's *A Nineteenth Century Childhood*; and Bertrand Russell on 'The Interior of the Atom'.

See also 'A Disillusioned Romantic' and 'A Prince of Prose' above; '*Lord Jim*', 'Mr Conrad's "Youth"', 'Mr Conrad's Crisis', *II VW Essays*; and 'Joseph Conrad', *IV VW Essays* and *CR 1*. Reprinted: *CDB, CE*. Reading Notes (Berg, xxv.)

2 – Thomas Otway (1652–85), author of *Venice Preserved* (1682) etc.

3 – *The Arrow of Gold* (1919), *The Rescue* (1920).

4 – *Youth* (1902), *Lord Jim* (1900), *The Nigger of the Narcissus* (1897).

5 – Conrad, *Some Reminiscences* (Eveleigh Nash, 1912), 'A Familiar Preface', p. 26.

6 – Conrad, *Notes on Life and Letters* (J. M. Dent & Sons, Ltd., 1921), 'Books,' p. 11.

7 – John Milton, *Samson Agonistes* (1671), 1. 1721 ff., spoken by Manoa:

> 'Nothing is here for tears, nothing to wail
> Or knock the breast, no weakness, no contempt,
> Dispraise, or blame; nothing but well and fair,
> And what may quiet us in a death so noble.'

8 – *Nigger of the Narcissus* (Dent, 1923), ch. iv, p. 90.

9 – *Ibid.*, ch. iii, p. 49, which has: 'glorious and obscure'.

10 – 'Falk' in *Typhoon* (Dent, 1923, p. 172).

11 – *Nigger of the Narcissus*, ch. v, p. 154.

12 – Henry James (1843–1916); Anatole France (1844–1924).

13 – *Chance* (1914).

The Compromise

None of the great Victorian reputations has sunk lower than that of Mrs Humphry Ward.[2] Her novels, already strangely out of date, hang in the lumber room of letters like the mantles of our aunts, and produce in us the same desire that they do to smash the window and let in the air, to light the fire and pile the rubbish on top. Some books fade into a gentle picturesqueness with age. But there is a quality, perhaps a lack of quality, about the novels of Mrs Ward which makes it improbable that, however much they fade, they will ever become picturesque. Their large bunches of jet, their intricate festoons of ribbon, skilfully and firmly fabricated as they are, obstinately resist the endearments of time. But Mrs Trevelyan's life of her mother makes us consider all this from a different angle. It is an able and serious book, and like all good biographies so permeates us with the sense of the presence of a human being that by the time we have finished it we are more disposed to ask questions than to pass judgements. Let us attempt, in a few words, to hand on the dilemma to our readers.

Of Mrs Ward's descent there is no need to speak. She had by birth and temperament all those qualities which fitted her, before she was twenty, to be the friend of Mark Pattison,[3] and 'the best person', in the opinion of J. R. Green, to be asked to contribute a volume to a history of Spain.[4] There was little, even at the age of twenty, that this ardent girl did not know about the Visigothic Invasion or the reign of Alfonso el Sabio. One of her first pieces of writing, 'A Morning in the Bodleian', records in priggish but burning words her scholar's enthusiasm: '. . . let not the young man reading for his pass, the London copyist, or the British Museum illuminator', hope to enjoy the delights of literature; that deity will only yield her gifts to 'the silent ardor, the thirst, the disinterested-ness of the true learner'.[5] With such an inscription above the portal, her fate seems already decided. She will marry a Don; she will rear a small family; she will circulate 'Plain Facts on Infant Feeding' in the Oxford slums; she will help to found Somerville College;[6] she will sit up writing learned articles for the *Dictionary of Christian Biography*; and at last, after a hard life of unremunerative toil, she will finish the book which fired her fancy as a girl and will go down to posterity as the author of a standard work upon the origins of modern Spain. But, as everyone knows, the career which seemed so likely, and would have been so honourable, was interrupted by the melodramatic success of *Robert Elsmere*.[7] History was entirely forsaken for fiction, and the Origins of Modern Spain became transmuted into the Origins of Modern France, a phantom book which the unfortunate Robert Elsmere never succeeded in writing.

It is here that we begin to scribble in the margin of Mrs Ward's life those endless notes of interrogation. After *Robert Elsmere* – which we may grant to have been inevitable – we can never cease to ask ourselves, why? Why desert the charming old house in Russell Square for the splendour and expenses of Grosvenor Place?[8] Why wear beautiful dresses, why keep butlers and carriages, why give luncheon parties and weekend parties, why buy a house in the country and pull it down and built it up again,[9] when all this can only be achieved by writing at breathless speed novels which filial piety calls autumnal, but the critic, unfortunately, must call bad? Mrs Ward might have replied that the compromise, if she agreed to call it so, was entirely justified. Who but a coward would refuse when cheques for £7,000 dropped out of George Smith's[10] pocket before breakfast, to spend the money as the great ladies of the Renaissance would have spent it, upon society and entertainment and philanthropy? Without her novel-writing there would have been no centre for good talk in the pretty room overlooking the grounds of Buckingham Palace.[11] Without her novel-writing thousands of poor children would have ranged the streets unsheltered. It is impossible to remain a schoolgirl in the Bodleian for ever, and, once you breast the complicated currents of modern life at their strongest, there is little time to ask questions, and none to answer them. One thing merges in another; one thing leads to another. After an exhausting 'At Home' in Grosvenor Place, she would snatch a meal and drive off to fight the cause of play centres in Bloomsbury. Her success in that undertaking involved her, against her will, in the anti-suffrage campaign.[12] Then, when the war came, this elderly lady of weak health was selected by the highest authorities to peer into shell-holes, and be taken over men-of-war by admirals. Sometimes, says Mrs Trevelyan, eighty letters were dispatched from Stocks in a single day; five hats were bought in the course of one drive to town – 'on spec., darling';[13] and what with grandchildren and cousins and friends; what with being kind and being unmethodical and being energetic; what with caring more and more passionately for politics, and finding the meetings of liberal churchmen 'desperately, perhaps disproportionately'[14] interesting, there was only one half-hour in the whole day left for reading Greek.

It is tempting to imagine what the schoolgirl in the Bodleian would have said to her famous successor. 'Literature has no guerdon for bread-students, to quote the expressive German phrase . . . only to the silent ardor, the thirst, the disinterestedness of the true learner, is she prodigal of all good gifts.'[15] But Mrs Humphry Ward, the famous novelist, might have rounded up her critic of twenty. 'It is all very well,' she might have said, 'to accuse me of having wasted my gifts; but the fault lay with you. Yours was the age for seeing visions; and you spent it in dreaming how you stopped the Princess of Wales's runaway horses, and were rewarded by "a command" to appear at Buckingham Palace.[16] It was you who starved my imagination and condemned it to the fatal compromise.' And here the elder lady undoubtedly lays her finger upon the weakness of her own work. For the depressing effects of her books must be attributed to the fact that while her imagination always attempts to soar, it always agrees to perch. That is why we never wish to open them again.

In Mrs Trevelyan's biography these startling discrepancies between youth and age, between ideal and accomplishment, are successfully welded together, as they are in life, by an infinite series of details. She makes it apparent that Mrs Ward was beloved, famous, and prosperous in the highest degree. And if to achieve all this implies some compromise, still – but here we reach the dilemma which we intend to pass on to our readers.

1–A review in the *N&A*, 29 September 1923, (Kp C242) reprinted in the *NR*, 9 January 1924, of *The Life of Mrs Humphry Ward* (Constable & Co., 1923) by her daughter Janet Penrose Trevelyan. 'Mrs Ward is dead;' VW had recorded in her diary on 10 April 1920, 'poor Mrs Humphry Ward; & it appears that she was merely a woman of straw after all – shovelled into the grave & already forgotten. The most perfunctory earth strewing even by the orthodox.' See also *I VW Diary*, 21 September 1919.

The same issue of the *N&A* contained LW's 'World of Books' column, subtitled 'Charming Memories', on *Early Memories: Some Chapters of Autobiography* by John Butler Yeats, and an article by T. S. Eliot on 'Andrew Marvell'. Reprinted: *B&P*. Reading Notes (Berg, xxv).

2–Mary Augusta Ward, *née* Arnold (1851–1920), was the daughter of Thomas Arnold and Julia Sorrell, and a niece of Matthew Arnold; she married Thomas Humphry Ward (d. 1926), fellow of Brasenose College, Oxford, in 1872.

3–Mark Pattison (1813–84), fellow, and ultimately rector, of Lincoln College, Oxford, a Newmanite until Newman became a Roman Catholic.

4–For the quotation, Trevelyan, ch. ii, p. 21; John Richard Green (1837–83), historian, and a friend of Leslie Stephen who was to edit his letters. Mrs Ward did not contribute a volume to the historical series referred to, edited by Edward Freeman.

5–For both quotations, Trevelyan, ch. ii, p. 22.

6–Mrs Ward circulated her leaflet on 'Plain Facts on Infant Feeding' in about 1876. She was joint-secretary of the fund-raising committee to establish Somerville College – or Hall as it was initially called – which was founded in 1879, and became an active member of its original Council.

7–*Robert Elsmere* (1888).

8–The Wards lived at 61 Russell Square, from 1881 until 1891 when they moved to 25 Grosvenor Place.

9–This was Stocks, near Tring in Hertfordshire, which the Wards obtained in 1892.

10–George Murray Smith, of Smith & Elder, Mrs Ward's publishers.

11–See Trevelyan, ch. x, pp. 188–9: 'As to the persons who came and went in that pretty room, looking out on the garden of Buckingham Palace, how is it possible to number or name them, or to recall the flavour of their long-vanished conversation? Many have, like their hostess, passed into the unknown: figures like Leslie Stephen, who wrote to her often, especially after his wife's death, and came at intervals to Grosvenor Place for a long *tête-à-tête*, his ear-trumpet between them ...'

12–Mrs Ward had opposed women's suffrage 'from her earliest days at Oxford, ever since the time when the first Women's Petition for the vote was brought to the House of Commons by Miss Garrett and Miss Emily Davies in 1866, and John Stuart Mill moved his amendment to the Reform Bill of 1867' (*ibid.*, ch. xii, p. 224), and was to campaign against it, through the Women's National Anti-Suffrage League, of which she was founder, until the cause was lost in 1918. Her unwillingness to play an active role in the campaign was based on practical rather than ideological grounds.

13–Trevelyan, ch. xiii, p. 256.

14–*Ibid.*, ch. viii, p. 151, quoting a letter to Bishop Creighton, 9 August 1898.

15–*Ibid.*, ch. ii, p. 22; the ellipsis marks the omission of: '; let not the young man reading for his pass, the London copyist, or the British Museum illuminator, hope to enter within the enchanted ring of her benignant influences;' – see n6 above.

16–For Mrs Humphry Ward's childhood daydreams, *ibid.*, ch. i, pp. 11–12.

Mr Bennett and Mrs Brown

The other day Mr Arnold Bennett, himself one of the most famous of the Edwardians, surveyed the younger generation and said: 'I admit that for myself I cannot yet descry any coming big novelist'.[2] And that, let us say in passing, is all to the good – a symptom of the respectful hostility which is the only healthy relation between old and young. But then he went on to give his reasons for this lamentable fact, and his reasons, which lie deep, deserve much more consideration than his impatience, which lies on the surface. The Georgians fail as novelists, he said, because 'they are interested more in details than in the full creation of their individual characters ... The foundation of good fiction is character-creating, and nothing else. To render secure the importance of a novel it is necessary, further, that the characters should clash with one another,'[3] or, of course, they will excite no emotion in the breast of the author or anybody else. None of this is new; all of it is true; yet here we have one of those simple statements which are no sooner taken into the mind than they burst their envelopes and flood us with suggestions of every kind.

The novel is a very remarkable machine for the creation of human character, we are all agreed. Directly it ceases to create character, its defects alone are visible. And it is because this essence, this character-making power, has evaporated that novels are for the most part the soulless bodies we know, cumbering our tables and clogging our minds. That, too, may pass. Few reviewers at least are likely to dispute it. But if we go on to ask when this change began, and what were the reasons behind it, then agreement is much more difficult to come by. Mr Bennett blames the Georgians. Our minds fly straight to King Edward.[4] Surely that was the fatal age, the age which is just breaking off from our own, the age when character disappeared or was mysteriously engulfed, and the culprits, happily still alive, active, and unrepentant, are Mr Wells, Mr Galsworthy,[5] and Mr Bennett himself.

But in lodging such a charge against so formidable a library we must do as painters do when they wish to reduce the innumerable details of a crowded landscape to simplicity – step back, half shut the eyes, gesticulate a little vaguely with the fingers, and reduce Edwardian fiction to a view. Thus treated, one strange fact is immediately apparent. Every sort of town is represented, and innumerable institutions; we see factories, prisons, workhouses, law courts, Houses of Parliament; a general clamour, the voice of aspiration, indignation, effort and industry, rises from the whole; but in all this vast conglomeration of printed pages, in all this congeries of streets and houses, there is not a single man or woman whom we know. Figures like Kipps or the sisters (already nameless) in *The Old Wives' Tale*[6] attempt to contradict this assertion, but with how feeble a voice and how flimsy a body is apparent directly they are stood beside some character from that other great tract of fiction which lies immediately behind them in the Victorian age. For there, if we follow the same process, but recall one novel, and that – *Pendennis*[7] – not one of the most famous, at once start out, clear, vigorous, alive from the curl of their eyelashes to the soles of their boots, half a dozen characters whose names are no sooner spoken than we think of scene after scene in which they play their parts. We see the Major sitting in his club window, fresh from the hands of Morgan; Helen nursing her son in the Temple and suspecting poor Fanny; Warrington grilling chops in his dressing-gown; Captain Shandon scribbling leaders for the *Pall Mall Gazette* – Laura, Blanche Amory, Foker;[8] the procession is endless and alive. And so it goes on from character to character all through the splendid opulence of the Victorian age. They love, they joke, they hunt, they marry; they lead us from hall to cottage, from field to slum. The whole country, the whole society, is revealed to us, and revealed always in the same way, through the astonishing vividness and reality of the characters.

And it was perhaps on that very account that the Edwardians changed their tactics. Such triumphs could scarcely be rivalled; and, moreover, triumphs once achieved seem to the next generation always a little uninteresting. There was, too (if we think ourselves into the mind of a writer contemplating fiction about the year 1900), something plausible, superficial, unreal in all this abundance. No sooner had the Victorians departed than Samuel Butler, who had lived below-stairs, came out, like an observant bootboy, with the family secrets in *The Way of All Flesh*.[9] It appeared that the basement was really in an appalling state. Though the saloons were splendid and the dining rooms portentous, the drains were of the most primitive description. The social state was a mass of corruption. A sensitive man like Mr Galsworthy could scarcely step out of doors without barking his shins upon some social iniquity. A generous mind which knew the conditions in which the Kippses and the Lewishams[10] were born and bred must try at least to fashion the world afresh. So the young novelist became a reformer, and thought with pardonable contempt of those vast Victorian family parties, where the funny man was always funny, the good woman always good, and nobody seemed aware, as they pursued their own tiny lives, that society was rotten and Christianity itself at stake. But there was another force which made much more subtly against the creation of character, and that was Mrs Garnett and her translations from Dostoevsky. After reading *Crime and Punishment* and *The Idiot*,[11] how could any young novelist believe in 'characters' as the Victorians had painted them? For the undeniable vividness of so many of them is the result of their crudity. The character is rubbed into us indelibly because its features are so few and so prominent. We are given the keyword (Mr Dick has King Charles's head; Mr Brooke, 'I went into that a great deal at one time'; Mrs Micawber, 'I will never desert Mr Micawber'),[12] and then, since the choice of the keyword is astonishingly apt, our imaginations swiftly supply the rest. But what keyword could be applied to Raskolnikov, Mishkin, Stavrogin, or Alyosha?[13] These are characters without any features at all. We go down into them as we descend into some enormous cavern. Lights swing about; we hear the boom of the sea; it is all dark, terrible, and uncharted. So we need not be surprised if the Edwardian novelist scarcely attempted to deal with character except in its more generalised aspects. The Victorian version was discredited; it was his duty to destroy all those institutions in the shelter of which character thrives and thickens; and the Russians had shown him – everything or nothing, it was impossible as yet to say which. The Edwardian novelists therefore give us a vast sense of things in general; but a very vague one of things in particular. Mr Galsworthy gives us a sense of compassion; Mr Wells fills us with generous enthusiasm; Mr Bennett (in his early work) gave us a sense of time. But their books are already a little chill, and must steadily grow more distant, for 'the foundation of good fiction is character-creating, and nothing else', as Mr Bennett says; and in none of them are we given a man or woman whom we know.

The Georgians had, therefore, a difficult task before them, and if they have failed, as Mr Bennett asserts, there is nothing to surprise us in that. To bring back character from the shapelessness into which it has lapsed, to sharpen its edges, deepen its compass, and so make possible those conflicts between human beings which alone rouse our strongest emotions – such was their problem. It was the consciousness of this problem and not the accession of King George,[14] which produced, as it always produces, the break between one generation and the next. Here, however, the break is particularly sharp, for here the dispute is fundamental. In real life there is nothing that interests us more than character, that stirs us to the same extremes of love and anger, or that leads to such incessant and laborious speculations about the values, the reasons, and the meaning of existence itself. To disagree about character is to differ in the depths of the being. It is to take different sides, to drift apart, to accept a purely formal intercourse for ever. That is so in real life. But the novelist has to go much further and to be much more uncompromising than the friend. When he finds himself hopelessly at variance with Mr Wells, Mr Galsworthy, and Mr Bennett about the character – shall we say? – of Mrs Brown, it is useless to defer to their superior genius. It is useless to mumble the polite agreements of the drawing room. He must set about to remake the woman after his own idea. And that, in the circumstances, is a very perilous pursuit.

For what, after all is character – the way that Mrs Brown, for instance, reacts to her surroundings – when we cease to believe what we are told about her, and begin to search out her real meaning for ourselves? In the first place, her solidity disappears; her features crumble; the house in which she has lived so long (and a very substantial house it was) topples to the ground. She becomes a will-o'-the-wisp, a dancing light, an illumination gliding up the wall and out of the window, lighting now in freakish malice upon the nose of an archbishop, now in sudden splendour upon the mahogany of the wardrobe. The most solemn sights she turns to ridicule; the most ordinary she invests with beauty. She changes the shape, shifts the accent, of every scene in which she plays her part. And it is from the ruins and splinters of this tumbled mansion that the Georgian writer must somehow reconstruct a habitable dwelling-place; it is from the gleams and flashes of this flying spirit that he must create solid, living, flesh-and-blood Mrs Brown. Sadly he must allow that the lady still escapes him. Dismally he must admit bruises received in the pursuit. But it is because the Georgians, poets and novelists, biographers and dramatists, are so hotly engaged each in the pursuit of his own Mrs Brown that theirs is at once the least successful, and the most interesting, generation that English literature has known for a hundred years. Moreover, let us prophesy: Mrs Brown will not always escape. One of these days Mrs Brown will be caught. The capture of Mrs Brown is the title of the next chapter in the history of literature; and, let us prophesy again, that chapter will be one of the most important, the most illustrious, the most epoch-making of them all.[15]

1 – A signed essay in the 'Literary Review' of the *New York Evening Post*, 17 November 1923, (Kp C240) reprinted in *N&A*, 1 December 1923, and *Living Age* (Boston), 2 February 1924. VW had broached the subject of this essay in her diary, as early as 19 June, at a time when she was busy writing *Mrs Dalloway* (1925): 'People, like Arnold Bennett, say I cant create, or didn't in J[acob]'s R[oom], characters that survive. My answer is – but I leave that to the Nation: its only the old argument that character is dissipated into shreds now: the old post-Dostoevsky argument. I daresay its true, however, that I haven't that "reality" gift. I insubstantise, wilfully to some extent, distrusting reality – its cheapness. But to go further. Have I the power of conveying the true reality? Or do I write essays about myself? Answer these questions as I may, in the uncomplimentary sense, & still there remains this excitement'. See also 'Character in Fiction' below; 'Books and Persons', 'Mr Galsworthy's Novel', 'The Rights of Youth', *II VW Essays*; 'What is a Novel?', *IV VW Essays*.

2 – Arnold Bennett (1867–1931), 'Is the Novel Decaying?', *Cassell's Weekly*, 28 March 1923 (reprinted in *M&M*, pp. 112–14): 'I have seldom read a cleverer book than Virginia Woolf's *Jacob's Room*, a novel which has made a great stir in a small world. It is packed and bursting with originality, and it is exquisitely written. But the characters do not vitally survive in the mind because the author has been obsessed by details of originality and cleverness. I regard this book as characteristic of the new novelists who have recently gained the attention of the alert and the curious, and I admit that for myself I cannot yet descry any coming big novelists.'

3 – *Ibid.*: 'To render secure the importance of a novel it is necessary, further, that the characters should clash one with another so as to produce strong emotion, first in the author himself and second in the reader. This strong emotion cannot be produced unless the characters are *kept* true throughout. You cannot get strength out of falsity. The moment the still small voice whispers to the reader about a character, "He wouldn't have acted like that," the book is imperilled. The reader may say: "This is charming. This is amusing. This is original. This is clever. This is exciting."

But if he also has to say, "It's not true," the success of the book cannot be permanent. | The foundation of good fiction is character creating, nothing else. The characters must be so fully true that they possess even their own creator. Every deviation from the truth, every omission of truth, necessarily impairs the emotional power and therefore weakens the interest. | I think that we have today a number of young novelists who display all manner of good qualities – originality of view, ingenuity of presentment, sound common sense, and even style. But they appear to me to be interested more in details than in the full creation of their individual characters. They are so busy with states of society as to half forget that any society consists of individuals, and they attach too much weight to cleverness, which is perhaps the lowest of all artistic qualities.'

4 – Edward VII (1841–1910), reigned from 1901.

5 – H. G. Wells (1866–1946); John Galsworthy (1867–1933).

6 – Arthur Kipps, hero of Wells's *Kipps* (1905); Constance and Sophia Baines are the sisters in Bennett's *The Old Wives' Tale* (1908).

7 – W. M. Thackeray (1811–63), *The History of Pendennis* (1848–50).

8 – Characters in *Pendennis*; Captain Shandon, first editor of the *Pall Mall Gazette* (the evening paper of that name was not founded until 1865; it was owned by George Smith and first edited by Frederick Greenwood); Laura Bell, illegitimate child adopted by Helen Pendennis; Blanche Amory, daughter of Lady Clavering and of the convict 'Col.Altamont'; Harry Foker, heir to 'Foker's Entire'.

9 – Samuel Butler (1835–1902), *The Way of All Flesh* (1903) – see '*The Way of All Flesh*' above.

10 – George Edgar Lewisham, in Wells's *Love and Mr Lewisham* (1900).

11 – Constance Garnett (1862–1946) translated the whole *oeuvre* of Fyodor Dostoevsky (1821–81), whose *Crime and Punishment* and *The Idiot* were first published in 1866 and 1879–80 respectively.

12 – For Mr Dick and King Charles's head, see *David Copperfield* (1849–50), ch. xiv, etc; for Mr Brooke, see George Eliot, *Middlemarch* (1871–2), ch. ii; and for Mrs Micawber's pledge of loyalty, *David Copperfield*, ch. 12 (Penguin, 1966, pp. 227–8).

13 – Rodion Romanovich Raskolnikov, hero of *Crime and Punishment*; Prince Lev Nicolaevich Mishkin, hero of *The Idiot*; Nikolay Vsevolodovich Stavrogin, hero of Dostoevsky's *The Possessed* (1872); Alyosha (Alexey Fyodorovich Karamazov), in Dostoevsky's *The Brothers Karamazov* (1872–80).

14 – George V (1865–1936), reigned from 1910.

15 – VW's essay prompted a series of responses in the N&A, though none from Arnold Bennett. See 'The Successors of Charles Dickens' by J. D. Beresford (1873–1947, novelist), *N&A*, 29 December 1923; 'First Catch Your Hare' by Logan Pearsall Smith (1865–1946, man of letters), *N&A*, 2 February 1924; and 'Why Only Dickens?' by Michael Sadleir (1888–1957, novelist and bibliographer), *N&A*, 9 February 1924. (The articles by Beresford and by Smith are reproduced in *M&M*, nos. 38 and 39.)

The Chinese Shoe

Lady Henry Somerset, her biographer says, 'came into the world with a far larger share of the joy of being alive'[2] than is the lot of most. If that were so, no woman was ever more completely defrauded of her rights. The Victorian age was to blame; her mother was to blame; Lord Henry was to blame; even the saintly Mr Watts[3] was forced by fate to take part in the general conspiracy against her. Between them each natural desire of a lively and courageous nature was stunted, until we feel that the old Chinese custom of fitting the foot to the shoe was charitable compared with the mid-Victorian practice of fitting the woman to the system. She was a lively child who enjoyed society. And here is an account of one of the most daring dissipations of her youth: 'If it is a *mild night* and you have not the shadow of a cold and you and Annie wrap up like *Mummies Hoods* over your heads and hats and veils and *grebe fur* round your throats *after your hood is put on* and you have the large carriage',[4] you may, as a very great indulgence, visit the night school and stay a few minutes. They had no education. Their politics, their friendships, their religion, their occupations from morning to night were dictated to them and enforced upon them in letter after letter, and scolding after scolding, by the most beautiful, the most generous, and the most exacting of mothers.

At last Lady Somers's work was complete, and her two daughters were fit to endure the rigours of English society at its most severe. Lady Isabel, however, had not been quite so effectively trained as her sister. There were corners and crannies still unswept by the harsh broom of convention. She had read Mill's *Liberty* in secret. In the American War she had come out, even at Eastnor, on the side of the North.[5] And, during her first season, when an aristocratic party was playing a game in which each had to say truthfully what was the desire of his or her heart, Isabel had the audacity to declare 'To live in the country and to have fifteen children' – that was what she wanted most. 'Of all the horrible indecent things for a young girl to say!' Lady Somers exclaimed when they went up to bed. 'What do you suppose they will think of the mother who has brought up such an indelicate daughter?'[6] Isabel cried herself to sleep. Yet everyone had laughed; she had thought herself such a success. And a success she must have been. Her letters are full of royalties and Lady Molesworth's ball tonight, Marlborough House next week, Lady

Westminster's on Monday, and Lady Wharncliffe's dinner tomorrow; while in the whole round of gaiety one name recurs again and again – that of Lord Lorne. Lord Lorne was clearly in love with her. One morning Lord Lorne called, and sat watching Mr Watts, who was painting Lady Isabel as he had painted her mother. Lady Isabel said she was tired, and asked to get down; but Mr Watts was obdurate; sit she must. At last, Lord Lorne, seeing no chance of a private talk, took his departure. Nothing had been said. Nothing now could be said. For almost directly, Queen Victoria sent for him, and informed him that she had 'arranged other plans for his happiness'.[7] It was a bitter blow to Lady Isabel, who refused a great many gentlemen for a great many reasons (one picked the turtle fat off her plate and ate it) before, in her second season, she agreed to marry Lord Henry Somerset. They were married in St George's, Hanover Square, and she carried a basket of snowdrops picked in his own garden by Lord Tennyson himself.[8]

Perhaps the most amusing pages in the book are three loose sheets written by the Duchess of Beaufort, Lord Henry's mother, to one of her sons.[9] The eighteenth century was still in full swing at Badminton. Anything might happen because nothing need be seen. When a gentleman fell drunk to the floor at dinner, sweeping the tablecloth and all the china with him, the Duchess never flickered an eyelid. When the Duke had his mistress's portrait sent down to Badminton, the Duchess observed that it was a fancy portrait, and proposed to hang it in the drawing room. Her family protesting, she hung it in the Duke's bedroom, remarking that it would 'be a pleasant surprise for him'. The only moral teaching Lady Henry received from her mother-in-law was to wear white kid gloves 'at all times in the house'.[10] Soon the famous catastrophe occurred, and Lady Henry was forced to take those proceedings against her husband which are still, Miss Fitzpatrick thinks, sending subterranean rumblings through the suburbs of Bournemouth. The gentleman who wrote charming drawing room songs was accused by his wife of a crime 'that was only mentioned in the Bible'.[11] For mentioning the sin, which some said she had invented, Lady Henry was cut by a large section of society. Mr Gladstone never invited her to his house again.[12] A man explained that his wife must cease to know her, not because she had been wrong, but because it was impossible for him to explain why she had been right. Thus, at twenty-seven Lady Henry saw herself 'stranded in a backwater'.[13] Although she met the man she wished to marry she refused to seek a divorce, retired to Eastnor Castle, and for the next seven years lived almost entirely alone. It was in these circumstances that she received her call to undertake that work among the inebriates for which she is chiefly known. But we have left ourselves no space to deal with these activities. Nor, indeed, do they occupy much in her biography. When you fit a woman into a shoe, any number of trifles – happiness, work, children – have to be left out.

1 – A review in the N&A, 17 November 1923, (Kp C240.1) of *Lady Henry Somerset* (Jonathan Cape, 1923) by Kathleen Fitzpatrick. Lady Henry Somerset, *née* Isabella Caroline Somers Cocks (1851–1921), a daughter of Virginia Pattle, and a first cousin of VW's mother. In 1872, she married Lord Henry Somerset (1849–1932), second son of the 8th Duke of Beaufort, comptroller of Queen Victoria's household, 1874–9, and MP for Monmouthshire, 1871–80, but discovering subsequently that he was homosexual, she renounced him publicly, and the couple were formally separated in 1878. She afterwards devoted her energies to the redemption of inebriate women, becoming in 1890 president of the British Women's Temperance Association.

The same issue of the N&A also contained LW's 'World of Books' column, on the Shrewsbury edition of Samuel Butler's works; and an article by Lytton Strachey, on 'Sir John Harrington'. See also *'Frances Willard', II VW Essays.*

2 – Fitzpatrick, ch. i, p. 11.

3 – For the culpability of the painter G. F. Watts (1817–1904), see below, and see, *ibid.*, ch. iv, p. 89.

4 – *Ibid.*, ch. iii, p. 73.

5 – Lady Isabel's sister: Lady Adeline (1852–1920), who married the 10th Duke of Bedford; J. S. Mill, *On Liberty* (1859); the American Civil War, 1861–5; Eastnor Castle in Herefordshire, home of the Somers family.

6 – Fitzpatrick, ch. iv, p. 83.

7 – *Ibid.*, p. 89; Queen Victoria (1819–1901).

8 – *Ibid.*, p. 92; Alfred, Lord Tennyson (1809–92).

9 – *Ibid.*, pp. 93–6.

10 – For the first quotation, *ibid.*, p. 99, and for the second, *ibid.*, p. 98.

11 – *Ibid.*, p. 106.

12 – *Ibid.*, p. 107: 'Some cut her because they knew only one side of the scandal, others cut her because there had been any scandal at all. She was never again invited to Mr Gladstone [1809–98]'s house. The Duchess of Bedford, her sister's mother-in-law, declined to meet her. Girls she had known were withdrawn from contact with her by their careful Mamas, and when they asked for an explanation they were told by these ignorant innocent women that "Isabel Somerset had invented a dreadful new sin".'

13 – *Ibid.*, p. 113.

Jane Austen at Sixty

VW's review in the *N&A*, 15 December 1923, (Kp C241) of *The Works of Jane Austen*. Ed. R. W. Chapman (5 vols. OUP, 1923), was later minimally revised and incorporated into 'Jane Austen', in *The Common Reader*; 1st series (1925). The reader is referred to *IV VW Essays*, where the later essay, together with variants in the form of footnotes, is printed in its place as part of *The Common Reader*.

1924

'The Poems, English and Latin, of Edward, Lord Herbert of Cherbury'

Lord Herbert of Cherbury is, of course, best known as the writer of the famous autobiography.[2] In the present volume Mr Moore Smith has collected his poetry, both English and Latin, which has hitherto appeared only in Professor Churton Collins's edition of 1881.[3] Professor Collins was remarkable for his zeal rather than for the accuracy of his scholarship, and there was room, therefore, for a new edition. The poems are now carefully edited, provided with notes and commentary, and produced with the invariable distinction of the Clarendon Press. As for their merits, Mr Moore Smith perhaps makes out a case for his view that they have been underestimated, but not many people will agree with him that 'in poetic feeling and art Edward Herbert soars above his brother George'.[4]

1 – A notice in the *N&A*, 19 January 1924, (Kp C242.1) of *The Poems, English and Latin of Edward, Lord Herbert of Cherbury* [1583–1648]. Edited by G. C. Moore Smith (OUP, 1923).

2 – Lord Herbert's *Autobiography* was first published by Horace Walpole in 1764; a further edition by Sir Sidney Lee appeared in 1886.

3 – J. Churton Collins, ed. *The Poems of Lord Herbert of Cherbury* (1881).

4 – Moore Smith, intro., p. xvii; among those cited as underestimating Edward, Lord Herbert's poetry is the reviewer's father, *ibid.*, p. xvi: 'But to Leslie Stephen [*National Review*, vol. xxxv, p. 671] again Herbert was a "third-rate poet" ...'; George Herbert (1593–1633).

Montaigne

VW's review in the *TLS*, 31 January 1924, (Kp C243) of the *Essays of Montaigne* trans. Charles Cotton, ed. William Carew Hazlitt (5 vols, Navarre Society, 1923) was later minimally revised for inclusion, under the same title, in *The Common Reader*: 1st series (1925). The reader is referred to *IV VW Essays*, where the revised version, together with variants in the form of footnotes, is printed in its place in *The Common Reader*.

The Lives of the Obscure

VW's essay in the *London Mercury*, January 1924, (Kp C244) was later revised for inclusion, under the title 'Taylors and Edgeworths', in *The Common Reader*: 1st series (1925). The reader is referred to *IV VW Essays*, where the revised version, together with variants in the form of footnotes, is printed in its place in *The Common Reader*.

'Glimpses of Authors'

Miss Ticknor's grandfather, the well-known Boston publisher, left her a legacy of many literary friends, and the entrée of many interesting houses. Some of the famous men had, provokingly enough, died before she met them; but she saw all the Dickens relics, and went to Earl's Court with his family. For obvious reasons, she never knew the great Coleridge, but she met Mr Ernest Coleridge under the clock in the British Museum. With Lady Ritchie she lunched, and she had tea with the grand-niece of Jane Austen.[2] Experienced readers of memoirs will be able to forestall the amiable and appreciative comments which these entertainments draw forth. Of first-hand information there is not much; but Dickens, it appears, used blue ink because blue ink dries instantly and he had an antipathy to blotting-paper. He also disliked pencils. Again, Jane Austen had a ring, which Miss Ticknor has seen, made of a single large turquoise, in a simple gold setting. In short, there is nothing scandalous, vulgar, or exciting in this kindly book.

1 – A notice in the *N&A*, 9 February 1924, (Kp C244.1) of *Glimpses of Authors* (Werner Laurie, 1924) by Caroline Ticknor, granddaughter of William Davis Ticknor (1810–64), ultimately of the publishing partnership Ticknor & Fields. See also 'Poe's Helen', *II VW Essays*.
2 – The references are to Ticknor, ch. i, 'Dickens [1812–70] in Boston', pp. 1–15; ch. xxiii, 'Memories of the Coleridge Family', pp. 293–303; ch. xxv 'Anne Thackeray Ritchie [1837–1919]', pp. 310–21; and ch. xxiv, 'Jane Austen [1775–1817]'s Grand Niece [identified as Mr Austen-Leigh's aunt]', pp. 304–9.

'Unpublished Letters of Matthew Arnold'

Even in these few letters Matthew Arnold stands out like a bust of the best Greek period, restrained, clear cut, aristocratic. It is both a relief and a surprise to come upon somebody who believed in the sovereignty of the intellect, was not afraid to quote Aristotle in his private letters,[2] and remained aloof from the squabbles and scandals of his contemporaries. One or two remarks upon his own poetry are of considerable interest. Writing about 1849, after *The Strayed Reveller* had appeared, he says: 'But as I feel rather as a reformer in poetical matters, I am glad of this opposition. If I have health and opportunity to go on, I will shake the present methods until they go down, see if I don't. More and more I feel bent against the modern English habit (too much encouraged by Wordsworth) of using poetry as a channel for thinking aloud, instead of making anything.'[3] He travels in France, and reflects: 'This is the worst of aristocracies, with all their merits – they are inaccessible to ideas . . . But our people's strong point is not intellectual *coup d'œil* any more than our aristocracy's, and this is our worst chance.'[4] In short, Matthew Arnold is Matthew Arnold, and that, we cannot help thinking, was a very good thing to be.

1 – A notice in the *N&A*, 16 February 1924, (Kp C244.2) of *Unpublished Letters of Matthew Arnold* [1822–88]. Edited by Arnold Whitridge (Yale University Press, 1923).
2 – E.g., Arnold, to Mrs Forster, concerning his poem 'Merope', 1858, p. 41.
3 – *Ibid.*, to the same, undated – probably 1849, the year of the publication of *The*

Strayed Reveller. Frazer's Magazine, May 1849, complained that the subjects treated in this volume were uninteresting, pp. 15–17.

4–*Ibid.*, to the same, Hotel [sic] du Luxembourg, Nismes [sic], 22 May 1859, p. 48.

'Arthur Yates: an Autobiography'

'... his two pet aversions were Bolshevism and motor-traffic',[2] writes Mr Blunt, in his introduction to Mr Yates's autobiography. Arthur Yates rode a race with a broken collar-bone, trained Cloister, never betted, roared with laughter when his stable-boys took a toss, dosed them liberally with brandy, bred outlandish beasts in his grounds; and could never help tipping a man down on his luck. The portrait, which is on familiar lines, is very simply drawn, but then Mr Yates was not a very complicated person.

1–A notice in the *N&A*, 16 February 1924, (Kp C244.3) of *Arthur Yates* [d. 1922] *Trainer and Gentleman Rider. An Autobiography.* Written in collaboration with Bruce Blunt (Grant Richards, 1924). Yates's steeplechaser Cloister won the 1893 Grand National.

2–Yates, intro., p. 29.

'Letters and Journals of Anne Chalmers'

The greater part of this book consists of the journal of a tour through England which Anne Chalmers took with her father, the great Dr Chalmers, and her mother in the summer of 1830. She was a sprightly girl, and her observations are full of fun. Now she is tickled to death by the conversation of Mr Bennett, who has circumnavigated the globe and will repeat what the Sandwich Islanders said to him.[2] Next she visits Coleridge and tries, unsuccessfully, to report what he said 'about the fugacious nature of consciousness and the extraordinary nature of man'.[3] Then she descends into a coal-pit; then she listens to a debate in the House of Commons; and then, quite unexpectedly, Mrs James[4] gives her Lord Byron's works – all of which events, miraculous to state, take place on a Tuesday! Eventually she married Mr Hanna. But her freedom of spirit seems to have survived, and the book, for those who like such old wives' tales, is full of amusement.

1—A notice in the N&A, 23 February 1924, (Kp C244.4) of *Letters and Journals of Anne Chalmers*. Edited by Her Daughter (Chelsea Publishing Co., 1922). Anne Chalmers (1813–91), eldest daughter of Rev. Dr Thomas Chalmers, sometime professor of Moral Philosophy at St Andrew's and professor of Divinity at Edinburgh University, and his wife Grace, *née* Pratt; she married in 1836 Rev. William Hanna.
2—Chalmers, 'The Journal of 1830', p. 118; the circumnavigator was a George Bennet.
3—*Ibid.*, p. 120.
4—Unidentified.

The Enchanted Organ

The enormous respectability of Bloomsbury was broken one fine morning about 1840 by the sound of an organ and by the sight of a little girl who had escaped from her nurse and was dancing to the music.[2] The child was Thackeray's elder daughter, Anne. For the rest of her long life, through war and peace, calamity and prosperity, Miss Thackeray, or Mrs Richmond Ritchie, or Lady Ritchie, was always escaping from the Victorian gloom and dancing to the strains of her own enchanted organ. The music, at once so queer and so sweet, so merry and so plaintive, so dignified and so fantastical, is to be heard very distinctly on every page of the present volume.

For Lady Ritchie was incapable at any stage of her career of striking an attitude or hiding a feeling. The guns are firing from Cremorne for the taking of Sebastopol, and there she sits scribbling brilliant nonsense in her diary about 'matches and fairy tales'. 'Brother Tomkins at the Oratory is starving and thrashing himself because he thinks it is right,' and Miss Thackeray is reading novels on Sunday morning 'because I do not think it is wrong'.[3] As for religion and her grandmother's miseries and the clergyman's exhortations to follow 'the one true way', all she knows is that it is her business to love her father and grandmother, and for the rest she supposes characteristically 'that everybody is right and nobody knows anything'.[4]

Seen through this temperament, at once so buoyant and so keen, the gloom of that famous age dissolves in an iridescent mist which lifts entirely to display radiant prospects of glittering spring, or clings to the monstrous shoulders of its prophets in many-tinted shreds. There are Mr FitzGerald and Mr Spedding coming to dinner 'as kind and queer and melancholy as men could be';[5] and Mrs Norton 'looking like a beautiful slow sphinx';[6] and Arthur Prinsep riding in Rotten Row with violets in his buttonhole – '"I like your violets very much", said I, and of course they were instantly presented to me'[7] – and Carlyle vociferating that a cheesemite might as well understand a cow as we human mites our maker's secrets;[8] and George Eliot, with her steady little eyes, enunciating a prodigious sentence about building one's cottage in a valley, and the power of influence, and respecting one's work, which breaks off in the middle;[9] and Herbert Spencer stopping a Beethoven sonata with 'Thank you, I'm getting flushed';[10] and Ruskin asserting that 'if you can draw a strawberry you can draw anything';[11] and Mrs Cameron paddling about in cold water till two in the morning;[12] and Jowett's four young men looking at photographs and sipping tumblers of brandy and water until at last 'poor Miss Stephen', who has been transplanted to an island where 'everybody is either a genius, or a poet, or a painter, or peculiar in some way', ejaculates in despair, 'Is there *nobody* commonplace?'[13]

'Poor Miss Stephen', bored and bewildered, staying with several cousins at the hotel, represented presumably the Puritanical conscience of the nineteenth century when confronted by a group of people who were obviously happy but not obviously bad. On the next page, however, Miss Stephen is significantly 'strolling about in the moonlight';[14] on the next she has deserted her cousins, left the hotel, and is staying with the Thackerays in the centre of infection. The most ingrained Philistine could not remain bored, though bewildered she might be, by Miss Thackeray's charm. For it was a charm extremely difficult to analyse. She said things that no human being could possibly mean; yet she meant them. She lost trains, mixed names, confused numbers, driving up to Down, for example, precisely a week before she was expected, and making Charles Darwin laugh – 'I can't for the life of me help laughing,' he apologised.[15] But then if she had gone on the right day, poor Mr Darwin would have been dying. So with her writing, too. Her novel *Angelica* 'went off suddenly to Australia with her feet foremost, and the proofs all wrong and the end first!!!'[16] But somehow nobody in Australia found out. Fortune rewarded the generous trust she put in it. But if her random ways were charming, who, on the other hand, could be more practical or see things when she liked more precisely as they were? Old Carlyle was a god on one side of his face, but a 'cross-grained, ungrateful, self-absorbed old nutcracker'[17] on the other. Her most typical, and, indeed, inimitable sentences rope together a handful of swiftly gathered opposites. To embrace oddities and produce a charming, laughing harmony from incongruities was her genius in life and in letters. 'I have just ordered,' she writes, 'two shillings' worth of poetry for ⟨my fisherman⟩ ... We take little walks together, and he carries his shrimps and talks quite enchantingly.'[18] She pays the old dropsical woman's fare in the omnibus, and in return the 'nice jolly nun hung with crucifixes'[19] escorts her across the road. Nun and fisherman and dropsical old woman had never till that moment, one feels sure, realised their own charm or the gaiety of existence. She was a mistress of phrases which exalt and define and set people in the midst of a comedy. With Nature, too, her gift was equally happy. She would glance out of the window of a Brighton lodging-house and say: 'The sky was like a divine parrot's breast, just now, with a deep, deep, flapping sea.'[20] As life drew on, with its deaths and its wars, her profound instinct for happiness had to exert itself to gild those grim faces golden, but it succeeded. Even Lord Kitchener and Lord Roberts and the South African War[21] shine transmuted. As for the homelier objects which she preferred, the birds and the downs and the old charwoman 'who has been an old angel, without wings, alas! and only a bad leg', and the smut-black chimney-sweeps, who were 'probably gods in disguise',[22] they never cease to the very end to glow and twinkle with merriment in her pages. For she was no visionary. Her happiness was a domestic flame, tried by many sorrows. And the music to which she dances, frail and fantastic, but true and distinct, will sound on outside our formidable residences when all the brass bands of literature have (let us hope) blared themselves to perdition.

1–A review in the N&A, 15 March 1924, (Kp C245) reprinted in the NR, 6 August 1924, of Letters of Anne Thackeray Ritchie [1837–1919]. With forty-two additional letters from her father William Makepeace Thackeray [1811–63]. Selected and edited by her daughter Hester Ritchie. With illustrations (John Murray, 1924).

The same issue of the N&A also contained LW's 'World of Books' column, on spring books; and articles by Clive Bell, on Harold Nicolson's Byron: the Last Journey; and J. M. Keynes, on 'The Franc'. See also 'Lady Ritchie' above, where there is a full biographical note, and 'Blackstick Papers', I VW Essays. Reprinted: Mom., CE.

2–See Ritchie, ch. i, pp. 1–2: 'Another impression remains to me of some place near

Russell Square, of a fine morning, of music sounding, of escaping from my nurse and finding myself dancing in the street to the organ with some other children.'

3 – For the first quotation, *ibid.*, Journal, 14 August 1855, p. 71; in the Crimean War, Sebastopol was finally stormed by the French and the Russians were forced to abandon it in September 1855; for the second and third quotations, *ibid.*, July–August, 1857, p. 107: 'I say to myself I cannot understand religion therefore I leave it alone and read novels on a Sunday because I do not think it wrong, while Brother Tompkins [sic] at the Oratory is starving and thrashing himself because he thinks it right.'

4 – For both quotations, *ibid.*, to W. M. Thackeray in America, Paris, 1852, p. 46, which has: 'and so I suppose everybody is right'. Miss Ritchie's grandmother: Anne Carmichael-Smyth, *née* Becher (d. 1864), widow of Richmond Thackeray (d. 1816).

5 – *Ibid.*, Journal, March–September, 1854, p. 64. Edward Fitzgerald (1809–83), author of *The Rubáiyát of Omar Khayyám* (1859); James Spedding (1808–81), Bacon scholar.

6 – *Ibid.*, Mrs [Emily, Lady] Tennyson, 1870: 'Last night I dined out and met De Lesseps, who said that Sarah Bernhardt first suggested the Suez Canal to him and that they can trace the March of the Egyptians, and that the Israelites crossed close by their present works. Lord Broughton and Mrs Norton were also there. She looked like a beautiful slow sphinx.' Caroline Elizabeth Sarah Norton, *née* Sheridan (1808–77), poet, wife of the Hon. George Chapple Norton.

7 – *Ibid.*, Journal, 3 March 1859, p. 109; Arthur Haldimand Prinsep, son of the Indian civil servant Henry Thoby Prinsep and Sarah Pattle; he became a major-general in the Bengal cavalry.

8 – *Ibid.*, 28 November 1873, p. 152: 'To see Mr Carlyle who said "A cheese-mite might as well attempt to understand a cow and the great universe of grass beyond it, as we human mites might expect to understand our making and our Maker's secrets."'

9 – *Ibid.*, to Richmond Ritchie, 1873: 'She said it was much better in life to face the very worst, and build one's cottage in a valley so as not to fall away, and that the very worst was this, that people are living with a power of work and of help in them, which they scarcely estimate. That we know by ourselves how very much other people influence our happiness and feelings, and that we ought to remember that we have the same effect upon them. That we can remember in our own lives how different they might have been if others, even good people, had only conducted themselves differently. ¶ This part I'm glad to say I couldn't follow, nor could I remember at the moment a single instance of any single person's misconduct. She said too we ought to be satisfied with immediate consequences, and respect our work ...' George Eliot (1819–80).

10 – *Ibid.*, to Richmond Ritchie, 10 January 1899, p. 248: 'two rather amusing things happened. One was I took Pinkie to call on Herbert Spencer. He was much pleased that she should play to him, but said the worst of Beethoven was he never knew when to leave off. The second movement of the sonata he stopped. "Thank you, I'm getting flushed, that will be quite enough. Thank you."'

11 – *Ibid.*, to George M. Smith, July 1876, p. 176.

12 – *Ibid.*, to the same, Freshwater, Easter, 1865, p. 128; Julia Margaret Cameron (1815–79), VW's great-aunt.

13–*Ibid.*, to Walter Senior, Freshwater, Easter, 1865, p. 126; Benjamin Jowett (1817–93), Master of Balliol College, Oxford; Caroline Emelia Stephen (1834–1909), VW's aunt.

14–*Ibid.*, p. 127.

15–*Ibid.*, Journal, 1882, p. 183; Charles Darwin (1809–82).

16–*Ibid.*, to Mrs Douglas Freshfield, Paris, 1875, p. 166, which has: '*first!!!*'. The novel was *Miss Angel* (1875).

17–*Ibid.*, to Reginald J. Smith, 25 July 1902, p. 260.

18–*Ibid.*, to Gerald Ritchie in India, Aldeburgh, 1887, p. 204.

19–*Ibid.*, 'Notes of Happy Things', p. 265, adapted.

20–*Ibid.*, to Richmond Ritchie, 10 January 1899, p. 249, which has no commas, and: 'flapping sort of sea'.

21–*Ibid.*, to Mrs Gerald Ritchie in India, Florence, 1900, pp. 254–5: 'Last night I lay thinking about our noble Dandies and "Cooks' Sons", and of that wise old man Lord Roberts forgetting his own overwhelming grief [at the death in action of his son Lt Frederick Roberts in 1899], to plan victory and moderation and success for his country. And then I thought of overriding, conquering Kitchener working with him so loyally, and the people waiting so courageously and patiently, and Zebul coming at last. I do thank God that life is not only bad and hard, but strong and kind and enduring.' Frederick Sleigh Roberts, 1st Earl Roberts of Kandahar (1832–1914) was Supreme Commander in South Africa and Horatio Herbert Kitchener, 1st Earl Kitchener (1851–1916), his Chief of Staff, during the South African or Boer War, 1899–1902.

22–For the first quotation, *ibid.*, to Lady Robert Cecil, 1 October 1908, p. 276; and for the second, *ibid.*, to Richmond Ritchie, March 1899, p. 252.

I was given the opportunity ...

I was given the opportunity to see a demonstration of a new colour film process by Mr Friese-Greene. The inventor's results probably compare favourably with other colour films, but they are very uneven in merit. The quiet-coloured scenes of English country are much the most successful; anything like a bright colour tends immediately to produce an oleographic effect. That is, of course, not peculiar to Mr Friese-Greene's process. It almost looks as if nature's brighter colours which harmonise pleasingly when seen in three dimensions acquire an unpleasantly garish quality when represented in two.

1–A paragraph in the 'From Alpha to Omega' column in the *N&A*, 5 April 1924, (Kp C245.1). The demonstration took place at the Holborn Empire on the afternoon of Tuesday, 25 March 1924, when Spectrum Films Ltd presented three colour films: *Moonbeam Magic*, *A Quest of Colour* and *The Dance of the Moods*, produced by a process invented by Claude Friese-Greene. According to *The Times* of 26 March, *A Quest of Colour* consisted of views of beauty spots and a series of famous English towns and castles, the 'most striking' of which were scenes of Aldershot with 'various regiments in full ceremonial uniform ... both standing still and on the march'. *The Dance of the Moods* showed 'a number of dancers from the Margaret Morris School of Dancing'.

The Patron and the Crocus

VW's essay in the *N&A*, 12 April 1924, (Kp C246) was later minimally revised for inclusion, under the same title, in *The Common Reader*: 1st series (1925). The reader is referred to *IV VW Essays*, where the revised version, together with variants in the form of footnotes, is reprinted in its place as part of *The Common Reader*.

Aesthetically speaking, the new aquarium . . .

Aesthetically speaking, the new aquarium is undoubtedly the most impressive of all the houses at the zoo. Red fish, blue fish, nightmare fish, dapper fish, fish lean as gimlets, fish round and white as soup plates, ceaselessly gyrate in oblong frames of greenish light in the hushed and darkened apartment hollowed out beneath the Mappin terraces. Scientifically, no doubt, the place is a paradise for the ichthyologist; but the poet might equally celebrate the strange beauty of the broad-leaved water plants trembling in the current, or the sinister procession of self-centred sea-beasts forever circling and seeking perhaps some minute prey, perhaps some explanation of a universe which evidently appears to them of inscrutable mystery. Now they knock the glass with their noses; now shoot dartlike to the surface; now eddy slowly and contemplatively down to the sandy bottom. Some are delicately fringed with a fin that vibrates like an electric fan and propels them on; others wear a mail boldly splashed with a design by a Japanese artist. That crude human egotism which supposes that Nature has wrought her best for those who walk the earth is rebuked at the aquarium. Nature seems to have cared more to tint and adorn the fishes who live unseen at the depths of the sea than to ornament our old, familiar friends, the goat, the hog, the sparrow, and the horse.

1–A paragraph in the 'From Alpha to Omega' column in the N&A, 19 April 1924, (Kp C246.1) on the new aquarium at the London Zoological Gardens, opened to the public on Monday, 7 April 1924.

'Anatole France, the Man and His Work'

It is no easy matter to write a great man's life and criticise his work when in the first place he is alive, and in the second you are his friend. Mr May's book, pleasantly and simply written as it is, shows signs of the inevitable constraint. To go deep would be to risk too many embroilments. He give us an outline of the life, and adds, rather gingerly, a discussion of the books. Both need a good deal of amplification at the reader's hands. But it is convenient to have the biographical facts so conveniently together, and, when it comes to criticism, Mr May provides material for argument. Several interesting and intimate photographs add to the book's charm.

1–A notice in the N&A, 3 May 1924, (Kp C246.11) of Anatole France [1844–1924], The Man and His Work (John Lane, 1924) by James Lewis May.

The Private View of the Royal Academy . . .

The Private View of the Royal Academy is not an occasion for passing aesthetic judgements. One thousand five hundred and sixty-three works of art are, it is true, exhibited, but on Friday the second these were sliced into innumerable segments by the moving bodies of perhaps twice that number of well-dressed and distinguished human beings. The mind was perpetually jerked from art to life, and from life back again to the hollyhock, the polar bear, and the death-bed. There is, of course, less division between art and life at Burlington House than elsewhere. H.M. the King, Lord Milner, and the Princess Bibesco, as depicted by Mr Sims, Sir William Orpen, and Mr John, inevitably recall the glories of our blood and State rather than suggest reflections upon form in the abstract.[2] At the Private View one tends to glance at the pictures as one turns the pages of an amplified and highly coloured illustrated newspaper devoted to the celebration of the British Empire in the persons of its generals, admirals, doctors, illustrious dead, inimitable fox-hounds, noblemen in orders, duchesses in jewels, and English squires upon English hacks. As a compliment to ourselves it is magnificent. As a contribution to art it requires a more serious and detailed examination than the private viewer can give.

1 – A paragraph in the 'From Alpha to Omega' column of the N&A, 10 May 1924, (Kp C246.2) on the private view on 2 May of the hundred and fifty seventh Royal Academy Exhibition, which was opened to the public on 5 May. See also 'The Royal Academy' above.
2 – Oil paintings: no. 132, Charles Sims RA (1873–1928), 'H.M. The King'; no. 110, Sir William Orpen RA (1878–1931), 'The Viscount Milner, KG, GCB, GCMG'; and no. 27, Augustus John RA (1878–1961), 'Princess Antoine Bibesco'.

Mr Benson's Memories

In order to appreciate Mr Benson's memories fully one should have been educated at Eton and Cambridge. One should have a settled income. One should have an armchair. One should have dined well. In this mood, and in these circumstances nothing can be pleasanter than to hear old stories of old dons; how Austen Leigh, for instance, once spat out a glass of wine at a railway station, which reminds us how very queer his pronunciation was; and so dallying to reminisce by the way, we reach the O. B., of course, and Stuart Donaldson, and divagate to the Cornishes, about whom we have our own favourite story to tell; praise Lady Ponsonby, most vigorous of old ladies; imitate Henry James; recollect Howard Sturgis; and wind up, when we are pleasantly kindled into mild self-approbation by the excellence of our friends, with a few speculations about Rupert Brooke.[2]

What would Rupert Brooke have become if he had lived? But it is significant of Mr Benson's methods and tastes that Rupert Brooke shoulders his way out of the golden circle in which the rest of his figures move. Mr Benson is mildly caustic about his poetry: 'some of the poems are undeniably ugly ... some of the love poems are even over-voluptuous'. Worst still, 'his feet and hands were somewhat large, and set stiffly on their joints; the latter had no expressiveness or grace, and his feet were roughly proportioned and homely'.[3] Mr Benson is far more at his ease in the society of people whose feet are shapely and diminutive, who exist rather than act, who, to quote his own phrase, 'give to the artistic and beautiful handling of life and its occasions the energy, the richness of perception, and the settled purpose that more directly practical natures reserve for their professional activities'.[4]

The scene that Mr Benson prefers is a large rambling house, filled with 'kindly unemphatic people',[5] whose whims and oddities are not pronounced enough to startle, but offer the appreciative observer hours and hours of delightful entertainment. Over it all he pours and pours endless words. The house is described; the servants are described; the dogs and the carriage horses are described; kindly glances, grave and tender tones are recalled; characters are skilfully and courteously adumbrated. Mr Benson is never incisive; the dinner table, or the tea table, or the high table, is always between him and his host to prevent intimacy. But in no other atmosphere could these well-bred, melancholy, distinguished Victorians appear so much at home. As we follow Mr Benson through this long, loitering journey among pleasant places and charming people, we are irresistibly reminded of another of his stories in another of his books – of an old dog of the Bensons which used to roam the fields open-mouthed, and once a woodcock flew in, and he put the bird gently and apologetically out unhurt. So Mr Benson has wandered, and the woodcocks have flown in, and he has put them out unhurt, as befits the son of an archbishop, who was educated at Eton, and lives at Cambridge.

1 – A review in the NA, 10 May 1924, (Kp C246.3) of Memories and Friends (John Murray, 1924) by A.C. [Arthur Christopher] Benson (1862–1925), man of letters, Master of Magdalene College, Cambridge, 1915–25. Educated at Eton College, where he also taught, 1885–1903, and at King's College, Cambridge, Benson had sufficient private means to accept an unpaid fellowship at Magdalene, to which he was elected in 1904. He was a son of Edward White Benson, archbishop of Canterbury, 1884–96, and Mary Sidgwick. See Editorial Note, p. xxv. Reading Notes (Berg, xix).
2 – Benson, 'Edward Compton Austen-Leigh [master at Eton, 1887–1905]', pp. 147–66; 'Oscar Browning [1837–1923, master at Eton, 1860–74; fellow of King's College, Cambridge]', pp. 128–46; 'Stuart Alexander Donaldson [d. 1915, sometime master at Eton; Master of Magdalene College, Cambridge, Vice-Chancellor, Cambridge University, 1912–13]', pp. 222–49; 'Blanche Warre-Cornish [née Ritchie, mother of Molly MacCarthy]', pp. 167–91; 'Lady Ponsonby [Emily Charlotte Mary, 1817–77, novelist]', pp. 54–71; 'Henry James [1843–1916]', pp. 192–204; 'Howard Sturgis [1855–1920, author of Tim (1891) and Belchamber (1904)]', pp. 265–96; 'Rupert Brooke [1887–1915]', pp. 323–33.

3 – For the first quotation, *ibid.*, ch. xviii, 'Rupert Brooke', p. 332, and for the second, *ibid.*, p. 327.
4 – *Ibid.*, Pref., p. vii, and ch. x, 'Blanche Warre-Cornish', p. 167.
5 – *Ibid.*, ch. i, 'Thomas Hare', p. 11, which has 'kindly, unemphatic'.

'Marie Elizabeth Towneley'

Sister Marie des Anges, in secular life Mary Towneley, was descended from the two ancient and wealthy families of Towneley and Tichborne. The lay reader will probably find the chief interest of this handsome and copiously illustrated biography in the psychological drama of a woman who had great possessions. She was a handsome girl, a keen rider to hounds, whose family legitimately expected her to live a brilliant life in their own brilliant world. Without a trace of the ascetic – for she was benevolent and warm-hearted and a trifle impatient – she left them to lead the life of a religious sister at Namur. There she never had a room to herself or enjoyed the luxury of blind or curtain. She cleaned the knife-machine and made the beds. Of her famous friends she never spoke, and only revealed her passion for riding by an occasional kindness to a horse. The vast wealth which she inherited on her brother's death she lavished upon buying houses and endowing schools for the benefit of the English province. The story is told simply, if with too much insistence upon coats and arms and noble pedigrees.

1 – A notice in the *N&A*, 7 June 1924, (Kp C246.31) of *Mary Elizabeth Towneley* [1846–1922] *(In religion Sister Marie des Saints Anges) Provincial of the English Province of The Sisters of Notre Dame of Namur. A Memoir.* With a Preface by His Lordship the Bishop of Southwark (Burns Oates & Washbourne Ltd., 1924).

'Unwritten History'

To sum up this stout, much illustrated volume in one word, it is the kind of book that the late King Edward[2] would have enjoyed in his bath. That was the feat which the *World* under Mr Hamilton's editorship satisfactorily accomplished. His book scores the same kind of success. It is dashing, splashing, spirited, a little broad in its humour, very cosmopolitan in its tone, and never for an instant stodgy, solemn, or highbrow. He has done everything that it is possible to do with a pen, and most things that can be done with a knife and fork. The story of his life, which is still in mid-career, reads like a gramophone record of good club talk. The talker has dined well, is in high feather, and reels off story after story. Some perhaps we have heard before. But it is worth letting the whole book run through one's fingers if only for the sake of one or two undoubted pearls. And the sands flow fast.

1–A notice in the N&A, 21 June 1924, (Kp C246.4) of *Unwritten History*. With sixteen illustrations (Hutchinson & Co., 1924) by Cosmo Hamilton (1879–1942), dramatist, novelist and sometime editor of the *World. A journal for men and women*, which ceased publication in 1922. See Editorial Note, p. xxv.
2–Edward VII (1841–1910).

'The Life and Last Words of Wilfrid Ewart'

The war has made us familiar with the type of book of which Mr Graham's is a good example. A young man impresses his friends with his powers, writes one novel of great promise, and is killed at the age of thirty. The friends then attempt to record what he was to them, and to adumbrate what he might have been to the world. Those who did not know him follow with sympathy, but necessarily with some bewilderment. Mr Ewart was a brilliant journalist; it is obvious from the quotations here made. He was also one of those reserved and fastidious characters who take long to mature. The book is mainly a record of experiments in the art of growing up. At the end, we do not feel that we know what he would have become, if the stray bullet wandering about Mexico that night had missed him. But it is a vivid record of possibilities, and, as usual, Mr Graham writes with an eager and transparent sentimentality which is very readable.

1–A notice in the N&A, 21 June 1924, (Kp C246.5) of *The Life and Last Words of Wilfrid Ewart* (G. P. Putnam's Sons, 1924) by Stephen Graham.
Wilfrid Herbert Gore Ewart (1892–1922) served through the war as a Captain in the Scots Guards; his works include *Practical Poultry-Keeping for Small-Holders* (1915) with James S. Hicks, *A Journey in Ireland* (1921), *Way of Revelation* (1921), and the posthumously published *When Armageddon Came. Studies in peace and war* (1933) and *Scots Guards* (1934). See Editorial Note, p. xxv.

'Robert Smith Surtees'

Very little excuse surely is needed for this life, which is largely an autobiography, of Surtees the famous sporting novelist. Characteristically, for Surtees was pleased to be a landowner and a magistrate with a 'taste for scribbling'[2] as he put it, his fragment of autobiography was mixed with notes taken on the bench, and thus escaped notice until Mr Cuming went into his papers. The fragments, incomplete as they are, are all to the good. They tell us how he came to London in 1825; how he hunted in Sussex and France; how he pretended to practise as a solicitor, 'but did not allow legal pursuits to interfere with his enjoyment of life';[3] how to beguile the dead winter of 1829, he began to write a semi-sporting novel, which was laughed at by his friends; how he got the *New Sporting Magazine* to accept him; how he created Jorrocks; inherited Hamsterley Hall, hunted the county at his own expense, stood for Parliament and failed; hated railways, and was in every way the model of that peculiarly British breed, the well-bred, well-read country gentleman, who by some freak of nature conceals a vein of genius in the seams of his mind. Since the words and doings of Jorrocks are still current coin, genius is not too strong a word to use of his creator, of whom we are glad to know what little we can.

1–A notice in the *N&A*, 21 June 1924, (Kp C246.6) of *Robert Smith Surtees (Creator of 'Jorrocks'), 1803–1864* by Himself and E. D. Cuming (Blackwood, 1924). See also 'Jack Mytton', *V VW Essays* and *CR 2*. See Editorial Note, p. xxv. Reading Notes (Berg, xix).
2–Surtees, 'Surtees Manuscripts', vi, p. 60, also, ch. iii, p. 154.
3–*Ibid.*, ch. i, p. 132, which has: '... we glean enough from his own writings and papers to assure us that he did not suffer legal pursuits to interfere seriously with his enjoyment of life'.

Thunder at Wembley

It is nature that is the ruin of Wembley; yet it is difficult to see what steps Lord Stevenson, Lieutenant-General Sir Travers Clarke, and the Duke of Devonshire could have taken to keep her out.[2] They might have eradicated the grass and felled the chestnut trees; even so the thrushes would have got in, and there would always have been the sky. At Earls Court and the White City, so far as memory serves, there was little trouble from this source. The area was too small; the light was too brilliant. If a single real moth strayed in to dally with the arc lamps, he was at once transformed into a dizzy reveller; if a laburnum tree shook her tassels, spangles of limelight floated in the violet and crimson air. Everything was intoxicated and transformed. But at Wembley nothing is changed and nobody is drunk. They say, indeed, that there is a restaurant where each diner is forced to spend a guinea upon his dinner. What vistas of cold ham that statement calls forth! What pyramids of rolls! What gallons of tea and coffee! For it is unthinkable that there should be champagne, plovers' eggs, or peaches at Wembley. And for six and eightpence two people can buy as much ham and bread as they need. Six and eightpence is not a large sum; but neither is it a small sum. It is a moderate sum, a mediocre sum. It is the prevailing sum at Wembley. You look through an open door at a regiment of motor-cars aligned in avenues. They are not opulent and powerful; they are not flimsy and cheap. Six and eightpence seems to be the price of each of them. It is the same with the machines for crushing gravel. One can imagine better; one can imagine worse. The machine before us is a serviceable type and costs, inevitably, six and eightpence. Dress fabrics, rope, table linen, old masters, sugar, wheat, filigree silver, pepper, birds' nests (edible, and exported to Hong Kong), camphor, bees-wax, rattans, and the rest – why trouble to ask the price? One knows beforehand – six and eightpence. As for the buildings themselves, those vast, smooth, grey palaces, no vulgar riot of ideas tumbled expensively in their architect's head; equally, cheapness was abhorrent to him, and vulgarity anathema. Per perch, rod, or square foot, however ferro-concrete palaces are sold, they too work at out six and eightpence.

But then, just as one is beginning a little wearily to fumble with those two fine words – democracy, mediocrity – Nature asserts herself where one would least look to find her – in clergymen, school children, girls, young men, invalids in bath-chairs. They pass quietly, silently, in coveys, in groups, sometimes alone. They mount the enormous staircases; they stand in queues to have their spectacles rectified gratis; to have their fountain-pens filled gratis; they gaze respectfully into sacks of grain; glance reverently at mowing machines from Canada; now and again stoop to remove some paper bag or banana skin and place it in the receptacles provided for that purpose at frequent intervals along the avenues. But what has happened to our contemporaries? Each is beautiful; each is stately. Can it be that one is seeing human beings for the first time? In streets they hurry; in houses they talk; they are bankers in banks, sell shoes in shops. Here against the enormous background of ferro-concrete Britain, of rosy Burma, at large, unoccupied, they reveal themselves simply as human beings, creatures of leisure, civilisation, and dignity; a little languid perhaps, a little attenuated, but a product to be proud of. Indeed they are the ruin of the Exhibition. The Duke of Devonshire and his colleagues should have kept them out.[3] As you watch them trailing and flowing, dreaming and speculating, admiring this coffee-grinder, that milk and cream separator, the rest of the show becomes insignificant. And what, one asks, is the spell it lays upon them? How, with all this dignity of their own, can they bring themselves to believe in that?

But this cynical reflection, at once so chill and so superior, was made, of course, by the thrush. Down in the Amusement Compound, by some grave oversight on the part of the Committee, several trees and rhododendron bushes have been allowed to remain; and these, as anybody could have foretold, attract the birds. As you wait your turn to be hoisted into mid-air, it is impossible not to hear the thrush singing. You look up and discover a whole chestnut tree with its blossoms standing; you look down and see ordinary grass scattered with petals, harbouring insects, sprinkled with stray wild flowers. The gramophone does its best; they light a horse-shoe of fairy-lamps above the Jack and Jill; a man bangs a bladder and implores you to come and tickle monkeys; boatloads of serious men are poised on the heights of the scenic railway; but all is vain. The cry of ecstasy that should have split the sky as the boat dropped to its doom patters from leaf to leaf, dies, falls flat, while the thrush proceeds with his statement. And then some woman in the row of red-brick villas outside the grounds comes out and wrings a dish-cloth in the backyard. All this the Duke of Devonshire should have prevented.

The problem of the sky, however, remains. Is it, one wonders, lying back limp but acquiescent in a green deckchair, part of the Exhibition? Is it lending itself with exquisite tact to show off to the best advantage snowy Palestine, ruddy Burma, sand-coloured Canada, and the minarets and pagodas of our possessions in the East? So quietly it suffers all these domes and palaces to melt into its breast; receives them with such sombre and tender discretion; so exquisitely allows the rear lamp of Jack and Jill and the Monkey-Teasers to bear themselves like stars. But even as we watch and admire what we would fain credit to the forethought of Lieutenant-General Sir Travers Clarke, a rushing sound is heard. Is it the wind, or is it the British Empire Exhibition? It is both. The wind is rising and shuffling along the avenues; the Massed Bands of Empire are assembling and marching to the Stadium. Men like pin-cushions, men like pouter pigeons, men like pillar-boxes, pass in procession. Dust swirls after them. Admirably impassive, the bands of Empire march on. Soon they will have entered the fortress; soon the gates will have clanged. But let them hasten! For either the sky has misread her directions, or some appalling catastrophe is impending. The sky is livid, lurid, sulphurine. It is in violent commotion. It is whirling water-spouts of cloud into the air; of dust in the Exhibition. Dust swirls down the avenues, hisses and hurries like erected cobras round the corners. Pagodas are dissolving in dust. Ferro-concrete is fallible. Colonies are perishing and dispersing in spray of inconceivable beauty and terror which some malignant power illuminates. Ash and violet are the colours of its decay. From every quarter human beings come flying – clergymen, school children, invalids in bath-chairs. They fly with outstretched arms, and a vast sound of wailing rolls before them, but there is neither confusion nor dismay. Humanity is rushing to destruction, but humanity is accepting its doom. Canada opens a frail tent of shelter. Clergymen and school children gain its portals. Out in the open under a cloud of electric silver the bands of Empire strike up. The bagpipes neigh. Clergy, school children, and invalids group themselves round the Prince of Wales in butter. Cracks like the white roots of trees spread themselves across the firmament. The Empire is perishing; the bands are playing; the Exhibition is in ruins. For that is what comes of letting in the sky.

1 – An essay in the *N&A*, 28 June 1924, (Kp C247) on the occasion of the British Empire Exhibition, April–October 1924 (extended into 1925), which the Woolfs visited on 29 May, and which *The Times*, 23 April, celebrated in a 'British Empire Section'. The same issue of the *N&A* contained LW's 'World of Books' column, on *A Book of Characters* compiled and translated by Richard Aldington. Reprinted: *CDB*. See Editorial Note, p. xxv.

2 – James Stevenson, Baron Stevenson of Holmbury, cr. Bart 1917 (1873–1926), adviser on commercial affairs to the Secretary of State for the Colonies and Chairman of the exhibition board; Lieutenant-General Sir Travers Clarke, the exhibition's chief administrative officer; Victor Christian William Cavendish, 9th Duke of Devonshire (1868–1938) was, as secretary of state for the colonies, 1922–5, and a former governor-general of Canada, 1916–22, deeply involved in the organisation of the exhibition, and its principal financial guarantor.

3 – For the Duke of Devonshire's view of the matter, see *The Times*, 6 June 1924: 'He considered all the present symptoms most promising ... An immense number of children were being imbued with something of the Imperial spirit. Greater than trade or commerce was the Imperial idea which underlay the whole Exhibition; and greater than trade ... must always be the principles of Liberty and Justice ...'

The Weekend

This is a very prettily printed little book, with a gay dust cover, and a dull binding, and a book marker with 'Have you forgotten the salt?' on one side, and 'Have you forgotten the corkscrew?' on the other, and good poems and bad poems and games and songs and recipes and quips and cranks and blank pages for more games and songs and quips and cranks – in short, the very book to hand to one's hostess in return for a candlestick on Saturday night with a blessing. Instead of reviewing the book, it may be more to the point to describe simply what fruit that blessing bore on Sunday.

The day was hot; breakfast late. Through the half-open door a woman's voice could be heard reciting:–

> I scarcely believe my love to be so pure
> As I had thought it was[2]

– an embarrassing statement (since the book was forgotten), and matters were scarcely mended by the horrid agony of being forced to guess, on entering the room, who wrote it. Happily there was present a retired governor of one of our eastern possessions, who, taking the volume from her hand as she read on, cried out that, whoever wrote it, Donne did not. There was, it seems, an iniquitous misprint on that page; and under cover of his fulminations eating became momentarily feasible. A sunburnt egg might be hooked into proximity with a spoon. But could one eat it? The indefatigable woman was off again reciting Shakespeare,[3] and the bold spirit has yet to be discovered who can crack an egg with intrepidity while Shakespeare is being read aloud. A tentative tapping came from some; others sat mute, bored, upright. However, the day was hot; the window open; the garden wide; escape possible. Roses, peonies, cauliflowers – we need not retail a list of garden produce at this season, nor make apology for that genial and pious spirit which, when the church bells ring to church, bids some of us resign ourselves to sleep. Only, the path was narrow; and people must walk up and down it two abreast. Even in the underworld of dreams it was impossible not to adumbrate some fantastic version of what the noise was all about. It was about poetry. First, that nobody could call that poetry; next, that everybody must admit this. Suddenly – and there the very dead must have wakened to see the wretched little book tossed and torn between a couple of infuriated readers – suddenly the word 'Emerson' rent the air. Emerson had been discovered among the laurels; couchant with Shelley and Keats; proclaimed by the anthologists the author of a 'great poem' – Emerson the American![4] Emerson the essayist! Worse was to come. A living rhymer, without even the varnish of death or antiquity to excuse the blasphemy, had intruded into the same holy spot. He too wrote 'great poems'. Since sleep was impossible, the morning might as well be wasted in argument; living against dead; classics against romantics; until the lunch bell rang, and dishevelled and bellicose the guests assembled to find their hostess, who had been to church, returned fresh for the pursuit. We were all to spend the afternoon, she said, playing games. *The Week-End Book*, of which she had regained possession, recommended Free Association Team Race, the Animal and the Stick Game, Famous People on Paper, Book Reviews,[5] and many others. Moreover, it provided recipes for sandwiches and cocktails. She proposed to take us all for a walk and to wind up, as the kind people suggested, with a little music.

As she ended, animation was to be observed in some quarters. Upon others the shades of night descended. One of those deep and for the most part hidden abysses between man and man had been uncovered. Tempers would soon be lost. Thunder was brewing; satire preparing. The beef was getting cold; the servant maid was jogging people's elbows, when the old gentleman, who had ruled the East and subdued, no doubt, countless mutinies and hordes of wild elephants, observed that in his experience the race is divided thus: there are the sociables and there are the solitaries. One party, he said, is every bit as good as the other. (Tension relaxed.) Indeed, he said, each is indispensable to the other. (Amenity was restored.) Here we have an instance, he continued, pointing to the book. (Plates circulated.) The sociables, for whom this facetious and altogether well-meaning little book was written, are admirable citizens, people of spirit, adventure, and good will. Let them take their book, sing their songs, play their games, mix their cocktails, admire their poems, in company. Meanwhile the solitaries, to whom he owned that he belonged, will do, he said (and seldom has human face looked so divine), precisely what they like. And what did we like, as we trooped after him out of doors? Everything in the whole world. Pigs and calves; cocks and hens; the smell of beans and the smell of straw; roses and tobacco; but not, we agreed, as we rambled off into the vast and glorious freedom of the universe, that book.

1–A review in the *TLS*, 3 July 1924, (Kp C248) of *The Week-End Book*. General editors: Vera Mendel, Francis Meynell; Music editor: John Goss (Nonesuch Press, 1924). See Editorial Note, p. xxv.

2–*Week-End Book*, 'Great Poems', John Donne, 'Love's Growth', p. 36, opening lines. Donne is also represented by: 'The Good-Morrow', p. 32; 'The Sun Rising', p. 33; 'Love's Deity', p. 34; 'The Dream', p. 35; 'The Ecstasy', pp. 36–8; 'Batter my heart, three personed god . . .', p. 39; and in the section 'Hate Poems' by 'The Curse', p. 130.

3–Shakespeare is represented by: 'Spring and Winter' ('When daisies pied and violets blue' and 'When icicles hang by the wall'), *ibid.*, pp. 28–9.

4–Ralph Waldo Emerson is represented by 'Days' ('Daughters of Time, the hypocritic Days'), *ibid.*, p. 69; Shelley by: 'Love's Philosophy' and 'To Night', p. 67; and in the section 'Hate Poems' by 'To Sidmouth and Castlereagh', pp. 118–19; Keats by 'Written in Fields' ('To one who has been long in city pent'), p. 68.

5–*Ibid.*, 'Play', pp. 234–5.

Stendhal

Stendhal's fame, since it depends upon a small but enthusiastic band whose attachment is not literary merely, but personal, will probably increase in England rather than lessen, and we do not doubt that this new and finely printed edition of his works will find room on many English shelves. In particular, we welcome the first volume of what the editors hope to make the definitive edition of the *Journal*. True, the first volume is no fair specimen of the rest. It is filled with a vast number of dry facts, annotations, and enumerations. He records the state of his health and the state of his purse. He is for ever going to the play and seeing so-and-so act. But he is pen-tied, congested, and callow. If he were not Stendhal, we might shirk the labour of adding up so many little facts into one sum total. But then he is Stendhal. He is that dry, scientific, amorous, complex, and strangely fascinating man who even in scraps tastes differently from other people, who even in this first volume forces us to try to fit the pieces of his puzzle together.

The first volume of the diary is kept by a composite human soul who is neither boy nor man, but a mixture of child and schoolmaster. The child writes down his doings day by day; the schoolmaster looks over his shoulder and makes his comment in the margin. In other words, Stendhal was set from the first upon mastering the art of life. With this end in view he takes notes and observes incessantly both what others do and what he does himself. For example, he must cure himself of the habit of blurting out his opinion just as nimbler-witted people are wishing to change the conversation. He has observed that simplicity is always popular; he must aim then at simplicity. In these early pages we seem to see him hard at work in the dim hour before the sun rises, examining the foundations upon which his life is to be built. Again and again he turns to examine the problems of literature. What are the qualities that go to make a first-rate comedy? And what is the difference between tragedy and comedy? And what are the elements of Shakespeare's greatness? Then life is taken up and turned round between his fingers. By what means can one ensure the greatest possible happiness in life? And which is more powerful – love of glory or love of women? By degrees the familiar features of his character begin to emerge: his ambition; his fastidiousness – 'Je pourrais faire un ouvrage qui ne plairait qu'à moi et qui serait reconnu beau en 2000'[2] – his passionate, yet scientific, research into the nature of love; his indefatigable curiosity as to the constituents of the human soul. 'C'est la connaissance de ce qu'il y a de plus caché au fond du cœur et de la tête que je veux acquérir.'[3] Meanwhile, the forerunners of that long procession of women which was to march through his life make their appearance – Adèle, Victorine, Mélanie.[4] His pen gathers strength and point as it fleshes itself upon these lovely creatures, who are at once the objects of his passionate love and of his scientific curiosity; he raves, he dissects, he tears them to pieces. Indeed, the process is at times so frank that the publishers have thought best to print certain passages on loose leaves, which can be burnt or bound, according to the wishes of the reader. For our own part Stendhal is Stendhal; and disinfects every page with the pungency of his own personal fascination.

1 – A review in the N&A, 5 July 1924, (Kp C249) of Stendhal: Journal. Texte établi et annoté par Henry Debraye et Louis Royer. Tome Premier, 1801–1805; Le Rouge et le Noir, two vols; Vie de Rossini. Suivie des Notes d'un Dilettante. Texte établi et annoté avec une introduction historique par Jules Marsan. Préface de Paul Bourget, two vols (Edouard Champion, 1923) by Stendhal, pseudonym for Henri Beyle (1783–1842) whose Vie de Rossini and Le Rouge et le Noir first appeared in 1823 and 1830 respectively; the original edition of his Journal was published in 1888. See also 'Stendhal', VI VW Essays. Reading Notes (Berg, xix). See Editorial Note, p. xxv.

2–*Journal*, 'Journal de mon troisième voyage à Paris 10 nivôse, dernier jour de l'année 1804', p. 206.

3–*Ibid.*, intro., p. v, quoting 'Journal du 7 juin 1810'.

4–*Ibid.*, p. xiii: 'Henri Beyle passe pour un séducteur professionel; cependant, peu de femmes, relativement, ont occupé son coeur entre 1802 et 1818. Citons-les: Victorine Mounier, Adèle Rebuffet, Mélanie Guilbert (Louason), Mina de Griesheim, Madame Daru, Angéline Bereyter, Angela Pietragrua.'

'Days That Are Gone'

Colonel la Terrière has lived to an age when, having no future, as he says, and very little present, the most congenial occupation is to record the joys of the past. And the Colonel is convinced that the joys of himself and of other 'very ordinary gentlemen' like him are over and done with for good. He was educated at Eton and Oxford. 'What Eton will become under the present radical revolution it is impossible to say.'[2] Possibly the people will destroy Eton, and then what he takes the liberty of thinking the finest product in the world, the English gentleman, will become extinct. 'Thank God, we've got rid of Lloyd George at last,' he exclaims, but not before we made 'the most colossal mistake in history'[3] – for so the Colonel said it was at the time, and so time has proved it to be – the Armistice. The Colonel's advice was disregarded upon another occasion with disastrous results. King Edward backed the wrong horse. We should have kept in with Germany. 'I hate the sight of a German, and even to hear anyone speak two words of their beastly language makes me sick, but my detestation of them doesn't blind me to facts.'[4] His comments upon the Labour Government are, unfortunately, squeezed into a postscript. As for Kitchener, he was not a man of the world; and as for Oscar Wilde, whom the Colonel encountered at Oxford: '"Great wits to madness oft are near allied" seems to hit off the poor chap. R.I.P.'[5] Let us echo R.I.P.

1–A notice in the *N&A*, 5 July 1924, (Kp C249.1) of *Days That Are Gone . . . Being the Recollections of some Seventy Years of the Life of a very ordinary Gentleman and his Friends in Three Reigns* (Hutchinson & Co., 1924) by Colonel B. De Sales La Terrière [1856–****] (Exon of the Yeomen of the Guard).

2–La Terrière, ch. vi, p. 55.

3–For the first quotation, *ibid.*, ch. xli, p. 286, and for the second, *ibid.*, p. 284. The coalition government formed during the war under David Lloyd George (1863–1945) fell in 1922.

4 – *Ibid.*, p. 285.

5 – Ramsay MacDonald led the first Labour government, Jan.–Nov. 1924. Lord Kitchener (1850–1916), whom Lloyd George succeeded as minister of war. For the quotation, La Terrière, ch. x, p. 76; La Terrière and Oscar Wilde (1854–1900) were contemporaries at Magdalen College. La Terrière is misquoting Dryden, *Absalom and Achitophel*, l. 163: 'Great wits are sure to madness near ally'd'.

'Before the Mast – And After'

The fascination of Sir Walter Runciman's book may best be conveyed by saying that, if one of Mr Conrad's sea captains had possessed a gift for writing, this is precisely the book he would have written. Here is a Conrad novel in the rough, before the master has thrown his cloak of many-coloured words over it. Sir Walter was an active seaman in the great days, which he admires and regrets, of the sailing ship. Benevolent legislation had then done little to remove what was removable of a sailor's hardships. Sir Walter climbed from cabin-boy to captain over the stoniest of roads. He was 'moulded into manhood under the rule of barely regulated ferocity'.[2] He has gone without food or water, been shot at by mutineers, ridden storms, and seen ships sink by his side, until, worn out by the buffetings of his friend and enemy, he retired, to become a highly successful shipowner. But Sir Walter would probably agree that it was the early life that was the best worth living, not only for its adventures, but for its encounters, for his book is full of various and wonderful men.

1 – A notice in the *N&A*, 12 July 1924, (Kp C250) of *Before the Mast – And After. The Autobiography of a Sailor and Shipowner* (Fisher Unwin, 1924) by Sir Walter Runciman, 1st Baron Runciman of Shoreston (1847–1937), chairman and founder in 1889 of the Moor Line Ltd. See Editorial Note, p. xxv.

2 – Runciman, ch. v, p. 103.

'The Truth at Last'

Mr Somerset Maugham, who introduces these recollections, says that it struck him as singular that Charles Hawtrey excelled in an art 'to which after all he was somewhat indifferent'.[2] His real interest, he goes on to say, was not in acting, but in life, particularly in that special department of life which centres in the race-course. Hawtrey made his first bet when he was an Eton boy, and it was the forerunner of a vast progeny. He became an actor as most men become bankers, barristers, or doctors – to make a living. And for the rest of his life the two interests intersect so closely and beat up such a dust of affairs between them that it is difficult to see any particular event very clearly. That is the weakness of much dramatic and sporting literature. It needs a born writer to breathe life into the innumerable details of ancient races and ancient plays. Hawtrey was only a perfunctory recorder – a hurried, good-tempered, rather breathless man setting down notes of what had happened to him and feeling, one can be sure, that all the spice went out of his story as he told it. Now and again he makes a little confidence – 'I am a steadfast believer in the efficacy of prayer'[3] – or tells a vivid story, but for the most part the book is a jumble of old race-cards and old play-bills, among which the reader must be prepared to do a little artful skipping for himself.

1–A notice in the N&A, 19 July 1924, (Kp C250.1) of The Truth at Last (Thornton Butterworths Ltd., 1924) by Charles Hawtrey (1858–1923), actor-manager and comedian, knighted in 1922.
2–W. Somerset Maugham (1874–1965); Hawtrey, intro., p. 7.
3–Ibid., ch. x, p. 119; Hawtrey prayed for the success of The Private Secretary, a play he adapted from the German of Von Moser, and his prayers were rewarded at the Globe Theatre in 1884.

Character in Fiction

It seems to me possible, perhaps desirable, that I may be the only person in this room who has committed the folly of writing, trying to write, or failing to write, a novel. And when I asked myself, as your invitation to speak to you about modern fiction made me ask myself, what demon whispered in my ear and urged me to my doom, a little figure rose before me – the figure of a man, or of a woman, who said, 'My name is Brown. Catch me if you can.'

Most novelists have the same experience. Some Brown, Smith, or Jones comes before them and says in the most seductive and charming way in the world, 'Come and catch me if you can.' And so, led on by this will-o'-the-wisp, they flounder through volume after volume, spending the best years of their lives in the pursuit, and receiving for the most part very little cash in exchange. Few catch the phantom; most have to be content with a scrap of her dress or a wisp of her hair.

My belief that men and women write novels because they are lured on to create some character which has thus imposed itself upon them has the sanction of Mr Arnold Bennett. In an article from which I will quote he says: 'The foundation of good fiction is character-creating and nothing else . . . Style counts; plot counts; originality of outlook counts. But none of these counts anything like so much as the convincingness of the characters. If the characters are real the novel will have a chance; if they are not, oblivion will be its portion . . .'[2] And he goes on to draw the conclusion that we have no young novelists of first-rate importance at the present moment, because they are unable to create characters that are real, true, and convincing.

These are the questions that I want with greater boldness than discretion to discuss tonight. I want to make out what we mean when we talk about 'character' in fiction; to say something about the question of reality which Mr Bennett raises; and to suggest some reasons why the younger novelists fail to create characters, if, as Mr Bennett asserts, it is true that fail they do. This will lead me, I am well aware, to make some very sweeping and some very vague assertions. For the question is an extremely difficult one. Think how little we know about character – think how little we know about art. But, to make a clearance before I begin, I will suggest that we range Edwardians and Georgians into two camps; Mr Wells, Mr Bennett, and Mr Galsworthy I will call the Edwardians; Mr Forster, Mr Lawrence, Mr Strachey, Mr Joyce, and Mr Eliot I will call the Georgians.[3] And if I speak in the first person, with intolerable egotism, I will ask you to excuse me. I do not want to attribute to the world at large the opinions of one solitary, ill-informed, and misguided individual.

My first assertion is one that I think you will grant – that every one in this room is a judge of character. Indeed it would be impossible to live for a year without disaster unless one practised character-reading and had some skill in the art. Our marriages, our friendships depend on it; our business largely depends on it; every day questions arise which can only be solved by its help. And now I will hazard a second assertion, which is more disputable perhaps, to the effect that on or about December 1910 human character changed.

I am not saying that one went out, as one might into a garden, and there saw that a rose had flowered, or that a hen had laid an egg. The change was not sudden and definite like that. But a change there was, nevertheless; and since one must be arbitrary, let us date it about the year 1910.[4] The first signs of it are recorded in the books of Samuel Butler, in *The Way of All Flesh* in particular; the plays of Bernard Shaw continue to record it.[5] In life one can see the change, if I may use a homely illustration, in the character of one's cook. The Victorian cook lived like a leviathan in the lower depths, formidable, silent, obscure, inscrutable; the Georgian cook is a creature of sunshine and fresh air; in and out of the drawing room, now to borrow the *Daily Herald*,[6] now to ask advice about a hat. Do you ask for more solemn instances of the power of the human race to change? Read the *Agamemnon*, and see whether, in process of time, your sympathies are not almost entirely with Clytemnestra. Or consider the married life of the Carlyles,[7] and bewail the waste, the futility, for him and for her, of the horrible domestic tradition which made it seemly for a woman of genius to spend her time chasing beetles, scouring saucepans, instead of writing books. All human relations have shifted – those between masters and servants, husbands and wives, parents and children. And when human relations change there is at the same time a change in religion, conduct, politics and literature. Let us agree to place one of these changes about the year 1910.

I have said that people have to acquire a good deal of skill in character-reading if they are to live a single year of life without disaster. But it is the art of the young. In middle age and in old age the art is practised mostly for its uses, and friendships and other adventures and experiments in the art of reading character are seldom made. But novelists differ from the rest of the world because they do not cease to be interested in character when they have learnt enough about it for practical purposes. They go a step further; they feel that there is something permanently interesting in character in itself. When all the practical business of life has been discharged, there is something about people which continues to seem to them of overwhelming importance, in spite of the fact that it has no bearing whatever upon their happiness, comfort, or income. The study of character becomes to them an absorbing pursuit; to impart character an obsession. And this I find it very difficult to explain: what novelists mean when they talk about character, what the impulse is that urges them so powerfully every now and then to embody their view in writing.

So, if you will allow me, instead of analysing and abstracting, I will tell you a simple story which, however pointless, has the merit of being true, of a journey from Richmond to Waterloo, in the hope that I may show you what I mean by character in itself; that you may realise the different aspects it can wear; and the hideous perils that beset you directly you try to describe it in words.

One night some weeks ago, then, I was late for the train and jumped into the first carriage I came to. As I sat down I had the strange and uncomfortable feeling that I was interupting a conversation between two people who were already sitting there. Not that they were young or happy. Far from it. They were both elderly, the woman over sixty, the man well over forty. They were sitting opposite each other, and the man, who had been leaning over and talking emphatically to judge by his attitude and the flush on his face, sat back and became silent. I had disturbed him, and he was annoyed. The elderly lady, however, whom I will call Mrs Brown, seemed rather relieved. She was one of those clean, threadbare old ladies whose extreme tidiness – everything buttoned, fastened, tied together, mended and brushed up – suggests more extreme poverty than rags and dirt. There was something pinched about her – a look of suffering, of apprehension, and, in addition, she was extremely small. Her feet, in their clean little boots, scarcely touched the floor. I felt that she had nobody to support her; that she had to make up her mind for herself; that, having been deserted, or left a widow, years ago, she had led an anxious, harried life, bringing up an only son, perhaps, who, as likely as not, was by this time beginning to go to the bad. All this shot through my mind as I sat down, being uncomfortable, like most people, at travelling with fellow passengers unless I have somehow or other accounted for them. Then I looked at the man. He was no relation of Mrs Brown's I felt sure; he was of a bigger, burlier, less refined type. He was a man of business I imagined, very likely a respectable corn-chandler from the North, dressed in good blue serge with a pocket-knife and a silk handkerchief, and a stout leather bag. Obviously, however, he had an unpleasant business to settle with Mrs Brown; a secret, perhaps sinister business, which they did not intend to discuss in my presence.

'Yes, the Crofts have had very bad luck with their servants,' Mr Smith (as I will call him) said in a considering way, going back to some earlier topic, with a view to keeping up appearances.

'Ah, poor people,' said Mrs Brown, a trifle condescendingly. 'My grandmother had a maid who came when she was fifteen and stayed till she was eighty' (this was said with a kind of hurt and aggressive pride to impress us both perhaps).

'One doesn't often come across that sort of thing nowadays,' said Mr Smith in conciliatory tones.

Then they were silent.

'It's odd they don't start a golf club there – I should have thought one of the young fellows would,' said Mr Smith, for the silence obviously made him uneasy.

Mrs Brown hardly took the trouble to answer.

'What changes they're making in this part of the world,' said Mr Smith looking out of the window, and looking furtively at me as he did do.

It was plain, from Mrs Brown's silence, from the uneasy affability with which Mr Smith spoke, that he had some power over her which he was exerting disagreeably. It might have been her son's downfall, or some painful episode in her past life, or her daughter's. Perhaps she was going to London to sign some document to make over some property. Obviously against her will she was in Mr Smith's hands. I was beginning to feel a great deal of pity for her, when she said, suddenly and inconsequently.

'Can you tell me if an oak tree dies when the leaves have been eaten for two years in succession by caterpillars?'

She spoke quite brightly, and rather precisely, in a cultivated, inquisitive voice.

Mr Smith was startled, but relieved to have a safe topic of conversation given him. He told her a great deal very quickly about plagues of insects. He told her that he had a brother who kept a fruit farm in Kent. He told her what fruit farmers do every year in Kent, and so on, and so on. While he talked a very odd thing happened. Mrs Brown took out her little white handkerchief and began to dab her eyes. She was crying. But she went on listening quite composedly to what he was saying, and he went on talking, a little louder, a little angrily, as if he had seen her cry often before; as if it were a painful habit. At last it got on his nerves. He stopped abruptly, looked out of the window, then leant towards her as he had been doing when I got in, and said in a bullying, menacing way, as if he would not stand any more nonsense.

'So about that matter we were discussing. It'll be all right? George will be there on Tuesday?'

'We shan't be late,' said Mrs Brown, gathering herself together with superb dignity.

Mr Smith said nothing. He got up, buttoned his coat, reached his bag down, and jumped out of the train before it had stopped at Clapham Junction. He had got what he wanted, but he was ashamed of himself; he was glad to get out of the old lady's sight.

Mrs Brown and I were left alone together. She sat in her corner opposite, very clean, very small, rather queer, and suffering intensely. The impression she made was overwhelming. It came pouring out like a draught, like a smell of burning. What was it composed of – that overwhelming and peculiar impression? Myriads of irrelevant and incongruous ideas crowd into one's head on such occasions; one sees the person, one sees Mrs Brown, in the centre of all sorts of different scenes. I thought of her in a seaside house, among queer ornaments: sea-urchins, models of ships in glass cases. Her husband's medals were on the mantelpiece. She popped in and out of the room, perching on the edges of chairs, picking meals out of saucers, indulging in long, silent stares. The caterpillars and the oak trees seemed to imply all that. And then, into this fantastic and secluded life, in broke Mr Smith. I saw him blowing in, so to speak, on a windy day. He banged, he slammed. His dripping umbrella made a pool in the hall. They sat closeted together.

And then Mrs Brown faced the dreadful revelation. She took her heroic decision. Early, before dawn, she packed her bag and carried it herself to the station. She would not let Smith touch it. She was wounded in her pride, unmoored from her anchorage; she came of gentlefolks who kept servants – but details could wait. The important thing was to realise her character, to steep oneself in her atmosphere. I had no time to explain why I felt it somewhat tragic, heroic, yet with a dash of the flighty, and fantastic, before the train stopped, and I watched her disappear, carrying her bag, into the vast blazing station. She looked very small, very tenacious; at once very frail and very heroic. And I have never seen her again, and I shall never know what became of her.

The story ends without any point to it. But I have not told you this anecdote to illustrate either my own ingenuity or the pleasure of travelling from Richmond to Waterloo. What I want you to see in it is this. Here is a character imposing itself upon another person. Here is Mrs Brown making someone begin almost automatically to write a novel about her. I believe that all novels begin with an old lady in the corner opposite. I believe that all novels, that is to say, deal with character, and that it is to express character – not to preach doctrines, sing songs, or celebrate the glories of the British Empire, that the form of the novel, so clumsy, verbose, and undramatic, so rich, elastic, and alive, has been evolved. To express character, I have said; but you will at once reflect that the very widest interpretation can be put upon those words. For example, old Mrs Brown's character will strike you very differently according to the age and country in which you happen to be born. It would be easy enough to write three different versions of that incident in the train, an English, a French, and a Russian. The English writer would make the old lady in to a 'character'; he would bring out her oddities and mannerisms; her buttons and wrinkles; her ribbons and warts. Her personality would dominate the book. A French writer would rub out all that; he would sacrifice the individual Mrs Brown to give a more general view of human nature; to make a more abstract, proportioned, and harmonious whole. The Russian would pierce through the flesh; would reveal the soul – the soul alone, wandering out into the Waterloo Road, asking of life some tremendous question which would sound on and on in our ears after the book was finished. And then there is the writer's temperament to be considered.* You see one thing in character, and I another. You say it means this, and I that. And when it comes to writing each makes a further selection on principles of his own. Thus Mrs Brown can be treated in an infinite variety of ways, according to the age, country, and temperament of the writer.

But now I must recall what Mr Arnold Bennett says. He says that it is only if the characters are real that the novel has any chance of surviving. Otherwise, die it must. But, I ask myself, what is reality? And who are the judges of reality? A character may be real to Mr Bennett and quite unreal to me. For instance, in this article he says that Dr Watson in *Sherlock Holmes* is real to him:[8] to me Dr Watson is a sack stuffed with straw, a dummy, a figure of fun. And so it is with character after character – in book after book. There is nothing that people differ about more than the reality of characters, especially in contemporary books. But if you take a larger view I think that Mr Bennett is perfectly right. If, that is, you think of the novels which seem to you great novels – *War and Peace, Vanity Fair, Tristram Shandy, Madame Bovary, Pride and Prejudice, The Mayor of Casterbridge, Villette*[9] – if you think of these books, you do at once think of some character who has seemed to you so real (I do not by that mean so lifelike) that it has the power to make you think not merely of it itself, but of all sorts of things through its eyes – of religion, of love, of war, of peace, of family life, of balls in county towns, of sunsets, moonrises, the immortality of the soul. There is hardly any subject of human experience that is left out of *War and Peace* it seems to me. And in all these novels all these great novelists have brought us to see whatever they wish us to see through some character. Otherwise, they would not be novelists; but poets, historians, or pamphleteers.

HP Essay: 'And then besides age and country there is the writer's temperament to be considered.'

But now let us examine what Mr Bennett went on to say – he said that there was no great novelist among the Georgian writers because they cannot create characters who are real, true, and convincing. And there I cannot agree. There are reasons, excuses, possibilities which I think put a different colour upon the case. It seems to to me at least, but I am well aware that this is a matter about which I am likely to be prejudiced, sanguine, and near-sighted. I will put my view before you in the hope that you will make it impartial, judicial, and broad-minded. Why, then, is it so hard for novelists at present to create characters which seem real, not only to Mr Bennett, but to the world at large? Why, when October comes round, do the publishers always fail to supply us with a masterpiece?

Surely one reason is that the men and women who began writing novels in 1910 or thereabouts had this great difficulty to face – that there was no English novelist living from whom they could learn their business. Mr Conrad is a Pole; which sets him apart, and makes him, however admirable, not very helpful. Mr Hardy has written no novel since 1895.[10] The most prominent and successful novelists in the year 1910 were, I suppose, Mr Wells, Mr Bennett, and Mr Galsworthy. Now it seems to me that to go to these men and ask them to teach you how to write a novel – how to create characters that are real – is precisely like going to a bootmaker and asking him to teach you how to make a watch. Do not let me give you the impression that I do not admire and enjoy their books. They seem to me of great value, and indeed of great necessity. There are seasons when it is more important to have boots than to have watches. To drop metaphor, I think that after the creative activity of the Victorian age it was quite necessary, not only for literature but for life, that someone should write the books that Mr Wells, Mr Bennett, and Mr Galsworthy have written. Yet what odd books they are! Sometimes I wonder if we are right to call them books at all. For they leave one with so strange a feeling of incompleteness and dissatisfaction. In order to complete them it seems necessary to do something – to join a society, or, more desperately, to write a cheque. That done, the restlessness is laid, the book finished; it can be put upon the shelf, and need never be read again. But with the work of other novelists it is different. *Tristram Shandy* or *Pride and Prejudice* is complete in itself; it is self-contained; it leaves one with no desire to do anything, except indeed to read the book again, and to understand it better. The difference perhaps is that both Sterne and Jane Austen were interested in things in themselves; in character in itself; in the book in itself. Therefore everything was inside the book, nothing outside. But the Edwardians were never interested in character in itself; or in the book in itself. They were interested in something outside. Their books, then, were incomplete as books, and required that the reader should finish them, actively and practically, for himself.

Perhaps we can make this clearer if we take the liberty of imagining a little party in the railway carriage – Mr Wells, Mr Galsworthy, Mr Bennett are travelling to Waterloo with Mrs Brown. Mrs Brown, I have said, was poorly dressed and very small. She had an anxious, harassed look. I doubt whether she was what you call an educated woman. Seizing upon all these symptoms of the unsatisfactory condition of our primary schools with a rapidity to which I can do no justice, Mr Wells would instantly project upon the window-pane a vision of a better, breezier, jollier, happier, more adventurous and gallant world, where these musty railway carriages and fusty old women do not exist; where miraculous barges bring tropical fruit to Camberwell by eight o'clock in the morning; where there are public nurseries, fountains, and libraries, dining rooms, drawing rooms, and marriages; where every citizen is generous and candid, manly and magnificent, and rather like Mr Wells himself. But nobody is in the least like Mrs Brown. There are no Mrs Browns in Utopia. Indeed I do not think that Mr Wells, in his passion to make her what she ought to be, would waste a thought upon her as she is. And what would Mr Galsworthy see? Can we doubt that the walls of Doulton's factory would take his fancy? There are women in that factory who make twenty-five dozen earthenware pots every day. There are mothers in the Mile End Road who depend upon the farthings which those women earn. But there are employers in Surrey who are even now smoking rich cigars while the nightingale sings. Burning with indignation, stuffed with information, arraigning civilisation, Mr Galsworthy would only see in Mrs Brown a pot broken on the wheel and thrown into the corner.

Mr Bennett, alone of the Edwardians, would keep his eyes in the carriage. He, indeed, would observe every detail with immense care. He would notice the advertisements; the pictures of Swanage and Portsmouth; the way in which the cushion bulged between the buttons; how Mrs Brown wore a brooch which had cost three-and-ten-three at Whitworth's bazaar; and had mended both gloves – indeed the thumb of the left-hand glove had been replaced. And he would observe, at length, how this was the non-stop train from Windsor which calls at Richmond for the convenience of middle-class residents, who can afford to go to the theatre but have not reached the social rank which can afford motor-cars, though it is true, there are occasions (he would tell us what), when they hire them from a company (he would tell us which). And so he would gradually sidle sedately towards Mrs Brown, and would remark how she had been left a little copyhold, not freehold, property at Datchet, which, however, was mortgaged to Mr Bungay the solicitor – but why should I presume to invent Mr Bennett? Does not Mr Bennett write novels himself? I will open the first book that chance puts in my way – *Hilda Lessways*.[11] Let us see how he makes us feel that Hilda is real, true, and convincing, as a novelist should. She shut the door in a soft, controlled way, which showed the constraint of her relations with her mother. She was fond of reading *Maud*;[12] she was endowed with the power to feel intensely. So far, so good; in his leisurely, surefooted way Mr Bennett is trying in these first pages, where every touch is important, to show us the kind of girl she was.

But then he begins to describe, not Hilda Lessways, but the view from her bedroom window, the excuse being that Mr Skellorn, the man who collects rents, is coming along that way. Mr Bennett proceeds:

The bailiwick of Turnhill lay behind her; and all the murky district of the Five Towns, of which Turnhill is the northern outpost, lay to the south. At the foot of Chatterley Wood the canal wound in large curves on its way towards the undefiled plains of Cheshire and the sea. On the canal-side, exactly opposite to Hilda's window, was a flour-mill, that sometimes made nearly as much smoke as the kilns and the chimneys closing the prospect on either hand. From the flour-mill a bricked path, which separated a considerable row of new cottages from their appurtenant gardens, led straight into Lessways Street, in front of Mrs Lessways' house. By this path Mr Skellorn should have arrived, for he inhabited the farthest of the cottages.[13]

One line of insight would have done more than all those lines of description; but let them pass as the necessary drudgery of the novelist. And now – where is Hilda? Alas. Hilda is still looking out of the window. Passionate and dissatisfied as she was, she was a girl with an eye for houses. She often compared this old Mr Skellorn with the villas she saw from her bedroom window. Therefore the villas must be described. Mr Bennett proceeds:

The row was called Freehold Villas: a consciously proud name in a district where much of the land was copyhold and could only change owners subject to the payment of 'fines', and to the feudal consent of a 'court' presided over by the agent of a lord of the manor. Most of the dwellings were owned by their occupiers, who, each an absolute monarch of the soil, niggled in his sooty garden of an evening amid the flutter of drying shirts and towels. Freehold Villas symbolised the final triumph of Victorian economics, the apotheosis of the prudent and industrious artisan. It corresponded with a Building Society Secretary's dream of paradise. And indeed it was a very real achievement. Nevertheless, Hilda's irrational contempt would not admit this.[14]

Heaven be praised, we cry! At last we are coming to Hilda herself. But not so fast. Hilda may have been this, that, and the other; but Hilda not only looked at houses, and thought of houses; Hilda lived in a house. And what sort of a house did Hilda live in? Mr Bennett proceeds:

It was one of the two middle houses of a detached terrace of four houses built by her grandfather Lessways, the teapot manufacturer; it was the chief of the four, obviously the habitation of the proprietor of the terrace. One of the corner houses comprised a grocer's shop, and this house had been robbed of its just proportion of garden so that the seigneurial garden-plot might be triflingly larger than the other. The terrace was not a terrace of cottages, but of houses rated at from twenty-six to thirty-six pounds a year; beyond the means of artisans and petty insurance agents and rent-collectors. And further, it was well built, generously built; and its architecture, though debased, showed some faint traces of Georgian amenity. It was admittedly the best row of houses in that newly settled quarter of the town. In coming to it out of Freehold Villas Mr Skellorn obviously came to something superior, wider, more liberal. Suddenly Hilda heard her mother's voice . . .[15]

But we cannot hear her mother's voice, or Hilda's voice; we can only hear Mr Bennett's voice telling us facts about rents and freeholds and copyholds and fines. What can Mr Bennett be about? I have formed my own opinion of what Mr Bennett is about – he is trying to make us imagine for him; he is trying to hypnotise us into the belief that, because he has made a house, there must be a person living there. With all his powers of observation, which are marvellous, with all his sympathy and humanity, which are great, Mr Bennett has never once looked at Mrs Brown in her corner. There she sits in the corner of the carriage – that carriage which is travelling, not from Richmond to Waterloo, but from one age of English literature to the next, for Mrs Brown is eternal, Mrs Brown is human nature, Mrs Brown changes only on the surface, it is the novelists who get in and out – there she sits and not one of the Edwardian writers has so much as looked at her. They have looked very powerfully, searchingly, and sympathetically out of the window; at factories, at Utopias, even at the decoration and upholstery of the carriage; but never at her, never at life, never at human nature. And so they have developed a technique of novel-writing which suits their purpose; they have made tools and established conventions which do their business. But those tools are not our tools, and that business is not our business. For us those conventions are ruin, those tools are death.

You may well complain of the vagueness of my language. What is a convention, a tool, you may ask, and what do you mean by saying that Mr Bennett's and Mr Wells's and Mr Galsworthy's conventions are the wrong conventions for the Georgians? The question is difficult: I will attempt a short cut. A convention in writing is not much different from a convention in manners. Both in life and in literature it is necessary to have some means of bridging the gulf between the hostess and her unknown guest on the one hand, the writer and his unknown reader on the other. The hostess bethinks her of the weather, for generations of hostesses have established the fact that this is a subject of universal interest in which we all believe. She begins by saying that we are having a wretched May, and, having thus got into touch with her unknown guest, proceeds to matters of greater interest. So it is in literature. The writer must get into touch with his reader by putting before him something which he recognises, which therefore stimulates his imagination, and makes him willing to co-operate in the far more difficult business of intimacy. And it is of the highest importance that this common meeting-place should be reached easily, almost instinctively, in the dark, with one's eyes shut. Here is Mr Bennett making use of this common ground in the passage which I have quoted. The problem before him was to make us believe in the reality of Hilda Lessways. So he began, being an Edwardian, by describing accurately and minutely the sort of house Hilda lived in, and the sort of house she saw from the window. House property was the common ground from which the Edwardians found it easy to proceed to intimacy. Indirect as it seems to us, the convention worked admirably, and thousands of Hilda Lessways were launched upon the world by this means. For that age and generation, the convention was a good one.

But now, if you will allow me to pull my own anecdote to pieces, you will see how keenly I felt the lack of a convention, and how serious a matter it is when the tools of one generation are useless for the next. The incident had made a great impression on me. But how was I to transmit it to you? All I could do was to report as accurately as I could what was said, to describe in detail what was worn, to say, despairingly, that all sorts of scenes rushed into my mind, to proceed to tumble them out pell-mell, and to describe this vivid, this overmastering impression by likening it to a draught or a smell of burning. To tell you the truth, I was also strongly tempted to manufacture a three-volume novel about the old lady's son, and his adventures crossing the Atlantic, and her daughter, and how she kept a milliner's shop in Westminster, the past life of Smith himself, and his house at Sheffield, though such stories seem to me the most dreary, irrelevant, and humbugging affairs in the world.

But if I had done that I should have escaped the appalling effort of saying what I meant. And to have got at what I meant, I should have had to go back and back and back; to experiment with one thing and another; to try this sentence and that, referring each word to my vision, matching it as exactly as possible, and knowing that somehow I had to find a common ground between us, a convention which would not seem to you too odd, unreal, and far-fetched to believe in. I admit that I shirked that arduous undertaking. I let my Mrs Brown slip through my fingers. I have told you nothing whatever about her. But that is partly the great Edwardians' fault. I asked them – they are my elders and betters – How shall I begin to describe this woman's character? And they said, 'Begin by saying that her father kept a shop in Harrogate. Ascertain the rent. Ascertain the wages of shop assistants in the year 1878. Discover what her mother died of. Describe cancer. Describe calico. Describe – ' But I cried, 'Stop! Stop!' and I regret to say that I threw that ugly, that clumsy, that incongruous tool out of the window, for I knew that if I began describing the cancer and the calico my Mrs Brown,* that vision to which I cling though I know no way of imparting it to you, would have been dulled and tarnished and vanished for ever.

That is what I mean by saying that the Edwardian tools are the wrong ones for us to use. They have laid an enormous stress upon the fabric of things. They have given us a house in the hope that we may be able to deduce the human beings who live there. To give them their due, they have made that house much better worth living in. But if you hold that novels are in the first place about people, and only in the second about the houses they live in, that is the wrong way to set about it. Therefore, you see, the Georgian writer had to begin by throwing away the method that was in use at the moment. He was left alone there facing Mrs Brown without any method of conveying her to the reader. But that is inaccurate. A writer is never alone. There is always the public with him – if not on the same seat, at least in the compartment next door. Now the public is a strange travelling companion. In England it is a very suggestible and docile creature, which, once you get it to attend, will believe implicitly what it is told for a certain number of years. If you say to the public with sufficient conviction, 'All women have tails, and all men have humps,' it will actually learn to see women with tails and men with humps, and

*HP Essay: 'if I began describing the cancer and the calico, my Mrs Brown'.

will think it very revolutionary and probably improper if you say 'Nonsense. Monkeys have tails and camels humps. But men and women have brains, and they have hearts; they think and they feel,' – that will seem to it a bad joke, and an improper into the bargain.*

But to return. Here is the British public sitting by the writer's side and saying in its vast and unanimous way, 'Old women have houses. They have fathers. They have incomes. They have servants. They have hot water bottles. That is how we know that they are old women. Mr Wells and Mr Bennett and Mr Galsworthy have always taught us that this is the way to recognise them. But now with your Mrs Brown – how are we to believe in her? We do not even know whether her villa was called Albert or Balmoral; what she paid for her gloves; or whether her mother died of cancer or of consumption. How can she be alive? No; she is a mere figment of your imagination.'

And old women of course ought to be made of freehold villas and copyhold estates, not of imagination.

The Georgian novelist, therefore, was in an awkward predicament. There was Mrs Brown protesting that she was different, quite different, from what people made out, and luring the novelist to her rescue by the most fascinating if fleeting glimpse of her charms; there were the Edwardians handing out tools appropriate to house building and house breaking; and there was the British public asseverating that they must see the hot water bottle first. Meanwhile the train was rushing to that station where we must all get out.

Such, I think, was the predicament in which the young Georgians found themselves about the year 1910. Many of them – I am thinking of Mr Forster and Mr Lawrence in particular – spoilt their early work because, instead of throwing away those tools, they tried to use them. They tried to compromise. They tried to combine their own direct sense of the oddity and significance of some character with Mr Galsworthy's knowledge of the Factory Acts, and Mr Bennett's knowledge of the Five Towns. They tried it, but they had too keen, too overpowering a sense of Mrs Brown and her peculiarities to go on trying it much longer. Something had to be done. At whatever cost of life, limb, and damage to valuable property Mrs Brown must be rescued, expressed, and set in her high relations to the world before the train stopped and she disappeared for ever. And so the smashing and the crashing began. Thus it is that we hear all round us, in poems and novels and biographies, even in

---

HP Essay: '–that will seem to it a bad joke, and an improper one into the bargain'.

newspaper articles and essays, the sound of breaking and falling, crashing and destruction. It is the prevailing sound of the Georgian age – rather a melancholy one if you think what melodious days there have been in the past, if you think of Shakespeare and Milton and Keats or even of Jane Austen and Thackeray and Dickens;[16] if you think of the language, and the heights to which it can soar when free, and see the same eagle captive, bald, and croaking.

In view of these facts, with these sounds in my ears and these fancies in my brain, I am not going to deny that Mr Bennett has some reason when he complains that our Georgian writers are unable to make us believe that our characters are real. I am forced to agree that they do not pour out three immortal masterpieces with Victorian regularity every autumn. But instead of being gloomy, I am sanguine. For this state of things is, I think, inevitable whenever from hoar old age or callow youth the convention ceases to be a means of communication between writer and reader, and becomes instead an obstacle and an impediment. At the present moment we are suffering, not from decay, but from having no code of manners which writers and readers accept as a prelude to the more exciting intercourse of friendship. The literary convention of the time is so artificial – you have to talk about the weather and nothing but the weather throughout the entire visit – that, naturally, the feeble are tempted to outrage, and the strong are led to destroy the very foundations and rules of literary society. Signs of this are everywhere apparent. Grammar is violated; syntax disintegrated, as a boy staying with an aunt for the weekend rolls in the geranium bed out of sheer desperation as the solemnities of the sabbath wear on. The more adult writers do not, of course, indulge in such wanton exhibitions of spleen. Their sincerity is desperate, and their courage tremendous; it is only that they do not know which to use, a fork or their fingers. Thus, if you read Mr Joyce and Mr Eliot you will be struck by the indecency of the one, and the obscurity of the other. Mr Joyce's indecency in *Ulysses*[17] seems to me the conscious and calculated indecency of a desperate man who feels that in order to breathe he must break the windows. At moments, when the window is broken, he is magnificent. But what a waste of energy! And, after all, how dull indecency is, when it is not the overflowing of a superabundant energy or savagery, but the determined and public-spirited act of a man who needs fresh air! Again, with the obscurity of Mr Eliot. I think that Mr Eliot has written some of the loveliest lines in modern poetry.[18]* 'But how intolerant he is of the old usages and

* *HP Essay:* 'I think that Mr Eliot has written some of the loveliest single lines in modern poetry'.

politenesses of society – respect for the weak, consideration for the dull! As I sun myself upon the intense and ravishing beauty of one of his lines, and reflect that I must make a dizzy and dangerous leap to the next, and so on from line to line, like an acrobat flying precariously from bar to bar, I cry out, I confess, for the old decorums, and envy the indolence of my ancestors who, instead of spinning madly through mid-air, dreamt quietly in the shade with a book. Again, in Mr Strachey's books, *Eminent Victorians* and *Queen Victoria*,[19] the effort and strain of writing against the grain and current of the times is visible too. It is much less visible, of course, for not only is he dealing with facts, which are stubborn things, but he has fabricated, chiefly from eighteenth-century material, a very discreet code of manners of his own, which allows him to sit at table with the highest in the land and to say a great many things under cover of that exquisite apparel which, had they gone naked, would have been chased by the men-servants from the room. Still, if you compare *Eminent Victorians* with some of Lord Macaulay's essays,[20] though you will feel that Lord Macaulay is always wrong, and Mr Strachey always right, you will also feel a body, a sweep, a richness in Lord Macaulay's essays which show that his age was behind him; all his strength went straight into his work; none was used for purposes of concealment or of conversion. But Mr Strachey has had to open our eyes before he made us see; he has had to search out and sew together a very artful manner of speech; and the effort, beautifully though it is concealed, has robbed his work of some of the force that should have gone into it, and limited his scope.

For these reasons, then, we must reconcile ourselves to a season of failures and fragments. We must reflect that where so much strength is spent on finding a way of telling the truth the truth itself is bound to reach us in rather an exhausted and chaotic condition. Ulysses, Queen Victoria, Mr Prufrock – to give Mrs Brown some of the names she has made famous lately – is a little pale and dishevelled by the time her rescuers reach her. And it is the sound of their axes that we hear – a vigorous and stimulating sound in my ears – unless of course you wish to sleep, when in the bounty of his concern, Providence has provided a host of writers anxious and able to satisfy your needs.

Thus I have tried, at tedious length, I fear, to answer some of the questions which I began by asking. I have given an account of some of the difficulties which in my view beset the Georgian writer in all his forms. I have sought to excuse him. May I end by venturing to remind you of the duties and responsibilities that are yours as partners in this business of writing books, as companions in the railway carriage, as fellow travellers with Mrs Brown? For she is just as visible to you who remain silent as to us who tell stories about her. In the course of your daily life this past week you have had far stranger and more interesting experiences than the one I have tried to describe. You have overheard scraps of talk that filled you with amazement. You have gone to bed at night bewildered by the complexity of your feelings. In one day thousands of ideas have coursed through your brains; thousands of emotions have met, collided, and disappeared in astonishing disorder. Nevertheless, you allow the writers to palm off upon you a version of all this, an image of Mrs Brown, which has no likeness to that surprising apparition whatsoever. In your modesty you seem to consider that writers are of different blood and bone from yourselves; that they know more of Mrs Brown than you do. Never was there a more fatal mistake. It is this division between reader and writer, this humility on your part, these professional airs and graces on ours, that corrupt and emasculate the books which should be the healthy offspring of a close and equal alliance between us. Hence spring those sleek, smooth novels, those portentous and ridiculous biographies, that milk and watery criticism, those poems melodiously celebrating the innocence of roses and sheep which pass so plausibly for literature at the present time.

Your part is to insist that writers shall come down off their plinths and pedestals, and describe beautifully if possible, truthfully at any rate, our Mrs Brown. You should insist that she is an old lady of unlimited capacity and infinite variety; capable of appearing in any place; wearing any dress; saying anything and doing heaven knows what. But the things she says and the things she does and her eyes and her nose and her speech and her silence have an overwhelming fascination, for she is, of course, the spirit we live by, life itself.

But do not expect just at present a complete and satisfactory present-ment of her. Tolerate the spasmodic, the obscure, the fragmentary, the failure. Your help is invoked in a good cause. For I will make one final and surpassingly rash prediction – we are trembling on the verge of one of the great ages of English literature. But it can only be reached if we are determined never, never to desert Mrs Brown.

1–An essay in the *Criterion*, July 1924, (Kp C251) substantially derived from a paper read to the Cambridge Heretics on 18 May 1924 (MHP, B 13, transcribed in Appendix III below), which had itself evolved from 'Mr Bennett and Mrs Brown' above. In the following October the essay was reprinted, with very minor revisions (indicated here in the footnotes), by The Hogarth Press and issued as a pamphlet:

'Mr Bennett and Mrs Brown' (The Hogarth Essays, First Series, No. 1), under which title it also appeared, in two instalments, in the 'Books' section of the *New York Herald Tribune*, 23 and 30 August 1925.

Arnold Bennett (1867–1931) made no reply in the *Criterion* to VW's essay, although invited to do so by the editor, T. S. Eliot; he did, however, renew his original attack, which had appeared in *Cassell's Weekly*, 28 March 1923 (see notes below), some years later, in 'Another Criticism of the New School', *Evening Standard*, 2 December 1926 (*M&M*, no. 58). See also *'Books and Persons'*, 'Mr Galsworthy's Novel', 'The Rights of Youth', *II VW Essays*; 'What is a Novel?', *IV VW Essays*; 'Edmund Gosse', *V VW Essays*; and see Editorial Note, p. ***.

2 – Bennett, 'Is the Novel Decaying?', *Cassell's Weekly*, 28 March 1923 (*M&M*, pp. 12–14), which has: 'The foundation of good fiction is character-creating and nothing else. To render secure the importance of a novel . . . [see 'Mr Bennett and Mrs Brown', n3, above]'.

3 – H. G. Wells (1866–1946), John Galsworthy (1867–1933), E. M. Forster (1879–1970), D. H. Lawrence (1885–1930), Lytton Strachey (1880–1932), James Joyce (1882–1941), T. S. Eliot (1888–1963). See Appendix III, which has: 'Before I begin I shd. say that when I speak of the Georgians I am speaking of such writers as Mr Joyce, Mr Lawrence, Mr Forster, Mr Strachey, Mr Eliot, Miss Sitwell, Miss Richardson . . .'

4 – VW's choice of year was not wholly arbitrary: Edward VII, who reigned from 1901, died on 6 May 1910, and was succeeded by George V (d.1936). The First Post-Impressionist Exhibition opened at the Grafton Galleries on 8 November 1910, the ramifications of which startling event were yet to be fully registered in her fiction.

5 – Samuel Butler (1835–1902), *The Way of All Flesh* (1903) – see *'The Way of All Flesh'* above. George Bernard Shaw (1856–1950), whose *Saint Joan* was first produced in 1923 in America and in England in 1924, the year in which the English ban on his *Mrs Warren's Profession* (1893) was lifted.

6 – The *Daily Herald* was established in 1912, as 'a spirited advocate of social reform, its chief concern being the welfare of the working classes' (*Newspaper Press Directory*).

7 – Aeschylus, *Agamemnon* (458 BC). For VW on Thomas (1795–1881) and Jane Welsh Carlyle (1801–86) see 'The Letters of Jane Welsh Carlyle', 'More Carlyle Letters', *I VW Essays*, and 'Geraldine and Jane', *V VW Essays* and CR2.

8 – Bennett, 'Is the Novel Decaying?': 'The Sherlock Holmes stories have still a certain slight prestige. Because of the ingenuity of the plots? No. Because of the convincingness of the principal character? No. The man is a conventional figure. The reason is the convincingness of the ass Watson. Watson has real life. His authenticity convinces everyone, and the books in which he appears survive by reason of him'. Sir Arthur Conan Doyle (1859–1930) first established Holmes and Watson in the pages of the *Strand Magazine* in 1891.

9 – L. N. Tolstoy, *War and Peace* (1865–72); W. M. Thackeray, *Vanity Fair* (1847–8); Laurence Sterne, *The Life and Opinions of Tristram Shandy* (1760–7); Gustave Flaubert, *Madame Bovary* (1856); Jane Austen, *Pride and Prejudice* (1813); Thomas Hardy, *The Mayor of Casterbridge* (1886); Charlotte Brontë, *Villette* (1853).

10–Joseph Conrad (1857–1924) was born in Poland, Teodor Jozef Konrad Korzeniowski; his most recent work of fiction was *The Rover* (1923). Thomas Hardy (1840–1928), whose last novel was *Jude the Obscure* (1895).

11–Arnold Bennett, *Hilda Lessways* (1911).

12–Alfred, Lord Tennyson, *Maud; A Monodrama* (1855).

13–Bennett, *Hilda Lessways* (Methuen & Co., 1911), bk 1, ch. i, pp. 8–9.

14–*Ibid.*, p. 9.

15–*Ibid.*, pp. 9–10, which has: 'triflingly larger than the others'; and begins a new paragraph at: 'Suddenly Hilda heard'.

16–William Shakespeare (1564–1616), John Milton (1608–74), John Keats (1795–1821), Jane Austen (1775–1817), W. M. Thackeray (1811–63), Charles Dickens (1812–70).

17–*Ulysses* was published in 1922; Harriet Weaver had approached The Hogarth Press with Joyce's manuscript in 1918 but it was both legally and, because of its size, practically impossible for them to publish.

18–Eliot's publications at this date included *Prufrock and Other Observations* (1917), and *Poems* (1919) and *The Waste Land* (1922), both of which were issued by The Hogarth Press, the latter in 1923.

19–*Eminent Victorians* (1918), *Queen Victoria* (1921).

20–Thomas Babington Macaulay (1800–59), whose essays were first published in a collected edition in 1843.

Joseph Conrad

VW's essay in the *TLS*, 14 August 1924, (Kp C252) was later minimally revised for inclusion, under the same title, in *The Common Reader:* 1st series (1925). The reader is referred to *IV VW Essays*, where the revised version, together with variants in the form of footnotes, is reprinted in its place in *The Common Reader*.

Editions-de-Luxe

A Midsommer Night's Dreame is a magnificently printed book, which possesses, in addition, a quality not always found with magnificence, that it is easy, luxurious, and delightful to read. That it is a trifle too broad for the ordinary size of human hands is the only criticism we have to make. The text is a reproduction of that of the first folio of 1623. Mr

Newdigate has directed the printing; Mr Paul Nash provided the illustrations; and Mr Granville-Barker has written the introduction.[2] This last is an extremely illuminating document, for in it Mr Granville-Barker, while showing us how the play was probably staged in Shakespeare's time, deals with some of the problems which beset a producer at the present day. In *A Midsummer Night's Dream* Shakespeare was at odds with the mechanism of the modern theatre. He allows only for a little dancing, and for a few simple costumes. If, however, the producer keeps strictly to Shakespeare's provisions, he may achieve far less effect than the same methods achieved in Shakespeare's day. To us, whose eyes and ears have grown used to a far more elaborate setting, simplicity may seem bareness, reticence may appear starvation. To add the measure of exaggeration which is right in the circumstances, while keeping in mind the fact that the play is a poetic play, and everything must serve, and nothing compete with, the poetry, is a highly ticklish undertaking. Moreover, in *A Midsummer Night's Dream* the music has to be considered, which raises problems of special subtlety, as well as the dress, and the exact shade of meaning which the actors are to be taught to put upon their lines. Following in Mr Barker's steps, we see that a good producer is called upon to be a learned and sensitive Shakespearean critic in addition to his other qualifications; and his introduction whets our taste for the play in the best way possible by exciting our curiosity and stimulating our intelligence before the curtain rises.

Mr Bax's three experiments in dramatic form are also produced in a dignified and luxurious style, with wide margins and coloured illustrations. But the splendour of the form makes us ask inevitably whether his simple charm, verging as it so often does upon prettiness and dexterity, is worthy of the setting. By introducing the word 'experiment' he has perhaps led us to expect something more drastic than the very mild attempts which he has here made to supplement the conventional dramatic method. But acted simply in a studio with attention to dress and gesture, his three plays will no doubt achieve, what is by no means despicable, a pleasant, tasteful, and well-bred entertainment.

1–A review in the *N&A*, 23 August 1924, (Kp C253) of *A Midsommer Night's Dreame*. With an introduction by Harley Granville-Barker (Ernest Benn, 1924) by William Shakespeare and *Studio Plays: Three Experiments in Dramatic Form*. With designs for costumes and one scene by Dorothy Mullock (Palmer, 1924) by Clifford Bax (1886–1962), author and playwright, a founder in 1919 of the Phoenix Society which sought to revive early English drama on the London stage.

2 – Mr Newdigate, otherwise unidentified. Paul Nash (1889–1946), artist, a contemporary at the Slade School, 1910–11, of Gertler, Nevinson, Spencer and Nicholson, perhaps best known at this date for his work as an official war artist. Harley Granville-Barker (1877–1946), author, actor, director and Shakespearean scholar, whose production of *A Midsummer Night's Dream* – and other Shakespeare plays – at the Savoy Theatre during the period 1913–14 was profoundly influential.

The cheapening of motor-cars

The cheapening of motor-cars is another step towards the ruin of the country road. It is already almost impossible to take one's pleasure walking, and only inevitable necessity impels the owners of children or dogs to venture their limbs upon what is now little better than an unfenced railway track. On the line itself there are at least rails and signals to ensure some kind of safety. But on the high road the procession of vehicles is irregular and chaotic, and the pedestrian has to depend upon the consideration and humanity of the motorist, who is in a position to dispense with both if it suits him. That it does suit him those who have lived on the verge of military operations this summer can testify – the approach of a military car being the signal among walkers and cyclists either to dismount and stand still or risk some perfectly wanton onslaught on the part of the military upon the common amenities of the King's highway. The English road, moreover, is rapidly losing its old character – its colour, here tawny-red, here pearl-white; its flowery and untidy hedges; its quiet; its ancient and irregular charm. It is becoming, instead, black as cinders, smooth as oilcloth, shaven of wild flowers, straightened of corners, a mere racing-track for the convenience of a population seemingly in perpetual and frantic haste not to be late for dinner.

1 – A paragraph contributed to the 'From Alpha to Omega' column in the *N&A*, 27 September 1924, (Kp C253.1).

The Woolfs first acquired a car – a second-hand Singer, for £275 – in July 1927 and became intrepid motorists: 'Soon we shall look back at our pre-motor days as we do now at our days in the caves' (*III VW Diary*, 10 August 1927). See Editorial Note, p. xxv.

Appreciations

Mr Priestley is an appreciator, not a critic. He fills an office of great public use in an age oppressed with new books, and stinted of time in which to read them. He helps us to get at what is worth having in our contemporaries, rescues some, like Maurice Hewlett, who have fallen into the background, traces the development of others, like Mr de la Mare, who are still in mid-career, and gives us, by means of apt quotations, the chance of gauging much more rapidly and effectively than we could otherwise have done Mr Saintsbury's view of criticism, or the main outlines of Mr Jacobs's fiction.[2] As an appreciator, Mr Priestley has qualities that make him both admirable and trustworthy. He is a patient and careful exponent; he writes fluently and lucidly; he subdues, if he possesses, any wish to cut capers or shoot rockets of his own; and, above all, he is a born admirer.

But there are no revelations in his pages, no surprises, none of those phrases which are, he says, 'keys to new treasure-chambers of literature'.[3] One may enjoy his very readable essay upon Mr de la Mare with *The Veil*[4] lying upon the table, and feel no curiosity to re-read the book by its light. Part of this is due, of course, to the inevitable difficulties of digging deep into contemporaries – that one meets them at dinner, that we have only incomplete fragments upon which to base our judgement, and that they stand too close on top of us to be seen in proportion. Then, again, many of these essays have had some not wholly critical purpose in view, which has led Mr Priestley to meander into biography and apology, while, being obviously in the self-conscious stage of authorship, he has wasted a good deal of time doing battle with 'people' – people who contribute to the 'Pale Review,' people, who, if you praise anyone, 'are ready to think that one has dowered So-and-so with every virtue known to letters'.[5] Yet making allowance for all this we cannot help feeling that Mr Priestley might have grazed a good deal closer to his subjects without doing them violence or losing them readers. He might have been a critic, not merely an appreciator.

For if, as Mr Priestley asserts, his nine figures – Messrs Bennett, de la Mare, Hewlett, Housman, Jacobs, Lynd, Saintsbury, Santayana, and Squire[6] are important (though 'it must not be understood that I necessarily consider the figures the most important in contemporary literature'),[7] they are worth taking seriously. They have no need to be wrapped in cocoons of cotton-wool. They can hold their own, not merely with their contemporaries, but with the masters in their own lines. But at this point Mr Priestley seems to back out of one half of the business of criticism, which is, as he says, 'to appreciate and compare' either with some phrase of disarming modesty, or with some vague statement that 'such introspection and quaint imagery take us back to Donne and the metaphysicals of the seventeenth century'[8] which leaves us uncertain whether he means that Mr Squire is as good a poet as Donne, or resembles Donne; and quite in the dark, when the essay is finished, as to where in the ranks of poets Mr Priestley would place him.

The result is, therefore, that though we get a sense of his nine figures in outline, we get no sense of them in detail. They remain unrelated; praised, but praised provisionally. We slip about in uncomfortable uncertainty whether Mr Lynd is a 'magnificent proseman' absolutely or comparatively – on a par with Hazlitt, or only infinitely superior to Mr Garvin.[9] Thus, when we come to sample the authors in the quotations which are liberally provided, we find ourselves as often as not at loggerheads with Mr Priestley, yet remaining quite unrepentant. For though he has arranged his matter so as to bring his figures into focus, he has left us to make up our minds about them for ourselves. In short, he has fulfilled the office of an appreciator, which is to stimulate our interest, particularly in our contemporaries, but left unattempted the business of a critic, which is to make us reconsider our opinions and test, if we do not accept, his values.

1–A review in the *N&A*, 27 September 1924, (Kp C254) of *Figures in Modern Literature* (John Lane, 1924) by J. B. Priestley (1894–1984), whose *The Good Companions* and *Angel Pavement* were published in 1929 and 1930, in which year VW wrote in her diary, 8 September: 'At the age of 50 Priestley will be saying "Why don't the highbrows admire me? It isn't true that I only write for money." He will be enormously rich; but there will be that thorn in his shoe – or so I hope. Yet I have not read, & I daresay shall never read, a book by Priestley ... And I invent this phrase for Bennett & Priestley "the tradesmen of letters".' Reading Notes (MHP, B 20).

2–Priestley, 'Maurice Hewlett's Later Verse and Prose', pp. 55–76. Maurice Henry Hewlett (1861–1923), poet, author of romantic fiction and essayist, upon whom VW wrote in 'War in the Village', *II VW Essays; ibid.*, 'Mr de la Mare', pp. 31–54. Walter de la Mare (1873–1956), poet, novelist and anthologist, upon whom VW wrote in 'The Intellectual Imagination', above, and 'Dreams and Realities', *II VW Essays; ibid.*, 'Mr George Saintsbury', pp. 144–64; George Edward Bateman Saintsbury (1845–1933), literary critic and historian, Professor of Rhetoric and English Literature at Edinburgh University, 1895–1915; 'Mr W. W. Jacobs', *ibid.*, pp. 103–23; William Wymark Jacobs (1863–1943), story-writer.

3 – *Ibid.*, 'Mr George Saintsbury', p. 145.

4 – Walter de la Mare, *The Veil* (1921).

5 – For the 'Pale Review', Priestley, 'Mr W. W. Jacobs', p. 103, and for the quotation, *ibid.*, 'Mr A. E. Housman', p. 101.

6 – *Ibid.*, 'Mr Arnold Bennett', pp. 3–30; Arnold Bennett (1867–1931), see 'Mr Bennett and Mrs Brown' and 'Character in Fiction' above. *Ibid.*, 'Mr A. E. Housman', pp. 77–102; A. E. Housman (1859–1936), author of *A Shropshire Lad* (1896), whose *Last Poems* had appeared in 1922. *Ibid.*, 'Mr Robert Lynd', pp. 124–43. Robert Wilson Lynd (1879–1949), literary journalist and essayist, upon whom VW wrote in 'A Book of Essays', *II VW Essays. Ibid.*, 'Mr George Santayana', pp. 165–87. George Santayana (1863–1952), speculative philosopher, author of *Life of Reason* (1905–6). *Ibid.*, 'Mr J. C. Squire', pp. 188–215. John Collings Squire (1884–1958), man of letters, editor of the *London Mercury*, 1919–34, upon whom VW wrote in 'Parodies', 'Imitative Essays' and 'Bad Writers', *II VW Essays*.

7 – *Ibid.*, author's note, unnumbered contents page.

8 – For the first quotation, *ibid.*, 'Mr George Saintsbury', p. 147 and for the second, 'Mr J. C. Squire', pp. 212–13, a complete sentence.

9 – For the quotation, *ibid.*, 'Mr Robert Lynd', p. 143. William Hazlitt (1778–1830). J. L. Garvin (1868–1947), editor of the *Observer*, 1908–42.

The Schoolroom Floor

Of writers there are two kinds: one builds neat architectural sentences, in which brick is placed upon brick, solid and symmetrical; the other flies and smudges with the flat of the thumb or the tip of the little finger; the one makes sentences, the other phrases; and it is to the phrase-makers that Mrs MacCarthy belongs. That orderly and accurate beginning – 'I was born in the eighties into a sheltered, comfortable, upper middle class, religious and literary circle'[2] – does not deceive us. A dozen lines lower down you will find her catching the Poet Laureate himself in her net – 'Lord Tennyson was living a deliciously sheltered life at Farringford, perplexed about immortality on the windy downs';[3] next, giving chase to her mother and aunts 'flitting up and down the wide staircase in white muslins, with camellias in their hair and Beethoven scores under their arms'.[4]

For Mrs MacCarthy was the daughter of Mrs – must we call her Kestell? – of Eton, and this little book is an attempt to envelope that dazzling and erratic butterfly and any other queer Victorian insects who may be on the wing in a veil of gauze. Rather tentative, rather apologetic, rather amateurish these sweeps of the net seem to be. It is only when the book is finished that we realize how beautifully with a fling of a phrase the insects have been caught. There they are, fluttering and feasting on their dahlias and their ivy blossoms – Mr Shorthouse asking for a hymn tune, Mr Oscar Browning sipping tea,[5] Mary Coleridge reading Browning aloud, the old Judge disrupting the whole assembly with his cough ('It is a geyser explosion, a thunderstorm, the collapse of a skylight, something quite unique in the volume of crashing sound'),[6] Herr Joachim taking Mrs Tallboys down to supper, Mr Henry James surveying the ballroom – there they are.[7]

But we must not mislead lovers of memoirs into supposing that Mrs MacCarthy has dished up the eminent Victorians once more. That may be Lord Tennyson's hat in the hall; those Mr Browning's boots; through the drawing-room door we may hear the reverberation of Mr Henry James, who, seeing the end of his sentence in the distance, with uplifted hand and rumbling fence of sound wards off intruders. But we are for the schoolroom. We run upstairs into the children's shabby quarters, where Evelina is making a garden of tattered flowers on the carpet, Mary lying on the floor 'chaunting idly and looking at things upside down',[8] while old Nurse ranges about threatening hair-brushes and inciting young ladies to virtuous employment. For it is Mrs MacCarthy's achievement to throw open the whole house and not merely the sanctuaries of the eminent and grown-up; to make us free of the rambling Victorian dwelling-place with its profusion of coal fires, its legions of starched housemaids, its trays, its cans, its lamps, its candles, its warbling aunts, its scrimmaging schoolboys, and above all its strange mistress, odd, speculative, absent-minded; brilliant, disconcerting, unaccountable – its Mrs Kestell, in short. That elusive figure with the Warden at her side trails and wanders through her daughter's pages. Now in the middle of her waltz tune she stops to dream; now inhales the sweetness of a peach; now, ignoring the bigwig to whom she should be listening, bears down upon some shy colleger and carries him off to read Sainte-Beuve aloud in the garden: '"So fascinating reading to Mr ——," she says presently re-entering the room. "He understands every *nuance*"';[9] now, snatching up her pen on the impulse of the moment, greets her little girl at the station with the news that the shepherd of Farringford is dead; quotes Clough; and explains the word 'fantastic'.[10]

Bulky, vigorous, and voluble, not so very eminent, full of agreeable eccentricities and dashed with a whimsical radiance – such are the Victorians if you lie with Mrs MacCarthy on the schoolroom floor.

1–A review in the *TLS*, 2 October 1924, (Kp C255) of *A Nineteenth-Century Childhood* (William Heinemann, 1924) by Mary [Molly] MacCarthy, *née* Warre-Cornish (1882–1953), daughter of Francis Warre-Cornish, Vice-Provost of Eton, 1893–1916, and Blanche, *née* Ritchie, and wife of the critic Desmond MacCarthy, to whom the book is dedicated. The volume had been serialised in eight parts in the *N&A*, 1 September 1923–14 June 1924. She had previously published a novel, *A Pier and A Band* (1918).

'By the way,' VW wrote to her on 2 October 1924 (*III VW Letters*, no. 1500), 'I've been reading your childhood over again with envy and delight, and even scribbled a wretched review for The Times. I thought I'd better make a breast of it; (clean breast it should be). I did it in a frightful hurry; and missed out all I wanted to put in, and did not convey in the least my envy and delight. Now you will be squirming with horror, like a toad one's half trodden on in the dark. But I detect in your tone a slight audacity which I take to mean that you have been considerably complimented, and find it rather refreshing. I thought old [A.C.] Benson rather good [for VW on 'Mr Benson's Memories' see above], considering what a foggy dew the poor man's mind is.' See Editorial Note, p. xxv.

2–MacCarthy, ch. i, p. 1.

3–*Ibid.*, Alfred, Lord Tennyson (1809–92).

4–*Ibid.*, p. 3.

5–For Joseph Henry Shorthouse (1834–1903), a Birmingham vitriol manufacturer and author of *John Inglesant* (1881), *ibid.*, ch. ii, p. 11; and for Oscar Browning (1837–1923), historian and Fellow of King's College, Cambridge, an Apostle, and a master at Eton from 1860 until his dismissal in 1875 following malicious gossip about ill-judged but probably innocent intimacies with his pupils, *ibid.*, p. 7.

6–For the poet Mary Coleridge (1861–1907) reading 'the "Flight of the Duchess" or some other poem' and from 'Artemis Prologizes' by Robert Browning (1812–89) and for the coughing but otherwise unidentified Judge, *ibid.*, ch. v, pp. 55–6.

7–For Joseph Joachim (1831–1907), the Hungarian virtuoso violinist, friend of Mendelssohn, Brahms and Schumann, and Mrs Tallboys, otherwise unidentified, *ibid.*, ch. x, p. 99; and for Henry James (1843–1916), *ibid.*, p. 98.

8–*Ibid.*, ch. i, p. 9. 'Evelina' conceals the identity of one or other of Mary's four sisters, possibly the eldest, Cecilia, who married Admiral Sir William Fisher.

9–Charles Augustin Sainte-Beuve (1804–69), *ibid.*, ch. vii, p. 77. .

10–*Ibid.*, ch. v, p. 53; Arthur Hugh Clough (1819–61).

Restoration Comedy

Of Mr Gosse's book, now enlarged, revised, and containing one poem not yet printed in Congreve's works, one may say what one may generally say of Mr Gosse's books; that it is competent, well-informed, and discreet; full of demure fun, pleasant phrases ('he passed through the literary life of his time as if in felt slippers'),[2] and good sense. The standard, of course, is not the highest. He does not create a character when he writes a biography; he does not penetrate to the depths when he writes a criticism. But his pages are completely free from the extravagance of the creative, or the turbidity of the profound. He enjoys to the full 'the charming pleasure of easy composition';[3] and Congreve, of whom little is known, and that mostly to his credit, is a subject well-suited to his urbane and skilful pen.

Mr Dobrée has attempted with marked success a more difficult task. He has tried to give us a general view of comedy in the period from Etherege to Farquhar,[4] and has succeeded in putting forward a variety of suggestive and interesting ideas from which we may proceed to further discovery on our own account. Chief among them are that Restoration comedy expressed 'not licentiousness, but a deep curiosity, and a desire to try new ways of living'; and that it was 'of English growth and would have existed substantially the same had Molière never lived'[5] – both sayings which lead us to put our Wycherley[6] and our Congreve to the test of reading afresh. Licentiousness is, of course, a chameleon quality which changes from age to age. Not so very long ago London playgoers had a chance of analysing their own attitude to the matter when *The Country Wife*[7] was performed. Of that twentieth-century audience few were shocked, but it is safe to say that some were bored. It became plain, indeed, as the favourite topic was harped upon, in scene after scene, joke after joke, that indecency loses its savour sooner, is less fertile and profound, than more normal topics once the shock of novelty has worn off. Yet it was obvious, too, that indecency was as essential a part of Wycherley's genius as the crust is of the loaf; nor can we agree with Mr Dobrée in making 'a deep curiosity and a desire to try new ways of living' the begetter of that peculiarly irresponsible and very English love of bawdry. We doubt, indeed, whether in the matter of indecency there is much to choose between the Elizabethan and Restoration comedy; save that Elizabethan indecency is put away from us and disguised by the poetry, and Restoration indecency brought home and laid bare by the prose.

But the change of subject in Restoration comedy is, of course, undeniable. And here Mr Dobrée makes a subtle distinction. The 'atmosphere' remained English; but the 'life' owed much to the French.[8] The French civility had penetrated into the English drawing room; the language was more expressive and the manners more refined. But the genius which gave colour and tone to the whole remained English, and far more closely related to the Elizabethan than to the French. No one, indeed, who compares *The Plain Dealer* with *Le Misanthrope*[9] can fail to be aware of some of the fundamental differences which separate the two races. Where the French suggest, the English explain; where the French generalise, the English particularise; where the French give us in Alceste[10] a type of man's disillusionment and the vanity of society, the English give us a burly sea captain who is far better fitted to polish off a Dutchman with his own fists than to stand apart and meditate the worthlessness of mankind.

Etherege, Wycherley, Dryden, Shadwell, Congreve, Vanbrugh,[11] and Farquhar are all dealt with in Mr Dobrée's book with a brevity which is full of point, though some contortions of wit are needed to keep the matter within the space, and we confess to thinking that those anti-quated weapons – rapier, singlestick, and bludgeon – as articles of comparison have served their day. But the book has the prime merit of lighting up a corner of the library which had grown, not altogether owing to our own fault, a little dim.

1 – A review in the *N&A*, 18 October 1924, (Kp C258) reprinted in the *NR*, 11 February 1925, of *Restoration Comedy, 1660–1720* (OUP, 1924) by Bonamy Dobrée and *The Life of William Congreve* [1670–1729] ... first published 1888, 2nd impression revised and enlarged (Wm Heinemann, 1924) by Edmund Gosse. See also 'Congreve' and 'Mr Gosse and his Friends' above; 'Congreve', *IV VW Essays*; and 'Congreve's Comedies: Speed, Stillness and Meaning', *VI VW Essays*. See Editorial Note, p. xxv. Reading Notes (*MHP*, B 20).

2 – Gosse, ch. v, p. 165: 'He passes through the literary life of his time as if in felt slippers, noiseless, unupbraiding, without personal adventures.'

3 – *Ibid.*, p. 167, after quoting Voltaire's *Lettres philosophiques* (1733) on Congreve: 'The anecdote is interesting and valuable, but perhaps we need not be so much disgusted at Congreve's attitude as Voltaire. We must remember that the incident occurred in 1726, very late in Congreve's life, when literary ambition, and, above all, the charming pleasure of easy composition, had long abandoned him. May not what Voltaire took to be vanity have been really modesty?'

4 – Sir George Etherege (1634?–91?); George Farquhar (1678–1707).

5 – For the first quotation, Dobrée, ch. ii, p. 22, and for the second, *ibid.*, ch. iv, p. 57: 'It seems fair to say that Restoration comedy was of English growth, that it would have existed substantially the same had Molière never lived, and our own theatres never been closed because stage-plays were "spectacles of pleasure, too commonly expressing lascivious mirth and levity".' Molière (Jean Baptiste Poquelin, 1622–73).

6 – William Wycherley (1640–1716).

7 – William Wycherley, *The Country Wife* (1675).

8 – For 'atmosphere', Dobrée, ch. iv, p. 48: '... the object of French comedy was something quite different from that of the English. The former aimed at atmosphere, the latter at acute characterization and high-flavoured speech', and *ibid.*, p. 51: 'English plays, therefore, never aimed at producing the same cool atmosphere as the

French'; and for 'life', *ibid.*, p. 54: 'We may say, in fact, that it was French life rather than French literary form that was reflected in our comedies through the medium of the court, in confirmation of which we may appeal to Dryden [and his dedication of *Marriage à la Mode* to Rochester].'

9 – Wycherley, *The Plain Dealer* (1677); Molière, *Le Misanthrope* (1666).
10 – Hero of *Le Misanthrope*.
11 – John Dryden (1631–1700); Thomas Shadwell (1642?–92); Sir John Vanbrugh (1664–1726).

It is strange as one enters the Mansard Gallery . . .

It is strange as one enters the Mansard Gallery today to think that once upon a time the London Group led the van and received into its devoted breast the most pointed arrows of ridicule and criticism. Last week out of a crowd of a hundred private viewers one only, and she elderly and infirm to boot, might be heard to giggle; the rest were able to concentrate their minds not upon their own dignity but upon the pictures – a change marvellous, but welcome. But the Group has not lost its sting in coming of age. It has grown able to practise easily what it once professed self-consciously. The good pictures are as good as, perhaps better than, ever. There is a very fine example of Mr Sickert;[2] Mr Thornton[3] proves himself an artist to be reckoned with seriously; Mr Mathew Smith[4] follows his own bent rather too pugnaciously, for there is danger that his marked personality may stereotype and confine him; Mlle Lessore[5] is exquisitely witty; Mrs Bell[6] illumines a whole wall, in spite of the drizzle outside, with a flower piece in which every rose seems instinct with brilliant life, yet seized in a moment of intense stillness; in a superb picture of red-hot pokers Mr Grant[7] makes us hope that he has reconciled the diverse gifts which for the last year or two have been tugging him asunder and puzzling his admirers. But the show is curiously unequal. The goodness of the good accentuates the mediocrity of the bad. And there are one or two problems. What is Mr Gertler doing?[8] we ask with the curiosity which that remarkable artist always arouses. What mood of dissatisfaction and experiment has him trapped at the moment? A curious stolidity marks his pictures this year. Considered as an end they are disappointing, as a stage in his progress interesting as usual.

1 – A paragraph in the 'From Alpha to Omega' column in the *N&A*, 18 October 1924, (Kp C255.1) on the 21st Exhibition of the London Group, at the Mansard Gallery, Heal & Son Ltd, 196 Tottenham Court Road, 13 October–8 November 1924. The London Group, to which Bloomsbury's painters belonged, had grown in 1913 out of the Camden Town and other smaller groups; its first exhibition was held at the Goupil Gallery in March 1914. VW had addressed the Group at a dinner on 31 March 1924, upon the retirement of their president Bernard Adeney (succeeded by Frank Dobson). She spoke on the unity of the arts (see *II VW Diary*, p. 300, n 7).

2 – Walter Sickert (1860–1942), No. 34 'Banco'.

3 – Alfred Thornton (1863–1939), No. 55 'Spring Landscape', No. 57 'King's Mill Stream', No. 74 'The Sluice, King's Mill', No. 80 'King's Mill, Painswick', No. 98 'Griffith's Farm, Stroud'.

4 – Matthew Smith (1879–1959), No. 56 'Pose Turque', No. 61 'Odalisque', No. 68 'Croquis de Nu', No. 71 'Odalisque Sleeping'.

5 – Thérèse Lessore (1884–1944, who in 1926 married Walter Sickert), No. 32 'Epsom. Watching the Oaks', No. 41 'The End of May', No. 43 'June in the Gardens', No 76 'The Fossetts at Islington'.

6 – Vanessa Bell (1879–1961), No. 9 'Roses and Apples', No. 12 'Nude', No. 16 'Farm Buildings'.

7 – Duncan Grant (1885–1978), No. 14 'Still Life', No. 28 'Pot of Flowers', No. 40 'The Pond', No. 49 'Red-Hot Pokers'.

8 – Mark Gertler (1891–1939), No. 18 'Head of a Young Girl', No. 39 'Ornamental Bird', No. 50 'Pond', No. 54 'Roses and Tapestry', No. 100 'The Toilet'.

Not the least pitiable victims . . .

Not the least pitiable victims of the deplorable summer that is dead are the aged men who, being past work in the fields, have been used to pick up a few shillings by scouring fields for mushrooms. The crop, always capricious, has in certain districts failed almost entirely this summer, and it is common to meet the village patriarch who tends the geese and the grandchildren, and sometimes cuts a little wood, listlessly poking in the grass and lamenting either that some smart fellow has been before him, or that the rain, which is favourable in moderation, has flooded the mushrooms out of the fields. Of the habits and nature of mushrooms, he can tell one little. Time out of mind they have grown in this field; never, so long as he can remember, have they been seen in that. Yet the fields appear in every way identical. Further, there are periods in their coming and going, ruled, according to him, by the moon, which has its finger in so many village pies. Two years ago the glut of mushrooms satiated the appetites of every breakfast-table for miles around, but this year a handful is considered fair exchange for a whole hatful of apples. But while the male pursuit of mushroom gathering has failed, the women and children have had a fine harvest of blackberries, for the sexes keep their stations scrupulously distinct – no man picking blackberries, no woman encroaching upon the mushroom preserves.

1 – A paragraph contributed to the 'From Alpha to Omega' column in the N&A, 18 October 1924, (Kp C255.2). See Editorial Note, p. xxv.

'Richard Hakluyt'

It is strange that this little volume should be the first devoted entirely to Richard Hakluyt, and stranger still that Hakluyt's solitary composition (for the great *Navigations* was of course a compilation), his *Discourse concerning Western Planting*, written in 1584, should have been left to the Americans to publish in 1877.[2] For Hakluyt was more than the first editor of the English travels; he was the first Secretary of State for the Colonies. It was he who foresaw the benefits of 'plantations' for our surplus population, and as a refuge for 'people forced to flee for the truth of God's word';[3] he who endeavoured to train sailors in the arts of navigation, and collected from all sorts of obscure sources, often at great trouble to himself, information useful to travellers. Moreover, he was the first to feel that responsibility for the moral and intellectual welfare of the savage which so many English statesmen have professed since. His aim, as he repeated, was not merely profit, but 'the saving of the souls of the poor and blinded infidels', the instilling into them of 'the sweet and lively liquor of the Gospel'.[4] All this is well brought out in Mr Watson's little biography, and corrects the too purely literary estimate which sees in him chiefly the man who may have inspired Shakespeare, and who has certainly got together some of the finest stories of sea travel in the language.

1 – A notice in the N&A, 25 October 1924, (Kp C255.3) of *Richard Hakluyt* (The Sheldon Press, 1924) by Foster Watson, D.Litt., Prof. Emeritus, University College of Wales, Aberystwyth. See also 'Sir Walter Raleigh', 'Trafficks and Discoveries', *II VW Essays*; 'The Elizabethan Lumber Room', *IV VW Essays* and *CR 1*. See Editorial Note, p. xxv. Reading Notes (MHP, B 20).
2 – *The Principal Navigations, Voyages, and Discoveries of the English Nation*

(1589; 1598–1600); the *Discourse* was published by the Maine Historical Society.
3–For the first quotation, Watson, ch. ix, p. 91, and for the second, *ibid.*, p. 94.
4–For the first quotation, *ibid.*, ch. viii, p. 88, and for the second, *ibid.*, ch. ix, p. 93.

'Smoke Rings and Roundelays'

The best tribute to the worth of Mr Partington's book is that we found ourselves so entertained by its contents and so spiritually made aware of the soul of tobacco that for a whole hour, engrossed in its pages, we neglected our pipe. The compilation had been made with considerable skill and variety. Poets, historians, memoir writers, and novelists have all contributed the praises or written the life story of the inspired leaf. Thus we learn how it is M. Nicot,[2] French Ambassador to Portugal in 1559, who is immortalised in nicotine; how stealthily the habit first took root under cover, like so many English habits, of its virtues rather than its charms; how 'a leaf or two being steept o'er night in a little white wine is a vomit that never fails in its operation';[3] how women smoked anciently as much as men; how the weed was banned in the prudish days of Victoria; how cigarettes were first seen in England about 1860;[4] how Van Klaes of Rotterdam smoked nearly five ounces of tobacco every day, and had his coffin lined with the wood of his old cigar-boxes, and his pipe and matches laid beside him – 'for one never knows what may happen'[5] – and at that point it became necessary to light up, which pipe, and it was the best of the day, we smoked and dedicated to the erudite Mr Partington.

1–A notice in the *N&A*, 25 October 1924, (Kp C255.4) of *Smoke Rings and Roundelays. Blendings from Prose and Verse Since Raleigh's Time* (Castle, 1924) compiled by Wilfred Partington, with woodcuts by Norman James. Reading Notes (MHP, B 20). See Editorial Note, p. xxv.
2–Jean Nicot, Lord of Villemain, Master of the Requests of the French King's household.
3–Partington, 'After Poring Upon a Book. James Howell, *Epistolae Ho-Elianae* (1650)', p. 160.
4–*Ibid.*, p. 127: "'It may fairly be concluded, I think," says G. L. Apperson in his *Social History of Smoking*, "that although about 1860 there may have been an occasional cigarette-smoker in England . . . yet it was not until a little later date that the small paper-enclosed rolls of tobacco became at all common among Englishmen . . .'"
5–*Ibid.*, 'King of Smokers', p. 104; Heer van Klaes (d. aetat 98).

'Memories of a Militant'

The great age of militancy and the vote is rapidly becoming dim, but it is still within living memory that one of the most picturesque champions of the cause was a factory girl who had actually worn shawl and clogs and was ready to go to prison any number of times. In her autobiography Miss Kenney throws light upon the make-up of a temperament which every revolution seems to create or bring to the surface. For Miss Kenney is not one of the rare thinkers who lead and inspire, but one of the more numerous class who follow and are inspired. 'I could not have reasoned the point why a cat drinks milk,' she writes, and she adds that, when she tried to read other books in order to write her own, she found that her 'clear thought did not flow freely',[2] and shut them up. Her devotion, it sometimes seems, was rather to Miss Pankhurst[3] than to a cause, and her book gives an account of their personal adventures and escapes rather than a history of the whole movement. But she is a singularly good witness-medium through which to behold those stirring days, because her enthusiasm is so unreflecting and her style so spontaneous. Strangely and incongruously she numbers Voltaire among her heroes.[4]

1 – A notice in the *N&A*, 8 November 1924, (Kp C256.1) of *Memories of a Militant* (Edward Arnold, 1924) by Annie Kenney (1879–1953), fifth of twelve children born to Horatio Nelson Kenney, cotton operative, and his wife Ann Wood. See Editorial Note, p. xxiv.
2 – For the first quotation, Kenney, ch. xxi, p. 180: 'There was I, head of a great Militant Movement, having final responsibility for a paper [*Votes for Women*], I who could not have reasoned the point of why a cat drank milk, jumping at conclusions about words, actions, speeches'; and for the second, *ibid*., ch. xv, p. 136, which has: 'it prevented clear thought from flowing freely'.
3 – (Dame) Christabel Pankhurst (1880–1958).
4 – Kenney, ch. iii, p. 22, first discovered Voltaire in an article in the pages of the *Rational Review* in Oldham Library. She quotes his view that: 'England is a country where thought is noble and free, unrestrained by any slavish fear. If I followed my own inclination I would take up my abode there with no other ideal than to learn to think' (ch. xv, p. 130).

'Peggy. The Story of One Score Years and Ten'

The Webling sisters were once little girls who recited at parties and roused the admiration of John Ruskin,[2] who presented Peggy with Johnson's dictionary, and Rosalind with a complete set of Byron's works bound in blue morocco. Indeed they met most of the celebrities of the late nineteenth century, and pressed the 'very warm and unusually soft hands' of Edward Prince of Wales.[3] But celebrities look a little garish in the homely light which this very friendly and unpretentious and engaging book sheds upon the Webling family. Time's wheel turns methodically, and brings nonentities to the top and sends the celebrated down. We are tired of the witticisms of Oscar Wilde,[4] but the sayings of Mrs Wilson, the dressmaker, enchant. The pink plush, she said, 'was so rebukey that it positively broke the needles'. And she said she would not work for 'any pompshous or precocious person'.[5] The Weblings were neither pompshous nor precocious. Mr Webling sold old silver, and his daughter lived a hand-to-mouth journalistic dramatic existence, in England and in Canada, the story of which is better worth reading, in all its garrulity and slippered ease, than nine novels out of a baker's dozen.

1 – A notice in the *N&A*, 8 November 1924, (Kp C256.2) of *Peggy. The Story of One Score Years and Ten* (Hutchinson & Co., 1924) by Peggy Webling, 'author of *Comedy Corner, The Fruitless Orchard* etc'. VW wrote in her diary on Friday, 17 October 1924: 'Did I put down my progress towards Perpetual Immortality (to quote one of Peggy Webling's wishes as a child – a [Books in] Brief I'm doing, or should be doing?)' See Editorial Note, p. xxiv.

2 – John Ruskin (1819–1900).

3 – For the quotation, Webling, ch. vi, p. 73: 'My small hand was lost in his, which was very warm and unusually soft for a man's, though his clasp was firm.' Edward, Prince of Wales (1841–1910), from 1901 Edward VII.

4 – For the tired witticisms of Oscar Wilde (1854–1900), both addressed to Ruskin, *ibid.*, ch. vi, pp. 70–1: 'Is not Peggy Webling a wave of delight from God?', and: 'Great Master is not Peggy Webling *too precious!*'

5 – For both quotations, *ibid.*, ch. iv, p. 38.

'The Antiquary'

There are some writers who have entirely ceased to influence others, whose fame is for that reason both serene and cloudless, who are enjoyed or neglected rather than criticised and read. Among them is Scott. The most impressionable beginner, whose pen oscillates if exposed within a mile of the influence of Stendhal, Flaubert, Henry James, or Chekhov, can read the Waverley novels one after another without altering an adjective. Yet there are no books perhaps upon which at this moment more thousands of readers are brooding and feasting in a rapture of silent satisfaction. *The Antiquary, The Bride of Lammermoor, Redgauntlet, Waverley, Guy Mannering, Rob Roy, The Heart of Midlothian*[2] – what can one do when one has finished the last but wait a decent interval and then begin again upon the first?

Uncritical and silent enjoyment – perhaps this implies that the Waverley novel reading habit has something vicious about it, that one keeps it private, does not wish to share it, nor feel altogether sure that one can defend it. What can be said, for instance, in favour of Scott's style? Every page of every masterpiece is watered down with long, languid Latin words: peruse, manifest, evince; the sea in the heat of a crisis is 'the devouring element'; a gull on the same occasion a 'winged denizen of the crag'.[3] But this only shows that Scott, like most great novelists, wrote in pages, not in sentences, and had at his command, and knew the season when to use, styles of different qualities, genteel penmanship included. These slips and slovenlinesses are pauses which give the reader breathing space and air the book. Moreover, it is only perfunctorily that one either notices or condemns them; read currently, in their places, as Scott uses them, they fulfil their purpose and merge perfectly with their surroundings. Let us compare Scott the slovenly with Stevenson[4] the precise, and it cannot be denied that though we get from Stevenson a much closer idea of a single object, we get from Scott an incomparably more vivid impression of the whole. The storm in *The Antiquary*, made up of all sorts of stage hangings and cardboard screens – 'denizens of the crags', 'clouds like disasters around a sinking empire'[5] – nevertheless roars and splashes and almost devours the group huddled on the crag; while the storm in *Kidnapped*,[6] with its conscientious detail and its neat dapper adjectives, is incapable of wetting the sole of a lady's slipper.

The much more serious charge against Scott is that he used the wrong pen, the genteel pen, not merely to fill in backgrounds and dash off a cloud piece, but to describe the intricacies and passions of the human heart. But what language to use of the Lovels and Isabellas, the Darsies, Ediths, and Mortons![7] As well talk of the hearts of seagulls and the passions and intricacies of walking-sticks and umbrellas; for indeed these ladies and gentlemen are scarcely to be distinguished from the winged denizens of the crag. They are equally futile; equally impotent; they squeak; they flutter; and a strong smell of camphor exudes from their poor dried breasts when, with a dismal croaking and cawing, they emit the astonishing language of their love-making.

'Without my father's consent, I will never entertain the addresses of anyone; and how totally impossible it is that he should countenance the partiality with which you honour me, you are yourself fully aware,' says the young lady. 'Do not add to the severity of repelling my sentiments the rigour of obliging me to disavow them,'[8] replies the young gentleman; and he may be illegitimate, and he may be the son of a peer, and he may be both one and the other, but it would take a far stronger inducement than that to make us care a straw what happens to Lovel and his Isabella.

But then, after all, we are not meant to care a straw. Having pacified his conscience as a magistrate by alluding to the sentiments of the upper classes in tones of respect and esteem, having vindicated his character as an artist by awakening 'the better feelings and sympathies of his readers by strains of generous sentiment and tales of fictitious woe',[9] Scott was quit both of art and of morals, and could scribble endlessly for his own amusement. Never was a change more emphatic; never one more wholly to the good. One is tempted indeed to suppose that he did it, half-consciously, on purpose – showed up the languor of the fine gentlemen who bored him by the immense vivacity of the common people whom he loved. Images, anecdotes, illustrations drawn from sea, sky, and earth, race and bubble from their lips. They shoot every thought as it flies, and bring it tumbling to the ground in metaphor. Sometimes it is a phrase – 'at the back of a dyke, in a wreath o' snaw, or in the wame o' a wave'; sometimes a proverb – 'he'll no can haud down his head to sneeze, for fear o' seeing his shoon';[10] always the dialogue is sharpened and pointed by the use of that Scottish dialect which is at once so homely and so pungent, so colloquial and so passionate, so shrewd and so melancholy into the bargain. And the result is strange. For since the sovereigns who should preside have abdicated, since we are afloat on a broad and breezy sea without a pilot, the Waverley novels are as unmoral as Shakespeare's plays. Nor, for some readers, is it the least part of their astonishing freshness, their perennial vitality, that you may read them over and over again, backwards and forwards, and never know for certain what Scott himself thought.

We know, however, what his characters thought, and we know it almost as we know what our friends think by supplementing what they say as they speak, by watching their faces, hearing their voices, by remembering, constructing, and putting two and two together. However often one may have read *The Antiquary*, Jonathan Oldbuck is made afresh each time. We notice different things, we make him up a little differently at every reading, and it is for this reason that Scott's characters, like Shakespeare's and Jane Austen's,[11] are never the same twice running. But Scott's characters have this disability; it is only when they speak that they are alive, for it is inconceivable that they ever sat down and thought, and as for prying into their minds or drawing inferences from their behaviour, he was far too true a gentleman to attempt it. 'Miss Wardour, as if she felt she had said too much, turned and got into the carriage'[12] – that is the furthest he will pursue Miss Wardour, and it is not very far. But this matters the less because the characters he cared for were by temperament chatterboxes; Edie Ochiltree, Oldbuck, Mrs Mucklebackit, talk incessantly; they turn and twist their characters as they talk, or, if they stop talking, it is only to act, which reveals them still further – active, able-bodied people as they are, out in all weathers, horsemen, soldiers, gipsy women, fishermen. By their talk and by their acts – that is how we know them.

But how far, then, can we know people if we know only that they say this and do that, if they never talk about themselves, and their creator lets them go their ways in complete independence of his supervision or interference? Are they not all of them, Ochiltrees, Antiquaries, Meg Merrilies, and Dandy Dinmonts,[13] merely bundles of humours and good humours, innocent, childish humours at that, who serve to beguile our dull hours and charm our sick ones, and are packed off to the nursery when the working day returns and our normal faculties crave something tough to set their teeth into? Indeed, the Waverley reader must admit, there is a simplicity in them; a sanity, a complete lack of subtlety which, just as the Scotch dialect charms and the coaches and the highwaymen allure, may be adventitious snares, charming us who have grown so used to a more sophisticated art. But first this chatter and gossip contain within them a host of observations, subtle, and profound enough should we trouble to spread them out; and next this transparent stream through which we see stones, weeds, and minnows at the bottom, becomes without warning the sea – the deep, the inscrutable, the universal ocean on which we put out with the greatest only. Thus it is in the cottage where Steenie Mucklebackit lies dead; the father's grief, the mother's irritability, the minister's consolations, all come together, tragic, irrelevant, comic, drawn, one knows not how, to make a whole, a complete presentation of life, which, as always, Scott creates carelessly, without a word of comment, as if the parts grew together without his willing it, and broke into ruin again without his caring.

For who taps at the door and destroys that memorable scene? The cadaverous Earl of Glenallan; the unhappy nobleman who, years ago, had married his sister in the belief that she was his cousin, in horror at which she had jumped off a cliff and left him to wear the sables for ever. Romance breaks in; the peerage breaks in, all the trappings of the undertaker and the heralds' office in combination. True, there is a sort of charm in these absurdities now that the dust is thick on them and the colours dim; but judged squarely we must admit them vapid and thin; tiresome in the ravelling and the unravelling; a ceremonious posturing with cloaks and swords upon a Gothic background. What, indeed, is more capricious than the romance of human relations? What changes more swiftly from year to year? And Scott with his formal, old-fashioned approach to the mysteries of the heart, was not the one to break the seals or loose the fountains. His romance is nature's romance. It is the romance of hunted men, hiding in woods at night; of brigs standing out to sea; of waves breaking in the moonlight; of solitary sands and distant horsemen; of violence and suspense. This survives; this, which is not so profound or so moving as the other, but if we remember the excitement of the moment, and the flying beauty of the landscape, and the abundance and the freedom and the groups round inn-tables and the talk – above all the talk – ostlers talking, old beggars talking, gipsies talking, postmistresses talking, as if they would talk their hearts out, how then can we deny him a place among the highest? And the only question to be decided is which to read next, *Waverley,* or *The Bride of Lammermoor?*

1–A signed essay in the *N&A,* 22 November 1924, (Kp C256) reprinted in the *NR,* 3 December 1924, based on *The Antiquary* (1816) by Sir Walter Scott (1771–1832). VW later substantially revised the essay and it subsequently appeared in the posthumous collection *The Moment* – see *VI VW Essays.* See also 'Scott's Character' above; 'Gas at Abbotsford', *VI VW Essays*; and see Leslie Stephen, 'Sir Walter Scott', *Hours in a Library* (1874 etc), and the *DNB* entry on Scott, also by Stephen.

The same issue of the *N&A* also contained LW's 'World of Books' column, on the works of Thomas Love Peacock. Reading Notes (Berg xxvi).

2 – Stendhal (Henri Beyle, 1783–1842); Gustave Flaubert (1821–80); Henry James (1843–1916); Anton Chekhov (1860–1904). *The Bride of Lammermoor* (1819), *Redgauntlet* (1824), *Waverley* (1814), *Guy Mannering* (1815), *Rob Roy* (1817), *The Heart of Midlothian* (1818).

3 – For the first quotation, Scott, *The Antiquary* (3 vols, Constable & Co., 1816), vol. i, ch. vii, p. 164: 'The father and daughter threw themselves into each other's arms, kissed and wept for joy, although their escape was connected with the prospect of passing a tempestuous night upon a precipitous ledge of rock, which scarce afforded footing for the four shivering beings, who now, like the sea-fowl around them, clung there in hopes of some shelter from the devouring element which raged beneath'; and for the second, *ibid.*, ch. viii, p. 170: 'Some attempt was made to hold communication between the assistants above, and the sufferers beneath, who were still clinging to their precarious place of safety; but the howling of the tempest limited their intercourse to cries, as inarticulate as those of the winged denizens of the crag, which shrieked in chorus, alarmed by the reiterated sound of human voices, where they had seldom been heard.'

4 – Robert Louis Stevenson (1850–94).

5 – Scott, vol. i, ch. vii, p. 149: 'The sun was now resting his huge disk upon the edge of the level ocean, and gilded accumulation of towering clouds, through which he had travelled the livelong day, and which now assembled on all sides like misfortunes and disasters around a sinking empire and falling monarch.'

6 – R. L. Stevenson, *Kidnapped* (1886).

7 – Lovel and Isabella Wardour, characters in *The Antiquary*; Darsie Latimer, character in *Redgauntlet*; Edith Ballenden and Henry Morton, characters in *Old Mortality* (1817).

8 – For the first quotation, Scott, vol. i, ch. xiii, p. 275, spoken by Isabella Wardour, which has 'could countenance'; and for the second quotation, *ibid.*, p. 274; spoken by Lovel, which begins: '"Forgive me, if I interrupt you, Miss Wardour – you need not fear my intruding upon a subject where I have been already severely repressed – but do not add to the severity . . ."'

9 – The source of this quotation has not been discovered.

10 – For the first quotation, Scott, vol. i, ch. vii, p. 160: '"I [Edie Ochiltree] hae lived to be weary o' life; and here or yonder – at the back o' a dyke, in a wreath o' snaw, or in the wame o' a wave, what signifies how the auld gaberlunzie dies!"' (The phrase 'at the back of a dyke' also occurs at *ibid.*, ch. xii, p. 265.) For the second quotation, *ibid.*, vol. ii, ch. x, p. 282: '". . . Ye'll hae heard o' the muckle kist o' gowd that Sir Arthur has fund down bye at St Ruth? – He'll be grander than ever now – he'll no can haud down his head . . ."'

11 – Jane Austen (1775–1817).

12 – Scott, vol. ii, ch. iv, p. 106, which begins: 'Lovel bowed low and coloured deeply, and Miss Wardour . . .'

13 – Meg Merrilies and Dandy Dinmont, characters in *Guy Mannering*.

Can neither war nor peace . . .

Can neither war nor peace teach the French to translate or even to spell English? Glancing through a catalogue of pictures the other day which was thoughtfully provided with translations into English and German, I came upon 'Le Dessert' translated 'Leavings', 'Le torso d'une jeune femme' translated 'Young woman's trunk', and so on and so on. No English proof-reader would dare pass such misquotations of Racine as we put up with whenever Shakespeare is quoted in French. But there is a charm in the arrogance of French illiteracy, which takes it for granted that all languages save one are the base dialects of savages.

1 – A paragraph contributed to the 'From Alpha to Omega' column in the N&A, 22 November 1924, (Kp C256.21) introduced: 'A correspondent writes:'. The offending catalogue has not been identified.

'These Were the Muses'

There is a fascination in faded women of letters which excuses any number of volumes devoted to the record of their careers, so that Miss Wilson has no need to apologise for resuscitating nine forgotten worthies,[2] beginning with Mrs Centlivre and ending with Sara Coleridge. But facts are stubborn things; they require a little coaxing before they will yield their virtue; and that coaxing Miss Wilson purposely refrains from giving them. The stories are told with singular flatness, doubtless with great accuracy, and with a very liberal allowance of quotation. But this method has been adopted with a particular end in view. It is in order that readers whose appetites are sated with modern fiction may take a helping of Mrs Sheridan, Lady Morgan, or Mrs Trollope. For such readers Miss Wilson's book may well prove useful; for those who prefer the women to their works it is a little unsatisfying. The music of those particular muses is after all grown a little dim. The ladies themselves, however, as the excellent illustrations prove, were one and all of quite exceptional beauty.

1 – A notice in the N&A, 22 November 1924, (Kp C256.3) of These Were the Muses

(Sidgwick & Jackson, 1924) by Mona Wilson, author and lifelong companion of the historian G. M. Young – neighbours for a period of Desmond and Molly MacCarthy at Oare in Wiltshire (see *III VW Letters*, no. 1348).

2 – Wilson's resuscitated worthies were: Susannah Centlivre (1667?–1723), Charlotte Lennox (1720–1804), Frances Sheridan (1724–66), Hester Chapone (1727–1801), Sydney, Lady Morgan (1783?–1859), Jane Porter (1776–1850), Frances Trollope (1780–1863), Mary Anne Kelly ('Eva'; 1826–1910) and Sara Coleridge (1802–52).

Indiscretions

It is always indiscreet to mention the affections. Yet how they prevail, how they permeate all our intercourse! Boarding an omnibus we like the conductor; in a shop take for or against the young lady serving; through all traffic and routine, liking and disliking we go our ways, and our whole day is stained and steeped by the affections. And so it must be in reading.* The critic may be able to abstract the essence and feast upon it undisturbed, but for the rest of us in every book there is something – sex, character, temperament – which, as in life, rouses affection or repulsion; and, as in life, sways and prejudices; and again, as in life, is hardly to be analysed by the reason.

George Eliot is a case in point. Her reputation, they say, is on the wane, and, indeed, how could it be otherwise? Her big nose, her little eyes, her heavy, horsey head loom from behind the printed page and make a critic of the other sex uneasy. Praise he must, but love he cannot; and however absolute and austere his devotion to the principle that art has no truck with personality, still there has crept into his voice, into text-books and articles, as he analyses her gifts and unmasks her pretentions, that it is not George Eliot he would like to pour out tea.† On the other hand, exquisitely and urbanely, from the chastest urn into the finest china Jane Austen[2] pours, and, as she pours, smiles, charms, appreciates – that too has made its way into the austere pages of English criticism.

But now perhaps it may be pertinent, since women not only read but sometimes scribble a note of their opinions, to enquire into their preferences, their equally suppressed but equally instinctive response to the lure of personal liking in the printed page.‡ The attractions and

* *Vogue*, NY: 'So it must be in reading.'
† *Vogue*, NY: 'pour his tea.'   ‡ *Vogue*, NY: 'Now perhaps it may be pertinent. . .'

repulsions of sex are naturally among the most emphatic. One may hear them crackling and spitting and lending an agreeable vivacity to the insipidity of weekly journalism. In higher spheres these same impurities serve to fledge the arrows and wing the mind more swiftly if more capriciously in its flight. Some adjustment before reading is essential. Byron is the first name that comes to mind. But no woman ever loved Byron; they bowed to convention; did what they were told to do; ran mad to order. Intolerably condescending, ineffably vain, a barber's block to look at, compound of bully and lap-dog, now hectoring, now swimming in vapours of sentimental twaddle, tedious, egotistical, melodramatic, the character of Byron is the least attractive in the history of letters.* But no wonder that every man was in love with him. In their company he must have been irresistible; brilliant and courageous; dashing and satirical; downright and tremendous; the conqueror of women and companion of heroes – everything that strong men believe themselves to be and weak men envy them for being. But to fall in love with Byron, to enjoy *Don Juan*[3] and the letters to the full, obviously one must be a man; or, if of the other sex, disguise it.

No such disguise is necessary with Keats. His name, indeed, is to be mentioned with diffidence lest the thought of a character endowed as his was with the rarest qualities that human beings can command – genius, sensibility, dignity, wisdom – should mislead us into mere panegyric. There, if ever, was a man whom both sexes must unite to honour; towards whom the personal bias must incline all in the same direction. But there is a hitch; there is Fanny Brawne. She danced too much at Hampstead, Keats complained.[4] The divine poet was a little sultanic in his behaviour; after the manly fashion of his time apt to treat his adored both as angel and cockatoo. A jury of maidens would bring in a verdict in Fanny's favour. It was to his sister, whose education he supervised and whose character he formed, that he showed himself the man of all others who 'had he been put on would have prov'd most royally'.[5] Sisterly his women readers must suppose themselves to be; and sisterly to Words-worth, who should have had no wife, as Tennyson should have had none, nor Charlotte Brontë her Mr Nicholls.[6]

To put oneself at the best post of observation for the study of Samuel Johnson needs a little circumspection. He was apt to tear the tablecloth to ribbons; he was a disciplinarian and a sentimentalist; very rude to women, and at the same time the most devoted, respectful and devout of their admirers. Neither Mrs Thrale,[7] whom he harangued, nor the pretty

Vogue, NY: 'and melodramatic'.

young woman who sat on his knee is to be envied altogether. Their positions are too precarious. But some sturdy matchseller or apple woman well on in years, some old struggler who had won for herself a decent independence would have commanded his sympathy, and, standing at a stall on a rainy night in the Strand, one might perhaps have insinuated oneself into his service, washed up his tea cups and thus enjoyed the greatest felicity that could fall to the lot of woman.*

These instances, however, are all of a simple character; the men have been supposed to remain men, the women women when they write.† They have exerted the influence of their sex directly and normally. But there is a class which keeps itself aloof from any such contamination. Milton is their leader; with him are Landor, Sappho, Sir Thomas Browne, Marvell.[8] Feminists or anti-feminists, passionate or cold – whatever the romances or adventures of their private lives not a whiff of that mist attaches itself to their writing. It is pure, uncontaminated, sexless as the angels are said to be sexless. But on no account is this to be confused with another group which has the same peculiarity. To which sex do the works of Emerson, Matthew Arnold, Harriet Martineau, Ruskin and Maria Edgeworth belong?[9] It is uncertain. It is, moreover, quite immaterial. They are not men when they write, nor are they women. They appeal to that large tract of the soul which is sexless; they excite no passions; they exalt, improve, instruct, and man or woman can profit equally by their pages, without indulging in the folly of affection or the fury of partisanship.

Then, inevitably, we come to the harem, and tremble slightly as we approach the curtain and catch glimpses of women behind it and even hear ripples of laughter and snatches of conversation. Some obscurity still veils the relations of women to each other. A hundred years ago it was simple enough; they were stars who shone only in male sunshine; deprived of it, they languished into nonentity – sniffed, bickered, envied each other – so men said.‡ But now it must be confessed things are less satisfactory. Passions and repulsions manifest themselves here too, and it is by no means certain that every woman is inspired by pure envy when she reads what another has written. More probably Emily Brontë was the passion of her youth; Charlotte even she loved with nervous affection; and cherished a quiet sisterly regard for Anne. Mrs Gaskell[10]

*Vogue, NY: 'sympathy. Standing at a stall on a rainy night in the Strand . . .'
†Vogue, NY: 'character. The men have been supposed to remain men, the women, women, when they write.'
‡Vogue, NY: 'enough. They were stars who shone on in male sunshine; deprived of it, they languished, into nonentity, sniffed, bickered and envied each other, so men said.'

wields a maternal sway over readers of her own sex; wise, witty and very large-minded, her readers are devoted to her as to the most admirable of mothers; whereas George Eliot is an Aunt, and, as an Aunt, inimitable.* So treated she drops the apparatus of masculinity which Herbert Spencer[11] necessitated; indulges herself in memory; and pours forth, no doubt with some rustic accent, the genial stores of her youth, the greatness and profundity of her soul. Jane Austen we needs must adore; but she does not want it; she wants nothing; our love is a by-product, an irrelevance; with that mist or without it her moon shines on.† As for loving foreigners, some say it is an impossibility; but if not, it is to Madame de Sévigné[12] that we must turn.

But all these preferences and partialities, all these adjustments and attempts of the mind to relate itself harmoniously with another, pale, as the flirtations of a summer compared with the consuming passions of a lifetime, when we consider the great devotions which one, or at the most two, names in the whole of literature inspire.‡ Of Shakespeare we need not speak. The nimble little birds of field and hedge, lizards, shrews and dormice, do not pause in their dallyings and sportings to thank the sun for warming them; nor need we, the light of whose literature comes from Shakespeare, seek to praise him. But there are other names, more retired, less central, less universally gazed upon than his. There is a poet, whose love of women was all stuck about with briars; who railed and cursed; was fierce and tender; passionate and obscene. In the very obscurity of his mind there is something that intrigues us on; his rage scorches but sets on fire; and in the thickest of his thorn bushes are glimpses of the highest heavens, and ecstasies and pure and windless calms. Whether as a young man gazing from narrow Chinese eyes upon a world that half allures, half disgusts him, or with his flesh dried on his cheek bones, wrapped in his winding sheet, excruciated, dead in St Paul's, one cannot help but love John Donne.[13] With him is associated a man of the very opposite sort – large, lame, simple-minded; a scribbler of innumerable novels not a line of which is harsh, obscure or anything but propriety itself; a landed gentleman with a passion for Gothic architecture; a man

---

*Vogue, NY: 'Mrs Gaskell wields a maternal sway over readers of her own sex; wise, witty, and very large-minded, she finds her readers as devoted to her as to the most admirable of mothers. Whereas'.

†Vogue, NY: 'Jane Austen we needs must adore, though she does not want it. She wants nothing; our love is a by-product, an irrelevance; with that mist, or without it, her moon shines on.'

‡Vogue, NY: 'All these preferences and partialities . . . the great devotion which one name, or at most two, in the whole of literature inspire.'

who, if he had lived today, would have been the upholder of all the most detestable institutions of his country, but for all that a great writer – no woman can read the life of this man and his diary and his novels without being head over ears in love with Walter Scott.[14]

1 – An essay in *Vogue,* late November 1924, (Kp C256.4) reprinted, with very minor, largely punctuational revisions, as 'Indiscretions in Literature', *Vogue,* New York, 1 June 1925. The English *Vogue* version bore the subtitle, which quotes a fragment from William Blake's 'Note-Book' of c.1793: '"Never Seek to Tell Thy Love, Love That Never Told Can Be" – But One's Feelings for Some Writers Outrun All Prudence'; and informed the reader that: 'Mrs Woolf is a daughter of the late Sir Leslie Stephen. *The Voyage Out, Night and Day,* 'Monday or Tuesday' and *Jacob's Room* are her principal works'. The article in American *Vogue* was subtitled: 'Wherein Our Affections or Disaffections For Writers Come Imprudently Forth'. See Editorial Note, p. xxiv.

2 – George Eliot (1819–80); Jane Austen (1775–1817).

3 – George Gordon, Lord Byron (1788–1824), *Don Juan* (1819–24).

4 – John Keats (1795–1821) and his doomed relationship with Fanny Brawne had been documented relatively recently in *John Keats. His Life and Poetry. His Friends Critics and After-Fame* (Macmillan & Co., 1917) by Sidney Colvin, wherein, e.g., pp. 330–1fn: 'Through the Dilkes, Miss Brawne was invited out a great deal, and as Keats was not in robust health enough to take her out himself (for he never went with her), she used to go with military men to the Woolwich balls and to balls in Hampstead; and she used to dance with these military officers a great deal more than Keats liked.'

5 – Shakespeare, *Hamlet,* V, ii, ll. 409–10, spoken by Fortinbras:

> 'Let four captains
> Bear Hamlet, like a soldier, to the stage;
> For he was likely, had he been put on,
> To have proved most royally: and, for his passage,
> The soldiers' music and the rites of war
> Speak loudly for him.'

6 – William Wordsworth (1770–1850) married Mary Hutchinson in 1802; Alfred, Lord Tennyson (1809–92) married Emily Sellwood in 1850; Charlotte Brontë (1816–55) married her father's curate, Rev. A. B. Nicholls, in 1854.

7 – Samuel Johnson (1709–84); Hester Lynch Thrale, *née* Salusbury, later Piozzi (1741–1821).

8 – John Milton (1608–74); Walter Savage Landor (1775–1864); Sappho (born c.612BC); Sir Thomas Browne (1605–82); Andrew Marvell (1621–78).

9 – Ralph Waldo Emerson (1803–82); Matthew Arnold (1822–88); Harriet Martineau (1802–76); John Ruskin (1819–1900); Maria Edgeworth (1767–1849).

10 – Emily Brontë (1818–48); Anne Brontë (1820–49); Elizabeth Cleghorn Gaskell (1810–65).

11 – Herbert Spencer (1820–1903).

12 – Madame de Sévigné (1626–96).

13–John Donne (1571–1631).
14–Sir Walter Scott (1771–1832).

Miss Ormerod

VW's essay in *Dial*, N.Y., December 1924, (Kp C257) based upon *Eleanor Ormerod, LL.D., Economic Entomologist, Autobiography and Correspondence of Eleanor Ormerod,* ed. Robert Wallace (John Murray, 1904), was included in the first American edition of *The Common Reader*: 1st series (1925). The reader is referred to *IV VW Essays* where the essay is reprinted in its place in *The Common Reader.*

Appendices

Appendices

APPENDIX I

Leonard Woolf's Obituary of Lady Ritchie

The obituary notice reprinted here was published in *The Times*, 28 February 1919, a week before VW's tribute to her aunt appeared in the *TLS* (see 'Lady Ritchie', p. 13). That it is by LW we have the authority of his wife's diary, in which she wrote on Friday, 7 March 1919: 'Lady Wolseley who seems a lady of the utmost distinction since she writes to the Editor of the Times in pencil, finds L's memoir of Aunt Anny "most admirable", & the delicacy of his touches "a proof of Genius in *him*". To balance this satisfactorily my article, according to B[ruce] R[ichmond, editor of the *TLS*], is received with acclamation in the office, at home, & in my Club'.

'Death of Lady Ritchie, Thackeray's Daughter'

We regret to announce the death on Wednesday, at the Porch, Freshwater, of Lady Ritchie, widow of Sir Richmond Ritchie and daughter of William Makepeace Thackeray.

When a near relation of some famous man of a former generation dies, it is customary to say that a link with the past has been broken: Lady Ritchie's death is the breaking of such a link, and much more. One cannot think of her merely as the daughter of Thackeray, because she was one of those rare examples, a child of a great writer inheriting much of her parent's genius. Though not many novel readers of this generation take down Miss Thackeray's *Old Kensington* from the mid-Victorian bookshelf, yet if they do, they will see at once that there is no exaggeration in applying the word 'genius' to its author. But if she deserved more fame and success than she achieved as a novelist, it was rather in her life and personality that the wayward spirit of genius showed itself.

The bare chronicle of her life was placid and, on the whole, singularly happy. She was born in 1837, the great novelist's eldest child. Before her sixth year, owing to Mrs Thackeray's mental breakdown, her father's marriage had become, as he described it, 'a wreck'. This fact profoundly influenced her early years. She and her sister, the only two children who survived, were sent to live at Paris with Thackeray's mother, who had married Major Smyth, the original of Colonel Newcome. In 1846 their father brought them back to live with him in the house in York Street, Kensington, where *Vanity Fair* was written. Lady Ritchie's books show clearly how these two homes, Paris and Kensington, divided and dominated her childhood. She lived, if one may use the expression, that chapter of the Apocrypha which praises famous men. Thackeray himself gave his two small daughters a companionship and intimacy which are usually impossible between parents and children, middle-age and childhood. And in Paris and Kensington almost every famous man and woman of the time came into their lives. Lady Ritchie herself in *Chapters From Some Memoirs* has made their figures live for us with astonishing vividness like the procession of our own fireside memories of the past; the dying Chopin playing in his bare and narrow room to the grim Scotch spinster who brought him the basket of food; Count D'Orsay sitting at the breakfast table and seeming 'to fill the bow-window with radiance as if he were Apollo'; Samuel Rogers 'standing in the middle of the room, taking leave of his hostess, nodding his head . . . a little like a Chinese mandarin with an ivory face'. As the children grew up there came the Carlyles and Dickens and Leech and Charlotte Brontë and George Eliot and Mrs Kemble and Kingsley, and a whole host of greater and lesser lights. So they lived among famous men until their father's death in 1863, and, indeed, after it. There was an extraordinarily strong affection between the two sisters, so strong that they were not separated by the marriage of the younger to Leslie Stephen in 1867. Miss Thackeray herself, in 1877, married her cousin, the late Sir Richmond Ritchie, by whom she had a son and a daughter.

Lady Ritchie published her first book, *The Story of Elizabeth* in 1863, and this was followed during the next twenty-two years by six other novels or volumes of stories. But she will probably be best remembered by her reminiscences. It was in that form of writing that her genius found its most suitable material. She had the rare power of not only feeling, but also of making others feel, how amusing and romantic her fireside memories were. *Old Kensington* is the best of her novels, because in it she is allowing this power full play, not in the world of facts, but of imagination. And the very qualities of her genius left her without that laborious concentration necessary for the production of so massive a work of art as the novel. Her manuscripts, made up of hastily written fragments pinned confusedly together, were the despair of her friends and publishers, and once when one of her novels was published in Australia the last chapter was printed in the middle of the book and nobody found it out. That fact shows her limitations more clearly than any criticism. She had her father's sentiment and shrewdness so admirably and so contradictorily combined that she continually verged on his besetting sins of sentimentality and cynicism and never fell into either; she had poetry and a lightness of wit and humour that made her conversation inimitable; and, lastly, she had that quality which made one of her severest friends say that she was the most sympathetic person he had ever met. But she never possessed that sense of facts, order, continuity, without which the production of a great work of art is impossible. Her mind was too quick and too light for the heavier and slower world in which she had to live. In conversation she fascinated and amused all who knew her, and yet what she said never seemed quite to fit in with what others were saying; it was, someone once remarked, as though she were singing her own beautiful but erratic tune just outside the circle of the other musicians.

Lady Ritchie was left a widow in 1912. Among various writings in which she commemorated her father, there should not be forgotten her contributions to the centenary edition of Thackeray's works; they contained, besides introductions which only his daughter could have written, a good many pieces unfinished or unpublished before.

APPENDIX II

Byron & Mr Briggs

This appendix reproduces a transcript of VW's typescript 'Byron & Mr Briggs' (MHP, B11d), the introductory chapter to a proposed book 'Reading'. First referred to in her diary entry for Monday, 23 May 1921, the book, which she appears to have begun writing in February–March 1922, was never completed in the form suggested here, but the ideas behind it were subsequently developed and recast until they evolved and emerged as *The Common Reader*: 1st series (1925). The chapter – although unpolished and in places almost impenetrably overgrown with emendations – is thus an especially valuable document.

A wholly admirable clean text version of 'Byron & Mr Briggs', to which I am greatly indebted, has been prepared by Professor Edward A. Hungerford and published in the *Yale Review*, vol. LXVIII, March 1979, no. 3. The opportunity has been taken here to include more exhaustively VW's second and third thoughts, where these have been intelligible. I have also indicated the points at which there arise words, phrases and passages I have failed to decipher with any certainty. I have not been able to trace Tom Briggs to a biographical source. No such work as *The Flame of Youth* is catalogued under Ella King Sanders. No one of the name Sylvia Reddish, described by VW as the author of *Thoughts at Dusk*, is catalogued.

The typescript consists of thirty-eight pages, thirty-seven numbered 1–37, with one unnumbered page inserted at the start of section '11'. VW's emendations are made in black ink, purple ink and lead pencil. Some passages are scored out with a blue pencil. I have not attempted to differentiate between these media in making the transcript. Additions and revisions are reproduced between ⟨angled brackets⟩ whether these occur in the heart of the text or (with some exceptions) its margins. Every effort has been made to divine and represent the sequence of her alterations, although this has sometimes been a matter of intelligent guesswork or, in the last resort, practicability. Cancelled words and passages are marked through with a fine line. All editorial interventions, including inserted page numbers and [?doubtful readings], are contained in square brackets, with the exception of the occasional quotation mark, added for clarity's sake. Single quotation marks are employed throughout. The footnotes are mine.

~~PREFACE~~
⟨Introductory. Byron & Mr Briggs⟩

The spring of 1922 was made memorable to me ⟨(if the egotism may be pardoned)⟩ by the appearance of a novel ~~called the Flame of Youth~~ by E. K. Sanders. called the Flame of Youth. On the cover the publishers drew attention to the fact that this was a first novel, and they pledged their faith that it was a good one. And so, drawing up to the fire (for the spring of 1922 was a cold one) ⟨~~for it was cold in March, 1922~~⟩ what could be easier ⟨for a reviewer⟩ than to run through the four hundred pages of sufficiently large ~~print?~~ ⟨type between tea & dinner.⟩ Almost automatically an impression of the book's worth would form during this process. And next morning, perhaps with labour, perhaps without, the impression would be floated onto paper and would be found to measure not less than two, but certainly not more than five, of what printers call Long Primer.

⟨But⟩ E. K. Sanders (whether man woman or child,⟨⟩) ~~or, as for some reason I supposed, a mulatto in hiding from the police~~ put an end to my career as a reviewer, ~~for ever~~. For I found myself at the end of two hours with no impression of the Flame of Youth; with no review to write next morning, ~~with no review to write next morning,~~ with nothing to seal ~~up~~ send off and deliver. ⟨without indeed having opened the volume⟩ Now there are repulsive books in which with spasmodic industry reviewers paste the long columns that once looked solid enough and were built with energy and hope. To these I referred in the belief that I [p.2] should find there some method ~~for~~ ⟨of for⟩ dealing with ⟨this first novel, this very promising first novel, as the publishers called it;⟩ ~~Sanders, whether man woman or child~~; for first novels, have come my way for many years, and many publishers have pledged their faith that they were ~~good one~~[s]. ⟨promising⟩

Hours passed; days went by; and, still reading in the faded book, I sought a method for dealing with the Flame of Youth; ~~but sought in vain~~.

II.

In England at the present moment books are published every day of the week and every week of the year. The stream sometimes dribbles and sometimes gushes. But it is continuous and many waters of all salts and ~~colours~~ ⟨savours⟩ go to make it. Indeed the weekly paper which deals most faithfully with modern literature has twenty seven divisions through which it filters the volumes that arrive at the office in a single week. One can say straight off that some of the books have nothing to do with literature. '⟨[⟩A Text book of practical chemistry, ⟨]⟩ 'Janes Fighting Ships' 'Lubricating and Allied Oils.' 'The Black problem'. 'Websters Royal Red Book'. '⟨[⟩Mrs Wilson's⟨]⟩ Cook Book.' 'Factory Administration and Cost Accounts.' 'Scurvy: Past and Present.' ⟨all⟩ these have nothing to do with literature. But even as I copy the names I ~~have my doubts~~; I fancy that if on a cold winters evening in a village inn one would feel kindly towards ⟨one found⟩ 'Janes Fighting Ships' ⟨on the window sill⟩ ⟨one would read it through;⟩ and though the Oils and the Factory Acts would always remain repulsive [*p.3*] under any circumstances short of imprisonment or a sea voyage arctic exploration⟨]⟩'The Black Problem' ~~would~~ and 'Scurvy: past and present' would certainly wile away an evening and give one ⟨~~something to think about~~⟩ ~~happy dreams~~.

In a country where literature is so rich and so various what wonder if the method of dealing with it is equally elastic? Granted that a poem differs essential[ly] from a text book of physics, there remain whole multitudes ⟨of volumes⟩ which cover ⟨wh. stretch fr. poetry to physics. poetry to science⟩ the ~~ground~~ between ~~them~~ and are neither one thing nor the other. Mr ~~Masefield~~ ⟨Conrad⟩ has written a poem ⟨novel⟩ called ~~Reynard~~ the Fox; ⟨The Rescue;⟩ that is pure literature; The Vicar of Wakefield has been reprinted; pure literature again. But some old Squire has rummaged in the family archives and produced a couple of volumes proving beyond a doubt that none of his race has ever ⟨done or said or thought anything ~~out of the way remarkable~~⟩ ⟨out of the way⟩ moved beyond the parish boundaries since the reign of William the Conqueror; and what is that? Miss Sylvia Reddish issues her Thoughts at Dusk. The Professors are always writing about Byron and Coleridge. Works of astonishing erudition come from America. Journalists collect

475

their journalism. Women travel in Mesopotamia and meet brigands. And as for biographies, they have become to the upper classes what plumes and black horses are to the lower – a show for the neighbours, something due to the dead. Yes; there is always a reason for writing a book; and often, surprisingly often, there is something of value in it. But what, I ask myself turning the pages of the [*p.4*] ~~faded~~ volume faded volume, what sort of value have they? and have the ~~got it~~ ⟨a value⟩ in common? and if I know what ~~their~~ ⟨this⟩ value is will it help me to decide ~~the~~ the value of E. K. Sanders novel – the Flames [*sic*] of Youth?

3

We are on the brink of a serious argument; but with a little circumspection, it may be possible to keep on the outskirts. The qualities that a book should contain in the abstract, the qualities that it does contain in the flesh, have been discussed and analysed from the times of Aristotle to the present moment. Aristotle, Dryden, Addison, Johnson, Coleridge, Boileau, ~~Diderot~~, ⟨Keats⟩ Sainte Beuve, Matthew Arnold, Taine, Anatole France, Remy de Gourmont – to go no further, have all said their say and said it (~~so~~⟨as⟩) one feels ~~as one~~ ⟨in⟩ reads⟨ing⟩ them) with a conviction which is only roused in men's minds, and conveyed to the minds of others⟨,⟩ when they have been ⟨looking⟩ ~~possessed of~~ ⟨on⟩ the truth. That this truth is never the same for two generations, or for two human beings, – let alone for two human beings of genius – is a fact which may be distressing, if you wish to get the matter settled once and for all; but has to be faced. ~~The Their~~ ⟨At anyrate⟩ difference⟨s⟩ of critical theory and ~~their~~ ⟨of ~~practice~~⟩ differences of ⟨critical judgment⟩ fact are by this time sufficiently notorious. Any parrot can repeat their blunders. ⟨~~the critics~~ the usual string of blunders⟩ Johnson ridiculed Tristram Shandy. Arnold thought Shelleys letters better than his poetry. Coleridge fell prostrate at the feet [*p.5*] of Mr Bowles. ~~Any~~ The parrot has said enough. ⟨~~Again,~~ Then,⟩ Any pig can sort the critics into schools. There is the biographic; the psychological; the socio-political; the historical; the aesthetic, the impressionist; ⟨the scientific⟩ the analytic. Doubtless there are more; but each can be traced back to some man of genius who was so convinced of the truth of what he saw that he imposed his conviction upon others. But the men who read in this way, with an overmastering bias in this that or the other direction⟨,⟩ are the critics. Pelt them with volumes taken from each of the twenty seven divisions into which modern literature is divided and they will somehow order them into conformity with a principle arrived at by reading, and reasoning ⟨,⟩ and the light of ⟨individual⟩ genius. But the reviewer never penetrated⟨s⟩ deep enough to lay hold upon a principle. Like a man in a shooting gallery⟨,⟩ he sees ~~the~~ books move steadily ~~past in~~ front of ⟨past⟩ him. Bang! He lets fly. The rabbit is missed; ~~he has only just time to reload before taking aim at the pheasant~~; but he has only ~~just time~~ to reload before taking aim at the pheasant.

Therefore it is useless to look in any scrap book of old reviews for a method. You may find a personality, but that is quite a different thing, and (with E.K. Sanders at the back of my mind) I should like to discover what the value of a reviewer is, taking it for granted that he has no method, but only a personality – that he is in short much nearer [*p.6*] the ordinary reader, of whom there are multitudes, than the critic of whom, with great luck, there is one in a century.

[4]

⟨But⟩ The common reader is ~~a person of some importance~~ ⟨a person of great importance.⟩ ⟨not to be despised.⟩ Indeed Dr Johnson rejoiced 'to concur with the common reader; for by the common sense of readers, uncorrupted ~~by~~ with literary prejudice, after all the refinements of subtilty and the dogmatism of learning, must be finally decided all claim to poetical honours.' In an age ~~which has no~~ ⟨without a⟩ critic, ⟨[⟩ and there is none to be found in England at the moment,⟨]⟩ literature both past and present must rest in the hands of the people who continue to read it. Milton is alive in the year 1922 ⟨& ~~looks as he does look~~⟩ ⟨& of a certain size & shape⟩ only because some thousands of unimportant people ⟨insignificant men & women⟩ are holding his page at this moment before their eyes.

But when Coleridge was lecturing about Shakespeare, or Dryden was writing about poetry, common opinion had an influence to guide it. You shut your shakespeare and went ~~off to Fleet Street~~ to hear ~~what~~ Coleridge had to say about him; you read the preface to [*hiatus in text of about half a line*] and your judgment of poetry was shaped accordingly. But to have this effect, an influence must be powerful. Acting first upon the scholars and reviewers it must by them be spread abroad among the multitude. In our time there are scholars by the score and reviewers by the thousand; but there is no critic to point the way. [*p.7*]

5

General statements are convenient ~~no doubt and sometimes~~ and no doubt sometimes they are true. But this one has in it obvious elements of falsehood should you descend from the general to the particular – should you look into the way in which reading is commonly done now, and not imagine how it was done a hundred years ago by old Mr Briggs who drove up from Kensington to hear Coleridge in snowy weather, only to find that Coleridge had forgotten the engagement. ⟨to come⟩

The truth is that reading is kept up because people like reading. The common reader is formidable and respectable and even has power over great critics and great masterpieces in the long run because he likes reading and will not let ⟨even⟩ Coleridge do his reading for him. How many thousands I know not, but certainly there are many thousands who never pick up a book on a bookstall for half a minute without getting a shock of ~~some sort~~. ⟨~~from~~ one kind or another⟩ ⟨some kind of shock from it⟩ Expose them to something violent, like King Lear, and the shock entirely obliterates Aristotle, Dryden, Addison, Johnson, Coleridge, Boileau, Diderot, Sainte-Beuve &c &c. The whole ~~lot of them are~~ ⟨hierarchy is⟩ powerless to unseat the judgment of an ignorant boy or girl who has read the play to the end. It is all very well, when the impression has spent itself, to take down Coleridge and Coleridge will delight ~~astound~~ and instruct, but only in the margin of the mind. It is I who have read the play. I hold it in my mind. ⟨~~brain~~⟩ I am [p.8] ~~in~~ directly in touch with Shakespeare. No third person can explain or alter or even throw much light upon ~~my~~ ⟨our⟩ relationship.

This ~~is~~ then ⟨is⟩ the very heart of the ~~whole~~ business – it is this which sends the blood running ⟨coursing⟩ through ~~literature~~. ⟨the whole of the old book & the new⟩ It is this which raises libraries and draws up out of the ~~barren~~ air myriads upon myriad of ⟨new⟩ books ⟨in the spring & the autumn⟩ But it is an unguided passion, voluntary ~~and~~ individual ⟨& lawless⟩ and thus capable of doing enormous harm as a glance at ~~current~~ ⟨contemporary⟩ literature ~~will~~ ⟨is bound to⟩ prove. ⟨Contemporary literature is confusing.⟩ ⟨Take the case of Mr Briggs for example (1795–1859)⟩ ~~Or~~ ⟨L⟩let us look back ⟨for a moment⟩ at ⟨the case of Tom⟩ ~~Mr~~Briggs (1795–1859) He was convinced by the eloquent Mr Coleridge that Measure for Measure was the most painful of Shakespeares plays 'likewise degrading to the character of the woman' ⟨;⟩ but next time he read Measure for Measure he had forgotten what Coleridge said ⟨!⟩ or his own ideas seemed fresher or his ~~own daughter~~ ⟨wife⟩ bounced into the ~~breakfast room~~ ⟨study & kissed him on the top of the head⟩ that very moment. At any rate Coleridges principles, elegant, profound ⟨,⟩ and original as they were, applied to old poetry, to poetry in general, and

Mr Briggs never once thought of Coleridge when he laid it down a few weeks later that this new book by Mr Keats was trash.

6

– And Briggs' grandchildren? He This spectacle maker of Cornhill with his taste for literature and his this loathing for Keats left a large number of descendants. Many have gone [*p.9*] out into the world and fought and conquered and made money and died rather honourably in obscure Indian villages with nothing but a copy of Dickens and or a little volume of Shakespeare to keep them company. A taste for reading is very hard to kill. At the same time, how are we to say what it amounts to in the flesh? Briggs the Colonel died with his Shakespeare; but never formulated his views upon the poetic drama. Briggs the stockbroker read Darwin; and burnt Swinburne. Mrs Brigg (who was a Grant from Dundee) knew the waverley novels by heart. That was enough for her. Between them. ⟨but⟩ She ⟨never⟩ could ⟨never⟩ abide George Eliot. Between them the different generations must have devoured half the London Library and the whole of Mudies. But as, But silently, vora-ciously, gluttonously, like ⟨as like a plague lot of of⟩ locusts and ⟨or⟩ caterpillars. As for leaving any record of their opinions save by crosses and notes of exclamation in the margin (which staffs of librarians are always engaged in rubbing out) that was ⟨,⟩ and that is ⟨,⟩ none of their business. They read ⟨then⟩ for pleasure; they still read ⟨now⟩ for pleasure; and if you catch them laying down the law in private about Mr Wells' latest or Mr Joyce's most outrageous, they do it violently enough; but always with a sort of shrug of the shoulders as if to say 'That's what I think. But who am I?'

It would be difficult to persuade the grandchildren of Briggs who knew Coleridge that ⟨[⟩their views matter; that they decide decide all claim to poetical honours; that they matter [*p.10*] ⟨Dr Johnson respec-ted them:⟩ they are common readers; that they decide all claim to poetical honours; [*unconstrued insertion*] that their views matter so much as to be gone into at some length and made the subject of a book by a distant relation.

Yet that was the conclusion to which my reading of old newspaper articles finally led me. The views of the grandchildren of Briggs matter; and I too am a grandchild of ⟨we reviewers are almost all of us⟩ ⟨descended fr the spectacle maker of Cornhill⟩ Briggs. True ⟨T⟩the genealogists might ⟨may⟩ dispute this claim; but if one has waited ⟨impatiently⟩ for three weeks to get Byrons letters from the library, ⟨&

~~swallowed them whole~~ [*undeciphered word*]⟩ then, according to my ~~reasoning,~~ ⟨definition⟩ one is a grandchild of Briggs.

[*There follow several densely entangled revisions, only some of which have proved legible enough to be transcribed in the next paragraph.*]

[7]

⟨But in order to define the method (the lack of method possibly) wh. will be used in the following pages.⟩ In order to cut short ⟨speed up the⟩ ⟨facilitate & quicken the argument⟩ ⟨& to apologise for all its faults⟩ further definition, ~~it may be~~ well ⟨will help⟩ to set down here a few impressions of Byron's letters by a spiritual descendant of Tom Briggs, that is to say by a common ~~reader, according to the description of Dr Johnson.~~ ⟨The common reader is important, yet he has never been considered⟩ ⟨The faults nature of the method will be apparent, & apology [*undeciphered word*]⟩

& reference ~~will be~~ more vivid

⟨X X X X X⟩

Byron was a fine old boy and wrote far better letters from abroad than his people had a right to expect. He should have stayed an undergraduate for ever, dominating his own group but strictly kept in order ⟨by Kinnaird & Hobhouse⟩ ~~But als~~; ⟨alas – my boy [? Hobby O]⟩ here are women; and he must needs be a man of the world, and learn the trade from that tight lipped hard faced prosaic peeress Lady [*p.11*] Melbourne who soon brought out the worst of him, ⟨–⟩ the dancing master and dandy, so proud of his conquests though so obviously ashamed of his foot. Caroline Lamb, insane but generous, would have made ⟨him⟩ a better wife ~~for him~~ than the mathematical Miss Milbanke. The big boy who limped off the field in a rage because he had been clean bowled for two or three runs needed what women call 'managing'. But what woman could give it him? He was dangerous ⟨; a treacherous lapdog.⟩ In the midst of sentiment down came the sledge hammer of fact. Who could be more unflinching and direct? Indeed one is inclined to wonder why he thought himself a poet. Presumably the fashion of the age dictated, and ~~he~~ ⟨Byron⟩ was impressed by fashions. Yet his description of the Wedderburne affair, proves ⟨, what his poetry [*two undeciphered cancelled words*] also hints,⟩ ~~what becomes more and more evident~~, that prose was his medium; satire his genius. He goes to Venice, and is there a single phrase to show that he saw it? Does he even momentarily abstract himself from the Countesses and the ⟨C⟩~~c~~arnivals to think, on the Lido, as Wordsworth thought in rustic Cumberland, how she had held the gorgeous East in fee, and men must mourn when even the showod [? shadow] of what once was great has passed away ⟨?⟩ No such phrase, with its aloofness, ~~and~~ contemplation, and solicitude for ~~the fate of mankind in general~~ ⟨the human fate⟩ is possible from ~~him~~ ⟨Byron⟩. All is immediate, personal, and of this world. Yet it would be difficult to rank Don Juan much lower than the Prelude or to forget hours spent racing before the wind through Byrons Cantos, when Wordsworths stanzas lay cold, unruffled, ~~and tasted~~ [*p.12*] ~~shadowed~~ and shut in ⟨& shadowed⟩ by the rocks of his own self-centredness.

Byron was a novelist – that is to say he came at his conception through his observation of actual life; whereas a poet ~~would~~ think⟨s⟩ of life in general, or ~~perhaps~~ so intensely of his own in particular as to include the general life. ⟨experience.⟩ This he ~~would~~ express⟨es⟩ in language exact and enduring. Byron on the other hand writes the perfection of prose. Compare, for example, his letters with the stiff and stilted compositions ~~of~~ by Shelley here, unfortunately⟨,⟩ placed beside them. Sir Timothey's conduct is (for the first time) understandable. ⟨intelligible.⟩ To have this prig for one's son ⟨, to⟩ ~~would have been infuriating~~; and to listen to his preachings intolerable. But Mary loved him (~~see page~~ —). She can hardly write for fury that a servant girl should slander him, and when she met ⟨meeting⟩ Mrs Hoppner in the street cut her dead. ~~But~~ ⟨A⟩ ~~all~~ this must have seemed rather extreme and a little bourgeois to Byron; ~~who was a snob~~. ⟨whose range was so wide, whose grasp was so vigorous who ~~was normally a snob~~ where blood was so blue⟩ And so he frittered his life away; and grew very bitter before the end, which was in the grand style, as the death of Ajax was ⟨;⟩ fate bowling him out before he ~~many many~~ ⟨made half the runs he ~~ought to have~~ shd. have made.⟩ and up fly our caps as he limps off the field in a rage. [*p.13*]

xxxxxxxxxxxxxxxxx

Let us pull this page to pieces, observing that ~~it was written quickly~~, not from notes but from recollection, and is an attempt to give an impression remaining in the mind an hour or two after finishing a book. ⟨]⟩ ⟨~~Well;~~⟩ Some reading is implied, more than could be expected of a working man, or of any but a very exceptional bank clerk. On the other hand, no Byron expert and no scholar ⟨c⟩would write so carelessly. A critic would have disregarded all the personalities and would have fixed upon the aesthetic problems here glimpsed and brushed aside. But it has, in spite of compression, one very marked and for our purposes very important characteristic. The reader has obviously ~~read~~ from the first page to the last, ⟨read⟩ with a view to ~~making~~ ⟨framing⟩ a whole. As each page is turned you can see him hastily rigging up, from ~~his~~ reading or experience, something to serve for background; roughly setting the characters in ⟨action⟩ ⟨motion⟩ ⟨deciding, ordering them⟩ [*undeciphered phrase*] relation⟨s⟩ ~~to each other~~; making a dart at their qualities; hazarding a guess at the character of literature; ⟨their ~~writing.~~⟩ and shaping the whole little world as it grows in his mind into ~~conformity~~ ⟨likeness⟩ with some conception which he derives partly from his ⟨time⟩ age (he is pagan, not Christian) partly from private experiences and qualities peculiar to himself. 'He', do we say? [*p. 14*] In the colour of each judgment, ⟨But it is obvious from⟩ in the shape of each sentence, ~~in~~ the tilt of the ~~whole, it is obvious~~ ⟨& atmosphere & proportion which⟩ that he is a woman. 'But Mary loved him'. The cat is out of the bag; ⟨() ⟨& since⟩ ~~and~~ no one can ~~put her back again~~ ()⟩ ⟨so long as the world lasts⟩ ⟨~~Catch her~~, put her back again, had better ~~have~~ be given the run of the house.⟩

But the writer's sex is not of interest; nor need we dwell upon the ~~qualities~~ peculiarities ⟨of temperament⟩ which ~~make~~ one person's reading of Byron's letters different from anothers. It is the quality they ~~all~~ have in common that is interesting – that ~~all readers~~ have ⟨the reading of ordinary readers has⟩ in common, that is to say, for it is clear that scholars and critics ⟨read⟩ ~~differently~~, in a way of their own.

8

To make a whole – ⟨it is⟩ that ~~is what~~ ⟨which⟩ we have in common. Our reading is always urged on by ~~that~~ instinct, ⟨to do that⟩, ⟨complete what we read,⟩ which is, for some reason, one of the most universal and profound ⟨of our instincts⟩ You may see it at work any night among the passengers in a third class railway carriage. – Is he related to the woman opposite? ~~In love then?~~ No they work in the same office. In love then? No; she wears a wedding ring. Going home then to the same suburb? Ah, yes. 'We shall meet on Tuesday'. A bridge party no doubt . . . . .' ⟨The man, reaching up for his despatch bag, says⟩ 'I'm sure it would pay to start another hotel there' from which it appears that they belong to a group of people in the habit of going to ~~the same golfing resort~~ St Andrews ⟨to play golf⟩ in the summer. [*p.15*]

Everyone ~~plays~~ [*undeciphered cancelled word*] ⟨plays⟩ this familiar game. Everyone feels the desire to add to a single impression ~~the~~ the others that go to complete it. ⟨[⟩ Here a mans face catches the attention; instinctively you give him character, relationships, occupation, habits desires, until some sort of completeness is attained ⟨achieved⟩ ⟨]⟩. It is as if ⟨as if you took advantage of every hint at life to live more fully yourself⟩ ⟨T⟩there were ⟨must be⟩ ⟨is⟩ something disagreeable to the mind in allowing any ⟨an⟩ impression ⟨wh. has struck it forcibly⟩ ⟨of any force⟩ to remain isolated. It must be at once completed by others; ⟨made into something⟩ ⟨made⟩ ⟨habitable be⟩ one must, for one's own comfort, have a whole in one's mind: fragments are unendurable. So it is in reading Byron's letters. There too⟨,⟩ in the impression quoted we see the same desire at work to complete, to supply background, significant relationship⟨,⟩ motive, while we are rounding the whole with a running commentary ⟨or significance of our own⟩ which flings out at the end, 'Fate bowled him unfairly. Up fly our caps, as he limps off the field in a rage.'

⟨The book is finished;⟩ So too, the train reaches Putney. Our fellow passengers get out, but not before we are fairly easy in our minds about them. They have their lives; they have their place in the scheme. – although we have to admit that our attention was intermittent, that we read a column in the evening newspaper, and that after the woman said 'We shall meet on Tuesday' a glaring red theatre shot up on the right; a backstreet in Wandsworth was illuminated; a splendid and miserable sight ⟨– think of the splendour & misery of ⟨her observation is⟩ of the hour –⟩ so ⟨&⟩ that the three dots which mark the interruption ⟨of this splendour & misery⟩ ⟨this [*undeciphered word*] truth & blue sky & children running in the road⟩ threw some strange significance upon the ⟨man's⟩ next remark that it would pay ⟨to make a new⟩ to start a hotel there. ⟨at St Andrews.⟩ [*p.16*]

started suddenly out of the distance,

9

It is hardly necessary to say that such wholes as these are extremely imperfect, ⟨&⟩ probably highly inaccurate. Very likely there was not a word of truth in our re-construction of the travellers lives. Certainly if we examine the fragment on Byrons letters we shall find slips enough in three or four ⟨five⟩ hundred words to infuriate a scholar. Byron did not make 'two or three runs'; Wordsworth did not live in 'rustic Cumberland'; when he wrote the sonnet ⟨On the Extinction of the Venetian Republic here made,⟩ here misquoted; The Prelude is not strictly speaking written in stanzas; and the use of metaphors to convey critical judgments is generally an attempt to conceal ⟨under some artificial flower⟩ vagueness and poverty of thought. That is all true; ⟨& to write of facts inaccurately is to impair the artistic value ⟨validity even,⟩ of

1802

your the writing⟩ and no one would be so foolish as not to wish it otherwise. ⟨to write is always To write of facts & not to⟩ But given our conditions, given our education, given it is inevitable; given above all those two instincts which are so deeply implanted in our souls – the instinct to complete; the instinct to judge. Give us a fragment and ⟨tho our materials are [? scant]⟩ we will make a whole of it; give us a book and ⟨though our minds are ill [undeciphered word]⟩ we will ⟨though⟩ judge it for ourselves.

⟨9⟩

Thus then ⟨in some such terms as these perhaps the⟩ the common reader is more or less ⟨maybe⟩ defined; but who shall say anything about his partner in the enterprise – this vast, bewildering, unsorted, uncharted, perpetually increasing and changing volume of literature? Twenty seven divisions⟨,⟩ we say⟨,⟩ have been driven through [p.17] the mass; but what if they are not water tight? if biography leaks through into poetry ⟨history⟩ and history into fiction, and criticism is stained with the juice of them all? In what sense can we possibly talk, even lazily, over the fire, of ⟨making⟩ a wholes⟨?⟩ And⟨T⟩to make [a] whole ⟨even⟩ of ⟨one man, Lord⟩ Byron, must we not have read some three hundred volumes, and a good many papers still waiting to be published?

[The typescript here seems to indicate the intended insertion of two paragraphs of dialogue, marked section '11' and typed on a separate unpaginated sheet. (No section '10' survives.)]

⟨11⟩

⟨'And what do you make of the Byron-Leigh controversy?' said old MacCallum Briggs settling down for a gossip with his cousin.

'That he had a child by his grandmother' replied Cherry, very inaccurately, but rather to the point.⟩

11

⟨For⟩ Happily nature provides means by which our minds very rapidly and perhaps unconsciously take what suits their constitutions and reject the rest. One mind will grasp fifty volumes of about Byron; another only one or part of one. But both will have their views; and each⟨,⟩ will have be true, according to the illusion which nature allows; ⟨will seem true⟩ to the beholder. Nor is it simply an illusion. When Johnson talked of the common sense of readers, he meant no doubt he meant that the faculty of knowing what to use, what to neglect, is well

developed among us, and can be trusted in the long run to whittle away
⟨wear down⟩ even the enormous deposits ~~of matter~~ which have heaped
themselves over a man like Byron, so that the average judgment of him
will be correct and will be formed by reading ~~a very small number of
books.~~ ⟨only a few books out of a very large number.⟩

This may be so; but we have still to face a problem which cannot be
shirked by anyone who reads even a few books about Byron. Even in the
hasty impression of his letters ~~already~~ quoted ⟨above⟩ the writer had to
face it, or at least to give an [*p.18*] agonised and terrified glance in its
direction. 'What am I to make of Byron's poetry? And where am I to
place it? Is it in my whole, or somehow outside it?

To have read and reached [*undeciphered word inserted*] out for ⟨&
read⟩ all that comes to hand about Byron, to have enjoyed to the full the
fun of making him up, ~~of seeing him in every possible aspect~~, of
imagining how he spoke ~~and~~ looked ~~and~~ dressed, and ⟨of⟩ getting at
him through Leigh Hunt, and at Leigh Hunt through his diary, and at
Moore through Mrs Moore, and at Mrs Moore through Mrs Lynn
Linton who will bring in Landor and Bath, and ~~who~~ Shelley and so back
to Byron, ~~and~~ running ⟨of racing on⟩ the scent with Lord Lovelace, and
⟨again⟩ Mr Edgcumbe until the lustres and pilasters of the Georgian
world seem vivid enough, and the ⟨huge⟩ ~~square~~ of St Marks has
shadows ~~of golden lions~~ ⟨sharp [?Ursine] shadows up⟩ on its pavement,
and the woods of Ravenna scents and darknesses – all this is nothing but
a random game, like that we play in railway carriages with people who
leave us at Putney. It is making up a whole; ⟨[? it is creating ~~lif~~ living
people, but only such]⟩ but only such a whole as we could live in
ourselves⟨;⟩ and imagine as the living place of others. It is a game; ⟨a
game too perpetually interrupted by life,⟩ yet in the middle ~~of it~~ will
come ⟨,⟩ ~~perhaps~~ more vividly and startlingly ⟨perhaps⟩ for the exercise
⟨,⟩ a sense of something ⟨very real⟩ outside, of something flung by
Byron or another into the outer air, where it exists, independently of the
~~people~~ ⟨man⟩ who made it, apart from the gay ⟨garrulous⟩ little society
which rattles and bangs on its way, ~~with so many entrances and exits~~
⟨with so many greetings & farewells⟩ of people ~~coming~~ ⟨getting in⟩ and
departing ⟨people getting out⟩ [*p.19*] to some quite unimaginable end.
What is this thing which ~~people make, which hundreds of years ago they
made, which keeps along side of us, outside the carriage window~~,
⟨[?flung] out as we travel, which keeps pace with us for thousands of
years,⟩ and draws our eyes to it with an irresistible fascination?

A book or two. There are not ~~very~~ many, and in every library they

as we
can
~~imagine~~
see of him
with
others

485

stand ~~alone~~, ⟨apart⟩ poems, plays⟨,⟩ novels, ⟨a little philosophy⟩ perhaps a few histories, not much affected by their neighbours ~~in the other compartments~~, unchanged by the triumphs of science, and never superseded by any new discovery in the art of writing. Few as they are, any one can possess them; and perhaps it was Sir John Lubbock who demonstrated that you can buy the whole of English literature, ~~splendid as it~~ is, ⟨the richest in the world,⟩ for two pound ten and store it in a packing case which has contained a month's supply of groceries for a family of eight. By such devices men of good will attempt again and again to persuade us that literature is as easy to read as it is ⟨beneficial in⟩ ⟨salutary to the reader⟩ its effects ~~are to possess~~. But let us try. Let us take a very short poem and see what sort of processes it stirs up in the mind of a common reader.

⟨X X X X X⟩

Western wind, when will thou blow
The small rain down can rain?
Christ, if my love were in my arms
And I in my bed again!*

⟨that is⟩ Passionate; direct.⟨;⟩ A cry, ~~which I cry too. . . . . Christ, if~~
[*p.20*] ~~my love were in my arms and I in my bed again! and it seems~~ to appl~~y~~⟨ies⟩ to ~~all~~ everything. Western wind, when will thou blow – how wistfully it begins, with a sort of weary delaying compared with the direct attack of the concluding lines – ~~Western wind – of course the~~ the alliteration ~~must~~ ⟨of course⟩ help⟨ing⟩ ~~And the~~ ⟨The⟩ 'small rain' is exquisite.⟨–⟩ the fine rain that comes on the western wind, blowing ~~white~~ ⟨[? washing]⟩ sheets over the orchards. Some sailor wrote it, far away looking towards England. 'Christ if my love were in my arms and I in my bed again!' ~~One finally~~ ⟨I must⟩ returns to the poem itself; not connecting it with rain⟨,⟩ or sailor ⟨,⟩ or any ⟨[⟩ individual ⟨]⟩ experience in particular. I cannot except by constantly repeating the poem ~~itself~~ ⟨as a whole⟩, keep in touch with the emotion. I am tempted directly I begin to analyse to get far away from what I feel. After reading it several times I cease to get any emotion. But later I shall think involuntarily of 'the small rain' ~~with curiosity~~, for it describes rain that I
[? I shall have seen but never thought of calling ~~small~~. ⟨I shall think repeat the

*Anon.

486

f ~~poem~~⟩ But if I say the poem through these details are merged in a whole;
1 in the direct shock of emotion which I receive, and cannot explain to
ae myself or communicate to others.
]

X X X X X [p.21]

12

That is not very satisfactory as an analysis. It amounts to little more
than saying, 'The poem impressed me. I cannot say why. Perhaps it was
this, that, or the other.⟨[⟩ It ~~suddenly comes into my head, here in this
third class railway carriage~~ and gives me a shock of emotion'. ⟨]⟩ ⟨– &
'emotion' is vague.⟩

Yet there again with the poem, as with Byron's letters, the mind is
trying to make a whole. ⟨In the first place⟩ It is trying to sort out ⟨lay
bare⟩ and sharpen its perceptions. It is trying to stop itself from thinking
irrelevantly. It is trying to refer its impressions as accurately ⟨closely⟩ as
possible to the poem itself.⟨[⟩ It feels that there is more in the four lines
read together than in any one taken separately.⟨]⟩ It is trying to grasp
the poet's conception entire. According to conditions and to education it
is trying to grade this 'shock of emotion' by comparing it with emotions
received from other poems. ⟨or by other means⟩ ⟨[⟩ It will ask, perhaps,
When was this written and ⟨what else⟩ did he write ~~more~~? It will try to
make sure of its pleasure by reading something ⟨notoriously good or
notoriously bad⟩ universally praised and testing the one with the other.
or by quoting it aloud to a second person and comparing
impressions.⟨]⟩ Thus gropingly, blunderingly fitfully, with inadequate
materials and imperfect instruments the common reader judges pure
literature to be good or bad, to be of a certain sort of goodness or
badness, and to have some relation to life. ⟨~~fit in somewhere, somehow~~⟩
[p.22] Finally it is trying ⟨to⟩ ~~using~~ ⟨e⟩ the materials thus extracted and
tested to make some sort of world which suits its constitution. But what
way does a reader attempt to make a world out of pure literature?

(At this point we part company, very respectfully, with critics and
scholars. In all that follows, 'we' refers to those who are neither one nor
the other.)

Perhaps ⟨we try to make a world out of literature in this way⟩ in
something of this fashion. Given the four lines of poetry quoted above,
the reader says straight off 'This is passionate and direct'⟨;⟩ for that is
the sensation which they rouse in him. And now instinctively he says
'But having felt passion I want to feel the opposite', He turns the page
and reads, shall we say ⟨,⟩ Chaucer's Ballade de Bon Conseyl.

> Flee fro the prees, and dwelle with sothfastnesse;
> Suffyce unto thy thyng though hit be smal.*

and the two different sensations, one direct and passionate, the other stern and solemn are placed together and form a [*undeciphered word inserted*] nucleus out there in the void. They form a nucleus to which other sensations ~~attach~~ ⟨can return & attach⟩ ~~themselves~~; and this process once begun goes on indefinitely. ⟨Consider the zigzagging of natural reading done in youth.⟩ From tragedy we turn to comedy from the subtle and strange to the simple and direct. Now we must read Chaucer; now Rousseau; now the songs of Campion now Wuthering Heights. One principle guides us in making our course and that is that the emotion roused in us by each play [*p.23*] poem or story must be so strong that it has the power first to absorb us and then to send us, by a natural reaction, in search of a different sensation – of a sensation which appears to complete the one originally felt. By these means we become masters of a vast body of emotion, which increases according to our capacity to feel, and grows more intense as we become better fitted to define it. ⟨We realise that Eng. lit is quite different fr. French⟩ [*undeciphered phrase inserted*].

But if this were true – that we get from literature the sequence of our own emotions ⟨]⟩ ⟨that we build up in books an image of our own emotions⟩ immensely enlarged and intensified – to read the classics would be an emotional orgy, requiring no more effort than a shop girl makes who dreams as she listens to the band in Hyde Park of making love by moonlight at Margate ⟨:⟩ ⟨it wd⟩ ~~and giving~~⟨e⟩ no deeper satisfaction ⟨than that⟩ ⟨We cannot [*undeciphered cancelled phrase*] whole truth by any means.⟩ ~~To speak truly,~~ ⟨For in the first place⟩ ⟨reading great books⟩ it is always an effort, often a disappointment, and sometimes ⟨a⟩ drudgery ~~of a repulsive nature~~ ⟨kind⟩ to read the great ~~works of great writers~~. ⟨In the second,⟩ It is an exaggeration to say (as we have said) that we get emotion ~~always~~ from every book we read. From the great writers we get sometimes no ~~shock of~~ emotion at all. ⟨Emotion⟩ It comes only after hard ~~preliminary~~ ⟨unemotional⟩ exercise of the brain. Nor when we get it does it refer to ourselves. 'It ⟨i.e.⟩ the emotion, seems to ⟨[?refer]⟩ apply to everything' says the commentator quoted above. ⟨~~For that reason it is~~ That is one ~~reason for our difficulty~~ cause for effort.⟩ It is a greater effort to feel for all lovers and for all partings than to feel for your own or a friends. It is a greater

---

*Geoffrey Chaucer, 'Truth. Balade de Bon Conseyl'.

effort to visualise [*p.24*] country in general, and wind in general, than some particular orchard under the blow of the south west ~~wind~~. ⟨breeze.⟩ Yet it is these general emotions and these nameless winds that prevail in Homer Virgil Dante and Shakespeare. The great writers require that we shall cease to be so-and-so, ~~in such-and-such a room~~; ~~and~~ ⟨but &⟩ shall retain only the truth of our emotions⟨,⟩ which we have in common with others – the stubborn truth which persists through all the ~~interruptions, frivolities~~ and insincerities of daily life and provides us with something of universal validity by which to test the love of Othello; the rage of Lear; the scorn of Hamlet; the humanity of Falstaff. ⟨But⟩ ⟨To concentrate & collect in this way is very ~~hard~~ exhausting.⟩

'~~But~~ these details, says the commentator ⟨,⟩ who had only four lines to consider, 'are merged in a whole'. And here we reach the final difficulty; ~~the gate of brass~~ which has shut in the faces of ~~som many~~ ⟨so many⟩ ~~eager~~ adventurers and sent them back ~~again~~ to ~~life~~ ⟨again to reviews⟩ and the music halls and ~~the~~ evening paper⟨s⟩ to lives and letters and autobiographies; to talk about the thing and not the thing itself. [*p.25*]

13

There is someone in the corner of the railway carriage, let us suppose, who has occupied him self with reading the newspaper, looking out of the window, and guessing from scraps of talk at the lives of his fellow passengers. Suddenly, this random ~~noisy~~ jumble and confusion of colour and sound becomes fixed, as if a circle were put round it, and a finger pointed at it and a voice said 'Thats it – *that*.'

The writer (for we are trying to imagine the process in a writer's mind) receives a shock; he sees that this is complete and somehow significant; and this completeness and significance can most properly be expressed in words. For the rest of the journey he does not read nor listen to the talk. ~~The question is~~ First he must get the impression more and more ~~as vivid as possible~~; ⟨~~exactly clear~~ precise;⟩ then he must consider how to express in words exactly what there is in his mind.

But directly we write we find ~~that we are chan~~ that we putting ourselves under the dominion of a law. The law of writing rules even ⟨this⟩ ⟨man⟩ last night's vision of a .Wandsworth street. There are the shaped sentences; the ancient ~~words~~; the words that tempt ~~us~~, as everything tempts us, ~~from the~~ strict course ⟨outline⟩ of our impression ⟨conception⟩; and yet ⟨⟨& yet we must be tempted.⟩⟩ ⟨we must feel everything⟩ And here perhaps the great writers whose vision is most proper for expression in words make their supreme felicities — their famous passages; the daffodils of Shakespeare; the faery casements of Keats. ⟨And the conception as a whole is greater than its details.⟩ [*p.25*]

But directly we write we find that we are putting ourselves under the dominion of a law. The law of writing rules even last night's vision of a Wandsworth street. There are the shaped sentences; the ancient words, the words that tempt us (as everything tempts us, and we must let ourselves be tempted) ⟨know temptation & conquer it⟩ from the strict outline of our conception. Yet it is to this ⟨conception,⟩ that we must remain faithful ⟨;⟩ ⟨to the finger pointing, & to the⟩ as the supreme felicities – Shakespeare's daffodils, the faery casements of Keats, are faithful, in spite of their sudden and astonishing beauty; to the design. ⟨not 'ornaments' they are always in their places⟩ ⟨but parts of the structure⟩ ⟨⟨The finger that points⟩⟩ ⟨[⟩ Reading would be easy enough if great books consisted of famous passages only; but there is always the vision as a whole controlling, compressing the triumphs of language, the daring flights of the mind.⟨]⟩ Thus it is not enough to rest in the enjoyment of some astonishing moment. One must gather all ⟨it all in⟩ beauty, explore every subtlety, ⟨the various changes⟩ ring each change of sound, and yet must subdue all this ⟨it⟩, as the poet subdued it, ⟨the⟩ to some larger design, to art itself; for that perhaps is the circle round the whole.

So it seems that its ⟨the⟩ emotions ⟨of poetry⟩ are not our private emotions, and that they are brought into conformity with some abstract principle which appears to have no more to do with emotion than law has to do with the old cab horse on the rank outside the law courts.

At any rate, when the writer in the railway carriage began to shape his story he neither read or listened to the [*p.26*] talk of the other passengers. He seemed withdrawn in abstraction from the rest.

Must we withdraw in abstraction from the rest if we are to follow this irresistible fascination of reading poetry, or can we honestly say that we make a world of literature and that this world is inseparable from the world of the hearth rug and of the pavement – ⟨the life as full, the control as drastic?⟩ that we pass from one to the other, live as fully in one as in the other, submit to the same sort of control, and altogether prove ourselves as full of energy and virtue when we read Shakespeare as when we are engaged at the full height of our powers in transacting the affairs of life? Perhaps we can get nearer the truth by throwing these abstractions into a concrete form ⟨,⟩ and imagining some scene of real existence ⟨,⟩ and tracing as far as we can the transitions from one world to another, from life to literature. ⟨The railway carriage will do ⟨do to begin with⟩ serve our purpose.⟩

14

It is boring to ~~spend~~ have to spend so much time in getting from place to place. Still we have been to the play; we are on our way home; we are in transition from one incident to the next and protected by the continuity of our personal affairs from the naked facts of the third class railway carriage full of people. True, we guess at them; we fling a thought after them; ⟨round them⟩ ⟨we try to rope them in, & extend our view⟩ but on entering the house we find at once that life has accumulated; the post has been; we tell our adventures; and are at the centre of our own existences. It is dull, ⟨humdrum⟩ [*p.27*] exacting, exciting and pleasant also – this sense of the pressure of the past, of the necessity of the future, and of the moment alive with all the colours of the past twelve hours. ⟨~~the positive, brilliant~~ colour⟩ ⟨Wed. Feb 1st⟩ Already as we go up stairs the next day is half shaped and lies in our minds with all the bloom on it of a thing which has not yet happened. But ~~the day~~ ⟨twelve hours have so stirred us;⟩ brewed in us so many ideas and emotions the aimlessness of travelling has ⟨so⟩ afflicted us, the pressure ⟨*undeciphered phrase inserted*⟩ ⟨things ~~passing~~ fleeting & ~~going~~ unrecorded, & unrealised⟩ upon us is so great that we long for some finality, something stated. ~~Why not try Herrick?~~ ⟨So we read:⟩

> In this little urn is laid
> Prudence Baldwin, once my maid;
> From whose happy spark here let
> Spring the purple violet.*

⟨And apace the dust is laid.⟩ ~~That does~~ it ⟨,⟩ ~~at once.~~ ⟨~~Ah, that is it⟩ It~~ ⟨That⟩ has been said, finished, and ⟨T⟩~~the mind rests on~~ the happy spark, the purple violet, ~~or rather~~ ⟨It revives⟩ revives ⟨the mind⟩ as if ⟨it had been⟩ given something definite after churning among vaguenesses, ~~and~~ ⟨S⟩~~so~~ delightful is it to feel accurately like this that we go on

> Though clock
> To tell how night draws hence, I've none,
> A cock
> I have to sing how day draws on:
> I have a maid, my Prew, by good luck sent,
> To save

*Robert Herrick, 'Upon Prew his Maid'.

> That little, Fates me gave or lent:
> A hen
> I keep, which, creeking day by day, [*p.28*]
> Tells when
> She goes her long white egg to lay,*

⟨[⟩ The long white egg in its cleanliness and exactitude is ~~what we have~~ missed all day;⟨]⟩ and so once more –

> ⟨[⟩ To gather flowers Sappha went,
> And homeward she did bring
> With in her Lawnie continent,
> The treasure of the Spring.⟨]⟩†

and again

> Here is a solemn fast we keep,
> While all beauty lies asleep
> Husht be all things; (no noise here)
> But the toning of a tear:
> Or a sigh of such as bring
> Cowslips for her covering.‡

No doubt Herrick wrote more perfect poems; and no doubt to read thus, somnambulistically, dwelling, like a man feeling in the dark, upon the purple violet, the long white egg,⟨[⟩ the lawnie continent ⟨]⟩ the toning of a tear, the cowslips for her covering, is not reading, but only striking notes one after another and letting each one sound. Still since the sounds are pure ⟨,⟩ echoes come back. ⟨return to us⟩ We are in ~~that~~ ⟨the⟩ world which has been made by reading passionately, ⟨or laboriously,⟩ fiercely, according to the needs of the moment. We can turn hither and thither, putting our hands in the dark upon the familiar landmarks, referring [*p.29*] to Horace perhaps for he too brought out the beauty of ~~substantial~~ ⟨actual⟩ things; to Marvell – it matters not very much to whom we refer. ⟨for we hope ⟨know⟩ already ~~proved~~ that ~~the quotation~~ the ~~em~~ literature ~~of this~~ has its relation to our day.⟩ ⟨for we have been here before, & ~~these words shed that~~ these ideas shed their comment on the day without [?deliberation]. The point is that we are stepping ⟨taking our way⟩ ⟨moving⟩ among words which generalise our emotions and without even indirectly glancing at them, ⟨are related to⟩ gently take them up into their proper places and set them down in the

*Robert Herrick, 'His Grange, or private wealth'.
†Herrick, 'The Apron of Flowers'.
‡Herrick, 'An Epitaph upon a Virgin'.

light of a profound and comprehensive gaze. And above and beyond this (though no doubt it forms the most exquisite part of the pleasure) is the irresistible fascination ⟨the indefinable fascination,⟩ inseparable from art itself.

⟨[Soles ~~reddire~~ occidere et reddire possunt:
Nobis cum semel occidid brevis lux
Nox ~~et~~ est perpetua una dormienda]⟩*

15

But life does not yield so gently to literature in the day time. Civilisation in the twentieth century has ⟨[⟩ done some thing to facilitate the processes of ~~always~~ appearing dressed and washed, educated and housed and fed and warmed; but it is not even now ~~at all~~ ⟨possible⟩ easy without constant friction and physical ~~activity to give scope~~ ⟨lavished upon us the means of giving scope⟩ to all those desires – for music, for pictures, for air and the country, for talk and friendship and solitude which are our natural endowment. The telephone]*p.30*] rings; the train starts. Appliances are in existence for projecting us into the heart of London, ⟨hither & thither – to the city, to Bond Street⟩ where the grain ~~is~~ ⟨sacks are⟩ dumped onto the decks of steamers, or for ~~setting~~ us down to ~~pace~~ ⟨lifting [us] out⟩ ⟨into⟩ the fashionable pavement of Bond Street, or for shutting thick doors and ~~setting~~ ⟨reducing the multitudinous city life to⟩ four fiddlers on a platform under ~~electric light~~, or for allowing us to draw in the pageantry of Hyde Park on a summers day, ⟨or for pressing our faces against some miserable window in a back street⟩ or for depositing us an hour or two later by some green pool where the gulls are dipping, and the sea anemones bow from side to side as the wave streams over them. –⟨t⟩~~T~~he catalogue is endless. And if, besides running over the things one can see and do, we conceive how inclination is ~~all the time~~ drawing⟨s⟩ us into contact with people, into liking and repulsion, ~~and~~ intimacy and separation, all ~~the culminations and regrets of ordinary existence~~, ⟨ups & downs &⟩ then it may well seem as we come in hot ~~all through~~ with the effort and exertion ⟨exhilaration of life,⟩ that books are ~~pale and~~ moon like, and ⟨literature⟩ but the hobby of elderly men. But as a matter of fact what is it that happens?

'~~Much of the explanation of Byron's fame must be attributed to the~~

*Catullus, v.

effect he had upon the other sex'. said Justin Adolphus Macready, ⟨Terence Hewet⟩ who was descended on his mother's side from Briggs of Cornhill.

Rose Shaw replied that she could understand even now that Byron was an extremely fascinating man. She could imagine how he did it too – his vitality, and his cloak, and then the desire to redeem him, Every woman would think it was [*p.31*]

⟨Here is a little party of ordinary people, sitting round the dinner table, & talking, about Byron⟩ ⟨gossiping; who will marry who; what the Prime Minister said, have you read Byron's letters⟩ 'Much of the explanation of ⟨One must remember how much of⟩ Byron's fame must be attributed to the effect he had upon the other sex ⟨women⟩' said Terence Hewet, who was descended on the mother's side, from Briggs of Cornhill.

⟨And⟩ Rose Shaw replied ⟨said⟩ that she could understand even now that Byron was an extremely fascinating man. She could imagine how he did it too – his vitality, his cloak, and then the desire to redeem him. Every woman would think that it was left for her &c &c. ⟨to do that⟩ Clarissa ⟨Mrs Dalloway⟩ confessed to a passion for Donne on the strength of his portrait chiefly 'and some of the poems if you read them aloud-alas! I cant get Dick to read aloud ⟨my husband never has time to read aloud to me now –⟩ though so difficult are extraordinarily moving.' ⟨,⟩ to which Mr Pepper politely ⟨bowed⟩ assented.

'And of course ⟨And then⟩ ⟨E⟩every woman is in love with Keats' said ⟨continued⟩ Clarissa Dalloway, only to draw from Julia Hedge the unexpected and obstinate assertion that she was entirely on Fanny's side, and no young woman of spirit could have been expected to tolerate for an instant his exacting conventional ways with women. ⟨of making love⟩

⟨–⟩ This is trivial gossip. ⟨–⟩ But let us wait a minute. ⟨–⟩ They went into Hewets sitting room, overlooking the river, and after admiring the lights on the water, they began, at least Hewet and Rose began, pulling out books which were much in need of a duster. He would fetch a duster, Hewet said, 'for you *will* wear such lovely clothes' and Rose perceiving that this rather melancholy man, whose taste she so much respected, [*p.32*] did not despise her for choosing that particular shade of hydrangea coloured silk, confessed that she disliked Tristram Shandy. But why? She thought that Sterne was insincere. She thought that Thomas Hardy was sincere. She thought that Mr W. E. Norris was sincere.

'Wait' she said holding up her finger, and it came out (but we need not follow the process) that she liked a sort of matter of fact directness in literature and did not want authors, at any rate novelists, to be telling you all about it. 'if you know what I mean'. But what did she mean? ~~Hewet~~ Standing at the bookcase Hewet ⟨,⟩ ⟨[⟩ who had a strange habit of holding some object before his eyes and lapsing (or rather thinking twenty dozen things in the course of a second; ⟨]⟩ wondered – took down Life's Little Ironies – opened it – ~~shut it~~ – observed that it was a copy of the first edition ⟨d.d. St John Hirst⟩ – wondered whether Rose could be trusted not to stand the coffee pot on it – decided that it was worth risking – wondered what on earth this ~~popinjay~~ delightful popinjay – ~~this popinjay with a heart, but had she a brain~~ – meant by sincerity – and ⟨so⟩, via Natasha presumably, ⟨landed⟩ upon to War and Peace.

'War and Peace' he said aloud, 'that is the most sincere book in the world.'

Clarissa Dalloway heard the statement, and thought it a little ⟨smiled thinking it too⟩ solemn; ~~so she told him not to go corrupting youth~~. ⟨though she had an Englishwoman's respect for literature⟩ She ~~had~~ promised to fetch ~~her~~ husband from the House at ten; ~~and~~ they were taking ~~Rose~~ Shaw to Mrs Durrants evening party [p.33]
⟨at wh.⟩ Clarissa Dalloway heard the statement, ⟨said it was time to go to Mrs D's party⟩ ⟨smiled, & sitting up said they must go⟩ ~~and smiled~~, thinking it a little too serious for life, ⟨smiled⟩ though she had an Englishwoman's respect for litrature.

'Come,' she ~~said to Rose. and they~~ went. Julia went. Mr Pepper and Hewet remained alone.

⟨[⟩ So far life and literature seem to help each other out.⟨]⟩ Rose Shaw and Hewet were using literature partly in order to make them understand each other. What does she mean by 'sincerity'? She will read Lifes Little Ironies and he perhaps will dip into Tristram Shandy. From this point they will go on building up side by side ⟨, he this chimney, she that, ~~outhouse~~⟩ a world in literature which will become (if she turns out a born reader ⟨as she may⟩ which remains to be seen) a great deal subtler ~~and more fully expressed~~ than the world of Mrs Durrants evening parties and the Houses of Parliament, and yet closely attached to it, and very interesting as a comment upon it ⟨upon them & their adventures⟩ ⟨their adventures there that very evening⟩ ~~Very likely that evening~~ Rose will say to Timmy Durrant 'Do you know a man called Hewet? He seems to read a great deal' and she will think as she sips her ice, what did she ~~did~~ mean⟨t⟩ ~~about~~ ⟨by⟩ sincerity.

At last, at last, old Pepper had gone ⟨,⟩ ~~though Hewet had taken pains not to let him see what an intolerable restraint his company~~ was. He was an old friend. He had mellowed. But still he could sit on till midnight speculating upon the possible [*p.34*] success of the Mount Everest expedition while Hewet was jarred all through because Mrs Dalloway had taken Rose Shaw ~~off~~ to the Durrants party. ⟨Yet⟩ He pressed Pepper to stay; he helped him on with his overcoat. But directly he was alone. . . . It is not necessary to imagine the turmoil in his mind. He sat up reading Shakespeare.

<h1 style="text-align:center">16</h1>

Anyone who is left alone in a tumultuous frame of mind is quite likely to ⟨sit up⟩ read ⟨ing⟩ Shakespeare, ~~choosing that~~ one of the plays ⟨It ~~is an effort. It is~~ One must make the plunge; it is an effort⟩ which most agrees or most contrasts with his mood. ~~However~~ ⟨but⟩ in ten minutes or so the personal cobwebs are blown clean away. The vigour of the language is too overwhelming ⟨to be missed⟩ ~~Read one of the less familiar plays – Troilus and Cressida~~ for instance, ⟨–⟩ Every ounce of energy is used up in realising the perpetual succession of images which coin even the thinnest pencilled thoughts on the borderlands of our consciousness into robust highly coloured shapes. ⟨bodies⟩ Merely to throw ourselves this way and that with the emotions of the different speakers gives the illusion of violent physical exercise. To seize the first phrases of each character as ~~they~~ ⟨it⟩ shoot ⟨s⟩ out ready primed with the qualities of the speaker and stow away ⟨makes⟩ their ⟨its⟩ meaning requires the utmost agility of imagination. The vitality, the intensity, the compression and pressure of ~~each~~ ⟨every⟩ page keep one on the stretch almost to the exclusion of comment, and as [*p.35*] for saying that this is 'ornament' or that 'structure' such phrases if we remember them float ~~far away~~ like feathers on the ~~blast of a~~ storm at sea. ⟨~~wind west gale~~ wind⟩ Yet suddenly, between the acts, the figure of Byron appears, ~~and~~ how tawdry, insincere and theatrical! What an enlargement ⟨expansion⟩ of understanding ⟨feeling⟩ we have undergone! ⟨not in himself but in his poetry⟩⟩

> The large Achilles, on his pressed bed lolling,
> From his deep chest laughs out a loud applause*

⟨⟨No, it is not Byron himself but his poetry.⟩⟩ ⟨There is a magnificence in this world.⟩⟩ These are the great men who have caught us up

---

*Shakespeare, *Troilus and Cressida*, I, iii, 162–3, spoken by Ulysses.

into their own world. And later as the weaving of character and incident thickens not only are we engaged in the perpetual thrust and parry of mood, but more loftily have risen to be spectators ⟨as well⟩; at the same time that we are actors, and are aware of the ~~sublimity of the conflict~~; of the inevitable catastrophe; aware, not at this point of 'art' or a 'circle round the whole' but of something ~~inexorable~~ in ~~life itself~~ ⟨fate⟩ which ~~compels obedience~~ ⟨~~exacts suffering~~⟩ ⟨controls emotion: opposes itself inexorably to human desires & life⟩ [*brief hiatus in text*] fate which opposes itself inexorably to human desires. And then ~~the last two acts crumble in our hands~~. ⟨–⟩ The inevitable catastrophe does not happen. What is the failure ⟨?⟩ ⟨Is it⟩ in construction here? ~~and~~ ⟨or⟩ the ornament, ⟨–⟩ is that perhaps excessive? or somehow unrelated to the conception? ~~And how~~ ⟨But⟩ in spite of the conflict between good and bad and the apparent triumph of cynicism, does do we feel so strongly tha[t] Shakespeare was on the side of ⟨. . . . virtue?⟩ [*p.36*]

There are a thousand questions arising from Troilus and Cressida in which we may become absorbed. But the main fact is plain enough. ⟨We have spent⟩ Two or three hours ~~have been spent~~ with our faculties at full tilt. We have exercised ~~our humour~~, our intellect, our sympathy, our scorn, our cynicism. The exercise has been continuous without interruption and always at ~~full~~ ⟨high⟩ pitch. It is ~~quite unlike~~ ⟨much more intense⟩ the ceremony and interruption, the ~~effort and~~ frustration of the dinner table. It is capable of laying sleep [*sic*] the miserable agitations which beset men left ~~to think~~ alone to think about some Rose Shaw who has gone to a party. But it is the natural culmination of the days work, and Troilus and Cressida which is a difficult ⟨&⟩ puzzling play, yet draws the sting of the ordinary man's misery and sweats out of him something impure.

Thus roughly we mark down a few of the emotions which have the most obvious relation to life. But it is clear that the greater part of what we feel when we read Shakespeare is incommunicable. So perhaps is the greater part of what we feel when we go for a country walk. There is a silence in life, a perpetual deposit of experience for which action provides no proper outlet and our own words no fit expression. ⟨[⟩ Hewet could never have told Rose Shaw what was in his mind when she left ⟨him⟩; for the moment's emotion mixed itself with the accumulated thoughts of years.⟨]⟩ And is this to be found in books – ⟨an expression of⟩ this most intimate life which is lived in solitude, and so alters the commonest sights of the country side that butterflies on the teasle compose in one pair of eyes a whole [*p.37*] chapter of life and for another remain nothing but butterflies on the teasle? Indeed it is strange how often Shakespeare ⟨ makes us⟩ penetrates here; ⟨anticipates whatever we are about to say!⟩ how ⟨how⟩ often again he will take some grain of emotion germ of emotion that we scarcely realised and show it in full flower elsewhere;⟨]⟩ how much indeed, that would die unexpressed and unshared and thus not fully felt in the privacy of our own minds becomes bolder, more rational, and infinitely more profound in poetry.

But with all this ⟨the constant⟩ use of the words feeling and emotion, of fascinations that are irresistible and yet ⟨alas⟩ indefinable, we may be ⟨may⟩ giving a handle ⟨an [undeciphered word]⟩ to the moralist who ⟨to⟩ objects that reading is self indulgence and that there is no lesson in all this language, ⟨&⟩ nothing in pure literature ⟨the word⟩ ⟨when we have made⟩ that imposes restraint and teaches morality ⟨a man or woman to be good.⟩ ⟨There are people who go to Chapel instead⟩ But then he has never read Shakespeare.

17

⟨But⟩ Like most clever and well educated men ⟨even⟩ Hewet wrote 'None' when he was asked to state his religion by on the Census paper. The silence of life was certainly not expressed for him in Westminster Abbey, or in Westminster Cathedral ⟨either⟩ Nevertheless when he was told by a bore ⟨didn't show it when bored⟩ by an old friend he did not show it. He had, therefore, some code of manners, some order and restraint in daily life, which he had come by ⟨acquired by some means⟩ ⟨somehow or other⟩ ⟨for himself⟩ —— But how, in these days of science, and opportunity and freedom do we come by codes, even of manners?

It would be unbecoming in a common reader to dogmatise, [p.38] may we not suppose that anyone who likes poetry perceives that there is a strictness in poets' minds; that they are orderly not lax; and that the discipline which is needed to create a poem is needed to understand it; and this independent of any teaching which it may please us to elicit? What is the lesson of Troilus and Cressida? Heaven knows. But 'fate opposes itself inexorably to human desires, and Shakespeare is on the side of virtue' – something like that remains with us, vague if we write it down, very powerful as we make it out and carry it with us.

⟨And so⟩ And now Mr Pepper is gone; and here is poor Terence Hewet half in love with Rose Shaw. Whole volumes have been written about Shakespeares view of love; but one still retains the impression that in his eyes love was important, not trivial. And so one with the rest of the day's work; death and suffering; humiliation ⟨love⟩ and desire. And so

498

The different worlds ~~melt into each other~~ ⟨merge into each other⟩ and to be for ever enlarging our spheres, with whatever materials come to hand, ~~and,~~ so as to live more fully and completely, ~~to find what restraint and discipline are needed for this purpose,~~ ⟨& with that end in view to find the necessary discipline & restraint⟩ this, however differently it is done, ~~seems to be the natural instinct of~~ ordinary people. As for having Shakespeare without a hearthrug, or a hearthrug without Shakespeare, that ⟨one⟩ is ⟨as⟩ unthinkable. ⟨as the other⟩

In the end, then, though we have found no method, the fact seems to emerge that the writers of England and the readers of England are necessary to one another. They cannot live apart. They must be for ever engaged in intercourse. It is a law of our [*p.39*] being and the proof of our descent from Briggs of Cornhill that we should somehow, anyhow, using ~~the~~ critics, scholars, the Lives and letters, gossip and journalism, fact and fiction, anything that comes handy, make out for ourselves what sort of book the Flame of Youth is by E. K. Sanders which is to be published on March 26th, 1922, price seven and sixpence. The publishers say it will be 'the talk of the season'. It is high time to begin the review.

APPENDIX III

Character in Fiction

What follows is a transcript of VW's heavily revised typescript 'Character in Fiction' (MHP, B13), a draft of her paper delivered to the Cambridge Heretics Society on Sunday, 18 May 1924. The paper itself, which derives in part from her essay 'Mr Bennett and Mrs Brown' (see p. 384), was published by T. S. Eliot in the *Criterion* of July 1924 (see p. 420).

Authorities on the subject vary, but it seems that the Heretics Society was founded in 1909 or 1911, and that the founders included the linguistic psychologist C. K. Ogden, president 1911–24 (his famous book *The Meaning of Meaning* was published in 1923), and the academic lawyer H. F. Jolowicz, with the economist Philip Sargant Florence, who succeeded Ogden as president, and the brilliant mathematician and philosopher F. P. Ramsey. It was a mixed society, and so rather advanced by the standards of the time, and it enjoyed a certain reputation for exclusivity. Members did not need *literally* to be heretics but when discussing religion they were not permitted to appeal to authority. Past speakers included Jane Harrison, G. B. Shaw, G. K. Chesterton, F. M. Cornford, and G. M. Trevelyan. Lytton Strachey and Roger Fry also read papers, the latter in 1927. The Heretics gathered on Sunday evenings at 8.30 and among a number of venues, a small, and therefore crowded, room in King's Parade was generally used in the early 1920s but not necessarily on this occasion.

The Woolfs travelled up to Cambridge on the afternoon of Saturday, 17 May, to stay with George ('Dadie') Rylands. They dined that night with J. M. Keynes, Rylands, Denis Robertson, and F.L. and 'Topsy' Lucas, probably at King's College, where, on the Sunday, they lunched, again with Rylands and also with Sebastian Sprott, with whom and others, including the eminent Heretic J. B. S. Haldane, they dined that night at the Cambridge Union, after which VW read her paper. (R. B. Braithwaite, another prominent Heretic, was also of the company on the Saturday and it is probable that he too heard VW's paper.)

VW later wrote of the event to Jacques Raverat, himself a Cambridge man: 'Two weeks ago I was in Cambridge, lecturing the heretics upon Modern Fiction. Do you feel kindly towards Cambridge? It was, as Lytton would say, rather "hectic"; young men going in for their triposes; flowering trees on the backs; canoes, fellows' gardens; wading in a slightly unreal beauty; dinners, teas, suppers; a sense, on my part, of extreme age, and tenderness and regret; and so on and so on. We had a good hard headed argument, and I respect the atmosphere, and I'm glad to be out of it' (*III VW Letters*, no. 1479, 8 June 1924).

The typescript consists of twenty-four pages, twenty-two numbered 1–22, and two further pages originally numbered 18 and 19 but renumbered 21 and 22 respectively and forming the conclusion to the paper. It is heavily amended throughout with numerous insertions and cancellations in purple ink, black ink (possibly also a third shade, dark blue ink) and in lead pencil. The principles upon which the transcript is made are the same as those employed and explained at Appendix II, 'Byron & Mr Briggs'.

Character in Fiction

It seems to me possible that I may be the only person in this room who has committed the folly of writing, or trying to write, or wishing to write, a novel. And when I ask myself ⟨as your invitation made me ask myself⟩ what demon whispered in my ear and urged me to my doom, a little ~~picture~~ ⟨figure⟩ always comes before me; the ~~picture~~ ⟨figure⟩ of a man, or of a woman, who says My name is Brown. Catch me if you can.

I do not think that I am the only writer who has this experience. Most novelists, if you asked them, would say I think that they are haunted in precisely the same way. Some character comes before them, some Brown, Smith or Jones, and says in the most seductive and charming way in the world, Come and catch me if you can. And so, led by this will o the wisp, they flounder through volume after volume, ~~year after year~~, spending the best years ⟨part⟩ of their lives ⟨in the pursuit⟩, and receiving for the most part very little cash in exchange; ~~in the attempt to snare this phantom~~ who dances just ahead ⟨o⟩f th⟨e⟩m. ⟨Few ~~Some~~ catch the phantom; most have to be contented with a scrap of her dress.⟩ ⟨or a lock of her hair⟩

My belief that men and women write novels because they are lured on to create some character which has thus imposed itself on them has the sanction of Mr Arnold Bennett. In an article from which I will quote he says 'The foundation of good fiction is character creating and nothing else . . . Style counts; plot counts; wide information counts; originality of outlook counts. But none of these counts anything like so much as the convincingness of the characters. If the characters are real the novel will have a chance; if they are not, oblivion will be its portion . . . .' And he goes on to draw a conclusion which is that we have ⟨no⟩ [p.2] young novelists of first rate importance at the present moment because for various reasons which do not seem to me ~~very convincing~~ ⟨quite satisfactory⟩ ⟨with wh. I will deal later⟩, they are unable to create characters which are real; true; and convincing.

This is the question which I want, with greater boldness than discretion, to discuss tonight. I want to make out what it is that we mean when we talk about 'character' in fiction. I should like too to say something about this question of reality which Mr Bennett raises. And I should like to suggest some reasons why the younger novelists fail to create characters, if, as Mr Bennett asserts, it is true that they fail they do [sic]. This will lead me, I am well aware to make ~~some~~ ⟨many⟩ very sweeping, and also some very vague assertions. For the truth is that the subject is an extremely difficult one. It might well fill a whole volume. I expect that there are professors in America who are even now making it the text of several volumes. But ⟨asking you to bear with me⟩ I will do my best. ⟨~~Who are I~~ Before I begin I shd. say that when I speak of the Georgians I am speaking of such writers as Mr Joyce, Mr Lawrence, Mr Forster, Mr Strachey, Mr Eliot, Miss Sitwell, Miss Richardson who are certainly un Edwardian tho' I have no reason to think that they wd. agree to what I say or particularly like to be grouped together.⟩

I have said that perhaps I am the only novelist present. But I am quite certain that everyone in this room is a judge of character. Indeed it would be impossible to live with any success without being a judge of character. This gift, or instinct, or faculty, – whatever it is, is one ⟨~~is the most~~⟩ that we use begin to use directly we get out of bed in the morning, and go on using more or less consciously all day long. We are always altering our conduct ~~at the dictation~~ ⟨according to its ~~verdict~~ report⟩ of our judgment of character. ~~According as~~ ⟨t⟩ it⟨s⟩ ⟨dictation⟩ ~~decrees~~ we make friends or enemies, we like or dislike people; we trust them with our money or we dont trust them; we marry them or we refuse to marry them. And here I will venture the first [*p.3*] of my sweeping statements. No generation since the world began has known quite so much about character as our generation. I am not saying that we are the best judges of character; for that unfortunately does not necessarily follow. What I do say is that the average man or woman today thinks more about character than his or her grandparents; character interests them more; they get closer, they dive deeper in to the real emotions and motives of their fellow creatures. There are scientific reasons why this should be so. If you read Freud you know in ten minutes some facts – or at least some possibilities – which our parents could not possibly have guessed for themselves. ⟨That is a very debatable point. ~~But~~ how much we can learn ~~from science~~ that is real know ~~from science & make~~ use ~~of from science~~ & make our own from science⟩ And then there is a ~~more~~ vaguer force at work – a force which is sometimes called the Spirit of the Age or the Tendency of the age. This mysterious power is taking us by the hand, I think, and making us look much more closely into the reasons why people do and say and think things, ⟨thus character⟩ ⟨shapes to her⟩ and diverting us ⟨from what they do⟩ from the adventures, the violent events, the actions in short, of the human race. ⟨That is one of the reasons I think we are so curiously different fr. our fathers; & why therefore our literature must be different.⟩ ⟨~~But the~~⟩.

that
people
change

However this may be, it is obvious that most people have to acquire a good deal of skill in character reading if they are to get through a single year of life without disaster. But this skill is acquired, I believe, before the age of twenty five or thirty. When they are mature, most people have learnt enough for practical purposes. They have learnt enough to keep them from making fools of themselves. They have made friends, and chosen wives and husbands. And in most cases, ~~they have had to take up~~ some They have taken [*p.4*] up some pursuit, like economics, or science, or trade, which absorbs the greater part of their energies; and ⟨inevitably⟩ this other branch of learning – this character mongering as ~~Jane Austen~~ ⟨Sterne⟩ called it I think – falls into disuse. That is ~~one of the reasons, it often seems to me,~~ ⟨perhaps⟩ why old people and elderly people, find it so difficult to make friends. They have long since ⟨ceased⟩ to be interested in character, and ⟨when⟩ a new ~~person~~ ⟨~~character~~ person⟩ ⟨appears, they try to make ~~it~~ him fit in with⟩ worries them a little. All they can do is to remember what once upon a time – twenty or thirty years ago – they felt for somebody else. ~~It annoys them to find that~~ ⟨They find – as is after all very likely – that the newcomer differs from the⟩ If your character does not resemble what [*sic*] the version of character which they once made out for themselves, they are annoyed; they are apt to call ~~you~~ ⟨him⟩ insolent, impertinent, bad mannered, and extremely uninteresting into the bargain. ~~But this is by the way.~~

Now novelists differ from the rest of the world because they do not cease to be interested in character when they have learnt enough about it for practical purposes. They go a step further. They feel that there is something permanently interesting in ~~a~~ character in itself. Like other people of course, they have their likes and dislikes; they have to decide in exactly the same way who is to be trusted, who ~~is~~ to be avoided, and who ~~is~~ to be married. But when all this ⟨practical⟩ business has been discharged, there is something about people which continues to seem to them of overwhelming importance in spite of the fact that it has no bearing whatever upon their comfort, happiness, or income. This is what I ~~want to~~ ⟨exerts its fascination⟩ I find it very difficult to explain – what this ⟨thing⟩ is and why it is ⟨interesting now⟩. So if you will allow me I will give you an account of a railway journey which ⟨Instead of giving you an analysis of character or trying to define what is called in textbooks the aesthetic emotion⟩ [*p.5*] I made the other day from Richmond to Waterloo. I shall try to make you see by describing a very ordinary and perhaps rather insignificant experience, what I mean by 'character in itself'.⟨[⟩ What I mean when I say that a novelist thinks differently about character from other people.⟨]⟩ and why, though the characters in question had no possible influence upon my own life, for good or for bad, still they gave me something which was for me ⟨& might have been for the world at large⟩ of very great importance. ⟨If you will use your imaginations very generously & indulgently you may also see in this anecdote the germ of the whole business of creating [character].⟩ ⟨This incident happened one night about two weeks ago. I was going up to London⟩ I was late. I ran down the stairs just as the train was going out, and jumped into the first carriage I came to. As I opened the door, I had a strange and rather uncomfortable feeling that I was interrupting a conversation between two people who were already sitting there. ~~Yet,~~ ⟨But⟩ I thought, they are too old for it to matter very much. I am not interrupting a newly engaged couple. No; the woman must have been sixty at least, and the man well over forty. They were sitting opposite each other, and the man had been leaning over and talking rather emphatically from the expression on his face – he was flushed. ~~They both looked at me, as if I disturbed them. and~~ sat back and became silent ⟨as if I had disturbed him in the middle of some very important remark⟩. The elderly lady whom I will call Mrs Brown ⟨seemed however relieved. She⟩, was one of those clean worn fresh-coloured old ladies whose extreme tidiness – every button in its place, every thing fastening, tied together, clean irreproachable – [*p.6*] suggests ⟨a more⟩ extreme poverty ⟨than rags & dirt⟩; one feels that they have one complete set of clothes which is ⟨kept carefully in a cupboard⟩ only worn on special occasions. There was something pinched about her – a look of suffering, of apprehension and in addition she was extremely small. Her feet in their clean little boots scarcely touched the floor. She had those pale blue eyes which remind one of ⟨peaceful⟩ afternoon⟨s⟩ skies in November; but they were not peaceful; they were strained, anxious, and at the same time enduring. I felt she had no body to support her; that she had to decide things for herself; and that having been ⟨deserted⟩ left a widow many years ago she had had an extremely anxious ⟨time⟩ life – she had had to educate and bring up an only son.

her kindred had

All this shot through my mind as I sat down, ~~as generally happens~~, ⟨being unable⟩ ⟨as⟩ I suppose when we are ~~travelling. We cannot settle~~ in for a short railway journey even without making up our ⟨my⟩ minds as to ⟨our⟩ my fellow travellers. Then I looked at the man. He was no relation of hers I felt sure. ⟨He was of a bigger, burlier, less refined type⟩ ~~He was obviously not at his ease~~. He was a man of business I imagined – a hard headed astute man from the North, who had knocked about a good deal, and not perhaps been very scrupulous in his dealings. Still he was not a ruffian; he was quite respectable; upright, ⟨dressed in blue serge⟩ according to his lights. ⟨But he was obviously not at his ease.⟩ But he had to settle some business or other with Mrs Brown. ~~It was~~ an unpleasant business, a secret business which they were not going to discuss in my presence. I pretended to read. ⟨but⟩ I knew ~~however~~ that this dodge would not take them in.

'Theyve had ⟨The Crofts have very⟩ bad luck with their servants' Mr Smith ⟨as I will call him⟩ said. ⟨In [*undeciphered word*] going back to something wh. had been said much earlier in the conversation, for the sake of saying something⟩ ⟨with a view to keeping up the conversation⟩ clearly making conversation. [*p.7*] 'Yes' said Mrs Brown, ~~a little condescendingly~~. 'My grandmother had a maid who came when she was fifteen and stayed till she was 80. (this was said to impress both [of] us I thought.)

'⟨Ah⟩ One doesnt often come across that sort of thing nowadays' said ~~Mr Brown~~. Smith
– he was conciliatory.

Then they were silent.

'Its an awful pity that they dont start a golf club there – I should have thought one of the young fellows would' said Mr B̶r̶o̶w̶n̶ ⟨Smith⟩ The silence made him uneasy.

Mrs Brown said something so low that I could not hear. ⟨She was not interested in the question of his golf club.⟩ 'What changes theyre making in this part of the world' said Mr Brown looking out of the window; ⟨&⟩ looking at me too. And now it began to seem to me quite plain ⟨fr. Mrs Browns silence, from the uneasy way in wh. Mr Smith talked⟩ that he had made Mrs Brown sell him her house against her will; or that he had some power ⟨over her⟩ which was disagreeable to her ⟨, that he⟩ o̶v̶e̶r̶ ̶h̶e̶r̶ ̶p̶r̶i̶v̶a̶t̶e̶ ̶a̶f̶f̶a̶i̶r̶s̶. Her son had got into debt perhaps; She was going to London to make some [disposition] of her property. Clearly she was in B̶r̶o̶w̶n̶s̶ ⟨Smiths⟩ hands. against her will. ⟨I felt a great deal of pity for her when,⟩

Suddenly she said,

'Can you tell me if an oak tree dies when the leaves have been eaten for two years in succession by caterpillars?'

She spoke quite brightly, rather precisely, ⟨with a cultivated [*undeciphered word*]⟩

B̶r̶o̶w̶n̶ ⟨Mr Smith⟩ was relieved to have a topic of conversation given him. yet ⟨a little put out &⟩ rather hurried. He told her a great deal very quickly about plagues of insects. He had a brother who kept a fruit farm in Kent. . [*p.8*] And then while he talked a very odd thing happened. Mrs Brown took out her little white handkerchief and began to dab her eyes. She was crying. But she went on listening quite composedly to what he was saying; and he went on talking, a little louder, as if he had seen her cry often before – as if it were a painful habit. Yet I thought it got on his nerves. He looked at the out of the window and said in a different voice, ⟨in a menacing even a bullying way⟩

speaking quite low and ⟨]⟩ leaning towards her as he had been doing when I got in

'So then referring to ⟨that matter we were discussing⟩ what we've been saying, it'll be all right George will be there on Tuesday. at eleven?'

'We shant be late' said Mrs Brown. ⟨She was frightened; but at the same time extremely dignified⟩

'that'll be all right' said Mr Smith rather uncomfortably. getting up, buttoning his coat, reaching his bag from the rack ⟨[– doing these things rather ostentatiously, to fill up the time, I thought. He made these preparations ⟨]⟩ as if he were in a great hurry to be gone; ⟨[⟩ as if his situation had become suddenly extremely uncomfortable;⟨]⟩ as if he had got what he wanted, and felt a little ashamed, and anxious to get out of the old ladys sight as soon as possible. The train stopped at Clapham Junction; Mr Smith had jumped out almost before it stopped. Mrs Brown and I were left alone together. She sat very still in her corner, small, tidy, clean, suffering keenly, and somehow rather queer. All this seemed to come pouring like a draught – like a smell of burning – from the corner where she sat. I mean it was very pungent and unmistakable the impression she made. At the same time of course, we were rattling into London. past great buildings, flaring lights, sudden glimpses [*There is no page nine in the typescript as it survives.*]

[*p.10*] to realise her character. to steep myself in her atmosphere. I had no time to explain why I felt it somehow tragic, heroic, yet with a dash of something flighty, ~~strange, something~~ ⟨& fantastic⟩ that made one wish to burst out laughing – before the train stopped. I watched her disappear, carrying her bag, in the ⟨vault⟩ vast blazing station. She looked very small, very tenacious, at once very frail and very heroic. And I have never seen her again, and I shall never know what became of her.

Now I have done my best to describe this incident which happened to me about a fortnight ago as accurately as I can. So far as I am able I have described the people, and written down exactly what they said. But directly I read over what I have written, I realise how very far it is from the whole truth; at best it is only one version of the truth. If anyone else had been with me, and described the same incident they would have described it quite differently. They would have noticed different things; from the same facts they would have drawn different conclusions. My Mrs Their Mrs Brown would have been quite a different person from my Mrs Brown I am sure. Therefore we must accept the fact I think that when two novelists look together at the same people – at the same incident – it is quite likely, indeed it is probable that they will come to the very opposite conclusions about them. One will notice what the other neglect; one think important what the other finds negligible. And here therefore we That is one of the perplexities one of the pitfalls of writing novels. A character which is real [*p.11*]

Now I have not told you this anecdote in order to make you realise the pleasures of travelling from Richmond to Waterloo. I hope you will not accuse me of telling it in order to display my own powers of observation and creation. What I want you to see in it is this; here is a character imposing itself upon another person. Here is Mrs Brown making someone begin almost automatically to write a novel about her. I think I might safely say that this is the way in which nine novels out of ten do begin. They begin with a character; that character suggests scenes and situations, and so from a single encounter we get a novel of thirty two chapters. ⟨It is the character which suggests everything else.⟩ But this is not as simple as it looks. I must recall what Mr Arnold Bennett says. He says that 'the foundation of good ~~charac~~ fiction is character creating and nothing else and he says that it is only if the characters are real that the novel has any chance of surviving; if they are not oblivion will be its portion.' It seems to me a very difficult thing to say what reality is. One of the A character may be real to Mr Bennett and quite unreal to me. For instance he says that Dr Watson in Sherlock Holmes is real to him; well, to me Watson is not real at all; he is a mere dummy; an amusing figure of fun. And so on, with book after book ⟨~~it is with~~ all [*two undeciphered words*]⟩ ⟨but especially with contemporary books⟩; people are always surprising ~~me~~ ⟨one⟩ by ⟨the character⟩ what they think real and ⟨the character⟩ what they think unreal. But if you take a larger view, I think Mr Bennett is perfectly right. If that is, you think of the novels which seem to you great novels – ~~we may agree to call~~ ⟨War & Peace⟩ Vanity Fair, David Copperfield, Jane Eyre, Pride and Prejudice, ~~The Antiquary; Jude the Obscure~~ ⟨The Mayor of Casterbridge⟩ – ~~great novels~~; if you think of these books, you do at once think of some character who has seemed [*p.12*] so real that it has the power not merely to make you think of it in itself, but of all sorts of other things ⟨through its eyes⟩, of religion, of landscape, of love, of the immortality of the soul, of ~~the relation~~ mans relation to the world.⟨[⟩ Yes, if a great novelist took ⟨had taken⟩ that little incident in the railway carriage, ~~and showed us~~ made us realise Mrs Brown, he would give us at the same time a complete view of human life ⟨work of art [?]⟩ ⟨as⟩ Tolstoy ~~does~~ that in War and Peace. Novelists are always attempting to do ~~it~~. And they always do it as I in my very rough sketch attempted to do it⟨]⟩, through character. There ⟨in my sketch⟩ was old Mrs Brown in her corner; there was the world outside her; there were the flying houses, the river, the beauty of the visible world, ⟨the fate to wh. she was travelling⟩ which in the hands of a great writer ~~becomes~~ the beauty of the is ~~brought into~~ relation with the ~~character~~ – makes a whole – makes a complete universe. ⟨a whole universe it seems to me was suggested by the old lady in the train⟩ But there is no need to argue the question further. I am sure we are all agreed with Mr Bennett that characters must be real. They are the germs from which the whole of the living body of the fiction springs.

But now I want to examine what Mr Bennett went on to say; he went on to say that there are no great novelists among the Georgian writers because they cannot create characters who are real, true and convincing. I think that Mr Bennett is only superficially right. I think that, being a man of some standing, age, and celebrity he has contented himself with a birds eye view ⟨of his juniors⟩, and has not troubled to ~~investigate~~ ⟨go into⟩ the truth of the matter ⟨very deeply⟩. ~~Anyhow,~~ I will now give you my views for what they are worth. ~~Again~~ I must ask you ~~nototo~~ accuse me of egotism, but ~~unless In~~ my view then, the ~~Georgian novel~~ men and women ~~who began~~ writing novel[s] about ~~the year~~ 1910 – or 11 had an ~~immensely~~ difficult task before ~~them.~~ [*p.13*] Anyhow let us consider the question as impartially as we can. Why is it so hard for novelists at the present moment to create characters which seem real not only to Mr Bennett but to the world at large? Why in short – for it comes to the same thing have we no great novelists among the younger generation? I will lay before you my own view, but it is of course a prejudiced view, a near sighted view, and I hope you will use your minds upon it and make it a large and long sighted view because you, as spectators, as readers, as ⟨the⟩ public, see most of the game, and ~~decide the~~ give the ~~verdict~~ ⟨prizes⟩ in the ~~long run~~ ⟨end⟩.

In my view then, the men and women who began writing novels in 1910 or thereabouts had an immensely difficult task before them. One of the chief difficulties was that there was no living English novelist from whom they could learn their business. (Mr Conrad is a Pole, which makes him not very helpful; and Mr Hardy stopped writing novels in 1895) The most prominent and successful novelists in the year 1910 were I suppose Mr Wells Mr Bennett and Mr Galsworthy. Now it seems to me that to go to these men and ⟨to⟩ ask ~~you to~~ them to teach you how to write a novel – how to create characters that are real – is precisely like going to a bootmaker and asking him to teach you how to make a watch. Do not let me give you the impression that I do not admire and enjoy their ~~work~~ ⟨books⟩ ⟨novels.⟩ which ~~They~~ seems to me of great value and indeed ⟨of great⟩ necessity. One must have boots. There are seasons when they matter much more than watches. To drop metaphor, I think that after the ⟨creative splendours⟩ [of the] Victorian ⟨age⟩ splendours it was quite necessary – not only for life but for literature that some one should write the books that Mr Wells and Mr Bennett and Mr Galsworthy have written. Yet, though I read these books with great excitement as they came out they left me with a strong feeling of disappointment. I felt that ⟨I⟩ was defrauded of something [*p.14*] that I needed in a novel; something that I had got from the great Russians and from the English

Victorians. I was always making up theories to account for my disappointment. At last I came to the conclusion that it was because Mr Wells
Mr Galsworthy and Mr Bennett had no power to create character⟨s⟩.
They were not interested in character itself. I was asking them for
watches and they were offering me boots.

To make this clearer ⟨to throw some light upon the predicament wh.
the Georgians found themselves in⟩, let us imagine Mr Wells, Mr
Bennett and Mr Galsworthy in the railway carriage with Mrs Brown. Mr
Wells with his extraordinarily active and speculative mind would look
out of the window, see the river, seize upon some wonderfully ingenious
idea ⟨be floated off upon some generous & stupendous idea⟩ – shall we
say about electric barges ⟨?⟩ ⟨shall we say⟩ barges propelled in some
hitherto unknown way so that ⟨miraculous barges able to bring⟩ food
grown in the Equator was delivered fresh and glowing in ⟨to⟩ Camberwell by eight o clock the next day ⟨morning⟩. What sport his
imagination would have ⟨!⟩ How he would revel in the adventure and
the colour and the detail of it all. You know how he sweeps one off ones
feet into some jolly and bright and beautiful Utopia where everyone is
happy and well ⟨good active & [ingenious ?]⟩ and rather like Mr Wells
⟨or Mr and Mrs Sidney Webb.⟩ ⟨But⟩ Nobody is in the least like Mrs
Brown. That poor old lady would have no place at all except indeed
unless indeed as she could be fitted up and refurbished ⟨up & made to
look like a good citizen ⟨robust & jolly & industrious⟩ of the Utopia of
the future –⟩ and made to enjoy life about a thousand years hence. But
sitting in the corner of the third class carriage, I do not think that Mr
Wells would waste a thought on her ⟨as she exists at the present
moment⟩ at all. And what would Mr Galsworthy see? I suspect that
Doultons factory would take his fancy. He would brood over all those
thousands of men and women engaged in making earthenware pots all
day long. He would invent some bitter [p.15] and very realistic story
about a girl who supported a mother by making fifteen thousand pots a
day; while the Manager lived in South Kensington, sent his sons to Eton,
and lunched on Sundays ⟨surrounded by his family⟩ off roast beef ⟨&
Yorkshire pudding⟩. I do not think that Mr Galsworthy in his indignation with the iniquities of the factory ⟨industrial⟩ system and the public
school system and the family system would even see Mrs Brown in her
corner. Mr Bennett alone of the three Edwardian novelists would keep
his eyes in the carriage. He indeed would observe every detail with
immense care. He would notice the advertisements, the pictures of
Swanage and Portsmouth, the way in which the stuffing of a the seat

bulges out between the buttons; how Mrs Brown wore a brooch which had cost three and ten at Whitworth's bazaar; and had mended both gloves – indeed the thumb of ⟨the left glove⟩ one had been replaced. And he would observe at length how this was the non stop train from Windsor which calls at Richmond for the convenience of middle class residents who can afford to go to the theatre but have not reached the social rank which owns ⟨can afford⟩ motor cars of their own. And so he would ~~actually~~ ⟨~~allow~~ approach⟩ reach Mrs Brown, would tell us how she had been left a little copyhold not freehold property in Datchet, which however was mortgaged to Mr ~~Skellorn~~ ⟨Bungay⟩ the solicitor But why ⟨should I⟩ invent Mr Bennett? I will read you a passage by Mr Bennett himself. ⟨He is describing a young girl, Hilda Lessways, – this is the way he ~~begins his~~ approaches her on page 8. She is at her bedroom window, expecting a visit from Mr Skellorn the agent who collects the rents.⟩ [*p.16*] Now all this seems to me to have nothing whatever to do with Hilda Lessways, ⟨Mr Skellorn⟩ Mrs Brown or any other human being whatsoever. No, I do not think that Mr Bennett with all his power of observation has once looked directly at poor Mrs Brown. There she sits in her corner of the railway carriage – that carriage which is travelling not from Richmond to Waterloo but from one age of English literature to the next – for Mrs Brown is eternal; Mrs Brown is human nature; Mrs Brown changes only on the surface; it is the novelists who get in and out – there she sits and not one of the Edwardian writers has so much as looked at her. They have looked, very powerfully, very searchingly, out of the window; at factories; at the decoration and upholstery of the carriage; at the circumstances and conditions of life, but not at life itself. And so they have developed a technique of novel writing which suits their purpose; they have made tools which do their business. ⟨But their tools are quite useless for ~~our~~ the ~~Georgian business~~ us.⟩

Now you may well complain of the vagueness of my language. What is a tool, you may ask; and what do you mean by saying that Mr Bennetts and Mr Galsworthys and Mr Wells's tools are the wrong kind of tools for the Georgians? ⟨[⟩ I wish I could invoke the help of professors here; for this is a very difficult matter to make plain. ⟨]⟩ But think of the passage which I have just read to you from Mr Bennett. That is a tool; that is a method for making you believe what we know of course is not true in fact, that Hilda Lessways is a real woman. By beginning his novel like that he is making use of a convention. All writers have to make use of conventions for conveying their meaning to the reader. Now it is [*p.17*] an enormous help to a writer to have a convention which is ready to use and fitting to use. – which helps him to express his meaning without distorting it. It would have been an enormous help to me if when I wished to convey to you my impression of that scene in the railway carriage I had had some one at hand to tell me where I was to begin. But I did not know where to begin. I just jumped in, and said how the impression was very pungent unmistakable, like a draught, like a smell of burning, and that all sorts of irrelevant and incongruous scenes rushed into my head. ⟨That is not the way to create a masterpiece.⟩ Now this is partly Mr Bennetts fault. He should have helped me; but he hindered me. I asked him – he is my elder and better – how shall I begin to describe this womans character? And he said 'Tell them how her father kept a drapers shop in Harrogate. Ascertain the rent and discover what her mother died of. Then let us approach the shop. Do you know the price of calico? We will begin with a scene in the ~~shop~~ ⟨basement⟩ –' Oh ⟨But⟩ I cried ⟨oh⟩ stop. Stop.

And I regret to say that I threw that ugly that clumsy, that misshapen and incongruous tool out of the window. Mr Bennett can use it; ~~but for~~ I knew that if I had started telling you all those facts my Mrs Brown would have escaped, disappeared, been utterly lost to me for ever.

That is what I mean by saying that the Edwardian tools are the wrong ones for us to use. They have laid an enormous stress upon the fabric of things, the appearance of things [;] they have given us a house, in the hope that we may be able to deduce the human being who lives there. And if you hold, as I hold that novels are ~~founded upon character, that is a very clumsy way of~~ [p.18] are about people and not about the houses they live in, that is the wrong way to set about it.

So you see one has to begin by throwing away the method that is in use at the moment. One is left facing ones subject without any method of conveying it to the reader. But one is never quite alone. The public is always with one, if not on the same seat still next door, in the next carriage so to speak. The public is a strange companion. ⟨composite creature:⟩ It is in England a very suggestible and apparently docile ~~creature~~ ⟨beast⟩; it will believe what it is told implicitly for a certain number of years. If you said to the public All women have tails and all men humps, it would actually learn to ~~see men with~~ ⟨see⟩ women with tails and men with humps; and you would think it a little indecent and very revolutionary if you said Nonsense. Not a bit of it. Monkeys have tails and camels humps. But men and women have neither; they have brains and they have hearts. ~~Still the British public has extreme good taste about literature; it is always right in the long run.~~ ⟨They wd. refuse to believe you; that they wd. think quite absurd & rather [*undeciphered word*] into the bargain⟩

But to return. Here is the British public sitting by ones side and saying in its vast and unanimous way Old women have houses. They have fathers. They have incomes. They have servants. They have hot water bottles. That is how we know that they are old women. Mr Wells and Mr Bennett and Mr Galsworthy have always taught us ~~that they have all these things.~~ that this is so. But ⟨now⟩ with your Mrs Brown ⟨– how are we to ~~know~~ believe in her –⟩ we do not even know whether her villa was called Balmoral or Albert Edward ⟨[?Stratford]⟩. How can she be alive? No; she is a mere figment of your imagination. And naturally they laugh. [*p.19*] They have been taught to look at people in that way. You cannot expect them to forget what they have been taught to ~~see~~ ⟨believe⟩ all in a minute.

It is a very difficult thing to go against what most people believe. It is extremely difficult to say 'This is what I feel' when you know that you are perhaps the only person who does feel like that. In private life of course one can be silent; one can be tactful; one can change the conversation. But a writer has to speak out. He has to say as truthfully as he can what he feels. It is his only chance of life. If he falsifies, from fear or politeness, he at once loses not perhaps his circulation but what I hope there is no exaggeration in calling his soul. But again – it is not a simple matter for a writer to tell the truth. It is not a simple matter to describe even an old lady in a railway carriage. All sorts of incongruous ideas rush in as I have said. But I will not bother you now with that very difficult and complex matter – how to tell the truth. For one thing I do not think that we Georgians yet know how ⟨to tell the truth⟩. Character, life, humanity, Mrs Brown, call it what you will, blows at us from every corner, so fresh, so strong, so different from what it has ever been before – that really we are knocked over by it; we cannot yet describe it, ⟨we cannot⟩ or tell the truth about it. If we could, then undoubtedly we should be great writers.

⟨And we are not great writers.⟩

But, as I said just now, it was extremely difficult for the men and women who began to write novels about the year 1910 to be even good writers; even; their task was much harder than the task most generations have had. ⟨[*undeciphered word*] [?was that change]⟩ There were these old tools I have been speaking [*p.20*] of. Many of ⟨the Georgians⟩ them spoilt their early work – I am thinking of Mr Forster and Mr Lawrence – simply because instead of throwing away those tools they tried to use them. They tried to compromise. They tried to combine their own direct sense of the oddity and intensity of some character with Mr Galsworthys knowledge of the factory acts and Mr Bennetts knowledge of the geography of the Five Towns. They tried it; but they had too keen, too overpowering a perception of Mrs Brown and her peculiarities to go on trying it much longer. Something had to be done. At whatever cost of life limb⟨,⟩ and damage to valuable property Mrs Brown must be rescued, expressed set in her right relations to the world, before the train stopped and she disappeared for ever. And so the smashing and crashing began. Thus it is that you get people like Mr Joyce for example breaking up the old traditional form of the novel which has existed since the days of Richardson and before. 'I will break up the language, the grammar; ⟨I will bring⟩ the whole substantial building ⟨down about my head⟩' he seemed to say 'if by so doing I can keep absolutely close to my idea of Mrs Brown – Mrs Bloom, I mean. Thus it is that we hear all round us ⟨in poems & novels & biographies & even in newspapers in essays⟩, the sound of breaking and falling and destruction. It is the prevailing sound of the Georgian age. – rather a melancholy one, if you think what melodious days there have been in the past – if you think of Shakespeare and Milton, or even of Dickens and Thackeray. But let us not discourage them. These poets and novelists and biographers are destroying and breaking up from the most honourable motives – their determination never to desert Mrs Brown – their determination to give back to literature whatever ⟨the vision of reality that is in them they liked⟩ [p.21] ⟨the⟩ vision of reality their may be ⟨that is theirs⟩. Fame, money, popularity are all to be sacrificed rather than that. But it takes great energy, great courage. For really, – I do not want to exaggerate – but really there is nothing more important than that ⟨Mrs Brown ⟨nothing more important than our vision of reality⟩ every hair of her head is sacred⟩

It is for these reasons then that while I have the greatest respect for my contemporaries I do not think them either the most fortunate or the most successful of generations. I think that there is [a] certain amount of truth in what Mr Bennett says that they are not yet able to make us believe that their characters are real. But as I have said I think that this is partly the fault of the public; I believe that the public has got to learn to see the truth; and has got to forget to see the falsehood. I believe that the Edwardian version of human nature was – for very good reasons which you know better than I do – economic reasons, social reasons – very superficial, very conventional, all mixed up with clay and stucco brick and mortar, empire and commerce, ⟨Utopias & factories & Five Towns⟩ ⟨problems in the 5 towns⟩ conditions and circumstances. ~~But~~ ⟨So⟩| it is quite plain |from ⟨for⟩ all these causes| that we cannot expect the Georgians to give us a series of complete masterpieces coming out year after year in succession such as the Victorians enjoyed. We must reconcile ourselves to a season of failures and fragments. Where so much strength is being spent on finding a way of ~~expressing~~ telling the truth the truth itself is bound to reach us in rather an exhausted and chaotic condition. Mr Joyces Ulysses is an example of what I mean. He has had to use so much strength in hacking his way through to ~~an idea~~ his idea, his Ulysses, that he is half tired out by the time he gets there. Much of his book is very [*lacuna in text*] [*p.22*] stuff in consequence. And so ⟨even with⟩ it is with a very different book – Eminent Victorians by Mr Strachey

[*The pagination of the typescript breaks down here, at p.22. Two further pages, originally numbered 18 and 19 and renumbered 21 and 22 respectively, now follow.*]

masterpieces coming out year after year such as the Victorians enjoyed. We must reconcile ourselves to a succession of failures and fragments. Where so much strength is being spent in finding a way of expressing the truth, the truth itself is bound to reach us in a rather exhausted, chaotic condition. Mr Joyces Ulysses is an example of what I mean. He has had to use so much strength in hacking his way through to his idea, his Ulysses, that he is tired out by the time he gets there. Much of the book is very poor stuff in consequence; but now and then it is of the highest value. And even with a book ~~like Queen Victoria by Mr Strachey~~ which being a history and not a novel needs less creative effort on the part of the author, even there it seems to me the effort which he has to make to bring out sharply an aspect of the ~~Queens character~~ ⟨these queer people⟩ which is quite a new one⟨,⟩ has been such a strain on him that the book has ~~not~~ ⟨neither⟩ the ~~force~~ or depth or richness which it would have had if it had been written [in] an age like the Victorian age when the method was used unconsciously, and all a writers strength went into his matter.

I will end by asking you as readers to exercise great forebearance ~~and~~ when you read these queer Georgian books Do not like Mr Bennett say oh theyre trying to be clever; they are showing off; and neglecting the profound and lasting truths of the human soul. Say rather; they are working without much praise and without much ⟨a great deal of desire⟩ pay, very hard and ⟨very⟩ honestly to lay bare those truths; to find them afresh. The results may be ugly; irritating; spasmodic, obscure. But we must forgive them; for unless they go through this drudgery [*p.22*] no great writer can be born.

For I will make one last, and one very rash prediction. We are on the threshold of a very great age in English literature; but we can only reach it if we ⟨are determined never to desert⟩ ~~cling fast to~~ Mrs Brown.

APPENDIX IV

Notes on the Journals

After a prolonged period of writing almost exclusively for the *TLS* (see *II VW Essays*, 1912–18), VW now found herself gaining a far wider range of journalistic outlets, in Britain and in the USA. This appendix provides background notes to the journals, and editors, concerned, as available from the *Newspaper Press Directory* (*NPD*), from biographical studies, including entries in the *DNB*, from newspaper obituaries, and from John Gross's classic *The Rise and Fall of the Man of Letters* (Weidenfeld & Nicolson, 1969). Against each periodical are also given details of VW's contributions.

Athenaeum

Founded in 1828, the *Athenaeum* languished for some years before briefly becoming – between the appointment in April 1919 of John Middleton Murry (1889–1957) as editor and its merger with the *Nation* (see below) on 19 February 1921 – a leading critical weekly. VW noted in her diary of 19 March 1919: 'Murry is much of a small boy still, I think, in spite of his tragic airs. I suspect his boast will come true; the *Athenaeum* will be the best literary paper in existence in 12 months.' Murry's contributors included Clive Bell, T. S. Eliot, E. M. Forster, Roger Fry, Wyndham Lewis, Lytton Strachey, Paul Valéry, Leonard Woolf, and Katherine Mansfield who had married Murry in 1918, and who reviewed novels, including, to its author's pain, VW's *Night and Day* in the issue for 21 November 1919. VW's contributions: *1919:* 'The Eccentrics' (25 April); 'The Soul of an Archbishop' (9 May): 'The

Anatomy of Fiction' (16 May): 'On Some of the Old Actors' (6 June): 'Is This Poetry?' (in collaboration with LW, 20 June): 'Forgotten Benefactors' (4 July): 'These Are the Plans' (1 August): 'The Royal Academy' (22 August): 'Wilcoxiana' (19 September): 'Maturity and Immaturity' (21 November): 'Behind the Bars' (12 December); *1920:* 'Pictures and Portraits' (9 January): 'English Prose' (30 January): 'Money and Love' (12 March): 'The Wrong Way of Reading' (28 May): 'Mr Kipling's Notebook' (16 July): 'A Character Sketch' (13 August): 'Solid Objects' (22 October – see *CSF*).

Criterion

A quarterly founded and edited by T. S. Eliot (1888–1963), the first issue of which appeared in October 1922 and included Eliot's poem 'The Waste Land' (to be republished by The Hogarth Press in the following September). The *Criterion* drew upon a wide range of American and European contributors. Literary in its original emphasis, it increasingly embraced social and political subjects dear to Eliot's heart. It was first financed by Lady Rothermere (d.1937), wife of the newspaper magnate, and then, from 1925, by the firm of publishers Faber & Gwyer (afterwards Faber & Faber) of which, that year, Eliot became a director. It continued to appear, as the *New Criterion,* the *Monthly Criterion,* and again the *Criterion,* until 1939. VW's contributions: *1923:* 'In the Orchard' (April – see *CSF*); *1924:* 'Character in Fiction' (July).

Daily Herald

A Labour newspaper established in 1912. Described in the *NPD* as 'a spirited advocate of social reform, its chief concern being the welfare of the working classes', the paper appeared during the First World War as the *Weekly Herald* under the editorship of the Labour leader George Lansbury (1859–1940) who, in 1920, recruited Siegfried Sassoon (1886–1967) as the revived daily's first literary editor. E. M. Forster (1879–1970) deputised for Sassoon during March–April 1920 and in the same year Sassoon was succeeded by the poet and musical critic W. J.

Turner (1889–1946). It is just possible that Forster commissioned the first of VW's *Herald* pieces (see *II VW Diary* 10 April 1920) and certain that Turner commissioned the second (see *II VW Letters*, no. 1163). VW's contributions: *1920:* 'A Good Daughter' (26 May); *1921:* 'George Eliot' (9 March).

Dial (N.Y.)

American literary and cultural journal edited from November 1919 by Scofield Thayer (1889–1982), a friend at Harvard and at Oxford of T. S. Eliot, whose 'London Letter' was a regular *Dial* feature. VW's contributions: *1923:* 'Mrs Dalloway in Bond Street' (July – see *CSF*); *1924:* 'Miss Ormerod' (December 1924).

Living Age (Boston)

American journal edited 1920–28 by the economist Victor S. Clark (1868–1946). VW had made her American début as an essayist in the pages of the *Living Age* in July 1908 (see *I VW Essays*, p. xv), when it reprinted her *Cornhill* essay on 'John Delane'. In the issue for 2 February 1924, it now reprinted from the *New York Evening Post Literary Review* 'Mr Bennett and Mrs Brown'.

London Mercury

A monthly founded in November 1919 by J. C. Squire (1884–1958) and edited by him until 1934. Eschewing politics and professing an undogmatic approach to literature and the arts, the *Mercury* set out, according to its own prospectus, to satisfy 'the current needs of all those who are intelligently interested in literature, in the drama, in the arts, and in music'. In fact it quite belligerently opposed modernism and all things 'highbrow', engaged in running warfare with Murry's *Athenaeum* and tended to favour a culture of cricket, Georgian verse and beery bonhomie. Something of this conflict may be gathered from VW's diary entry of 31 January 1920: 'According to Squire the A[thenaeum] denies everything. It is a frost of death for all creative activity. Now the London Mercury provides a very fertile soil. He pressed me to write for the London Mercury. The A. is winning itself a bad name, on account of its hard sceptical tone. I tried to explain to Squire that there is such a thing as honesty & a high standard; his retort is & there are such things as poetry & enthusiasm.' VW's contributions: *1920:* 'An Unwritten Novel' (July – see *CSF*); *1924:* 'The Lives of the Obscure' (January).

Nation & Athenaeum

Created in 1921 when the *Nation*, a Liberal weekly owned by the Rowntree Trust, absorbed the *Athenaeum* (see above). The journal was edited until 1923 by H. W. Massingham (1860–1924), who had been editor of the *Nation* since its foundation in 1907. It was acquired in 1923 by a consortium of Liberals led by Maynard Keynes (1883–1946), under whose chairmanship the economist Hubert Henderson (1890–1952) succeeded Massingham as editor, and LW became literary editor, a post he held until 1930. LW contributed a weekly 'World of Books' column to the paper's literary pages. VW's contributions: *1923:* 'To Spain' (5 May): 'Romance and the Heart' (19 May): 'Laetitia Pilkington' (30 June): 'Mr Conrad: A Conversation' (1 September): 'The Compromise' (29 September): 'Mr Bennett and Mrs Brown' (17 November; first published in the *New York Evening Post Literary Review*), 'The Chinese Shoe' (17 November), 'Jane Austen at Sixty' (15 December); *1924:* 'The Poems ... of Edward Lord Herbert of Cherbury*' (19 January): '*Glimpses of Authors*' (9 February): '*Unpublished Letters of Matthew Arnold*' (16 February): '*Arthur Yates: An Autobiography*' (16 February): '*Letters and Journals of Anne Chalmers*' (23 February): 'The Enchanted Organ' (15 March): 'I was given the opportunity ...' (5 April): 'The Patron and the Crocus' (12 April): 'Aesthetically speaking ...' (19 April): '*Anatole France, the Man and His Work*' (3 May): 'The Private View of the Royal Academy ... (10 May): 'Mr Benson's Memories' (10 May): '*Marie Elizabeth Towneley*' (7 June): '*Unwritten History*' (21 June); '*The Life and Last Words of Wilfrid Ewart*' (21 June): '*Robert Smith Surtees*' (21 June): 'Thunder at

Wembley' (28 June): 'Stendhal' (5 July): *Days That Are Gone* (5 July): *Before the Mast – And After* (12 July): *The Truth at Last* (19 July): 'Editions-de-Luxe' (23 August): 'The cheapening of motor-cars . . .' (27 September): 'Appreciations' (27 September): 'Restoration Comedy' (18 October): 'It is strange as one enters the Mansard Gallery . . .' (18 October): 'Not the least pitiable victims . . .' (18 October): *Richard Hakluyt* (25 October): *Smoke Rings and Roundelays* (25 October): *Memories of a Militant* (8 November): 'Peggy. *The Story of One Score Years and Ten*' (8 November): *The Antiquary* (22 November): 'Can neither war nor peace . . .' (22 November): *These Were the Muses* (22 November).

New Republic (N.Y.)

American weekly edited during the period 1914–24 by Philip Littell (1868–1943) who co-published a number of VW's contributions to British journals and whose paper was to become her chief outlet in America. (Clive Bell was also a regular contributor.) VW's contributions (all reprinted from N&A): *1923:* 'To Spain' (6 June); *1924:* 'The Compromise' (9 January): 'The Enchanted Organ' (6 August): 'The Patron and the Crocus' (7 May): *The Antiquary* (3 December).

New Statesman

A weekly founded by Sidney and Beatrice Webb, G. B. Shaw and other members of the Fabian Society in 1913, and edited until 1931 by Clifford Sharp (1883–1935). Desmond MacCarthy (1877–1952), who succeeded J. C. Squire (see *London Mercury*) as the journal's literary editor in 1920, described the *Statesman* as being: 'out to improve the world, to correct the injustices of the social system, to stick up for the have-nots' (*Humanities*, 1953). As 'Affable Hawk' he contributed a weekly 'Books in General' column to the paper's literary pages. In addition to book reviewing, he also engaged VW to write dramatic criticisms. VW's contributions: *1920:* 'A Talk About Memoirs' (6 March): *The Higher Court* (17 April): 'Body and Brain' (5 June): 'The

Cherry Orchard' (24 July): 'Gorky on Tolstoy' (7 August): 'The Intellectual Status of Women' (9 and 16 October, correspondence with 'Affable Hawk' – see *II VW Diary*, App. III); *1921:* 'Congreve' (2 April): 'Ethel Smyth' (23 April): 'Trousers' (4 June); *1922:* 'Jane Austen Practising' (15 July); *1923:* 'An Impression of Gissing' (30 June).

New York Evening Post Literary Review

Established in 1920 by the critic Henry Seidel Canby (1878–1961) and edited by him until 1924, when he and others created the celebrated *Saturday Review of Literature*. VW's contribution: *1923:* 'Mr Bennett and Mrs Brown' (17 November).

Times Literary Supplement

Still under the editorship of Bruce Lyttelton Richmond (1871–1964), who had taken over the newly founded paper in 1902, the *TLS* now became gradually less and less a source of reviewing work for VW and increasingly, as she wished, an outlet for full-length essays or 'leaders'. VW's contributions: *1919:* 'The War from the Street' (9 January): 'Small Talk About Meredith' (13 February): *'The Tunnel'* (13 February): 'Lady Ritchie' (6 March): *'Sylvia and Michael'* (20 March): *'Within the Rim'* (27 March): 'Dickens by a Disciple' (27 March): 'Washington Irving' (3 April); 'Modern Novels' (10 April): 'The Novels of Defoe' (24 April): *'The Obstinate Lady'* (1 May): *'Java Head'* (29 May): 'Joseph Addison' (19 June); *'The Way of All Flesh'* (26 June): 'A Positivist' (17 July): 'Horace Walpole' (31 July): 'Herman Melville' (7 August): 'The Russian Background' (14 August): 'A Real American' (21 August): *'Sonia Married'* (28 August): *'September'* (25 September): 'Mr Gosse and His Friends' (2 October): *'Madeleine'* (9 October): 'Landor in Little' (16 October): 'Dostoevsky in Cranford' (23 October): 'Winged Phrases' (30 October): 'Real Letters' (6 November): 'The Limits of Perfection' (6 November): 'George Eliot' (20 November): 'Watts-Dunton's Dilemma' (11 December): 'The Intellectual Imagination' (11 December): 'Memories of Meredith' (18 December): *'Gold and Iron'*

(25 December); *1920:* 'An American Poet' (29 January): 'Cleverness and Youth' (5 February): 'Mr Norris's Method' (4 March): 'Men and Women' (18 March): 'Freudian Fiction' (25 March): *'The Letters of Henry James'* (8 April): 'An Imperfect Lady' (6 May): 'An Old Novel' (27 May): *'The Mills of the Gods'* (17 June): 'A Disillusioned Romantic' (1 July): 'The Pursuit of Beauty' (8 July): 'Pure English' (15 July): 'A Born Writer' (29 July): 'John Evelyn' (28 October): 'Jane Austen and the Geese' (28 October): 'Postscript or Prelude?' (2 December): 'Pleasant Stories' (16 December): 'A Flying Lesson' (23 December); *1921:* 'Revolution' (27 January): 'Mr Norris's Standard' (10 February): 'Henley's Criticism' (24 February): 'A Prince of Prose' (3 March); 'Scott's Character' (28 April): 'Gothic Romance' (5 May): 'Patmore's Criticism' (26 May): 'A Glance at Turgenev' (8 December): 'Fantasy' (15 December): 'Henry James' Ghost Stories' (22 December); *1922:* 'Dostoevsky the Father' (12 January): 'On Re-reading Novels' (20 July): 'Modern Essays' (30 November): 'Eliza and Sterne' (14 December); *1923:* 'How It Strikes a Contemporary' (5 April); 'Sir Thomas Browne' (28 June); *1924:* 'Montaigne' (31 January): 'The Weekend' (3 July): 'Joseph Conrad' (14 August): 'The Schoolroom Floor' (2 October).

Vogue (London)

Fashion magazine founded in 1909 by the American firm Condé Nast and dynamically edited during the period 1922–6 by Dorothy Todd, who broadened *Vogue*'s cultural appeal by publishing articles by or about avant-garde writers, artists and performers. For VW it was certainly an interesting and potentially lucrative departure, the 'ethics' of which were to precipitate her into an amusing 'wrangle' with the American man of letters Logan Pearsall Smith; she was driven to protest: 'I say Bunkum. Ladies' clothes and aristocrats playing golf don't affect my style; and they would do his a world of good . . . What he wants is prestige: what I want, money' (*III VW Letters*, no. 1524, to Jacques Raverat, 24 January 1925; and see nos. 1525, 1527). VW's contribution: *1924:* 'Indiscretions' (late November; reprinted as 'Indiscretions in Literature', *Vogue*, N.Y., 1 June 1925).

Woman's Leader and the Common Cause

A weekly created in 1920, in amalgamation with the monthly *Common Cause* (founded in 1909), and edited during the period 1920–3 by Ray Strachey (1887–1940). Its sole policy, was, in its own statement, 'to advocate a real equality of liberties, status and opportunities between men and women. So far as space permits, however, it will offer an impartial platform for topics not directly included in the objects of the women's movement, but of special interest to women.' VW's contribution: *1920:* 'The Plumage Bill' (23 July).

Bibliography

For bibliographical details concerning Virginia Woolf's writings and for related biographical works see under Abbreviations, p. xxix.

WORKS OF REFERENCE
Virginia Woolf's Reading Notebooks (Princeton University Press, Princeton, New York, 1983) by Brenda R. Silver

Virginia Woolf's Literary Sources and Allusions. A Guide to the Essays (Garland, New York, 1983) by Elizabeth Steele

Virginia Woolf's Rediscovered Essays. Sources and Allusions (Garland, New York, 1987) by Elizabeth Steele

CRITICAL STUDIES
Victorian Bloomsbury. The Early Literary History of the Bloomsbury Group. Volume One (Macmillan Press, London, and St Martin's Press, New York, 1987) by S. P. Rosenbaum

Virginia Woolf and the Real World (University of California Press, 1986) by Alex Zwerdling

INDEX

This index has been compiled upon the same principles as those employed and outlined in the previous volumes of *The Essays*. Thematic entries have been included under the following heads: Aristocracy; Biography; Character; Civilisation; Contemporaries; Conversation; Criticism; Edwardians; Essay, the; Genius; Georgians; Letters; Life itself; Literature; Modernism; Moment, the; Painting; Poetry; Prose; Reading; Realism; Reality; Reviewers; Semi-transparency; Victorian Era (and Victorians); Women.